ASTER FAMILY FLOWER

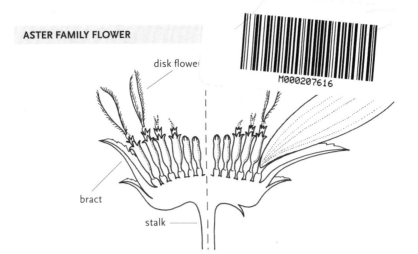

disk flower

bract

stalk

INFLORESCENCES

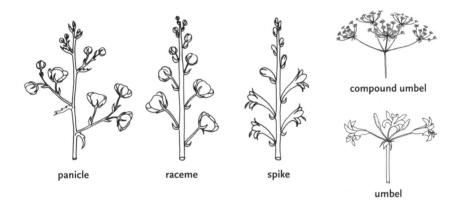

panicle

raceme

spike

compound umbel

umbel

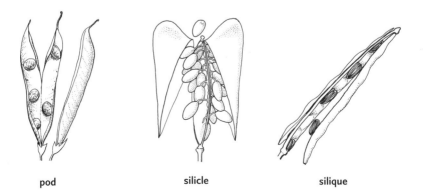

pod

silicle

silique

WILDFLOWERS
of TEXAS

Michael Eason

TIMBER PRESS FIELD GUIDE

Dedicated to my parents, Jack and Betty Eason. Thank you for taking me camping and introducing me to the wonders of the natural world.

Page 1: *Penstemon baccharifolius* growing on exposed limestone cliffs along the Pecos River in Val Verde County. Pages 2–3: A field of two of the most common springtime roadside flowers, *Lupinus texensis* and *Castilleja indivisa*, in Llano County. Pages 4–5: *Physaria fendleri* and *Stenandrium barbatum* along a limestone ridge in Brewster Country. Page 6: *Agave lechuguilla* with blooming *Castilleja rigida*. Pages 62–63: *Allium kunthii*. Page 185: *Zinnia grandiflora*. Page 291: *Silene laciniata* subsp. *greggii*. Pages 318–319: *Clematis carrizoensis*. Page 395: *Phacelia congesta*. Page 461: *Asclepias asperula*. Page 463: *Packera tampicana*. Page 469: *Clematis reticulata*. Page 507: *Streptanthus cutleri*.

Published in 2018 by Timber Press, Inc.
The Haseltine Building
133 S.W. Second Avenue, Suite 450
Portland, Oregon 97204-3527
timberpress.com

Printed in China
Cover design by Patrick Barber
Text design by Laura Shaw
Series design by Susan Applegate

Library of Congress Cataloging-in-Publication Data

Names: Eason, Michael, author.
Title: Wildflowers of Texas / Michael Eason.
Other titles: Timber Press field guide.
Description: Portland, Oregon: Timber Press, Inc., 2018. | Series: Timber Press field guide | Includes bibliographical references and index.
Identifiers: LCCN 2017046010 | ISBN 9781604696462 (flexibind)
Subjects: LCSH: Wild flowers—Texas—Identification.
Classification: LCC QK188 .E27 2018 | DDC 582.1309764—dc23 LC record available at https://lccn.loc.gov/2017046010

ISBN 13: 978-1-60469-646-2

CONTENTS

INTRODUCTION

Texas is a vast state. At nearly 269,000 square miles, it is second only to Alaska in size and comparable to Florida in plant diversity. With nearly 6000 taxa in the state's flora, you could spend a lifetime exploring and learning about the plants within its borders. Coastal Texas offers dune species; South Texas has sabal palm groves and night-blooming cereus cactus that can be several meters tall. Pine woodlands, orchids, and pitcher plants are found in East Texas, while extensive stands of yucca and ocotillo dominate in the arid lands of West Texas. Oak-juniper-pine woodlands char-acterize the upper elevations of the sky islands. Grasslands and canyon lands sweep through the Panhandle, and, of course, wildflowers line the country roads in Central Texas. Texas is fortunate to have such floral diversity. Not only is it aesthetically pleasing, it also offers a wide range of habitats for fauna.

The scope of this book primarily covers herbaceous flowering angiosperms. Trees, shrubs, cacti, grasses, sedges, rushes, and nonflowering plants (ferns and fern allies) are not covered. Occasionally, a few woody vines are included as well as semiwoody

Salvia lycioides on the south rim of the Chisos Mountains, with a panoramic view of the Sierra Quemada below.

ACKNOWLEDGMENTS

The completion of this work would not have been possible without the assistance and generosity of many people.

Many of the photographs were taken on private property throughout Texas and beyond. I am grateful to landowners who permitted me access to their properties. Their dedication to the conservation and protection of their lands is rarely acknowledged, but without these stewards, much of our natural history would be lost. While it would be impossible to list all the property owners, ranch managers, and stewards who allowed access, I do thank each and every one of them for their generosity and openness in allowing me and others access to their lands to document and research the flora of Texas.

Thank you to Duane T. Corley, who allowed access to his property in Montgomery County as well his ranch in northern Mexico. I was able to photograph many aquatic and wetland species in Montgomery County with ease. The ranch in northern Mexico allowed me to photograph many species which are uncommon or rare in Texas, including *Bouchea linifolia*, *Gomphrena haageana*, and *Haplophyton crooksii*.

Thanks to Hardy Jackson, his mother, Nora Nell Jackson, and his late father, Richard Jackson, for wonderful meals, conversation, lodging, and access to their property in Starr County, while photographing plants in the Lower Rio Grande Valley. I first met the Jackson family in 2008 and have remained friends with them through the years. I am especially grateful for Hardy's time chauffeuring me and my dog, Roemer, to various ranches in Starr County, and for allowing Roemer to chase deer and rabbits and play with Rosie. Roemer is forever thankful.

Other land owners I would like to thank include Steve Bentsen (Starr County), Gary and Clare Freeman (Jeff Davis County), Lloyd and Emma Hampton (Lampasas County), Harry Miller (Presidio County), Elizabeth Rogers (Brewster County), Hiram and Liz Sibley (Pecos County), and Edie Stewart (Montgomery and Brooks Counties).

I would like to give my appreciation to the folks at The Nature Conservancy. Many species photographed in the Davis Mountains were taken on their Davis Mountain Preserve. Additional plants were photographed at Dolan Falls, Independence Creek, and Southmost Preserves.

I would like to thank several people who spent time with me in the field and from whom I learned quite a bit when first starting a career in botany: Burr Williams, previously with the Sibley Nature Center; Wynn Anderson, now retired from the University of Texas at El Paso; Patty Manning, formerly with Sul Ross State University; and Ad and Gertrud Konings, authors of *Cacti of Texas in Their Natural Habitat*.

Several people graciously contributed images for this book. Thank you, Layla Dishman, Sonnia Fajardo Hill, and Rosanna Ohlsson-Salmon. Numerous species would not have been included without their contributions. Additionally, I would like to thank Matt Buckingham and Shirley Powell for last-minute image substitutions and needs as well as landscape images.

Thank you to Theodore and Nancy Haywood, whose support and understanding allowed this book to be completed. Thanks to Martin Simonton for photographing *Helianthus grosseserratus*, saving me a 20-hour round trip to East Texas; for assistance in finding *Nymphaea ampla*; and for numerous trips throughout Texas and northern Mexico to seek out plants.

Special thanks to Tonya Beard for editing, proofreading (several times), and suggesting changes in format and content as well as for help in resolving the excruciating dilemma of selecting color groups. In addition, I would like to thank Tonya for her patience, especially during the final few months of this project.

Thank you to Turner Collins of Evangel University for properly identifying the two questionable species of *Orobanche*, and to Michael Powell for his assistance in the herbarium at Sul Ross State University.

I would like to acknowledge several people who read over various documents and gave their input and suggested changes. Martin Terry, Martin Simonton, and Dallas Baxter, thank you for taking time to look over the species descriptions and other documents, and for your suggestions and encouragement throughout the process. Thanks to Nathan Carroll, who developed a database of the flora of Texas in 2007 and supplied me with various species lists as I began my research. Lori Gola, thank you for your patience while taking my portrait that sweltering day in Central Texas; I am sure I was a difficult subject.

At Timber Press I would like to thank Juree Sondker, with whom I first worked on this project. I was a bit apprehensive about undertaking such a project on my own and little did I know at the time how much work would actually be involved. Thanks also to Andrew Beckman, whose patience was tested during the final stages of this work after I went well beyond my deadline. Thanks to Sarah Milhollin, who reviewed thousands of images, some twice. Additionally, I would like to thank Linda Willms and Julie Talbot for editing the manuscript, culling nearly 15,000 words and catching many mistakes my bleary eyes could not.

Thank you, Steve Muzos, professor at Austin Community College. It was in your field biology class that my interest in plants was reignited. I remember having to create our own dichotomous keys, a skill I still use to this day when performing vegetation surveys. Other professors who encouraged me include Robert Koehn, formerly of Texas State University; and Martin Terry and James Zech, both of Sul Ross State University and who both advised me to pursue this project. And I would like to thank Flo Oxley. I am forever grateful for her support and guidance during my employment at the Lady Bird Johnson Wildflower Center, as well as her confidence in me while working with her and in undertaking this task.

I would also like to thank the numerous people whose passion for plants led them down a similar path and who have published field guides. I believe the first field guide my family purchased outside of the *Golden Guide* series was *Roadside Wildflowers of Texas* by Howard Irwin and Mary Motz Wills. This book led to numerous local and statewide field guides covering both the flora and fauna of Texas. I still own and treasure each field guide I've ever purchased, even those early Golden Guides.

And finally, I would like to thank the readers of this book. I hope you learn as much from it as I did in researching and writing it, and that this work continues to be a valuable resource for years to come.

species, such as plumed tiquilia (*Tiquilia greggii*), as they fall into a gray area called subshrubs. Because Texas covers a large area and consists of such a variety of habitats, every effort has been made to ensure equal representation throughout the ecoregions and geographic areas of Texas. Of course, some locales have more plant diversity, and thus have more species represented here.

I have also endeavored to include a wide range of plant families, and within larger families, examples of each genus. For the sake of space, many species had to be omitted; just a quarter of the state's herbaceous and semiwoody angiosperms are included. Nonetheless, a conscious effort was made to incorporate species that have not been included in other field guides.

Both native and introduced species are described, as all of these are now part of the region's flora. When Europeans arrived in the area now known as Texas, they brought plants for medicinal, aesthetic, and agricultural uses. Over time, these plants have escaped and naturalized. Other species were accidental introductions—unintentionally spread via seed mixes or other sources of contamination. New species continue to arrive, whether as garden escapees or seeds inadvertently spread through human activity. The majority of species included in this book are common plants that can be found throughout Texas—roadside wildflowers, if you will. Uncommon species, such as *Echeveria strictiflora*, are also included, as well as rare plants.

Some less-showy species have also been described. When one hears the term "wildflower" one immediately thinks of a large blousy flower that can be seen, and often identified, while traveling down the high-

The rare lady's slipper orchid (*Cypripedium kentuckiense*) can be found in a few East Texas locations.

way at 80 miles per hour. However, many of Texas's wildflowers do not fall into this category. These plants, with small or insignificant flowers, are included here, with special attention given to the species I am most often asked to identify.

A reference that many still use is *The Manual of the Vascular Plants of Texas* by Correll and Johnston (Texas Research Foundation, 1970). While it is out of print and difficult to find, used copies do become available. For readers wishing to take their botanizing to the next level, this book is a wealth of information and has historic value as well. *The Flora of North Central Texas* (Botanical Research Institute of Texas, 1999), is another wonderful reference. It was the first botanical tome

I purchased as an undergraduate, and many years later I still use it. Please see the bibliography at the back for other print resources.

Online resources can be helpful, too. For the most current nomenclature and complete maps, I prefer BONAP (The Biota of North America Program) and ITIS (Integrated Taxonomic Information System). Others prefer to use The Plant List or Tropicos, although these can disagree from time to time. Another source is the USDA PLANTS Database; although it is known to have errors and somewhat outdated nomenclature, it is an excellent resource for user-friendly maps, and many species do have illustrations or photographs. In this book, I have elected to use the most updated nomenclature according to ITIS, and have included synonyms for some of the recent changes.

HOW TO USE THIS BOOK

Wildflowers of Texas was written as a field guide to assist in the identification of herbaceous and semiwoody flowering plants and vines within the borders of Texas. It covers 1170 species. Each species is illustrated with a color photograph and features the plant's Latin name, family, common name, typical habitat(s), bloom time, frequency of occurrence, a short description of the plant's morphology (including growth cycle), and its general location range. In nearly all descriptions, the maximum range is given for height, length, and width. As plants do not always reach their maximum growth, these measurements should be taken with a grain of salt. In some cases, when photographs and full text descriptions are not warranted, additional species are mentioned along with differences in features, also called characters, between similar species, differences in subspecies, or varieties within a species.

Flower Color

This book is arranged by flower color, coded by colors along page edges. Sometimes a flower's color is hard to determine. The age of the bloom, lighting, and personal opinion can all have an influence on certain colors. What one person sees as red, another may see as dark pink or orange. Different shades of blue and purple can yield similar debate. If a plant in question cannot be found in one section, try looking in a section of related colors.

The White to Green Flowers section includes white flowers that may be tinged pink, purple, or blue, but overall, upon first glance, they appear white. In addition, this group includes green or greenish yellow flowered plants. Many milkweeds (*Asclepias*) are found in this section. The Yellow to Orange Flower section is fairly straightforward. The Red to Brown Flowers section includes obvious red flowers as well as brown, maroon, or reddish brown flowers. The Pink to Light Purple Flowers section includes distinctly pink flowers as well as those in lighter shades of purple. The last group, Purple to Blue Flowers, houses the darker shades. Plants in these last two groups can be difficult to differentiate by hue and color intensity; consult both groups if necessary to identify a plant.

Photographs

Wildflower photographs were selected to show important characters of each plant. In nearly all cases, the plant was photographed in flower, which is typically the feature one relies upon when identifying a plant, or what one first observes when confronted with an unknown species. The photograph, along with the text description, general location, and habitat, should all be considered when identifying a plant. In some cases, additional images are included to show different flower colors, fruits, or leaves.

Plant Families and Latin Names

Within each color group the plants are arranged alphabetically by family, then by genus. This arrangement was done out of simplicity and partially to avoid the splitting of families or genera within the same color group. For example, this keeps all the yellow-flowered plants in the sunflower family together. As you become more familiar with this book, and plant families, you'll simply go to the front of the color group for the Asteraceae, to the middle for the Lamiaceae, and to the back for the Verbenaceae. Of course, this means learning the plant families and their characteristics, which can be found in the chapter covering plant families. (You can also find plants by flower color and photographs, but knowing the plant families to which they belong can reveal interesting connections.)

Latin names, or binomials, are the first names listed for each plant. The first word indicates genus and the second is species (also known as specific epithet), such as in *Phlox drummondii*. Both are italicized. Occasionally, the abbreviation "var." or "subsp." follows, and an additional name is added, such as with *Phlox drummondii* subsp. *drummondii*. "Subsp." refers to a subspecies and "var." refers to a variety.

The unique Latin name can be used anywhere, and even if a person is not familiar with that particular name, they may recognize the genus or family. Additionally, binomials are often descriptive of the plant, can give some insight into the plant's origins, reference the person who first discovered or described the species, or identify the person who was honored by the name. In *Tetraneuris linearifolia*, the specific epithet *linearifolia* indicates linear leaves, while *Argemone chisosensis* hints at the location of this species, the Chisos Mountains, and the genus *Engelmannia* honors botanist George Engelmann.

Common Names

In each description, the common name is listed after the family name. Plants can have one or many common names; for sake of space here, we have listed no more than three common names per plant.

Why are Latin names used primarily instead of common names? Latin names are more precise. The same common name can be used for several different plants, or a single plant may have many common names. Regional vernacular is often a factor. For instance, to many Texans, the common name bluebells refers to *Eustoma exaltatum*, a member of the Gentianaceae. A Californian, however, might think it refers to *Phacelia campanularia*, which is in the Hydrophyllaceae.

Habitat

Following the common name is a brief list of the types of habitat where a plant can be found. Most plants are widespread and have no preference, while others are more selective. If a plant is common along roadsides, that is noted. Many plants tend to occur in disturbed areas. These disturbed areas could be overgrazed pastures, areas that frequently flood, roadsides, or other sites where the soil is disrupted. Additionally, some species tend to be more prevalent around areas of human habitation—cities, towns, or suburban developments. That too is noted. Sometimes favored habitat found in a specific part of the state is included in the location range.

ACKNOWLEDGMENTS

The completion of this work would not have been possible without the assistance and generosity of many people.

Many of the photographs were taken on private property throughout Texas and beyond. I am grateful to landowners who permitted me access to their properties. Their dedication to the conservation and protection of their lands is rarely acknowledged, but without these stewards, much of our natural history would be lost. While it would be impossible to list all the property owners, ranch managers, and stewards who allowed access, I do thank each and every one of them for their generosity and openness in allowing me and others access to their lands to document and research the flora of Texas.

Thank you to Duane T. Corley, who allowed access to his property in Montgomery County as well his ranch in northern Mexico. I was able to photograph many aquatic and wetland species in Montgomery County with ease. The ranch in northern Mexico allowed me to photograph many species which are uncommon or rare in Texas, including *Bouchea linifolia*, *Gomphrena haageana*, and *Haplophyton crooksii*.

Thanks to Hardy Jackson, his mother, Nora Nell Jackson, and his late father, Richard Jackson, for wonderful meals, conversation, lodging, and access to their property in Starr County, while photographing plants in the Lower Rio Grande Valley. I first met the Jackson family in 2008 and have remained friends with them through the years. I am especially grateful for Hardy's time chauffeuring me and my dog, Roemer, to various ranches in Starr County, and for allowing Roemer to chase deer and rabbits and play with Rosie. Roemer is forever thankful.

Other land owners I would like to thank include Steve Bentsen (Starr County), Gary and Clare Freeman (Jeff Davis County), Lloyd and Emma Hampton (Lampasas County), Harry Miller (Presidio County), Elizabeth Rogers (Brewster County), Hiram and Liz Sibley (Pecos County), and Edie Stewart (Montgomery and Brooks Counties).

I would like to give my appreciation to the folks at The Nature Conservancy. Many species photographed in the Davis Mountains were taken on their Davis Mountain Preserve. Additional plants were photographed at Dolan Falls, Independence Creek, and Southmost Preserves.

I would like to thank several people who spent time with me in the field and from whom I learned quite a bit when first starting a career in botany: Burr Williams, previously with the Sibley Nature Center; Wynn Anderson, now retired from the University of Texas at El Paso; Patty Manning, formerly with Sul Ross State University; and Ad and Gertrud Konings, authors of *Cacti of Texas in Their Natural Habitat*.

Several people graciously contributed images for this book. Thank you, Layla Dishman, Sonnia Fajardo Hill, and Rosanna Ohlsson-Salmon. Numerous species would not have been included without their contributions. Additionally, I would like to thank Matt Buckingham and Shirley Powell for last-minute image substitutions and needs as well as landscape images.

Thank you to Theodore and Nancy Haywood, whose support and understanding allowed this book to be completed. Thanks to Martin Simonton for photographing *Helianthus grosseserratus*, saving me a 20-hour round trip to East Texas; for assistance in finding *Nymphaea ampla*; and for numerous trips throughout Texas and northern Mexico to seek out plants.

Special thanks to Tonya Beard for editing, proofreading (several times), and suggesting changes in format and content as well as for help in resolving the excruciating dilemma of selecting color groups. In addition, I would like to thank Tonya for her patience, especially during the final few months of this project.

Thank you to Turner Collins of Evangel University for properly identifying the two questionable species of *Orobanche*, and to Michael Powell for his assistance in the herbarium at Sul Ross State University.

I would like to acknowledge several people who read over various documents and gave their input and suggested changes. Martin Terry, Martin Simonton, and Dallas Baxter, thank you for taking time to look over the species descriptions and other documents, and for your suggestions and encouragement throughout the process. Thanks to Nathan Carroll, who developed a database of the flora of Texas in 2007 and supplied me with various species lists as I began my research. Lori Gola, thank you for your patience while taking my portrait that sweltering day in Central Texas; I am sure I was a difficult subject.

At Timber Press I would like to thank Juree Sondker, with whom I first worked on this project. I was a bit apprehensive about undertaking such a project on my own and little did I know at the time how much work would actually be involved. Thanks also to Andrew Beckman, whose patience was tested during the final stages of this work after I went well beyond my deadline. Thanks to Sarah Milhollin, who reviewed thousands of images, some twice. Additionally, I would like to thank Linda Willms and Julie Talbot for editing the manuscript, culling nearly 15,000 words and catching many mistakes my bleary eyes could not.

Thank you, Steve Muzos, professor at Austin Community College. It was in your field biology class that my interest in plants was reignited. I remember having to create our own dichotomous keys, a skill I still use to this day when performing vegetation surveys. Other professors who encouraged me include Robert Koehn, formerly of Texas State University; and Martin Terry and James Zech, both of Sul Ross State University and who both advised me to pursue this project. And I would like to thank Flo Oxley. I am forever grateful for her support and guidance during my employment at the Lady Bird Johnson Wildflower Center, as well as her confidence in me while working with her and in undertaking this task.

I would also like to thank the numerous people whose passion for plants led them down a similar path and who have published field guides. I believe the first field guide my family purchased outside of the *Golden Guide* series was *Roadside Wildflowers of Texas* by Howard Irwin and Mary Motz Wills. This book led to numerous local and statewide field guides covering both the flora and fauna of Texas. I still own and treasure each field guide I've ever purchased, even those early Golden Guides.

And finally, I would like to thank the readers of this book. I hope you learn as much from it as I did in researching and writing it, and that this work continues to be a valuable resource for years to come.

INTRODUCTION

Texas is a vast state. At nearly 269,000 square miles, it is second only to Alaska in size and comparable to Florida in plant diversity. With nearly 6000 taxa in the state's flora, you could spend a lifetime exploring and learning about the plants within its borders. Coastal Texas offers dune species; South Texas has sabal palm groves and night-blooming cereus cactus that can be several meters tall. Pine woodlands, orchids, and pitcher plants are found in East Texas, while extensive stands of yucca and ocotillo dominate in the arid lands of West Texas. Oak-juniper-pine woodlands char-

acterize the upper elevations of the sky islands. Grasslands and canyon lands sweep through the Panhandle, and, of course, wildflowers line the country roads in Central Texas. Texas is fortunate to have such floral diversity. Not only is it aesthetically pleasing, it also offers a wide range of habitats for fauna.

The scope of this book primarily covers herbaceous flowering angiosperms. Trees, shrubs, cacti, grasses, sedges, rushes, and nonflowering plants (ferns and fern allies) are not covered. Occasionally, a few woody vines are included as well as semiwoody

Salvia lycioides on the south rim of the Chisos Mountains, with a panoramic view of the Sierra Quemada below.

species, such as plumed tiquilia (*Tiquilia greggii*), as they fall into a gray area called subshrubs. Because Texas covers a large area and consists of such a variety of habitats, every effort has been made to ensure equal representation throughout the ecoregions and geographic areas of Texas. Of course, some locales have more plant diversity, and thus have more species represented here.

I have also endeavored to include a wide range of plant families, and within larger families, examples of each genus. For the sake of space, many species had to be omitted; just a quarter of the state's herbaceous and semiwoody angiosperms are included. Nonetheless, a conscious effort was made to incorporate species that have not been included in other field guides.

Both native and introduced species are described, as all of these are now part of the region's flora. When Europeans arrived in the area now known as Texas, they brought plants for medicinal, aesthetic, and agricultural uses. Over time, these plants have escaped and naturalized. Other species were accidental introductions—unintentionally spread via seed mixes or other sources of contamination. New species continue to arrive, whether as garden escapees or seeds inadvertently spread through human activity. The majority of species included in this book are common plants that can be found throughout Texas—roadside wildflowers, if you will. Uncommon species, such as *Echeveria strictiflora*, are also included, as well as rare plants.

Some less-showy species have also been described. When one hears the term "wildflower" one immediately thinks of a large blousy flower that can be seen, and often identified, while traveling down the high-

The rare lady's slipper orchid (*Cypripedium kentuckiense*) can be found in a few East Texas locations.

way at 80 miles per hour. However, many of Texas's wildflowers do not fall into this category. These plants, with small or insignificant flowers, are included here, with special attention given to the species I am most often asked to identify.

A reference that many still use is *The Manual of the Vascular Plants of Texas* by Correll and Johnston (Texas Research Foundation, 1970). While it is out of print and difficult to find, used copies do become available. For readers wishing to take their botanizing to the next level, this book is a wealth of information and has historic value as well. *The Flora of North Central Texas* (Botanical Research Institute of Texas, 1999), is another wonderful reference. It was the first botanical tome

I purchased as an undergraduate, and many years later I still use it. Please see the bibliography at the back for other print resources.

Online resources can be helpful, too. For the most current nomenclature and complete maps, I prefer BONAP (The Biota of North America Program) and ITIS (Integrated Taxonomic Information System). Others prefer to use The Plant List or Tropicos, although these can disagree from time to time. Another source is the USDA PLANTS Database; although it is known to have errors and somewhat outdated nomenclature, it is an excellent resource for user-friendly maps, and many species do have illustrations or photographs. In this book, I have elected to use the most updated nomenclature according to ITIS, and have included synonyms for some of the recent changes.

HOW TO USE THIS BOOK

Wildflowers of Texas was written as a field guide to assist in the identification of herbaceous and semiwoody flowering plants and vines within the borders of Texas. It covers 1170 species. Each species is illustrated with a color photograph and features the plant's Latin name, family, common name, typical habitat(s), bloom time, frequency of occurrence, a short description of the plant's morphology (including growth cycle), and its general location range. In nearly all descriptions, the maximum range is given for height, length, and width. As plants do not always reach their maximum growth, these measurements should be taken with a grain of salt. In some cases, when photographs and full text descriptions are not warranted, additional species are mentioned along with differences in features, also called characters, between similar species, differences in subspecies, or varieties within a species.

Flower Color

This book is arranged by flower color, coded by colors along page edges. Sometimes a flower's color is hard to determine. The age of the bloom, lighting, and personal opinion can all have an influence on certain colors. What one person sees as red, another may see as dark pink or orange. Different shades of blue and purple can yield similar debate. If a plant in question cannot be found in one section, try looking in a section of related colors.

The White to Green Flowers section includes white flowers that may be tinged pink, purple, or blue, but overall, upon first glance, they appear white. In addition, this group includes green or greenish yellow flowered plants. Many milkweeds (*Asclepias*) are found in this section. The Yellow to Orange Flower section is fairly straightforward. The Red to Brown Flowers section includes obvious red flowers as well as brown, maroon, or reddish brown flowers. The Pink to Light Purple Flowers section includes distinctly pink flowers as well as those in lighter shades of purple. The last group, Purple to Blue Flowers, houses the darker shades. Plants in these last two groups can be difficult to differentiate by hue and color intensity; consult both groups if necessary to identify a plant.

Photographs

Wildflower photographs were selected to show important characters of each plant. In nearly all cases, the plant was photographed in flower, which is typically the feature one relies upon when identifying a plant, or what one first observes when confronted with an unknown species. The photograph, along with the text description, general location, and habitat, should all be considered when identifying a plant. In some cases, additional images are included to show different flower colors, fruits, or leaves.

Plant Families and Latin Names

Within each color group the plants are arranged alphabetically by family, then by genus. This arrangement was done out of simplicity and partially to avoid the splitting of families or genera within the same color group. For example, this keeps all the yellow-flowered plants in the sunflower family together. As you become more familiar with this book, and plant families, you'll simply go to the front of the color group for the Asteraceae, to the middle for the Lamiaceae, and to the back for the Verbenaceae. Of course, this means learning the plant families and their characteristics, which can be found in the chapter covering plant families. (You can also find plants by flower color and photographs, but knowing the plant families to which they belong can reveal interesting connections.)

Latin names, or binomials, are the first names listed for each plant. The first word indicates genus and the second is species (also known as specific epithet), such as in *Phlox drummondii*. Both are italicized. Occasionally, the abbreviation "var." or "subsp." follows, and an additional name is added, such as with *Phlox drummondii* subsp. *drummondii*. "Subsp." refers to a subspecies and "var." refers to a variety.

The unique Latin name can be used anywhere, and even if a person is not familiar with that particular name, they may recognize the genus or family. Additionally, binomials are often descriptive of the plant, can give some insight into the plant's origins, reference the person who first discovered or described the species, or identify the person who was honored by the name. In *Tetraneuris linearifolia*, the specific epithet *linearifolia* indicates linear leaves, while *Argemone chisosensis* hints at the location of this species, the Chisos Mountains, and the genus *Engelmannia* honors botanist George Engelmann.

Common Names

In each description, the common name is listed after the family name. Plants can have one or many common names; for sake of space here, we have listed no more than three common names per plant.

Why are Latin names used primarily instead of common names? Latin names are more precise. The same common name can be used for several different plants, or a single plant may have many common names. Regional vernacular is often a factor. For instance, to many Texans, the common name bluebells refers to *Eustoma exaltatum*, a member of the Gentianaceae. A Californian, however, might think it refers to *Phacelia campanularia*, which is in the Hydrophyllaceae.

Habitat

Following the common name is a brief list of the types of habitat where a plant can be found. Most plants are widespread and have no preference, while others are more selective. If a plant is common along roadsides, that is noted. Many plants tend to occur in disturbed areas. These disturbed areas could be overgrazed pastures, areas that frequently flood, roadsides, or other sites where the soil is disrupted. Additionally, some species tend to be more prevalent around areas of human habitation—cities, towns, or suburban developments. That too is noted. Sometimes favored habitat found in a specific part of the state is included in the location range.

Bloom Time

The bloom times given follow the seasons. Few species flower during the winter months (December–March); those that do are typically farther south and may bloom year-round, as long as conditions allow. Species that are widespread and considered weedy tend to have longer bloom times. Of course, the species in question may be blooming in the Panhandle during the summer, but producing seed farther south. Spring (March–June) typically offers some of the best wildflower shows throughout the state. During 2015, because of ample rains the year prior, the Big Bend region had one of the best spring wildflower blooms in decades. Summer (June–September) brings heat, but it can also bring summer rains, especially in West Texas where the monsoon rains are a welcomed event. Many summer-only and early fall blooming species rely upon these summer rains. Fall (September–December) brings cooler temperatures, and rainfall in coastal and eastern regions. Again, many species will continue to bloom as long as freezing temperatures are kept at bay.

Listed bloom times are typical, but there are often exceptions. Bluebonnets have been noted in flower as late as October or as early as January, and many fall species can be triggered into blooming during the spring (although typically with shorter bloom time and less intensity). In some areas, such as the sky islands, plants bloom with regular consistency during the summer and fall months.

Plants are also opportunistic. When conditions are right, which typically means well-timed rains, vast numbers of wildflowers may appear in just a few days after a heavy rain. Perhaps the best example of this is the rain lily; populations with thousands of individuals flower after adequate rains.

Occurrence

Descriptions note whether a plant is common, locally common, uncommon, or rare. Common plants are typically found throughout Texas or in a large area of the state, in various habitats, and are easily seen along roadsides. Locally common plants, while they may be widespread and found in great numbers, are more selective in their habitat preference or soil type. Uncommon plants may be widespread throughout the state, or within a region, but occur in limited numbers due to habitat preference, soil type, or other factors. Rare plants have limited distribution and their numbers are usually low. However, a plant listed as rare in Texas may occur in vast numbers outside of Texas.

Description, Growth Cycle, Measurements, and Location Range

Plant descriptions cover basic characters. First, an overall description is given. This encapsulates the gestalt, or general first impressions of the plant, as well as its growth cycle and general size or height. Next, leaves are described, including leaf arrangement, size, shape, and margin morphology. In some cases, other identifying qualities are given such as whether or not the leaves are pilose, glaucous, or have stinging hairs. Floral, or inflorescence, descriptions mention size, shape, color, and any other features to assist in identification. Finally, additional qualities are described, depending upon the species in question. Often the fruits or seeds are described, as in some species these are very distinctive.

For those new to botany, the descriptive language can be intimidating. Some of the words may be unfamiliar to readers, and some are peculiar. Honestly, I still have to look up definitions from time to time. I have elected to use more botanical language than what is typically found in other field guides. As you learn these terms, you will see they accurately describe plant characters without having to define the term each time it is used.

Each plant's growth cycle is noted in the description as annual, biennial, perennial, or a combination of the three. The shortest lived are annuals. These plants germinate, flower, produce seed, and die within one year. Biennials have a two-year cycle. During their first year, they germinate and typically form a rosette of leaves and substantial roots. During the second year they flower, produce seed, and finally die. Perennials are long-lived. Many herbaceous plants will bloom and produce seed their first year. Some will continue this process for many years; others, like various *Penstemon* species, may be short-lived and die after a few years. Long-lived perennials may not bloom each year and instead wait until conditions are optimal for flower and seed production. Some plants will be perennial farther south, where freezing temperatures are uncommon, but considered an annual in northern areas of Texas.

Measurements are given in inches and feet. Ranges of height and length are not typically given; instead, the maximum sizes are listed. When the maximum measurement listed is much greater than a normal

specimen, it is noted. Plants can be variable in their morphology; environmental factors can have a direct effect on growth and should be taken into account. Generally, leaves on the lower portion of the stem will be larger than those above. Plants growing in shade tend to be taller and leggier, and have larger leaves than the same species growing in full sun. Although plants in shade may have fewer flowers, or the inflorescence may be stunted, there tends to be less influence from environmental factors on the size of the flowers.

A brief summary of where the species can be found is included. For simplicity, five general areas of Texas are used to describe where in the state a particular plant can be found. South Texas is generally south of San Antonio, west to Val Verde County, and east to Gonzalez County. North Texas consists of the Panhandle, south to Midland-Odessa. West Texas spans from El Paso to Val Verde County and north to Midland County. East Texas includes the lands east of I-35, south to the Coastal Bend. Central Texas includes the remainder. Of course, each of these geographic regions can cover several ecoregions, which is discussed in the next chapter.

Central Texas and East Texas have approximately 600 species represented in this field guide. West Texas, including the Chihuahuan Desert, has about 575 species. South Texas has around 450 species, and North Texas has approximately 300 representatives.

If the plant is widespread, general areas are given, such as "found throughout state, absent in northern Panhandle." These geographic areas are used for simplicity and because their names are more recognizable than some ecoregions. In a few cases, city or county names are used to designate ranges. When plants are not widespread and just found in one or two ecoregions, those areas are named. For uncommon or rare plants that are found in just a few counties, the county names are listed.

Putting It All Together

When it comes to identifying a plant, it is important to take as many factors as possible into account. Begin by observing every aspect of the plant. What color are the flowers and how many petals or lobes are present? Are the flowers radial or bilateral? Look at all the leaves—basal, lower and upper stem leaves, and bracts, if they are present. Are the leaves clasping? Sessile? Or do they have petioles? If petiolate, how long are the petioles and do they vary in length throughout the plant? What type of hairs are present? Are the hairs just found on the lower side of the leaf, or if along the stem, are they just at the nodes? Look at the sepals—how many are there and what is their length compared to the flower? Not all elements are needed to make a positive identification, and different attributes will be needed between families and genera.

In some cases, measurements are needed. If time and weather allow, this can be done in the field. If not, and you have permission to collect, get into the habit of taking herbarium (voucher) specimens. Record the date, location, associated species, habitat, soil type, and geology in a field notebook. The pressed plants can be accurately measured at home when you have more time. These specimens, with the associated data, can then be donated to a local herbarium.

There is no secret formula for identifying plants. However, I do believe that learning plant family characteristics will greatly increase your enjoyment of spotting wildflowers. It will take time and patience, but in the end, it is well worth it.

CLIMATE, GEOGRAPHY, AND ECOREGIONS

Elevation

As you traverse Texas from Beaumont, elevation 20 feet, to El Paso along I-10, the elevation increases gradually while precipitation decreases. Coastal Texas consists mostly of prairies, although much of it is now used for grazing and agriculture. Riparian areas follow the rivers, creeks, and drainages, opening into various bays along the coast.

As I-10 moves through San Antonio, you begin to notice a change in both vegetation and elevation. At this point the Edwards Plateau begins and elevation rises from roughly 700 feet in San Antonio proper to 1200 feet by the time you reach Boerne. Limestone hills, junipers, and oaks become the norm.

Traveling farther west, the vegetation become sparse and elevation increases to approximately 3000 feet in Fort Stockton, 4000 in Van Horn, decreasing slightly to 3800 feet in El Paso. North from Fort Stockton, the elevation increases to approximately 4800 feet by the time you reach the northwestern New Mexico border.

While these changes in elevation and other environmental factors have an effect on vegetation types and on what species may be present in any given area, it is not as dramatic as what you would see if traveling a much shorter distance. Nowhere else in Texas is this more evident than in Big Bend National Park.

At an elevation of approximately 1900 feet at the end of Hot Springs Road, you are surrounded by desert. Stark limestone dotted with diminutive cacti, prickly pear, ocotillo, and creosote dominates this area of the park. A mere 20 air miles into the Chisos Basin, you are at 7000 feet elevation and in an oak-juniper-pinyon pine woodland. Along the way, you would have passed through sotol stands, grasslands, and mixed shrublands, each with its own suite of plant species.

While elevation is not an issue throughout most of Texas, it is an issue in the sky islands. Certain species only occur above 5000 feet or so. Many species occur below this elevation. When warranted, the plant descriptions in this book will note whether a plant is found in low (below 3500 feet), mid (3500 to 5000 feet), or upper elevations (more than 5000 feet) of the Chihuahuan Desert.

Precipitation and Temperature

Average precipitation decreases as you move across the state from east to west, less so from south to north. Southeast Texas receives the most rainfall with up to 5 feet or more per year, far West Texas, less than 10 inches per year. Brownsville records 24 or more inches, while Lubbock obtains just under 20 inches.

The temperature differences are less dramatic and most noticeable during the

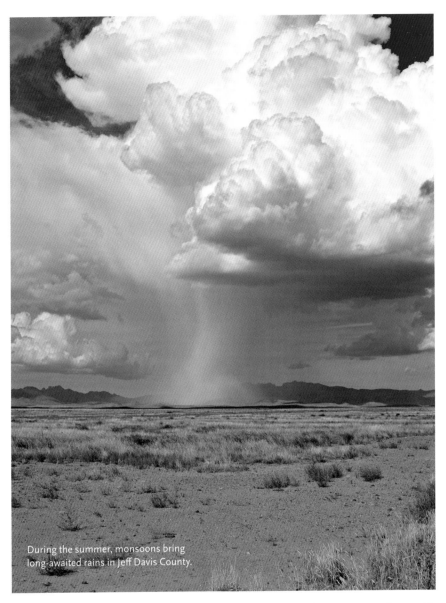

During the summer, monsoons bring long-awaited rains in Jeff Davis County.

winter months. The Panhandle, West Texas, and North-Central Texas typically see the coldest temperatures. Prolonged periods of freezing weather are common.

Both rainfall and temperature along with other environmental factors influence the plants found in any particular region.

Ecoregions

Ecoregions are large areas of land dictated by environmental and ecological parameters, such as soil types, geologic substrate, rainfall and other climate factors, and topography. On the whole, the community of plants within an ecoregion is definable, albeit in a generalized manner. Within the ecoregions different plant communities occur, again dependent upon environmental and ecological factors. It is hard to define the edges of ecoregions, as areas of integration occur and plant species can be mixed in these areas. Knowledge of the ecoregions and the plant species found within them will assist you in identifying plant species.

Plants span ecoregions. A plant common in coastal grassland may extend north into the Great Plains or farther. Texas is geographically in the middle of the United States. The southern tip is subtropical, the northern Panhandle easily sees temperatures drop below zero. The flora is diverse—nearly 6000 taxa, as stated, or about a quarter of the flora of the United States.

Several maps describe the ecoregions found in Texas. One of the most commonly used maps is Omernik's Level III ecoregion map (revised by US EPA in 2004) which divides Texas into 12 ecoregions. This map is further divided into Level IV ecoregions, giving a more detailed view of plant communities. The Nature Conservancy's map lists 11 ecoregions, combining areas such as the Panhandle into the Southern Short Grass Prairie and dividing eastern Texas into two ecoregions, with other differences evident as well. Gould's vegetation map lists 10 regions and probably has the most familiar names, such as the Trans-Pecos, East Texas Piney Woods,

and Post Oak Savanna. This book will use terms from each of these maps, although in the majority of cases, they are used as a general place reference and not as a definitive range limitation.

While terms like "ecoregions," "plant communities," or "vegetation types" may be new to some readers, anyone who has traveled throughout Texas has undoubtedly recognized ecoregions. In a quick weekend trip from Central Texas to Port Aransas, one crosses several ecoregions—the limestone hills of the Edwards Plateau, the clay soils of the Blackland Prairie, the sandy soils of the Post Oak Savanna, and finally the open grasslands of the Coastal Prairie, before arriving on the barrier islands. The following is a brief description of the ecoregions found in Texas. I will be using the ecoregion names in Gould's vegetative map and reference names from other maps.

Blackland Prairies
(Southern Tallgrass Prairie)

The Blackland Prairies have suffered greatly from overgrazing and agricultural use. They extend from the north-central portion of the state, from the Red River south to San Antonio, bordered on the west by the Edwards Plateau and the Cross Timbers, and on the east by the Post Oak Savanna, with an additional pocket from De Witt County northeast to Grimes County, which is surrounded by Post Oak Savanna. The mapping, and name, tends to remain the same on various maps.

The eastern portions average 40 inches of rain per year, while the western regions average about 30 inches annually. As the name suggests, this region is dominated by prairie species. The most common

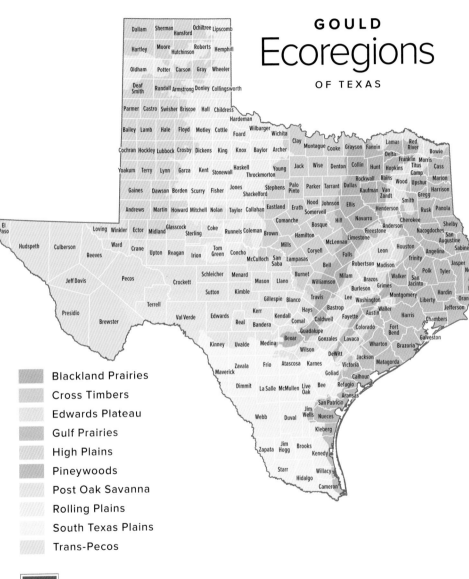

GOULD
Ecoregions
OF TEXAS

Dallam Sherman Hansford Ochiltree Lipscomb
Hartley Moore Hutchinson Roberts Hemphill
Oldham Potter Carson Gray Wheeler
Deaf Smith Randall Armstrong Donley Collingsworth
Parmer Castro Swisher Briscoe Hall Childress
Hardeman
Bailey Lamb Hale Floyd Motley Cottle Foard Wilbarger Wichita
Cochran Hockley Lubbock Crosby Dickens King Knox Baylor Archer Clay Montague Cooke Grayson Fannin Lamar Red River Bowie
Yoakum Terry Lynn Garza Kent Stonewall Haskell Throckmorton Young Jack Wise Denton Collin Hunt Hopkins Delta Franklin Titus Morris Camp Cass
Gaines Dawson Borden Scurry Fisher Jones Shackelford Stephens Palo Pinto Parker Tarrant Dallas Rockwall Kaufman Van Zandt Rains Wood Upshur Marion Harrison
Andrews Martin Howard Mitchell Nolan Taylor Callahan Eastland Erath Hood Johnson Somervell Ellis Henderson Smith Gregg Panola
Loving Winkler Ector Midland Glasscock Sterling Coke Runnels Coleman Brown Comanche Hamilton Bosque Hill Navarro Freestone Anderson Cherokee Rusk Shelby
El Paso Hudspeth Culberson Reeves Ward Crane Upton Reagan Irion Tom Green Concho McCulloch San Saba Mills Coryell McLennan Limestone Leon Houston Trinity Nacogdoches San Augustine Sabine Angelina
Jeff Davis Pecos Crockett Schleicher Menard Mason Llano Burnet Williamson Lampasas Bell Falls Robertson Madison Walker San Jacinto Polk Tyler Jasper Newton
Presidio Terrell Val Verde Edwards Sutton Kimble Gillespie Blanco Travis Lee Washington Grimes Montgomery Liberty Hardin Orange
Brewster Kinney Uvalde Medina Kerr Real Bandera Kendall Comal Hays Bastrop Caldwell Guadalupe Fayette Colorado Waller Austin Harris Fort Bend Chambers Jefferson
Zavala Frio Atascosa Karnes Bexar Wilson Gonzales Lavaca DeWitt Jackson Wharton Brazoria Galveston
Maverick Dimmit La Salle McMullen Live Oak Bee Goliad Victoria Matagorda Calhoun Refugio Aransas
Webb Duval Jim Wells Nueces San Patricio Kleberg
Zapata Jim Hogg Brooks Kenedy
Starr Hidalgo Willacy Cameron

	Blackland Prairies
	Cross Timbers
	Edwards Plateau
	Gulf Prairies
	High Plains
	Pineywoods
	Post Oak Savanna
	Rolling Plains
	South Texas Plains
	Trans-Pecos

TEXAS PARKS & WILDLIFE

grass species include little bluestem (*Schizachyrium scoparium*) and Indian grass (*Sorghastrum nutans*) in the uplands, and switchgrass (*Panicum virgatum*) in the riparian areas and drainages. Common herbaceous flowering plants include salvias, penstemons, and silphiums. Few intact areas remain. However, many of the plants can be found along county roadsides throughout the region, often occurring in vast numbers. In the Fayetteville area, between Highways 71 and 290, there are vast stands of *Echinacea atrorubens*, *Onosmodium bejariense*, and *Camassia scilloides* to be found.

Cross Timbers (Cross Timbers and Southern Tallgrass Prairie)

Covering more than 16.5 million acres, this ecoregion spans from the Red River south to the Edwards Plateau, bordered on the west by the Rolling Plains and to the east by the Blackland Prairie.

Canyons, escarpments, prairies, and rolling hills are present; the highest elevation is approximately 1500 feet in the southwest portion of the range, the lowest is approximately 500 feet on the eastern side. Rainfall is greatest to the east, averaging 35 inches per year, to 25 inches in the west. Low temperatures are often well below freezing; ice and snow storms are not uncommon.

Geology consists of sandstone and limestone, with varying soil types and depths throughout the region, allowing for a wide array of plant communities. Tree species include blackjack oak (*Quercus marilandica*), post oak (*Quercus stellata*), mesquite (*Prosopis glandulosa*), Ashe juniper (*Juniperus ashei*), and hackberry (*Celtis laevigata*). Dominant grasses include little bluestem

An open field of mixed wildflowers adjacent to a riparian area dominated by hardwood trees and shrubs.

(*Schizachyrium scoparium*) and sideoats grama (*Bouteloua curtipendula*). A wide array of herbaceous flowering plants can be found in this region, including the shooting star (*Dodecatheon meadia*) and false foxglove (*Agalinis densiflora*). The rare Glen Rose yucca (*Yucca necopina*) is found in the northern portion of this region, typically on limestone outcrops and in sandy grasslands.

Edwards Plateau

The Edwards Plateau, which covers about 24 million acres in the central portion of the state, is well known for its spring wildflower displays. It ranges from the Pecos River in the west, where it meets the Trans-Pecos, east to Williamson County, where it joins the Cross Timbers. To the south it is bordered by both the South Texas Plains and the Blackland Prairies. The northern border is confined by the High Plains, Rolling Plains, and partially by the Cross Timbers; there is an isolated pocket of the Edwards Plateau in Nolan and Taylor Counties. On some maps, the western edge is called the Stockton Plateau.

This area is also called the Hill Country; however, this general term covers a much larger area extending farther north. Spring-fed creeks are found throughout the region; deep limestone canyons, rivers, and lakes (reservoirs) are common. This junction of surrounding ecoregions has led to a rather high number of endemic, or isolated species throughout the region. Ashe juniper, perhaps the most common woody species found throughout the region, has increased over the years, along with other woody species, replacing savannas. Additional woody species include various species of oak, with live oak

Coreopsis basalis among granite outcrops in Mason County.

(*Quercus fusiformis*) being the most common; sycamores (*Platanus occidentalis*) and bald cypress (*Taxodium distichum*) border waterways. Pockets of madrones (*Arbutus xalapensis*), Texas pinyon pines (*Pinus remota*), bigtooth maples (*Acer grandidentatum*), and other oddities are found.

The Llano Uplift, an area of granite found in and around Llano County, gives us another suite of plants to view. The best area to see this formation is Enchanted Rock State Park, located between Fredericksburg and Llano. A quick hike reveals several species of ferns, more common farther west, growing along various cactus species in the shallow soils that form in low areas of the granite. Spring, late sum-

Bald cypress (*Taxodium distichum*) and ferns line Hamilton Creek in Travis County. These protected, water-rich canyons hold many species not found on the plateau above.

Dolan Falls on the Devil's River in Val Verde County. Spring-fed waters flow through limestone canyons.

mer, and fall are the best times for wild-flower viewing in the Edwards Plateau.

Gulf Prairies (Western Gulf Coastal Plain, Gulf Coast Prairies and Marshes)

This low-elevation region of Texas extends inland from the barrier islands, about 60 or so miles, and stretches from Browns-ville to Louisiana. In total, it covers about 9.5 million acres, with a high point of 150 feet in elevation. More than 1000 species of plants can be found in this region. On the southern end, species more common in Mexico (such as *Sabal mexicana*) and Central America occur.

The barrier islands provide us with dune systems, and clay flats to the inland side, which have species found in these areas alone. Many plants here, such as *Ipomoea pes-caprae* (beach morning glory), can be found throughout tropical regions of the globe; I've encountered the same species on the beaches of Guam.

Once inland, vast marshes and wet prairies occur. Occasionally, oak (*Quercus fusiformis*) groves can be found. Common grasses include species of *Bothriochloa*, *Paspalum*, and *Sporobolus*; eastern gamagrass (*Tripsacum dactyloides*); and switchgrass (*Panicum* species). Many rivers and creeks cut through the Gulf Prairies, and along these riparian areas various species of trees, *Sabal minor*, and other plants adapted to clay soils can be found. Due to overgrazing, farming, and fire suppression, woody species such as mesquite (*Prosopis glandulosa*) and huisache (*Acacia farnesiana*), and invasive species such as china-berry (*Melia azedarach*), Brazilian pepper (*Schinus terebinthifolius*), and Chinese tal-low (*Sapium sebiferum*) have increased and displaced our native flora.

Gayfeather and switchgrass on a coastal prairie in Harris County.

High Plains
(Southern Short Grass Prairie)

The High Plains covers the western portion of the Panhandle and spans 20 million acres of a mostly level plateau of clay soils over a caliche layer. It is bordered on the east by the Rolling Plains, which also divides the northern portion along the Canadian River drainage. To the south it is bordered by the Edwards Plateau and Trans-Pecos.

There is little change in elevation, mostly ranging between 3000 and 4000 feet. This is the coldest area of Texas, with the northern portion recording temperatures at or below 0 degrees Fahrenheit during winter; snow and ice storms are not uncommon. Rainfall is low as well, ranging from 12 inches per year in the west to 25 inches annually in the east.

Primarily grasslands, this region is also called the Southern Short Grass Prairie; other non-technical names for this region include the Llano Estacado and the Staked Plains. It was said the area was so lacking in trees and other landmarks that stakes were placed in the ground in order to assist in navigating across a rather flat landscape. Other sources state it was so named because a person would have to put a stake in the ground to secure a horse, as there were no trees. Dominant grasses included buffalo grass (*Bouteloua dactyloides*) and blue grama (*B. gracilis*). Various habitats include playas, grasslands, canyonlands, and sandhills. Mesquite (*Prosopis glandulosa*) and yucca (*Yucca glauca*) often dominate lands that were once grasslands. To the south, Havard's oak (*Quercus havardii*) dominates the dune systems along with other sand-loving species. In canyons and along rivers, you can find cottonwoods, soapberries, and a few species of oaks. This area is rich in history; farming and ranching forever changed the landscape.

The coastal dunes host many species found only along the barrier islands, including South Padre Island, shown here.

Ipomoea leptophylla is common during spring in open areas of the High Plains.

Pineywoods
(West Gulf Coast Coastal Plain,
Upper Western Gulf Coastal Plain)

This is the easternmost ecoregion found in Texas. It is bordered on the east by Louisiana, to the west by the Post Oak Savanna, and to the south by the Gulf Prairies.

Maximum elevation reaches 500 feet and soils are mostly sandy and acidic. Average rainfall can be more than 50 inches per year. The topography is generally rolling hills; lowlands include swamps, bogs, and marshes.

Pine, including longleaf pine (*Pinus palustris*), and hardwood forests dominate, with many woody understory species.

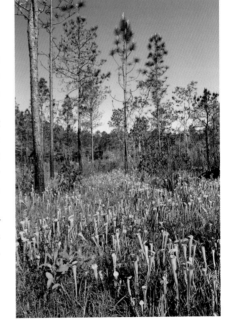

Hillside seepage bog with *Sarracenia alata* in Newton County.

Bracken fern (*Pteridium aquilinum* var. *pseudocaudatum*) dominates the understory in this pine forest in Angelina County.

Cow lily (*Nuphar advena*) and bald cypress (*Taxodium distichum*) at Caddo Lake in Marion County.

Blueberries (*Vaccinium* species) grow wild, as do native *Rhododendron* species and both species of pawpaw (*Asimina*). Here you will find orchids, pitcher plants, and numerous rare plants, such as *Hibiscus dasycalyx*, *Yucca cernua* (which has a global distribution of two counties), and *Trillium texanum*, the Texas trillium. Perhaps the area with the greatest plant diversity in East Texas is the Big Thicket, located in the southern region of East Texas. A visit to the Big Thicket National Preserve reveals numerous plant species found nowhere else in Texas. The northern portion tends to be drier but still harbors numerous rare species and more plants not found elsewhere in the state. Caddo Lake, which spans the Texas-Louisiana border in Northeast Texas, offers bald cypress swamps, acres of lilies and cow-lilies, and other aquatics such as American featherfoil (*Hottonia inflata*).

The flora of the Pineywoods is unique in Texas and more similar to the flora of states farther east.

Post Oak Savanna

The Post Oak Savanna covers 8.5 million acres of rolling hills extending from the Oklahoma border southwest to the South Texas Plains. It is bordered on the west by the Blackland Prairie and the Edwards Plateau, to the east by the Pineywoods and the south Gulf Prairies.

Annual rainfall averages 35 to 45 inches throughout the region, with higher averages to the east. A wide variety of hardwood trees are found, including several species of oaks, elms, and, in the Bastrop area, loblolly pine (*Pinus taeda*). In the open savannas, grasses and forbs dominate; the most common grass is little bluestem. As with other areas of Texas, ranching and

Nymphaea odorata covers the surface of this man-made pond in Tyler County.

agriculture, as well as fire suppression, have allowed woody species to encroach on the once-open savannas.

Rolling Plains

The Rolling Plains covers the eastern portion of the Panhandle, bordered to the west by the High Plains, to the south by the Edwards Plateau, and to the east by the Cross Timbers.

Mostly rolling hills, with occasional steep terrain, it is dissected by various river and creek valleys. Elevation ranges from 800 to 3000 feet, the lower portions occurring in the east. Rainfall is greatest in the east, at 30 inches per year; the west gets only 22 inches annually. Most rain events happen in the spring and late summer. Much of the original tall grasslands is now gone, invaded by short grasses and mesquite, which

are typical in overgrazed areas. Woody species still dominate lowlands, valleys, and riparian areas, as well as rocky hilltops. Here as in other areas of the state, ranching, farming, and fire suppression have had a negative impact on the flora.

South Texas Plains
(Southern Texas Plains, Tamaulipan Thornscrub, Rio Grande Plains)

This is an area south of the Edwards Plateau, bordered on the east by the Gulf Prairies and the southern ends of the Blackland Prairie and Post Oak Savanna; the western and southern border is the Rio Grande. It covers approximately 20 million acres of flat to rolling hills; the highest elevation is 1000 feet.

Rainfall averages 16 inches a year in the west and up to 35 inches annually in

An overgrazed field in the southern region of the Rolling Plains. Lacking in grasses, the area is now dominated by mesquite and a host of wildflowers.

the eastern portion; most of the rain falls during late spring and early summer. The southern part of the region rarely experiences freezing temperatures, and citrus groves can be found in the lower valley. The dominant woody species include mesquite (*Prosopis glandulosa*), various species of *Acacia*, and a myriad of other small, thorny trees and shrubs.

This area, especially the southern region, is rich in cacti and holds the rare star cactus, *Astrophytum asterias*. Numerous other rare species occur here; some are isolated to the inland sand sheets and others, such as the longflower tuberose (*Manfreda longiflora*), are farther south in the gypseous soils of Starr and Hidalgo Counties.

Farming, ranching, and fire suppression have adversely affected flora in the South Texas Plains. Woody vegetation has increased in some places, while other areas of thorn scrub have been removed for agriculture. Lands close to the Rio Grande have suffered greatly due to agricultural practices. The once dominant *Sabal mexicana*, which used to cover an estimated 40,000 acres along the mouth of the river and farther upstream, is now rare. In fact, when the Rio Grande was first named, it was called El Rio de las Palmas (river of palms). The palm, and its associated species, can still be found in protected areas south of Brownsville and farther upstream around Quemado, with isolated plants along the banks of the river and within resacas. Invasive species are numerous. The most aggressive species along the Rio Grande are the giant cane (*Arundo donax*) and salt cedar (*Tamarisk* species), which cover the banks of the river and other

Cenizo (*Leucophyllum frutescens*) in full bloom during the summer of 2013 in Val Verde County. In this area, three ecoregions merge: South Texas Plains, Edwards Plateau, and the Chihuahuan Desert.

waterways. Introduced grasses such as buffelgrass (*Pennisetum ciliare*), ubiquitous and often a seemingly endless monoculture in overgrazed areas, and King Ranch bluestem (*Bothriochloa ischaemum* var. *songarica*) often outcompete low-growing cacti and herbaceous plants, decreasing diversity. Many plants of the South Texas Plains are unique to the region. With spring rains, late spring and early summer are ideal times for wildflower viewing.

Trans-Pecos (Chihuahuan Desert)

The Trans-Pecos region is perhaps the most breathtaking area of Texas. This area is also referred to as the Chihuahuan Desert, although the Chihuahuan Desert extends farther east, technically. The Trans-Pecos is a typical basin-range system—there is vast elevation change and a myriad of vegetation types; in fact, it is the most botanically diverse area of Texas. The indicator species for this ecoregion is *Agave lechuguilla*; however, other species such as *Fouquieria splendens* and *Larrea tridentata* are often used. There are various maps that give different boundaries for the Chihuahuan Desert ecoregion, but in Texas it generally spans the entire area west of the Pecos River, and covers a small portion east of the Pecos from Loving south into Val Verde County. The underlying substrate and soil type vary throughout the region. Limestone and igneous soils are common, as are gypseous soils. Rainfall averages around 13 inches per year, with most of the precipitation falling during the summer monsoons.

The sky islands give rise to stands of *Cupressus arizonica* (Arizona cypress),

Spanish moss (*Tillandsia usneoides*) hangs from the overstory trees in Santa Ana National Wildlife Refuge in Hidalgo County.

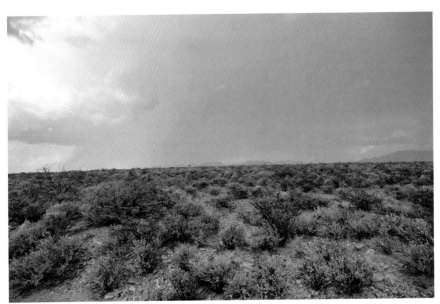

Open desert shrublands. Mariola (*Parthenium incanum*), creosote (*Larrea tridentata*), mesquite (*Prosopis glandulosa*), and acacia dominate lowlands between mountain ranges in the Trans-Pecos.

A view of the Chisos Basin. The upper elevations of the sky islands in West Texas offer oak-pine-juniper woodlands and numerous species not found in the surrounding basins.

Pinus ponderosa (ponderosa pine), and the occasional remnant colonies of *Populus tremuloides* (aspen). Pinyon-oak-juniper woodlands dominate upper elevations, mixed grass and shrublands flourish at mid elevations, and open, sparse desert vegetation populates lower elevations. In these lower elevations are vast stands of ocotillo, creosote, and other shrubby plants. Many rare species can be found throughout this region, whether in the higher elevations of the sky islands, or in the lower elevations, where species may be dependent on a particular soil or substrate.

VIEWING WILDFLOWERS

No matter where you live in Texas, it is always a short trip to find wildflowers, as there are numerous national, state, and local lands to visit. However, for many (myself included), it is more about the route than the destination.

The state is blessed with miles upon miles of roads, some of which are less traveled than others. Along these byways, if you slow down and occasionally stop, you can find a wide variety of plants between the pavement and the fence line.

To cover all of Texas's public and private lands is not the intent of this book. Plenty of websites and other guides will help you find your way. You do not need to travel far to find wildflowers. Even in urban areas, plants can grow in harsh environments—often in places you wish they would not, such as your garden.

Parks and Public Places

Texas is primarily a privately owned state. What does that mean? Less than 10 per-

Pinto Canyon Road in Presidio County cuts through grasslands in the upper portion before entering canyons and lower desert. Drives like this offer opportunities to view a vast array of plants.

cent of land in the state is available to the public; the rest is in private ownership. If you do not have permission from the land owner to access property, do not enter. Public lands include national, state, and local parks; wildlife management areas; recreational areas; national seashores, grasslands, and forests; and the like. Often, a fee is required for entry to public lands.

When visiting these areas, follow the rules set forth by each institution, as they tend to vary between sites and agencies. Some allow overnight camping, others do not. Some have staffed facilities, others do not (or staff may be seasonal).

Do your research and plan ahead. Many parks and recreational areas provide species lists, either online or onsite. I've found these to be valuable resources when visiting new areas.

Safety

It would be impossible to cover all the safety issues that can arise when exploring nature. Concerns in swampy areas of East Texas will be vastly different from those in the arid mountains of West Texas. The best and simplest advice is to be aware of your surroundings and your own limitations.

Whether you pull off on the side of the road or hike a trail in a park, each situation has its own challenges that may lead to injury or discomfort. Keep a small first aid kit with you, one that can easily fit in the glove compartment or under the seat of your vehicle, and that can be tossed into a small pack for light hiking.

For overnight backpacking trips, find a first-aid kit that best suits your needs and alter it with any additional medications. It is highly advisable to take a course in first aid, CPR, or even wilderness first aid. Additionally, just as you have a first aid kit for yourself, you should have one for your vehicle as well. This may include a tire patch kit, extra belts, jumper cables, extra oil, water, and so on. You should know where your car jack is and how to use it.

If you are taking a remote route or one you do not usually travel, let someone else know where you are going and how long you plan to be gone. Remember, not every place you visit will have cell phone service or a coffee shop. There are many areas within the state that are considered remote, and it may be several hours until another vehicle happens to pass your way.

Photography

Whether you use the camera on your phone or a digital SLR or something in between, a few basic tips may help when later relying upon photographs to identify a plant. Take clear, close-up photographs of the plant's flowers, leaves, and stems as well as an image of overall habit. If the plant is in fruit, a photo can be helpful. Take images from different angles, including the underside of leaves and the back and side of the flowers.

Balanced lighting is also helpful. If it is very sunny, try to apply shade to the subject. Many camera shops sell sun shades for such purposes, but a large hat, or even the shade of another person, can help. If it is too shady, learn how to use the flash on your camera.

Additionally, it is helpful to keep a record of where you are. This is especially important if you happen to stop several times along the road or visit many sites in one day. I've worked with people who write the location down in their field journal and take a photograph of the journal prior to photographing at each stop. Many cameras now come with GPS; if you have this option, make sure it is always enabled.

Double-check your images. Zoom in to check clarity and focus. This is best done in the shade. If you are using a camera that uses memory cards, keep an extra card with you. Do not delete images in the field. It is best to wait until you have downloaded and viewed the photographs on your computer.

Additional Resources

The bibliography in the back of this book, as well as the websites and databases mentioned earlier, are valuable resources when identifying plants. At one point, I had to document my botanical library, one that had been building for quite some time. For Texas alone, I had acquired more than 100 books. Many are local field guides. Some are old with out-of-date nomenclature, but of great historical value. Several are often used, most are not, but all have their own importance. I referenced quite a few while writing this book, including many books that cover the flora of the neighboring states or regions.

When you come across a plant you do not know, you may think about what it is not. You may recognize the plant as a dicot, ruling out monocots, and if you know it is not in the Asteraceae, Fabaceae, or Lamiaceae, all very large families, you've just decreased the unknowns drastically. Eventually, through elimination, the unknown always turns into a known, and it is always the last place you look. The next time you come across the same or similar species,

you will know where to begin, building your own internal reference library. Each time you read through several descriptions you are learning the flora, whether you realize it or not, a little bit each time. Of course, you could just ask someone, or post an image on the internet for others to tell you, but what fun is that?

Other resources include local and online herbariums. Online herbaria now provide images of the species and scanned images of specimens, as well as descriptions and locations. Writing this book would not have been possible without these last two resources. I was able to peruse herbaria (swbiodiversity.org) throughout the United States and Mexico without having to leave the comfort of my home office. That said, you should be wary of online information. Double- and triple-check different reputable websites and databases. I have encountered numerous errors, both in descriptions and in images online. Some of these were simply misidentifications; others were errors in images that were uploaded to databases under the wrong species name.

And finally, if learning about your local flora is indeed a passion, consider joining your local chapter of the Native Plant Society of Texas (npsot.org), the Texas Master Naturalist program (txmn.org), or other like-minded organizations. These groups offer field trips (usually led by a knowledgeable botanist or biologist), presentations, and volunteer opportunities, all of which can help you discover more about the local flora and fauna.

PLANT FAMILIES

Two groups of flowering plants are included in this book, the monocotyledons and the dicotyledons. Monocotyledons, or monocots, have one leaf when they germinate, while the dicotyledons, or dicots, have 2. Monocots have foliage with parallel venation, and their floral parts are in multiples of 3. Dicots have foliage venation other than parallel and the number of their floral parts varies.

This basic but essential division is the first step in identifying plants. The ability to eliminate many families with just a few characters will greatly reduce the time spent trying to identify an unknown species.

The next step is knowing characteristics of plant families. This takes time and effort, but eventually you will be able to walk through a field and recognize a malvaceous flower from several feet away. Of course, by looking at plants, or images, over and over, you can come to the same conclusion, but the ability to explain to someone else which characters led you to that conclusion will be a great asset.

The following are brief descriptions of the plant families found in this book. Since plant families can span states, countries, and continents, only the relevant characters that apply to the plants covered in this book are mentioned.

Monocots

ALISMATACEAE—WATER-PLANTAIN FAMILY. A global family of 11 genera and about 80 species of aquatic herbaceous plants, mostly in tropical and subtropical regions, with a number of species extending into temperate regions. Three genera are found in Texas, 2 are included here: *Echinodorus* with 2 species, *Sagittaria* with 10. *Echinodorus* species have burlike fruiting heads, *Sagittaria* species do not. Within genus *Sagittaria*, leaf morphology can be used to identify some species, but for the others, flower morphology will be needed. Aquatic or marginal herbaceous annuals or perennials, stoloniferous or with corms. Leaves basal, simple, and with long petioles, blades usually large. Flowers in terminal, leafless scapes, inflorescence usually a raceme, flowers actinomorphic, with 3 petals and 3 sepals. Ovaries are superior, fruits are nutlets, combined into a single, congested, rounded head.

AMARYLLIDACEAE—AMARYLLIS FAMILY. A family of bulb-producing herbaceous plants in approximately 1600 genera, widely distributed, primarily in tropical and subtropical regions. This family contains many economically important ornamentals and vegetables. Texas has many representative genera, several of which are described here. Herbaceous, bulbous perennials with simple, linear or grasslike or straplike basal leaves, margins entire. Flowers on leafless scapes, solitary or in umbels, actinomorphic, with 6 tepals. Ovaries are superior (*Allium*) or inferior, fruits are dry capsules.

ARACEAE—ARUM FAMILY. A family of 3200 species in 110 genera of global distribution, the majority of species in tropical and subtropical regions. This diverse group includes large, terrestrial plants such as taro (*Colocasia*), which is widely used as food, various ornamentals, and the aquatic duckweeds (*Lemna, Wolffia*), which are the world's smallest flowering plants. Texas has many representative genera, several of which are covered in this book. Herbaceous terrestrial or floating aquatic perennials. Leaves variable, simple or compound, basal with long petioles, or a floating rosette. Flowers in a spadix, surrounded by a spathe or not (*Orontium*), numerous or solitary (*Pistia*). Ovaries are superior or inferior, fruits are berries or utricles (*Orontium*).

ASPARAGACEAE—ASPARAGUS FAMILY. Once a small family, now large with 114 genera and approximately 2900 species distributed globally. It includes many members formerly in the Liliaceae and all members of the Agavaceae. Representative genera in Texas include *Agave, Dasylirion,* and *Yucca,* as well as numerous herbaceous plants, many of which are described here. Herbaceous perennials, some semisucculent or with fleshy leaves. Leaves simple, sometimes grasslike, margins entire; in some genera, all leaves are basal. Flowers actinomorphic, with 6 tepals. Ovaries are superior or inferior, fruits are capsules or berries.

BROMELIACEAE—BROMELIAD FAMILY, PINEAPPLE FAMILY. A family of 56 genera and approximately 2600 species, mostly found in the Americas, with one species in western Africa. Texas has 2 genera: the terrestrial *Hechtia* and the epiphytic *Tillandsia*. Only the latter is represented here. Herbaceous, epiphytic perennials. Leaves silvery gray, simple, spirally arranged. Flowers solitary and sessile (*Tillandsia usneoides*) or few to numerous on a slender scape, actinomorphic. Ovaries are superior, fruits are capsules.

COLCHICACEAE—COLCHICUM FAMILY. A family of 18 genera and approximately 275 species, distributed mostly outside of the Americas. The sole representative in Texas is the genus *Uvularia*. Herbaceous, rhizomatous perennial. Leaves alternate, simple, perfoliate. Flowers in terminal inflorescences, bell-shaped, actinomorphic with 6 tepals. Ovaries are superior, fruits are capsules.

COMMELINACEAE—SPIDERWORT FAMILY. A family of 40 genera and approximately 650 species with distribution primarily in subtropical and tropical regions. This family is well represented in Texas and includes genera *Commelina, Tinantia,* and *Tradescantia*. Herbaceous perennials, often semisucculent or fleshy. Leaves simple, alternate, margins entire. Flowers in terminal or axillary cymes, actinomorphic or zygomorphic (*Tinantia*), with 3 sepals and 3 petals. Ovaries are superior, fruits are capsules.

HYDROCHARITACEAE—TAPE-GRASS FAMILY, FROG-BIT FAMILY. Freshwater and salt-water aquatics in 17 genera and approximately 76 species that are widely distributed. Most of the marine species are found in the Indian and Pacific Oceans, while the freshwater species are mainly in the Northern Hemisphere.

This family includes many popular aquarium plants, such as hydrilla, which has been introduced to Texas waterways. Several genera are found in Texas, but only *Limnobium* is included here. Herbaceous, aquatic, stoloniferous aquatic perennial. Leaves simple, basal only, margins entire, petiolate. Flowers on separate scapes, 3 sepals, 3 petals, actinomorphic. Ovaries are inferior, fruits are berrylike.

HYPOXIDACEAE—STAR-GRASS FAMILY. A small family of 9 genera and approximately 150 species, primarily in tropical and subtropical regions in the Southern Hemisphere, with a few species found in the Northern Hemisphere. *Hypoxis* is the sole genus in Texas and is represented here by 2 species. Herbaceous perennial with grasslike, simple leaves. Flowers in terminal racemes or umbels at the end of a short scape, actinomorphic, 6 tepals, yellow. Ovaries are inferior, fruits are capsules.

IRIDACEAE—IRIS FAMILY. A family of 70 genera and approximately 2000 species, most of them found in tropical Central and South America and Africa. The Iridaceae is composed of primarily terrestrial perennials, although a few *Iris* species are found in wet soils, often on banks, occasionally slightly submersed. Texas has several genera, 5 of which are covered here. Herbaceous perennials, rhizomatous or from bulbs or corms, with simple, grasslike or straplike leaves. Flowers actinomorphic with 3 petals and 3 sepals, small, or large and showy, terminal, solitary or numerous. Ovaries are inferior, fruits are capsules.

LILIACEAE—LILY FAMILY. A family mostly of the Northern Hemisphere, with approximately 18 genera and 750 species, many ornamental. Included here are genera *Erythronium* and *Lilium*. Herbaceous, bulbous perennials. Leaves simple with entire margins, basal or whorled. Flowers solitary on scapes or in umbels, actinomorphic, floral parts in multiples of 3. Ovaries are superior, fruits are capsules.

MAYACACEAE—BOG-MOSS FAMILY. A monotypic family with 6 species found mostly in the Americas and one found in southern Africa. The single U.S. species, *Mayaca fluviatilis*, occurs in East Texas. Herbaceous aquatic or terrestrial perennial. Leaves simple, spirally arranged, margins entire. Flowers solitary, actinomorphic, occurring in leaf axils. Ovaries are superior, fruits are capsules.

MELANTHIACEAE—DEATH CAMUS FAMILY. A family of 16 genera and approximately 170 species with distribution primarily in the Northern Hemisphere, represented here by 3 genera: *Schoenocaulon*, *Toxicoscordion*, and *Trillium*. Herbaceous, rhizomatous or bulbous perennials. Leaves simple, spirally arranged, margins entire. Flowers in racemes or solitary (*Trillium*), actinomorphic, with 3 sepals and 3 petals. Ovaries are superior, fruits are capsules.

NARTHECIACEAE—BOG ASPHODEL FAMILY. A small family of 5 genera and 36 species distributed in eastern North America, western Europe, and Southeast Asia. Three genera occur in the United States; one, *Aletris*, is found in Texas. Herbaceous perennial. Leaves simple, arranged in a rosette, margins entire. Flowers small, yellow, numerous, in a terminal spike, actinomorphic, floral parts in multiples of 3. Ovaries are superior, fruits are capsules.

ORCHIDACEAE—ORCHID FAMILY. The world's largest flowering plant family has 800 genera and approximately 20,000 species, with global distribution in a variety of habitats. Vast morphological diversity is found in this family, but the flowers are zygomorphic, often showy and modified, and there are thousands of dustlike seeds. Numerous genera are found throughout Texas, with the majority of species in East Texas. Herbaceous perennials, primarily terrestrial, with one semiaquatic species and many saprophytes. Roots enlarged, tuberous, in some species rhizomatous. Leaves absent or single or many, simple, varying from slender and grasslike to oval or round, margins entire. Flowers zygomorphic, with 3 petals and 3 sepals, in some cases highly modified. Ovaries are inferior, fruits are capsules, seeds are tiny (often less than ½ millimeter long) with a honeycomb outer shell that aids in wind dispersal and in strength.

PONTEDERIACEAE—PICKEREL-WEED FAMILY. A small family of freshwater aquatics with 9 genera and 33 species, mainly found in tropical and subtropical regions. Texas has 3 representative genera: *Eichhornia*, an introduced invasive, and *Pontederia* and *Heteranthera*, 2 native genera which are both included here. *Heteranthera* has one perennial species; the others are annual and often occur in ephemeral pools in remote locations. Their seeds are small and are often transported when they become trapped in mud on the feet of birds. Aquatic herbaceous annuals or perennials, rooted or floating. Leaves simple, basal or alternate, grasslike or broad, petiolate or sessile. Flowers solitary to numerous on spikes, actinomorphic or zygomorphic, floral parts in multiples of 3. Ovaries are superior, fruits are capsules.

TOFIELDIACEAE—FALSE ASPHODEL FAMILY. A small family, primarily found in the Northern Hemisphere, with 4 genera and 29 species. *Triantha racemosa*, the single species in Texas, is rare in the Big Thicket. Herbaceous, rhizomatous perennial with simple, grasslike leaves. Flowers in racemes, actinomorphic, with 6 tepals. Ovaries are superior, fruits are capsules.

XANTHORRHOEACEAE—DAYLILY FAMILY, ALOE FAMILY, GRASS-TREE FAMILY. A family of 40 genera and 900 species found throughout the tropics and temperate regions and encompassing the Asphodelaceae, which includes the aloes; the Hemerocallidaceae, daylilies; and the original family, Xanthorrhoeaceae, which is from Australia. Members of this expanded family are used as ornamentals and have escaped cultivation. There are no native species in North America. Occasionally aloes will escape and persist in far southern Texas. One representative of the family is included here; it is an introduced ornamental. Herbaceous, rhizomatous perennial with simple, grasslike leaves. Flowers in terminal cymes, usually 2 per scape, large, showy, actinomorphic. Ovaries are superior, fruits are capsules.

Dicots

ACANTHACEAE—ACANTHUS FAMILY. Of the 66 species within 13 genera, the species that occur in Texas are primarily terrestrial, with a few growing in shallow waters or on the banks of waterways and bodies of water. They are widespread throughout the state, occurring in each ecoregion. In addition to the herbaceous plants covered in this book, there are a few woody shrubs in western Texas, primarily in the Chihuahuan Desert. Leaves are simple, opposite, margins usually entire or toothed; leaf surfaces can be densely pubescent, glandular, or smooth. The flowers are variable, but all are bilabiate. In *Ruellia*, the flowers are 5-petaled and lobed, with a long tube; in the other genera the tube is reduced and the lobes, either 2 or 4, are deeply divided. Fruits are dehiscent, flattened capsules, usually 2-seeded.

AIZOACEAE—ICEPLANT FAMILY. A small family of 12 genera spread throughout the world and represented in Texas by 2 genera, *Sesuvium* and *Trianthema*, both included here. Of the species described here, pantropical *S. portulacastrum* is the most common and can be found along the barrier islands from Mexico to Louisiana. Succulent or semisucculent annuals or perennials, typically found along coastal areas or in areas with saline soils. Plants are low growing, usually prostrate or ascending. Leaves simple, opposite, with entire margins and glabrous surfaces. Flowers actinomorphic, with 5 tepals, pink to bluish purple.

AMARANTHACEAE—AMARANTH FAMILY. The family is large with 170 genera or so, since the recent inclusion of the Chenopodiaceae (goosefoot family). While economically important genera belong to the family, many of the plants are weedy and found in disturbed areas. Among the species represented in Texas,

Gomphrena haageana is by far the showiest, *Salsola tragus*, tumbleweed, the most infamous. Herbaceous annuals to shrubby perennials. Leaves opposite or alternate, simple, with various margins; in some cases succulent or semisucculent. Flowers either solitary or in clustered cymes or spikes, actinomorphic, with male and female flowers on separate plants or on the same plant, small, often not showy aside from the spiked inflorescences of *Gomphrena*.

APIACEAE—CARROT FAMILY. A large family with more than 400 genera that include economically important species such as the wild carrot (*Daucus carota*) and numerous herbs and spices. Many of the Old World species have been introduced and have become quite weedy in areas. In Texas, they are widespread, occurring throughout the state and well represented in each region. Often, fruit morphology is helpful when identifying species; for example, in some species the fruit are flattened, in others they may be round or ovoid. Herbaceous annuals, biennials, or perennials. Leaves highly dissected, often fanlike, or prickly (*Eryngium*), or simple (*Centella*, *Hydrocotyle*), mostly alternate, occasionally opposite. Flowers are small, 5-petaled, and in umbels, compound umbels, or crowded spikelike heads (*Eryngium*). Ovaries are inferior, fruits are schizocarps.

APOCYNACEAE—DOGBANE FAMILY. Recently, the Asclepidiaceae was moved into the Apocynaceae, which now has about 400 genera worldwide. Several genera are common in Texas. *Asclepias*, the most common of these, can be found in every region; in some cases, 5 or more species can be found in a single county. Perennial herbaceous to semishrubby plants or prostrate to high-climbing, twining vines with milky sap. The leaves are simple, opposite, occasionally whorled in *Asclepias*, margins are generally entire or wavy. Flowers are actinomorphic, with floral parts in multiples of 5, large and showy (*Telosiphonia*) or small (*Cynanchum*), funnel-shaped, bell-shaped, or rotate. Ovaries are superior, fruits are dehiscent follicles with flattened seeds attached to a silky coma, which aids in wind dispersal.

APODANTHACEAE—STEM-SUCKER FAMILY. A small family consisting of 2 or 3 genera worldwide. Here in Texas it is represented by one species, *Pilostyles thurberi*. The plants are stem parasites on various semiwoody species in the Fabaceae and are found in western Texas. Only the flowers are visible outside the host plant; flowers are small with reddish brown scales on the exterior and with creamy interiors, urn-shaped, often resembling a fungus or insect eggs.

ARISTOLOCHIACEAE—BIRTHWORT FAMILY, DUTCHMAN'S PIPE FAMILY, ARISTOLOCHIA FAMILY. A small family with up to 12 genera worldwide, represented by *Aristolochia* in Texas. This is a primitive family, with highly modified, tubular flowers. In addition to their unusual flower morphology and anatomy, these species are pollinated by small saprophagous flies of various families that are attracted to the flowers' scent, which is akin to decaying organic matter. The flies, once inside, are trapped for a day or so, then allowed to escape, hopefully covered in pollen, after the fine hairs that line the inside of the calyx

and tube have deteriorated. Prostrate to erect herbaceous perennials or vining perennials, with alternate, simple leaves. The flowers are strongly zygomorphic; instead of petals they have a highly modified calyx, consisting of 1) a limb, the opening, which is covered in fine hairs; 2) a tube; 3) a utricle, which holds the stamens and pistil (gynostemium); and 4) an ovary. Fruits are 3-chambered capsules, with triangular black seeds.

ASTERACEAE—COMPOSITE FAMILY, SUNFLOWER FAMILY. This is the largest dicot family with more than 1600 genera worldwide. The family is further divided into subfamilies, and within subfamilies, tribes. In Texas, it is represented by numerous and diverse genera that include herbaceous annuals and perennials, woody shrubs, and vines. It is an easy family to recognize, but species identification can be a challenge. Leaves are variable—alternate, opposite, or rarely whorled—simple (rarely compound) and can be variously lobed. The inflorescences are heads, or capitulums, with radial symmetry, and usually consist of numerous florets of different types. Perhaps the most common is the radiate head, which consists of an outer ring of ray florets and numerous disc florets (*Helianthus* and many other genera). Other combinations of florets occur, such as a lack of disc florets with fertile ray, or ligulate, florets, or simply with just disc florets. Fruits vary in morphology, but all are achenes; some are large and angled, others slender and long with a modified pappus (which aids in dispersal), still others are flat (*Verbesina*).

BERBERIDACEAE—BARBERRY FAMILY.
A small family with 2 native representative genera in Texas: *Mahonia*, a woody shrub, and *Podophyllum*, an herbaceous perennial. Only the latter is included in this book. Herbaceous, rhizomatous perennial with simple, alternate leaves. Flowers actinomorphic, solitary or in panicles, floral parts in multiples of 4 or 6. The fruit is a fleshy berry with numerous seeds.

BIXACEAE—ACHIOTE FAMILY. A very small family with one representative genus in the United States, *Amoreuxia*. An herbaceous perennial from woody rootstock. Leaves opposite, palmately lobed, stipules are present. Flowers large, showy, 5-petaled, slightly zygomorphic, stamens numerous. The fruit is a large, ovate multichambered capsule.

BORAGINACEAE—BORAGE FAMILY.
A large, well-known family with about 150 genera worldwide. In Texas, there is a higher concentration of this family in West and South Texas. Usually herbaceous annuals or perennials, with one woody species, *Cordia boissieri*, a small tree which occurs in far southern Texas. The one succulent, glabrous species, *Heliotropium curassavicum*, is found on saline soils along the coast or on inland salt flats and gypseous soils. Plants in this family typically have alternate leaves, occasionally opposite below, stems and leaves are covered with stiff hairs (with one exception), and leaf margins are usually entire. Flowers are in terminal scorpioid cymes, 5-lobed, with fused petals, actinomorphic, usually white, white with yellow centers, yellow, or pale blue.

BRASSICACEAE—MUSTARD FAMILY.
This well-known family has about 340 species worldwide and includes many familiar culinary species. Representative genera include *Cardamine*, *Physaria*, and *Streptanthus*. The distinctive fruits and flower structure are key characters in identifying this family in the field. In Texas, the Brassicaceae are annual to perennial herbaceous plants with simple, alternate leaves and entire to variously lobed margins. One introduced species has compound leaves (*Nasturtium officinale*). Flowers are usually in a raceme or corymb and have 4 petals, 4 sepals, and 6 stamens. Yellow and white flowers dominate; however, blue, orange, and purple flowers occur frequently in some genera. The fruit is a siliqua or silicula; the only difference between the two is the relative length of the fruit. Fruit morphology varies from long and slender to flat and heart-shaped or globose.

CABOMBACEAE—WATER-SHIELD FAMILY.
A small family of 2 genera and 6 species found in temperate and tropical areas. Both genera are found in Texas, each with one species. A single species, *Brasenia schreberi*, is represented in this book. The Cabombaceae are aquatic, rhizomatous perennials. Leaves are submersed and opposite with short petioles (*Cabomba*) or floating and alternate with long petioles *(Brasenia)*. Flowers are solitary on long peduncles, actinomorphic, trimerous. Ovaries are superior; fruits are achene-like in *Brasenia* and follicle-like in *Cabomba*.

CAMPANULACEAE—BELLFLOWER FAMILY, LOBELIA FAMILY. A small family of 90 or so worldwide genera. In Texas, it is represented by a few genera, the most common being *Lobelia*, which is found throughout the state. Plants in this family are herbaceous annuals or perennials with alternate, simple leaves. Flowers are variable, actinomorphic or zygomorphic, and occur in racemes or cymes, floral parts in multiples of 5. In *Campanula* and *Triodanis*, the flowers are bell-shaped with fused petals and 5 lobes; in *Lobelia*, the flowers are strongly 2-lipped.

CARYOPHYLLACEAE—CARNATION FAMILY. A family with about 86 genera found throughout the world, including common and recognizable plants such as carnations and dianthus. In Texas, the family is represented by several genera including the showy *Silene*. This family includes herbaceous annuals and perennials. Leaves are opposite, simple, with entire margins, and often clasping to perfoliate. Flowers can be solitary or, more commonly, in cymes or raceme-like cymes, with 5 free petals, actinomorphic. The tips of the petals are often fringed or lobed, sometimes deeply. Ovaries are superior, fruits are capsules.

CELASTRACEAE—STAFF TREE FAMILY, BITTERSWEET FAMILY. A worldwide family consisting of approximately 96 genera. In Texas, it mostly consists of woody shrubs (*Euonymus*, *Maytenus*, and *Mortonia*) and a few herbaceous genera (*Lepuropetalon*, *Parnassia*). The herbaceous plants are annuals or perennials, with basal leaves only. Leaves are simple with entire margins. Flowers are 5-petaled, actinomorphic. Ovaries superior or partially inferior, fruits are capsules.

CISTACEAE—ROCKROSE FAMILY. A small family with worldwide distribution of 8 genera, represented in Texas by *Helianthemum* and *Lechea*. Herbaceous perennials or subshrubs with alternate, opposite, or whorled simple leaves and entire margins. Flowers showy or not, actinomorphic, solitary or in cymes, with 5 sepals and 3 or 5 petals. Ovaries are superior, fruits are capsules.

CLEOMACEAE—SPIDER-FLOWER FAMILY. A small family with about 11 genera mainly spread throughout warmer regions and represented in Texas by *Cleomella* and *Polanisia*. Plants are aromatic (typically spice-scented) and usually sticky to the touch. Herbaceous annuals with trifoliolate, alternate leaves covered with glandular hairs. Flowers in racemes, strongly zygomorphic, with 4 clawed petals. Ovaries are superior, fruits are capsules. Plants are typically spice-scented.

CONVOLVULACEAE—MORNING GLORY FAMILY. A large family with nearly 2000 species spread throughout the globe. Well-known genera include *Convolvulus* and *Ipomoea*, bindweeds and morning glories, respectively. *Ipomoea* is widely planted as an ornamental and has escaped cultivation in some areas. Many ornamentals are cultivars and hybrids and their identification to species can be troublesome, as they may not be included in available keys. This group includes herbaceous annuals and perennials as well as annual and perennial vines, some vines clambering, others high-climbing and twining. Leaves are simple, alternate, margins entire or lobed, sometimes deeply, appearing palmate. Flowers are usually showy, actinomorphic, shaped like a bell or funnel or trumpet, with 5 lobes. Fruits are 4-chambered, dehiscent capsules with seeds that are typically large.

CRASSULACEAE—STONECROP FAMILY.
A large family of succulents with 1500 species distributed around the world. The most recognizable genera, including *Echeveria*, *Sedum*, and *Sempervivum*, are commonly sold as houseplants. However, the native species found in Texas are generally uncommon to rare, aside from a handful of species. Plants in Texas are succulent or not, herbaceous annuals or perennials, succulents with mostly basal leaves in a rosette, stem leaves alternate, simple, margins entire. Flowers in cymes, actinomorphic, with 5 sepals and 5 petals, small in most genera, large in *Echeveria*.

CUCURBITACEAE—CUCUMBER FAMILY.
A large family with worldwide distribution of about 120 genera that include economically important plants such as pumpkins, squash, and other pepos. Occasionally watermelons (*Citrullus lanatus* var. *lanatus*) or cantaloupes (*Cucumis melo*) will be found in the wild, usually in parks or along roadsides. Plants in this family are prostrate or climbing, annual or perennial vines with alternate, simple leaves, margins entire or heavily lobed; tendrils are produced in leaf axils. Flowers are either solitary or in inflorescences originating from leaf axils, actinomorphic, with separate male and female flowers, each with 5 petals and 5 sepals, showy in some species, greatly reduced in others, petals fused or not, flowers rotate or funnel- to bell-shaped. Ovaries are inferior, fruits are berries and can be fleshy, hard-skinned, or single-seeded and covered in burs.

DROSERACEAE—SUNDEW FAMILY.
A small but widespread family consisting of 3 genera and up to 180 species. Represented in Texas by the genus *Drosera*. Often found in large numbers, scattered throughout open, wet, sandy soils with poor nutrients. Carnivorous, herbaceous, annual or perennial, small, often only a couple inches in diameter. Leaves in rosettes, typically red with obvious glandular hairs throughout. Flowering stem a scape, with one to many actinomorphic, 5-petaled flowers.

ERICACEAE—HEATH FAMILY. A large, widespread family with more than 4000 species throughout the world. Economically important food crops as well as horticultural plants are found in this family. In Texas, there are woody plants such as madrone (*Arbutus xalapensis*), blueberry and huckleberry (*Vaccinium* species), and one herbaceous species (*Monotropa uniflora*). No other plant in Texas resembles *M. uniflora*, an herbaceous, mycotrophic perennial lacking chlorophyll and leaves. Flowers terminal, solitary, actinomorphic, and bell-shaped. Fruits are capsules.

EUPHORBIACEAE—SPURGE FAMILY, EUPHORBIA FAMILY. A large, widespread family with diverse characters, consisting of approximately 6300 species worldwide. Economically important plants such as tapioca (*Manihot esculenta*) and candelilla (*Euphorbia antisyphilitica*), the local plant used for wax, are found in this family. In addition, many species from Africa have horticultural value and are often mistaken as members of the family Cactaceae, which they superficially resemble. The majority of Texas plants are either herbaceous annuals or perennials or weak shrubs, the remaining few are geophytes. Leaves are (mostly) alternate or clustered, simple or palmately lobed, or reduced, with entire, toothed, or lobed margins. The sap can be white, clear, or red, usually caustic, but in some species the sap is used as an antiseptic. Inflorescences vary, and some species have solitary flowers; male and female flowers are separate. The distinguishing feature of some genera is the cyathium, a specialized arrangement of male and female flowers surrounded by bracts; this structure is easily mistaken for a flower. In *Jatropha* and *Cnidoscolus*, the flowers are more typical in appearance at first glance; however male and female flowers are separate. In other genera, such as *Acalypha*, there are either separate male and female plants, or male flowers are separated from female flowers on the same plant. In such cases, if the flowers are along the same spike, the male flowers are typically above the female flowers. Flowers in this latter group are relatively bland, with the little color there is coming from the styles or stamens. Fruits in all genera are capsules with 1 or 3 seeds; capsules often split under pressure and disperse the seeds as they dehisce.

FABACEAE—PEA FAMILY, LEGUME FAMILY. Another large and diverse family with close to 20,000 species worldwide. Economically important food crop species are found in this group as well as ornamentals and species used for timber, medicines, and a myriad of other purposes. Woody species in Texas include mesquite (*Prosopis glandulosa*), acacias (*Vachellia*), and numerous other native and introduced species. Three subfamilies are represented in Texas, easily distinguished by flower morphology.

Woody, herbaceous, or vining annuals or perennials. Leaves alternate, usually pinnate or bipinnate, sometimes trifoliolate, occasionally simple, margins entire. Flowers zygomorphic or actinomorphic, sometimes pealike with a banner, 2 lateral wings, and a keel (*Baptisia, Clitoria, Dalea, Lupinus*), other times clustered in rounded or cylindric heads (*Mimosa*), or 5-petaled with one petal unequal (*Chamaecrista, Hoffmannseggia, Senna*). Fruits are legumes or loments.

GENTIANACEAE—GENTIAN FAMILY. The family comprises 87 genera with about 1600 species. The well-known bluebell (*Eustoma exaltatum*) is included in this family. Plants in Texas are herbaceous annuals or perennials, with simple, opposite leaves that have entire margins. Flowers are in terminal or axillary cymes, actinomorphic, with 4 or (usually) 5 petals and are shaped like a funnel, bell, or tube. Ovaries are superior, fruits are capsules, with numerous, tiny seeds.

GERANIACEAE—GERANIUM FAMILY. A small family of 5 or 6 genera with about 800 species distributed worldwide, including the well-known ornamentals, geraniums (*Pelargonium*). In Texas, the family is represented by 2 genera, *Erodium* and *Geranium*. Herbaceous annuals, biennials, or perennials with alternate leaves, margins lobed and/ or deeply dissected. Flowers solitary or in cymes, actinomorphic, bell-shaped, 5-petaled. Ovaries are superior, fruits are schizocarps, dividing into mericarps often with highly modified awns that move in response to changes in humidity.

HYDROLEACEAE—HYDROLEA FAMILY.
This is a monotypic family with 11 species distributed throughout warmer regions. Texas has 2 species in East Texas and one in Cameron County; these are generally found in wet areas. Herbaceous or shrubby perennial with spiny stems, alternate and simple leaves with entire or serrate margins. Flowers are actinomorphic, bell-shaped, 5-petaled, arranged in corymbs. Ovaries are superior, fruits are rounded capsules.

HYDROPHYLLACEAE—PHACELIA FAMILY. A small family of 15 genera and 300 species with distribution in the Americas. *Phacelia* (bluecurls) is perhaps the best-known genus in Texas. This family is closely related to the Boraginaceae, and often the two can be confused; however, the fruits of the Boraginaceae are schizocarps, not capsules. Herbaceous annuals, biennials, or perennials with simple, alternate leaves. Flowers occur in scorpioid cymes, with the uppermost flowers opening as the coil unfurls, flowers actinomorphic, bell- or funnel-shaped, 5-lobed. Fruits are dehiscent capsules.

HYPERICACEAE—MANGOSTEEN FAMILY. A family of 6 genera and approximately 600 species with wide distribution, primarily in the Northern Hemisphere. *Hypericum*, the only genus in Texas, has 20 species in the eastern half of the state and is represented here with 4 species. Herbaceous or shrubby perennials, with simple, opposite leaves. Flowers actinomorphic, with 4 or 5 petals and numerous stamens, flowers borne terminal or solitary or in cymes, yellow. Ovaries are superior, fruits are capsules.

KRAMERIACEAE—RHATANY FAMILY.
A single-genus family consisting of 18 species spread throughout the Americas. The majority of species are small shrubs, with one herbaceous vine (*K. lanceolata*) represented here. A hemiparasitic, prostrate vine with simple, alternate leaves. Flowers showy, solitary, zygomorphic, 5-petaled, with 4 upper petals and one lower. Ovaries are superior, fruits are single-seeded capsules, usually with spines or barbs, which can be an identifying character in the woody species.

LAMIACEAE—MINT FAMILY. A large, worldwide family with more than 200 genera and 6800 species. This family is well known for its culinary and ornamental uses, and many cultivars exist. In Texas, the species are herbaceous or semiwoody, annuals or perennials, with square stems, opposite, simple leaves, margins variable. Flowers occur in terminal spikes, compact or loose, or clustered in upper leaf axils, have fused petals, are bilabiate, zygomorphic, rarely appearing actinomorphic, and can be quite large (*Salvia*) or small (*Hedeoma*), lips lobed or unlobed. Ovaries are superior, fruits are nutlets or stones, usually 4 per ovary.

LENTIBULARIACEAE—BUTTERWORT FAMILY, BLADDERWORT FAMILY. A small family with 3 genera and 300 species distributed worldwide. Two genera are represented in Texas, *Utricularia* and *Pinguicula*, both carnivorous and typically found in soils or waters that are nutrient-poor, such as bogs or swamps. *Utricularia gibba*, the most widespread species in Texas, is often found along the muddy banks of or floating in the waters of spring-fed creeks in Central

Texas. Herbaceous annuals or perennials, aquatic or terrestrial, basal leaves with secretory glands (*Pinguicula*), highly modified leaves used to capture small invertebrates (*Utricularia*). Flowers solitary or in racemes, bilabiate, strongly zygomorphic. Fruits are dehiscent capsules.

LINACEAE—FLAX FAMILY. A small, but economically important family consisting of 8 genera and about 180 species with worldwide distribution. *Linum* is the sole representative in Texas with more than 20 species found throughout the state. Herbaceous annuals or perennials with alternate or opposite leaves, typically sessile, with entire margins. Flowers in panicles, actinomorphic, with 5 petals that are not fused. Ovaries are superior, fruits are capsules.

LINDERNIACEAE—LINDERNIA FAMILY, FALSE-PIMPERNEL FAMILY. A small family of approximately 13 genera and 200 species with worldwide distribution, represented in Texas by one genus, *Lindernia*. The plants in this family used to be grouped in Scrophulariaceae, which was recently divided into several other families. Herbaceous annuals or biennials, with simple, opposite leaves. Flowers solitary, bilabiate, zygomorphic, with fused petals. Ovaries are superior, fruits are capsules.

LOASACEAE—ROCK-NETTLE FAMILY, STICK-LEAF FAMILY. A family of 20 genera and approximately 300 species, with showy flowers, mostly found in the Americas. Represented in Texas by 3 genera. Herbaceous annuals or perennials, with one species slightly shrubby. Leaves simple, opposite or alternate, margins lobed, toothed or entire, surfaces with hairs, sometimes stinging hairs (*Cevallia*). Flowers in clustered heads or racemes, with usually 5 sepals and petals, and numerous stamens, actinomorphic. Ovaries are inferior, fruits are dehiscent capsules, opening at the tip.

LOGANIACEAE—LOGANIA FAMILY. A small family of 15 genera and 350 species with worldwide distribution, represented in Texas by 2 genera, one of which is included here. Herbaceous annuals with simple, opposite leaves and entire margins. Flowers actinomorphic, in terminal cymes, 5-petaled. Ovaries are semi-inferior, fruits are capsules.

LYTHRACEAE—LOOSESTRIFE FAMILY. The family comprises 32 genera and about 600 species with worldwide distribution. Popular ornamentals are found in this family, such as crepe myrtle and pomegranate, which will occasionally escape cultivation in Texas. Several genera are represented here. Herbaceous annuals or perennials, some somewhat shrubby, with simple, alternate or opposite leaves and entire margins. Flowers actinomorphic or zygomorphic, 4- or 5-petaled. Ovaries are superior or inferior, fruits are capsules.

MALPIGHIACEAE—MALPIGHIA FAMILY. A family of approximately 1300 species worldwide, mostly in the Southern Hemisphere. One woody shrub and several herbaceous plants are found in Texas. Herbaceous to slightly woody perennials, one vinelike. Leaves simple, opposite, with entire or toothed margins. Flowers in racemes or cymes, actinomorphic, with 5 free petals which are clawed; the flowers look like propellers. Ovaries are superior, fruits are dry schizocarps, and winged in *Cottsia*.

MALVACEAE—MALLOW FAMILY, HIBISCUS FAMILY. This well-known, economically important family is widespread with about 2000 species and 115 genera. It includes ornamental genera such as *Hibiscus* and *Alcea*, as well as the fiber crop cotton (*Gossypium* species), which will occasionally escape in Texas. Recently, members of the Stericulaceae (*Ayenia*, *Hermannia*, *Melochia*) were moved into the Malvaceae. Numerous genera are found in Texas, with the heaviest concentration in the southern and western parts of the state. The flowers can be showy or relatively small. Annual or perennial herbaceous plants, or somewhat woody (*Hibiscus*, *Sphaeralcea*). Leaves alternate, simple, entire to deeply lobed. Flowers actinomorphic, with 5 petals united at the base, the petals usually overlapping and rolled when in bud. Ovaries are superior, fruits are dry capsules.

MARTYNIACEAE—UNICORN-PLANT FAMILY, DEVIL'S CLAW FAMILY. A small family with 5 genera and 16 species found in the Americas, formerly in the Pedaliaceae. Texas has one representative genus, *Proboscidea*, with several species, mostly found in the western portion of the state. Large herbaceous annual or perennial (one species), with simple, alternate leaves, margins lobed or entire, leaves and stems glandular-pubescent. Flowers in racemes, either extending beyond foliage or hidden below, showy, zygomorphic, tubular with bell-shaped openings that are 5-lobed. Ovaries are superior, fruits are distinctive capsules with 2 (or more) long, hooked horns extending and spreading as the capsule opens.

MELASTOMATACEAE—MELASTOMA FAMILY. A large family with global distribution of 4500 species. Texas has one representative genus, *Rhexia*, which is confined to the eastern portion of the state. Herbaceous perennials with simple, opposite leaves marked by conspicuous venation consisting of 3–7 veins running parallel to the leaf margins. Flowers showy, in cymes, actinomorphic, and with a distinctive, vase-shaped hypanthium that remains after flowering as the capsule. Ovaries are superior.

MENYANTHACEAE—BOG BEAN FAMILY. A small family of 5 genera and 60 species with global distribution. Represented in Texas by one genus, *Nymphoides*. Leaves superficially similar to the Nymphaeaceae, but the flower morphology easily distinguishes the families. Floating aquatic or rooted-in-mud herbaceous perennial with simple, basal and alternate leaves, margins entire. Flowers actinomorphic, showy, with fused petals and 5 lobes. Ovaries are superior, fruits are capsules.

MOLLUGINACEAE—CARPET WEED FAMILY. A small family of approximately 10 genera and 90 species with wide distribution. Two genera are represented in Texas and included in this book: *Glinus* and *Mollugo*. Herbaceous annuals or perennials, somewhat succulent, leaves alternate or opposite, occasionally whorled, or appearing so, margins entire. Flowers actinomorphic, with 5 tepals. Ovaries are superior, fruits are capsules.

NELUMBONACEAE—LOTUS FAMILY. A monotypic family of aquatic plants with 2 species. Both occur in Texas; one is an introduction and is found naturally in eastern Asia and Australia. Aquatic emergent, rhizomatous perennials with large, alternate, simple, peltate leaves. Flowers solitary, actinomorphic, large, and held well above water's surface on long peduncles, 20–30 petals. Ovaries are superior, fruits are large nutlets within a distinctive, woody receptacle.

NITRARIACEAE—NITRARIA FAMILY. A small family of 3 genera and 19 species with wide distribution typically in arid regions. Texas has one genus and 2 species, one of which (*Peganum mexicanum*) is the only member of this genus native to the New World. Herbaceous perennials, erect or prostrate. Leaves simple, alternate, lobed, margins entire. Flowers solitary from leaf axils, actinomorphic, with 5 petals. Ovaries are superior, fruits are capsules.

NYCTAGINACEAE—FOUR O'CLOCK FAMILY. An economically important family with numerous ornamentals widely distributed in 30 genera and approximately 400 species. Texas has several genera represented, with many West Texas species adapted to specific soil types. Herbaceous annuals or perennials, some weakly woody near the base, others with fleshy stems and leaves. Leaves opposite, simple, margins entire. Flowers actinomorphic, petals absent, perianth shaped like a bell or funnel or trumpet. Ovaries are superior, fruits are achenes, often winged or modified to aid in dispersal.

NYMPHAEACEAE—WATER LILY FAMILY. A family with global distribution of 6 genera and 60 species of aquatic perennials. Represented in Texas by 2 genera and 5 species, with the occasional introduction of persisting nonnative species. Aquatic perennials with simple, floating or slightly emergent leaves, attached to a rhizomatous root, which in some cases may be quite large and starchy. Flowers actinomorphic, large, showy, solitary, petals numerous. Ovaries are inferior in *Nymphaea*, superior in *Nuphar*, fruits are spongy berries.

OLEACEAE—OLIVE FAMILY. A family of 25 genera and about 550 species with global distribution. Includes the economically important genus *Olea* (olive) and several ornamentals. The family is comprised of primarily woody species, a few of which are in Texas, along with a handful of herbaceous plants. *Menodora* is represented here. Herbaceous perennials with simple, opposite leaves, margins entire. Flowers actinomorphic, with fused petals and 5 lobes, funnel- or trumpet-shaped, yellow. Fruits are capsules.

ONAGRACEAE—EVENING PRIMROSE FAMILY. A widely distributed family with 18 genera and 650 species. In Texas, the family is represented by several familiar genera with large, showy flowers. Herbaceous annuals or perennials with simple, opposite or alternate leaves, margins entire or toothed or lobed. Flowers solitary or in inflorescences, small or large and showy, actinomorphic or zygomorphic, numerous floral parts in multiples of 2–7. Ovaries are inferior, fruits are dehiscent capsules.

OROBANCHACEAE—BROOMRAPE FAMILY. A large family comprising 90 genera and more than 2000 species with global distribution. This family was relatively small until recent adjustments moved many genera to it from Scrophulariaceae, including the paintbrushes

(*Castilleja*) and false-foxgloves (*Agalinis*). The Orobanchaceae are either hemiparasitic or holoparasitic and attach to the roots of the host plant. *Orobanche* species are parasitic on various species of Asteraceae, while *Castilleja* species parasitize grass, and *Epifagus* uses beech as its host. Herbaceous annuals or perennials, with scalelike, nonphotosynthetic leaves or opposite or alternate photosynthetic, simple leaves; margins entire or lobed. Flowers in spikes or solitary, zygomorphic, bilabiate, with lower lip 3-lobed and upper lip 2-lobed. Ovaries are superior, fruit are capsules with small seeds that are dispersed by wind.

OXALIDACEAE—WOOD SORREL FAMILY. With only 5 genera in this family, it is surprising that it has about 900 species dispersed worldwide. The family is represented here by the genus *Oxalis*. Herbaceous, bunching, stoloniferous perennials, leaves usually trifoliolate. Flowers actinomorphic, yellow or rose or purple, with 5 free petals that are curled when in bud. Fruit is an explosive capsule.

PAPAVERACEAE—POPPY FAMILY. A family of approximately 920 species in 41 genera, primarily found in the Northern Hemisphere and including opium poppy (*Papaver*) and numerous ornamentals. Recently the Fumariaceae was added to this family. Texas has several representatives and one new addition, *Hunnemannia fumariifolia*, which is included here. *Corydalis* has highly modified flowers that differ dramatically from the typical flowers found in the remaining genera. However, the leaf morphology of *Corydalis*, *Eschscholzia*, and *Hunnemannia* is quite similar.

Herbaceous annuals or perennials. Leaves simple, usually lobed or dissected, alternate and/or basal, stems with latex. Flowers solitary or in racemes, zygomorphic or actinomorphic, showy or small, with 5 petals. Fruit is a capsule.

PASSIFLORACEAE—PASSION FLOWER FAMILY. A family with 16 genera and approximately 700 species, primarily distributed in the Americas and southern Africa. The family includes many ornamentals, and several species are cultivated for their fruit. Texas has one genus, *Passiflora*, with many species found throughout the state. The distinctive flower morphology of this family allows for easy identification in the field. Perennial, tendrilled vines with alternate, simple leaves, some deeply lobed. Flowers occur in leaf axils, actinomorphic, with 3–8 sepals and an equal number of petals, or the petals are absent; filaments numerous, occurring between the petals and the 5 stamens, often brightly colored, in some species green or cream colored; style 3-branched. Ovaries are superior, fruits are many-seeded, fleshy, edible berries.

PHRYMACEAE—PHRYMA FAMILY. A small family with about 6 genera worldwide. Many members of the Scrophulariaceae were recently moved to Phrymaceae. The family is represented here with 2 genera, *Mazus* and *Mimulus*. Herbaceous annuals or perennials. Leaves opposite and simple, margins lobed or toothed or serrate. Flowers solitary or in terminal racemes, zygomorphic, bilabiate, lower lip 3-lobed, upper lip 2-lobed. Fruit are capsules that split lengthwise to release the seeds.

PHYTOLACCACEAE—POKEWEED FAMILY.
A small family of 4 genera and 31 species mostly spread throughout the Americas, southern Africa, and Asia. Of the 4 genera found in Texas, one is an introduced vine; two others, *Phytolacca* and *Rivina*, are included here. The flowers in this family are not very showy and often small. However, the fruits are relatively large and numerous. Herbaceous perennials with simple, alternate leaves, entire to undulate margins. Flowers in racemes, actinomorphic, small, with 4 or 5 sepals. Ovaries are superior, fruits are berries.

PLANTAGINACEAE—PLANTAIN FAMILY.
After the influx of many species from Scrophulariaceae and other families, Plantaginaceae is large, with 94 genera and approximately 1900 species. Because this family is now quite variable, it is best to know the characteristics of the genera within. Herbaceous annuals or perennials, some moderately woody at the base, with a few aquatic species (*Callitriche*) and small climbing herbaceous vines. Leaves simple, opposite or whorled, margins variable. Flowers variable, bilabiate and zygomorphic (*Penstemon*) or actinomorphic, flora parts 4–8. Ovaries superior; fruit is a capsule.

POLEMONIACEAE—PHLOX FAMILY. A family of 20 genera and approximately 350 species, mostly found in the Northern Hemisphere; however, in the Americas, its range extends to the southern tip of South America, generally along the west coast. The family is well known for its showy flowers; many members are used for ornamentals. Texas is home to a handful of genera, 3 of which are included here. Herbaceous annuals or perennials. Leaves simple, alternate or opposite, with various margins. Flowers are zygomorphic (*Ipomopsis*) or actinomorphic (*Phlox*), typically trumpet-shaped and 5-lobed. Ovaries superior; fruit is a capsule.

POLYGALACEAE—MILKWORT FAMILY.
Widespread globally, with 10 genera and 1000 species. Represented here with one diverse genus, *Polygala*. The flowers in this family are often small and are surprisingly beautiful when viewed with a hand lens. Herbaceous annuals or perennials, occasionally with woody bases. Leaves simple, alternate, margins entire. Flowers in terminal or axillary, spikelike racemes, zygomorphic, with the 2 lateral sepals enlarged and petal-like and with 3 petals, the lowest round (typically) and referred to as the keel. Ovaries superior; fruit is a capsule.

POLYGONACEAE—BUCKWHEAT FAMILY.
A large family with about 50 genera and 1100 species spread globally, absent only in the Russian Arctic and portions of Australia. Common genera in this family include *Eriogonum*, *Polygonum*, and *Rumex*, all of which are included here. Herbaceous annuals or perennials, simple leaves, basal in some, otherwise alternate. Flowers in terminal racemes or cymes, actinomorphic, with 3 to 6 tepals. Ovaries superior; fruits are achenes.

PORTULACACEAE—PURSLANE FAMILY.
A widespread family with about 30 genera and 500 species. Includes economically important ornamental plants as well as edible species. Three of the several representative genera in Texas are included here. Herbaceous annuals or perennials, some semisucculent,

with opposite or spirally arranged simple leaves, margins entire, blades often fleshy. Flowers terminal, solitary or in panicles, actinomorphic, with 5 petals that are generally free to the base. Ovaries are superior or inferior (*Portulaca*), fruits are capsules.

PRIMULACEAE—PRIMULA FAMILY. A family of 21 genera and about 900 species spread globally. Many of the species are cultivated for ornamental use. Three genera are included here, one of which is introduced. Herbaceous annuals or perennials. Leaves simple, basal or opposite, margins entire. Flowers in axillary clusters or in a terminal umbel at the end of a slender scape, actinomorphic, 5-petaled. Ovaries superior; fruit is a capsule.

RANUNCULACEAE—BUTTERCUP FAMILY. A family of approximately 2500 species in 60 genera with global distribution. This family is well known for its ornamentals, including some Texas natives—*Aquilegia, Clematis, Delphinium, Ranunculus*—with a wide variety of characters. Herbaceous annuals or perennials or perennial vines, leaves opposite, simple or compound, margins variable. Flowers solitary or in cymes or racemes, actinomorphic (*Ranunculus, Anemone*) or zygomorphic (*Delphinium*), sepals usually 5. Ovaries are superior, fruits are achenes, often modified as in *Clematis*.

RESEDACEAE—MIGNONETTE FAMILY. A small family with 6 genera and 70 species mostly in Eurasia and northern Africa. For some time, the genus *Oligomeris* was thought to be an introduction to North America, given that the rest of the members of this family occurred in the Old World; however, it now appears *Oligomeris* is native in Central America, north into the American Southwest, including Texas. *Reseda* is introduced, and one species, *R. lutea*, has been reported from Texas. Herbaceous annuals or short-lived perennials with simple leaves, margins entire. Flowers in dense spikes, sessile, actinomorphic, with 2–4 sepals, and with 2 or 3 petals free or attached at base. Ovaries superior; fruits are angled, roundish capsules.

ROSACEAE—ROSE FAMILY. Well-known and economically important for both its ornamentals and its fruit, this family has about 5000 species in 104 genera distributed throughout the world. The family is very diverse, but flower morphology typically remains the same, and the ability to recognize the flower will assist in field identification. Two herbaceous genera are included here, *Geum* and *Duchesnea*. Herbaceous perennial with alternate, compound, trifoliolate leaves, margins serrate to dentate. Flowers actinomorphic, 5-petaled, petals free. Ovaries are superior, fruits are achenes, numerous, either dry or surrounded by a fleshy receptacle.

RUBIACEAE—MADDER FAMILY. With more than 13,000 species in 615 genera, this is the 4th-largest plant family, occurring globally, with most of the diversity in subtropical and tropical regions. Numerous representative genera are found in Texas, many of which are included here. Herbaceous annuals or perennials with simple, opposite leaves, occasionally whorled. Flowers actinomorphic, corolla tubular, floral parts in multiples of 4 or 5. Ovaries are inferior, fruits are capsules or berries.

RUTACEAE—CITRUS FAMILY. An economically important family comprised of many edible fruits and herbs. There are about 1700 species in 158 genera, mostly in tropical and subtropical regions, with a few expanding into temperate areas. Texas is home to about 10 genera, including several with woody plants (*Zanthoxylum, Ptelea*); 2 herbaceous genera are included here, *Ruta* and *Thamnosma*. Herbaceous perennials with alternate, simple or compound leaves, margins entire. The leaves are aromatic and have glandular surfaces, which cause dermatitis in some individuals. Flowers in cymes or racemes, actinomorphic, with 5 sepals and 5 petals. Ovaries are superior, fruits are capsules.

SAPINDACEAE—SOAPBERRY FAMILY. A family of about 1900 species and 145 genera with global distribution which now includes Aceraceae (maple family) and Hippocastanaceae (buckeye family). This family includes trees, shrubs, and vines, all of which are found in Texas, and the family is represented in this book by a single species, *Cardiospermum halicacabum*. Herbaceous perennial vine with alternate, compound leaves, margins toothed. Flowers in racemes, actinomorphic, with 4 sepals and 4 petals. Ovaries superior; fruit is an inflated pod with 3 cells, each holding one seed.

SARRACENIACEAE—PITCHER PLANT FAMILY. A small family of carnivorous plants with 3 genera and 20 species, all found in the Americas. The family is represented in Texas by one species, *Sarracenia alata*, which is included here. There is no mistaking this distinctive plant, typically found in nutrient-poor soils of East Texas. Herbaceous, rhizomatous perennial with modified leaves, forming liquid-holding pitchers which trap insects. Flowers solitary on a slender scape, arising directly from the rhizome, actinomorphic, floral parts in multiples of 5. Ovaries are superior, fruits are rounded capsules.

SAURURACEAE—LIZARD'S TAIL FAMILY. A small family with 4 genera and 6 species in North America and eastern Asia. Two genera with one species each are found in Texas: *Anemopsis californica* in the far western part of the state and *Saururus cernuus* in the eastern portion. Both prefer wet habitats. Herbaceous perennials, rhizomatous and stoloniferous, with simple, alternate leaves, margins entire. Flowers in dense spikes, actinomorphic, small, perianth absent; the white coloration comes from the bracts (*Anemopsis*) or floral parts (*Saururus*). Ovaries are superior, fruits are schizocarps (*Saururus*) or capsules (*Anemopsis*).

SCROPHULARIACEAE—FIGWORT FAMILY. Once a large family that included penstemons and other well-known ornamentals that have now been moved to other families. However, many well-known genera still remain. Included here are *Buddleja* and *Verbascum*. Herbaceous biennials to semi-woody perennials, with simple leaves, margins entire or toothed. Flowers in axillary clusters or terminal spikes, actinomorphic or zygomorphic, 4- or 5-lobed. Ovaries are superior, fruits are capsules.

SOLANACEAE—NIGHTSHADE FAMILY, POTATO FAMILY. A global family comprising approximately 90 genera and 2000 or more species of economically important food crops, tobacco, ornamentals, and many toxic species. Texas representatives of this family include woody species such as the wolfberries (*Lycium*). However, most plants in Texas are herbaceous. Seven genera are included in this book. Herbaceous annuals or perennials, one somewhat vine-like, leaves simple, alternate, margins entire to lobed. Flowers actinomorphic, 5-lobed, in terminal or axillary inflorescences or solitary shaped like a funnel, star, trumpet, or tube. Ovaries are superior, fruits are berries or capsules.

SPHENOCLEACEAE—CHICKENSPIKE FAMILY. A monotypic family with one species, *Sphenoclea zeylanica*, distributed primarily in the Southern Hemisphere and introduced in the New World. Herbaceous annual, with simple, alternate leaves, margins entire, stem hollow. Flowers in dense spike, actinomorphic, white, bell-shaped. Ovaries are semi-inferior, fruits are capsules.

URTICACEAE—NETTLE FAMILY. A family with global distribution of 1700 species in 43 genera. Four representative genera are in Texas, 3 of which are included here. Herbaceous annuals or perennials, stems and leaves dotted with calcium oxalate crystals, many with stinging hairs, alternate or opposite, simple, margins entire to toothed. Flowers in axillary terminal clustered cymes or panicles, or solitary, small, actinomorphic, male and female flowers separate. Ovaries are superior, fruits are capsules.

VERBENACEAE—VERVAIN FAMILY. A family with approximately 110 species in 34 genera, primarily found in the Americas, southern Africa, southern Europe, and Asia. Texas has numerous representatives, with a few semiwoody species, including the popular ornamental genus *Lantana*. Herbaceous annuals or perennials, some semiwoody. Leaves opposite, simple, in some species heavily lobed or dissected, margins entire, serrate, or toothed. Flowers in terminal or axillary spikes, numerous, rarely few, tubular or trumpet-shaped, zygomorphic or actinomorphic, 5-lobed. Ovaries are superior, fruits are schizocarps.

VIOLACEAE—VIOLET FAMILY. A family of 22 genera and approximately 900 species with global distribution. While most people are familiar with the ornamental violets, this family also includes trees, shrubs, and vines, mostly in subtropical or tropical areas. Texas has 2 representative genera, *Viola* and *Hybanthus*. Herbaceous perennials, often rhizomatous or stoloniferous, and plants acaulescent, or nearly so in *Viola*. Leaves simple, opposite, alternate or basal, margins variable, blades lobed in some species. Flowers solitary, showy in *Viola*, small in *Hybanthus*, 5-petaled, zygomorphic. Ovaries are superior, fruits are capsules.

ZYGOPHYLLACEAE—CALTROP FAMILY. A widespread family with 24 genera and approximately 275 species, mostly in arid regions. Several genera occur in Texas, including the woody shrubs *Larrea tridentata* (creosote) and *Guaiacum angustifolium* (Texas lignum-vitae), and the noxious *Tribulus terrestris* (goathead). Herbaceous annuals or perennials with opposite, compound leaves. Flowers solitary, actinomorphic, 5-petaled. Ovaries are superior, fruits are schizocarps.

GLOSSARY

acaulescent Stemless, or no apparent stem above ground; opposite of caulescent, which means with a stem

achene A dry, one-seeded indehiscent fruit, as in the family Asteraceae

actinomorphic In flowers, radial symmetry; flowers (or heads) can be divided equally more than once, as in the genus *Helianthus*

acuminate As in leaves; tapering to a point

annual A plant that germinates, grows, flowers, and sets seed within one year

apex Tip; farthermost point away from the base; as in leaves

apical tooth A small, single point at the tip of a petal

apiculate In leaves, tip terminating in a sharp point

appressed As in hairs; pressed closely to surface of stem or leaves

ascending As in stems; growing horizontally, then erect

auriculate As in leaves; eared, bases of leaves wrapping around stems

axil Where a leaf or petiole joins the stem

axillary Originating from the axil of a leaf

banner Posterior, and usually the uppermost, petal of a pea flower

berry A type of fleshy, indehiscent fruit, as in the genus *Capsicum*

bilabiate In flowers, two lips which may be variously lobed. E.g., the genus *Salvia*

bilateral In flowers, one even division of flower

bipinnate Twice pinnate

biternate In leaves, twice ternate

bract A modified leaf, found below flowers or inflorescences or where stems branch, differing in size, shape, and occasionally color from the stem and basal leaves of the plant, as in *Euphorbia bicolor*

bristle Stiff, straight hairs; may be found on stems, leaves, achenes, or ocreas

bulb An underground storage organ

calyx (pl. calyces) The sepals, collectively

canescent Downy hairs, usually white

capsule A dry, dehiscent fruit with few or many seeds

cespitose As in plant habit; tufted, clumped

character Morphological features used to identify a plant, such as leaf shape or length, flower color, petal number, and other features

ciliate As in leaf margins; lined with hairs

cleft A small cut or notch to about halfway to the base or midrib

cleistogamous Self-fertilizing flowers that do not open; usually small and inconspicuous

connate Fused, as in petals or leaves

convolute As in petals or leaves; overlapping

cordate As in leaves; heart-shaped

corm The swollen base of a stem; fleshy, used for storage

corolla The petals of a flower

corymb A flat-topped inflorescence with a central stem and pedicels of unequal length to where the flowers are all of the same height

crenate As in leaf margins; scalloped or rounded teeth

crenulate Minutely crenate

cuneate As in leaf bases; wedge-shaped

cyathium (pl. cyanthia) A type of inflorescence, typical of the genus *Euphorbia*, with separate but clustered male and female flowers surrounded by bracts; on the whole, the structure resembles a flower

cyme A determinate inflorescence with the main stem and lateral stems ending in a flower

decumbent Of stems; lying along the ground with the stem ascending

dehiscent In fruits, opening at maturity

deltate As in leaves; resembling the Greek letter delta, or an equilateral triangle

dentate As in leaf margins; toothed

denticulate Finely dentate

dioecious Of plants; male and female flowers on separate plants

disc floret The central flowers of a capitulum, as in the genus *Helianthus*

discoid A type of inflorescence within the Asteraceae that is composed of disc florets only

emarginate As in leaf tips; rounded, notched at the tip, usually at midvein

emersed In leaves or flowers, rising above the water's surface

entire As in a leaf margin, not lobed or otherwise altered

ephemeral Short lived, as in bodies of water or plants

epiphyte Of a plant; growing on another plant without obtaining nutrients or water, as in the genus *Tillandsia*

erect Upright

falcate Sickle-shaped

fascicled As in leaves; bundled

filament Stalk of the stamen

filiform As in leaves; threadlike

fleshy Thick and juicy, succulent

floret Small individual flower, as in the Asteraceae

foliolate Having leaflets, as in a compound leaf

follicle A dry, dehiscent fruit, splitting along one side, as in the genus *Asclepias*

funiculus A fleshy, threadlike appendage attached to a seed

galea In flowers, upper lip helmet-shaped, as in the genus *Scutellaria*

gibbose As in leaves; swollen on one side

glabrate Becoming glabrous or nearly glabrous

glabrous As in leaves or stems; hairless, smooth

glaucous As in leaf or stem surface; blue-green in color

glutinous Sticky, viscid, gluelike

gynostegium A floral structure found in the genus Asclepias; the crown of the stamens

hastate As in leaves; blade triangular in outline with basal lobes pointing outward

head In flowers; a compact inflorescence with few or many flowers, as in the Asteraceae

hemiparasitic A plant that is partially parasitic, obtaining only some of its nutrients and/or water from the host plant, as in the genus *Castilleja*

hirsute Rough, long hairs

hispid Erect, rigid hairs

holoparasitic A plant that is wholly parasitic, obtaining all its nutrients and water from the host plant, as in the genus *Orobanche*

hypanthium In flowers, a structure, tubular or cuplike, consisting of the calyx, corolla, and stamens, as in the family Onagraceae

indehiscent Not splitting open at maturity

inferior ovary Ovary below the sepals, petals, and stamens

inflorescence The arrangement of flowers on a plant

involucre A whorl of bracts at the base of a flower, covering the flower when in bud

involute In leaves, margins rolled upward

keel In a pea flower, the two lower petals, typically fused and enclosing the stamens and pistil

lacerate In petals, a torn or cut appearance

lacinate As in petals; cut into slender lobes

lanceolate In leaves or petals, shaped like a lance, tapering to a point at the ends

lateral As in petals; those on the side

lax Loose

leaflets The final segments of a compound leaf

legume A dry, dehiscent fruit that splits along two sides, as in the family Fabaceae; legumes may open under pressure, expelling the seeds, as in the genus *Lupinus*, or the fruit may gradually open, releasing the seeds slowly, as in the genus *Senna*

ligulate A fertile floret with long, petal-like appendage, as in the genus *Lygodesmia*

linear As in leaves; narrow in relation to length, sides parallel

limb As in flowers; the upper spreading portion of a flower with joined petals, as in the Convolvulaceae

lip As in flowers; in orchids it refers to a modified petal used to attract insects; in other species, the general term is used to describe a division of flower (upper lip, lower lip). Lips are usually lobed, as in the genus *Salvia*.

lobe In flowers or leaves; divisions along the margin, usually rounded

lomas Small hills

loment A pod breaking into one-seeded joints, typically found in the Fabaceae

lyrate As in leaves, lyre-shaped, a terminal lobe followed by smaller lateral lobes which are deeply lobed

monotypic Containing only one taxon of the next lower rank, as in the family Hydroleaceae

mucronate As in leaf tips; terminating in a sharp point

muricate Studded with short, rough points, as are the fruits of *Matelea reticulata*

mycoheterotroph A plant which obtains its nutrients from fungus, which in turn is attached to another vascular plant

nutlet A small nut, as found in the genus *Salvia*

oblique As in leaves; with unequal sides

oblanceolate In leaves, lance shaped, with the thin end attached to the petiole; reversed lanceolate shape

oblong As in leaves; an elongated blade with parallel sides, longer than wide, rounded at both ends

obovate Reversed ovate, stem attached to tapered end

ocrea A thin, papery sheath, with or without cilia or bristles, of 2 or more stipules, found at the junction of stems, as in the genus *Persicaria*

opposite In leaves or flowers, arranged in pairs at the same level

orbicular As in leaves; round or nearly so

oval In leaves or petals, nearly round

ovary Female organ that develops into fruit

ovate As in leaves; egg-shaped, with the larger end at the base

pandurate In leaves, fiddle-shaped; narrow in the middle

panicle A branching raceme; the flowers are on pedicels

papilionaceous Like a butterfly, as in flowers; a flower with a banner, keel, and two lateral wings, characteristic of the subfamily Papilionoideae of the family Fabaceae

parasite A plant that obtains all or part of its nutrition from another plant

pectinate In leaves, resembling the teeth of a comb or the skeleton of a fish

pedicel The stalk of a flower

peduncle The stalk of an inflorescence

peltate In leaves, shield-shaped; petiole attached to middle of leaf rather than at the base, as in the genus *Nelumbo*

perfoliate In leaves, the base of the leaf wrapped around the stem, so it appears that the stem passes through the leaf

perianth The collective term for the corolla and calyx, used when the two are similar

petal In flowers, one segment of the inner whorl surrounding fertile organs

petiole In leaves, the stalk of a leaf

phyllary (pl. phyllaries) Bract (or bracts) forming the involucre or head in the family Asteraceae

pilose Soft, straight, and spreading hairs

pinnate In leaves, leaflets arranged along a central axis, typically in pairs, may be even-pinnate or odd-pinnate, the latter with a terminal leaflet

pinnatifid In leaves, deeply lobed with lobes not reaching midvein

pistillate In flowers, female; lacks stamens

plicate In leaves, wrinkled appearance

poricidal Opening by pores, as in a capsule

prickle A stiff, pointed growth from the stem, leaf, or calyx of a plant

prostrate In stems, spreading along the ground without rooting at the nodes

pubescent Covered with short, soft hairs; downy; also used as a general term to define presence of hairs

raceme An unbranched, indeterminant inflorescence with stalked flowers

rachis An axis of a compound leaf, spike, or raceme

radial As in flowers; spreading, or arranged from a central point, as with species of *Helianthus*

radiate As in the family Asteraceae, with ray florets spreading from a central point

ray floret A small individual flower in the Asteraceae with a long outer extension that is often three-lobed; found along the outer portion of the head

recurved As in petals, bent backwards

reflexed As in flowers; curved backward or downward

reniform As in leaves; kidney-shaped

repand With an undulate margin

reticulate Net veined

revolute In leaves, margins rolled downward

rhizome/rhizomatous An underground stem which produces shoots and roots from its nodes; a vegetative means of reproduction

rhombic Diamond-shaped

rosette As in leaves; clustered at ground level, often round

rotate Of flowers; rounded corolla with no tube

sagittate Shaped like an arrowhead

salverform As in flowers; a flower with a corolla tube that abruptly spreads open. The tube does not flare along its length; it generally keeps the same diameter from the base to the opening of the limb.

samara An indehiscent winged fruit

scandent With a climbing nature

scape A leafless flower stalk originating directly from the roots

schizocarp A dry, dehiscent fruit formed from more than one carpel, breaking apart

when mature, as in the genus *Tribulus*

scorpioid As in flowers; an inflorescence curled at the end, uncurling as the flowers develop, as found in the genus *Phacelia*

sepal In flowers, one of the nonfertile segments of the outer whorl, surrounding the fertile organs, may be green or brightly colored

serrate In leaf margins, similar to dentate, but teeth are pointed and irregular, like a saw

sessile In leaves and flowers, without a petiole or pedicel, attached directly to stem or rachis

silicula A short siliqua, less than twice as long as wide

siliqua In fruits, a dry, dehiscent fruit, more than twice as long as wide, splitting along two lines, with an inner septum

sinuate As in leaves; strongly wavy

spadix In flowers, an inflorescence with a stout axis, usually with many small, crowded flowers, often fleshy or succulent, as in the genus *Colocasia*

spathe In flowers, a large, leafy bract which covers an inflorescence, as in the genus *Dracontium*

spatulate Spoon-shaped, broad at the tip, slender at the base, as in leaves or petals

specific epithet The second word in the scientific name of a plant, denoting species

spike Inflorescence consists of a central main stem with flowers directly attached to the stem

spine As in stems or leaves, a sharp, thin, pointed extension

spiral In leaves or flowers, arranged in a coiled manner along a central axis, as in the genus *Spiranthes*

spur In flowers, a cone-shaped or tubular outgrowth from the base of a perianth, usually containing nectar, as in the genus *Aquilegia*

stamen Male organ which bears pollen and includes both the filament and anther

standard The upper petal in a papilionaceous flower; occasionally inverted as in the genus *Clitoria*

stolon An aboveground, prostrate stem, rooting at the nodes, and often producing erect shoots and leaves at nodes

striated With visible longitudinal lines or grooves

strigose With stiff, straight, appressed hairs

succulent As in leaves or stems; fleshy, as in the genus *Echeveria*

superior ovary Ovary above the sepals, petals, and stamens

tendril A modified leaf, leaflet, or stipule; slender and occasionally forked, used in vining plants to assist in climbing

tepal In flowers, a collective term used when sepals and petals are similar, as in the genus *Zephyranthes*

terete Round in cross section

terminal In leaves or stems, at the end; for example, a terminal leaflet or terminal bud

ternate In leaves, in groups of 3, usually applied to leaflets

throat Opening of flowers with fused petals or sepals

thyrse In flowers, a type of inflorescence in which the main stem is indeterminant and with determinant lateral branches; a raceme with lateral cymes

tomentose In leaves and stems, a dense covering of short, matted hairs

trichome A hairlike growth from the epidermal layer

trifoliolate A compound leaf consisting of 3 leaflets

truncate As in leaf bases; square to petiole

tube As in flowers; a cylindric structure formed by fused petals or sepals

tuber A short, thickened underground stem with many buds

umbel In flowers, an inflorescence in which the flower stalks arise from the top of the peduncle and all the stalks are about the same length

undulate As in leaf margins; weakly wavy

urceolate Of flowers or fruits, shaped like an urn or vase

venation Arrangement of veins in a leaf

verrucose Warty, bumpy

villose A type of pubescence consisting of long, soft hairs; shaggy

viscid Sticky, adhesive; usually associated with pubescence covering leaves, stems, fruits, or other parts of a plant

wings As in flowers of the family Fabaceae, the two outer (lateral) petals; in stems, petioles, or fruit, thin, membranous extensions

woolly A type of pubescence, densely covered with long, matted hairs

zygomorphic Of flowers, bilateral symmetry

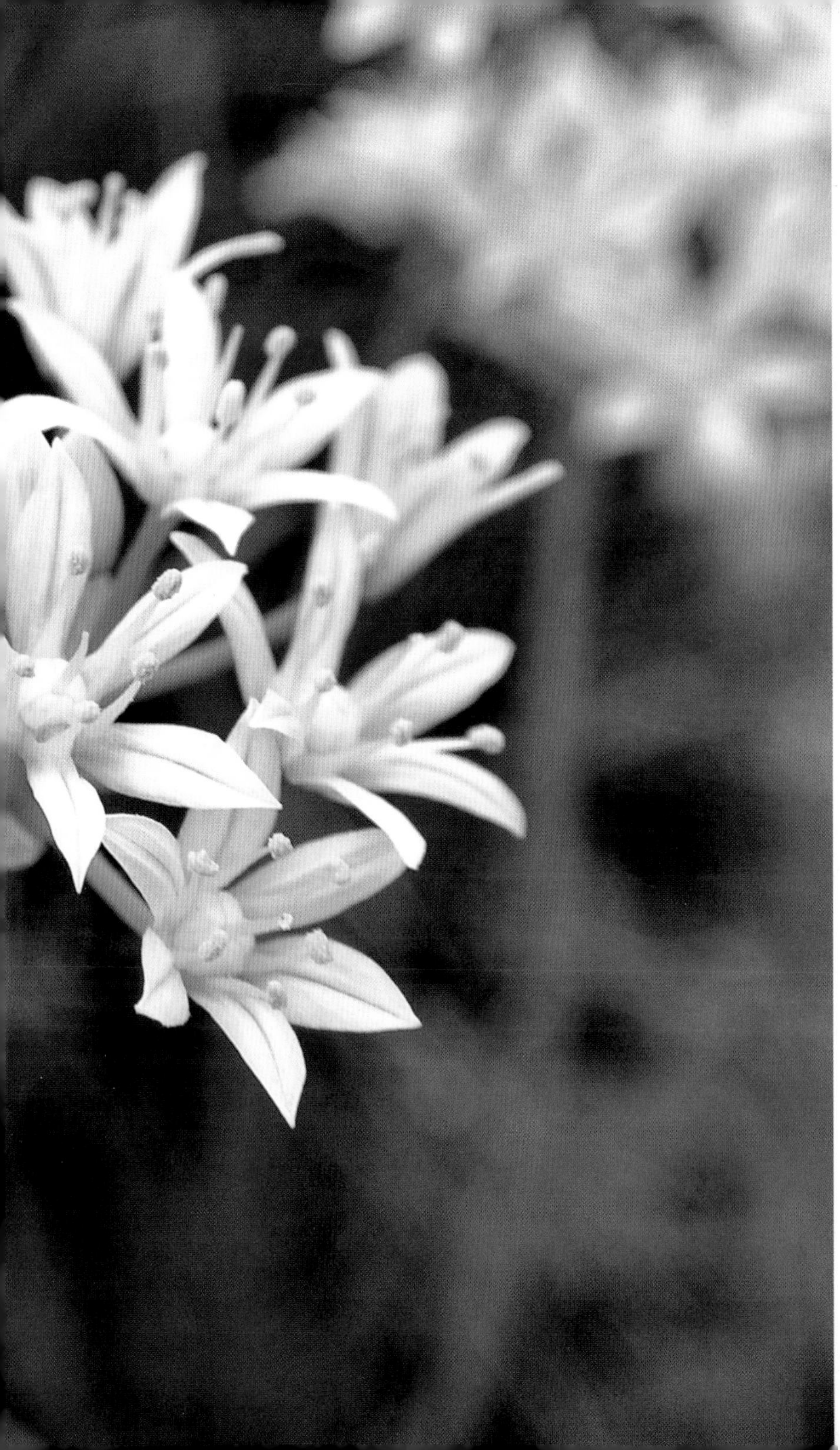

WHITE TO GREEN FLOWERS

Carlowrightia arizonica   ACANTHACEAE
Arizona wrightwort
Rocky soils, boulder outcrops, mesas.
Spring, summer, fall. Uncommon.

An erect, branching perennial with slender stems to 24 inches tall, usually shorter. Leaves opposite, oblong to linear-lanceolate, to 1 inch long and less than ¼ inch wide. Flowers in leaf axils, bilateral, to about 1 inch wide, white, 4-lobed, upper lobe with reddish purple venation and a yellow patch in center. Currently known from just Brewster and Presidio Counties. Look for this species in dry rocky slopes around Big Bend Ranch State Park and along River Road from Lajitas to Presidio. Flowers as early as mid-March, continuing through fall if weather permits. Genus named after Charles Wright, a botanist who collected in Texas during the mid-1800s.

Hygrophila lacustris   ACANTHACEAE
Gulf swampweed
Marshes, streams, roadside ditches and other wet areas. Spring, summer, fall. Locally common.

An erect, rhizomatous perennial to 30 inches tall with quadrangular stems. Leaves lanceolate, to 4¾ inches long and 1 inch wide. Flowers clustered in leaf axils, small, white to yellowish, lower lip with 3 lobes, upper lip with 2 lobes. Found in Southeast Texas. Often forms large colonies. Genus name of Greek origin and refers to water-loving (*hygro-phila*) nature of this genus.

Justicia americana   ACANTHACEAE
American water willow
Shallow waters of creeks, rivers, and streams, occasionally in man-made waters. Spring, summer, fall. Common.

An erect, rhizomatous aquatic perennial to nearly 3 feet tall, typically shorter, with slender unbranched stems. Leaves linear to lanceolate, to 6 inches long and 1 inch wide. Flowers in spikes extended on peduncles arising from leaf axils, 1 inch wide, white, upper lobe often tinged pink, lower lobe often with purple spots. Forms colonies covering large areas in shallow waters and extending out of main water channel to adjacent banks. Found throughout central portion of state.

Echinodorus cordifolius ALISMATACEAE
Creeping burhead, lance-leaf burhead
Marshes, swamps, ponds, roadside ditches and other
low, wet areas. Spring, summer, fall. Common.

A stout, rhizomatous perennial to nearly 3 feet tall when
flowering. Leaves on petioles to 18 inches long, ovate to
elliptic, to 12 inches long and 7 inches wide. Flowers in
decumbent racemes, to 15 at each whorl along raceme,
3-petaled, white, to 1 inch wide, with distinct greenish
yellow anthers and pistils. Found in wetlands from South
Texas north to Oklahoma and east to Louisiana. Most
often seen along coast in low areas that hold water. Only
species of *Echinodorus* with a decumbent raceme, making
it easy to identify.

Sagittaria lancifolia ALISMATACEAE
Bulltongue arrowhead, lance-leaf sagittaria,
duck potato, wapato
Marshes. Summer, fall. Locally common.

An erect, rhizomatous perennial to 6+ feet tall when flowering. Leaves emersed, on petioles that are triangular in
cross section and to 20+ inches long, ovate or elliptic, to
14 inches long and 6½ inches wide, margins entire. Flowers in racemes to 2 feet long, on peduncles to 4 feet long,
white, to 1½ inches wide, 3-petaled. Found in Southeast
Texas, close to coast. A few collections have been made
farther inland.

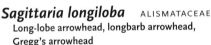

Sagittaria longiloba ALISMATACEAE
Long-lobe arrowhead, longbarb arrowhead,
Gregg's arrowhead
Edges of rivers, stream, ponds, and lakes,
ephemeral waters, roadside ditches and other low,
wet areas. Spring, summer, fall. Common.

An erect, stoloniferous perennial to 3+ feet tall when in
flower. Leaves strongly sagittate, to 10 inches long and 6
inches wide, lobes often slender, basal lobes longer than
upper. Flowers in racemes to 16 inches long, on peduncles to 2+ feet long, white, 3-petaled, to 1¼ inches wide.
Widespread throughout state, frequent along coast and in
Panhandle, less common elsewhere. Photographed specimen was located in Kinney County.

Sagittaria papillosa ALISMATACEAE
Nipplebract arrowhead
Marshes, swamps, roadside ditches.
Spring, summer, fall. Common.

A rhizomatous, herbaceous perennial to more than 3 feet tall. Leaves elliptic to ovate, to 22 inches long including triangular petiole, which is to 14 inches long. Flowers in 30-inch-long racemes of 4 to 10 whorls, up to 15 flowers per whorl, white, 3-petaled, just over 1 inch wide. Frequent in Southeast Texas, south along coast to Corpus Christi area.

Sagittaria platyphylla ALISMATACEAE
Delta arrowhead
Marshes, bogs, swamps, roadside ditches and other shallow bodies of water. Spring, summer, fall. Common.

A stoloniferous perennial to 5 feet tall, lacking rhizomes, but with corms. Leaves submersed and emersed. Submersed leaves grasslike, to 10 inches long and ¼ inch wide. Emersed leaves linear-ovate to ovate, 2–6½ inches long and to 2¼ inches wide, with triangular petioles to 27 inches long, usually much shorter. Flowers in 2-foot-long racemes of up to 9 whorls, to 10 flowers per whorl, white, 3-petaled, ½ inch wide. Found from Central to East Texas in low, wet areas. Absent in western Texas and Panhandle.

Alternanthera caracasana AMARANTHACEAE
Washerwoman, khakiweed, mat chaff flower
Pastures, desert washes, creek and river beds, manicured parks, lawns, agricultural areas and other disturbed places. Summer, fall. Common.

A prostrate to procumbent annual with villous to glabrous stems to 20+ inches long. Leaves opposite, sessile, rhombic-ovate to oval or obovate, to 1 inch long and ¾ inch wide, bases tapering, margins entire, tips rounded, surfaces green and glabrous. Flowers clustered in leaf axils, less than ¼ inch wide, white to off-white to tan, tepals spine-tipped and prickly. A common lawn weed. Widespread throughout Texas.

Alternanthera philoxeroides
AMARANTHACEAE
Alligator weed
Bogs, swamps, margins of lakes and ponds, wet ditches
and other wet areas. Spring, summer. Common.

An introduced, aquatic to semiterrestrial, prostrate to
ascending, stoloniferous and mat-forming perennial with
glabrous, branching, hollow stems to 3+ feet long. Leaves
opposite, sessile, linear to lanceolate, to 4½ inches long
and ¾ inch wide, margins entire, tips acute, surfaces glabrous. Flower clusters axillary or terminal, on slender
peduncles to 3 inches long, clusters rounded and to about
¾ inch wide, individual flowers about ⅛ inch wide, tepals
usually 4, white to silver. Frequent in waters of Southeast
Texas, less frequent elsewhere in eastern half of state.

Alternanthera sessilis   AMARANTHACEAE
Sessile joyweed
Bottomlands, bayous. Summer, fall. Rare.

An introduced, aquatic or semiterrestrial annual to perennial with ascending to creeping stems to 18+ inches long.
Leaves opposite, on short petioles, linear-lanceolate to
ovate-oblong, to 3¼ inches long and ¾ inch wide, margins entire to serrate, tips acute. Flowering heads sessile
in upper leaf axils, to ¼ inch wide, 1–4 heads per axil.
Flowers dense, bracts white, tepals white. Similar to *Alternanthera philoxeroides*, but not nearly as robust and with
smaller, sessile flowers. Currently known from Liberty
and Galveston Counties, most likely in other areas within
this region.

Atriplex acanthocarpa   AMARANTHACEAE
Burscale, saltbush, hardy saltbush
Open shrublands, thornscrub, lomas, saltflats.
Spring, summer, fall. Locally common.

An erect perennial with heavily branching stems to
3 feet tall and wide. Leaves opposite below, alternate
above, subsessile or on short petioles, oblong-ovate or
obovate-spatulate, to 2 inches long and 1 inch wide, margins entire or dentate or undulate. Male and female flowers on separate plants, inconspicuous. Male flowers along
leafy spikes, in clusters less than ¼ inch thick. Female
flowers clustered in axils or in racemes to 10 inches long.
Two varieties occur in state: var. *coahuilensis* in South
Texas and var. *acanthocarpa* in West Texas. Both prefer
silty, saline soils. Use vegetative plant parts, not flowers,
to accurately identify species.

Atriplex semibaccata   AMARANTHACEAE
Creeping saltbush, berry saltbush
Floodplains, marshes, saltflats, open shrublands, roadsides, agricultural areas and other open, disturbed sites. Spring, summer, fall. Uncommon.

An introduced, decumbent to prostrate perennial with branching stems to 3 feet long, forming plants to 4+ feet wide. Leaves alternate, spatulate, obovate to elliptic, to 1½ inches long and ⅓ inch wide, margins dentate to entire. Male and female flowers on separate plants, inconspicuous. Male flowers in small, terminal clusters. Female flowers either solitary or in small clusters in leaf axils. Fruits fleshy, red, rhombic, and a distinguishing character of species. Found in saline soils from El Paso to Brownsville.

Blutaparon vermiculare   AMARANTHACEAE
Silverhead, silverweed, saltweed
Dunes, beaches, and other coastal areas with salty-sandy soils. Winter, spring, summer, fall. Locally common.

A prostrate perennial with glabrous, often red, branching stems to 6 feet long. Leaves opposite, sessile, fleshy, linear to oblanceolate, to 2 inches long and about ½ inch wide, margins entire, surfaces glabrous. Inflorescence round to cylindric, to about ½ inch wide, with numerous flowers, surrounded by white to pink bractlets that turn silver when mature. Found along the lower coast. Specific epithet means "little worm," referring to the habit of this species.

Froelichia floridana   AMARANTHACEAE
Florida snake-cotton, plains snake-cotton, snake-cotton
Fields, meadows, prairies, open brush and woodlands, roadsides. Summer, fall. Common.

An erect annual with a single, sometimes weakly branched, stout stem to about 5 feet tall and covered in soft, sticky hairs. Leaves opposite, on short petioles, lanceolate to oblanceolate to oblong, to 4 inches long and ¾ inch wide, margins entire, surfaces sparsely pubescent. Inflorescence a terminal spike, to 4 inches long, with 1–3 shorter, lateral spikes. Flowers arranged in 5 spirals along spike and hidden in woolly-white hairs, small, cone-shaped, maturing to a vaselike shape, petals absent, calyx cream or pink. Widespread across state. Genus name honors Josef Aloys Frölich, an early 19th-century German botanist.

Froelichia gracilis AMARANTHACEAE
Slender cottonweed, slender snake-cotton, snake-cotton
Fields, meadows, prairies, open brush and woodlands,
roadsides, railroad rights-of-way and other disturbed
areas. Winter, spring, summer, fall. Common.

An erect annual or short-lived perennial with several
stems branching from base to nearly 3 feet tall and covered with soft, silky, grayish white hairs. Leaves opposite,
sessile, mostly in lower third of plant, linear to lanceolate to elliptic, to 4 inches long and ⅓ inch wide, margins
entire. Flowers arranged in small 3-spiraled spikes, with
woolly-gray pubescence. Found throughout state.

Gomphrena serrata AMARANTHACEAE
Arrasa con todo
Open brush and woodlands, roadsides, urban and
suburban areas. Winter, spring, summer, fall. Uncommon.

A prostrate to decumbent annual to perennial with
pubescent stems to nearly 3 feet long. Leaves sessile or on
short petioles, obovate to oblong, margins entire, surfaces
with silky hairs. Inflorescences terminal, to ½ inch wide,
slightly round to cylindric, consisting of numerous flowers surrounded by white bractlets, sometimes tinged with
pink or red. Found along coast as well as inland where
sandy soils exist.

Kochia scoparia subsp. *scoparia*
(*Bassia scoparia*)
AMARANTHACEAE
Burningbush, Mexican firebush, Mexican fireweed
Along waterways and banks of bodies of
water, pastures, roadsides and other disturbed
areas. Spring, summer, fall. Common.

An erect, introduced annual, heavily branched and variable in size to 6 feet tall. Stems pubescent when young,
glabrous with age. Leaves alternate, sessile, linear to lanceolate, to 2½ inches long and ¼ inch wide, margins
entire to ciliate. Flowers in 2-inch-long racemes originating in leaf axils, small, less than ¼ inch wide, generally
green to yellow-green, petals absent. Common throughout Panhandle and West Texas, sparse in Central Texas.
Absent in southern and eastern portions of Texas.

Salsola tragus AMARANTHACEAE
Tumbleweed, Russian thistle, prickly Russian thistle
Fields, pastures, grasslands, shrublands,
urban and suburban areas, farms, ranches,
roadsides. Summer, fall. Common.

An introduced, erect annual, heavily branched from
base, forming plants 5+ feet wide, rounded when full and
mature, otherwise they may be wispy. Stems to 4 feet tall,
reddish to maroon and striated when older, green and
glabrous when young. Leaves alternate, linear to filiform,
to 2 inches long, tips pointed, prickly. Flowers in leaf
axils, creamy white with pink centers or pink to greenish,
small, less than ¼ inch wide. Found in western half of
Texas, spreading elsewhere.

Allium canadense var. *canadense*
AMARYLLIDACEAE
Wild onion, Canada onion, meadow garlic
Meadows, fields, woodlands, roadsides.
Winter, spring, summer. Common.

A bulbous perennial to 20 inches tall when in flower.
Leaves shorter than scape, about ¼ inch wide, margins
entire. Solitary scapes can reach 20 inches tall. Umbel
produces up to 10 flowers, each ¼ inch wide, fragrant,
white, sometimes tinged with pink. Fruits or seeds are
rarely produced by this variety; instead small bulbils are
formed, replacing pedicels. Found throughout most of
Texas. Absent in Chihuahuan Desert region. Both bulbs
and bulbils are edible and have a pleasant onion flavor.

Allium kunthii AMARYLLIDACEAE
Kunth's onion
Open, rocky hillsides and mountain
slopes. Summer, fall. Common.

A bulbous perennial, clustered, with short rhizomes and
a scape to 12 inches tall. Leaves are flat and channeled, to
8 inches long and ⅛ inch wide, sheathed, with sheaths
not above soil level. Scape gives rise to umbel consisting
of up to 20 star- to urn-shaped white flowers that may be
tinged with pink, each ¼ inch in diameter. Found in Chihuahuan Desert region of Texas, usually on rocky limestone slopes, but does occur on other substrates.

Crinum americanum   AMARYLLIDACEAE
Southern swamp lily, seven sisters, crinum
Marshes, stream banks, swamps. Winter,
spring, summer, fall. Rare.

A bulbous perennial with large, erect leaves and a scape
to 4 feet. Basal leaves to 4 feet tall but typically shorter, 1–3
inches wide, strap-shaped, margins scabrous. Flowers
2–7 per umbel, large, white, 10 inches in diameter, with
floral tubes about 6 inches long. Found in a few counties
from Coastal Bend to Louisiana.

Crinum bulbispermum   AMARYLLIDACEAE
Hardy swamp lily, crinum
Roadsides, feral gardens, bar ditches, old
homesteads, cemeteries, other disturbed
areas. Spring, summer. Uncommon.

An introduced, bulbous perennial with a scape to 30
inches tall. Leaves strap-shaped, 3 feet long and about 2
inches wide. Flowers funnel-shaped, white to pink to red,
to 4½ inches long and just over 4 inches wide. A common pass-along plant that often escapes cultivation and
becomes naturalized. Found throughout eastern portion
of state from Coastal Bend north to Dallas area.

Hymenocallis liriosme   AMARYLLIDACEAE
Spiderlily, western marsh spider-lily, Texas spider-lily
Marshes, ponds, swamps, bar ditches and
other low, wet areas. Spring. Common.

An erect perennial from a nonrhizomatous bulb, to 2 feet
tall when flowering. Leaves deciduous, 5–8 per bulb, to
2 feet long and ½–1¾ inches wide, strap-shaped to lanceolate, slightly channeled, leatherlike to the touch. Flowers 3–5 in scapes equal to or slightly shorter than leaves,
white with yellow centers, to 7 inches in diameter, with
6 long thin tepals extending beyond corona (giving rise
to common name spiderlily). Found from Coastal Bend
northeast into and throughout East Texas. Often cultivated. Genus name is Greek for "beautiful membrane."
Specific epithet, also Greek, means "fragrant."

71

Hymenocallis occidentalis AMARYLLIDACEAE
**Northern spider-lily, woodland spider-lily,
Carolina spider-lily**
Low, seasonally flooded forests, clay flats,
meadows. Summer, fall. Uncommon.

An erect perennial from a nonrhizomatous bulb, to 30
inches tall when in flower. Leaves deciduous, oblanceolate, channeled with petiole-like bases, not leatherlike
to the touch, occasionally withering prior to flowering.
Flowers about 7 in a 24-inch-tall scape, large, white with
yellow centers, to 6 inches in diameter, with 6 narrow
tepals that extend beyond the corona. Two species of
Hymenocallis occur in Texas and their ranges overlap;
differences in leaf morphology and habitat easily distinguish them. Found in floodplains and seasonally flooded
woods in East Texas. Specific epithet means "of the west."

Nothoscordum bivalve AMARYLLIDACEAE
Crow-poison
Fields, meadows, grasslands, open brush
and woodlands, roadsides and other open
areas. Spring, summer, fall. Common.

An erect, bulbous perennial to 16 inches. Leaves
sheathed, basal, linear, to 12 inches, margins entire.
Scapes solitary, to 16 inches tall, with an umbel of about
6 flowers, to about ⅜ inch wide, radial, on stalks ¾–2
inches long, tepals white to cream, elliptic, to ⅜ inch
long, tips pointed, outer tepals yellow at base and with a
purple stripe. Found throughout Texas. Weak in upper
Panhandle. Absent in far West Texas.

Zephyranthes candida AMARYLLIDACEAE
Fairy lily, autumn zephyrlily, Peruvian swamp lily
Suburban and urban areas, old homesteads, roadsides
and other disturbed areas. Summer, fall. Locally common.

An introduced, bulbous perennial to 10+ inches tall,
spreading via bulbs, clumping. Basal leaves grasslike, to
6 inches long and ⅛ inch wide. Spathe to 1¾ inches long.
Flowers radial, solitary, white to pink, 2 inches wide,
3 sepals and 3 petals of equal size and shape. Native to
South America. Widely available in the nursery trade.
Most common in and around Southeast Texas; sporadic
elsewhere.

Zephyranthes chlorosolen (*Cooperia drummondii*)
AMARYLLIDACEAE
Rain lily, evening rain lily, evening star rain lily
Prairies, fields, woodlands, open areas,
roadsides. Spring, summer, fall. Common.

A bulbous perennial with a scape to 12 inches tall. Leaves
dull green, somewhat glaucous, about ¼ inch wide and to
12 inches long, rubbery. Spathe to 2 inches long. Flowers
white, occasionally tinged pink, trumpet-shaped, erect, to
2 inches wide, with floral tube to 4¾+ inches long. Fruits
3-chambered capsules with flat, black seeds stacked
within. Widespread throughout state. Absent in upper
Panhandle. Weak in East Texas.

Zephyranthes drummondii
(*Cooperia pedunculata*)   AMARYLLIDACEAE
Cebolleta, prairie lily
Fields, meadows, grasslands, prairies, open
brush and woodlands, roadsides and other open
areas. Spring, summer, fall. Common.

An erect, bulbous perennial to 12+ inches tall when in
flower. Leaves basal, dull green to bluish green, to 12
inches long and ⅓ inch wide, rubbery. Spathe to 2 inches
long. Flowers white, occasionally with pink streaks along
outside, funnel-shaped, to 3¾ inches long and 2 inches
wide, floral tube to 1¾ inches long. Fruits 3-chambered
capsules with flat, black seeds stacked within. Found in
open areas of Central Texas, south to Coastal Bend, west
to Val Verde County, into, but weak in, East Texas.

Ammi majus   APIACEAE
**Large bullwort, false bishop's weed, false
Queen Anne's lace**
River and creek banks, floodplains, roadside ditches
and other low, wet areas. Spring. Common.

An erect, branching annual with stout, glabrous stems
to 3+ feet tall. Leaves alternate, oblong, to 8 inches long
and 5¾ inches wide, pinnate or ternate, leaflets lanceolate, bases cuneate, margins serrate, tips acute to obtuse.
Flowers in terminal or axillary compound umbels,
numerous, white, 5-petaled, petals unequal. Found in
South Texas, northeast to Louisiana, less common farther
north into Edwards Plateau and to Red River.

Ammoselinum butleri   APIACEAE
Butler's sandparsley
River and creek floodplains and bottomlands,
woodlands. Spring. Uncommon.

An erect annual, branching from base, with glabrous
stems to 12+ inches tall. Plants variable in size, often
reaching just a few inches in height. Leaves alternate,
on petioles more than 1 inch long, oblong, biternate, to
1 inch long and ¾ inch wide, lobes linear, tips obtuse,
surfaces glabrous. Flowers in sessile umbels in upper
leaf axils, small, 5-petaled, white. Found in shady areas.
Sporadic throughout South Texas, north into Oklahoma,
east to Harris County.

Bifora americana   APIACEAE
Prairie bishop
Fields, meadows, grasslands, prairies, open
brush, woodlands. Spring. Common.

An erect, slender annual with branching stems to 28+
inches tall. Leaves alternate, ovate-oblong, to 2 inches
long and 1¼ inches wide, ternate, leaflets pinnate and
then again lobed, ultimate lobes threadlike, surfaces
glabrous. Stems and branches terminating in compound umbels with numerous small, white, 5-lobed
flowers. Fruits distinctively paired. From Red River in
North-Central Texas south to Coastal Bend, and from
Val Verde County east to Hardin County, most common
in southern and eastern Edwards Plateau.

Bowlesia incana   APIACEAE
Hoary bowlesia, hairy bowlesia, miner's lettuce
Brush and woodlands, thickets, rocky outcrops,
ledges, among boulders, urban and suburban
areas, roadsides. Spring. Common.

A prostrate or decumbent annual with pubescent or
glabrous, branching stems to 2 feet long. Leaves opposite, oval, to 1¼ inches long and 1¾ inches wide, palmately lobed, 5–7 lobes entire or dentate. Flowers in
umbels originating from axils, peduncles to ¾ inch
long, no more than 6 flowers per umbel, white often
purple-tinged, small and inconspicuous. Found throughout South Texas, north to Red River, east into Louisiana,
west to Presidio County; spreading. Common in residential areas.

Centella asiatica (*C. erecta*)   APIACEAE
Erect centella, erect spadeleaf
Wet meadows, savannas, edges of waterways
and bodies of water, roadside ditches and other
low, wet areas. Spring, summer. Common.

A low-growing, creeping, rhizomatous perennial, often forming small colonies. Underground stems to several inches long, plants less than 8 inches tall. Basal leaves on petioles to 6 inches long, erect, cordate to ovate, to 2+ inches long and 1 inch wide, bases cordate, margins entire to toothed, tips rounded. Flowers in umbels, on peduncles usually shorter than tallest leaves, small, 1/16 inch wide, white, sometimes tinged pink. Frequent in wet soils of Southeast Texas, becoming less common farther west. Often, only erect leaves seen emerging from soil.

Chaerophyllum tainturieri   APIACEAE
Wild chervil, hairy fruit chervil
Fields, meadows, grasslands, prairies, open
brush, woodlands. Spring. Common.

An erect, slender annual with pubescent stems, branching from base, to 20+ inches tall. Leaves alternate, on petioles to 6 inches long, bipinnate, ovate, to 3¼ inches long and 2½ inches wide, secondary divisions pinnatifid, ultimate lobes elliptic, to ⅛ inch long and 1/16 inch wide. Flowers in loose, compound umbels originating from upper leaf axils, small, 5-petaled, white. Fruits ribbed, glabrous, to ¼ inch long. Found throughout Texas, but absent in Panhandle and far southern Texas.

Cicuta maculata   APIACEAE
Spotted cowbane, water hemlock, suicide root
Riparian areas, marshes. Spring, summer. Common.

An erect biennial or short-lived perennial with stout, branching, glabrous stems to 6 feet tall, often reddish purple, lower stem hollow. Leaves alternate, petiolate, once or twice odd-pinnate, lower leaves to 18 inches long and 8 inches wide, upper leaves smaller, leaflets 3–7, oblong-elliptic, to 4 inches long and 1¼ inches wide, bases wide-tapering, margins dentate, tips acute. Inflorescences in terminal compound umbels to 6 inches wide, umbellets with up to 15 flowers. Each flower to ⅛ inch wide, 5-petaled, white. Frequent in East and Central Texas, less common in Panhandle. Absent elsewhere. Toxic to humans.

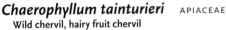

Daucus carota   APIACEAE
Wild carrot, Queen Anne's lace, bird's nest
Fields, grasslands, meadows, open brush and
woodlands, roadsides, rights-of-way and other
open areas. Spring, summer, fall. Common.

An introduced, erect, branching biennial with stems
to 5 feet tall. Leaves alternate, bipinnate-pinnatifid, to 4
inches long and 2 inches wide, segments linear to rhombic, to ⅜ inch long and less than ¼ inch wide, bases
sheathed to stem, tips acute to pointed, blades airy, lacy,
lower surface pubescent. Flowers in terminal compound
umbels on peduncles to 20 inches long, umbels flat, to 5
inches wide, flowers white, numerous, 5-petaled, about
⅛ inch wide. Often with single reddish purple flower in
umbel center. Found in eastern third of Texas, occasionally farther west.

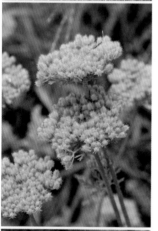

Daucus pusillus   APIACEAE
American wild carrot, rattle-snake weed
Fields, meadows, grasslands, open brush
and woodlands, roadsides and other open
areas. Spring, summer. Common.

An erect annual with glabrous, reddish brown stems,
branching from base or weakly above, to 30+ inches
tall. Leaves alternate, mostly in lower half, few along
stems, oblong to 4 inches long and 3 inches wide, 2- or
3-pinnatifid, final lobes linear, tips acute. Flowers in terminal compound corymbs, white, 5-petaled, about ⅛
inch wide. Bracts just below inflorescence are similar
to, but smaller than, leaves. Widespread in open areas
throughout state. Weak in Panhandle.

Eryngium heterophyllum   APIACEAE
Mexican thistle
Mountain grasslands, open brush and
woodlands, rocky slopes, roadsides and other
open areas. Summer. Locally common.

An erect, branching perennial with stout, glabrous stems
to 24+ inches tall. Basal leaves oblanceolate, to 5 inches
long, margins dentate, with long, thin spines, tips acute.
Lower stem leaves alternate, sessile, pinnatifid, stiff, margins entire, tips pointed. Upper stem leaves opposite,
rigid, palmately parted, tips pointed. Flowering heads
terminal, white and tinged blue, to ¾ inch tall and ½
inch wide, with rigid white bracts below. Found in mid to
upper elevations in Big Bend region.

Eryngium yuccifolium APIACEAE
Rattlesnake-master, button snake root
Prairies, grasslands, open woodlands. Summer. Common.

An erect, stout perennial with glabrous, branching stems
to 5+ feet tall. Basal leaves stiff, linear, to 3 feet long and
1½ inches wide, margins with short spines. Stem leaves
similar, smaller. Flowering heads in branching cymes,
roundish oval, to 1 inch wide, greenish white, bracts
ovate-lanceolate, not lobed, stiff, tips pointed. Found in
open areas throughout eastern third of Texas. Genus
name of Greek origin; means sea holly.

Hydrocotyle bonariensis APIACEAE
Largeleaf pennywort, salt pennywort, sombrerillo
Coastal areas, dunes, marshes, roadsides.
Spring, summer, fall. Common.

A creeping perennial, rooting at nodes, with glabrous,
slender stems. Leaves peltate, petiole to 15 inches long,
blades round to ovate, to 4 inches in diameter, margins
lobed. Flowers in umbels held well above leaves, numerous, small, white, 5-petaled. Found along Gulf Coast.
Specific epithet refers to Buenos Aires; the species is
widely distributed in coastal areas of the Americas.

Hydrocotyle umbellata APIACEAE
**Manyflower marshpennywort, common pennywort,
ombligo de Venus**
Banks of ponds, lakes, streams, rivers, roadside ditches
and other low, wet areas. Spring, summer, fall. Common.

A prostrate or floating perennial, rooting at nodes,
with glabrous, slender stems. Leaves round, peltate,
on petioles usually shorter than 16 inches long, margins crenate. Flowers in umbels held well above leaves,
numerous, small, white, 5-petaled. Found in wet areas,
including lawns, from Val Verde County east into
Louisiana, north into Oklahoma and south throughout
coastal Texas.

Hydrocotyle verticillata APIACEAE
Whorled marshpennywort
Banks of creeks, lakes, ponds, rivers,
roadside ditches, irrigated areas and other
wet areas. Spring, summer. Common.

A prostrate, creeping perennial with glabrous, slender stems, rooting at nodes. Leaves peltate, on petioles usually shorter than 10 inches long, round, to 2½
inches in diameter, crenately lobed, 8–13 lobes per leaf.
Flowers in axillary inflorescences, spikelike, to 7 inches
long, whorled along rachis, well spaced, white to cream,
5-lobed, small. Found throughout Texas, in wet soils,
including residential lawns. Absent in Panhandle.

Scandix pecten-veneris APIACEAE
Venus' comb, crow-needles
Fields, pastures, grasslands, prairies, roadsides
and other open areas. Spring. Uncommon.

An introduced, erect annual, branching from base, with
stems to 15+ inches tall. Leaves alternate, bipinnate, to
6 inches long and 3 inches wide, lobes linear, margins
entire, tips acute. Flowers in terminal or lateral umbels
on short peduncles, white, 5-petaled, petals unequal.
Fruits linear to oblong, to ¾ inch long with a 3-inch-long
beak. Found in Harris County and surrounding counties,
with other populations occurring in Austin and Dallas–
Fort Worth areas. Elongated fruits are distinctive.

Spermolepis echinata APIACEAE
Bristly scaleseed
Fields, pastures, prairies, grasslands, open
brush and woodlands, roadsides and other
open areas. Spring. Common.

A low-growing, spreading annual with glabrous stems
and leaves to 16 inches tall. Leaves alternate, ovate, to
1 inch long and ¾ inch wide, biternate, lobes slender,
threadlike, tips pointed. Flowers white, small, 5-petaled,
in umbels on peduncles to nearly 3 inches long, umbels
with 14 rays, rays to ⅝ inch long. Fruits oval, ¹⁄₁₆ inch
long, covered in short bristles. Widespread throughout
Texas. Weak in Panhandle and western Edwards Plateau.

Torilis arvensis APIACEAE
Spreading hedge parsley, field hedge parsley, common hedge parsley
Fields, pastures, grasslands, open brush and woodlands, roadsides, suburban and urban areas. Spring. Common.

An introduced, erect, slender annual with branching, pubescent stems to 24 inches tall. Leaves alternate, ovate-lanceolate, 2- or 3-pinnate, ultimate lobes linear. Stems terminating in compound umbels to 3 inches wide. Flowers numerous, small, white, 5-petaled. Fruits oblong, covered in hooked bristles which aid in dispersal. Frequent throughout Edwards Plateau, west into Brewster County, southeast to Houston, and north into Oklahoma; spreading elsewhere.

Apocynum cannabinum APOCYNACEAE
Dogbane, Indian hemp, prairie dogbane
Prairies, fields, meadows, open brush and woodlands, roadsides and other open areas. Spring, summer. Common.

An erect, multistemmed perennial with branching, glabrous, light green to red stems to 3+ feet tall. Leaves opposite, sessile or on petioles ¼ inch long, elliptic to oblong, to 3½ inches long and 1 inch wide, margins entire. Numerous flowers occur in panicles at end of primary stems or lateral stems, white to cream, about ¹⁄₁₀ inch wide and about as long. Widely distributed across state, aside from South Texas, where it is absent. Genus name of Greek origin and means "free from" (*apo*) "dogs" (*kuon*), hence the common name dogbane, as the sap was used as dog poison.

Asclepias amplexicaulis APOCYNACEAE
Clasping milkweed, blunt-leaved milkweed, sand milkweed
Meadows, fields, prairies, open woodlands, roadsides and other open areas. Spring, summer. Common.

An erect perennial with a single stem to 3 feet tall. Leaves opposite, sessile, ovate to oval, to 5 inches long and 2 inches wide, bases cordate and clasping, margins entire to wavy, tips rounded but may have a sharp point. Inflorescences solitary and terminal, held well above foliage, consisting of up to 80 flowers, pedicels to 2 inches long. Flowers to ½ inch long, petals reflexed, greenish, often tinged with rose or pink, crown tannish to pink, horns slightly shorter than hoods. Found mostly in East Texas, extending south below Edwards Plateau.

Asclepias asperula APOCYNACEAE
Antelope horns, green flowered milkweed
Grasslands, prairies, sparse brushlands,
open woodlands, roadsides and other open
areas. Spring, summer, fall. Common.

An erect to spreading perennial with 1–10+ pubescent
stems to 2 feet long. Leaves opposite with short petioles,
linear to lanceolate, to 8 inches long and 3 inches wide,
margins entire, blades folded, pubescent. Flowers in solitary, terminal, compact inflorescences to 4 inches wide,
on stalks to 3½ inches long or sessile, greenish yellow,
often tinged with maroon or purple, corolla forming a
5-parted bowl, hood purplish with a cream or pale green
tip. Found everywhere except in South and East Texas.

Asclepias emoryi APOCYNACEAE
Emory's milkweed
Fields, prairies, open brush and woodlands, roadsides
and other open areas. Spring, summer, fall. Uncommon.

An ascending to decumbent perennial with a single
stem, branching from base, to 10+ inches long. Leaves
opposite, oblong-lanceolate, to 4 inches long and 1½
inches wide, margins wavy to entire. Flowers in umbels
along middle to upper stem, about 10 per umbel, corolla
5-lobed, creamy white to dingy green, often with brownish purple stripes, lobes reflexed, hood pale green ending
in white. Found in South Texas, north into Edwards Plateau and southern Panhandle.

Asclepias engelmanniana APOCYNACEAE
Engelmann's milkweed
Fields, prairies, grasslands, open brush and woodlands,
roadsides. Spring, summer. Uncommon.

An erect perennial with a single, unbranched glabrous
stem to 4+ feet tall. Leaves alternate, sessile, linear, to 10
inches long and ⅓ inch wide, margins entire, surfaces
glabrous. Upper leaves may appear opposite. Flowers
in tight, rounded umbels in middle to upper portion of
stem, sessile or on peduncles to 1½ inches long, greenish yellow or creamy yellow, often tinged purple, 5-lobed,
curved with tips ascending. Follicles glabrous, lanceolate,
to 5 inches long, tapering to a point. Found throughout
Central Texas, north through Panhandle and Oklahoma,
west into Chihuahuan Desert.

Asclepias glaucescens   APOCYNACEAE
Nodding milkweed
Woodlands, canyons, rocky hillsides, mountain
creek beds. Summer, fall. Uncommon.

An erect, multi- or single-stemmed, unbranched
perennial to 30+ inches tall, with glabrous leaves and
stems. Leaves opposite, sessile, often angled upward,
ovate-elliptic, to 6½ inches long and 2¾ inches wide,
margins entire, surfaces waxy to the touch. Flowers in
2½-inch-wide umbels in upper portion of stem, about
1 inch wide, corolla 5-lobed, greenish yellow, hood yellowish tan. Follicles to 6 inches long, glabrous, elliptic.
Found in upper elevations in mountains of West Texas,
north into New Mexico, south into Mexico.

Asclepias latifolia   APOCYNACEAE
Broadleaf milkweed
Fields, prairies, grasslands, open shrub
and woodlands, roadsides and other open
areas. Spring, summer, fall. Common.

An erect, single- to multistemmed, rhizomatous perennial to 3+ feet tall, with glabrous, glaucous leaves and
stems. Leaves opposite, rounded to broadly elliptic, to 5½
inches long and 4 inches wide, bases rounded to slightly
cordate, margins entire, tips rounded to truncated.
Flowers in umbels in middle to upper portion of stems,
5-lobed, pale green to greenish yellow, reflexed, hood
white, yellowing with age. Follicles smooth, thick, to 3¾
inches long. Found in Panhandle, south into Edwards
Plateau, southwest into Chihuahuan Desert.

Asclepias linearis   APOCYNACEAE
Thin-leaved milkweed, slim milkweed
Grasslands, prairies, edges of marshes.
Spring, summer, fall. Locally common.

An erect, rhizomatous perennial with pubescent stems,
branching from base, to 2+ feet tall. Leaves opposite,
sessile, 2 or 3 per node, linear, to 3¾ inches long, margins entire. Flowers in umbels in upper portion of stem,
peduncles to ¾ inch long, pale green to greenish white,
corolla 5-lobed, reflexed, hood white. Follicles slender,
smooth, to 4 inches long. Found from South Texas northeast to Houston, mostly along coast. However, can be
found inland, around seasonally wet areas.

Asclepias longifolia APOCYNACEAE
Longleaf milkweed

Grasslands, prairies, open areas in pine woodlands, swamps, wet savannas, roadside ditches and other open, wet areas. Spring, summer. Uncommon.

An ascending to erect perennial with slender, pubescent stems to 2+ feet tall. Leaves alternate, sessile, linear to lanceolate, to 7 inches long and ½ inch wide, margins entire. Flowers in umbels in upper portion of stem, peduncles to 2½ inches long, inflorescences rounded with about 40 slender flowers, corolla heavily reflexed, greenish yellow to pale yellow with brownish red to maroon tips, hood brownish red to maroon. Follicles slender, to 4¾ inches long and ½ inch wide. Uncommon in Southeast Texas, rare in Northeast Texas.

Asclepias obovata APOCYNACEAE
Pineland milkweed

Oak-pine or mixed pine woodlands, adjacent fields, savannas, meadows, roadsides and other open areas. Spring, summer, fall. Locally common.

An erect perennial with a single, unbranched or weakly branched, slightly tomentose stem to 3+ feet tall. Leaves opposite, oval to oblong, to narrowly ovate above, to 3¼ inches long and 1¾ inches wide, bases rounded to truncate, margins entire to wavy, tips rounded to acute. Flowers in umbels 1½ inches wide in upper stem, about ½ inch long, corolla 5-lobed, lobes greenish yellow, reflexed, hood spreading, tannish yellow, often with tinges of red or pink. Follicles to 4¾ inches long. Found in Southeast Texas, north into Oklahoma.

Asclepias oenotheroides APOCYNACEAE
Zizotes milkweed

Prairies, fields, grasslands, open shrub and woodlands, desert grass and sparse shrublands, creek and river banks, roadsides and other open areas. Spring, summer, fall. Common.

An ascending to erect perennial with single or multiple stalks, branching from base, to 20+ inches long. Leaves and stems tomentose. Leaves opposite, on petioles ¾ inch long, ovate to lanceolate to oblong, to 4¾ inches long and 2½ inches wide, bases truncate to tapering, margins entire to wavy, tips rounded to pointed. Flowers in clusters in middle to upper stem, corolla creamy white to yellowish green to pale yellow, reflexed heavily or slightly, hood tannish green to green with white tip, elongated. Widespread; absent in Piney Woods.

Asclepias perennis APOCYNACEAE
Aquatic milkweed, white swamp milkweed
Swamps, bogs, palmetto groves, roadside ditches and
other low, wet areas. Spring, summer. Locally common.

An ascending to erect perennial with multiple,
unbranched, glabrous to pubescent stems. Leaves
opposite, on petioles to ¾ inch long, narrow-elliptic to
ovate-elliptic, to 5 inches long and 1½ inches wide, bases
attenuate, margins entire, tips tapering to point. Flowers
in umbels to 2½ inches wide in upper portion of stem, up
to 50 per umbel, corolla 5-lobed, white to pink, reflexed
with ascending tips, hood white, hooks extending well
beyond hood. Follicles smooth, lanceolate, to 3 inches
long. Found in Southeast Texas, from Louisiana border
southwest to Coastal Bend.

Asclepias prostrata APOCYNACEAE
Prostrate milkweed
Open grass and brushlands. Spring. Rare.

A prostrate perennial with stems to 16 inches long, radiating from a central rootstock. Opposite leaves, triangular to deltoid-lanceolate to 1¾ inches long, short petiolate
to nearly sessile, margins wavy, bases truncate to weakly
cordate, tips acute. Flowers few, usually 4 or 5 in umbels
held just above stem, to 1 inch long with cream-white
hoods extending beyond pale green hooks, the 5 pale
green reflexed lobes have ascending tips. Follicles elliptic,
to 2 inches long. Rare, but found in sandy-silty soils close
to Rio Grande in Starr, Hidalgo, and Zapata Counties.

Asclepias stenophylla APOCYNACEAE
**Slimleaf milkweed, narrowleaf milkweed,
narrowleaf green milkweed**
Prairies, grasslands, fields, meadows, woodland
openings. Spring, summer. Uncommon.

An erect perennial with 1 or 2 stems to 2+ feet tall, stems
pubescent in upper portion, glabrous on lower. Leaves
alternate, occasionally appearing opposite, sessile or
nearly so, linear, to 7 inches long and ¼ inch wide, margins entire to revolute, tips pointed, surfaces slightly
pubescent. Flowers in umbels originating from leaf axils
in middle to upper stem, to 25± per umbel, 5-lobed, pale
greenish white to pale yellow, reflexed, hood white. Follicles slender, tapering at both ends, glabrous to slightly
pubescent, to 5 inches long and ⅓ inch wide. Found
in eastern third of Texas, north into Panhandle and
Oklahoma.

Asclepias subverticillata APOCYNACEAE
Horsetail milkweed, poison milkweed
Grasslands, fields, open shrublands, canyon
bottoms. Spring, summer, fall. Common.

An erect, rhizomatous perennial with slender, branching stems to 4+ feet tall. Leaves whorled in 3s or 5s, or opposite above, subsessile, linear, to 4¾ inches long and less than ¼ inch wide, margins entire to revolute, blades often folded, tips pointed. Flowers in umbels in middle to upper portion of stem, to 20± in loose clusters, 5-lobed, greenish white to greenish yellow, hood white. Follicles slender, to 4¾ inches long, glabrous. Frequent in Chihuahuan Desert, with isolated collections elsewhere. Grows in and along low areas that collect water during monsoon seasons. Often forms large colonies.

Asclepias texana APOCYNACEAE
Texas milkweed, white milkweed
Oak-juniper and oak-pine-juniper woodlands,
canyons, creek bottoms, mountain slopes.
Spring, summer. Locally common.

An erect, multistemmed, branching perennial with stems to 2+ feet tall. Leaves opposite, on petioles to ½ inch long, oval to oblong-elliptic, bases obtuse to tapering, margins entire, tips pointed. Flowers in umbels in upper portion of stems, to about 20 per umbel, corolla 5-lobed, lobes reflexed, tips ascending and flared, both corolla and hood white. Follicles slender, to 3¾ inches long, tapering at both ends, smooth. Found in two separate areas of Texas: southern and eastern Edwards Plateau and mountains of Big Bend region.

Asclepias variegata APOCYNACEAE
**Redring milkweed, white-flowered milkweed,
red-neck milkweed**
Mixed woodlands, thickets, roadsides.
Spring, summer. Uncommon.

An erect perennial with an unbranched, pubescent stem to 3+ feet tall. Leaves opposite, on petioles to 1¼ inches long, oblong to ovate, to 6 inches long and 3 inches wide, bases rounded to acute, margins entire to wavy, tips rounded to pointed. Flowers in compact terminal or axillary umbels, 35± per rounded 3-inch-wide umbel, on peduncles to 2 inches long, 5-lobed, corolla reflexed, hood and corolla white with red ring at base of hood. Follicles slender, tapering to point on free end, to 5 inches long and ¾ inch wide, glabrous to softly pubescent. Found in the eastern fourth of Texas.

Asclepias verticillata   APOCYNACEAE
Whorled milkweed
Grasslands, prairies, fields, open shrub
and woodlands, roadsides and other open
areas. Spring, summer. Common.

An erect, rhizomatous perennial with slender, branching,
slightly pubescent stems to 3+ feet tall. Leaves whorled,
4–6 per node, subsessile, linear, to 3 inches long and ⅒
inch wide, blades ascending to erect, margins entire to
revolute, tips pointed. Flowers in umbels in upper portion of stem, 20± per 1½-inch-wide umbel, pale greenish
white, corolla reflexed with ascending tips, hood white.
Follicles slender, lanceolate, to 4 inches long and ½ inch
wide, smooth. Widely distributed across state; frequent in
eastern half of Texas.

Asclepias viridiflora   APOCYNACEAE
Green-comet milkweed, wand milkweed, green milkweed
Grasslands, prairies, fields, open shrub and
woodlands, roadsides. Spring, summer. Common.

An erect, typically single-stemmed perennial with an
unbranched, stout, pubescent stem to 2+ feet tall. Leaves
opposite, sessile or on petioles ⅓ inch long, stiff, variable
from slightly round-oval to lanceolate, to 5 inches long
and 1½ inches wide, bases tapering, margins entire and
wavy, tips rounded to pointed. Flowers in tight, rounded
umbels in upper stem, to 50± per umbel, greenish yellow,
corolla 5-lobed, extremely reflexed, parallel with pedicel,
hood light brownish purple with dusty white edge. Follicles lanceolate, smooth, to 5 inches long and ¾ inch wide,
tapering to point on free end. Widely scattered.

Asclepias viridis   APOCYNACEAE
Green milkweed, green antelope horns
Fields, prairies, grasslands, open shrub and woodlands,
roadsides and other open areas. Spring, summer. Common.

An ascending to erect or decumbent perennial with a
glabrous, single stem branching from base, to 2 feet
long. Leaves alternate on petioles to ⅓ inch long, ovate to
oblong-lanceolate, to 4¾ inches long and 2 inches wide,
bases truncate to round, margins entire, tips rounded
to blunt. Flowers in crowded umbels which are terminal or in upper axils of stem, 5-lobed, cream to greenish yellow, lobes ascending, hood deflexed, purplish red
with white tips. Follicles thick, ovate, tapering to point on
free end. Widespread in eastern half of Texas, north into
Oklahoma.

Cynanchum barbigerum APOCYNACEAE
Bearded swallow-wort, thicket threadvine
Open shrub and woodlands, thickets, roadsides,
fence lines. Spring, summer, fall. Common.

A twining, climbing perennial vine with glabrous to
slightly pubescent stems to 8+ feet long. Leaves opposite,
on petioles ⅓ inch long, linear to elliptic-lanceolate, to 2
inches long and ¼ inch wide, bases rounded, margins
revolute, tips pointed. Flowers in corymbs originating
from leaf axils, on peduncles to ½ inch long, with up to 5
creamy white or white, 5-lobed, bell-shaped flowers, lobes
linear, obviously pubescent on inner surface, recurved.
Follicles smooth, lanceolate to 2 inches long. Found in
southern Edwards Plateau, south into Mexico.

Cynanchum laeve APOCYNACEAE
Honeyvine, blue vine, sand vine
Fields, brush and woodlands, roadsides, fence
lines. Spring, summer, fall. Common.

A twining, climbing perennial vine with glabrous to
slightly pubescent stems to 10+ feet long. Leaves opposite, on petioles to 1¾ inches long, triangular-lanceolate
to deltate, to 3¼ inches long and 2 inches wide, bases
cordate, margins entire, tips pointed. Flowers in umbels
from leaf axils, peduncles to 1 inch, 25+ per umbel, white
to greenish white, 5-lobed with lobes slender. Follicles
smooth, lanceolate, angled, to 6 inches long. Widespread
throughout Central Texas, north into Oklahoma, east into
Louisiana.

Cynanchum maccartii APOCYNACEAE
MacCart's swallow-wort
Thickets, brushlands, edges of woodlands, rocky
outcrops. Spring, summer, fall. Uncommon.

A twining, climbing perennial vine with glabrous,
branching stems to 8+ feet long. Leaves opposite, linear
to lanceolate, bases cuneate to rounded, margins entire to
slightly revolute, tips pointed. Flowers in clusters of 10+
on essentially sessile corymbs, corolla white to greenish
white to cream, 5-lobed with lobes ovate to lanceolate, glabrous. Follicles smooth, thin to 1¾ inches long. Found in
South Texas, north into Edwards Plateau.

Cynanchum pringlei   APOCYNACEAE
Pringle's swallow-wort
Rocky slopes, outcrops, canyons, open brush and
woodlands. Spring, summer. Uncommon.

A twining, climbing perennial vine with glabrous to
slightly pubescent, brownish red, branching stems to 6+
feet long. Leaves opposite, linear-oblong to lanceolate,
to about ¾ inch long, bases tapering to truncate, margins revolute, tips pointed. Flowers in small clusters in
leaf axils, urn-shaped, creamy white, corolla 5-lobed with
lobes spreading or slightly so, interior pubescent. Follicles glabrous, lanceolate, to 1¾ inches. Found in Chihuahuan Desert. Similar to *Cynanchum barbigerum*, but
with smaller flowers, reddish brown stems, and generally
smaller overall; their ranges do not seem to overlap.

Cynanchum racemosum   APOCYNACEAE
Talayote
Brush and woodlands, creek and river banks, roadsides,
fence lines. Spring, summer, fall. Common.

A twining, climbing perennial vine with glabrous
to slightly pubescent, branching stems to 15+ feet
long. Leaves opposite, on petioles to 2 inches long,
triangular-lanceolate to ovate, to 3½ inches long and 2¾
inches wide, bases heavily cordate with rounded lobes,
margins entire to slightly wavy, tips pointed. Flowers
in racemes originating from leaf axils, 10± per raceme,
greenish white to cream-colored, 5-lobed, lobes short,
recurved. Follicles smooth, rounded-lanceolate, to 5
inches long and 1½+ inches wide. Widespread. Found
throughout Central Texas, south to coastal Texas and into
Mexico, west into Big Bend region.

Funastrum cynanchoides   APOCYNACEAE
Fringed twinevine, twine vine, climbing milkweed vine
Thickets, creek and river banks, shrub and woodlands,
canyons, fence lines. Spring, summer, fall. Common.

A twining, climbing perennial vine to 10+ feet long,
with glabrous leaves and stems and a pungent,
burnt-rubber odor. Leaves opposite, on petioles to ¾
inch long, ovate-lanceolate to triangular-lanceolate or
linear-lanceolate, to about 3 inches long, bases cordate,
margins entire. Flowers in umbels from leaf axils, on
peduncles to 2 inches long, to 20± per umbel, corolla
5-lobed, lobes ovate, creamy white to greenish white,
sometimes tinged reddish purple. Lacking to absent in
eastern third of state.

Funastrum torreyi   APOCYNACEAE
Torrey's twinevine
Rocky slopes, creek banks, ridges, rocky outcrops and other rocky, wooded areas. Spring, summer. Uncommon.

A twining, climbing perennial vine with pubescent leaves and stems to 6+ feet long. Leaves opposite, on petioles to ½ inch long, ovate-lanceolate to ovate-triangular, bases cordate, margins entire, tips pointed. Flowers in umbels originating from leaf axils, 20± per umbel, peduncles to 1½ inches long, corollas 5-lobed, star-shaped, creamy white with reddish purple centers. Occurs in Brewster and Presidio Counties. Pubescent stems and leaves differentiate this species from *Funastrum cynanchoides*.

Matelea gonocarpos   APOCYNACEAE
Angle-pod milkweed vine
Wooded riparian areas, woodlands, thickets. Spring, summer. Common.

A twining, climbing perennial vine with pubescent stems to 15+ feet long. Leaves opposite, on petioles to 3 inches long, ovate-elliptic, bases cordate, tips pointed. Flowers in umbels originating from leaf axils, star-shaped, corolla lobes linear to lanceolate, green throughout, occasionally with darker color (brown, maroon) radiating from center. Follicles heavily angled, lacking warty protuberances of other milkweeds. Occurs in woodlands, around perennial streams, or in protected canyons, with deep soils and heavy tree cover. Found mostly in eastern portion of state; other occurrences in Central and South Texas. Specific epithet means "angled fruit," hence the common name.

Matelea parviflora   APOCYNACEAE
Small flower milkvine
Grasslands, open shrub and woodlands. Spring, summer. Uncommon.

A prostrate, creeping vine with pubescent leaves and stems to 20 inches long. Leaves opposite, on petioles to ½ inch long, triangular, to 2 inches long and nearly as wide, bases cordate or rounded or truncate, margins entire to wavy. Flowers on erect racemes about 6 inches tall, green, shiny, corolla lobes ovate and reflexed, each flower about ½ inch in diameter. Found in sandy soils of South Texas, often in open areas in woodlands and brushlands.

Matelea parvifolia   APOCYNACEAE
Spearleaf milkvine
Desert scrub, canyons, rocky outcrops.
Winter, spring, fall. Rare.

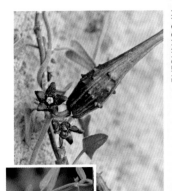

A twining, climbing perennial vine to 4 feet long, with
pubescent stems and leaves. Leaves opposite, ovate to lanceolate, to about ¾ inch long and ⅜ inch wide, bases cordate or sagittate. Flowers in umbels originating from leaf
axils, 5-lobed, lobes spreading, green to greenish brown
to dark maroon, about ¼ inch wide and as long. Follicles
lanceolate, to 1½ inches long, maroon or green, surface slightly muricate. Known to occur in Presidio and
Brewster Counties.

Matelea producta   APOCYNACEAE
Texas milkvine
Open shrub and woodlands. Spring, summer. Uncommon.

A twining, climbing vine with several stems to 6+ feet
long. Stems and leaves pubescent. Leaves on petioles
to 1½ inches long, triangular, to 3½ inches long and 2
inches wide, bases cordate, margins entire and slightly
wavy, tips pointed. Flowers in short umbels originating from leaf axils, green, somewehat bell-shaped, about
½ inch in diameter and nearly as long. Follicles to 4
inches long and smooth. Found in Chihuahuan Desert
region of Texas, usually in open brush and woodlands, or
among boulders or rocky outcrops, using other plants for
support.

Matelea reticulata   APOCYNACEAE
Pearl milkweed vine, green milkvine, net-veined milkvine
Riparian areas, woodlands, shrublands.
Spring, summer. Common.

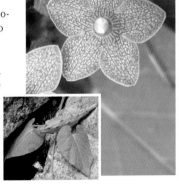

A twining, climbing perennial vine with stems to 12+
feet long, stems and leaves softly pubescent. Leaves opposite, generally triangular-ovate, to 4½ inches long and to
3¼ inches wide, bases cordate, tips tapering to a point.
The star-shaped green flowers with 5 ovate to obovate
corolla lobes appear in loose clusters from the leaf axils.
Perhaps the most remarkable feature of this plant is the
netted pattern on the flowers, surrounding a shiny
pearl-like center, which makes for easy identification. Follicles to 5 inches, slender, and covered in
warty protuberances. Abundant throughout Central Texas, becoming less common farther south to
Mexico and west into the Big Bend region.

Seutera angustifolia
(*Cynanchum angustifolium*)   APOCYNACEAE
Coastal swallowwort, vine milkweed
Coastal prairies, marshes, thickets. Spring,
summer, fall. Locally common.

A twining, climbing vine with stems to 10+ feet long.
Leaves opposite, on short petioles, linear, to 3¼ inches
long and ¼ inch wide, bases tapered, margins entire,
tips pointed. Flowers in cymes on short peduncles, 20±
per cyme, white to greenish white, with 5 slender lobes.
Found along coastal Texas from Mexico to Louisiana.

Telosiphonia hypoleuca   APOCYNACEAE
Davis Mountain rocktrumpet
Rocky slopes, open shrub and woodlands.
Summer, fall. Uncommon.

An erect, multistemmed perennial with reddish brown
stems to 16 inches tall. Leaves opposite, on short petioles,
oblong to linear, to 3¾ inches long and ¾ inch wide, margins entire, surfaces green above, white to silver pubescence below. Flowers funnel-shaped, white, to 3 inches
long and 2 inches wide, 1–3 per stem, opening in the evening and closing in the morning, or remaining open if
overcast. Grows at higher elevation in mountains of Big
Bend region, primarily on igneous substrate. Less common than *Telosiphonia macrosiphon*, but easily distinguished by its slender leaves.

Telosiphonia macrosiphon   APOCYNACEAE
**Rocktrumpet, longtube trumpet flower,
plateau rocktrumpet**
Rocky open brushlands, rocky outcrops,
canyons. Spring, summer, fall. Common.

An erect, multistemmed perennial with reddish brown
stems to 16 inches tall. Leaves opposite, on short petioles
to ⅜ inch long, ovate to slightly round, to 2½ inches long
and 1¾ inches wide, bases rounded to cordate, margins
wavy and occasionally revolute, leaf surfaces with flattened
hairs. Flowers solitary, white, sometimes pink-tinged,
funnel-shaped, to 6 inches long and 2½ inches wide, opening in early evening, closing after sunrise. Found throughout Chihuahuan Desert region, east into Edwards Plateau
on either igneous or limestone substrate. Grows on slopes
or in flats. *Telosiphonia lanuginosa* found from Laredo
south to Hidalgo County. *Telosiphonia brachysiphon* rare in
Franklin Mountains of El Paso County.

Arisaema dracontium ARACEAE
Green dragon, dragon-root
Woodlands, thickets, stream banks, riparian
areas. Spring, summer. Uncommon.

An erect perennial with single flowering stalk, to
2½ feet tall. One compound leaf, to 2 feet wide, with 13
elliptic leaflets, each to 8 inches long. Each plant produces a single greenish yellow spathe enclosing
a spadix, which is where the numerous, inconspicuous flowers are held. When in flower, the
spadix extends above the spathe, to 10 inches.
Typically found in shady areas with rich, moist
soils in Central Texas, east to Louisiana, north
into Oklahoma. While widespread and seemingly common in these areas, its limited habitat
makes it uncommon.

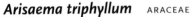

Arisaema triphyllum ARACEAE
Jack-in-the-pulpit, Indian-turnip
Bogs, swamps, wet woodlands. Spring. Uncommon.

An erect perennial with single flowering stalk to 24+
inches tall, bearing 1 or 2 leaves per plant and a single
inflorescence. Leaf 3-foliolate, leaflets ovate to rhombic,
to 7 inches long and 3 inches wide. Inflorescence to 3½
inches long and 2 inches wide, with a green to reddish
brown spathe loosely surrounding the spadix , which is
where the numerous, inconspicuous flowers are held.
The top of the spathe curves over the top of the spadix,
somewhat resembling a pitcher plant. Primarily found in
eastern fourth of Texas, occasionally farther west.

Pistia stratiotes ARACEAE
Water lettuce, water cabbage, shellflower
Streams, rivers, lakes, ponds, swamps and other
bodies of water. Summer, fall. Locally common.

An introduced, stemless, floating aquatic perennial with
thick, soft leaves, to 12 inches wide; producing vegetative offsets. Leaves wedge-shaped, to 6 inches long and
half as wide at tip, spongy and soft to the touch, forming
rosette (thus the common name, water lettuce). Flowers
and spathe minuscule, occurring at base of inner leaves,
white to pale green. Persistent in warmer waterways
throughout Texas, from southern Edwards Plateau south
to coast; in some areas can clog waterways or cover small
ponds.

Maianthemum racemosum   ASPARAGACEAE
**False spikenard, Solomon's plume,
large false Solomon's seal**
Deciduous woodlands. Spring, summer. Uncommon.

An erect to arching, rhizomatous perennial with stems to 4+ feet tall. Leaves alternate, on short petioles or sessile to clasping, elliptic to ovate, to 7 inches long and 3¼ inches wide, bases rounded to tapering, margins entire, tips acute. Flowers radial, to 250 in terminal panicles, small, ⅛ inch wide and as long, with 6 tepals. Subspecies *amplexicaule* is found in mountains of the Big Bend region and Guadalupe Mountains in West Texas and has clasping leaves, while subspecies *racemosum* is located in northeast corner of Texas and has leaves on petioles.

Manfreda longiflora   ASPARAGACEAE
Runyon's tuberose, longflower tuberose, amole de rio
Tamaulipan Thornscrub. Summer. Rare.

A rhizomatous perennial with tuberous roots and a bulbous stem. Leaves fleshy, linear, to 8 inches long and ½ inch wide, spreading from a central stem, margins toothed, blades with dark, reddish brown spots. Flowers in spikes to 20 inches tall, cream to white, fading to brick red as they age, to 1½ inches long and just over 1 inch wide, filaments included within the tube, a distinguishing character between this species and the closely related *Manfreda maculosa*. Found in a few counties in deep South Texas in undisturbed thornscrub. Usually seen when in flower as spikes extend above surrounding vegetation.

Manfreda maculosa   ASPARAGACEAE
Spice lily, American aloe, false aloe
Mesquite and acacia shrubland. Spring,
summer, fall. Common.

A rhizomatous perennial with fleshy roots and subterranean stem. Leaves fleshy, succulent, linear-lanceolate, to 15 inches long and 1 inch wide, margins toothed, blades channeled, spotted reddish brown, in varying degrees of density. Flowers in scapes to 4 feet tall, white fading to pink or brick red as they age, filaments extending beyond mouth of tube, which distinguishes this species from *Manfreda longiflora*. Found strictly in South Texas, south of San Antonio. Widely available in the nursery trade; a great addition to home landscapes.

Manfreda virginica   ASPARAGACEAE
Rattlesnake master, Virginian agave, false aloe
Fields, meadows, open forests and woodlands.
Spring, summer, fall. Common.

A semisucculent perennial with cylindric rhizomes,
basal leaves, scape to 4 feet. Leaves oblanceolate to
linear-lanceolate, to 16 inches long and 2½ inches wide,
succulent or semisucculent, erect or lax, margins toothed
or entire, spotted or not. Flowers borne on final 2 feet of
4-foot-tall scapes, up to 30 per scape, perianth greenish
yellow, often tinged red and bearing long anthers, which
are more noticeable than tepals and perianth. Widespread
in East Texas south to Corpus Christi area. Tends to prefer open slopes.

Polygonatum biflorum   ASPARAGACEAE
Giant Solomon's seal, smooth Solomon's seal, sealwort
Riparian areas, woodlands, canyons. Spring. Uncommon.

An erect, arching, rhizomatous perennial with stems to
5+ feet tall. Leaves alternate, sessile, lanceolate to elliptic, to 8 inches long and 3 inches wide, margins entire,
tips acute, leaf venation prominent. Flowers in hanging,
drooping racemes originating from leaf axils, white to
greenish yellow, to 1 inch long. Found primarily in East
Texas, along wooded creek and river banks and slopes,
from Red River in Northeast Texas south to Hardin
County. Also found in Guadalupe Mountains in West
Texas, where they were previously known as *Polygonatum
cobrense*.

Achillea millefolium   ASTERACEAE
Yarrow, milfoil, common yarrow
Meadows, fields, woodlands, shrublands, roadsides and
other disturbed areas. Spring, summer. Common.

An erect perennial to 2+ feet tall, with a single or few
stems that may or may not be branched. Leaves on petioles or sessile, pinnately divided 1–3 times and looking
fernlike. Basal leaves to 12 inches long. Upper leaves usually ⅓ this length. Flowers white, in terminal corymbs, to
100 per head, small, white to pink ray florets and numerous white to grayish white disc florets. A highly variable
species. Found throughout most of the state. Weakest in
the southern and western portions. Widely sold in nurs-
eries, along with its Old World cousin; both have escaped
and hybridized with naturally occurring populations.

Ageratina rothrockii ASTERACEAE
Rothrock's snakeroot
Canyons, mountain drainages and wooded
slopes, among boulders in mountainous,
shaded areas. Summer, fall. Uncommon.

An erect to ascending, rhizomatous perennial with slender, branching stems to 30+ inches tall. Leaves opposite,
on petioles to 3 inches long, lanceolate to ovate, to 2½
inches long and 1¼ inches wide, bases truncate to tapering, margins serrate to crenate, tips acute. Flowering
heads in loose, terminal corymbs, ray florets absent, disc
florets white and numerous. Found in Trans-Pecos region
above 4000 feet. Longer petioles and more herbaceous
habit separates it from other *Ageratina* species found in
West Texas.

Ambrosia cheiranthifolia ASTERACEAE
**Rio Grande ragweed, South Texas ragweed,
South Texas ambrosia**
Fields, prairies, open shrublands.
Spring, summer, fall. Rare.

An erect, rhizomatous perennial with stems to 16 inches
tall, forming small colonies. Leaves opposite on lower
stem, alternate above, sessile, oblong-lanceolate to oblanceolate, to about 2 inches long, margins entire, surfaces
with short, appressed hairs, young leaves may be slightly
pinnately lobed. Small, greenish male and female flowers
occur separately on terminal inflorescence, male flowers
extending above clustered female flowers below. Found
in a handful of counties along southern coast, south of
Coastal Bend region.

Anthemis cotula ASTERACEAE
Stinking chamomile, mayweed, dog fennel
Fields, roadsides, disturbed areas.
Spring, summer, fall. Common.

A foul-scented, introduced annual with branched stems
to 20 inches tall, sometimes taller. Leaves alternate, to
2 inches long and 1¼ inches wide, pinnately lobed 1 or
2 times. Solitary and terminal flowering heads held on
peduncles above foliage, ray flowers white, disc florets
to 15, greenish yellow. Widely introduced in eastern portion of Texas, west to eastern edge of Chihuahuan Desert,
south to Mexico. Absent in Panhandle. Readily escapes
cultivation and may be found around urban and suburban areas.

Aphanostephus ramosissimus ASTERACEAE
Lazy daisy, plains dozedaisy, plains lazydaisy
Fields, meadows, open shrublands, roadsides and
other open areas. Spring, summer. Common.

An annual with slender, branched stems to 18 inches tall.
Leaves alternate, simple, oblanceolate to linear. Lower
leaves deeply pinnatifid. Upper leaves shallowly pinnatifid to entire. Flowering heads solitary on peduncles above
foliage. Ray flowers thin and white, to 40. Disc florets
yellowish and numerous. Found throughout majority of
state. Absent in East Texas.

Arnoglossum ovatum ASTERACEAE
Ovateleaf cacalia, ovateleaf Indian plantain
Woodlands, savannas, fields, meadows, roadsides and
other low, wet areas. Spring, summer, fall. Common.

An erect, weakly rhizomatous perennial with a glabrous
stem to 8 feet tall, although usually much shorter. Basal
leaves membranous, ovate to lanceolate-linear, to nearly
12 inches long, margins entire. Stem leaves similar in
shape to basal leaves, but not as large and with short petioles. Flowers in terminal corymbs, 5 disc florets, cream to
greenish white, ray flowers absent. Size of plant and size
and shape of leaves variable. Found in Southeast Texas,
from Matagorda County east to Louisiana, and as far
north as Angelina County. Range overlaps with *Arnoglossum plantagineum*, but 2 species can easily be identified
by characters mentioned.

Arnoglossum plantagineum ASTERACEAE
Indian plantain, prairie plantain, groovestem
Indian plantain
Prairies, fields, meadows, pastures, open riparian areas
and other damp soils. Spring, summer, fall. Common.

An erect, weakly rhizomatous perennial with an angled
stem to 3 feet tall. Firm basal leaves broadly elliptic,
to 7 inches long, entire or sinuate margins. Lower and
mid-level leaves along stem are attached with petioles and
have entire or finely serrate margins. Uppermost leaves
generally smaller and narrower than lower leaves. White
to greenish white flowers occur in terminal corymbs and
have only disc florets. Found throughout central and eastern portions of state.

Artemisia ludoviciana ASTERACEAE

Silver wormwood, white sage, silver sage
Fields, meadows, prairies, woodlands, shrublands, rocky
outcrops and slopes, roadsides. Summer, fall. Common.

An erect, rhizomatous perennial with aromatic,
silver-white to gray-green foliage and stems, often forming small colonies. Leaves linear to elliptic, to 4⅓ inches
long and 1½ inches wide, margins entire to lobed to pinnatifid. Flowers in single or branched terminal inflorescences, ray florets absent, disc florets cream to pale yellow. Found throughout state. Weak in East Texas. Four
subspecies are known: *albula*, in far West Texas, has
heads in panicles; *ludoviciana*, mostly in the Panhandle, has entire leaf margins; *mexicana*, loosely dispersed
throughout Texas, has revolute, entire margins; *redo-
lens*, also in West Texas, has revolute leaf margins, lobed
leaves, and pubescent leaf undersides.

Bidens pilosa (*B. alba*) ASTERACEAE

Spanish needles, beggar-ticks, hairy beggar's ticks
Roadsides, creek and river banks and other disturbed
areas. Winter, spring, summer, fall. Uncommon.

An introduced, erect perennial with branching stems
to 2+ feet tall. Leaves opposite, on petioles to 2½ inches
long, ovate to lanceolate, to 4 inches long and 1 inch wide,
sometimes pinnately lobed, margins serrate or entire.
Flowering heads solitary, numerous yellow disc florets,
ray florets absent or to 8, white to pink. Scattered populations throughout state. Native to tropical Central and
South America.

Boltonia diffusa ASTERACEAE

Smallhead doll's daisy
Disturbed areas, edges of woodlands.
Summer, fall. Common.

An erect, stoloniferous perennial with slender, branching
stems to 3+ feet tall. Leaves alternate, linear to lanceolate, to 4½ inches long and ½ inch wide. Flowering heads
in panicles, 100+, each head about ½ inch wide, with 40
white to lilac ray florets and 100+ disc florets. Found in
eastern third of Texas.

Chaetopappa asteroides   ASTERACEAE
Arkansas leastdaisy
Open grass brush and woodlands, roadsides and
other open areas. Spring, summer, fall. Common.

An erect annual with weak, branching stems to 10+
inches tall. Leaves alternate, linear to oblanceolate, to ¾
inch long and ¹⁄₁₀ inch wide, margins entire, surfaces
rough. Flowering heads solitary at ends of stems, each
head about ½ inch wide, ray florets white to light blue and
to 18 per head, disc florets yellow and to 25 per head. Two
varieties: *grandis* in Lower Rio Grande Valley, *asteroides* in
Central Texas, north into Oklahoma, east to Louisiana.

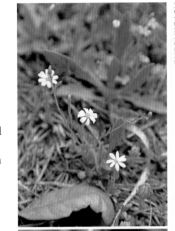

Chaetopappa effusa   ASTERACEAE
Spreading leastdaisy
Rocky outcrops, cliffs, ledges, open areas in oak-juniper
woodlands. Spring, summer, fall. Locally common.

An erect perennial with slender, branching stems to 30+
inches tall. Leaves alternate, oblong to lanceolate, to ¾
inch long and ½ inch wide, margins entire. Flowering
heads solitary at ends of stems, with 9 white ray florets
and to 7 yellow disc florets, each head about ½ inch wide.
Found on limestone in southwestern portion of Edwards
Plateau, often growing in shallow soils.

Chaptalia texana   ASTERACEAE
Silverpuff, Texas silverpuff, nodding lettuce
Grasslands, fields, open brush and woodlands.
Spring, summer. Uncommon.

An erect perennial with flowering stems to 14+ inches
tall. Basal leaves obovate to elliptic, to 8 inches long, margins lobed or toothed, lower surface of leaves tomentose,
upper surface glabrous. Flowering heads solitary, nodding, on peduncles to 14 inches long, florets numerous
and creamy white. Found on limestone soils from Brewster County east along southern edge of Edwards Plateau.

Chaptalia tomentosa   ASTERACEAE
Woolly sunbonnets
Bogs, wet meadows, open areas in pine woodlands
and forests. Spring, summer, fall. Uncommon.

An erect perennial with flowering stems to 8+ inches tall.
Basal leaves elliptic to obovate, to 7 inches long, margins
toothed, lower surface of leaves densely tomentose, upper
surface green. Flowering heads solitary, on peduncles to
8 inches long, heads erect with numerous florets, creamy
white above, purple-tinged below. Found in damp soils in
Big Thicket region of East Texas. Genus named after Jean
Antoine Chaptal, an 18th-century professor of chemistry.

Chloracantha spinosa   ASTERACEAE
Spiny aster, Mexican devilweed
Banks of waterways, marshes, ditches, canals and
other low, wet areas. Spring, summer, fall. Common.

An erect perennial with branching, often thorny, stems
to 4+ feet tall. Leaves alternate, oblanceolate, to 1½ inches
long, margins entire, occasionally toothed. Flowering
heads solitary or in loose panicles, each head about ½
inch wide with 30 white ray florets and 70 yellow disc
florets. Found throughout majority of state. Absent in
Northeast Texas. Weak in Panhandle. Prefers disturbed
areas and is quite common along coast and inland river
drainages.

Conyza canadensis (*Erigeron canadensis*)
ASTERACEAE
Horseweed, Canadian horseweed, conyza
Fields, meadows, creek and river banks, urban and
suburban areas, roadsides and other disturbed
areas. Spring, summer, fall. Common.

An erect annual with a single, branching, pubescent
stem to 6+ feet tall. Leaves oblanceolate to linear, to 4
inches long and ½ inch wide, margins entire to toothed.
Flowering heads in terminal panicles, hundreds of heads
per panicle, each head ¼ inch long and ⅛ inch wide with
30 creamy white to light tan disc florets and 40± inconspicuous ray florets. Found throughout Texas.

Diaperia candida (*Evax candida*)   ASTERACEAE
Silver pygmy cudweed, silver rabbit tobacco
Fields, prairies, meadows, pastures, roadsides
and other open areas. Spring. Common.

An erect, silky annual with a single stem, occasionally
branching from base, to 10 inches tall, silvery gray stem
and leaves. Leaves alternate, oblanceolate to obovate, to
½ inch long and ⅛ inch wide, margins entire, tips acute.
Inflorescences in racemes or spikes, often hidden or surrounded by upper leaves. Flowers inconspicuous, to less
than ⅛ inch wide and tall, to 5 florets per head, creamy
white to yellowish tan. Found throughout eastern half of
Texas, from Dallas area, south to Coastal Bend, east into
Louisiana. Additional populations in far South Texas.

Diaperia prolifera   ASTERACEAE
Big-head rabbit tobacco
Open areas with shallow soils. Spring,
summer, fall. Common.

An erect, silky annual with 2–10 stems to 6 inches tall,
plant overall grayish green to silvery. Leaves alternate,
oblanceolate to obovate, to ½ inch long and ⅛ inch
wide, margins entire, tips pointed. Flowering heads in
a divided, rounded cyme, surrounded by upper leaves.
Heads inconspicuous, to about ¼ inch wide, often hidden by hairs, to 40± per cluster. Found throughout central portion of Texas, north into Panhandle and eastern
Oklahoma. Absent in far western, far southern, and deep
East Texas.

Diaperia verna   ASTERACEAE
Spring rabbit tobacco
Open grasslands, brush and woodlands,
prairies, playas, roadsides and other open
areas. Spring, summer. Common.

An erect, silvery annual with 10 stems, branching from
base and at ends, to 6 inches tall, plant overall greenish
gray. Leaves alternate, oblanceolate to obovate, to ½ inch
long and ¼ inch wide, margins entire, tips pointed. Flowering heads (often obscured by upper leaves) in divided
rounded cymes, each head rounded to ⅛ inch wide, to 5
florets per head, inflorescences creamy white, pubescent.
Most common species of rabbit tobacco; found in nearly
every county in Texas.

Eclipta prostrata   ASTERACEAE
False daisy, yerba de tago, tattoo plant
Edges of bogs, ponds, marshes, bar ditches and in
other low, wet areas or in areas with poorly drained
soils. Winter, spring, summer, fall. Common.

A prostrate, short-lived perennial with reddish stems,
branched at base, to 3 feet long, with occasional branching throughout; may appear to be erect if other vegetation
is around to support its clambering habit. Leaves opposite, on petioles or sessile, lanceolate to linear, to 5 inches
long and about 1 inch wide, margins serrate to slightly
entire, upper leaf surface has visible, appressed hairs.
Flowers on short pedicels, usually 1–3 per pedicel, with
numerous white ray and disc florets, each flower about ⅓
inch in diameter. Widespread throughout Texas.

Erechtites hieraciifolius   ASTERACEAE
American burnweed
Creek and river banks, low areas, grasslands, open
areas in woodlands, roadsides and other open,
disturbed areas. Summer, fall. Common.

An erect, usually glabrous, single-stemmed annual to 6+
feet tall. Leaves alternate, on short petioles to nearly sessile, ovate to lanceolate, to 8 inches long and 3¼ inches
wide, margins serrate to slightly entire to lobed. Upper
leaves clasping. Flowering heads few or to 20+ in corymbs, each head urn-shaped, narrow at top, about ¾ inch
long, consisting of few to 100+ white to pale yellow florets.
Found in eastern third of Texas.

Erigeron philadelphicus   ASTERACEAE
Philadelphia fleabane, fleabane daisy
Prairies, fields, grasslands, open shrub
and woodlands, roadsides and other open
areas. Spring, summer. Common.

An erect annual to weak perennial with single or multiple stems to 30+ inches tall. Basal leaves obovate to oblanceolate, to 5+ inches long and 1+ inch wide, margins serrate to crenate, blades pubescent. Upper leaves similar to
basal, smaller and clasping. Flowering heads either solitary or to 35 in corymbs, each head about 1 inch wide and
consisting of 250+ white ray florets and numerous yellow
disc florets. Found in eastern half of Texas, from Coastal
Bend north into Oklahoma.

Erigeron procumbens   ASTERACEAE
Corpus Christi fleabane, Boca Chica daisy
Coastal and inland dunes, lomas, coastal grasslands,
roadsides. Spring, summer. Common.

A prostrate perennial, rooting at nodes and with stems
to 18+ inches long. Basal leaves oblanceolate to spatulate
to cuneate, to 3 inches long and 1 inch wide. Stem leaves
similar, but usually with serrate or crenate margins.
Flowering heads solitary, on erect peduncles to 10 inches
tall, each head about ¾ inch wide and with 350 white ray
florets and numerous yellow disc florets. Found on back
side of coastal dunes and mudflats along Texas coast.
Also found farther inland in open, wet soils.

Erigeron pulchellus   ASTERACEAE
Hairy fleabane
Woodlands, creek and river bottoms,
roadsides. Spring, summer. Uncommon.

An erect, rhizomatous perennial with pubescent stems to
2+ feet tall. Basal leaves oblanceolate to obovate to slightly
spatulate, to 6 inches long and 1½ inches wide, margins
dentate. Upper leaves similar, smaller, clasping. Flowering heads solitary or in corymbs, each head about 1 inch
wide and with 80+ white or light blue or pink ray florets
and numerous yellow disc florets. Found in eastern third
of Texas, north into Oklahoma, east into Louisiana.

Eupatorium leucolepis   ASTERACEAE
Justiceweed, white-bracted thoroughwort
Wet meadows, bogs, marshes, woodlands.
Summer, fall. Uncommon.

An erect, rhizomatous perennial with a single, weakly
branched, slightly pubescent stem to 3+ feet tall. Leaves
opposite, sessile, lanceolate-oblong to linear-oblong,
to 2¼ inches long and ½ inch wide, bases rounded to
cuneate, margins entire to serrate, upper leaf surface
rough, lower surface softly pubescent. Flowering heads in
corymbs, slightly open to crowded, with numerous individual heads about ¼ inch wide, disc florets white and
about 5 per head, ray flowers absent. Found in far eastern
Texas, in sandy soils within pine forests.

Eupatorium rotundifolium ASTERACEAE
Roundleaf thoroughwort
Prairies, grasslands, woodlands, forests,
roadsides. Summer. Uncommon.

An erect, rhizomatous perennial with branching stems
to 3+ feet tall. Leaves opposite, sessile or nearly so, deltate to rounded to ovate, to 2+ inches long and 1¾ inches
wide, bases rounded to truncate, margins crenate to serrate. Flowering heads in corymbs. Individual heads about
¼ inch wide with about 5 white disc florets, ray florets
absent. A variable species found in eastern third of Texas,
in wet or damp soils.

Facelis retusa ASTERACEAE
Annual trampweed, trampweed
Urban and suburban areas, roadsides and other
disturbed sites. Spring. Uncommon.

An introduced annual with leafy stems to 12+ inches tall,
decumbent branches arising from base of main stem.
Leaves alternate, sessile, spatulate to lance-linear, to ¾
inch long and ⅛ inch wide, margins entire to revolute,
tips truncate with short point, lower leaf surface gray
tomentose, upper surface green and glabrous. Flowering heads in spikes, florets with white to purple feathery
bristles extending from calyx. Found mostly in Southeast
Texas, north into Oklahoma, west to Edwards Plateau,
spreading.

Fleischmannia incarnata ASTERACEAE
Pink thoroughwort
Thickets, woodlands, river and stream banks, floodplains,
swamps, ditches. Fall, winter. Uncommon.

An erect to lax or sprawling perennial with branching
stems to 5+ feet tall. Leaves opposite, on petioles to 1½
inches long, triangular, bases truncate, margins serrate
to crenate. Flowering heads in loose corymbs, each head
about ⅜ inch wide in white, purple, pink, or lavender.
Typically found in wet soils from South Texas northeast into Louisiana and north into Oklahoma. Named in
honor of Gottfried Fleischmann (1777–1850), a German
professor of botany.

Florestina tripteris ASTERACEAE
Sticky florestina
Fields, meadows, open brushlands, roadsides and other open areas. Winter, spring, summer, fall. Uncommon.

An erect annual with slender, branching stems to 2 feet tall. Leaves opposite below, alternate above, on petioles, simple to 5-lobed, oblong to ovate, margins entire. Flowering heads in corymbs, each head about ⅜ inch wide with 30+ white disc florets, ray florets absent. Typically found in open, disturbed sites in South Texas, north into western Edwards Plateau and eastern Chihuahuan Desert.

Gaillardia aestivalis var. *winkleri*
ASTERACEAE
Winkler's blanket flower, white fire-wheel, Winkler's fire-wheel
Pine-oak woodlands. Spring, summer, fall. Rare.

An erect perennial with a single, heavily branched stem to 2 feet tall. Leaves on petioles to 1¼ inches long, elliptic to spatulate, to 2⅓ inches long and just under 1 inch wide. Flowers to 2½ inches in diameter, on peduncles to 8 inches long, 15± ray florets white to rose to pink, disc florets creamy yellow and numerous. Only occurs in Tyler, Hardin, and Newton Counties in Big Thicket area of East Texas and can be located in sandy soils.

Hymenopappus artemisiifolius
ASTERACEAE
Old plainsman
Fields, meadows, grasslands, prairies, open shrub and woodlands, roadsides and other open areas. Spring, summer. Common.

An erect, slender, single-stemmed, branching biennial to 3+ feet tall. Leaves alternate, primarily basal, with a few along lower stem, oblong to lanceolate, simple or once pinnately lobed, to 8+ inches long and to 1¼ inches wide, lobes slender and to ¾ inch long and ¼ inch wide, margins entire. Flowering heads discoid, to 60 per stem, in terminal corymbs, to 60 disc florets per head. Variety *artemisiifolius* has white to purple-tinged flowers and is found in eastern half of Texas, from Edwards Plateau east into Louisiana, north into Oklahoma. Variety *riograndensis* has yellow to reddish flowers and is found in South Texas.

Hymenopappus scabiosaeus ASTERACEAE
Carolina woollywhite
Fields, grasslands, prairies, open shrublands, roadsides
and other open areas. Spring, summer. Common.

An erect biennial with slender to stout, leafy stems to
4+ feet tall. Basal leaves on petioles, pinnate or bipinnate, to 10 inches long, with lobes variable, linear, to ¾
inch long and ⅛ to ⅓ inch wide, margins entire to revolute, tips rounded to acute. Stem leaves sessile, similar
to basal leaves in shape, but smaller, with thinner lobes.
Flowering heads discoid, to 100 per stem, in terminal corymbs, heads white, to 80 disc florets per head. Similar to
Hymenopappus artemisiifolius, but Carolina woollywhite
is larger, basal leaves are not simple, and disc florets are
white, not otherwise. Widespread in various habitats
throughout state.

Iva annua ASTERACEAE
Annual sumpweed, annual marsh elder, marsh elder
Marshes, edges of ponds, lakes, creeks, and rivers, wet
meadows and grasslands, roadside ditches and other low
areas with wet or damp soils. Summer, fall. Common.

An erect annual with branching stems to 4+ feet tall.
Leaves alternate, deltate-ovate or elliptic-lanceolate, to 4+
inches long and 2 inches wide, bases tapering to truncate,
margins toothed, tips acute to obtuse, surfaces rough.
Flowering heads in terminal and lateral spikes, heads
discoid, numerous, about ⅛ inch wide, flowers greenish
white. Found throughout eastern half of Texas.

Marshallia caespitosa ASTERACEAE
Barbara's buttons, puffballs
Fields, meadows, open brush and woodlands, roadsides
and other open areas. Spring, summer. Common.

An erect, slender perennial with unbranched stems
to 2 feet tall. Basal leaves on petioles, linear to elliptic to oblanceolate, to 5½ inches long and ½ inch wide,
3-nerved. Flowering heads solitary, about 1¼ inches wide,
on 12-inch-long peduncles that may be branched, each
head consisting of numerous white to lavender disc florets. An early spring flower. Found throughout Edwards
Plateau, south to Coastal Bend, east to Louisiana, and
north into Oklahoma. Named in honor of Henry Marshall, an American botanist.

Melampodium cinereum ASTERACEAE
Hoary blackfoot daisy
Sparse grass and scrubland, fields, roadsides and other open areas. Winter, spring, summer, fall. Locally common.

An erect to lax, rounded perennial with branching stems to 10 inches tall. Leaves oblong to linear, to 2 inches long and ½ inch wide, margins entire and may be pinnately lobed. Flowering heads on peduncles to 2¼ inches, each head about 1 inch wide, ray florets white and 7–13 per head, disc florets to 50 and yellow. Found in open, rocky to gravelly soils from Val Verde County, south to Brownsville. Similar to *Melampodium leucanthum*, but generally smaller, with more ray florets and with longer hairs on stems and leaves.

Melampodium leucanthum ASTERACEAE
Blackfoot daisy
Open brush and woodlands, fields, grasslands, roadsides and other open areas. Spring, summer, fall. Common.

An erect to lax perennial with weak branching stems to 20 inches tall. Leaves lanceolate to linear, 1½ inches long and ⅜ inch wide, pinnately lobed, margins entire. Flowering heads on peduncles to 2½ inches long, each head 1 inch wide, 8± white to creamy white (occasionally purple-tinged) ray florets and numerous yellow disc florets. Widespread across Edwards Plateau, west into New Mexico and north into Panhandle. Range overlaps with *Melampodium cinereum* around Val Verde County, where hybrids can be expected.

Mikania scandens ASTERACEAE
Climbing hempweed, climbing hempvine
Riparian areas, floodplains, edges of tanks, ponds and other bodies of water. Spring, summer, fall. Uncommon.

A twining, climbing perennial vine with angled or winged stems to 10+ feet long. Leaves opposite, on petioles to 2 inches long, deltate to triangular, to 4 inches long, bases weak to strong cordate, margins crenate, dentate to undulate, tips acute. Flowers in dense corymbs, about 5 inches in diameter, each head about ¼ inch wide with 4 white to pinkish disc florets. Mostly found in eastern third of state, southwest to Mexico, although uncommon south of Coastal Bend.

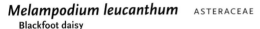

Parthenium confertum   ASTERACEAE
False ragweed
Fields, pastures, meadows, grasslands, open
brush and woodlands, roadsides and other open
areas. Spring, summer, fall. Common.

An erect biennial with branching stems to 28 inches tall.
Leaves alternate, ovate to rounded to elliptic, to 6 inches
long and 1 inch wide. Lower leaves pinnatifid to lyrate,
hirsute. Upper leaves 1- or 2-pinnatifid, lobes entire,
hirsute. Flowering heads in open panicles, radial to 14
inches wide, white to cream, numerous disc florets and 5
small pistillate florets forming a star along edges. Found
throughout Chihuahuan Desert, west into Edwards Plateau, south to Brownsville.

Parthenium integrifolium   ASTERACEAE
Wild quinine
Fields, meadows. Spring, summer. Rare.

An erect, rhizomatous perennial with slender, glabrous,
branching stems to 3 feet tall. Basal leaves in a rosette, on
petioles, lanceolate to ovate, to 6 inches long and 4 inches
wide, margins serrate, tips acute. Upper leaves alternate,
similar to basal, but smaller. Inflorescences in terminal panicles, each head ⅓ inch wide, flowers clustered or
open. Ray florets white, 5 per head, inconspicuous. Disc
florets numerous and white. Found in northeast corner of
Texas, which is southwestern extent of its range.

Perityle bisetosa var. *bisetosa*   ASTERACEAE
Twobristle rockdaisy, twospike rockdaisy
Limestone ledges, outcrops, canyons, and
cliffs. Spring, summer, fall. Rare.

An erect, rounded perennial with branching stems to 4
inches tall, stems radiating from a central woody base.
Leaves opposite or alternate, lanceolate to ovate, to ¾ inch
long, bases tapering, margins entire to weakly serrate,
tips acute, blades thick and leathery. Flowering heads solitary and terminal, ¼ inch wide, ray florets white and to
17 florets per head. Found in Pecos and Brewster Counties, on open limestone substrate, often growing in cracks
and fissures.

Pinaropappus roseus   ASTERACEAE
Rock lettuce
Fields, open brush and woodlands, rocky slopes, roadsides
and other open areas. Spring, summer. Common.

An erect annual with thin stems to 18 inches tall. Leaves
sessile, linear to lanceolate, to 4¾ inches long and ½ inch
wide, margins entire or occasionally toothed. Single flowering head about 1½ inches wide on a slender, leafless
stalk to 18 inches tall, 40± white ligulate florets tinged
pink or lavender. Found throughout Central Texas, radiating outward wherever limestone soils are present.

Psathyrotopsis scaposa   ASTERACEAE
Naked turtleback
Sparse desert scrub. Spring, summer, fall. Uncommon.

A small, erect perennial to 16 inches tall when in flower.
Leaves alternate, mostly basal, rounded-deltate to lanceolate, to 2¼ inches long and 1½ inches wide, margins serrate or crenate, surfaces somewhat tomentose. Flowering heads either solitary or in weak corymbs on leafless
stems, each head about ¼ inch wide, ray florets absent,
disc florets numerous, creamy white to yellow. Found in
Chihuahuan Desert at lower elevations, usually in creosote scrub.

Silphium albiflorum   ASTERACEAE
White rosinweed
Grasslands, savannas, fields, prairies, open
brushlands, roadsides and other open areas.
Spring, summer. Locally common.

An erect perennial with thick, rough, terete stems to 30
inches tall. Leaves alternate, sessile or on petioles, deltate
to elliptic to linear to rhombic, to 16 inches long and 10
inches wide, pinnately lobed 1 or 2 times, bases cuneate
to truncate, margins toothed or entire, tips pointed,
surfaces rough, scabrous. Flowering heads radial, in
racemes, each head with up to 30 white ray florets and
100+ white disc florets, flowers to 3+ inches wide. Found
on limestone soils throughout Central Texas, a Texas
endemic.

Stevia serrata ASTERACEAE
Saw-tooth candyleaf
Oak-pine woodlands. Summer, fall. Uncommon.

An erect, leafy-stemmed perennial to 3 feet tall. Leaves alternate, sessile, lanceolate to linear, to 2¾ inches long, margins sparsely serrate. Flowering heads in corymbs, with 5 white (or rarely pink or purple) florets per head, each floret 5-lobed and funnel-shaped. Found in upper elevations of Davis Mountains, reported from the Chisos Mountains. One of 3 species of *Stevia* in Texas.

Symphyotrichum ericoides ASTERACEAE
Heath aster
Prairies, grasslands, fields, open brush and woodlands, roadsides and other open areas. Summer, fall. Common.

An ascending to erect rhizomatous perennial with single or multiple branching stems to 2+ feet tall. Leaves alternate, linear, to 3 inches long and ¼ inch wide, margins entire, surfaces pubescent. Upper leaves smaller than lower. Flowering heads solitary to more than 100 per stem, each head about ½ inch wide with 20± white ray florets and numerous disc florets. Found throughout state, but weak in East Texas and absent in South Texas.

Tridax procumbens ASTERACEAE
Tridax daisy, coatbuttons, cadillo chisaca
Urban areas, feral fields, vacant lots, roadsides, railroad rights-of-way and other disturbed areas. Winter, spring, summer, fall. Locally common.

An introduced, procumbent to ascending perennial with stems to 3 feet long. Leaves opposite, on petioles to ¾ inch long, deltate to lanceolate to ovate, pinnately or palmately lobed, to 1½ inches long and half as wide, margins roughly toothed or entire. Flowering heads on peduncles to 12 inches long, each head with 3–8 ray florets and 40–80 yellow disc florets. Native to tropical Americas, *Tridax* is a recent introduction (ca. 1990s) and can be found in far South Texas from Starr County south to Cameron County, north to Coastal Bend. Introductions throughout state are likely, as this plant has been noted in Austin area.

Verbesina microptera ASTERACEAE
Texas crownbeard
Shrublands, woodlands, prairies, roadsides and
other open areas. Spring, summer. Common.

An erect, single-stemmed perennial with winged stems,
to 6+ feet tall and 3 feet wide. Leaves alternate, deltate
to lanceolate, to 10 inches long and 6 inches wide, with
toothed to nearly entire margins. Flowering heads in
loose, terminal panicles, each head approximately ½
inch in diameter, with white ray and disc florets. Found
in South Texas, south of Edwards Plateau, usually growing in sandy-loam soils. Specific epithet means "small
winged," referring to stems.

Verbesina virginica ASTERACEAE
Frostweed, iceplant, Virginia crownbeard
Woodlands, floodplains, bottomlands,
thickets. Summer, fall. Common.

An erect, single-stemmed, unbranched perennial to 8+
feet tall, with winged stems. Leaves alternate, lance-ovate
to lance-linear, to 9 inches long and 4¾ inches wide, margins coarsely toothed to sinuate, surfaces rough. Flowering heads numerous in terminal corymbs, each cluster to
6 inches in diameter, with 7 white ray florets and 15 white
disc florets per head. Found from western Central Texas
east into Louisiana, north into Oklahoma and south to
Coastal Bend. Common names frostweed and iceplant
come from delicate ice formations that form on lower
stem during season's first freeze.

Xanthium strumarium ASTERACEAE
Cocklebur, fox-bur
Creek and river beds, washes, drainages,
edges of ponds and lakes, roadsides and other
seasonally wet areas. Summer, fall. Common.

An erect, single-stemmed, weakly branched annual with
reddish stems to 4+ feet tall. Leaves alternate, on petioles
to 8 inches long, cordate to ovate, to 8 inches long and 6
inches wide, margins coarsely dentate or lobed, upper
surfaces rough. Flowers in spikes from leaf axils or terminal, to 4 inches long, male flowers below with white
anthers, otherwise green, female flowers above, green.
Fruits are burs, about 1 inch long, with recurved barbs.
Found throughout state.

Zinnia acerosa ASTERACEAE
Desert zinnia, shrubby zinnia, southern zinnia
Open grass, brush and woodlands, rocky
slopes and hillsides, rocky outcrops, ledges.
Spring, summer, fall. Common.

An erect to prostrate, rounded, branching perennial with
greenish gray, pilose stems to 11 inches tall. Leaves opposite, sessile, linear, to ¾ inch long and ¹⁄₁₆ inch wide, margins entire, tips pointed, surfaces rough. Solitary flowering heads on peduncles to 1¾ inches long, radial, each
head to ¾ inch wide with 4–7 white ray florets and to 13
yellow disc florets. Common throughout Chihuahuan
Desert, locally common in Starr County.

Podophyllum peltatum BERBERIDACEAE
Indian apple, may-apple, wild mandrake
Deciduous woodlands, fields, meadows, river and
creek banks. Spring, summer. Locally common.

An erect, rhizomatous perennial with a single stem to 24
inches long. Large, opposite leaves on petioles to 6 inches
long are round, 5- to 6-lobed, to 12 inches long and wide,
with margins dentate to entire. Nonflowering stems produce just one leaf which is larger and with more lobes
than flowering stems. Single, nodding, white flowers in
leaf axil and on short pedicels, to 1½ inches wide, with
6–9 petals. Occasionally populations of pink-flowered
plants can be found. Found in deep East Texas. Prefers
rich, damp soils.

Buglossoides arvensis BORAGINACEAE
False gromwell, corn gromwell
Fields, meadows, grasslands, open brush and woodlands,
urban and suburban areas, roadsides and other open,
disturbed areas. Spring, summer, fall. Common.

An introduced, erect annual or biennial with pubescent,
branching stems to 2+ feet tall. Leaves alternate, sessile,
oblanceolate to oblong-linear, to 1½ inches long and ¼
inch wide, margins ciliate, blades pubescent. Small flowers occur in leaf axils at ends of stems, white, 5-lobed,
about ¼ inch wide. Found throughout majority of state.
Absent in Chihuahuan Desert and far South Texas, but
spreading.

Cordia podocephala   BORAGINACEAE
Texas manjack, white cordia
Open brush and woodlands, canyon bottoms,
open rocky slopes, occasional roadsides.
Spring, summer, fall. Uncommon.

An erect, shrubby perennial with occasionally branching stems to 2+ feet tall. Leaves alternate, lanceolate to oblanceolate, to 3¾ inches long and 1 inch wide, bases acute, margins serrate to toothed, tips acute to obtuse. Stems terminating in a peduncle to 8 inches long. Flowers in a compact roundish head, numerous, white, funnel-shaped, only a few open on any given day. Scattered throughout South Texas, into northern Mexico. Named after Valerius Cordus, a 16th-century German botanist and physician.

Cryptantha crassipes   BORAGINACEAE
Terlingua creek cat's-eye
Sparse, gypseous-clay flats. Winter, spring. Rare.

A rounded, mounding perennial to 10 inches tall when in flower. Several short stems, often hidden by dense leaves, from a woody caudex. Basal leaves numerous, linear-lanceolate to linear-spatulate, involute, to 2½ inches long and ¼ inch wide, margins entire, tips acute, surfaces silvery pubescent. Stem leaves similar, alternate, becoming smaller up the stem. Flowers in terminal clusters, salverform, 5-lobed, white with yellow centers, just over ⅓ inch wide. Found only in Brewster County, in a small area north of Terlingua and Study Butte, in extremely xeric conditions.

Cryptantha palmeri   BORAGINACEAE
Palmer's cryptantha
Open desert scrub, rocky outcrops, roadcuts.
Spring, summer. Uncommon.

An erect perennial with several pubescent stems to 16 inches tall, leaves and stems grayish green. Basal leaves oblanceolate, to 6 inches long and ¼ inch wide. Stem leaves alternate, spatulate to oblong, blades grayish green with longer, visible, stiff hairs. Stems terminating in several scorpioid cymes consisting of numerous 5-lobed flowers, each flower about ⅓ inch wide, white with a yellow center. Found throughout Chihuahuan Desert, on limestone, south to Maverick County and east into western Edwards Plateau.

Heliotropium angiospermum
BORAGINACEAE
Scorpion-tail
Grasslands, fields, open brush and woodlands,
roadsides and other open areas. Winter,
spring, summer, fall. Common.

An erect to decumbent, annual to short-lived perennial
with branching stems to 30+ inches tall. Leaves alternate, on petioles to ⅓+ inch long, ovate to lanceolate, to
2½ inches long and 1 inch wide, bases rounded, margins
entire to ciliate, tips rounded to acute, upper blade surface gibbose. Stems terminating in scorpioid inflorescences with numerous 5-lobed flowers, each flower about
¼ inch wide, white with a yellow center. Found throughout South Texas into Mexico.

Heliotropium confertifolium
BORAGINACEAE
Leafy heliotrope
Sparse, open desert scrub and open shrublands.
Spring, summer, fall. Uncommon.

An erect to spreading woody perennial with leafy,
branching stems to 5 inches long, slightly mat-forming.
Leaves alternate, crowded, mostly appearing at ends of
stems, lanceolate, less than ¼ inch long, margins entire
and ciliate, tips pointed, clustered leaves appearing over-
lapped like roof shingles. Flowers terminal, 5-lobed, to
about ¼ inch wide, white with a yellow center. Found on
limestone, from Presidio County south to Brownsville, in
counties bordering the Rio Grande.

Heliotropium convolvulaceum
BORAGINACEAE
Fragrant heliotrope, phlox heliotrope
Open grass and brushlands, desert dunes, roadsides
and other open areas. Spring, summer, fall. Common.

An erect to ascending annual with branching, pubescent stems to 16+ inches tall. Leaves alternate, on short
petioles, lanceolate to ovate, to 1¾ inches long and about
½ inch wide, bases rounded, margins entire to revolute, tips acute, surfaces with short flat hairs. Flowers funnel-shaped, corolla white with a yellow throat,
5-lobed, to almost 1 inch wide. Found in sandy soils from
Chihuahuan Desert north into Panhandle, becoming less
common in North-Central Texas.

Heliotropium curassavicum BORAGINACEAE
Seaside heliotrope, salt heliotrope, cola de mico
Dunes, salt flats, open grass and brushlands,
marshes, edges of waterways and bodies of water.
Winter, spring, summer, fall. Common.

A prostrate, rhizomatous perennial with thick, semisucculent, branching, glaucous stems to 18+ inches long.
Leaves alternate, sessile, oblanceolate, to 2 inches long,
margins entire, tips rounded, surface glabrous, blade
thick. Stems terminating in scorpioid cymes. Flowers
5-lobed, less than ¼ inch long, white with a yellow that
fades and darkens with age. Widespread throughout
Texas, frequent along coast and in Chihuahuan Desert,
where it is often found in and around areas with saline
soils. Seeds are often water dispersed.

Heliotropium greggii BORAGINACEAE
Gregg's heliotrope, fragrant heliotrope
Open grass and brushlands, desert scrub,
roadsides and other open areas. Winter
(occasionally), spring, summer, fall. Common.

A prostrate to decumbent, rhizomatous perennial with
branching stems to 6+ inches long. Leaves alternate, sessile or on short petioles, lanceolate to linear, to ½ inch
long, bases acute to truncate, margins revolute, tips
pointed, midvein prominent, surfaces silvery pubescent. Flowers in terminal cymes, elongating with age,
white with yellow center, 5-lobed, to about ½ inch wide.
Found throughout West Texas, east to western portion of
Edwards Plateau.

Heliotropium molle BORAGINACEAE
Soft heliotrope
Grasslands and desert scrub in river floodplains
and valleys. Spring, summer. Uncommon.

A decumbent, rhizomatous perennial with occasionally branched, gray-pubescent stems to 12 inches long.
Leaves alternate below, opposite above, on petioles to 1½
inches long, ovate to lanceolate, to 2 inches long and ¾
inch wide, bases oblique, margins crenate, tips acute to
obtuse, leaf surfaces villose. Stems terminating in scorpioid cymes. Flowers white with a yellow center radiating
out along centers of 5 lobes. Found in Presidio and Brewster Counties, usually in silty soils along the Rio Grande.

Heliotropium tenellum BORAGINACEAE
White heliotrope, pasture heliotrope
Grasslands, fields, pastures, open brush
and woodlands, roadsides and other open
areas. Spring, summer, fall. Common.

An erect, open annual with leafy, branching stems to 18+
inches tall. Leaves alternate, to 2 inches long, on petioles
to ¼ inch long, linear, bases narrowing, margins revolute, tips acute, surfaces with soft, flattened, silvery hairs.
Flowers loosely spaced in terminal, elongated cymes,
white with yellow throat, 5-lobed, less than ¼ inch wide.
Frequent in southwest Edwards Plateau. Less common
north into Oklahoma, east to Louisiana, south to Coastal
Bend.

Onosmodium bejariense BORAGINACEAE
Marbleseed
Grasslands, prairies, open brush and woodlands,
canyons, roadsides. Spring, summer. Common.

An erect, branching perennial with stems to nearly 3 feet
tall, leaves and stems covered in stiff hairs. Leaves alternate above, basal below, lanceolate, 5+ inches long and ½
inch wide, margins entire, blades with prominent veins.
Stems terminating in scorpioid cymes. Flowers tubular,
white, about 1 inch long, 5-lobed, each lobe erect and connate, surrounding style. Found throughout eastern portion of state, extending west into Edwards Plateau, south
to Coastal Bend.

Capsella bursa-pastoris BRASSICACEAE
Shepherd's purse
Urban and suburban areas, fields, grasslands, open
brush and woodlands, roadsides and other open,
disturbed areas. Spring, summer. Common.

An introduced, erect annual with pubescent stems to
2 feet tall. Basal leaves oblong, to 4 inches long and 2
inches wide, margins entire, pinnately lobed, lyrate, or
dentate. Stem leaves sessile, oblong, lanceolate, or linear,
to 2 inches long and ½ inch wide. Flowers small, 1/16 inch
long, numerous on slender racemes, with 4 white petals.
Fruits are deltoid silicles with a cordate tip. This common
lawn weed is frequently found throughout Texas.

Cardamine bulbosa BRASSICACEAE
Spring cress, bulbous bittercress
Meadows, savannas, fields, grasslands, creek
and river bottoms, woodlands and other low,
wet areas. Spring, summer. Common.

An erect, rhizomatous perennial with glabrous to slightly
pubescent unbranched stems to 2 feet tall. Lower leaves
on petioles to 4 inches long, cordate to ovate, to 5 inches
long, margins entire, repand, or dentate. Upper leaves
ovate to oblong to linear-lanceolate, to 2½ inches long and
1 inch wide, margins similar to lower leaves. Flowers in
terminal racemes, each flower to ½ inch wide with 4 white
to pink petals on pedicels to ½ inch long. Found in eastern third of Texas in low wet areas, often in sandy soils.

Cardamine concatenata BRASSICACEAE
Pepper root, cutleaf toothwort
Rich, mixed woodlands and forests, on
slopes, near creeks. Spring. Rare.

An erect, rhizomatous perennial with pubescent, occasionally glabrous, unbranched stems to 16 inches tall.
Lower leaves trifoliolate, to 8 inches long, leaflets oblong,
lanceolate to linear, to 2½ inches long, bases cuneate,
margins dentate to 3-lobed. Two to three upper leaves
whorled, or opposite, trifoliolate, similar to lower leaves
otherwise. Flowers in terminal racemes, with 4 white
to pink petals, oblanceolate, spreading or not. Found in
deep East Texas.

Eruca vesicaria BRASSICACEAE
Rocket, garden rocket, arugula
Roadsides, urban and suburban areas,
agricultural fields and other disturbed areas.
Spring, summer, fall. Locally common.

An introduced, erect, branching annual with glabrous
leaves and stems to 3+ feet tall. Basal leaves on petioles 2
inches long, oblanceolate, pinnately divided, to 6 inches
long and 2 inches wide, lobe margins entire to dentate.
Upper leaves similar, subsessile, smaller. Flowers in
racemes, on pedicels to ½ inch long, each flower to nearly
2 inches wide, 4-petaled, creamy white with purple veins.
First introduced in late 19th century, now spread throughout most of the western United States. Found from
Cameron County northwest to El Paso, common along
stretches of highway during wet years.

Nasturtium officinale BRASSICACEAE
Watercress
Edges of waterways and bodies of water,
marshes, roadside ditches and other wet areas.
Winter, spring, summer, fall. Common.

An introduced, prostrate to decumbent, rhizomatous perennial with glabrous, fleshy stems to 3+ feet long. Leaves alternate, on petioles, compound, to 6+ inches long, with 3–9 leaflets, each leaflet oval to ovate to round or lanceolate, bases obtuse, margins entire, tips obtuse. Flowers in terminal racemes, numerous, white, 4-petaled, ¼ inch wide. Fruit is a slender siliqua to ⅝ inch long. Found in Central Texas, west to New Mexico, and north into Panhandle and Oklahoma. Less common in East Texas. Absent in South Texas.

Nerisyrenia camporum BRASSICACEAE
Bicolored fanmustard
Desert washes, desert scrub. Winter,
spring, summer, fall. Common.

An erect perennial with pubescent to glabrous, branching stems to 2 feet tall. Leaves alternate, sessile or appearing so, oblanceolate or obovate to spatulate, to 1¾ inches long and ¾ inch wide, bases tapering, margins entire, dentate, or repand, tips acute to obtuse. Flowers radial, in terminal racemes, 4-petaled, white to pink to lavender, to 1 inch wide. Found throughout Chihuahuan Desert, south to Starr County, generally following the Rio Grande.

Nerisyrenia linearifolia BRASSICACEAE
White Sands fanmustard
Open desert scrub, flats, roadsides.
Spring, summer, fall. Uncommon.

An erect, pubescent perennial with stems to 16 inches tall. Leaves alternate, linear to 3 inches long and ¼ inch wide, margins entire, tips acute to obtuse. Flowers in terminal racemes to 12 inches long, numerous, radial, white, fading to lavender, 4-petaled, to 1 inch wide. Fruits are slender, to 1¼ inches long. Found in gypseous soils from El Paso west to Midland-Odessa area, south to Terrell County. Leaf morphology seperates this species from *Nerisyrenia camporum*.

Synthlipsis greggii BRASSICACEAE
Gregg's keelpod
Open thornscrub, sparse grass and brushlands,
gravelly to rocky slopes and hillsides.
Winter, spring, fall. Locally common.

An erect annual with single or multiple pubescent stems
to 24 inches tall. Basal leaves on petioles 2 inches long,
obovate to spatulate, to 4 inches long and 2 inches wide,
bases cuneate to truncate, margins pinnately lobed to
sinuate, tips acute, surfaces pubescent. Stem leaves similar but smaller, sessile or nearly so. Flowers in terminal
racemes, radial, white, 4-petaled, to about ¾ inch wide.
Fruits are flattened, ovate to round, to ½ inch long and
¼ inch wide. Typically found in gypseous soils, from
Hidalgo County upstream to Maverick County. Also
found in Big Bend region north to Culberson County.

Thelypodium texanum BRASSICACEAE
Texas thelypody
Desert washes, creeks, desert scrub.
Winter, spring. Locally common.

An erect annual with glabrous, branching stems to 18+
inches tall. Basal leaves on 1-inch-long petioles, oblanceolate to spatulate, to 6+ inches long and 1¾ inches wide,
pinnately lobed, lobe margins dentate to entire. Stem
leaves similar but smaller, becoming linear. Flowers in
racemes, clustered at apex, actinomorphic, to about ¼
inch long, white, 4-petaled. Stem elongating after flowering. Fruits long, thin. Found in open, rocky to gravelly
areas, primarily on limestone, in Chihuahuan Desert.

Thelypodium wrightii BRASSICACEAE
Wright's thelypody
Rocky outcrops, open mountain slopes, canyons.
Spring, summer, fall. Locally common.

An erect biennial, with glabrous, branching stems to 8+
feet tall. Basal leaves lanceolate, to 10 inches long and 2½
inches wide, pinnately lobed to lyrate, margins entire to
dentate. Upper leaves on short petioles, lanceolate to linear, to 3½ inches long and ½ inch wide, margins entire
to dentate. Flowers in racemes on slender pedicels to ½
inch long, actinomorphic, to ½ inch wide, white to lavender, 4-petaled. Raceme elongating after flowering. Fruit
is a thin silique to 3 inches long. Found among boulders,
often in shady areas of Chihuahuan Desert. Frequent
along scenic loop in Jeff Davis County.

117

Tillandsia recurvata   BROMELIACEAE
Ball moss
Woodlands, shrublands, riparian areas.
Spring, summer. Common.

An epiphytic perennial to about 6 inches in diameter with gray or silver foliage. Flowers nondescript, on slender scapes, extending well beyond foliage. Widespread throughout southern half of Texas, from Brewster County east to Louisiana, south into Mexico. Often seen in older live oaks (*Quercus fusiformis*), but also known to occur in a variety of species, as well as power lines, cliff faces, and barbed wire.

Tillandsia usneoides   BROMELIACEAE
Spanish moss
Established woodlands, forests, riparian areas.
Spring, summer. Locally common.

An epiphytic, hanging perennial to 15+ feet long with much-branched, fine, silver foliage and with nondescript sessile flowers appearing in leaf axils. Most often seen hanging on large trees, power lines, fences, and other objects and is more common in East Texas; farther west it is usually found in riparian habitats. Specific epithet is a reference to *Usnea*, a genus of lichen, which Spanish moss resembles. An iconic plant of the South, Spanish moss has various uses and was once mixed with horse hair and used as stuffing in furniture and car seats.

Cerastium brachypodum   CARYOPHYLLACEAE
Short-stalk chickweed, mouse ear chickweed
Fields, meadows, grasslands, open brush and woodlands, roadsides and other open areas. Spring, summer. Common.

An erect, glandular-pubescent, slender annual with a single or multiple stems, occasionally branching, to 8 inches tall. Leaves opposite, lanceolate to elliptic, to 1¼ inches long and ⅓ inch wide, margins entire, tips acute, blades pubescent. Flowers in terminal cymes, with 3–30 flowers per cyme, white, 5 lobed petals. Found in the central portion of Texas, from Coastal Bend north into Oklahoma; isolated collections in Panhandle.

Cerastium glomeratum CARYOPHYLLACEAE
Sticky mouse-ear chickweed
Fields, pastures, agricultural areas, roadsides and other
disturbed areas. Winter, spring, summer, fall. Common.

An introduced, erect or ascending, glandular-pubescent,
slender annual with single or multiple stems, branching
below, to 18 inches tall. Leaves opposite, sessile. Basal and
lower leaves oblanceolate or obovate, occasionally spatulate, to 1 inch long and ½ inch wide, margins entire, tips
pointed, surfaces with long, white hairs. Upper leaves
ovate to elliptic-ovate, otherwise similar. Flowers in terminal, clustered cymes, 3–50 flowers per cyme, white,
to ⅜ inch wide, 5-petaled, petals slender and divided
approximately ⅕ their length. Found throughout eastern
third of Texas, west into Edwards Plateau.

Silene stellata CARYOPHYLLACEAE
Starry campion, widow's frill
Mixed, open woodlands, floodplains.
Summer. Uncommon.

An erect perennial with several unbranched stems to 30
inches tall. Leaves opposite on upper and lower stem, in
whorls of 4 mid-stem, sessile, elliptic to lanceolate, to 4
inches long and 1½ inches wide, margins entire. Flowers solitary or to 3 per branch, on panicles originating
from central stem, white, about ¾ inch in diameter, with
5 deeply lobed petals, each petal with 8–12 lobes. Found
in northeastern portion of state, with historic collections
farther southwest into Central Texas.

Lepuropetalon spathulatum CELASTRACEAE
Petiteplant
Wet savannas, meadows, grasslands and other
low, wet areas. Winter, spring. Uncommon.

A small, glabrous winter annual less than ¾ inch in
diameter, forming a tiny, rounded tuft. Leaves alternate,
spatulate, to ⅓ inch long, margins entire, tips obtuse,
surfaces glandular. Flowers solitary, occurring near ends
of stems, white, with 5 sepals less than ⅛ inch long and
5 minute and inconspicuous petals much smaller than
sepals. Found in sandy, wet soils in the eastern third of
Texas. Less common farther west to Edwards Plateau and
often overlooked because of its diminutive size.

Parnassia asarifolia   CELASTRACEAE
Kidneyleaf grass of Parnassus
Bogs associated with sphagnum moss.
Late summer, fall. Rare.

An erect perennial, consisting of mostly basal leaves, to
20 inches tall when flowering. Basal leaves on petioles 6
inches long, reniform, to 2¾ inches long, margins entire
to undulate. Stem leaves similar but smaller, sessile.
Flowers solitary and terminal on a scape to 16 inches tall,
5-petaled, radial, to 1⅜ inch wide, petals clawed, white
with distinctive darker greenish gray venation. Found in
northeastern Texas.

Polanisia dodecandra subsp. *trachysperma*   CLEOMACEAE
Clammyweed, redwhisker clammyweed
Fields, grasslands, open shrublands, washes, creek
and river banks and beds, roadsides and other open,
disturbed areas. Spring, summer, fall. Common.

An erect annual with a single, branching stem to 2 feet
tall, stems and leaves with sticky-glandular hairs. Leaves
alternate, trifoliolate, leaflets oval to oblong, to 1½ inches
long and ½ inch wide, margins entire to ciliate. Upper
leaves not compound. Flowers in terminal racemes, bilateral, white, 4-petaled, petals spatulate to cordate, clawed,
with 12 red to reddish purple stamens, about 1 inch long
and spreading. Found throughout majority of Texas.
Absent in southern and far western Texas.

Polanisia erosa subsp. *erosa*   CLEOMACEAE
Large clammyweed
Open shrub and woodlands, grasslands, fields, roadsides
and other open areas. Spring, summer, fall. Common.

An erect annual to 2 feet tall with branching, glandular stems. Leaves alternate, trifoliolate, leaflets linear to
oblanceolate, to 1½ inches long and ¼ inch wide, margins
entire, blades often folded upward. Flowers numerous, in
terminal racemes to 10 inches long, bilateral, 4-petaled,
petals clawed, white or tinged pink, 2 large petals at 10
and 2 o'clock positions (roughly), 2 smaller petals usually at 4 and 7 o'clock positions, petals deeply divided into
9 thin lobes. Found in eastern third of Texas. Grows in
open areas with sandy soils. Less common farther west
and south. Subspecies *breviglandulosa*, which has yellow
flowers, is found from Corpus Christi south into Mexico.

Polanisia uniglandulosa   CLEOMACEAE
Mexican clammyweed, hierba del coyote
River and creek beds, washes, drainages, open grass, brush
and woodlands, roadsides. Spring, summer. Uncommon.

An erect, glandular annual, either branched or
unbranched to 30+ inches tall. Leaves alternate, trifoliolate, leaflets elliptic to oblanceolate, to 1¾ inches long
and ¾ inch wide, bases rounded to cuneate, margins
entire, tips acute, surfaces glandular. Flowers in terminal
racemes, white, 4-petaled, petals with a long narrow claw
to 1¼ inches long. Up to 25 reddish pink stamens extend
in various directions, stamens to 2 inches long. Primarily
found in Chihuahuan Desert region, growing in mountain creek beds and other disturbed areas.

Convolvulus equitans   CONVOLVULACEAE
Bindweed, Texas bindweed
Prairies, fields, roadsides and other disturbed
areas. Spring, summer, fall. Common.

A twining or spreading perennial vine with pubescent
stems to 6+ feet long. Leaves alternate, variably shaped,
often dependent upon sun exposure, from ovate to
triangular-lanceolate to slender-oblong with large basal
lobes, to 3 inches long and 1½ inches wide, margins
entire, wavy, toothed, or 1- to 3-lobed at base. Flowers
funnel-shaped, on pedicels to 1 inch long from leaf axils,
solitary, or rarely to 3, about 1¼ inches wide and as long,
white to pink, sometimes with a red or rose center, distinctly 5-angled. Found throughout Texas. Weakest in
eastern portion.

Dichondra argentea   CONVOLVULACEAE
Silver ponyfoot, dichondra
Rocky slopes, open desert scrub, canyons,
escarpments. Spring, summer. Uncommon.

A prostrate, trailing, mat-forming perennial, rooting at
nodes, with branching, pubescent stems to 18 inches
long, rarely more than 2 inches high. Leaves alternate,
evenly spaced along stem, on erect petioles to ½ inch
long, reniform, ½ inch wide and long, margins wavy,
blades and petioles covered in silvery white pubescence.
Flowers inconspicuous, solitary, bell-shaped, about ⅛
inch wide, cream-colored, 5-lobed, on short pedicels originating in leaf axils. Found in Chihuahuan Desert.

Dichondra brachypoda   CONVOLVULACEAE
New Mexico ponyfoot
Mountain forests and woodlands, canyons,
drainages. Summer. Locally common.

A prostrate, trailing, mat-forming perennial to 7 inches
tall, rooting at nodes, with branching, pubescent stems
to 18+ inches tall. Leaves alternate, evenly spaced along
stem, on petioles to ¾ inch long, reniform, to 1¾ inches
long and 2 inches wide, bases can be strongly cordate,
margins entire, occasionally wavy, blades green and
fuzzy. Flowers solitary on short pedicels from leaf axils,
nodding when in fruit, bell-shaped, 5-lobed, greenish
cream. Located in Chihuahuan Desert, at mid to upper
elevations and usually in shade of oaks, junipers, pines,
and other large trees. Common along Scenic Loop in Jeff
Davis County.

Dichondra carolinensis   CONVOLVULACEAE
Carolina ponysfoot, ponysfoot
Urban and suburban areas, woodlands, and banks
of creeks, rivers, and ponds. Spring. Common.

A prostrate, creeping, mat-forming perennial with pubescent stems, rooting at nodes, to 4 inches high. Leaves
alternate, evenly spaced along stem, on petioles, reniform, to 1 inch long and as wide, margins entire. Flowers
solitary on short pedicels from leaf axils, about ⅛ inch
wide, bell-shaped, 5-lobed, creamy white, surrounded by
larger, green, fuzzy sepals. A common lawn weed. Widely
distributed in eastern half of state. Spreading because of
accidental human transport.

Evolvulus sericeus   CONVOLVULACEAE
Silver dwarf morning glory, white evolvulus
Grasslands, fields, prairies, open brush
and woodlands, roadsides and other open
areas. Spring, summer, fall. Common.

An erect to prostrate perennial with silky, pubescent
stems to 12+ inches long. Leaves alternate, lanceolate to
ovate to elliptic, to 1 inch long and ⅓ inch wide, green,
densely pubescent below, less so above, bases tapering,
margins with visible silvery white hairs, tips acute, blades
often folded. Flowers solitary, sessile or on short peduncles originating from leaf axils, rotate to bell-shaped,
white to pale blue, to ½ inch wide. Common throughout
Central Texas, south into Mexico, east to Louisiana. Less
common west into Chihuahuan Desert.

Ipomoea amnicola   CONVOLVULACEAE
Redcenter morning-glory
Fields, brushlands, roadsides and other disturbed
areas. Winter, spring, summer, fall. Locally common.

An introduced, twining, climbing perennial vine
with glabrous stems to 15+ feet long. Leaves alternate, glabrous, heart-shaped, to 4¼ inches long and
about three-fourths as wide, bases cordate, margins
entire. Flowers on umbels at end of long pedicels,
funnel-shaped, 3–12±, white or pink to rose with dark red
centers, to 1½ inches long and to 2 inches wide. Native
of Paraguay. First collection in Texas (1920s) was from
Lower Rio Grande Valley, where species is still common
today, north along coastal counties to Corpus Christi
area. Specific epithet of Latin origin and means "dwelling
near the river," referencing the species's native habitat.

Ipomoea imperati   CONVOLVULACEAE
Beach morning-glory
Beaches, dunes. Winter, spring, summer, fall. Common.

A prostrate perennial vine with stems, rooting at nodes,
to 20+ feet long. Leaves variable from linear-lanceolate
to oblong-ovate to oblong, to 2½ inches long and 1½
inches wide, bases slightly cordate to squarish to angled,
margins entire to 3- to 7-lobed, tips round to notched,
blades leathery to the touch, folded. Flowers solitary, to
2¾ inches long and nearly as wide, funnel-shaped, white
with a yellow throat. Found in state's barrier islands, frequently mixed with *Ipomoea pes-caprae*. Pantropic. Seed
is covered in tiny, light-colored hairs, which aid in floatation and distribution.

Ipomoea lacunosa   CONVOLVULACEAE
**Whitestar, whitestar morning-glory, small white
morning glory**
Thickets, brush and woodlands, creek and
river banks. Summer. Common.

A twining, climbing annual vine with slender, pubescent
stems to 7+ feet long. Leaves alternate, on petioles, cordate to hastate to 3-lobed, to 4 inches long and 2 inches
wide at base, bases strongly cordate, margins entire, tips
acute. Flowers on long peduncles originating from leaf
axils, to 3, funnel-shaped, white to pink, to 1 inch long
and ¾ inch wide. Found in shady areas in eastern third of
Texas, often growing in low areas adjacent to creeks and
rivers.

123

Ipomoea pandurata   CONVOLVULACEAE
Wild sweet potato, man of the earth, manroot
Thickets, open brush and woodlands, fence lines
and other open areas. Spring, summer. Common.

A climbing, twining perennial vine, with glabrous to
pubescent, reddish purple stems to 20+ feet long, sprawling in open areas. Leaves alternate, on petioles 4 inches
long, cordate to ovate or 3-lobed, to 4+ inches long and 3¾
inches wide, margins entire. Inflorescences on peduncles originating from leaf axils, to 5 flowers per peduncle, funnel-shaped, white with rose to reddish purple centers, 5-lobed, to 3 inches wide. Most common in eastern
quarter of Texas. Less common in North-Central Texas,
Edwards Plateau, and south of Coastal Bend.

Ipomoea tenuiloba   CONVOLVULACEAE
Spiderleaf
Rocky slopes and mountain summits.
Summer, fall. Uncommon.

A prostrate perennial vine with glabrous stems to 2+ feet
long from tuberous roots. Leaves on petioles to 1½ inches
long, round, deeply palmately lobed, lobes 5–9, linear,
to 2¾ inches long and to ¼ inch wide, bases cordate,
margins entire. Flowers funnel- to trumpet-shaped, to
3½ inches long and 1½ inches wide, white to pale pink.
Found at higher elevations in rocky outcrops and slopes
in sky islands of Chihuahuan Desert. Specific epithet
means "thin lobed."

Merremia dissecta   CONVOLVULACEAE
Alamo vine, cut-leaf morning-glory, wood rose
Open shrub and woodlands, stream and river
banks, roadsides, fence lines and other open
areas. Spring, summer, fall. Common.

A glabrous, twining, climbing perennial vine with stems
to 15+ feet long. Leaves on petioles to 2¾ inches long,
palmately lobed, leaflets 5–7, lanceolate, margins dentate
to pinnately lobed. Flowers solitary or in small groups
on peduncles to 4 inches long, pedicels to 1 inch long,
about 2 inches in diameter and as long, funnel-shaped,
white with a deep red center. Found throughout southern
two-thirds of Texas, with heaviest concentration south of
San Antonio. Native to Texas.

Stylisma pickeringii var. pattersonii
CONVOLVULACEAE
Pickering's dawnflower, Pickering's morning-glory
Open fields, grasslands, brush and woodlands.
Spring, summer, fall. Locally common.

A prostrate, trailing vine with several densely pubescent stems to 6+ feet long, stems radiating from a central rootstock. Leaves sessile, linear, to 2½ inches long, margins entire. Flowers on peduncles roughly the same length as leaves, white, funnel-shaped to about 1 inch wide. Widely scattered in open areas with sandy soils from Coastal Bend, northeast into Louisiana and north into Oklahoma. Named in honor of Charles Pickering, a 19th-century American naturalist.

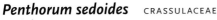

Penthorum sedoides CRASSULACEAE
Ditch stonecrop
Swamps, floodplains, muddy banks of rivers or ponds, and other wet areas. Summer, fall. Common.

An herbaceous perennial with pink or reddish stems to about 2 feet tall, typically unbranched but may be branched in upper portions. Leaves sessile or on petioles to ⅓ inch long, elliptic to ovate, to 4 inches long and 1 inch wide, margins serrate. Flowers develop in cymes originating from upper stems, to 7 flowering stalks radiating outward, each flower ¼ inch in diameter, greenish white, forming reddish pink capsules when mature. Widespread in eastern portion of state and easily found in wet soils, especially floodplains.

Sedum cockerellii CRASSULACEAE
Cockerell's stonecrop
Rocky outcrops, slopes, boulders and cliff faces. Summer. Rare.

A low-growing, mat-forming succulent perennial several inches wide with reddish flowering stems to 8 inches long. Basal leaves oblong-spatulate, to ¾ inch long and less than ¼ inch wide, tips acute. Stem leaves alternate, oblanceolate-elliptic or spatulate, to ¾ inch long. Flowers in cymes at tops of flowering shoots, tinged or streaked white to pink, 5-petaled, to ¼ inch wide. Found in upper elevations of Davis and Franklin Mountains, usually on or around wet, shady slopes or rock crevices.

125

Sedum wrightii CRASSULACEAE
Wright's stonecrop
Protected cliff faces, canyon walls, boulder outcrops. Summer, fall. Uncommon.

An herbaceous perennial succulent forming a mat to 1 foot in diameter, usually smaller. Basal leaves obovate to elliptic, to ½ inch long. Leaves along flowering stems to ⅓ inch or slightly longer. Flowering stems to 5 inches long, erect or decumbent, cymes compact, sometimes branched. Flowers ¼ inch wide, white, as few as one to as many as 20 per cyme. Found in higher elevations of mountain ranges in West Texas, on north-facing or protected slopes in pine-oak woodlands. Usually associated with various species of *Selaginella*, *Cheilanthes*, and *Notholaena*.

Cyclanthera stenura CUCURBITACEAE
Trans-Pecos cyclanthera
Canyons, ravines, rocky outcrops, cliffs, among boulders, fence lines. Spring, summer, fall. Uncommon.

A climbing, annual vine with glabrous stems to 10+ feet long. Tendrils 2-branched if present. Leaves alternate, on petioles to 1 inch long, 3-foliolate with side leaflets deeply lobed, almost appearing 5-foliolate, middle leaflet to 2 inches long, lanceolate, margins serrate. Male flowers in racemes to 6+ inches long, originating from leaf axils, white, about ¼ inch wide. Female flowers originating from leaf axils as well, on short peduncles, inconspicuous. Fruits about 1 inch long, green, elliptic, and covered with short spines. Found in mid to upper elevations in mountains of Big Bend region.

Sicyos microphyllus CUCURBITACEAE
Little leaf bur cucumber
Rocky outcrops, cliffs, ridges, banks and drainages of mountain streams. Fall. Uncommon.

A climbing or trailing annual vine with pubescent or glabrous stems to 10+ feet long. Leaves alternate, pentagonal to 5-lobed, to 4 inches long and 5 inches wide, margins occasionally toothed. Male flowers to 16, in racemes to 7 inches long, originating from leaf axils, greenish white, about ¼ inch wide. Female flowers inconspicuous, on short peduncles originating from same axils as male flowers. Fruits oval-shaped, spiny pepos to about ⅓ inch long. Found in upper elevations in Davis Mountains. Easily seen during fall, if adequate rainfall permits, along Scenic Loop in Jeff Davis County.

Monotropa uniflora ERICACEAE
Indian pipe, ghost plant, corpse plant
Rich oak-pine forest and woodlands.
Spring, summer. Uncommon.

An erect, mycoheterotrophic perennial with white to
pink to red flowering stalks to 12 inches tall, covered with
leaflike scales to ⅜ inch long. Leaves and stems absent.
Flowers solitary, white, occasionally tinged pink or red,
to about 1 inch long and ½ inch wide, becoming erect
after pollination and (with stalk) turning black. Species
lacks chlorophyll. Its roots intermingle with the hyphae
of macrofungi, and the fungi are in a mycorrhizal rela-
tionship with a photothetic species. *Monotropa uniflora*
obtains nutrients from both the fungi and the photothetic
plant. Found in East Texas in deep shade.

Acalypha gracilens EUPHORBIACEAE
Slender threeseed mercury
Fields, meadows, grasslands, open shrub and
woodlands, urban and suburban areas and other
disturbed sites. Summer, fall. Common.

An erect annual with a slender, pubescent stem, which
may be branched at base, to 24 inches tall. Leaves alternate, on petioles ¾ inch long, lanceolate or linear, to 2½
inches long and ¾ inch wide, bases tapering, margins
entire to crenate, tips acute, blades pubescent. Inconspicuous flowers in axillary spikes to just over 1 inch
long, with pubescent, leafy bracts. Male flowers above on
greenish yellow to red part of spike, female flowers below.
Fruits 3-seeded capsules to about ⅛ inch long. Found
throughout Southeast Texas, west into Edwards Plateau,
north into Oklahoma.

Acalypha ostryifolia EUPHORBIACEAE
Pineland threeseed mercury, hophornbeam copperleaf
Fields, pastures, open brush and woodlands,
urban and suburban area, roadsides and other
disturbed areas. Summer, fall. Common.

An erect annual with a branching, angular stem to 30+
inches tall. Leaves alternate, on petioles, ovate to cordate,
bases rounded or cordate, margins serrate, tips pointed.
Male and female flowers separate, not showy. Male flowers
in spikes to 2 inches long originating from leaf axils lower
on stem. Female flowers originate from terminal leaf axils
and are held above foliage. Fuzzy appearing female spike
crowded with 3-chambered, 3-seeded capsules. Male flowers greenish yellow. Found throughout state.

Cnidoscolus texanus   EUPHORBIACEAE
Texas bull-nettle, mala mujer, treadsoftly
Pastures, fields, grasslands, open shrub
and woodlands, roadsides and other open
areas. Spring, summer. Common.

An erect perennial with branching stems to 20 inches tall
and to 3 feet wide, stems and leaves with stinging hairs.
Leaves alternate, round, to 6 inches wide and as long, palmately lobed, 3–5 lobes, ovate, margins sinuate or dentate
or slightly lobed. Flowers in terminal cymes held above
leaves, male and female on same plant and similar in
appearance, with white 5-lobed corollas (males occasionally 4-lobed) to 1 inch long and to 2 inches wide. Found in
sandy or sandy-loam soils throughout eastern two-thirds
of Texas, from upper Panhandle south into Mexico, east
into Louisiana.

Croton monanthogynus   EUPHORBIACEAE
Dove weed, prairie tea
Fields, pastures, grasslands, open brush, roadsides and
other open areas. Spring, summer, fall. Common.

An erect, rounded, branching annual with stems to
20+ inches tall. Leaves alternate, occasionally opposite
near top, on petioles to ½ inch long, lanceolate-oblong,
to 2 inches long and ¾ inch wide, margins entire, tips
rounded, upper leaf surface green and pubescent, lower
surface woolly-white with star-shaped hairs. Male and
female flower separate, small, developing in upper leaf
axils. Male flowers white, petal-like bracts. Female flowers green. Fruits are egg-shaped capsules to ¼ inch long.
Widespread throughout Texas. Weak in Panhandle.

Euphorbia antisyphilitica   EUPHORBIACEAE
Candelilla
Sparse desert scrub. Winter, spring,
summer, fall. Locally common.

An erect, rhizomatous, multistemmed perennial with
slender, waxy, glaucous stems to 24+ inches tall. Leaves
alternate, sessile, linear, to $1/_{16}$ inch long. Cyathia along
upper stems with 5 petal-like wings, white with reddish
brown bases, to ¼ inch wide. Numerous male flowers
surround a single female flower with a branching style,
pink to red. Primarily found on limestone, in Chihuahuan Desert and in Lower Rio Grande Valley.

Euphorbia bicolor   EUPHORBIACEAE
Snow on the prairie
Grasslands, prairies, fields, pastures, roadsides
and other open areas. Summer, fall. Common.

An erect, single-stemmed, branching annual with glabrous to pubescent stems to 3+ feet tall. Leaves alternate, ovate to elliptic, to 3 inches long, bases sessile,
margins entire to ciliate, tips acute to obtuse, blades glabrous. Cyathia terminal with leafy bracts below. Bracts
glaucous with white margins to nearly entirely white,
linear to oblanceolate, to 2½ inches long and ¼ inch
wide, tips acute. Cyathium with numerous male flowers,
one female flower, 5 petal-like appendages. Fruits are
3-chambered capsules. Found throughout eastern third
of state, from Coastal Bend north into Oklahoma.

Euphorbia cordifolia
(*Chamaesyce cordifolia*)   EUPHORBIACEAE
Heartleaf spurge, heartleaf sandmat, roundleaf spurge
Open grass, brush and woodlands, roadsides and
other open areas. Summer, fall. Common.

A prostrate annual with numerous glabrous, reddish
brown stems, from a central taproot, to 20+ inches
long, stems and leaves with milky latex. Leaves opposite, on short petioles, elliptic-round to oblong-ovate, to
½ inch long, bases cordate, margins entire, tips obtuse
to rounded. Cyathia solitary along stem, mostly toward
ends, somewhat egg-shaped, with 5 white, bractlike
appendages that look superficially like petals, to ⅛ inch
wide. Found in open, sandy soils from Rio Grande Valley
into North-Central Texas, east into Louisiana.

Euphorbia corollata   EUPHORBIACEAE
Flowering spurge
Open brush and woodlands, riparian areas.
Spring, summer, fall. Common.

An erect, slender, airy perennial to 28+ inches tall with
single- or multistemmed branching in upper portions.
Leaves alternate, sessile, linear-oblong, to 2½ inches long
and ½ inch wide, margins entire, tips obtuse, surfaces
glabrous. Individual male and female flowers. Cyathia
in terminal panicles, with 5 petal-like bracts, and either
male or female flowers in center. Found in eastern third
of state, from Coastal Bend north into Oklahoma.

Euphorbia davidii EUPHORBIACEAE
David's euphorbia
Fields, pastures, grasslands, open brush and
woodlands, roadsides and other open areas.
Spring, summer, fall. Locally common.

An introduced, erect, branching annual with pubescent stems to 20 inches tall. Leaves opposite, on petioles,
lanceolate to elliptic, to 2½ inches long, bases tapering,
margins crenate-serrate, tips acute, surfaces pubescent.
Flowers in terminal clusters, individual flowers inconspicuous. Male and female flowers separate. Fruits are
3-chambered capsules, pale green, pubescent. Found in
disturbed areas in Panhandle, south into Edwards Plateau, west through Chihuahuan Desert. Spreading.

Euphorbia dentata EUPHORBIACEAE
Toothed spurge
Fields, pastures, grasslands, open brush and woodlands,
canyons, riparian areas. Spring, summer, fall. Common.

An erect, weakly branching annual with pubescent stems
to 24 inches tall. Leaves opposite or alternate along stems,
whorled near inflorescences, on petioles to ¾ inch long,
ovate-lanceolate to linear-lanceolate, to 3 inches long and
1 inch wide, bases wedge-shaped, margins dentate, tips
acute, leaf surfaces glabrous. Flowers in terminal clusters
to 2 inches wide, inconspicuous. Bracts below flowers
are similar to leaves, but smaller, often white near base,
color extending to tips. Fruits large, conspicuous, green,
3-chambered capsules. Found throughout state in various habitats, often becoming weedy.

Euphorbia eriantha EUPHORBIACEAE
Beetle spurge
Sparse desert scrub. Winter, spring, summer. Uncommon.

An erect, slightly pubescent annual with branching
stems to 20 inches tall. Leaves alternate, upper leaves
nearly opposite, on petioles to ¼ inch long, linear to
linear-lanceolate, to 3 inches long and ¼ inch wide, margins entire but uneven and slightly involute, tips acute,
leaf surfaces with scattered, visible, appressed hairs.
Flowers in terminal clusters, male and female flowers
separate, both small and inconspicuous. Fruits are obvious, 3-chambered capsules, egg-shaped, with dense covering of silvery white hairs. Found in Big Bend region,
north into Culberson County.

Euphorbia maculata
(*Chamaesyce maculata*)   EUPHORBIACEAE
Spotted sandmat
Open grass, brush and woodlands, washes,
creek and river beds, roadsides and other open,
disturbed areas. Summer, fall. Common.

A prostrate, mat-forming annual with multiple pubescent
stems from a central root, to about 18 inches in diameter, stems and leaves with milky latex. Leaves opposite, on
short petioles, oblong, to ¾ inch long and ¼ inch wide,
bases asymmetric, margins entire or weakly toothed,
blades often with a dark patch on upper surface. Flowers in leaf axils, solitary or in clusters, male and female
flowers separate but within same inflorescence to ⅛ inch
wide. Cyathium urn-shaped, with white or red petal-like
bracts. Found throughout state.

Euphorbia marginata   EUPHORBIACEAE
Snow on the mountain
Grasslands, prairies, fields, pastures, roadsides
and other open areas. Summer, fall. Common.

An erect, single-stemmed, branching annual with glabrous to pubescent stems to 3+ feet long. Leaves alternate, sessile, ovate to elliptic, to 3 inches long, margins
entire to ciliate, tips acute to obtuse, blades glabrous.
Cyathia terminal with leafy bracts below. Bracts glaucous
with white margins to nearly entirely white, lanceolate,
tips acute. Cyathium with numerous male flowers, one
female flower, and 5 white, petal-like appendages. Fruits
are 3-chambered capsules. Found throughout western
two-thirds of state.

Euphorbia missurica
(*Chamaesyce missurica*)   EUPHORBIACEAE
Prairie sandmat
Open grass, brush and woodlands, roadsides and
other open areas. Spring, summer. Common.

An ascending to erect annual with multiple, slender, reddish brown, glabrous stems to 3 feet tall. Leaves opposite, on short petioles, linear to oblong, to 1 inch long and
¼ inch wide, bases asymmetrical, margins entire and
slightly involute, tips rounded. Cyathia solitary in upper
portions of stems, with white or pink bractlike petals, to
about 3⁄16 inch wide. Found throughout state, often in disturbed soils.

Jatropha dioica   EUPHORBIACEAE
Leather-stem, toothbrush plant, sangre de drago
Open brush and thornscrub, rocky outcrops, ledges and other open, dry areas. Winter, spring, summer. Common.

An erect, somewhat rhizomatous ephemeral perennial with thick, leathery, reddish brown, mostly leafless stems to 3+ feet long. Leaves fascicled, spatulate or linear or palmately lobed, to 2 inches long, bases tapering, margins entire, tips round. Male and female flowers on separate plants. Male flowers in clustered cymes, either terminal or along stem, white to creamy white, often tinged pink or red. Female flowers bell-shaped, solitary. Both flowers less than ¼ inch long. Throughout South Texas, north into southern Edwards Plateau, west into Chihuahuan Desert.

Ricinus communis   EUPHORBIACEAE
Castor-bean, castor-oil plant, higuerilla
River and creek bottoms and banks, edges of rivers and other low, wet areas. Spring, summer. Locally common.

An introduced, erect, stout annual with ascending stems to 10+ feet tall. Leaves alternate, peltate on long petioles, palmately 7- to 9-lobed, to 20 inches long and wide, margins serrate, tips pointed. Flowers in terminal inflorescences, nonshowy. Male flowers lower on inflorescence, with numerous, cream-colored, branching stalks attached to anthers, 5 obvious green sepals. Female flowers above male, style 3-parted with forked, red to cream parts. Fruits are 3-chambered capsules. Found throughout Texas.

Stillingia sylvatica   EUPHORBIACEAE
Queen's delight
Fields, pastures, grasslands, open brush and woodlands, roadsides. Spring, summer. Common.

An erect to ascending, multistemmed, leafy perennial with branching, glabrous stems to 28+ inches tall, older, larger specimens forming a roundish, dense shrub. Leaves alternate, nearly sessile, lanceolate to oblanceolate, to 3+ inches long and ½ inch wide, margins serrate to crenulate, tips and bases acute. Flowers terminal in spikes, inconspicuous, reduced. Female flowers below, male above. Fruits are capsules, 3-celled, rounded, to ½ inch long. Widespread throughout Texas, most common in East Texas.

Stillingia texana   EUPHORBIACEAE
Texas queen's delight, Texas toothleaf
Fields, meadows, grasslands, open shrub and woodlands, roadsides and other open areas. Spring. Common.

An erect, multistemmed, branching perennial to 18 inches tall, stems originating from central rootstock, larger individuals forming a small, rounded shrub. Leaves alternate, sessile or nearly so, linear to lanceolate, to 3 inches long, bases tapering, margins serrate or crenulate, tips acute. Flowers in terminal spikes, inconspicuous, reduced. Male flowers above, female below. Male portion of spike is yellow when in flower. Fruits are 3-chambered capsules, rounded, to about ⅜ inch long. Found on limestone soils throughout Edwards Plateau and surrounding regions.

Stillingia treculiana   EUPHORBIACEAE
Trecul's toothleaf, sanar toda
Open brushlands, thickets, disturbed areas. Spring. Uncommon.

An erect, branching, leafy perennial to 20+ inches tall, with glabrous stems. Leaves alternate, sessile, oblong to obovate-oblong, to 1¾ inches long and ¾ inch wide, bluish green to green, waxy, and generally contorted or twisted, bases tapering, margins dentate, tips pointed or rounded. Flowers in terminal spikes, nonshowy. Female flowers below, male flowers above, well-spaced, creamy. Fruits are rounded capsules, about ¼ inch wide and long. Found from South Texas north into western Edwards Plateau. Sap is used as an antiseptic.

Tragia ramosa   EUPHORBIACEAE
Noseburn, desert tragia, branched noseburn
Fields, pastures, grasslands, meadows, open brush and woodlands, roadsides and other open areas. Spring, summer, fall. Common.

An erect, multistemmed perennial with slender branching stems to 16 inches tall, leaves and stems covered with visible, stinging hairs. Leaves alternate, on petioles ¾ inches long, lanceolate to ovate, to ¾ inch long, margins toothed, tips acute, blades commonly folded upward. Flowers in short racemes originating from upper stem, opposite leaves or terminal, small, petals absent. Male and female flowers separate. Female solitary on raceme, with divided red style; male with recurved sepals and yellow anthers. Absent in deep East Texas and along coast.

133

Tragia urticifolia EUPHORBIACEAE
Nettleleaf noseburn
Fields, pastures, open brush and woodlands, roadsides and other open areas. Spring, summer, fall. Common.

An erect to trailing, multistemmed, slender perennial with stems to 20 inches long, leaves and stems with stinging hairs. Leaves alternate, on short petioles to nearly sessile, ovate-lanceolate to triangular-lanceolate, to 2 inches long and 1¼ inches wide, bases cordate, margins serrate, tips acute. Flowers in racemes originating from upper stem or terminal, nonshowy, greenish yellow, one female flower per raceme (which is closer to stem), male flowers numerous. Found in eastern third of Texas, in sandy, open soils, west into Edwards Plateau.

Baptisia alba FABACEAE
White wild indigo, white false indigo
Grasslands, prairies, open shrub and woodlands, river and creek slopes, roadsides and other open areas. Spring, summer. Locally common.

An erect, shrubby perennial with weakly branched, reddish brown, glabrous stems to 6 feet tall. Leaves alternate, trifoliolate, ovate to oblanceolate, to 2 inches long and ¾ inch wide, bases tapering, margins entire, tips pointed. Stems terminating in spikelike racemes to 24 inches long. Flowers white, often with purple-brown blotches, papilionaceous, to about 1 inch long, banner somewhat angled forward, margins rolled backward, lateral wings not spreading and appearing inflated. A species primarily found in eastern fourth of state.

Dalea candida FABACEAE
White prairie clover
Fields, meadows, grasslands, prairies, open brush and woodlands, roadsides and other open areas. Spring, summer. Common.

An erect perennial from a woody base with branching, glabrous stems to 3+ feet tall. Leaves alternate, pinnate, to 2 inches long, 5–9 leaflets, each leaflet oblong or linear-oblanceolate, to 1¼ inches long, margins entire, tips acute to mucronate. Stems terminating in dense spikes to 4 inches tall, elongating after flowering. Flowers white, bilateral, less than ⅛ inch wide and as long, papilionaceous. Found throughout state; most common in Panhandle and Chihuahuan Desert.

Dalea cylindriceps FABACEAE
Sandsage prairie clover, dense-flowered prairie clover
Grasslands, open shrublands. Spring,
summer. Uncommon.

An erect perennial with glabrous stems, occasionally
branching, to 24+ inches tall. Leaves alternate,
pinnate, with 7–9 leaflets, each leaflet oblanceolate to oblong-elliptic, to 1 inch long. Flowers in
terminal, dense spikes to 7+ inches long, bilateral, white to pink, to ¼ inch long, somewhat
papilionaceous, with lower petals that would normally form keel not united. Found in sandy soils
of the Trans-Pecos and east to Midland-Odessa
area.

Dalea multiflora FABACEAE
Roundhead prairie clover, round headed dalea
Grasslands, prairies, fields, meadows, open
brush and woodlands, roadsides and other
open areas. Spring, summer. Common.

An erect perennial with glabrous, branching stems
to 2+ feet tall. Leaves alternate, pinnate, to 1¾ inches
long, smaller leaves in upper branches. Leaflets 3–9,
linear-oblong to linear-oblanceolate, to ½ inch long, margins entire to involute, tips obtuse or mucronate, lower
surfaces with glands. Flowers in terminal spikes or originating from upper leaf axils, spikes rounded, compact.
Flowers numerous, crowded, white, papilionaceous, less
than ¼ inch wide and long. Found throughout Central
Texas, south to Coastal Bend, west to Pecos River, north
into Oklahoma, and east to Houston area.

Sophora nuttalliana FABACEAE
Silky sophora
Grasslands, prairies, open valleys and canyon
bottoms, and other low, flat areas. Spring,
summer. Uncommon to locally common.

An ascending to erect, spreading, rhizomatous perennial
with flowering stems to 12 inches tall, leaves and stems
with a soft, silky pubescence. Leaves alternate, compound
with 8± leaflets per leaf, to about 3 inches long, leaflets to
about ⅓ inch long, margins entire, blades typically folded
revealing silky underside. Flowers on stems terminating in racemes to nearly 4 inches long, papilionaceous,
creamy white, extending beyond lavender calyx. Found in
the Trans-Pecos, north into Panhandle.

135

Tephrosia onobrychoides FABACEAE
Multibloom hoarypea
Fields, pastures, grasslands, open brush and
woodlands, roadsides. Spring. Common.

A decumbent or reclining perennial from a woody base,
with many pubescent stems to 30+ inches long. Leaves
alternate, pinnate, to 9 inches long, with 13–25 leaflets,
each leaflet linear-oblanceolate to elliptic, to 2 inches long
and ⅝ inch wide, bases rounded, margins entire, ciliate, tips mucronate. Flowers on uncrowded racemes to 12
inches tall, papilionaceous, white, turning red with age,
banner erect, cleft, wings spreading. Found in sandy soils
in eastern half of Texas, from Coastal Bend north into
Oklahoma, east into Louisiana.

Tephrosia virginiana FABACEAE
Devil's shoestring, goat's rue, Virginia tephrosia
Meadows, fields, open brush and woodlands,
roadsides. Spring. Common.

An erect pubescent perennial from a woody base, with
multiple stems, rarely branched, to 30 inches tall. Leaves
alternate, pinnate, to 5¾ inches long, with 9–31 leaflets,
each leaflet elliptic to linear-oblong, to 1¼ inches long,
margins entire, tips mucronate, surfaces visibly pubescent. Flowers in 4-inch-long racemes, nearly 1 inch long,
papilionaceous, banner erect, cream to pale yellow, wings
and keel pinkish red. Found throughout eastern third
of Texas. Bicolored flowers, thinner leaflets, and erect
nature distinguish this species.

Trifolium lappaceum FABACEAE
Burdock clover, lappa clover
Urban and suburban areas, roadsides and other
open, disturbed areas. Spring. Locally common.

An introduced, decumbent to erect annual with pubescent stems, branching from base to 10+ inches long.
Leaves alternate, 3-foliolate leaflets, obovate to oblanceolate, to ¾ inch long and less than ¼ inch wide, bases
tapering, margins minutely dentate, ciliate, tips rounded.
Flowers in rounded spikes originating from leaf axils,
ascending to erect, barely extending beyond pubescent
bractlets, papilionaceous, white to cream, turning pink
throughout the season, banner and lateral wings enclosing keel. Found in Southeast Texas. Recently found in
Northeast Texas, along Red River; expect elsewhere.

Vicia caroliniana FABACEAE
Carolina vetch, wood vetch, pale vetch
Woodlands. Spring. Uncommon.

An erect, slender perennial with trailing or climbing
stems to 3+ feet long. Leaves alternate, pinnate, to 4
inches long, leaflets ovate, to about ¾ inch long and ¼
inch wide, bases rounded, margins entire, tips pointed,
terminal tendril branched. Flowers in axillary racemes
to 3½ inches long, numerous, papilionaceous, white to
rarely pink, keel blue-tipped, to about ½ inch long, banner erect. Uncommon to rare in East Texas to eastern
edge of Edwards Plateau. Prefers deciduous woodlands,
usually growing on slopes near creeks or streams.

Obolaria virginica GENTIANACEAE
Virginia pennywort, pennywort
Hardwood forests. Spring. Uncommon.

An erect single-stemmed, mycoheterotrophic perennial
with simple or weakly branched stems to 4 inches tall.
Leaves opposite, sessile, cuneate-obovate, to ¾ inch long,
margins entire, tips obtuse. Scalelike leaves found at
base of plant. Flowers solitary or in groups of 3, terminal
and in leaf axils, white, 4-lobed, lobes about ¼ inch long.
Found in deep East Texas in Jasper, Angelina, and Sabine
Counties. Common in eastern United States.

Limnobium spongia HYDROCHARITACEAE
Frog's-bit, American spongeplant, Cajun water-lettuce
Ponds, swamps, ditches, stagnant waters, muddy
banks and flats and other slow-moving or still waters.
Spring, summer, fall. Uncommon to locally common.

An acaulescent, stoloniferous, aquatic perennial, floating or rooted in mud. Basal leaves only, on petioles to 6+
inches long, oval-cordate, to 3 inches long and as wide,
bases cordate, margins entire, tips obtuse, blades glabrous and spongy to the touch, lower surface may be
yellow-green to purple. Male and female flowers on separate plants, occasionally on same plant. Male flowers on
pedicels to 4 inches long with 3 oblong sepals, 3 linear
petals, 6–12 stamens, white, to about 1 inch wide. Female
flowers similar, on pedicels to 1½ inches and with 6–9
styles. Uncommon in eastern third of state.

pea family
FABACEAE

gentian family
GENTIANACEAE

tape-grass family
HYDROCHARITACEAE

Nama carnosum   HYDROPHYLLACEAE
Sand fiddleleaf
Open grass, brush and desert scrublands.
Spring, summer. Uncommon.

An erect or ascending perennial with branching, leafy
stems to 16 inches tall. Leaves alternate, densely crowded,
linear, to 1¼ inches long, margins revolute. Flowers in
crowded terminal cymes, often hidden by and barely
extending beyond leaves, white, about ⅓ inch long,
tubular to funnel-shaped or elongated urn-shaped, with
5 lobes, radial. Found on sandy-gypseous soils in the
Trans-Pecos, from Reeves County to Hudspeth County.

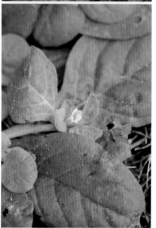

Nama jamaicense   HYDROPHYLLACEAE
Jamaicanweed
Canyons, rocky outcrops, creek and river banks,
open brush and woodlands, thickets, roadsides and
other open areas. Spring, summer. Common.

A prostrate to ascending annual with branching stems
from a central rootstock, to 16+ inches long, forming
small mats, leaves and stems pubescent. Leaves alternate,
occasionally opposite, spatulate to obovate, to more than 3
inches long and 1½ inches wide, bases tapering, margins
entire, tips rounded. Small, white, 5-lobed flowers occur
singly in upper leaf axils, to ¼ inch long, tubular. Found
throughout Central Texas, south to coast and into Mexico.
Prefers shady areas with moist soils.

Phacelia rupestris   HYDROPHYLLACEAE
Rock phacelia, white-flowered phacelia
Rocky outcrops, canyons, among boulders,
ridges, open brush and woodlands. Spring,
summer, fall. Locally common.

An erect, lax, branching annual to biennial, with
soft-pubescent leaves and stems to 2 feet tall. Leaves alternate, ovate, to 4 inches long and 1¾ inches wide, pinnately lobed, often deeply, final margins entire to lobed.
Stems terminating in scorpioid cymes. Flowers white,
bell-shaped. Similar to *Phacelia congesta*, but with white
flowers and a rounded habit. Common among boulders
in West Texas. Specific epithet means "living on rocks or
cliffs," an indication of habitat preference.

Agastache micrantha LAMIACEAE
White giant hyssop
Mountain woodlands and forests. Summer, fall. Common.

A heavily aromatic, erect, branched perennial to 2 feet tall, leaves and stems covered in fine hairs. Leaves sometimes on petioles, deltate-lanceolate, to 1 inch wide and 2½ inches long, margins serrate. Small white flowers, barely ⅛ inch in diameter, appear on terminal spikes to 7½ inches long. Found growing in wooded areas and among rocky outcrops and boulders in higher elevations of West Texas mountain ranges.

Hyptis alata LAMIACEAE
Cluster bushmint, musky mint
Swamps, marshes, bar ditches, wet meadows and other low, wet areas. Summer, fall. Locally common.

An erect, single-stemmed perennial to 5 feet tall with an unusual, slightly pleasing, musky mint aroma. Leaves opposite, ovate to linear-lanceolate, to 6 inches long and 2 inches wide, margins roughly serrate. Flowers numerous, white, often dotted with purple, to about ¼ inch long, in clusters at end of 2-inch-long peduncles arising from leaf axils, lower lip much reduced and deflexed, upper lip consisting of 4 lobes, vegetative portions of inflorescence often tinged with white pubescence. Genus name from Greek *huptios*, "turned back," referring to lower lip. Only native *Hyptis* species in Texas. Can be found in southeastern portion of state, east into Louisiana.

Lycopus rubellus LAMIACEAE
Taperleaf water horehound, stalked water horehound, water horehound
Marshes, swamps, bogs, wet meadows, roadside ditches and other low, wet areas. Summer, fall, early winter. Common.

An erect, rhizomatous perennial with branching stems to 3 feet tall. Leaves opposite, on petioles to 1 inch long, lanceolate to elliptic, to 4 inches long and 1½ inches wide, bases tapering, margins widely dentate to entire, tips acute. Flowers in clusters in axils of middle and upper leaves, white, less than ¼ inch long, bilabiate. Lower lip 3-lobed with a broad middle lobe, upper lip notched to slightly 2-lobed. Found in eastern third of Texas.

139

Marrubium vulgare LAMIACEAE
Horehound, white horehound
Pastures, roadsides and other disturbed areas,
grasslands, open brush and woodlands, river and
creek bottoms. Spring, summer, fall. Common.

An introduced, erect, branching, perennial with
woolly-white leaves and stems to 3 feet tall, aromatic.
Leaves opposite, on petioles to ¾ inch long, round to
ovate, to about 2 inches long and wide, margins crenate,
upper leaf surfaces wrinkled. Flowers white, bilabiate, in
clusters in upper axils of stems, about ¼ inch long. Lower
lip 3-lobed with a broad middle, upper lip erect. Found
throughout Central Texas, west into New Mexico, occasional elsewhere. Often occurs in overgrazed pastures.

Monarda fruticulosa LAMIACEAE
Shrubby horsemint, spotted beebalm, shrubby beebalm
Grasslands, meadows, fields, pastures, open brush and
woodlands. Winter, spring, summer. Locally common.

An erect, shrubby perennial with heavily branched stems
to 2+ feet tall. Leaves opposite, sessile to subsessile, linear, to 1⅓ inches long, bases tapering, margins entire,
occasionally toothed at tip, tips acute. Stems terminating in short spikes with evenly spaced, roundish flowering heads. Flowers bilabiate, white to pink with darker
spots along inside. Lower lip 3-lobed, upper lip slightly
notched, curving, and about same length as lower lip.
Exterior of corolla with long, visible hairs. Floral bracts
dusty white with a pink tinge. Found in sandy soils of
South Texas.

Monarda lindheimeri LAMIACEAE
Lindheimer's beebalm
Edges of woodlands, thickets, roadsides.
Spring, summer. Uncommon.

An erect, rhizomatous perennial with either unbranched
or branching stems to 30+ inches tall. Leaves opposite,
ovate to lanceolate, to 3 inches long and ¾ inch wide,
bases truncate, margins serrate, tips pointed. Upper
leaves sessile. Lower leaves on petioles ¼ inch long.
Stems terminating in a single, rounded flowering head
consisting of numerous creamy white, bilabiate flowers, lower lip elongated, 3-lobed with center lobe thin
and curved to a point, upper lip thin, stamens projecting
beyond lip, bracts greenish white. Found in shaded areas
in eastern third of Texas.

Pycnanthemum albescens LAMIACAEAE
Whiteleaf mountain mint
Woodlands, meadows, thickets. Summer, fall. Common.

An erect, branching perennial with pubescent stems to 4+ feet tall. Leaves opposite, on short petioles to nearly sessile, ovate to lanceolate, to 2¾ inches long and 1 inch wide, bases tapering to rounded, margins serrate, tips acute, all but lowest leaves with a greenish white hue. Flowering heads roundish, occurring at ends of stems or in upper leaf axils, on short peduncles, numerous, small, bilabiate, white to light pink with darker spots, lower lip 3-lobed, upper lip notched. Found in eastern fourth of Texas. Foliage has a pleasant, pungent mint aroma.

Pycnanthemum muticum LAMIACEAE
Clustered mountainmint, hairy mountainmint
Woodlands. Summer, fall. Uncommon.

An erect perennial with a single pilose stem, branching at ends or occasionally in upper portion of main stem, to 40+ inches tall. Leaves opposite, on short petioles to nearly sessile, ovate to lanceolate, to 3¼ inches long and 1½ inches wide, bases cordate to rounded, margins serrate to entire, tips pointed. Flowers in corymbs at ends of stems, clustered in roundish heads with leafy, white bracts below, small, less than ¼ inch long, bilabiate, white to very pale pink, with dark purple spots inside throat and along lobes, lower lip 3-lobed. Currently known from Montgomery and Harris Counties in Southeast Texas and Dallas County in North-Central Texas.

Pycnanthemum tenuifolium LAMIACEAE
Narrowleaf mountainmint, slender mountainmint
Wet meadows, grasslands, fields and pastures, marshes, open brush and woodlands, roadsides and other wet, open areas. Spring, summer, fall. Common.

An erect perennial with branching stems, mostly above, to 3+ feet tall. Leaves opposite, linear to 2¾ inches long and ¼ inch wide, bases tapering, margins revolute, tips acute. Stems branching and terminating in roundish flowering heads, forming a dense corymb, each head with numerous white to light pink, bilabiate flowers, throats and inside of lobes with purple spots. Lower lip 3-lobed, middle lobe longer than lateral, all equally wide, upper lobe notched. Found in eastern fourth of Texas.

Teucrium cubense   LAMIACEAE
Coast germander, small coastal germander
Grasslands, creek and river bottoms, palm
groves and other low, wet areas. Winter,
spring, summer, fall. Locally common.

An erect annual to perennial with multiple branching
stems to 2+ feet tall. Basal leaves on petioles, oblong
to obovate, to about 1½ inches long, margins lobed,
crenate or entire. Upper leaves similar, opposite, smaller
and variously lobed. Flowers on short stalks in upper leaf
axils, bilabiate, white, with prominent purple venation,
lower lip 3-lobed with middle lobe greatly enlarged, upper
lip reduced. Found from El Paso southeast to Cameron
County and along coast from Mexico to Louisiana; isolated populations elsewhere.

Teucrium laciniatum   LAMIACEAE
Cut-leaf germander
Grasslands, fields, prairies, open brush
and woodlands, roadsides and other open
areas. Spring, summer. Common.

An erect perennial with stems to 10 inches tall. Leaves
opposite, pinnately lobed 2–8 times, lobes entire or once
again lobed, to 2 inches long and less than ¼ inch wide,
ultimate margins entire to slightly revolute, tips pointed.
Flowers at ends of stems, bilabiate, white to cream, to
1 inch long, lower lip 3-lobed with middle lobe greatly
enlarged, upper lip reduced. Found throughout Edwards
Plateau, west to El Paso and north into Oklahoma and
Panhandle. Forms colonies.

Erythronium albidum   LILIACEAE
Trout lily, white trout lily, dog-tooth violet
Woodlands, forests, scrub oak thickets, bottomlands
and floodplains. Spring. Uncommon.

An erect (when in flower), bulbous perennial to 8 inches
tall. Basal leaves, one in nonflowering plants or 2 in flowering plants, elliptic to lanceolate, to 6 inches long and 2
inches wide, bases tapering, margins entire, tips acute,
blades mottled purple-brown and gray-green. Flowers solitary, to 2 inches long, nodding at end of a scape
to 8 inches long, 6-petaled, white to pink or lavender,
recurved. Found from eastern Edwards Plateau north
into Oklahoma and east to Louisiana. One of earliest species to flower in spring. Often found in small colonies.

Mentzelia humilis   LOASACEAE
Stickleaf
Open desert scrub and grasslands.
Spring, summer. Locally common.

An erect perennial with white, branching stems to 24+ inches tall. Leaves opposite, sessile, linear to linear-lanceolate, to 2¾+ inches long, lobes distinctive, resembling teeth of a comb. Flowers terminal or from axillary peduncles, white, to 2 inches wide, petals linear, stamens numerous. Found in Chihuahuan Desert from Hudspeth County east to Ward County, on gypseous soils.

Mentzelia strictissima   LOASACEAE
Grassland blazing star
Grasslands, prairies, meadows and other open areas. Spring, summer, fall. Uncommon.

An erect, branched perennial with a single stem to 3 feet tall. Leaves linear to lanceolate, to 4 inches long, margins toothed, surfaces rough to the touch. Flowers white, opening later in afternoon, 2 inches in diameter, petals linear to oblanceolate. Prefers sandy soils. Found in southwestern portion of short grass prairie in Midland-Odessa area, west to New Mexico.

Mitreola petiolata   LOGANIACEAE
Lax hornpod, miterwort
Banks of streams, rivers, lakes, and ponds, wet savannas, roadside ditches and other low, wet areas. Spring, summer, fall. Common.

An erect annual with glabrous, branching stems to 28+ inches tall. Leaves opposite, on short petioles, ovate-elliptic to ovate-lanceolate, to 3¼ inches long, bases tapering, margins entire, tips obtuse to acute. Flowers in terminal cymes, white, 5-petaled, radial, less than ¼ inch wide. Fruits are small capsules with 2 horns, hence the common name. Found in wet, damp soils from East Texas west to Val Verde County, south to Coastal Bend, north into Oklahoma.

143

Herissantia crispa   MALVACEAE
Bladdermallow, curly bladder mallow, curly abutilon
Thickets, brushlands, canyons, ravines, desert
washes. Winter, spring, summer, fall. Uncommon.

An erect to prostrate, spreading perennial with branching, pubescent stems to 2 feet long. Leaves on petioles to 2 inches long, ovate to triangular, bases cordate, margins serrate to dentate, tips pointed. Flowers 5-petaled, white with a yellow-green center, about ¾ inch wide. Fruits hang on withering pedicels below leaves, are green when young and mature brown, outer walls accordion-like, thin, and papery. Found from El Paso south to Cameron County. In West Texas, prefers rocky canyons; in South Texas, found among thornscrub. In some areas has a lax vining habit; in others somewhat erect and spreading.

Hibiscus aculeatus   MALVACEAE
Big thicket hibiscus, pineland hibiscus, comfort root
Banks of creeks and ponds and other wet,
open areas. Spring, summer, fall. Rare.

An erect perennial to 3+ feet tall with leaves and stems covered in rough hairs. Leaves ovate, split into 3–5 parts, to 4 inches long and 5 inches wide, bases cuneate to cordate, margins crenate to serrate. Petioles on lower leaves can be two-thirds length of blade or longer; petioles on upper leaves shorter. Solitary, funnel-shaped flowers appear in axils of upper leaves, white to pale yellow with red throats, to 3 inches long and 2 inches wide. Known from Hardin County. Specific epithet means "prickly" or "thorny."

Hibiscus dasycalyx   MALVACEAE
Neches River rose mallow
Marshes, seasonally wet soils, edges of slow-
moving bodies of water. Summer. Rare.

An erect perennial to 7 feet tall, usually shorter, with glabrous stems and leaves. Leaves alternate, triangular to ovate, deeply 3-lobed, to 5 inches long and wide, bases cordate to truncate, margins roughly toothed. Solitary flowers, cream to white with dark reddish purple centers, to 6 inches wide and nearly as long. Specific epithet of Greek origin and means "hairy" (*dasys*) "calyx" (*calyx*). Found in a few counties in central East Texas; available in the nursery trade and may be introduced elsewhere.

Hibiscus laevis   MALVACEAE

Rose mallow, halberdleaf rose mallow, military hibiscus
Margins of lakes, slow-moving rivers,
floodplains, ditches, canals and other open,
wet areas. Spring, summer, fall. Common.

An erect perennial with glaucous stems to 8+ feet
tall. Leaves variable from ovate to triangular to
lanceolate-ovate, on petioles 3½ inches long, 3- to
5-lobed, to 7 inches long and nearly as wide, bases cordate to truncate, margins serrate to dentate, leaf surfaces
glabrous. Flowers solitary, in axils of upper leaves, on
pedicels to 4 inches long, funnel-shaped, white or rose
or pink, deeper red within throat. Common throughout
coastal Texas, from Coastal Bend to Louisiana, north into
Oklahoma. Isolated populations in Central Texas.

Hibiscus trionum   MALVACEAE

Flower-of-an-hour, rosemallow, Venice mallow
Roadsides, urban and suburban areas and other areas
of human habitation. Summer, fall. Uncommon.

An introduced, prostrate to sprawling annual with
branching, pubescent stems to 2 feet long and as tall.
Leaves alternate, to 3 inches long and 2 inches wide,
3-lobed with primary lobes again lobed, margins entire,
crenate, or dentate. Flowers solitary, originating from
leaf axils, 5-petaled, radial, white to cream with deep reddish purple centers, to about 2 inches wide. Occasional
throughout Texas. Photograph shows specimen at 5900
feet in Davis Mountains, along a drainage.

Proboscidea louisianica subsp. *louisianica*

MARTYNIACEAE
Devil's claw, ram's horn, unicorn plant
Agricultural fields, washes, river bottoms, roadsides
and other disturbed areas. Summer, fall. Common.

An annual to 3+ feet tall and 5+ feet wide. Leaves on
long petioles, ovate, to 10 inches wide, surfaces highly
viscid-pubescent. Flowers in racemes above foliage, white
to light pink, darker spots on lobes and into interior of
tube, sometimes forming lines. Fruits dry dehiscent pods
that split open when mature. Recurved claws of fruit
attach themselves to large mammals, which disperse
seeds. Widely dispersed across Texas. Absent in deep East
Texas and far West Texas.

Schoenocaulon texanum   MELANTHIACEAE
Greenlily, Texas feathershank
Fields, meadows, open brush and woodlands,
rocky hillsides and slopes, ridges, roadsides and
other open areas. Spring, summer. Common.

An erect, bulbous perennial to 24+ inches tall when in
flower. Basal leaves grasslike, to 2 feet long and ¼ inch
wide, sheathed at base, arching. Scape to 20 inches tall.
Flowers in terminal, crowded racemes to 12 inches long,
to 250± per raceme, ⅓ inch wide, tepals green and fleshy,
stigmas white. Found in Chihuahuan Desert west into
Edwards Plateau and south to Coastal Bend. Can occur in
vast numbers in fire-managed or properly timed mowing
regimes.

Toxicoscordion nuttallii (*Zigadenus nuttallii*)
MELANTHIACEAE
Nuttall's death camus
Fields, prairies, grasslands, open brush
and woodlands. Spring. Common.

An erect, bulbous perennial with stems to 20+ inches
tall. Leaves on lower stem only, sheathed, grasslike, to 18
inches long and ¾ inch wide. Flowers in terminal panicles, up to 60 per panicle, creamy white, radial, 6 tepals,
ovate, to ¾ inch wide. Found in eastern Central Texas,
north into Oklahoma. Weak farther west, south, and east.

Trillium texanum (*T. pusillum* var. *texanum*)
MELANTHIACEAE
Texas wakerobin
Wet woodlands. Spring. Rare.

An erect, rhizomatous perennial with 1 or 2 scapes to
8+ inches tall. Leaves absent. Scapes slender, 8+ inches
tall, topped by 3 leaflike bracts. Bracts sessile or on short
petioles, oblong to lanceolate, to 3¼ inches long and 1¼
inches wide, margins entire, tips obtuse, blades with
obvious venation, upper surface green and lower surface
brownish maroon. Flowers solitary, on short pedicels, 3
sepals, green, oblong-lanceolate, to 1¼ inches long and ⅜
inch wide, 3 petals, white maturing to pink, to 1¼ inches
long and ⅝ inch wide. Scattered populations occur in
Northeast Texas, south into Jasper County. Colonial.

Nymphoides aquatica MENYANTHACEAE
Floating heart, banana lily, banana plant
Ponds, slow-moving bodies of water.
Spring, summer. Locally common.

A submersed aquatic perennial with floating leaves. Leaves on petioles to 10+ inches long, reniform to round, to 6 inches wide and long, bases heavily cordate, margins entire. Upper leaf surfaces yellow-green and often with reddish brown edges. Lower surfaces pitted and darker in color. Flowers 5-petaled, radial, white with yellow centers, margins wavy, apex of petal mucronate, pedicels to 3¼ inches long. Found in Southeast Texas with scattered collections elsewhere in Texas; when present, often in large numbers.

Glinus radiatus MOLLUGINACEAE
Spreading sweetjuice, sweetjuice, Louisiana sweetjuice
River floodplains, wet fields and meadows, edges of ephemeral bodies of water. Summer, fall. Uncommon.

An introduced, prostrate annual with branching, tomentose stems to 20 inches long radiating from a central root. Leaves in whorls, spatulate or obovate or elliptic, to 1 inch long and ½ inch wide, bases cuneate, margins entire, tips rounded or acute or notched. Flowers in clusters to 11, in leaf axils along stem, with 5 erect sepals, reddish brown and tomentose on outer surface, creamy to pink on inner surface. Seeds reddish brown with a distinct fleshy, threadlike appendage. A small, often-overlooked plant found in Central Texas, east to Louisiana, south to the coast and into Mexico, north into Oklahoma. Absent in West Texas and the Panhandle.

Mollugo verticillata MOLLUGINACEAE
Carpetweed, Indian chickweed
Disturbed areas. Winter, spring, summer, fall. Common.

A prostrate to ascending annual with glabrous, branching stems to 8+ inches long. Leaves in whorls of up to 8, sessile, linear to oblanceolate, to 1½ inches long and ¼ inch wide, bases tapering, margins entire, tips acute. Inflorescences on pedicels to ½ inch long originating from leaf axils, to 5 flowers per axil, radial, to ¼ inch wide, with 5 white sepals, petals not present. A common weed of disturbed areas. Found throughout Texas.

Peganum harmala   NITRARIACEAE
Peganum, Syrian rue, African rue
Disturbed areas, roadsides. Spring,
summer, fall. Common.

An intorduced, upright, multibranched, rounded perennial to 16 inches tall and 3 feet wide, from a large, deep
root. Stems and leaves pubescent to glabrous. Leaves
alternate, highly dissected, dark green and somewhat
fleshy to the touch. Flowers white, about 1½ inches
wide, 5-petaled. Fruits are 3-chambered capsules, with
50 seeds per chamber. Introduced and classified as an
invasive species. Originally from Middle East and North
Africa. First noted in New Mexico during 1920s; has since
spread west to California and north to Washington. Easily
found in overgrazed fields in West Texas, where it thrives
in the intense heat of summer.

Abronia fragrans   NYCTAGINACEAE
**Fragrant white sand verbena, fragrant verbena,
prairie snowball**
Grasslands, scrublands. Spring, summer, fall. Uncommon.

A moderately branched, erect perennial to 3 feet tall, with
leaves and stems covered in glandular hairs. Leaves opposite, ovate to lanceolate, to 4½ inches long and 3 inches
wide, margins entire to undulate. Flowers to 80 in a single, rounded head, white sometimes tinged with shades
of pink, about 1 inch long and ⅓ inch wide. Grows in
sandy soils of West Texas and Panhandle, also in sand
dunes around the Monahans area during spring and
summer if rains allow.

Acleisanthes crassifolia   NYCTAGINACEAE
Texas trumpets
Grass and shrublands, occasional roadsides.
Spring, summer, fall. Rare.

A procumbent, branching perennial with pubescent
stems to 20+ inches long. Leaves opposite, on petioles ¾
inch long, ovate to deltate-ovate, to 2¾ inches long and
1 inch wide, bases rounded, margins entire to undulate,
tips acute or pointed or obtuse, upper surface with obvious white coloration along primary veins. Flowers solitary in upper leaf axils, funnel-shaped, white to cream, to
2 inches long. Found in South Texas, south of Del Rio in
counties that border the Rio Grande. Grows in open limestone soils within *Leucophyllum frutescens* shrublands.

148

Acleisanthes longiflora   NYCTAGINACEAE
Angel trumpets, yerba de la rabia
Roadsides, grasslands, shrublands, disturbed areas.
Late winter, spring, summer, fall. Common.

A heavily branched, sprawling perennial from a single
rootstock to 3 feet wide. Leaves opposite, triangular to
lanceolate, to 1¾ inches long and 1⅓ inches wide, margins entire, blades semisucculent. Flowers solitary, elongated, funnel-shaped, to 7 inches long and ¾ inch wide,
white, occasionally tinged pink. Found in South, West,
and Central Texas, but some collections have been made
farther east and north into Panhandle. Grows in various
soil types, but generally prefers open areas.

Acleisanthes obtusa   NYCTAGINACEAE

Berlandier's trumpets, vine four o'clock
Shrublands, grasslands. Spring, summer, fall. Common.

A heavily branched perennial vine often to 6+ feet long
when supported. Leaves opposite, deltate, to 2½ inches
long and 1½ inches wide with flat to undulate margins.
Flowers funnel-shaped, white to light pink, to 2½ inches
long and ¾ inch wide, solitary or in 2- to 5-flowered
cymes. Found in various soil types throughout South
Texas, from Kinney County south to Cameron County,
east to Calhoun County. Not uncommon to see this species growing on lomas near the barrier islands.

Mirabilis longiflora   NYCTAGINACEAE
Long-flowered four o'clock, fairy trumpets
Rocky slopes, among boulders, ledges, woodlands,
shrublands. Summer, fall. Uncommon.

An erect, branching perennial with several minutely
pubescent stems to 5+ feet tall. Leaves opposite, cordate
or deltate to ovate-lanceolate, to 5¾ inches long and 3¼
inches wide, bases rounded to cordate to truncate, margins entire, tips tapering to a point, blade surfaces with
small, sticky hairs. Flowers in terminal compact cymes
or originating from upper leaf axils, to 6+ inches long,
elongated, funnel-shaped, white with tubular part tinged
lavender, green, or blue. Found in Big Bend region, in
shady areas at mid to upper elevations.

Nymphaea ampla NYMPHAEACEAE
White water lily, white lotus, sacred white lotus
Marshes, ephemeral pools and other slow-moving
bodies of water. Spring, summer. Rare.

An aquatic, rhizomatous perennial with floating suborbicular leaves. Heavily veined leaves are green above and purple below, both surfaces often covered with darker spots, margins dentate. Flowers white, to 7 inches in diameter, occurring above water's surface on peduncles. Species was only known from 2 collections in Kinney County until Martin Simonton and I made a collection in July 2015, the first in more than 100 years. Currently, this is the only known population of this species in Texas, but it is expected to be elsewhere and may be confused with *Nymphaea elegans*. Widespread in Mexico and the Caribbean.

Nymphaea odorata subsp. *odorata*
NYMPHAEACEAE
White water lily, alligator bonnet, ninfa acuática
Ponds, marshes, lakes, slow-moving bodies
of water. Spring, summer, fall. Common.

An aquatic, rhizomatous perennial with floating leaves. Roundish leaves are to 10 inches in diameter, green above and tinged reddish purple below, with entire margins, sometimes with a narrow sinus. Fragrant white flowers, to 7½ inches in diameter, are usually floating, rarely extending above water's surface. Found in eastern third of state, usually occurring in large colonies that can cover the surface of small ponds. Most freeze tolerant of our 4 species.

Oenothera albicaulis ONAGRACEAE
**Whitest evening primrose, white-stemmed evening
primrose, prairie evening primrose**
Fields, pastures, grasslands, open brushlands,
roadsides and other open areas. Spring. Common.

An erect to decumbent annual with villose stems to 20 inches long. Stem leaves alternate, on petioles to 1½ inches long, elliptic to oblanceolate, to 4 inches long and 1 inch wide, pinnatifid to sinuous, bases tapering, ultimate margins entire or toothed, tips acute. Basal leaves larger than stem leaves. Flowers white, to 3¼ inches wide, 4-lobed, lobes heart-shaped. Widespread and locally common, especially with adequate winter rains, from Panhandle south throughout Chihuahuan Desert.

Oenothera engelmannii   ONAGRACEAE
Engelmann's evening primrose
Open grass and shrublands, dunes, roadsides and other
open, sandy areas. Spring, summer. Uncommon.

An erect, typically single-stemmed, weakly branched
annual to 24+ inches tall, stems covered with long, soft
hairs. Leaves alternate, sessile, lanceolate, to 2½ inches
long, margins sinuate-dentate, tips acute, blades pubescent. Hypanthium to 1¼ inches long. Flowers white,
fading pink, with a yellowish green center, to 1¼ inches
wide, petals heart-shaped. Found in Panhandle south to
Chihuahuan Desert and northern Edwards Plateau.

Oenothera glaucifolia (*Stenosiphon linifolius*)
ONAGRACEAE
False gaura, flax leaved stenosiphon
Rocky hillsides, outcrops, grasslands, drainages, roadsides
and other open, rocky areas. Summer. Common.

An erect, single- to multistemmed, airy perennial with
unbranched or weakly branched, glabrous stems to 8+
feet tall. Leaves alternate, lanceolate to 2½ inches long
and ¾ inch wide, margins entire, tips pointed, surfaces glabrous, somewhat glaucous. Flowers in terminal, crowded spikes, white, 4-petaled, petals to ¼ inch
long, distinctly clawed. Primarily found on limestone
soils, often in colonies. Frequent in Panhandle, eastern
Edwards Plateau, and North-Central Texas. Less common
farther east and west into Culberson County.

Oenothera kunthiana   ONAGRACEAE
Kunth's evening primrose
Open grass, brush and woodlands, washes and
drainages, roadsides and other open, sandy to
gravelly areas. Winter, spring. Common.

An erect, branching annual with nearly glabrous stems to
16 inches tall. Leaves alternate, on petioles to ¾ inch long,
lanceolate to oblanceolate to elliptic, to 3¾ inches long
and 1 inch wide, bases tapering, margins sinuate, pinnatifid, or entire, tips acute. Hypanthium to ¾ inch long.
Flowers white to pink, often with darker venation and
yellow centers, 4-petaled, to 1½ inches wide. Found from
South Texas north into Edwards Plateau and west into
Chihuahuan Desert.

151

Oenothera rosea   ONAGRACEAE
Rose evening primrose, rose sundrops
Drainages, open brush and grasslands, desert
washes. Spring, summer. Uncommon.

An erect, well-branched, rhizomatous perennial with
reddish brown to green stems to 16 inches tall. Leaves
alternate, on petioles to 1 inch long, elliptic to ovate, to
2 inches long and 1 inch wide, bases wedge-shaped to
tapering, margins nearly entire to sinuate-pinnatifid, tips
acute to obtuse. Hypanthium to ⅓ inch long. Flowers in
a loose raceme, white to rose-pink, often with pale yellow
centers and darker veins, 4-petaled, to 1 inch wide. Found
in sandy or gravelly soils, from Hudspeth County southwest to Cameron County, occasional in South-Central
Texas.

Habenaria repens   ORCHIDACEAE
Green spider orchid, bog orchid, water spider bog orchid
Marshes, ponds, bogs, wet meadows, slow-moving
streams. Summer, fall. Locally common.

An erect to decumbent, terrestrial or aquatic perennial
to 3 feet tall, typically much shorter. Leaves alternate,
sheathed, grasslike, lanceolate to linear, to 10 inches long
and 1¾ inches wide, margins entire. Flowers in dense
racemes of 50± per raceme, with 3 light green, ovate
sepals to about ⅓ inch long. Petals greenish, divided, lip
3-lobed with middle lobe wider and shorter than outer
two. Small flowers look like tiny green spiders. Found
throughout eastern fourth of Texas; additional populations in Cameron County and east of San Antonio.

Malaxis unifolia   ORCHIDACEAE
Green adder's mouth orchid
Pine woodlands and forests, bogs, baygalls.
Spring, summer. Uncommon.

An erect perennial with glabrous, green stems to 20
inches tall. One leaf, occasionally 2, ovate, to 4 inches
long and 2 inches wide, sheathed. Racemes with few to
150+ flowers on pedicels to ½ inch long. Flowers green,
about ⅛ inch wide, sepals oblong-elliptic, petals linear and recurved, lip 3-lobed, deltate to cordate-ovate or
oblong-elliptic. Uncommon to rare in eastern fourth of
Texas from Houston area north into Oklahoma. Found
on wooded slopes near waterways.

Platanthera nivea ORCHIDACEAE
Snowy orchid
Pine savannas, meadows. Spring, summer. Uncommon.

An erect perennial with stems to 3 feet tall. Leaves few, to
3 per plant, linear to linear-lanceolate, to 12 inches long
and ¾ inch wide. Flowers in dense spikes, white, not
fringed, lower sepal broader than lateral, lateral sepals
spreading, slightly twisted, petals linear to oblong. Lip
linear-elliptic to oblong, to about ⅓ inch long, erect and
slightly curved backward. Found in Southeast Texas,
from Houston area northeast to Newton County.

Spiranthes brevilabris ORCHIDACEAE
Texas lady's tresses, short lipped ladies' tresses
Fields, meadows, roadsides and other
open areas. Winter, spring. Rare.

An erect, slender, single-stemmed perennial to 16 inches
tall. Basal leaves oval to oblanceolate, to 2½ inches long
and ¾ inch wide. Flowers in a pubescent, spiraled spike,
9± per turn, creamy white to pale yellow, sepals thin and
to 3⁄16 inch long, lateral sepals distinct and appressed, petals linear to lanceolate-oblong and as long as sepals. Lip
ovate to oblong, to 3⁄16 inch long and ⅛ inch wide, upper
margin crisped and lacerate, middle of lip yellow. Found
in Southeast and Northeast Texas. Small flowers, crisped
margin, and appressed sepals distinguish this species.

Spiranthes cernua ORCHIDACEAE
Nodding lady's tresses
Meadows, fields, prairies, open woodlands, roadsides
and other open areas. Summer, fall. Common.

An erect, slender perennial with stems to 25 inches
tall. Leaves mostly basal, on petioles to ¼ inch long,
linear-lanceolate to oblanceolate or obovate or elliptic,
to 10 inches long and ¾ inch wide. Flowers in a spiraled, pubescent spike, 4± per turn, white to greenish
white, nodding, sepals and petals to ½ inch long, lateral
sepals distinct and appressed to slightly spreading. Petals linear-lanceolate, lip somewhat joined to petals, ovate
to linear-lanceolate, to ⅜ inch long, margins crenulate or
lacerate or entire. Found in eastern half of Texas, from
Coastal Bend north. Can be quite variable. Longer flowers, joined lip and petals, and number of flowers per turn
help in identification.

Spiranthes ovalis   ORCHIDACEAE
Lesser ladies' tresses, October ladies' tresses
Woodlands, thickets. Fall, winter. Uncommon.

An erect, slender perennial to 16 inches tall. Leaves basal, and/or along lower half of stem, oblanceolate to 6 inches long and ¾ inch wide. Flowers white, in tightly spiraled, pubescent spikes, 3± per turn, sepals distinct, spreading, linear, to ¼ inch long. Petals lanceolate, to ¼ inch long, lip ovate and less than ¼ inch long, margins crisped. Found from Galveston Bay area north into Oklahoma, east to Louisiana.

Spiranthes praecox   ORCHIDACEAE
Giant ladies' tresses, grass-leaved ladies' tresses, greenvein lady's tresses
Fields, meadows, coastal plains, open woods, roadsides and other open areas. Winter, spring. Uncommon.

An erect, slender perennial to 30+ inches tall. Basal leaves linear-lanceolate, to 10 inches long and 2 inches wide. Flowers white, in weakly pubescent spikes, 4–7 per turn, sepals distinct to ⅜ inch long, lateral sepals clasping, petals linear, to ⅜ inch long. Lip oblong, slightly longer than sepals and petals, margins toothed or wavy, veins raised and green, obvious. Mostly found in Southeast Texas, with range extending. Less common west to Bastrop County and north to Oklahoma. Green veins along lip aid in identification.

Spiranthes vernalis   ORCHIDACEAE
Spring ladies' tresses, grass-leaved ladies' tresses
Meadows, fields, open brushlands, dunes, lomas, roadsides and other open areas. Spring, summer. Common.

An erect perennial with slender flowering stems, to 24+ inches tall. Basal leaves to 5, linear-lanceolate, to 10 inches long and ½ inch wide, keeled. Flowers in pubescent spikes, 3–7+ per turn, nodding to ascending, white to cream, sepals distinct to ⅜ inch long, lateral sepals spreading. Petals oblong, slightly shorter than sepals, lip ovate, shorter than petals, creamy yellow in center or with brownish orange spots. Found along coastal Texas, extending north in eastern third of state, east to Louisiana.

Tipularia discolor ORCHIDACEAE
Cranefly orchid, crippled cranefly
Deciduous or mixed woodlands. Spring. Uncommon.

An erect, slender perennial with stems to 20+ inches
tall. Leaves solitary, ovate, to 4 inches long and 3 inches
wide, lower surface deep purple, upper surface green
with purple spots, appearing in fall, withering by spring.
Flowers in a raceme to 20+ inches tall, green to yellow to greenish purple, to 50 per raceme, sepals
oblong-elliptic to ⅓ inch long. Petals linear-oblong
to linear-oblanceolate, slightly shorter than sepals,
lip to ⅓ inch long, with 2 basal lobes, spur to 1 inch
long. Found in rich soils in eastern fourth of Texas.

Bellardia trixago OROBANCHACEAE
Trixago bartsia, Mediterranean linseed, sticky bellardia
Fields, open shrublands, roadsides, agricultural fields
and other disturbed areas. Spring. Locally common.

An introduced, erect annual with stems to 12+ inches tall.
Leaves opposite, lanceolate, to 2 inches long and ¼ inch
wide, bases clasping, margins toothed. White to pink
flowers, about ¾ inch wide, 2-lipped, are arranged in a
dense, terminal spike to 3 inches long. Lower lip white
and divided into 3 lobes, upper lip folded and usually
tinged pink. Originally noted in Texas during early 1970s;
has spread rapidly throughout Southeast Texas and north
to Dallas-Fort Worth area.

Orobanche uniflora OROBANCHACEAE
One-flowered broomrape
Woodlands. Spring. Uncommon.

An erect, parasitic perennial with 1 to several leafless,
pubescent stems to 8 inches tall when in flower. Stem
covered with small, oval to ovate, appressed scales. Flowers solitary, to 1 inch long, nodding, 5-lobed, faded white
to purple to lilac, sometimes with a yellow patch at base
of lower middle lobe. Tiny wind-dispersed seeds can
travel great distances. Found from West Texas to Louisiana, north into Oklahoma. Apparently absent in South
Texas.

Argemone albiflora   PAPAVERACEAE
White prickly poppy, devil's fig, white thistle
Fields, meadows, prairies, open brush and
woodlands, roadsides and other open areas.
Spring, summer, fall. Common.

An erect annual to biennial, typically single-stemmed to
6 feet tall, with prickles throughout and yellow sap. Lower
(basal) leaves on petioles, lobed, with prickles along veins
on upper side of leaf, to 8 inches long and 2½+ inches
wide. Upper leaves without petioles, smaller, lobed to a
lesser extent, prickles not present on veins. Large, terminal white flowers are 4± inches across, with 150+ yellow
stamens. Widespread throughout Texas, occurring in disturbed habitats such as overgrazed fields and in dry, gravelly creek bottoms.

Argemone chisosensis   PAPAVERACEAE
Chisos prickly poppy
Open fields, brushlands, roadsides.
Spring, summer, fall. Common.

An erect, weakly branched biennial to perennial with
prickly stems to nearly 3 feet tall. Lower leaves to 6+
inches long, lobed. Upper leaves shorter, with fewer
lobes. Prickles on lower surface of leaves. Flowers terminal, white to lavender, to 4 inches broad, with 150+ stamens. Found in open areas in western portion of state
from Val Verde County, west to El Paso.

Sanguinaria canadensis   PAPAVERACEAE
Bloodroot
Mixed woodlands and forest. Spring. Uncommon.

An erect, rhizomatous perennial with glabrous stems to
12 inches tall when flowering. Basal leaves only, oval to
round, to 5 inches in diameter, palmately lobed, margins
scalloped to undulate to lobed, upper surface glaucous.
Flowers solitary, on a scape about 6 inches long, white
to pink, 1½ to 3 inches wide, with as many as 16 petals.
An early spring bloomer. Often occurs in small colonies.
Found in deep East Texas.

Passiflora filipes PASSIFLORACEAE
Slender passionflower, yellow passionflower
Sabal palm groves and resacas along the lower Rio
Grande. Spring, summer, early fall. Locally common.

A perennial vine to 8+ feet long, often clambering over
small shrubs and trees. Leaves shallowly 3-lobed, glabrous, darker above and lighter below. Flowers white to
cream, sometimes tinged green, about ¾ inch in diameter. Known from far southern tip of Texas in Cameron
and Hidalgo Counties among *Sabal mexicana* and associated species found along resacas. Food source for helico-
nian butterflies.

Passiflora tenuiloba PASSIFLORACEAE
Birdwing passionflower, slender-wing passionflower
Desert scrub, open brush and woodlands, canyons, edges
of washes, rocky outcrops. Spring, summer, fall. Common.

A twining, climbing perennial vine, with slender stems
to about 6 feet long. Leaves alternate, shaped like bird
wings, the outer 2 lobes much larger than center, linear to lanceolate, upper surfaces dark green to nearly
purple, glabrous. Flowers about ½ inch wide, greenish
yellow. Fruits are marble-sized berries, turning deep
purple-black when ripe. Found throughout Central Texas,
west to the Big Bend Region, and south into Mexico. Like
other species of *Passiflora*, birdwing passionflower is an
important food source for butterflies.

Mazus pumilus PHRYMACEAE
Japanese mazus
Urban and suburban areas, roadsides and other
disturbed areas. Spring, summer, fall. Uncommon.

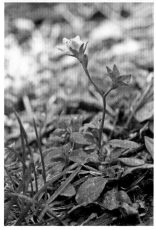

An introduced, prostrate to ascending to erect annual
with glabrous or slightly pubescent stems to 12 inches
long, rooting at nodes. Basal leaves on petioles,
obovate-spatulate to ovate-oblanceolate, to 2½ inches
long, bases cuneate, margins toothed to pinnately lobed.
Stem leaves similar, opposite, becoming sessile. Flowers
in terminal racemes, to 20 per raceme, bilabiate, white
to purple to blue with a white throat and yellow spots,
about ⅓ inch wide. Lower lip 3-lobed, outer lobes larger
than middle (which is often cleft), upper lip reduced and
notched, slightly erect. Found in eastern half of state. Prefers wet or damp habitats. Does quite well in residential
lawns and gardens.

Phytolacca americana PHYTOLACCACEAE
Pokeweed, pokeberry, poke
Open brush and woodlands, roadsides, pastures, disturbed areas. Spring, summer. Common.

An erect, branching perennial with glabrous stems to 8+ feet tall, stems green, turning red with age. Leaves alternate, on petioles to 1 inch long, ovate to lanceolate, to 12 inches long and 5 inches wide, bases cordate, margins entire, tips pointed. Flowers in loose 1-foot-long racemes, numerous, white, ¼ inch wide, petals absent, 5 sepals. Fruits deep purple when mature, about ¼ inch wide. Found throughout Central Texas, east into Louisiana, north into Oklahoma, and south to Coastal Bend.

Bacopa monnieri PLANTAGINACEAE
Water hyssop, coastal water hyssop, herb-of-grace
Stream and river banks, edges of ponds and lakes, ephemeral waters, low, wet areas. Spring, summer, fall. Common.

A prostrate to slightly ascending, mat-forming perennial with branching stems to 2+ feet long. Leaves opposite, spatulate to ovate, ¾ inch long, margins entire to slightly serrate at ends. Flowers solitary, originating from upper leaf axils, bell-shaped, white to pale blue, to ⅓ inch wide, bilabiate, upper lip 2-lobed, lower lip 3-lobed. Found in southern half of Texas.

Bacopa rotundifolia PLANTAGINACEAE
Disc water hyssop, round leaf water hyssop
Banks of streams, rivers, lakes, ponds, and other bodies of water, shallow pools, roadside ditches and other low, wet areas. Spring, summer, fall. Uncommon.

A prostrate to ascending, mat-forming perennial or semi-aquatic with floating leaves and stems to 1+ foot long. Leaves opposite, round to elliptic, to 1¼ inches long and about as wide, bases clasping, margins entire. Flowers on short pedicels originating from leaf axils, white, bell-shaped, ⅓ inch wide, bilabiate, upper lip 2-lobed, lower lip 3-lobed. Common in coastal Texas, occasional elsewhere.

Gratiola neglecta   PLANTAGINACEAE
Clammy hedge hyssop
Banks of ponds, lakes, and streams, wet woodlands, grasslands, fields and roadside ditches. Spring. Common.

An erect annual with pubescent, branching stems to 10+ inches tall. Leaves opposite, sessile. Upper leaves lance-olate or oblanceolate or ovate, to 1¾ inches long and ½ inch wide, margins entire to slightly dentate, tips acute. Lower leaves linear, similar in other aspects. Flowers solitary from upper leaf axils, on pedicels to 1 inch long, white, tubular, bilabiate, ⅓ inch long. Upper lip 2-lobed, lower lip 3-lobed, each lobe notched. Found throughout eastern third of Texas. Prefers wet or damp soils.

Gratiola virginiana   PLANTAGINACEAE
Roundfruit hedge hyssop
Shallow waters along edges of waterways, ditches, clay ponds within woodlands and forests. Spring. Common.

An erect, glabrous annual to biennial, with branch-ing stems to 18+ inches tall, stems often reddish brown. Leaves opposite, sessile, lanceolate-elliptic to oblong-obovate, to 2¾ inches long, margins undulate to serrate, tips acute. Flowers originating from upper leaf axils, on pedicels to ¼ inch long, white to cream, tubular, arching, bilabiate. Upper lip entire, lower 3-lobed, lobes notched. Found in eastern third of Texas, close to or in shallow waters.

Mecardonia acuminata   PLANTAGINACEAE
Axil flower
Wet grasslands, fields, prairies, bogs, swamps, roadside ditches and other low, wet areas. Summer. Common.

An erect or ascending, glabrous perennial with branch-ing stems to 24+ inches tall. Leaves opposite, on short petioles to sessile, oblanceolate to oblong-lanceolate, to 1¾ inches long, bases tapering, margins serrate to toothed, tips acute to rounded. Flowers on 1¾-inch-long pedicels originating from upper leaf axils, tubular, white tinged pink or purple, to about ⅜ inch long, bilabi-ate. Upper lip 2-lobed, erect, interior of upper lip visibly pubescent, lower lip 3-lobed, protruding. Found in wet soils throughout eastern third of Texas. Less common west into Edwards Plateau.

Penstemon albidus PLANTAGINACEAE
White penstemon, white-flower beardtongue
Fields, pastures, grasslands, prairies, roadsides
and other open areas. Spring. Common.

An erect perennial with rough, pubescent stems to 24+
inches tall. Leaves opposite, sessile, linear to lanceolate,
to 3½ inches long and ¾ inch wide, margins entire, tips
acute. Flowers in terminal racemes, bell-shaped, white to
pink, bilabiate. Upper lip 2-lobed, lower lip 3-lobed, lobe
margins often wavy, interior of tube streaked brownish
purple. Common in Panhandle, less common farther
south into northern Edwards Plateau.

Penstemon ambiguus PLANTAGINACEAE
Sand penstemon, pink plains penstemon
Open brush and grasslands. Spring,
summer. Locally common.

An erect perennial with pubescent or glabrous, branching stems to 2+ feet tall. Leaves opposite, sessile, linear, to 1 inch long and ¼ inch wide, margins entire,
tips acute. Flowers numerous, in terminal racemes,
trumpet-shaped, white to pink, to 1¼ inches long, bilabiate. Upper lip 2-lobed, reflexed, lower lip 3-lobed and projecting, tube curved. Found in sandy soils in Panhandle
and western Trans-Pecos.

Penstemon digitalis PLANTAGINACEAE
**Foxglove penstemon, smooth white penstemon,
Arkansas wedding bouquet**
Fields, grasslands, open brush and woodlands,
roadsides and other open areas. Spring. Uncommon.

An erect, leafy perennial with glabrous stems to 3+ feet
tall. Leaves opposite, sessile, lanceolate, to 5 inches long
and 2 inches wide, margins toothed or slightly entire,
tips acute. Basal leaves shorter, on petioles, ovate to lanceolate. Flowers in terminal racemes, white, tubular, to 1
inch long, bilabiate. Lower lip 3-lobed, upper lip 2-lobed,
lobes similar. Occasional in northeastern Texas, south to
the Houston area. Common outside Texas and often sold
as an ornamental; expect elsewhere.

Penstemon guadalupensis PLANTAGINACEAE
White beardtongue, white penstemon,
Guadalupe penstemon
Fields, grasslands, savannas, open brush and woodlands,
roadsides and other open areas. Spring. Uncommon.

An erect perennial with pubescent to glabrous stems to
16 inches. Leaves opposite, sessile, linear to lanceolate, to
3 inches long and ¾ inch wide, margins entire to toothed,
tips acute. Flowers in terminal racemes, bell-shaped,
to ¾ inch long, white to pink, often with purple streaks
inside tube, tube somewhat inflated, bilabiate. Lower
lip 3-lobed, upper lip 2-lobed, lobes erect, broad. Found
throughout Edwards Plateau, north into southern Panhandle. Uncommon, but can occur in large numbers.

Penstemon laxiflorus PLANTAGINACEAE
Nodding penstemon, loose-flowered penstemon,
nodding beardtongue
Grasslands, fields, open brush and woodlands,
roadsides and other open areas. Spring. Common.

An erect perennial with slender, pubescent to glabrous
stems to 24+ inches tall. Leaves opposite, sessile, lanceolate to linear, to 5 inches long and ¾ inch wide, margins
toothed, tips acute. Flowers in terminal racemes, white
to pink with purple streaks, tubular, to 1¼ inches long,
often nodding, bilabiate. Upper lip 2-lobed, lobes erect,
lower lip 3-lobed and projecting, visibly bearded within.
Common throughout eastern third of Texas, less common in eastern Edwards Plateau.

Plantago aristata PLANTAGINACEAE
Bottlebrush Indianwheat, largebracted plantain
Pastures, fields, open grass, brush and
woodlands, roadsides and other open areas.
Spring, summer, fall. Common.

An erect annual with pubescent leaves and stems to 16
inches when flowering. Basal leaves only, linear to oblanceolate, to 8 inches long and ⅜ inch wide, margins entire,
tips acute, lower surface of blades with long white, scattered hairs. Scape to 10 inches tall. Spike terminal, to 6
inches long, with long white hairs throughout, bracts
along spike linear, pubescent, to 1¼ inches long, ascending. Flowers sessile, inconspicuous, creamy to dirty
white with a reddish brown center, ⅛ inch wide and long.
Found in sandy, open, often abused soils of eastern third
of Texas.

161

Plantago helleri PLANTAGINACEAE
Heller's plantain
Pastures, fields, open grass, brush and
woodlands, roadsides and other open
areas. Spring, summer. Common.

An erect annual with villose leaves and stems, to
10 inches tall when flowering. Basal leaves only,
linear-oblanceolate, to 8 inches long and ⅜ inch wide,
margins entire, tips acute. One or more scapes per plant,
each to 8 inches long. Flowering spikes to 1¾ inches long,
bracts linear and to ¼ inch long. Flowers crowded on
spike, about ¼ inch wide, conspicuous, petals overlapping, translucent, creamy to dirty white with a reddish
brown center. Found throughout Central Texas, west to
Hudspeth County.

Plantago hookeriana PLANTAGINACEAE
Tallow weed
Fields, pastures, grasslands, open brush
and woodlands. Spring. Common.

An erect annual with woolly pubescent leaves and stems,
to 10 inches tall when in flower. Scapes and spikes usually
extending beyond leaves, occasionally equaling leaves.
Basal leaves spreading to erect, linear to oblanceolate, to
12 inches long and ¾ inch wide, margins entire to loosely
dentate. Spikes to 4 inches long, bracts barely noticeable
and not surpassing calyx. Flowers inconspicuous, translucent, creamy to dirty white with reddish brown center, 4-petaled, to ¼ inch wide. Found throughout Texas.
Absent in Panhandle and North Texas.

Plantago lanceolata PLANTAGINACEAE
English plantain, ribwort
Pastures, fields, roadsides, urban and suburban areas
and other disturbed places. Spring, summer. Common.

An introduced, erect, glabrous to pubescent biennial
or perennial to 2+ feet tall when in flower. Basal leaves
only, arching, lax, lanceolate to oblanceolate, to 18 inches
long, margins entire to toothed, tips acute, surfaces distinctly ribbed, usually with 5 prominent veins. Scapes to
20 inches tall. Spikes to 4 inches long at end of flowering
season, white styles extending from spike, bracts extending just beyond calyx with a translucent tip. Flowers
dense along spike, inconspicuous, creamy to dirty white
with brown veins down center of petals. Widespread
throughout Texas. A common weed of lawns and areas of
human habitation.

Plantago major   PLANTAGINACEAE
Common plantain, llantén
Pastures, fields, roadsides, urban and suburban areas
and other disturbed places. Spring. Common.

An introduced, erect perennial with large, glabrous to
weakly pubescent leaves and stems, to 16+ inches tall.
Basal leaves only, on long petioles, arching, lax, not erect,
ovate to elliptic, to 12 inches long including petiole, margins undulate to dentate or serrate, tips rounded, con-
spicuously 5-veined, thick and glabrous to the touch.
Scapes shorter than leaves. Spikes elongating to 8 inches
throughout the season, bracts shorter than calyx. Flowers
crowded, inconspicuous, to $1/16$ inch wide. White styles
are thick and numerous, and often most-noted feature.
Widespread throughout Texas; a common weed in maintained areas, drainages, and vacant lots.

Plantago rhodosperma   PLANTAGINACEAE
Redseed plantain
Fields, pastures, grasslands, prairies, open
brush and woodlands, roadsides and other
open areas. Spring. Common.

An erect to ascending annual with grayish green pubescence, to 16 inches wide and 12 inches tall when in flower.
Basal leaves only, spreading, flat to ascending, oblanceolate, to 12 inches long and 2 inches wide, margins toothed
to entire, tips rounded. Scapes to and equaling leaves.
Spikes to 8 inches long at end of season, bracts shorter
than calyx. Flowers creamy tan, with darker stripes down
middle of petals. Found throughout state. Absent in
Northeast Texas.

Scoparia dulcis   PLANTAGINACEAE
Licorice weed, bitterbroom, sweetbroom
Open woodlands, roadsides, disturbed
areas. Spring, summer, fall. Common.

An erect, glabrous annual with heavily branching, slender stems to 3+ feet tall. Leaves opposite to whorled, on
short petioles, ovate to elliptic-lanceolate, to 1½ inches
long and ¾ inch wide, bases narrower, margins serrate to entire, tips acute. Solitary flowers from upper leaf
axils, on pedicels to 1 inch long, white to light lavender,
less than ¼ inch wide, 4-lobed with lower lobe slightly
smaller than other 3 and heavily bearded. Found in sandy
soils of Southeast Texas.

163

Veronica peregrina   PLANTAGINACEAE
Purslane speedwell, necklace weed
Wet areas. Winter, spring. Common.

An erect, glabrous annual with stems, typically branching from base, to 12+ inches tall. Leaves opposite, linear-oblong, to ¾ inch long and ¼ inch wide, margins entire to dentate, tips rounded. Upper leaves sessile, lower leaves on petioles ¼ inch long. Stems terminating in bracted racemes. Flowers white, bilateral, less than ¼ inch long and as wide, 4-lobed with one lobe of unequal size. Found throughout Texas.

Polygala alba   POLYGALACEAE
White milkwort
Fields, prairies, grasslands, open brush and woodlands, rocky hillsides and slopes. Spring, summer. Common.

An erect, slender perennial with numerous, wispy, glabrous stems to 16 inches tall. Leaves alternate and opposite to whorled, to ½ inch long, upper leaves linear, lower leaves spatulate, stem leaves nearly appressed. Flowers in terminal spikelike racemes, to 3½ inches long, numerous, crowded, less than ¼ inch wide, white with greenish yellow centers. Lateral sepals petal-like and appearing as wings, the 5 petals condensed into a short tube. Found in western two-thirds of state, often occurring in small populations.

Polygala leptocaulis (*P. appendiculata*)
POLYGALACEAE
Swamp milkwort
Wet savannas, grasslands and fields, open piney woods, roadside ditches and other low, wet areas. Spring. Uncommon.

An erect, slender annual with glabrous, branching stems to 20 inches tall. Leaves alternate, occasionally opposite, sessile, linear, to 1 inch long, margins revolute, tips pointed. Flowers in terminal racemes to 4 inches long, either crowded or loosely arranged, small, to ¼ inch wide, white to purple or rose, sepal wings spreading, the 5 petals condensed. Found in wet to damp soils in Southeast Texas, occasionally farther north in East Texas.

Polygala verticillata   POLYGALACEAE
Whorled milkwort
Prairies, grasslands, fields, post-oak and
pine woodlands, roadsides and other open
areas. Spring, summer. Common.

An erect, single-stemmed annual with glabrous, branching stems to 16+ inches tall. Leaves whorled, occasionally alternate, sessile, linear to elliptic, to 1¼ inches long
and ¼ inch wide, bases tapering, tips pointed. Flowers in crowded, conical, terminal racemes, greenish
white, occasionally with pink or purple spots, to ⅛ inch
wide, lateral petal-like sepals obovate-oval. One of the
most widespread milkworts. Found in sandy soils from
lower coastal plain north into Oklahoma and east into
Louisiana.

Eriogonum annuum   POLYGONACEAE
Annual wild buckwheat
Grasslands, fields, prairies, open shrub and
woodlands. Spring, summer, fall. Common.

An erect annual with a single, tomentose, branching
stem to 5+ feet tall. Leaves alternate, petioles on basal
leaves ½ inch long but ¼ inch long on upper leaves,
oblanceolate to oblong, to 2¾ inches long and ½ inch
wide, margins entire, surfaces tomentose. Flowers in terminal cymes, bell-shaped, white, less than ¼ inch, clustered in groups of 10± along cyme. Widespread throughout Texas. Absent in South Texas and along coast. Often
occurring in vast numbers during years of adequate,
well-timed rains.

Eriogonum longifolium   POLYGONACEAE
Longleaf buckwheat
Fields, grasslands, open shrub and woodlands, roadsides
and other open areas. Spring, summer, fall. Common.

An erect, branching perennial with stems to 2+ feet tall,
stems and leaves glabrous to tomentose. Basal leaves on
petioles 6 inches long, lanceolate to oblong, to 8 inches
long and 1½ inches wide, margins entire, lower surface
tomentose, upper glabrous. Stem leaves alternate, sessile, similar in shape to basal leaves but smaller. Small
flowers evenly spaced in terminal, open cymes, to ¼ inch
long, bell-shaped, interior yellow-green with 6 spreading
tepals, exterior tomentose, silvery white. Found throughout majority of state. Absent in South Texas. Often occurring in large numbers.

Eriogonum suffruticosum   POLYGONACEAE
Bushy buckwheat
Sparse desert scrub. Spring. Rare.

An erect, much-branched, rounded perennial with slightly tomentose, woody stems to 18 inches tall and 18 inches wide. Leaves clustered at ends of stems, elliptic, to ¾ inch long and ¼ inch wide, bases tapering, margins revolute, tips pointed, surfaces tomentose. Inflorescence a tight, terminal cyme to 1½ inches long, flowers about ⅓ inch wide. Six tepals, outer 3 rounded, inner 3 oblanceolate to spatulate, creamy white to yellowish, with brownish red stripes down centers of tepals. Found in Chihuahuan Desert, in limestone soils.

Persicaria hydropiperoides   POLYGONACEAE
Swamp smartweed, water pepper
Banks of waterways and bodies of water, roadside ditches and other low, wet areas. Spring, summer, fall. Common.

An ascending or decumbent, rhizomatous perennial with glabrous, branching stems to 3+ feet tall. Leaves alternate, lanceolate to linear-lanceolate, margins pubescent, tips pointed, surfaces glabrous or slightly pubescent, blade without dark patch on upper surface. Ocrea brown, to 1 inch long, with bristles to ⅜ inch long. Flowers in terminal spikes to 3¼ inches long, radial, white to rose, about ¼ inch wide, with 5 tepals. Widespread throughout Texas. The ocrea is a key character in identifying *Persicaria* species.

Rumex crispus   POLYGONACEAE
Dock, curly dock, yellow dock
Pastures, fields, creek and river bottoms, edges of waterways and bodies of water, urban and suburban areas, agricultural fields, roadsides and other disturbed areas. Spring, summer, fall. Common.

An erect, leafy perennial with glabrous, branching stems to 3+ feet tall. Leaves alternate, lanceolate to lanceolate-linear, to 12 inches long and 2½ inches wide, bases wedge-shaped, truncate, or cordate, margins entire, undulate, and crisped, tips acute. Flowers in terminal panicles, numerous, 10–25 per whorl, nondescript, to ¼ inch long, with 6 tepals, greenish yellow. Widespread throughout state in disturbed soils or in areas that flood.

Rumex hastatulus POLYGONACEAE

Heart-wing sorrel, heart-wing dock, wild sorrel
Creek and river bottoms, fields, meadows,
open woodlands, roadsides and other open
areas. Spring, summer. Common.

An erect annual to short-lived perennial with single
or multiple branching, glabrous stems 18+ inches tall.
Leaves alternate, ovate to oblong-lanceolate to lanceolate,
to 3 inches long and ¾ inch wide, bases hastate, eared,
margins entire, tips acute to obtuse. Flowers in terminal
panicles in upper third of stem, hundreds in whorls of
6±, each flower less than ¼ inch long with 6 tepals, green
to reddish brown. Widespread in eastern third of state.
Often found in disturbed areas. Distinctive hastate leaves
are easiest way to identify this species.

Claytonia virginica PORTULACACEAE

**Spring beauty, Virginia spring beauty,
eastern spring beauty**
Prairies, wetlands, woodlands,
bottomlands. Spring. Common.

An erect perennial from a tuber, with semisucculent
stems to 6 inches tall. Leaves opposite, linear to lanceolate, to 5 inches long and ¼ inch wide, margins entire,
surfaces glabrous. Flowers about ⅓ inch wide, with 5
white to pink petals, each lined with darker pink stripes,
erect when open, nodding when closed. Found in eastern
third of Texas. Only *Claytonia* species in state. One of earliest spring flowers.

Primula meadia (*Dodecatheon meadia*)
PRIMULACEAE

Shooting star, roosterhead, prairie pointers
Prairies, grasslands, open shrub and
woodlands. Spring. Uncommon.

An erect, glabrous perennial to 20 inches tall when in
flower. Basal leaves only, oblong or oblanceolate, to 6
inches long and 2½ inches wide, margins
entire, tips rounded or with a short point.
Flowers in terminal umbels with 25+ per
umbel, white to pink, each flower with 5
severely reflexed petals to more than 1 inch
long. Found in northeast portion of Texas,
near Oklahoma border; isolated collections
in northeast Travis County.

buckwheat family
POLYGONACEAE

purslane family
PORTULACACEAE

primula family
PRIMULACEAE

Samolus ebracteatus   PRIMULACEAE
Limewater brookweed
Springs, river and creek banks, beaches.
Spring, summer, fall. Common.

An erect to ascending perennial with glaucous leaves and stems to 2 feet tall. Leaves sessile or with tiny petioles, spatulate, to 6 inches long, margins entire, tips rounded. Tiny, ¼-inch-wide flowers are white to pink and occur in terminal, airy racemes. Plants growing in open, sunny conditions tend to have leaves crowded at the base, while plants growing in shadier sites have elongated stems with leaves continuing up the stem. Widespread in Texas. Always found around water sources, whether that be salt or fresh water.

Samolus valerandi   PRIMULACEAE
Seaside brookweed
Springs, river and creek banks, marshes and other wet areas. Spring, summer, fall. Common.

An erect or ascending perennial with glabrous leaves and stems to 30+ inches tall when in flower. Leaves sessile or on petioles, obovate to spatulate to elliptic, to 6 inches long, margins entire, tips rounded. Numerous, small, ¼-inch-wide white flowers occur in terminal panicles to 8+ inches long. Inflorescence may be shortened to an inch or so. Found throughout state. More common than *Samolus ebracteatus*.

Anemone caroliniana   RANUNCULACEAE
Carolina anemone, wind flower
Prairies, meadows, open woods, roadsides and other open areas. Spring. Common.

A rhizomatous perennial, to 24 inches tall when flowering. Basal leaves 1–3 per plant, 1- or 2-ternate, terminal leaflet with 2 or 3 clefts, lateral leaflets pinnately lobed. Flowers solitary, white to pink to lavender to blue, occurring well above leaves, sepals to 30 and sometimes with pubescent lower side. Found in eastern Edwards Plateau, north to Oklahoma and into Panhandle, south to Corpus Christi area. Genus name from Greek *anemos*, which means "wind," referring to the dispersal of the seed.

Clematis drummondii   RANUNCULACEAE
Old man's beard, Texas virgin's bower, barbas de chivato
Roadsides, fence lines, open fields, prairies.
Spring, summer, fall. Common.

A perennial vine to 10+ feet long. Leaves are pinnately 5-
to 7-foliolate, simple and trilobed, leaflets to 1 inch long.
Flowers greenish white to cream, spreading sepals to ½
inch long. Unlike other *Clematis* species, *C. drummondii*
does not have showy flowers and is often overlooked until
it has gone to seed. Achene, with slender tails to 4 inches
long, is covered in fine hairs and gives species its common name. Found throughout Texas. Weak in eastern
portion of state. Grows along fence lines and on smaller
shrubs. Named after Thomas Drummond (1793–1835),
who collected specimens in Texas in the early 1830s.

Clematis terniflora   RANUNCULACEAE
Sweet autumn clematis, yam-leaved clematis
Urban and suburban areas, homesteads,
parks. Summer, fall. Uncommon.

A high-climbing, introduced vine with stems to 18+ feet
long. Leaves pinnately 3- to 5-foliate, leaflets ovate to lanceolate to deltate, to 2½ inches long and 1⅓ inches wide,
margins entire. Flowers in clusters of to 12, in cymes or
compound cymes, white, sepals spreading. Achene with
feathery tail to 2⅓ inches long. Naturalized species often
found near water. Documented in several counties in
East Texas as well as Travis and Bexar Counties in Central Texas.

Clematis virginiana   RANUNCULACEAE
Virgin's bower, devil's darning-needle
Streams, edges of woodlands and swamps, anywhere
with wet soils. Summer, fall. Uncommon.

A large climbing vine with glabrous stems to 20 feet
long. Leaves 3-foliolate, leaflets ovate to lanceolate, 3½
inches long and 3 inches wide, margins entire to coarsely
toothed, surfaces glabrous above, pilose below. Flowers in
panicles, numerous, white to cream, sepals wide spreading and to ½ inch long. Achenes with tails to 1¼ inches
long. Found in East Texas, mostly in counties on Louisiana border.

Oligomeris linifolia   RESEDACEAE
Desert spike, flaxleaf whitepuff
Open desert grass and scrub, washes, dunes and other
open areas. Winter, spring, summer, fall. Locally common.

An erect annual with stems to 15 inches tall. Leaves alternate or fasciculate, on petioles less than 2 inches long and
never exceeding length of blade, linear to lanceolate, to 2
inches long and ¹⁄₁₀ inch wide, margins entire. Flowers in
dense spikes, tiny, ¹⁄₁₀ inch wide, white, inconspicuous.
Once thought to be introduced, now thought to be native,
and only member of family in North America. Found in
Texas in Chihuahuan Desert. Additional populations in
far South Texas in and around Starr County. Often grows
in gypseous soils.

Geum canadense   ROSACEAE
White avens
Woodlands, thickets, meadows.
Spring, summer. Common.

An erect perennial with leafy, branching, glabrous to
downy stems to 3+ feet tall. Basal leaves to 10 inches long,
simple or pinnate with 5 main leaflets. Upper leaves
3-lobed or trifoliolate, to 3½ inches long and 3¾ inches
wide, margins serrate. Flowers white, 5-petaled, about
½ inch wide, on inflorescences containing to 15 flowers.
Found in riparian and other shady areas in Central Texas,
east to Louisiana, north into Oklahoma. Absent in Panhandle, West and South Texas.

Diodia teres   RUBIACEAE
Poorjoe, rough buttonweed
Meadows, fields, open grass, brush and woodlands,
roadsides and other open areas. Summer. Common.

A spreading or ascending to erect, single-stemmed
annual with angled, pubescent stems to 12 inches long
which may be weakly branched. Leaves opposite, sessile,
linear to lanceolate or linear-oblong, to 1½ inches long
and ¼ inch wide, margins revolute, tips acute to pointed,
blades at nearly right angles to stem with prominent central vein. Flowers either solitary or in clusters in leaf axils,
small, to ¼ inch long, funnel-shaped, 4-lobed, white to
pink with lobe tips often darker. Found throughout South
Texas, north into Oklahoma, east into Louisiana.

170

Diodia virginiana   RUBIACEAE
Virginia buttonweed, large buttonweed, poorjoe
Fields, meadows, grasslands, prairies, open
brush and woodlands, roadsides and other
open areas. Spring, summer. Common.

A spreading, procumbent perennial with 4-angled, villose branching stems to 2+ feet long. Leaves opposite, sessile, elliptic-oblanceolate or linear-lanceolate, to 1½ inches
long, margins entire to minutely serrate, tips acute.
Flowers originating in leaf axils, solitary, white, 4-lobed,
trumpet-shaped, to ⅜ inch wide. Found throughout
eastern third of Texas. Less common south to Cameron
County.

Galium aparine   RUBIACEAE
Stickywilly, catchweed bedstraw, goose-grass
Fields, grasslands, prairies, brush and woodlands, thickets,
coastal areas, urban and suburban areas, roadsides, fence
lines and other disturbed sites. Spring, summer. Common.

A reclining, often clambering annual with hirsute,
angled stems to 3+ feet long. Leaves whorled, sessile,
linear-oblanceolate, to 2¾ inches long, bases tapering,
margins entire, tips rounded, mucronate, surfaces rough
to the touch. Flowers on short pedicels originating from
leaf axils, 4-petaled, white, less than ¼ inch wide. Widespread throughout eastern two-thirds of Texas. Also
reported from El Paso County. Common weed in disturbed areas.

Galium virgatum   RUBIACEAE
Southwest bedstraw
Fields, grasslands, river and creek banks and floodplains,
canyons, brush and woodlands. Spring. Common.

An erect, single-stemmed annual with angular stems to
16+ inches tall, stems with scattered, stiff hairs. Leaves
whorled, oblong, to ⅜ inch long, margins toothed, with
stiff hairs, tips acute, surfaces bristly. Solitary flowers
sessile or nearly so in leaf axils, small, creamy white to
pale yellow, 4-lobed. Widespread throughout state. Weak
in Panhandle. Genus name of Greek origin, meaning
"bedstraw."

Hedyotis acerosa var. *acerosa*   RUBIACEAE
Needleleaf bluet
Open grass and brushlands, desert scrub, rocky
slopes, hillsides. Spring, summer. Uncommon.

An erect to ascending, low-growing perennial with
numerous branching stems to 12 inches tall. Leaves
opposite or whorled, threadlike, thin, to ½ inch
long, numerous. Flowers terminal or in leaf axils,
trumpet-shaped, white or pink or violet, 4-lobed, to ½
inch long. Typically found in sparsely vegetated areas, on
open limestone in western half of state, from Eagle Pass
north into lower Panhandle and throughout Chihuahuan
Desert.

Houstonia micrantha   RUBIACEAE
Southern bluet, small bluet, star violet
Fields, pastures, prairies, maintained lawns and
other areas, roadsides. Winter, spring. Common.

A small, erect annual with slender, glabrous stems to 4
inches, occasionally cespitose. Leaves opposite, sessile,
spatulate to ovate, to ⅜ inch long and ¼ inch wide, bases
tapering, margins entire, tips rounded. Flowers terminal,
trumpet-shaped, white, 4-lobed, to ⅛ inch long and wide.
Most common in eastern fourth of Texas, occasionally
west to eastern Edwards Plateau and Coastal Bend. Often
overlooked.

Mitchella repens   RUBIACEAE
Partridge-berry, two-eyed berry, running box
Woodlands, forests. Spring, summer. Locally common.

A trailing, mat-forming perennial with numerous
branching stems, mats often several feet wide. Leaves
opposite, on short petioles, ovate to round, to 1 inch long
and nearly as wide, bases rounded to cordate, margins
entire, tips obtuse, surfaces glabrous and often with
lighter venation on primary veins. Flowers paired in leaf
axils, trumpet-shaped, white, 4-lobed, to ½ inch long,
lobes visibly pubescent. Fruit is a red, oval-shaped drupe,
¼ inch long. Found in East Texas, often forming large
mats on small knolls or ridges.

Oldenlandia boscii RUBIACEAE
Bosc's mille graines, Bosc's bluet
Edges of ponds, lakes, rivers, and streams, wet
savannas and grasslands, roadside ditches and
other low, wet areas. Spring, summer. Common.

A prostrate, spreading annual with glabrous, branching stems to 12 inches long. Leaves opposite, sessile, linear to linear-oblanceolate, to 1 inch long, margins entire,
tips acute, surfaces nearly hairless. Flowers solitary or in
small clusters in upper leaf axils, funnel-shaped, 4-lobed,
white, less than ⅛ inch wide. Found in eastern Texas,
west into Edwards Plateau and to Coastal Bend, where it
becomes less common.

Oldenlandia corymbosa RUBIACEAE
Flattop mille graines, diamond flower
Urban and suburban areas. Summer. Rare.

An introduced, erect or spreading annual with glabrous,
branching stems. Leaves opposite, sessile, linear to lanceolate, to 1½ inches long and ¼ inch wide, bases tapering,
margins rough, tips acute to obtuse, pointed. Flowers
solitary or in small cymes, on peduncles to ¾ inch long,
originating from upper leaf axils, small, to ⅛ inch wide,
trumpet-shaped, 4-lobed, white with tinges of pink. A
pantropic weed. Found in Texas in Harris County.

Oldenlandia uniflora RUBIACEAE
Clustered mille graines, oneflower oldenlandia
Banks of waterways and bodies of water, roadside ditches
and other low, wet areas. Spring, summer. Common.

An erect, spreading annual with angled, branching stems
to 24 inches tall, stems with white hairs. Leaves opposite,
on short petioles, ovate to ovate-elliptic, to 1 inch long,
bases tapering, margins hirsute, tips acute. Flowers in
clusters, rarely solitary, in upper leaf axils, rotate, 4-lobed,
white, ⅛ inch long and wide. Found in wet, sandy soils of
Southeast Texas, west to eastern and southeastern edge of
Edwards Plateau, to Guadalupe County.

Richardia brasiliensis   RUBIACEAE
Tropical Mexican clover, Brazilian calla-lily, white-eye
Open brush and scrub oak woodlands,
prairies, dunes, lomas, roadsides and other
open areas. Spring, summer. Common.

An introduced, prostrate, branching annual to perennial with villose stems to 12 inches long. Leaves opposite, ovate to elliptic, to 1¾ inches long and ¾ inch wide,
bases tapering, margins entire to ciliate, tips slightly
acute, blades rough to the touch. Flowers in leaf axils,
funnel-shaped, with typically 6 lobes (occasionally 5),
white, tinged pink to purple. Found from South Texas
northeast into Louisiana.

Stenaria nigricans   RUBIACEAE
Diamondflowers
Open fields, pastures, grass, brush and woodlands,
rocky hillsides, slopes, outcrops and ridges, roadsides
and other open areas. Spring, summer. Common.

An erect, ascending or procumbent perennial with glabrous, branching stems to 20 inches tall. Leaves opposite,
sessile, linear to lanceolate, to 1¾ inches long and less
than ¼ inch wide, margins entire or revolute, with stiff
hairs, tips acute. Flowers in open, leafy cymes, numerous, funnel-shaped, 4-lobed, white, pink, or light purple,
to ⅓ inch long and wide. Widespread throughout state.
Absent only in Lower Rio Grande Valley and southern
Panhandle to Midland-Odessa.

Cardiospermum halicacabum
SAPINDACEAE
Balloon vine, love in a puff, heart seed
Open brush and woodlands, banks of
waterways and bodies of water, fence lines.
Spring, summer, fall. Common.

An introduced, annual to perennial climbing vine with
branching stems to 10+ feet long. Leaves alternate, triangular to deltate, biternate, to about 5 inches long and 3½
inches wide, lobes lanceolate, margins toothed. Flowers
in small clustered corymbs, less than ¼ inch in diameter, with 4 white sepals. Fruits inflated, to about 1½
inches in diameter, with 3 round black seeds and a white,
heart-shaped point of attachment. Widespread throughout eastern half of state, from Brownsville north into
Oklahoma.

Anemopsis californica   SAURURACEAE
Yerba mansa
Springs, marshes, seeps and other wet
areas. Spring, summer. Uncommon.

A stoloniferous, erect to spreading perennial to 12 inches
tall, stolons several feet long, usually forming small colonies. Leaves elliptic to oblong, on petioles equaling and
often exceeding length of blade, to 6 inches long, bases
cordate to obtuse, margins entire, tips rounded. Flowers
small, white, held above foliage in 1¾-inch-long spikes,
large white bracts below spike. Only a few collections
made in Texas. Found around perennial springs and
seeps in mountains of West Texas and other perennial
waters in Panhandle.

Saururus cernuus   SAURURACEAE
Lizard's tail, breastweed, water dragon
Marshes, bogs, floodplains and other low,
wet areas. Spring, summer. Common.

A weakly erect, rhizomatous perennial with zigzag stems
to 4 feet tall. Leaves alternate, on petioles shorter than
leaf blades, to 6 inches long and 3½ inches wide, bases
cordate, margins entire to slightly wavy. Flowers in spikes
to 7 inches long, originating from axils of upper leaves,
solitary, only about ¼ inch long. Produces one seed per
flower. Genus name of Greek origin and means "lizard" (*sauros*) and "tail" (*urus*). Specific epithet means
"drooping."

Buddleja racemosa   SCROPHULARIACEAE
Wand butterfly-bush
Rocky outcrops, cliffs, canyons, roadcuts and
other open, rocky areas. Spring. Uncommon.

An erect, woody perennial with weakly branched, glabrous stems to 2 feet tall. Leaves opposite, on petioles
to ¼ inch long, ovate-oblong to triangular-lanceolate, to
4 inches long and 1¼ inches wide, bases hastate, margins crenate to dentate, tips obtuse, lower surface of
blade white-gray tomentose and upper surface green
and glabrous. Flowers in terminal racemes to 12 inches
long, in loosely spaced, rounded clusters about ⅓ inch
in diameter. Clusters opposite along raceme and on
short, sometimes subsessile petioles, each flower small,
creamy white to yellow, 4-lobed. Found along southern
edge of Edwards Plateau, on limestone cliffs, ledges, and
escarpments.

Capsicum annuum   SOLANACEAE
Chile piquin, bird pepper, cayenne pepper
Woodlands, brushlands, riparian areas, fence
lines. Spring, summer, fall. Common.

An erect perennial (annual in colder areas), with branching stems to about 3 feet tall. Leaves opposite, on petioles,
ovate to lanceolate, to 2½ inches long and ½ inch wide,
margins entire, tips acute. Flowers originating from leaf
axils, white, star-shaped, 5-lobed, to ½ inch in diameter.
Fruits ovoid to globose berries, green when young, turning red when mature. Found throughout South-Central
Texas, east to Houston area. Common in nursery trade;
expect elsewhere, as it will naturalize.

Datura stramonium   SOLANACEAE
Jimson weed
Roadsides, urban and suburban areas, river and
creek beds. Spring, summer, fall. Uncommon.

An introduced, erect annual from a single branching
stem to 3 feet tall and as wide. Leaves ovate, on petioles
about half as long as blade, oblong or elliptic, to 8 inches
long and 6 inches wide, bases cordate to cuneate, margins deeply dentate or lobed. Flowers in upper leaf axils,
to 4 inches long and 2 inches wide, funnel-shaped, white,
may be tinged lavender, with dark purple centers. Fruits
remain erect through maturity, seeds black. Scattered
throughout state, with heaviest concentration in Central
to East Texas. A garden escapee.

Datura wrightii   SOLANACEAE
Datura, sacred datura, jimson weed
Creek and river beds, desert washes and drainages,
roadsides. Spring, summer, fall. Common.

An erect perennial to over 4 feet wide, branching from
base, stems softly pubescent to over 4 feet tall. Leaves
alternate, ovate to cordate, to 6 inches long and 4 inches
wide, bases asymmetric, margins entire to undulate,
lower side of leaves softly pubescent. Flowers on short
pedicels in upper leaf axils, white sometimes tinged lavender, to 7 inches long and 4 inches wide. Fused corolla
has 5 weakly shallow lobes with short tines at junction of
lobes. Fruits nodding at maturity, seeds brown. Flowers
open in late afternoon or just prior to sunset and remain
open throughout evening.

Nicotiana obtusifolia SOLANACEAE
Desert tobacco, coyote tobacco, tabaco de coyote
Rocky outcrops and among boulders, canyons,
desert washes, thornscrub, open brushlands.
Spring, summer, fall. Uncommon.

An erect biennial to perennial with simple or branching, viscid-pubescent stems to 3+ feet tall. Leaves
alternate, lower leaves obovate-oblong, upper leaves
elliptic-lanceolate, to 8 inches long and 2½ inches wide,
bases tapering or clasping (upper leaves), margins entire
to wavy, tips rounded to acute, blades pale green, tacky.
Flowers well-spaced in loose terminal racemes, greenish cream, tubular to bell-shaped, 5-lobed, to 1 inch long
and ⅓ inch wide. Found in Chihuahuan Desert, east into
Edwards Plateau, south to Cameron County.

Nicotiana repanda SOLANACEAE
Fiddle-leaf tobacco, wild tobacco, tabaco cimarron
Creek and river banks and floodplains,
among boulders, wooded canyons, ravines.
Winter, spring, summer. Uncommon.

An erect, leafy annual with slender stems to 3+ feet tall,
stems and leaves tacky. Leaves alternate, on winged petioles. Lower leaves larger, obovate to 8 inches long and 4
inches wide, bases tapering, margins wavy, tips rounded
to acute. Upper leaves ovate, clasping. White flowers in
terminal, loose, open racemes, funnel-shaped with slender tubes to 2½ inches long, corolla to 1¾ inches wide,
star-shaped, 5-lobed with lobes divided about half their
length. Flowers opening around dusk, closing after sunrise. Most common in South Texas.

Physalis acutifolia SOLANACEAE
Sharpleaf groundcherry, Wright's groundcherry
Rio Grande floodplain, agricultural fields, roadsides,
drainages, sparse desert scrub. Summer. Rare.

An erect, branching annual to 12+ inches tall. Leaves
alternate, on winged petioles to 2½ inches long, lanceolate to ovate, to 3½ inches long, bases tapering, margins
dentate, tips acute to rounded. Flowers solitary, on long
pedicels originating from leaf axils, creamy white with
yellow centers, rotate, to 1 inch wide. Rare, but can occur
in vast numbers in disturbed fields along the Rio Grande
in El Paso County, south into Hudspeth County.

Solanum carolinense SOLANACEAE
Carolina nightshade, common nightshade
Fields, pastures, open woodlands, roadsides and other
open, disturbed areas. Spring, summer, fall. Common.

An erect, rhizomatous, branching perennial with spiny
stems to 3 feet tall, leaves and stems with star-shaped
hairs. Leaves alternate, on petioles to 1¼ inches long,
ovate to ovate-elliptic, to 4¾ inches long, margins shallowly lobed or large-toothed, leaf surfaces with spines
along veins. Flowers in racemes, white to lavender, rotate,
5-lobed, distinctly star-shaped, tips of lobes somewhat
reflexed. Fruits are yellow berries when mature, green
when young. Common and problematic in East Texas,
occasionally westward. Prefers sandy soils.

Solanum jamesii SOLANACEAE
Wild potato, James's nightshade
Mountainous woodlands, canyons,
drainages. Summer, fall. Uncommon.

An erect, spreading, stoloniferous, tuberous perennial
with heavily branched, glabrous stems to 18 inches long.
Leaves alternate, pinnate, to 6 inches long, leaflets 7–9,
lanceolate to linear-oblong, and to 2½ inches long, margins entire. Flowers white, green stripes at base following midveins of lobes, star-shaped, to about 1 inch wide,
with 5 lobes pointed, reflexed, and divided to base. Found
in Chihuahuan Desert, from Jeff Davis County to El Paso
County.

Solanum ptychanthum SOLANACEAE
West Indian nightshade, black nightshade
Brush and woodlands, thickets, rocky outcrops, ledges,
among boulders, river and creek banks, disturbed
areas. Winter, spring, summer, fall. Common.

An erect, much-branched annual with glabrous stems
to 3+ feet tall. Leaves alternate, ovate to oval-lanceolate,
to 4 inches long, bases tapering, rounded or truncate,
margins entire to sinuate or toothed, tips acute. Flowers in umbels originating from middle to upper leaf
axils, white, occasionally tinged lavender or purple,
star-shaped, with 5 reflexed lobes, to ½ inch wide when
fully opened and not reflexed. Fruits are black, ¼+
inch wide. Found in southern half of Texas, from Jeff
Davis County east into Louisiana, occasionally north to
Oklahoma.

Solanum triquetrum SOLANACEAE
Texas nightshade, hierba mora
Brush and woodlands, rocky outcrops, ledges,
escarpments, among boulders, fence lines.
Winter, spring, summer, fall. Common.

An erect, rhizomatous, shrubby or scandent perennial,
with glabrous stems to 6+ feet tall. Leaves alternate,
deltate-cordate or hastate, 2½ inches long if hastate, 3–5
lobes with middle lobe lanceolate to linear. Flowers in
umbels originating in upper leaf axils, white, star-shaped,
to ½ inch wide, with reflexed lobes divided to base. Fruits
round, red berries to ⅓ inch wide. Found throughout
southern half of Texas from Culberson County east.
Absent in Panhandle and eastern fourth of Texas.

Sphenoclea zeylanica SPHENOCLEACEAE
Chickenspike, gooseweed, wedgewort
River bottoms, floodplains, bar ditches and other low,
wet areas. Summer, fall. Uncommon to locally common.

An introduced, erect, branching annual with glabrous,
hollow stems to 3+ feet tall. Leaves alternate, on petioles
to ¾ inch long, elliptic, to 4¾ inches long and 2 inches
wide, margins entire. Tiny white to green flowers borne
on a short spike about 3 inches long. Found primarily in
Southeast Texas. Considered an agricultural nuisance,
especially in rice fields. Specific epithet means "from
Ceylon," a reference to native range or where species was
originally collected.

Triantha racemosa TOFIELDIACEAE
Coastal false asphodel
Wet meadows and savannas, pine
barrens, bogs. Summer. Rare.

An erect, rhizomatous perennial with glandular stems
to 28+ inches tall. Leaves to 3 near base of plant, grasslike, to 14 inches long and ¼ inch wide. Flowers in open
racemes, to 80 per raceme, radial, to ½ inch wide, with
6 white oblong tepals. Ovary superior, style 3-branched.
Found in open, wet areas from Tyler County south to Jefferson County. Specific epithet derived from Latin word
racemus, indicating the type of inflorescence, a raceme.
The word was originally used to describe a cluster of
grapes, eventually becoming raycin, or what is known
today as raisin.

179

Boehmeria cylindrica   URTICACEAE
Small-spike false nettle, false nettle
Marshes, bogs, seeps, river and creek banks, areas
with wet or damp soils. Spring, summer. Common.

An erect perennial with glabrous, branching stems to
3 feet tall. Leaves opposite, on long petioles, ovate to
ovate-lanceolate, to 4 inches long and 2½ inches wide,
bases rounded to acute, margins serrate, tips acute, leaf
surface may be wrinkled, upper leaf surface with 3 distinct veins. Male and female flowers on separate plants.
Flowers in angled spikes originating from leaf axils,
small, greenish white, petals absent, male flowers with
4 stamens, female flowers tubular. Found throughout
East Texas and lower Edwards Plateau to Terrell County.
Uncommon in upper Panhandle.

Parietaria pensylvanica   URTICACEAE
Hammerwort, pellitory, Pennsylvania pellitory
Shaded creek and river banks, canyons, ledges, among
boulders, within the shade of trees and large shrubs, urban
and suburban areas, other shady areas. Spring. Common.

An ascending or reclining slender annual with branching, angled, pubescent stems to 12 inches long. Leaves
alternate, on petioles, lanceolate, to 3½ inches long and
¾ inch wide, bases cuneate, margins entire to undulate,
tips obtuse, surfaces pubescent, upper leaf surface with 3
distinct veins. Flowers occur in bracted clusters in upper
leaf axils, green, inconspicuous, small. Found throughout Texas. Weak in Panhandle south to Midland-Odessa.

Urtica chamaedryoides   URTICACEAE
Heartleaf nettle, ortiguilla
Brush and woodlands, palm groves, river banks,
floodplains, swamps, bogs, canyons, rocky slopes, ledges,
roadside ditches. Spring, summer, fall. Common.

An erect to reclining, branching annual with slender stems to 28 inches tall, stem with stinging bristles.
Leaves opposite, on petioles to 3 inches long, ovate to
round, upper leaves becoming lanceolate, to 3¼ inches
long and 2½ inches wide, bases rounded to cordate, margins serrate, tips acute to rounded. Flowers in small
rounded clusters at end of short peduncles originating
from leaf axils, 4 clusters per node, inconspicuous, inflorescences greenish. Found throughout South and Central
Texas, east into Louisiana and north into Oklahoma.

Urtica urens   URTICACEAE
Burning nettle, dog nettle, ortiga
Fields, pastures, open brush and woodlands,
roadsides and other open, disturbed areas.
Winter, spring, summer. Uncommon.

An introduced, erect or ascending annual with stems to
24+ inches tall, stems with stinging bristles. Leaves opposite, elliptic, rounded-ovate or ovate-oblong, to 1¾ inches
long and 1¼ inches wide, bases cuneate to slightly cordate, margins serrate, surfaces wrinkled to warty, upper
surface with 3 distinct veins. Flowers in rounded heads
on short peduncles originating from leaf axils, creamy
white to pale yellow, small. Inflorescences can be numerous, hiding stem. From Southeast Texas to lower coast.
Introduced from Eurasia.

Glandularia quadrangulata   VERBENACEAE
Beaked vervain
Fields, meadows, open brushlands, roadsides and other
open, disturbed areas. Winter, spring, summer. Common.

A prostrate to ascending, branching annual to short-lived
perennial with pubescent stems to 10 inches tall, stems
rooting at nodes. Leaves opposite, ovate, to 1¼ inches
long, twice divided and either pinnatifid or 3-cleft, bases
cuneate, tapering, margins revolute, tips obtuse to acute.
Flowers in terminal, sessile spikes, white with occasional
tinges of pink or blue or lavender, trumpet-shaped, ⅛
inch wide, 5-lobed, lobes unequal. Found in Chihuahuan
Desert region, south to Cameron County and throughout
South Texas; occasional elsewhere.

Lantana achyranthifolia   VERBENACEAE
Brushland lantana, caraquito blanco, Mexican marjoram
Shrublands, canyons, thickets, thornscrub, rocky
outcrops, ledges, mesas and other open, gravelly to rocky
areas. Winter, spring, summer, fall. Locally common.

An erect, shrubby perennial with branching stems to 6+
feet tall, stems with stiff, white hairs. Leaves opposite, on
petioles to ½ inch long, triangular-ovate to lanceolate, to
3¼ inches long and 2 inches wide, bases acute, margins
serrate, tips acute, blade surfaces rough. Flowers in round
spikes originating from upper leaf axils and elongating
when in fruit, on peduncles to 5½ inches long, bilateral,
white, turning lavender or purple with age, 4-lobed with
lower lobe larger. Found throughout South Texas, northwest to El Paso. Occasional collections made elsewhere.

181

Phyla lanceolata   VERBENACEAE
Northern frog-fruit
Margins of ponds, lakes, creeks, and rivers,
marshes, roadside ditches and other low, wet
areas. Spring, summer, fall. Common.

A procumbent to ascending perennial with simple or
branched stems, rooting at nodes, to 24+ inches long.
Leaves opposite, sessile or on short petioles, oblong to
lanceolate, to 3 inches long and 1¼ inches wide, bases
tapering, margins serrate, tips acute. Flowers in compact spikes originating from leaf axils, surpassing leaves,
numerous, white tinged pink and with darker centers,
bilateral, 4-lobed with lower lobe larger than other 3.
Widespread throughout state. Frequent in eastern third.
Uncommon elsewhere. Absent in the Trans-Pecos.

Phyla nodiflora   VERBENACEAE
Frog-fruit, common frog-fruit, Texas frog-fruit
Margins of waterways and bodies of water,
shaded woodlands, rocky outcrops, among
boulders, roadside ditches and other low, wet
areas. Winter, spring, summer, fall. Common.

A prostrate perennial with branching stems, rooting at
nodes, to 3+ feet long. Leaves opposite, on short petioles
or sessile, spatulate to obovate, to 3 inches long and 1 inch
wide, bases cuneate, margins serrate in distal half, tips
rounded to obtuse. Flowers in rounded spikes originating
from leaf axils and elongating to 1 inch long, on peduncles to 4¾ inches, numerous, bilateral, white to pink with
darker centers, 4-lobed with lower lobe generally larger
than other 3. Most common species of *Phyla* in Texas.

Tetraclea coulteri   VERBENACEAE
Coulter's wrinklefruit
Open brush and desert scrub, open desert grasslands,
rocky slopes and hillsides, roadsides and other
open areas. Spring, summer, fall. Common.

An erect, spreading, branching perennial with slender, pubescent stems to 16+ inches tall. Leaves opposite, sessile or on short petioles, ovate to 1½ inches long
and ¾ inch wide, margins dentate or entire on lower
leaves, tips acute and pointed. Flowers in upper leaf
axils in 3-flowered cymes, bilateral, trumpet-shaped,
cream-colored, often red-tinged, the 5 lobes unequal.
Found throughout Chihuahuan Desert, east into the
Edwards Plateau, south to Hidalgo County.

Hybanthus verticillatus   VIOLACEAE
Baby slippers, nodding green violet
Fields, meadows, prairies, grasslands, open brush and
woodlands, riparian areas. Spring, summer, fall. Common.

An erect, rhizomatous perennial from a woody base with
multiple leafy stems to 16 inches tall. Leaves opposite
below, alternate above, linear, elliptic, or lanceolate, to 2
inches long and ⅓ inch wide, bases gradually narrowing,
margins entire or ciliate, tips pointed. Flowers on slender peduncles originating from leaf axils, small, just over
¼ inch long, with 4 petals. Upper and 2 lateral petals ⅛
inch long, lower petal ¼ inch long, petals greenish white
to cream or yellow, upper 3 petals usually tinged purple.
Found throughout state, aside from far eastern Texas.

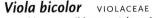

Viola bicolor   VIOLACEAE
Field pansy, wild pansy, Johnny jump-up
Fields, meadows, open brush and woodlands, urban
and suburban areas, roadsides. Spring. Common.

An erect to ascending annual with branching stems to
6 inches tall. Basal leaves round, on long petioles. Stem
leaves alternate, obovate to linear-oblanceolate, to 2
inches long, bases tapering to a point, margins crenate.
Flowers solitary, produced on slender stalks, each flower
about ½ inch wide with 5 petals, each petal white to
cream to blue-violet with dark veins, the lower petal with
a yellow patch near base, lateral petals somewhat pubescent. Common in northeastern portion of state, occasional elsewhere.

Viola lanceolata   VIOLACEAE
Lance-leaved violet, bog white violet
Bogs, wet meadows, banks of ponds, lakes, streams,
and other low, wet areas. Spring. Uncommon.

A stemless, stoloniferous, rhizomatous perennial with
stolons reaching 12 inches long. Leaves on petioles to
5 inches long, erect to ascending, lanceolate to elliptic
to linear, up to 5 inches long and 1 inch wide, margins
entire or lacerate near tip. Flowers solitary, white, ½ inch
wide, on reddish brown, glabrous pedicels up to 6 inches
long, 5-petaled with upper 2 petals reflexed, lateral petals
may have purple veins, lower petal with distinct purple
veins. Found in Southeast Texas, often in rich woodlands.

Viola primulifolia   VIOLACEAE
Primrose-leaved violet

Mixed pine woodlands and forests, wooded
bogs, stream banks. Spring. Uncommon.

A stemless perennial to 5 inches wide and 8 inches tall
when in flower. Basal leaves on petioles to 5+ inches
long, ovate to cordate, to 3½ inches long and 2 inches
wide, bases cordate, margins serrulate to crenulate, tips
rounded. Flowers solitary, on peduncles to 8 inches tall,
white, 5-petaled, lower 3 petals with dark, purple veins.
Found throughout East Texas, west into Bastrop County.

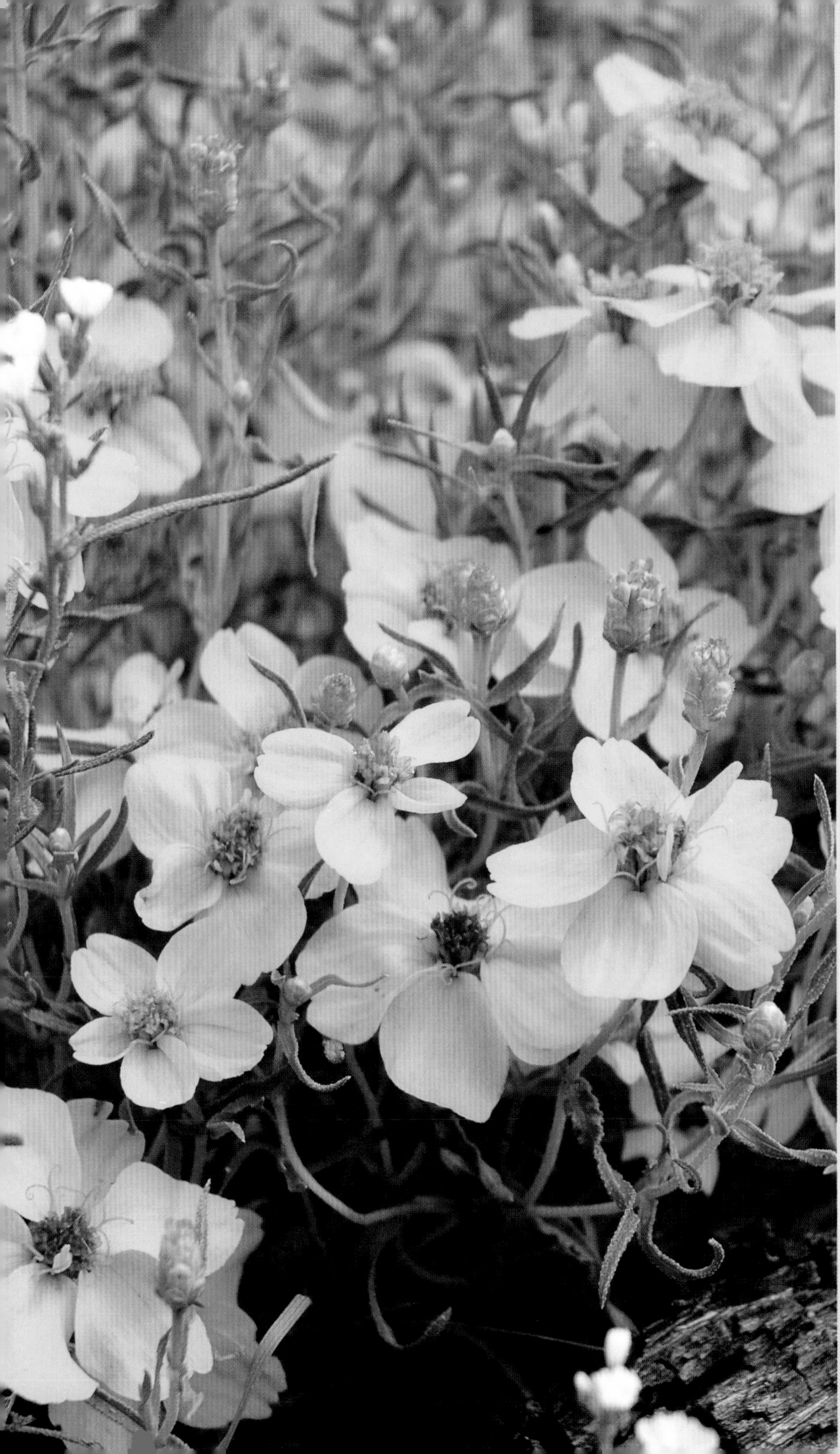

Thunbergia alata ACANTHACEAE
Black-eyed Susan vine
Fields, meadows, disturbed areas. Spring. Uncommon.

An introduced, pubescent perennial vine to 3+ feet long. Leaves ovate, on petioles to 3 inches long, blade to 3 inches long, margins entire or toothed, surfaces pubescent. Flowers 5-lobed, yellow-orange with a dark brownish red center, to 1½ inches wide. Long established in various areas throughout Texas, but not common. Most often found growing around old homesteads, gardens, and nursery centers. Genus named after Carl Peter Thunberg (1743–1828), a Swedish doctor and botanist.

Suaeda conferta AMARANTHACEAE
Beach seepweed, tufted sea-blite
Salt flats, dunes, open soils. Spring,
summer, fall. Locally common.

A prostrate to decumbent, mat-forming perennial, several feet wide, stems glabrous, reddish brown, to 8 inches tall, often zigzagged at ends. Leaves alternate, linear to elliptic, to ⅝ inch long, succulent. Flowers crowded in leaf axils, small, to ⅛ inch wide, sepal interior yellow, sepal exterior greenish blue. Found in saline soils of coastal Texas from Houston area south into Mexico as well as in the counties bordering the Rio Grande, from Maverick County south to Cameron County.

Tidestromia lanuginosa AMARANTHACEAE
Honeymat, woolly tidestromia
Desert scrub, grasslands, dunes, roadsides and other
sparse, open areas. Spring, summer, fall. Common.

A decumbent, prostrate or ascending annual with reddish, softly pubescent, often yellowish gray stems to 24 inches long. Leaves ovate, round, or lanceolate, to 1¼ inches long and nearly as wide, bases tapering to round, tips acute to rounded. Lower leaves alternate or opposite, on petioles. Upper leaves opposite, sessile. Flowers in clusters in upper leaf axils, small, about 1/16 inch wide, yellow, with downy leafy bracts just below and surrounding flower clusters. Common throughout western half of Texas and along coast into Louisiana; occasional farther east.

Allium coryi   AMARYLLIDACEAE
Yellow-flowered onion, Cory's wild onion
Rocky slopes, drainages, fields. Spring. Locally common.

A bulbous perennial with scape to 12 inches tall. Leaves flat to channeled, ⅛ inch wide and nearly as long as scape. Flowers in terminal umbels, 25 per umbel, urn-shaped, about ¼ inch broad, with 3 sepals and 3 petals. Sole species of yellow-flowered onion in Texas. Recorded from a few counties in Big Bend region. During years of well-timed and plentiful precipitation, it can be found growing along roadsides in West Texas. In other years, it may seem nonexistent. Named after Victor Louis Cory, an American botanist who collected in Texas in the early 1900s.

Habranthus tubispathus   AMARYLLIDACEAE
Copper lily, Rio Grande copperlily
Grasslands, fields, prairies, roadsides and other open areas. Summer, fall. Common.

An erect, bulbous perennial to 12 inches tall when in flower. Basal leaves few, linear to lanceolate, typically shorter than scape. Flowers solitary, at end of a slender scape with a spathe to 1 inch long, copper-yellow with a reddish brown center and veins, to 1 inch long, funnel-shaped, with 3 sepals and 3 petals similar in shape and color. Common after adequate, well-timed rains along coastal Texas from Coastal Bend northeast to Galveston Bay, inland to Edwards Plateau and north to Dallas–Fort Worth. Unclear whether species is native or introduced.

Zephyranthes longifolia   AMARYLLIDACEAE
Cebolleta, copper zephyrlily
Desert scrub and open brushlands, gravelly slopes, river floodplains, low areas. Summer, fall. Common.

An erect, bulbous perennial to 12+ inches tall. Leaves few, basal only, linear, to 8 inches long. Flowers solitary at end of scapes, lemon-yellow, about ¾ inch long and about 1 inch wide but width variable, with 3 sepals and 3 petals, obovate-elliptic, not fully spreading. Petals and sepal ending with short, blunt tip, spathe to 1¼ inches long, papery, membranous. Common throughout its range in Chihuahuan Desert, north into southern Panhandle; prefers sandy soils.

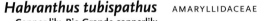

Zephyranthes pulchella AMARYLLIDACEAE
Showy zephyrlily
Coastal plains, swales, roadside ditches and low,
wet areas. Spring, summer, fall. Uncommon.

An erect, bulbous perennial to 12+ inches tall. Leaves
few, basal only, to 9 inches long, linear. Flowers solitary at
end of scapes, yellow, about 2 inches wide, with 3 sepals
and 3 petals, both elliptic-lanceolate, spreading, spathe
to 1¾ inches. Located in South Texas, generally south of
San Antonio, east to Harris County and into Louisiana.
During the course of photographing plants for this book,
this species was found in northern Kinney County, well
out of its documented range.

Polytaenia texana APIACEAE
Texas prairie parsley
Fields, grasslands, prairies, open brush and
woodlands, roadsides. Spring, summer. Common.

An erect, stout biennial with branching stems to 4 feet
tall. Leaves alternate, ovate to oblong, to 5 inches long and
4 inches wide, ternate, leaflets pinnate, bases cuneate,
ultimate margins lobed, tips obtuse. Flowers in terminal
and axillary compound corymbs on peduncles to 2 inches
long, yellow, numerous, small, 5-petaled. Fruits flat,
winged to ⅜ inch long. Found throughout Central Texas,
south to Coastal Bend, into East Texas. Absent in deep
East Texas. Often occurring in large numbers.

Pseudocymopterus montanus
(*Cymopterus lemmonii*) APIACEAE
Alpine false spring parsley
Mountain woodlands and forests. Summer. Uncommon.

An erect perennial with slender flowering stems to
30 inches tall. Leaves mostly basal, erect to arching,
ovate-oblong, 1- to 3-pinnate, to nearly 8 inches long
including petiole, ultimate lobes thin, linear to lanceolate, margins entire, tips acute. Stem leaves similar,
smaller. Inflorescence a terminal compound umbel, to
2½ inches broad with a rounded top, at end of a slender
peduncle to 30 inches long. Flowers small, numerous,
crowded, yellow, 5-petaled. Found in upper elevations of
Davis and Guadalupe Mountains in West Texas; common
throughout southwestern United States.

188

Tauschia texana APIACEAE
Texas umbrellawort
Thickets, woodlands, riparian areas,
floodplains. Winter, spring. Rare.

An acaulescent, glabrous perennial to 16 inches tall.
Leaves oblong, pinnate, to 6 inches long and 1¾ inches
wide, leaflets ovate, margins entire, tips rounded to acute.
Inflorescence a compound umbel on a peduncle to 16
inches long, held well above leaves. Flowers yellow, small,
5-petaled. Grows in alluvial soils along rivers and creeks
and other drainages in southern stretches of Blackland
Prairie and Post Oak Savanna, east to Houston area.

Zizia aurea APIACEAE
Golden zizia, golden Alexanders
Meadows, fields, savannas, open woodlands, roadsides
and other open areas. Spring, summer. Common.

An erect, branching perennial with glabrous stems to
30 inches tall. Leaves alternate, on petioles, odd-pinnate
with 5 leaflets. Each leaflet lanceolate, ovate, cordate, or
oblong, to 3 inches long and 2 inches wide, bases tapering to lobed, margins serrate, tips acute to obtuse. Stems
terminating in compound umbels, each to 3 inches wide.
Flowers numerous, yellow, 5-petaled, about ⅛ inch wide.
Found in eastern fourth of Texas, often along wooded
roadsides.

Asclepias tuberosa APOCYNACEAE
Butterfly weed, orange milkweed, butterfly milkweed
Woodlands, fields, prairies, thickets, brushlands,
canyon bottoms. Spring, summer, fall. Common.

An ascending to erect perennial with single to multiple branching, pubescent, leafy stems 30 inches
tall. Leaves alternate, sessile or subsessile, linear to
lanceolate-oblong, to 3½ inches long and ¾ inch wide,
bases cordate to truncate, margins entire, tips pointed.
Flowers in umbels in upper axils of stems, each umbel
to 2½ inches wide with up to 25 flowers. The 5-lobed,
reflexed corolla and hood are bright orange. Fruits slender, oval follicles, tapering at both ends, smooth, to 6
inches long and ¾ inch wide. Found in eastern half of
Texas, from Coastal Bend north into Oklahoma and
northern Panhandle. Additional populations occur in
Davis and Guadalupe Mountains in West Texas.

189

Haplophyton crooksii   APOCYNACEAE
Cockroach plant, hierba de la cucaracha
Rocky slopes, canyons, ravines. Spring, summer, fall. Rare.

An erect perennial with branched stems to 2 feet tall, stems covered with stiff, straight, appressed hairs. Leaves alternate, sessile or on short petioles, hirsute, linear to lanceolate, to 1⅓ inches long and about ½ inch wide, margins entire, ciliate. Bright yellow flowers, with 5 oval petals, about ¾ inch wide, occur at ends of stems, either solitary or in small groups. Found in West Texas at lower to mid elevations. Sap can be used as insecticide or repellent, hence the common name.

Trachelospermum difforme   APOCYNACEAE
Climbing dogbane
Open woodlands, riparian areas.
Spring, summer. Uncommon.

A twining, low-climbing perennial woody vine with branching, brownish red stems to 35+ feet long. Leaves opposite, on petioles to ½ inch long, variable from elliptic to linear to ovate, to 4¾ inches long and 3 inches wide, filled with milky sap, bases rounded, margins entire, tips pointed. Inflorescence a raceme with lateral cymes. Flowers numerous, creamy yellow to white, trumpet-shaped, about ¼ inch wide and twice as long. Found in eastern portion of state, around ponds, creeks, rivers and other waterways.

Colocasia esculenta   ARACEAE
Elephant's ear, taro, dasheen
Banks of rivers, streams, creeks, ponds, lakes, and other bodies of water. Spring, summer, fall. Common.

An introduced, stoloniferous, stemless perennial, from an underground corm, to 6 feet tall. Leaves peltate, on petioles longer than leaves, ovate to slender cordate, to 28 inches long and 16 inches wide, margins entire and wavy, basal lobes rounded. Flowers in a 14-inch-long spadix surrounded by an orange spathe. Origin is unknown, most likely from southeastern Asia. Widely cultivated for food and used as an ornamental. Has escaped cultivation and can be found throughout state.

Orontium aquaticum ARACEAE
Golden-club, neverwet
Shallow ponds, lakes, slow-moving streams,
bogs, swamps. Spring, summer. Rare.

An aquatic, rhizomatous perennial to 24 inches tall when
in flower. Leaves emergent or floating depending upon
depth of water, on petioles often longer than blades,
oblong-elliptic, to 12 inches long and 4 inches wide, margins entire. Flowers at tip of a 2-foot-long spadix, spathe
absent, numerous, tiny, yellow, giving the common name
golden-club. Found in a few counties in Southeast Texas.

Echeandia chandleri ASPARAGACEAE
Lila de los llanos, lily of the prairie, Chandler's craglily
Coastal plains. Spring, summer. Rare.

An erect perennial from corms, with grasslike leaves and
a flowering stalk to nearly 4 feet tall. Basal leaves to 20
inches long and ½ inch wide, linear to narrowly elliptic, margins entire, often with short hairs. Upper leaves
similar to basal, but half as long and wide. Flowers in a
branched raceme to 30 inches tall, yellow, with 3 sepals
and 3 petals, about 1½ inches in diameter, anthers not
joined. Found in a few counties along the lower coast
from Nueces County into Mexico. Similar in habit to
Echeandia texensis, but anthers in *E. texensis* are joined.
Genus named after Pedro Echeandía, a late 18th- to early
19th-century Mexican botanist.

Echeandia flavescens ASPARAGACEAE
Torrey's craglily, crag lily
Desert upper-elevation grasslands, open
woodlands. Summer. Uncommon.

An erect perennial with grasslike basal leaves, plants to
2 feet tall when in flower. Basal leaves linear, to 16 inches
long, margins denticulate, ciliate. Upper leaves similar to basal, about one-third their length, tapering to a
point. Typically 1 or 2 inflorescences, which may or may
not be branched, to 2 feet tall. Yellow flowers, 3 per node,
just over 1 inch in diameter. Only *Echeandia* species in
mountains of West Texas; found along woodland edges,
or in open areas at higher elevations. Isolated populations
in Edwards Plateau. Specific epithet of Latin origin and
means "yellowish" or "becoming yellow."

Echeandia texensis ASPARAGACEAE
Lily de los lomas, lily of the hills, Texas crag lily
Open areas within coastal scrubland. Spring, fall. Rare.

An erect perennial with grasslike basal leaves and an inflorescence to 3+ feet tall. Basal leaves to 9 per plant, linear to elliptic, to 2 feet long and ¾ inch wide, margins denticulate. Upper leaves similar to basal, tapering to a point, about one-third length of basal leaves. Flowers in branched, panicle-like racemes to 3 feet tall, yellow, with 3 sepals and 3 petals (which may be reflexed), about 1 inch in diameter, anthers joined. Known to occur on clay hills (lomas) along lower Texas coast in Cameron County. Similar to *Echeandia chandleri*, but distinct differences in anther morphology make the species easy to identify.

Manfreda sileri ASPARAGACEAE
Siler's tuberose
Mesquite and acacia shrubland.
Spring, summer. Uncommon.

A perennial with globose rhizomes and underground stem. Leaves spreading, lax, in a rosette to 3 feet in diameter, each leaf straplike, primarily green with varying degrees of dark brown to purple spotting, to 18 inches long and nearly 2 inches wide, margins toothed. Depending upon location or amount of sunlight, leaves can be flat in heavy shade or channeled and undulate in full sun. Scape to 7 feet tall, with final 12 inches bearing crowded yellow, funnel- to bell-shaped flowers, filaments erect. Found in South Texas shrublands. Similar to *Manfreda variegata* but filaments are not wide-spreading in *M. sileri*, and *M. variegata* usually has maroon flowers.

Schoenolirion croceum ASPARAGACEAE
Swamp candle, sunnybells
Wet savannas and fields, bogs, wet-marshy
pinelands. Spring. Uncommon.

An erect, bulbous perennial with flowering scapes to 12+ inches tall. Basal leaves 3–7 per plant, grasslike, to 12+ inches long. Scapes slender, terminating in an open raceme, pedicels to ¾ inch long. Flowers yellow, with 6 tepals, oblong-elliptic, with a distinct green stripe along outside surface, ovary superior, stigma unlobed. Found in wet, sandy soils from Newton County, west to Bastrop County.

Amblyolepis setigera   ASTERACEAE
Huisache daisy, butterfly daisy, honey daisy
Grasslands, fields, open areas, roadsides.
Winter, spring, summer, fall. Common.

An erect, weakly branched annual to about 20 inches tall.
Leaves alternate, glabrous. Lower leaves sessile and oblanceolate, middle and upper leaves clasping stem and ovate,
margins entire. Flowering heads solitary, terminal. Ray
florets yellow, to about ¾ inch long and deeply toothed.
Disc florets yellow, numerous, to about ¼ inch long.
Widespread throughout central portion of state, south
into Mexico, west into eastern Chihuahuan Desert and
north into Panhandle. Absent east of Edwards Plateau.

Bahia absinthifolia   ASTERACEAE
Bahia, hairyseed bahia, yerba raton
Open shrublands, rocky slopes, roadsides, other
open areas. Winter, spring, summer, fall. Common.

A perennial with erect to spreading stems, branching
from base, to 16 inches tall. Leaves variable, lanceolate,
with entire to toothed margins or ternately lobed, lobes
linear to oblong, 2 inches long and ¾ inch wide. Flowering heads in terminal branches, with 5 heads per branch,
each head to 2 inches broad with 13 yellow ray florets and
80+ disc florets. Found from El Paso south to Brownsville. Grows in various habitats and soil types.

Bahia pedata   ASTERACEAE
Bluntscale bahia
Grasslands, fields, meadows, open shrublands and
woodlands. Spring, summer, fall. Common.

An erect annual with a single stem to 3½ feet tall. Leaves
variable, predominantly alternate, with opposite leaves
uppermost along stem, largest leaves to 4⅓ inches long,
margins entire. Lower leaves 1- or 2-ternately lobed; upper
leaves simple, or 1-ternately lobed. Flowering heads solitary, about 1 inch wide, on terminal peduncles, with 15
yellow ray florets and 80+ yellow disc florets. Found in
westernmost portion of Texas, west of Pecos River, and
in northern Panhandle. Genus named after Juan Fran-
cisco Bahi (1775–1841), a Spanish botany professor and
naturalist.

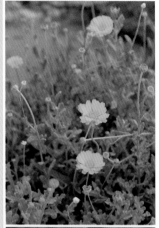

Baileya multiradiata   ASTERACEAE
Desert marigold, desert baileya, paper daisy
Desert washes, open shrublands, rocky
slopes, sparse grasslands, other open areas.
Winter, spring, summer, fall. Common.

An erect, multistemmed, woolly perennial to 3 feet tall.
Leaves on petioles 1½ inches long, ovate, palmately or
pinnately lobed, 4 inches long and 2 inches wide. Flowering heads solitary, on 12-inch-long peduncles, bright yellow, about 2 inches in diameter. Widespread throughout
West Texas, west of Pecos River, with no preference to soil
type or elevation. Blooms all year throughout its range
and is available in the nursery trade.

Berlandiera betonicifolia   ASTERACEAE
Green eyes, Texas green eyes, broochflower
Openings and edges of oak-pine woodlands.
Spring, summer, fall. Common.

An erect perennial with branched stems to 3½ feet tall.
Coarse, ovate leaves are to 4 inches long and half as wide,
but extremely variable in size, margins serrate or crenate.
Flowering heads to 2 inches wide in panicles or corymbs
held above leaves. Ray florets are deep yellow to orangish yellow, while disc florets are red to maroon. Found in
eastern portion of state, growing in shady to partial shady
areas with sandy loam soils. Genus named after Jean
Louis Berlandier, a French-Swiss physician who collected
plants in Texas and Mexico during early to mid-1800s.

Berlandiera lyrata   ASTERACEAE
Chocolate flower, chocolate daisy, lyreleaf daisy
Grasslands, prairies, open shrublands, roadsides and
other open areas. Spring, summer, fall, winter. Common.

An erect to decumbent perennial with multiple, leafy
stems to 2 feet long. Leaves alternate, oblanceolate or
spatulate, sometimes lyrate to pinnatifid, to 6+ inches
long, margins scalloped. Flowering heads in loose corymbs, each head to 2 inches wide. Ray florets 8± per head,
yellow-orange, underside with reddish purple veins, disc
florets numerous and reddish brown. Found in western portion of state, from Panhandle south to southern
Edwards Plateau, west into New Mexico and northern
Mexico.

Berlandiera pumila   ASTERACEAE
Soft green-eyes
Prairies, fields, grasslands, open shrub
and woodlands, roadsides and other open
areas. Spring, summer. Common.

An erect, multistemmed perennial with branching stems
to 3+ feet tall. Leaves alternate, on petioles to 1 inch
long, oblong or oval or ovate, up 3 inches long and about
three-fourths as wide, bases truncate, margins crenate,
blades velvety. Flowering heads in panicles, each head
about 2 inches wide, with 8± yellow-orange ray florets and
numerous reddish brown disc florets. Widespread in eastern third of Texas, from Coastal Bend north into Oklahoma, east to Louisiana.

Bidens aristosa   ASTERACEAE
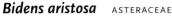
Tickseed sunflower
Grasslands, prairies, woodlands, marshes, roadsides
and other open areas. Summer, fall. Common.

An erect annual with leafy, branching stems to 2 feet
tall. Leaves opposite, on petioles to 1¼ inches long, lanceolate to linear, to 4 inches long and 1¼ inches wide, 3-
to 7-lobed, margins serrate, ciliate. Flowering heads in
corymbs, on peduncles to 3+ inches long, each head to 2
inches wide with 8± yellow ray florets and to 40+ yellow
disc florets. Found in eastern third of Texas.

Bidens bipinnata   ASTERACEAE
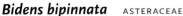
Spanish needles
Fields, brush and woodlands, forests.
Summer, fall. Common.

An erect annual with glabrous, angular, weakly branched
stems to 5 feet tall. Leaves opposite, on petioles to 2
inches long, 2- to 3-pinnate, to 8 inches long and 4 inches
wide, lobes ovate to lanceolate, margins dentate. Flowering heads solitary, each head about ¼ inch wide. Ray
florets lacking or to 5 per head, yellow, ⅛ inch long. Disc
florets numerous, orange-yellow. Distributed throughout state. Absent in far South Texas. Weak in Panhandle,
Central and West Texas.

Bidens tenuisecta ASTERACEAE
Slimlobe beggarticks
Fields, meadows, woodlands. Summer, fall. Rare.

An erect annual with a single branching stem to 16+ inches tall. Leaves opposite, deltate to ovate, to 2 inches long and 1½ inches wide, 1- to 3-pinnate, lobes linear, margins entire or ciliate. Flowering heads solitary, to ½ inch wide, with to 6 yellow ray florets per head, or absent, and 20± yellow disc florets. Found in Culberson County, Guadalupe Mountains National Park.

Borrichia frutescens ASTERACEAE
Bushy seaside tansy, sea daisy, sea ox-eye
Dunes, lomas, salt marshes, river banks.
Spring, summer. Common.

An erect, rhizomatous perennial with branching, resinous stems to 4+ feet tall. Leaves opposite, stiff, obovate to oblanceolate, to 4 inches long and 1½ inches wide, bases toothed, margins dentate to serrate, surfaces pubescent. Flowering heads solitary, on peduncles to 2¾ inches long, each head ¾ inch wide. Yellow ray florets to 30 per head, disc florets 75 and brown. Primarily found along coastal Texas; however, can be inland in saline soils to Webb County and in desert marshes in Pecos County.

Bradburia pilosa ASTERACEAE
Soft goldenaster
Fields, prairies, roadsides and other open areas. Spring, summer. Common.

An erect annual with a single, branching, pubescent stem to 30+ inches tall. Basal leaves oblanceolate, to 4 inches long and 1 inch wide, margins entire to dentate, surfaces pilose. Upper leaves linear to elliptic, becoming smaller farther up stem, margins entire to slightly dentate. Flowering heads solitary or numerous, on peduncles to 2¾ inches long, each head about 1 inch wide, with 16± yellow ray florets and numerous yellow disc florets. Found throughout eastern third of Texas, from Coastal Bend north into Oklahoma, east to Louisiana. Not found on Edwards Plateau.

Brickellia eupatorioides ASTERACEAE
False boneset
Fields, prairies, open brush and woodlands, roadsides
and other open areas. Spring, summer, fall. Common.

An erect, much-branched perennial with stems to 4+ feet
tall. Leaves opposite, occasionally alternate, sometimes
on petioles to ½ inch long, lanceolate, linear to oblong, to
4 inches long and 1½ inches wide, margins entire, dentate, or revolute. Flowering heads in panicles or corymbs,
each head ½ inch long and ¼ inch wide, with 35 pale yellow to greenish yellow to pink to maroon disc florets, ray
florets absent. Widespread throughout most of state; lacking in South Texas and Coastal Plain.

Calyptocarpus vialis ASTERACEAE
Straggler daisy, horseherb
Urban and suburban areas, oak-juniper woodlands.
Winter, spring, summer, fall. Common.

A prostrate to decumbent perennial with branching
stems to 18+ inches long, spreading from a central rootstock. Leaves opposite, on short petioles, ovate to deltate
to lanceolate, margins toothed, surfaces rough. Flowering heads solitary from upper leaf axils, each head about
¼ inch wide with to 8 orange-yellow ray florets and to 20
yellow disc florets. A common lawn weed. Often found in
shade of oaks and other deciduous trees. Expect to find
across most of Texas. Absent in Panhandle.

Centaurea melitensis ASTERACEAE
Malta star-thistle, tocalote
Fields, pastures, brush and woodlands, roadsides and
other disturbed areas. Spring, summer. Common.

An introduced, erect annual with single or multiple
branching, prickly stems to 3 feet tall. Lower and basal
leaves oblong to oblanceolate, to 6 inches long, margins
entire to dentate or pinnately lobed. Upper leaves alternate, linear to oblong, to 2 inches long, margins entire to
dentate. Flowering heads solitary or in small corymbs,
each head about ⅓ inch wide and with numerous yellow florets, involucre bracts with spines less than ¾ inch
long. This noxious weed is frequent throughout Central
Texas, west into New Mexico, south into Mexico. Often
displaces native species.

197

Centaurea solstitialis ASTERACEAE
Yellow starthistle, Barnaby starthistle
Fields, pastures, roadsides and other disturbed
areas. Summer, fall. Locally common.

An introduced, erect annual with a single stem branching from base, to 3 feet tall. Leaves alternate. Lower leaves linear to oblong, to 5 inches long, margins lobed. Upper leaves smaller, margins entire. Flowering heads solitary, occasionally in open clusters, to ¾ inch wide, disc florets numerous and yellow, ray florets absent, involucre bracts with central spines more than ¾ inch long. Similar to *Centaurea melitensis*, but roundish in shape and with longer spines on flowering heads. Found along I-35 corridor, from Dallas–Fort Worth south to San Antonio, spreading along roadsides and expected elsewhere in state.

Coreopsis basalis ASTERACEAE
Golden-wave, goldenmane tickseed
Fields, meadows, grasslands, prairies, open
brush and woodlands, roadsides and other
open areas. Spring, summer. Common.

An erect annual with branching stems to 2+ feet tall. Leaves opposite, found on lower ¾ of plant, on petioles 1½ inches long on lower leaves, shorter to sessile on upper leaves, pinnately lobed with 9+ lobes, each lobe linear to elliptic, to 2 inches long and ¾ inch wide. Flowering heads on peduncles to 6 inches long, either solitary or in loose corymbs. Individual heads about 1¾ inches wide with 8± yellow ray florets, often with a brownish red or maroon base of varying widths, tips of ray florets lobed or dentate, disc florets reddish brown, numerous. Found throughout Central Texas, east to Houston area, north to nearly Oklahoma, and into South Texas.

Coreopsis gladiata (*C. linifolia*) ASTERACEAE
Texas tickseed
Wet savannas, fields and prairies, roadside ditches
and other low, wet areas. Summer, fall. Uncommon.

An erect perennial with slender, branching stems to 2+ feet tall. Leaves alternate or opposite, elliptic or lanceolate or linear, to 4 inches long and 1 inch wide, occasionally lobed, margins entire. Flowering heads either solitary or in loose corymbs held on slender peduncles to 4+ inches long, each head about 2 inches wide with 8± lobed, yellow ray florets and numerous reddish brown disc florets. Found in far Southeast Texas, north to Caddo Lake area.

Coreopsis intermedia   ASTERACEAE
Goldenwave tickseed
Fields, meadows, open brush and woodlands,
roadsides. Spring, summer. Rare.

An erect perennial with glabrous, branching stems to
2+ feet tall. Leaves opposite, upper leaves sessile, lower
leaves on petioles 1½ inches long, oblong to ovate, to 3
inches long and ¾ inch wide, margins entire. Flowering heads solitary or in loose corymbs on peduncles to
10 inches long, each head about 1¾ inches wide with 8±
lobed, yellow ray florets and numerous yellow disc florets.
Found in open areas of East Texas, north into Arkansas
and Oklahoma, east into Louisiana.

Coreopsis lanceolata   ASTERACEAE
Lanceleaf coreopsis, lanceleaf tickseed, sand coreopsis
Fields, prairies, grasslands, roadsides and other
open areas. Spring, summer, fall. Common.

An erect, multistemmed perennial with branching stems
to 3+ feet tall. Basal leaves on petioles 4 inches long, elliptic to oblanceolate, with 3–5 lobes, to 6 inches long and
1 inch wide, margins entire. Upper leaves opposite, sessile, similar to basal leaves in shape but smaller. Flowering heads solitary on peduncles to 12 inches long. Each
head to 3 inches wide with 8± yellow, 4-lobed, dentate ray
florets, and with numerous yellow disc florets. Found in
eastern third of Texas.

Coreopsis nuecensoides   ASTERACEAE
Rio Grande tickseed, crown tickseed, sand coreopsis
Prairies, fields, grasslands, open mesquite and oak
woodlands, roadsides. Spring. Locally common.

An erect perennial with multiple, branching stems to 16+
inches tall. Leaves mostly basal, on petioles 3 inches long,
to 3 inches long and 1½ inches wide, with 3–5 lobes, each
lobe rounded to ovate to lanceolate, middle lobe larger,
margins entire. Upper leaves similar to basal but smaller,
opposite, and sessile. Flowering heads solitary at end of
slender peduncles to 6 inches long, each head to 2 inches
wide, with 8± ray florets. Each floret 3-lobed, yellow with
yellow-orange base, often with red flecks near base, disc
florets numerous, yellow-orange. Found along coastal
plain from Cameron County to Liberty County.

Coreopsis tinctoria ASTERACEAE
Goldenwave, golden tickseed, plains coreopsis
Fields, prairies, grasslands, open brush
and woodlands, roadsides and other open
areas. Spring, summer. Common.

An erect annual with a single branching stem to 3+ feet
tall. Leaves alternate, sometimes opposite, to 6 inches
long and 4 inches wide, 1- to 3-pinnate, with linear to
lanceolate lobes. Flowering heads solitary or in loose
corymbs on peduncles to 6+ inches long, each head to 2
inches wide. Ray florets 8± per head, yellow with red to
reddish brown bases, the darker color covering to half the
floret. Disc florets numerous, red to reddish brown. Most
widespread *Coreopsis* species in Texas. Found throughout state.

Engelmannia peristenia ASTERACEAE
Engelmann's daisy, cutleaf daisy
Fields, meadows, grasslands, open brush
and woodlands, roadsides and other open
areas. Spring, summer, fall. Common.

An erect, branching, multistemmed perennial with
rough leaves and stems to 24+ inches tall. Leaves alternate, sessile above, on petioles below, oblong to lanceolate, pinnate to bipinnate, lower leaves to 12 inches long,
margins entire or toothed, tips rounded. Flowering heads
in open terminal corymbs, each head 1¼ inches wide.
Ray florets yellow, notched, curling backward at ends
throughout day, to 9 per head. Disc florets yellow, numerous. Widespread throughout Texas. Weak to absent in
deep East Texas.

Gaillardia aestivalis ASTERACEAE
Lanceleaf blanket flower, prairie gaillardia
Grasslands, meadows, prairies, open woodlands and
forests, other open areas. Spring, summer, fall. Common.

An erect perennial with a single, much-branched stem to
2 feet tall. Leaves alternate, on petioles to 1¼ inches long,
elliptic to spatulate, to 2⅓ inches long and just under 1
inch wide. Flowering heads 2½ inches in diameter on
peduncles to 8 inches long. Ray florets to 15 per head,
yellow to cream to red or a mixture of these colors. Disc
florets numerous, brown or rusty brown. Widespread
throughout state, lacking in far western region and weak
in Panhandle. Frequent in open areas, especially along
roadsides, late spring into summer.

Gaillardia coahuilensis ASTERACEAE
Bandanna daisy, Mexican fire-wheel
Open shrublands, sparse grasslands, roadsides
and other open areas. Spring, summer. Rare.

An erect annual with a single branching stem to 2+ feet
tall. Leaves alternate, ovate to lanceolate, to 3 inches long
and 1 inch wide. Lower leaves on petioles just over 1 inch
long, margins lobed or toothed. Upper leaves lacking
petioles to point of clasping, margins entire. Flowering
heads to 2 inches in diameter, on peduncles to 8 inches
long. Ray florets to 13, yellow to orange along the outer
portion, yellow to red along inner. Disc florets numerous,
from yellow to red. Rare in Texas but easily found around
Langtry during years with well-timed rains. Ranges from
Brewster County, south into Maverick County, and prefers limestone soils.

Gaillardia multiceps ASTERACEAE
Gyp Indian blanket, onion blanketflower
Open shrublands, sparse grasslands, roadsides, other
open areas. Spring, summer, fall. Locally common.

An erect perennial, branching from a woody base to 18
inches tall. Leaves occurring predominantly in lower half
of plant, linear to thinly spatulate, to 2¼ inches long and
about ⅓ inch wide. Flowering heads about 1½ inches in
diameter, solitary, on peduncles 4+ inches long, ray florets yellow, disc florets numerous, yellow with brownish purple tips. Found on gypseous soils throughout the
Trans-Pecos. Often seen along roadsides south of Guadalupe Mountains. Specific epithet means "multiheaded."

Gaillardia pinnatifida ASTERACEAE
Red dome blanketflower, blanket flower, yellow gaillardia
Grasslands, open desert brush, canyons,
washes, roadsides, other open areas.
Spring, summer, fall. Common.

An erect perennial, occasionally rhizomatous, with stems
to 20 inches tall. Leaves mostly basal or restricted to lower
third of plant, on petioles 2 inches long, oblanceolate
to spatulate, 4¼ inches long and to 1 inch wide, bristly
to pubescent, margins pinnatifid, occasionally toothed
or entire. Flowering heads to 2 inches in diameter, on
peduncles to 10+ inches long. Ray florets absent or to 15
per head, yellow, but may have red at tip or base of floret.
Disc florets numerous, usually yellow with purple tips.
Frequent in western portion of state and throughout Panhandle. Absent elsewhere in Texas.

201

Grindelia lanceolata   ASTERACEAE
Narrowleaf gumweed, fall gumweed
Prairies, grasslands, fields, open brush and woodlands, roadsides, other open areas. Summer, fall. Common.

An erect biennial or perennial with glabrous, branching stems to 5+ feet tall, leaves and stems glandular, sticky to the touch. Leaves triangular, ovate to lanceolate or linear, to 4 inches long and ¾ inch wide, margins serrate to dentate. Flowering heads in corymbs, each head about 1½ inches wide, with 35± yellow-orange ray florets and numerous disc florets the same color. Found mostly in Central Texas, north into Oklahoma, southeast to Houston area.

Grindelia squarrosa   ASTERACEAE
Curlycup gumweed, curlytop gumweed
Fields, meadows, grasslands, open brushlands, roadsides, other open areas. Summer, fall. Common.

An erect biennial or perennial with sticky-glandular stems to 3+ feet tall. Leaves alternate, oval, ovate, spatulate, lanceolate or linear, to 3 inches long and to 1½ inches wide, bases clasping, margins crenate to serrate, tips acute or obtuse. Flowering heads in loose to crowded corymbs, each head to 1¼ inches wide, ray florets yellow, to 30+ per head, disc florets yellow, numerous. Most common gumweed in Texas. Absent only in eastern fourth and southern portion of state.

Helenium amarum var. *amarum*
ASTERACEAE
Bitterweed, yellow sneezeweed, yellowdicks
Fields, meadows, pastures, grasslands, open brush and woodlands, roadsides, other open areas. Spring, summer, fall. Common.

An erect, much-branched, leafy annual to 2 feet tall. Basal leaves linear to ovate, margins entire or slightly toothed. Upper leaves linear, to 3 inches long, entire. Flowering heads numerous, often more than 100 per plant, in panicles, each head to 1 inch wide, ray florets 8± and yellow, disc florets numerous and yellow. Found in eastern half of state, often in disturbed areas.

Helenium amarum var. badium

ASTERACEAE
Bitterweed
Fields, meadows, pastures, grasslands, open
brush and woodlands, roadsides, other open
areas. Spring, summer, fall. Common.

An erect, much-branched, leafy annual to 2 feet tall.
Basal leaves linear to ovate, margins pinnatifid, upper
leaves linear, to 3 inches long, entire. Flowering heads
numerous, often more than 100 per plant, in panicles,
each head to 1 inch wide, with 8± yellow ray florets and
numerous reddish brown disc florets. Found in eastern
half of state. Almost identical to var. *amarum*; however,
var. *badium* has brown disc florets and slightly different
leaf morphology.

Helenium drummondii   ASTERACEAE

Fringed sneezeweed
Woodlands, bogs, edges of swamps,
creeks, ponds, roadside ditches, areas with
damp soils. Spring. Uncommon.

An erect perennial with a single slender, unbranched,
winged stem to 2 feet tall. Basal leaves obovate to oblanceolate, 8+ inches long, margins entire, occasionally undulate or serrate. Middle and upper leaves similar, thinner.
Flowering heads solitary, at end of peduncles to 12 inches
long, each head about 3 inches wide and ¾ inch tall, with
30± yellow and toothed ray florets and hundreds of yellow
disc florets. Found in Southeast Texas.

Helenium elegans   ASTERACEAE

Pretty sneezeweed
Creek and river beds, washes, ditches, pond banks,
other wet areas. Spring, summer, fall. Common.

An erect, branched annual with glabrous, winged stems
to 4+ feet tall. Leaves alternate, sessile, lanceolate to elliptic to linear, to 3+ inches long, margins entire, serrate,
toothed, or lobed. Flowering heads in panicles, often
100+ per plant, each head about 1 inch wide. Ray florets
up to 17, lobed, yellow to reddish brown or yellow at tips
and reddish brown at base, reddish brown disc florets in
the hundreds. Found in Central Texas, west into Chihuahuan Desert.

Helenium flexuosum   ASTERACEAE
Purplehead sneezeweed
Creek and river banks, wet savannas, fields and
grasslands, roadside ditches and other low,
wet areas. Spring, summer, fall. Common.

An erect perennial with a single, winged, branching
stem. Leaves sessile, to 3 inches long and 1 inch wide.
Basal leaves oblanceolate to spatulate, margins entire or
serrate. Middle leaves becoming lanceolate. Upper leaves
linear, margins entire. Flowering heads in panicles, each
head about 1 inch wide. Ray florets to 14, lobed, yellow to
reddish brown to purple. Disc florets numerous, purple.
Found in eastern third of Texas.

Helenium microcephalum   ASTERACEAE
Little-head sneezeweed
Creek and river beds and banks, edges of ponds,
floodplains, roadside ditches, marshes, playas and
other low, wet areas. Spring, summer, fall. Common.

An erect annual with a single, winged, branching stem to
4+ feet tall. Leaves alternate, sessile, elliptic, to 3 inches
long, margins serrate to undulate. Flowering heads
rounded, in panicles, to 300+ heads per plant, each head
about ⅜ inch wide. Ray florets up to 13, yellow to red or
yellow and red, lobed, ¼ inch long, deflexed. Disc florets
numerous, green to brownish red. Widely distributed
across state. Absent in far eastern Texas. Usually an indicator of wet soils.

Helianthus angustifolius   ASTERACEAE
Swamp sunflower, narrowleaf sunflower
Wet savannas, floodplains, river bottoms, roadside
ditches and other low, wet areas. Fall. Common.

An erect perennial with a branching, pubescent stem to
5+ feet tall. Leaves opposite and alternate, sessile, lanceolate to linear, to 6 inches long and ¼ inch wide, bases
cuneate, margins entire to revolute, upper surfaces with
stiff hairs. Flowering heads numerous, to 2 inches wide,
on peduncles to 6 inches long, each head with up to 20
yellow ray florets and numerous dark brown disc florets.
Found in eastern third of Texas, around water or in wet
soils, occasionally in dry areas. Prefers shaded areas such
as edges of woodlands. Narrow leaves and a late bloom
period aid in identification.

Helianthus annuus   ASTERACEAE
Common sunflower
Fields, open brush and woodlands, roadsides,
fallow fields, urban and suburban areas and other
disturbed areas. Summer, fall. Common.

An erect annual with a stout, single branching stem to
9+ feet tall. Stem reddish brown with short, stiff hairs.
Leaves alternate, on petioles to 7 inches long, lance-ovate
to ovate, bases cuneate to cordate, margins serrate, lower
surface of blade rough. Flower heads numerous, to 6+
inches in diameter, with 15+ yellow ray florets and 150+
reddish brown or yellow disc florets. Found in just about
every county in Texas.

Helianthus argophyllus   ASTERACEAE
Silverleaf sunflower
Prairies, grasslands, fields, open shrublands.
Spring, summer. Common.

An erect perennial with a branching stem to 9+ feet tall,
leaves and stems covered with long silver to white hairs.
Leaves alternate, on petioles to 4 inches long, ovate to
lance-ovate, to 10 inches long and 8 inches wide, bases
truncate to slightly cordate, margins entire to serrulate,
leaf surfaces tomentose, soft to the touch. Flowering
heads to 3½+ inches wide, with 20± yellow ray florets and
numerous reddish brown disc florets. Found in sandy
soils along Texas coast from Mexico north to Houston
area, inland following San Antonio and Guadalupe River
drainages. Specific epithet refers to silvery (*argo*) leaves
(*phyllus*).

Helianthus ciliaris   ASTERACEAE
Blueweed, Texas blueweed, blueweed sunflower
Banks of ponds, canals, rivers, and creeks,
roadside ditches, agricultural fields, other
disturbed areas. Summer, fall. Common.

An erect, rhizomatous perennial with glabrous or glaucous stems to 30 inches tall. Leaves opposite, sessile,
linear to lanceolate, to 3 inches long and ¾ inch wide,
bases cuneate, margins entire or serrate, ciliate, blades
glaucous and glabrous to pubescent. Flowering heads on
peduncles to 5 inches long, several, each head about ¾
inch wide, ray florets yellow and up to 18, disc florets reddish brown and 35+. Widely considered a weed. Found in
western half of state, from Brownsville north into Panhandle and west to El Paso; prefers wet soils.

205

Helianthus debilis ASTERACEAE
Cucumberleaf sunflower, beach sunflower
Grasslands, fields, open brush and woodlands,
dunes, roadsides and other open areas.
Spring, summer, fall. Common.

An erect to decumbent, much-branched annual with
pubescent stems to 6 feet tall. Leaves alternate, on petioles to 2½ inches long, deltate to ovate, to 5½ inches long
and 5 inches wide, bases cordate or truncate or cuneate,
margins serrate to slightly entire, blades glabrous to
pubescent. Flower heads on peduncles to 18 inches long,
each head to 2½ inches wide, with up to 20 yellow ray florets and more than 30 red or yellow disc florets. Found in
sandy soils from Brownsville north to southern edge of
Edwards Plateau, northeast into Louisiana. Specific epithet means "weak," referring to decumbent stems.

Helianthus grosseserratus ASTERACEAE
Sawtooth sunflower
Prairies, fields, open brush and woodlands, roadsides,
ditches and other open areas. Summer, fall. Uncommon.

An erect, rhizomatous perennial with glabrous to pubescent branching stems to 10+ feet tall. Leaves opposite
below, alternate above, on petioles to 2 inches long, lanceolate to lance-ovate, to 12 inches long and 3½ inches
wide, bases cuneate, margins serrate. Flowering heads
to 4 inches wide, on peduncles to 4 inches long, 3+ per
peduncle, occasionally solitary, each head with up to 20
yellow ray florets and more than 100 yellow disc florets.
Dispersed erratically across state, with clusters around
Conroe, north of Dallas, and sporadic collections elsewhere. Tends to prefer wet soils.

Helianthus hirsutus ASTERACEAE
Hairy sunflower
Fields, open brush and woodlands,
roadsides. Summer, fall. Common.

An erect, rhizomatous perennial with pubescent stems
to nearly 6 feet tall. Leaves opposite, on petioles to ¾ inch
long, lanceolate to ovate, to 7 inches long and 3 inches
wide, bases truncate or rounded or cordate, margins
serrate to entire. Flowering heads to 7, on peduncles to
2 inches long, each head to 2 inches wide with up to 15
yellow ray florets and more than 40 yellow disc florets.
Found in eastern third of state, with additional populations in southeastern portion of Edwards Plateau.

Helianthus maximiliani ASTERACEAE
Maximilian sunflower
Drainages, creek banks, roadside ditches, other
seasonally wet areas. Summer, fall. Common.

An erect, rhizomatous perennial with rough stems to
9+ feet tall. Leaves alternate, on petioles to ¾ inch long,
lanceolate, to 11 inches long and 2 inches wide, bases
cuneate, margins entire to serrulate. Flowering heads on
peduncles to 4 inches long, each head to 2½ inches wide,
with up to 25 yellow ray florets and 75+ yellow disc florets.
Common throughout Central Texas, becoming less common both east and west. Absent in South Texas. Grows in
areas with wet soils, such as depressions and swales.

Helianthus mollis ASTERACEAE
Ashy sunflower, downy sunflower
Prairies, fields, meadows, open brush and
woodlands, roadsides. Summer, fall. Uncommon.

An erect, rhizomatous perennial with branching, pubescent stems to 5+ feet tall; leaves and stems with a gray,
downy appearance. Leaves opposite, sessile, lanceolate to
ovate, to 5½ inches long and 2½ inches wide, bases round
to cordate, margins entire to serrulate. Flowering heads
on peduncles to 5 inches long, each head about 2 inches
wide, with up to 22 yellow ray florets and more than 75
yellow disc florets. Found mainly in eastern third of state,
with heaviest concentration in Southeast Texas and near
Oklahoma border. Tends to grow in small colonies.

Helianthus petiolaris ASTERACEAE
Plains sunflower, prairie sunflower
Prairies, open shrublands, roadsides, other
open areas. Summer, fall. Common.

An erect, multistemmed perennial with branching,
rough, pubescent stems to nearly 6 feet tall. Leaves alternate, on petioles to 1½ inches long, lanceolate to deltate to
ovate, to 6 inches long and 3 inches wide, bases cuneate
to truncate, margins entire, occasionally serrate, sometimes slightly cordate. Flowering heads on peduncles to
6+ inches long, each head about 2 inches in diameter,
with up to 30 yellow ray florets and 50+ reddish purple
disc florets. Widespread and common throughout Panhandle and Chihuahuan Desert regions of Texas. Weak
in Edwards Plateau and northward.

Heliomeris longifolia   ASTERACEAE
Longleaf false goldeneye, southern goldeneye
Desert shrublands, oak-pine woodlands,
roadsides. Summer, fall. Locally common.

An erect annual with reddish brown, branching stems to 3+ feet tall, stems with short, flat hairs. Leaves opposite, occasionally alternate toward ends of stems, lanceolate to linear, to 6 inches long and ⅓ inch wide, margins ciliate to entire, surfaces with rough hairs. Flowering heads on short peduncles, with up to 14 yellow ray florets (notched at tip) and more than 50 yellow disc florets. Common at elevations above 4000 feet in mountains of West Texas.

Heterotheca canescens   ASTERACEAE
Hoary golden aster, hairy golden aster
Rocky outcrops, prairies, fields, open
brushlands, roadsides and other open areas.
Spring, summer, fall. Common.

An erect, rhizomatous perennial with multiple, canescent branching stems to 2 feet tall. Lower leaves on petioles, oblanceolate, to 1½ inches long and ¼ inch wide, bases cuneate, margins entire, surfaces densely covered with silver hairs. Upper leaves shorter, sessile, linear. Flowering heads to 1 inch wide, solitary or in corymbs, with up to 22 narrow yellow ray florets and up to 50 yellow disc florets per head. Widely spread throughout most drier parts of Texas, in various habitats. Absent in East Texas.

Hymenopappus flavescens   ASTERACEAE
Yellow plainsman, collegeflower
Fields, grasslands, prairies, open brushlands, roadsides
and other open areas. Spring, summer. Common.

An erect biennial with slender or stout, branching stems to 3+ feet tall. Leaves alternate. Basal leaves bipinnate, to 6 inches long, lobes linear, ¾ inch long and ⅓ inch wide. Stem leaves similar, smaller, lobes thinner and numerous. Flowering heads in terminal corymbs, to 100 heads per stem, ray florets absent, disc florets golden yellow to pale yellow and up to 40 per head. Found throughout Panhandle and Chihuahuan Desert, often occurring in large numbers.

Hymenoxys texana ASTERACEAE
Prairie dawn, Texas prairie dawn
Open fields, meadows, prairies. Spring. Rare.

A small, erect, slender annual with single or multiple, branched or unbranched stems to 4+ inches tall. Basal leaves oblanceolate to spatulate, 3- to 5-lobed, to 1 inch long, bases tapering, margins entire to dentate, tips rounded. Stem leaves sessile, linear-lanceolate, to ½ inch long, margins entire to slightly lobed, tips acute. Flowering heads terminal, solitary or in panicles, each head ⅓–½ inch wide. Ray florets, 3-lobed, pale yellow, 6–8 per head, less than ¹⁄₁₆ inch long. Disc florets to 75+ and yellow. Found in Houston and Fort Bend Counties, in sparse vegetation with sandy, saline soils.

Krigia cespitosa ASTERACEAE
Common dwarf dandelion, weedy dwarf dandelion
Fields, pastures, open brush and woodlands, urban and suburban areas, roadsides and other open spaces. Winter, spring, summer. Common.

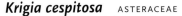

An erect or ascending annual with branching stems to 16+ inches tall. Stem leaves alternate, on petioles or sessile or clasping, oblanceolate to linear, to 6 inches long, margins entire or toothed, tips acute to obtuse. Basal leaves petiolate, oblanceolate to linear, to 6 inches long, margins entire or weakly toothed or lobed. Flowering heads solitary on slender peduncles. Heads radial, with up to 35 yellow florets. A common weed of lawns and manicured areas. Found in eastern half of Texas, west to Val Verde County.

Krigia dandelion ASTERACEAE
Potato dandelion, dandelion, potato dwarfdandelion
Fields, pastures, grasslands, open brush and woodlands, roadsides and other open spaces. Spring. Common.

An erect, rhizomatous perennial with glabrous stems to 20 inches tall. Basal leaves only, on winged petioles, linear to lanceolate or oblanceolate, to 9 inches long, margins entire or toothed or pinnately lobed, tips acute to obtuse, surfaces glabrous. Flowering heads solitary on slender peduncles arising directly from base. Heads radial with up to 34 yellow to yellow-orange florets. Found in eastern fourth of Texas, occasional farther west.

Lindheimera texana   ASTERACEAE
Texas star, Lindheimer daisy, Texas yellow star
Fields, meadows, open brush and woodlands, roadsides
and other open areas. Spring, summer. Common.

An erect annual with branching, hirsute stems to 3+ feet
tall. Leaves opposite above, alternate below, sessile, lanceolate to ovate, to 5 inches long, margins toothed to crenate below, entire above. Heads solitary or in small terminal clusters, to 1¼ inches wide with 5± bright yellow
ray florets and numerous dull yellow disc florets. Found
throughout Central Texas from Coastal Bend north into
Oklahoma, west to Pecos River, east to Houston. Named
in honor of Ferdinand Jacob Lindheimer (1801–1879),
a Texas plant collector known as the Father of Texas
Botany.

Packera glabella   ASTERACEAE
Butterweed
Woodlands, banks of streams and rivers,
meadows, roadside ditches and other
open, wet areas. Spring. Common.

An erect annual or biennial with a single, pinkish purple stem to 28+ inches tall. Stems hollow and glabrous.
Basal leaves obovate to oblanceolate, to 6 inches long and
1¼ inches wide, occasionally lobed, bases tapering, margins undulate to crenate. Stem leaves alternate, similar to
basal but smaller and clasping. Flowering heads, to 30, in
terminal umbels. Heads to 1 inch broad with up to 13 yellow ray florets and numerous yellow-orange disc florets.
Common throughout eastern third of Texas.

Packera obovata   ASTERACEAE
Roundleaf ragwort
Meadows, banks and slopes of streams, hillsides,
woodlands, roadsides. Winter, spring. Common.

An erect, stoloniferous and rhizomatous perennial with
glabrous stems to 20+ inches tall. Basal leaves on petioles, ovate or obovate or nearly round, to 4 inches long
and 3½ inches wide, bases tapering or rounded, margins
dentate or crenate or serrate. Stem leaves similar, smaller,
and clasping. Flowering heads in terminal corymbs.
Heads to ¾ inch wide with up to 13 yellow ray florets and
50+ yellow-orange disc florets. Widely dispersed in Texas;
most common in eastern third, with populations in
southern Edwards Plateau and northern portion of South
Texas; isolated populations in Culberson County.

Packera plattensis ASTERACEAE
Prairie groundsel, prairie ragwort
Prairies, meadows, open brush and woodlands,
roadsides and other open areas. Spring. Common.

An erect, rhizomatous biennial or perennial with tomentose or glabrous stems to 24+ inches tall. Basal leaves on
petioles, elliptic-ovate or slightly lyrate, to 3 inches long
and 1¼ inches wide, margins crenate or dentate or pinnately lobed, bases tapered to rounded. Stem leaves similar, smaller. Flowering heads in terminal corymbs. Heads
to 1 inch wide with 8–10 yellow ray florets and numerous
orange-yellow disc florets. Frequent in Edwards Plateau
and North-Central Texas, uncommon farther west and
into Panhandle; absent in South Texas and eastern fourth
of state.

Packera tampicana ASTERACEAE
Yellowtop, Great Plains ragwort, butterweed
Stream and river banks, open brush and woodlands,
pastures, fields, meadows, roadsides and other
open, disturbed areas. Spring. Common.

An erect, single- to multistemmed annual with glabrous
stems to 20+ inches tall. Basal leaves petiolate, oblanceolate to spatulate, pinnately lobed, to 6 inches long and
1¼ inches wide, ultimate margins entire or crenate or
dentate or lobed. Stem leaves similar, smaller, clasping.
Flowering heads in terminal corymbs with 8–13 yellow
ray florets and numerous yellow-orange disc florets. Most
common *Packera* species found in Texas, widespread
throughout state in various habitats. Weak to absent in
Panhandle. Prefers disturbed areas.

Pectis angustifolia ASTERACEAE
Limoncillo
Open desert scrub, grasslands, flatlands and
basins, roadsides. Summer, fall. Common.

A low-growing, prostrate to erect, branching annual with
glabrous stems to 8 inches tall and as wide. Leaves opposite, linear to 2 inches long, less than ⅛ inch wide, tips
acute, margins revolute with equally spaced yellow dots
along edges, upper surface with distinct ridge down middle, 2–5 pairs of bristles toward base of the leaf. Crushed
leaves produce lemony citrus scent. Flowering heads in
congested cymes. Heads with up to 8 yellow ray florets
and to 20 yellow disc florets. Frequent in Chihuahuan
Desert, less common west into Edwards Plateau and
south to Hidalgo County.

211

Pectis papposa   ASTERACEAE
Common cinchweed
Open desert scrub, grass and brushlands, flatlands and basins, roadsides. Spring, summer, fall. Common.

An erect or ascending, rounded, well-branched annual with glabrous to slightly pubescent stems to 12 inches tall and as wide. Leaves opposite, sessile, linear, to 2¾ inches long and less than 1/16 inch wide, margins revolute, gland-dotted along margin, tips acute, leaf bases with 1–3 pairs of bristles. Flowering heads in open or congested cymes. Heads with up to 8 yellow ray florets and to 34 yellow disc florets. Found in open areas in Chihuahuan Desert. Similar to *Pectis angustifolia*, but *papposa* is distinguished by leaf length, spicy scent of crushed leaves, and number of bristles.

Pericome caudata   ASTERACEAE
Tail-leaf pericome, mountain twin-leaf, yellow mistflower
Mountain woodlands and forests.
Summer, fall. Uncommon.

An erect, much-branched perennial with pubescent stems to 5+ feet tall. Leaves opposite, deltate to narrowly triangular, to nearly 3 inches long and 1½ inches wide, margins toothed, bases truncate, tips tapering to a point. Flowering heads in corymbs, ray florets absent, disc florets bright orange-yellow and to 70 per head. Found in upper elevations in mountains of West Texas, north into New Mexico, south into Mexico.

Perityle parryi   ASTERACEAE
Parry's rock daisy
Rocky slopes, cliffs, creek banks. Winter, spring, summer, fall. Uncommon.

An erect, rounded, heavily branched shrubby perennial with villose stems to 30 inches tall and as wide. Leaves opposite and alternate, on petioles to 2 inches long, cordate to slightly reniform, to 1¾+ inches long and to 2 inches wide. Leaf margins dentate, laciniate, undulate, and often shallowly 3-lobed. Flowering heads solitary or in loose few-flowered corymbs, ray florets yellow and to 20± per head, disc florets yellow and numerous to 100. Found on both limestone and igneous substrate, either growing directly in soil or on rock faces in Brewster and Presidio Counties; can be seen in Big Bend National Park and along River Road upstream from Lajitas.

Perityle rupestris var. *rupestris* ASTERACEAE
Leafy rock daisy
Igneous cliffs, rocky outcrops, ledges,
canyons. Spring, summer, fall. Rare.

An erect, often rounded, heavily branched perennial
with pubescent stems to 10+ inches tall. Leaves alternate,
ovate-cordate, reniform or triangular, to ¾ inch long and
wide, margins serrate, surfaces soft and pilose. Flowering
heads solitary or in short corymbs, each head to ⅓ inch
wide, ray florets absent, disc florets yellow and to 12 per
head. Found on igneous substrate in upper elevations of
Chihuahuan Desert.

Porophyllum scoparium ASTERACEAE
Trans-Pecos poreleaf
Washes, drainages, creek banks, open desert
scrub. Spring, summer, fall. Locally common.

An erect, branching, multistemmed perennial with
slender, glaucous stems to 3+ feet tall; often forming a
dense, rounded shrub. Leaves opposite, sessile, slender,
threadlike, to 1½ inches long, margins entire, tips acute.
Flowering heads solitary or in terminal corymbs, to ½
inch long and ⅓ inch wide, ray florets absent. Disc florets
numerous, yellow to yellow-orange, occasionally tinged
reddish brown or maroon. Found in Chihuahuan Desert
region, often in gravelly soils.

Pyrrhopappus carolinianus ASTERACEAE
Carolina desert-chicory
Fields, grasslands, prairies, open brush and
woodlands, roadsides and other open, disturbed
areas. Spring, summer. Common.

An erect, branching annual with a scapelike stem to
20+ inches tall when in flower. Leaves alternate, lanceolate, to 8 inches long and ½ inch wide, margins dentate,
occasionally pinnately lobed. Flowering heads in loose
corymbs, occasionally solitary. Heads radial to 2 inches
broad, ligulate florets only, pale yellow, to 150+ florets
per head. Found throughout eastern third of Texas, from
Coastal Bend north into Oklahoma; a common lawn
weed easily found in urban and suburban areas.

Rayjacksonia phyllocephala ASTERACEAE
Gulf Coast camphor daisy, camphor daisy
Open brushlands, salt flats, dunes. Spring,
summer, fall, occasionally winter. Common.

An annual to 3 feet tall with somewhat woody base, heavily branched. Leaves oblong to oblanceolate, 1½ inches long and ½ inch wide, margins coarsely serrate. Flowering heads in upper axils, sessile or nearly so. Surrounding leaves surpassing heads. Heads to 2 inches broad with yellow ray and disc florets. Found along the coast from Mexico to Louisiana, occasionally farther inland in sandy soils. A host plant for *Orobanche ludoviciana*.

Rudbeckia amplexicaulis ASTERACEAE
Clasping coneflower
Banks of creeks, ponds, rivers, lakes, marshes,
ephemeral pools, roadside ditches and other
low, wet areas. Spring, summer. Common.

An erect, branching annual with a single, glabrous, glaucous stem to 3+ feet tall. Leaves alternate, elliptic, lanceolate, oblong, or ovate, to 6 inches long and 2½ inches wide, margins entire to serrate to crenate, bases clasping. Flowering heads solitary or in open corymbs. Heads to 1½ inches tall and nearly as wide. Ray florets yellow, with maroon to reddish brown spots at the base, to 10+ per head. Disc florets numerous, brown. Clasping coneflower grows in eastern half of Texas; expect elsewhere, as this species was photographed in eastern Edwards County.

Rudbeckia grandiflora ASTERACEAE
Large coneflower, rough coneflower
Prairies, fields, meadows, open woodlands, roadsides
and other open areas. Spring, summer. Common.

An erect perennial to 4+ feet tall when in flower, hairs (usually stiff) typically lacking on lower stem and present above. Roots fibrous. Leaves elliptic to lanceolate to ovate, to 6 inches long and 4 inches wide, margins entire or weakly serrate, bases rounded to cuneate, surfaces with stiff, straight, appressed hairs. Basal leaves on long petioles, upper leaves on short petioles to sessile. Flowering heads usually solitary, terminal, to 3+ inches long with 25 yellow ray florets and greenish yellow to maroon disc florets numerous (in the hundreds). Common in eastern Texas. Named in honor of Olaus Rudbeck (1630–1702) a Swedish professor of medicine.

Rudbeckia hirta   ASTERACEAE
Brown-eyed Susan, black-eyed Susan
Fields, prairies, meadows, open brush and
woodlands, roadsides. Spring, summer. Common.

An erect annual to perennial with branching stems to
nearly 3 feet in height, stems leafy below, pubescent in
upper stem. Lower leaves oblanceolate, upper leaves elliptic, margins entire to serrate at tips, stiff hairs throughout.
Flowering heads solitary or to 5 in loose corymbs. Heads
with 16 yellow to yellow-orange ray florets, often with a
maroon spot at base, or floret may be mostly maroon.
Brownish purple disc florets 500+. Widespread throughout eastern half of Texas, expected elsewhere as this species is commonly included in wildflower seed mixes.

Rudbeckia maxima   ASTERACEAE
Great coneflower, cabbage coneflower, giant coneflower
Wet fields, savannas, prairies, open brush and
woodlands, roadside ditches and other wet
areas. Spring, summer. Locally common.

An erect, rhizomatous perennial with glaucous leaves
and stems to 8+ feet tall. Basal leaves large, fleshy, cab-
bagelike, elliptic to ovate, to 20+ inches long and 6 inches
wide. Stem leaves elliptic to ovate, leathery, reducing in
size up the stem, margins entire to dentate. Flowering
heads either solitary or in corymbs. To 20 yellow ray florets, to 3⅓ inches long and ½ inch wide, lax. Reddish
brown to maroon disc florets in the hundreds. Found in
eastern third of Texas, often forming large colonies.

Rudbeckia scabrifolia   ASTERACEAE
Roughleaf coneflower
Hillside bogs, seeps. Spring, summer, fall. Rare.

An erect, rhizomatous perennial with glabrous stems to
6+ feet tall. Leaves alternate, elliptic to lanceolate, blades
scabrous. Basal leaves on petioles 14 inches long, to 10+
inches long and 6 inches wide, margins serrate or entire
and/or undulate, bases rounded or tapering, tips acute.
Stem leaves becoming sessile, to 5 inches long, reduced
in length farther up the stem. Flowering heads, 2–11 in
loose panicles. Heads to 1 inch tall and ¾ inch wide, ray
florets to 15 and yellow, disc florets to 400+. Found in hillside pitcher plant bogs in mixed pine-hardwood forest of
deep East Texas.

215

Rudbeckia texana   ASTERACEAE
Texas coneflower
Prairies, fields, pastures, grasslands, openings in
woodlands, roadside ditches and other low, wet
areas. Spring, summer. Locally common.

An erect, rhizomatous perennial with stems to 6+ feet
tall. Basal leaves on long petioles, elliptic to lanceolate,
to 6 inches long and 3¾ inches wide, margins entire to
serrate, bases cuneate, tips acute, surfaces leathery and
somewhat glaucous. Stem leaves similar, smaller, sessile.
Flowering head solitary or to 5 in loose corymbs. Heads
with up to 16 yellow, lax ray florets, to 2 inches long; 500+
brownish red disc florets. Found in Southeast Texas,
often in large colonies.

Sanvitalia ocymoides   ASTERACEAE
Yellow creeping zinnia
Open fields, meadows, brushlands, thornscrub, and
other open areas. Summer, fall. Locally common.

A procumbent to erect annual with stems to 8 inches tall,
branching from base, leaves and stems visibly pubescent. Leaves approximately 1½ inches long and half as
wide, oblanceolate to obovate, margins entire. Flowering heads ½ inch in diameter with 5–20 yellow ray florets and numerous brown disc florets. Often overlooked
because of its size; however, it can be locally common in
open grasslands in far South Texas, and seems to prefer
slightly disturbed areas with clay soils. Genus name honors Federico Sanvitali, an 18th-century Italian naturalist and professor. Specific epithet is of Greek origin and
means "leaves of basil" (*ocimum*).

Senecio ampullaceus   ASTERACEAE
Texas ragwort
Fields, pastures, meadows, open brush
and woodlands, fence lines, roadsides and
other open areas. Spring. Common.

An erect annual with a single, glabrous stem, branching
when in flower, to 2+ feet tall. Leaves alternate, on petioles to sessile, ovate-lanceolate, to 3½ inches long and
1¼ inches wide, margins dentate to entire, bases tapering, tips acute. Flowering heads to 1½ inches wide in
corymbs, with 8± yellow ray florets and numerous yellow disc florets. South Texas north to Oklahoma, east to
Louisiana.

Senecio flaccidus   ASTERACEAE
Threadleaf ragwort
Open brush, canyons, drainages, roadsides and
other open areas. Summer, fall. Common.

An erect, multistemmed, branching perennial to 3 feet,
leaves and stems tomentose. Leaves alternate, sessile or
nearly so, lobes linear and to 4 inches long, threadlike,
margins entire or slightly toothed toward pointed tips.
Flowering heads in terminal corymbs. Ray florets yellow and 8 or 13 or 21 per head, disc florets numerous and
orange-yellow. Found in open areas, in rocky to gravelly
soils, from Maverick County north throughout Panhandle and west into New Mexico, essentially covering western third of Texas.

Senecio vulgaris   ASTERACEAE
Common groundsel
Open, disturbed sites. Spring. Uncommon.

An erect, single-stemmed, introduced annual to 20
inches, stem typically tomentose when young. Leaves
alternate, ovate to oblanceolate, to 4 inches long and
1 inch wide, lobed, final margins dentate, visibly pubescent with a prominent reddish brown central vein. Flowering heads in loose corymbs with up to 20 heads per, ray
florets absent, disc florets numerous and yellow. Uncommon but widespread throughout Texas around areas of
human disturbance such as parks and residential areas.

Silphium asteriscus   ASTERACEAE
Starry rosinweed
Prairies, meadows, open brush and woodlands,
riparian areas, roadsides. Summer, fall. Common.

An erect, multistemmed perennial with glabrous or
rough stems to 6+ feet tall. Leaves variable, opposite or
alternate, lanceolate to ovate, to 10 inches long and
2 inches wide, margins entire, tips acute, blades rough.
Inflorescences in terminal racemes. Flowering heads to
3+ inches broad, with up to 20 yellow ray florets and to
120 yellow-orange disc florets. Found in Edwards Plateau, east into Louisiana and north into Oklahoma; often
grows around perennial and seasonal waterways.

Silphium laciniatum   ASTERACEAE
Compass plant
Prairies, fields, grasslands, roadsides and other
open areas. Summer, fall. Uncommon.

An erect, multistemmed perennial with rough, scabrous
stems to 6+ feet tall. Basal leaves mostly. Leaves sessile
or petiolate, linear or ovate to rhombic, to 18 inches long
and 12 inches wide, deeply pinnately lobed 1 or 2 times,
margins entire to toothed, tips acute, surfaces rough, scabrous. Inflorescences in terminal, branching racemes.
Flowering heads to 4 inches wide, with 40± yellow ray
florets and hundreds of yellow disc florets. Uncommon
throughout eastern half of Texas.

Silphium radula   ASTERACEAE
Roughstem rosinweed
Prairies, fields, grasslands, roadsides and
other open areas. Summer. Common.

An erect perennial with a single, rough stem to 3+ feet
tall, long white hairs visible against dark, brownish red
stems. Basal leaves petiolate, lanceolate to ovate, to 8½
inches long and 3¼ inches wide, margins entire or dentate, bases tapering, tips acute. Stem leaves smaller,
sessile. Upper portion of raceme lacking leaves, open.
Flowering heads radial, with 18± yellow ray florets and
numerous yellow disc florets. Found in eastern third of
Texas, south to Coastal Bend, north into Oklahoma.

Simsia calva   ASTERACEAE
Awnless bush sunflower, bush sunflower
Prairies, open brush and woodlands, riparian
areas, rocky outcrops, canyons, roadsides.
Winter, spring, summer, fall. Common.

An erect perennial with multiple branching stems to 4+
feet tall. Leaves opposite, on winged petioles, ovate to deltate, occasionally 3-lobed, to 3 inches long and 2½ inches
wide, margins entire or dentate, bases cordate to cuneate,
leaf surfaces scabrous. Upper leaves occasionally perfoliate. Flowering heads solitary or to 3 on a peduncle to 8
inches long, each head about 1½ inches wide with 20±
yellow ray florets and 90+ yellow disc florets. Found in
Central Texas south to Mexico, west to Big Bend region.

218

Smallanthus uvedalius (*S. uvedalia*)
ASTERACEAE
Hairy leafcup, bear's foot, yellow leafcup
Edges of woodlands, thickets, creekbanks.
Spring, summer, fall. Uncommon.

An erect perennial, typically single-stemmed with slight
branching, to 5 feet tall. Leaves opposite, on petioles to
6 inches long, deltate to ovate, 3- to 5-lobed, to 15 inches
long and as wide, margins dentate. Flowering heads solitary or in loose corymbs, each head about 2 inches wide,
to 13± yellow ray florets and numerous yellow disc florets.
Loosely scattered in eastern third of Texas. U.S. Forest
Service roads in and around Montgomery County and
from Bastrop State Park to Buescher State Park are ideal
viewing spots during summer months.

Solidago caesia ASTERACEAE
Blue-stemmed goldenrod
Woodlands. Summer. Uncommon.

An erect to arching perennial with slender, glabrous,
unbranched or weakly branched stems to 3 feet, stems
turning glaucous throughout the season. Leaves alternate, sessile, lanceolate, to 6 inches long and 1¼ inches
wide, margins serrate, occasionally entire, tips acute,
upper surface of blades with prominent midvein. Flowering heads usually numerous, clustered in axils of mid
to upper leaves or in terminal panicle. Heads radial with
1–6 yellow ray florets and 6± yellow disc florets, to ¼ inch
wide. Found in East Texas, in and around Big Thicket.

Solidago odora ASTERACEAE
**Fragrant goldenrod, sweet goldenrod,
anise-scented goldenrod**
Meadows, savannas, grasslands, brush and woodlands,
woodland openings, roadsides. Summer. Common.

An erect, arching perennial with stems to 4+ feet tall.
Leaves alternate, sessile, oblanceolate above, lanceolate to
ovate below, to 4½ inches long and ¾ inch wide, margins
entire, tips acute, bases rounded, producing a distinctive
anise scent when crushed. Flowering heads in terminal
panicles with 350+ heads, ray florets yellow and 4± per
head, disc florets yellow and 4± per head. Found in sandy
soils in eastern fourth of Texas, less common west and
south to Coastal Bend.

Solidago rigida   ASTERACEAE
Stiff goldenrod
Fields, meadows, grasslands, open brush and
woodlands, roadsides. Summer. Common.

An erect, rhizomatous perennial with stout, pubescent
stems to 4+ feet tall, branching may occur in upper portion of stems. Leaves alternate, sessile above, on petioles
below, oval to oblanceolate, to 4 inches long, margins serrate or entire, tips obtuse. Flowering heads numerous,
terminal either from main stem or lateral stems, to ½
inch wide, with up to 13 yellow ray florets and to 35 yellow
disc florets. Frequent in Northern Blackland Prairie and
surrounding regions, south to coastal plains, occasional
elsewhere.

Solidago sempervirens   ASTERACEAE
Seaside goldenrod
Coastal plains, grasslands, dunes,
marshes. Summer, fall. Common.

An erect or ascending, rhizomatous perennial with single or multiple glabrous stems to 6+ feet tall. Leaves alternate, sessile above, on petioles below, slender to elliptic
to lanceolate, to 2½ inches long and ⅜ inch wide, margins entire, tips acute to obtuse, blades fleshy. Flowering heads numerous, in panicles, to ½+ inch wide, often
several hundred per plant. Ray florets yellow and 7–11 per
head, disc florets yellow and 10–16 per head. Found from
Mexico to Louisiana, inland along coastal plains, often in
large colonies.

Taraxacum officinale   ASTERACEAE
Common dandelion
Urban and suburban areas, overgrazed
pastures, roadsides and other disturbed areas.
Winter, spring, summer, fall. Common.

An introduced perennial, from a taproot, to 16 inches
tall when in flower. Basal leaves in a rosette, horizontal
to slightly erect when in flower, oblanceolate to obovate,
to 16 inches long and 4 inches wide, margins lobed to
toothed, lobes lanceolate to triangular. Flowering heads
solitary at ends of peduncles to 16 inches, to 1½ inches
wide, 100+ yellow ligulate florets. Widespread throughout
state, a common weed of lawns.

Tetragonotheca ludoviciana   ASTERACEAE
Louisiana nerveray, Louisiana square-head
Open oak woodlands, shrublands, meadows, prairies, other open areas. Spring, summer. Uncommon.

An erect, multistemmed perennial to 3+ feet tall, branching in upper portions of stems. Leaves opposite, sessile, oblong to ovate, 3¾ inches long and 3½ inches wide, margins toothed. Flowering heads terminal, either solitary or in loose corymbs. Heads to 1½ inches in diameter with 12± yellow ray florets and numerous disc florets. Found in sandy soils in eastern portion of state, east into Louisiana with isolated populations in Bastrop and Dallas–Fort Worth areas. An obvious characteristic of species in this genus is captured in the genus name, which translates to "four-angled container," referring to the quadrangular involucres.

Tetragonotheca repanda   ASTERACEAE
Showy nerveray
Fields, meadows, prairies, open woodlands, roadsides and other open areas. Spring, summer. Common.

An erect, multistemmed perennial to 2 feet tall; stems weakly branched above. Leaves mostly basal, on long petioles, ovate-lanceolate to rounded-deltate, to 4¾ inches long and 2¾ inches wide, margins roughly toothed and wavy. Upper leaves opposite, if present, and similar to basal, but smaller and petiole length decreases farther up stem. Inflorescences terminal, either solitary or in loose clusters. Flowering heads to 3 inches broad, with 16–21± yellow ray florets and numerous disc florets. Grows in sandy soils south of San Antonio.

Tetragonotheca texana   ASTERACEAE
Square bud daisy, nerve-ray, Texas square-head
Open woodlands, fields, meadows, roadsides and other open areas. Spring, summer, fall. Common.

An erect, single- to multistemmed perennial to 2 feet tall, weakly branching in upper portions of stem. Leaves opposite, sessile to connate-perfoliate above, on petioles below, oblong or ovate or lanceolate, 4 inches long and 1½ inches wide, margins incised to pinnatifid and/or undulate. Flowering heads solitary at end of long peduncles. Heads approximately 1¾ inches wide with 8–15 yellow ray florets and numerous brownish red disc florets. Found in southern portion of Edwards Plateau, west into Chihuahuan Desert; isolated populations in South Texas.

221

Tetraneuris linearifolia ASTERACEAE
**Four-nerved daisy, slender-leaf bitterweed, fineleaf
fournerved daisy**
Rocky hillsides, sparse grass and shrublands,
roadcuts and roadsides, other open areas.
Winter, spring, summer, fall. Common.

An erect perennial with branching stems to 16+ inches
tall. Leaves spatulate to oblanceolate, to 3 inches long and
¼ inch wide, margins entire or weakly dentate or lobed.
Flowering heads solitary, or in weak corymbs, on peduncles to 8 inches long. Heads about 1 inch wide, with 20±
yellow, 3-lobed ray florets and numerous yellow disc florets. Widespread throughout state. Absent in far eastern
Texas and northern Panhandle.

Thelesperma filifolium ASTERACEAE
Greenthread, stiff greenthread, plains greenthread
Fields, grasslands, prairies, open brush
and shrublands, roadsides and other open
areas. Spring, summer, fall. Common.

An erect, slender perennial with a single, branching stem
to 2+ feet tall. Leaves opposite, typically 3-lobed, lobes linear to filiform, to 2 inches long and ⅒ inch wide. Flowering heads solitary or in corymbs, individual heads about 2
inches wide. Ray florets 8±, yellow, 3-lobed, seldom with
reddish brown bases. Disc florets numerous and reddish
brown. Common throughout state. Absent in far eastern
Texas. Occasionally occurring in large numbers along
roadsides.

Thelesperma longipes ASTERACEAE
Longstalk greenthread
Desert scrub, open, rocky slopes, ledges,
outcrops. Spring, summer. Locally common.

An erect, bunching perennial with flowering stems to
16+ inches tall, leaves crowded in lower third of plant.
Leaves opposite, lobed, lobes linear to 1 inch long, margins entire, tips acute. Flowering heads solitary at end of
peduncles to 12+ inches long, ray florets absent, yellow
disc florets numerous to ¼ inch wide. Found throughout
Chihuahuan Desert, west into Edwards Plateau. Often
grows on limestone roadcuts, usually many individuals
present.

Thelesperma simplicifolium ASTERACEAE
Slender greenthread
Fields, grasslands, savannas, open brush and
woodlands, roadsides. Spring, summer. Common.

An erect perennial with slender stems to 16+ inches tall.
Leaves opposite, sessile, pinnately lobed, lobes linear to
1¾ inches long and less than ¹⁄₁₆ inch wide. Flowering
heads solitary, to 2 inches wide. Ray flowers yellow, 8 per
head, petals 3-lobed. Disc florets yellow and numerous.
Common throughout Central Texas, west into Chihuahuan Desert, south to Lower Rio Grande Valley, north
into Panhandle.

Thymophylla acerosa ASTERACEAE
Pricklyleaf dogweed
Open grass and shrublands, desert scrub, rocky slopes,
flats, roadsides. Winter, spring, summer, fall. Common.

An erect to spreading, branching perennial, often
rounded, to 10 inches tall and as wide, leaves and stems
glabrous to slightly pubescent. Leaves opposite, sessile, linear to ¾ inch long, margins entire, tips acute to
pointed. Flowering heads solitary, sessile or on short
peduncles, ray florets yellow and 8± per head, yellow
disc florets to 25+ with heads to ⅝ inch wide. Common throughout Chihuahuan Desert and into western
Edwards Plateau, north into southern Panhandle.

Thymophylla micropoides ASTERACEAE
Woolly pricklyleaf
Rocky outcrops, slopes, exposed bedrock.
Winter, spring, summer, fall. Uncommon.

A spreading, prostrate to ascending perennial with soft,
woolly leaves and stems to 6 inches tall. Leaves alternate, spatulate, to 1 inch long and ¼ inch wide, margins
entire or toothed. Flowering heads solitary and terminal
with leaves just below heads. Heads ⅓ inch wide with
15 bright yellow ray florets and numerous orange-yellow
disc florets. Found in shallow soils on limestone bedrock
in southwestern portion of Edwards Plateau and eastern
portion of Chihuahuan Desert.

Thymophylla pentachaeta ASTERACEAE
Parralena
Open grass and brushlands, flats, rocky-
open hillsides, roadsides and other open
spaces. Spring, summer, fall. Common.

An erect, wispy, branching, somewhat rounded annual
or short-lived perennial to 8 inches tall. Leaves opposite,
sessile, pinnate with 5–11 linear lobes, to 1 inch long, tips
pointed, blades stiff. Flowering heads solitary on peduncles to 4 inches long. Heads to ½ inch wide, ray florets
yellow to yellow-orange with 12–21 per head, yellow disc
florets to 80 per head. Found throughout South Texas,
north into lower Panhandle, west into Pecos County.

Thymophylla setifolia ASTERACEAE
Texas pricklyleaf
Open shrub and woodlands, rocky slopes, canyons, other
rocky areas. Winter, spring, summer, fall. Uncommon.

An erect, much-branched perennial to 8+ inches tall and
10 inches wide, leaves and stems with a white pubescence. Leaves opposite, linear to about ⅓ inch, multilobed
with lobes linear and entire. Flowering heads on short
peduncles held above foliage. Heads ¼ inch wide with 9±
yellow ray florets and multiple orange-yellow disc florets.
Found in West Texas, on limestone soils, from Val Verde
to Culberson County.

Tragopogon dubius ASTERACEAE
Yellow salsify, goat's beard, oyster plant
Roadsides, urban and suburban areas, feral fields,
other disturbed areas. Spring, summer. Common.

An introduced, erect annual or biennial with a single
branching stem to 3 feet tall. Leaves alternate, linear to
10 inches long, margins entire, bases clasping. Flowering heads solitary on slender, glaucous peduncles. Heads
2½ inches in diameter, with numerous yellow ray florets.
Achenes slender to 1 inch or longer in length, large feathery pappus to 3 inches wide. Yellow salsify is native to the
Old World, now widespread throughout West Texas and
Panhandle. Genus name of Greek origin and translates
to "goat's beard." Edible; roots taste like oysters, hence the
common name oyster plant.

Trixis californica ASTERACEAE
Trixis, American threefold, American trixis
Desert shrublands, rocky slopes, canyons, washes and
desert flats. Winter, spring, summer, fall. Common.

An erect, leafy perennial, heavily branched to 3+ feet tall.
Leaves alternate, linear to lanceolate, to 4⅓ inches long
and 1 inch wide. Flowering heads terminal, usually in a
loose panicle or corymb. Each head consists of to 25 fertile yellow florets, outer lip distinctly 3-lobed. Frequent
in Chihuahuan Desert, at lower to mid elevations close
to the Rio Grande; however, a few collections have been
made in Maverick and Starr Counties. Genus name of
Greek origin (*trixos*) and means "threefold," referring to
the 3-cleft corolla.

Trixis inula ASTERACEAE
Tropical threefold, Mexican threefold, trixis
Tamaulipan Thornscrub, thickets, roadsides.
Spring, summer, fall. Locally common.

An erect, heavily branched perennial to 6+ feet tall
if supported. Leaves alternate, on short petioles,
linear-lanceolate, to 6½ inches long, margins entire to
denticulate, margins and midveins on leaf underside
occasionally with observable hairs. Flowering heads in
terminal panicles or corymbs. Heads to ¾ inch wide with
8 to 15 yellow florets, outer lips distinctly 3-lobed. Found
at southern tip of Texas, from Jim Hogg County east to
coast and south into Mexico. Limited in its U.S. range,
but is common in the thornscrub and thickets that dominate this region.

Varilla texana ASTERACEAE
Saladillo, Texas varilla, varilla
Tamaulipan Thornscrub. Spring, summer. Locally common.

An erect, slightly rhizomatous perennial to 16 inches in
height, branching heavily from base. Leaves semisucculent, alternate, linear, roughly 1 inch long and ¹⁄₁₀ inch
wide, margins entire. Flowering heads solitary, terminal on slender and glabrate peduncles to 8 inches long.
Heads rounded and to ½ inch wide with numerous
golden yellow florets, ray florets absent. Found in South
Texas, from Maverick County south to Hidalgo County,
on gypseous-clay soils; numerous plants present. Common name *saladillo* means "salted," in reference to edible
leaves' salty taste.

Verbesina encelioides   ASTERACEAE
Cowpen daisy, butter daisy, golden crownbeard
Fields, meadows, pastures, roadsides and other
open, disturbed areas. Summer, fall. Common.

An erect, branched annual to 4 feet tall and nearly as
wide. Leaves alternate, deltate to lanceolate, to 4¾ inches
long and 2 inches wide, margins coarsely toothed. Flowering heads terminal, solitary or few per stem. Heads to
2 inches wide, with 150± yellow disc florets and 12+ yellow ray florets. Widespread throughout Texas and commonly grows in overgrazed areas. Genus name translates
to "resembling verbena." Specific epithet means "resembling encelia."

Verbesina nana   ASTERACEAE
Little crownbeard, dwarf crownbeard
Desert scrub, silty flats, roadsides and other
disturbed areas. Spring, summer, fall. Common.

A slightly erect perennial to 8 inches in height, branching from base. Leaves opposite, sometimes alternate, deltate to rhombic, margins toothed. Flowering heads solitary or few on short peduncles. Yellow-orange heads to
1½ inches in diameter with 150± disc and 16± ray florets.
Found mostly in western portion of state, with a few collections in Panhandle. Specific epithet means "dwarf,"
referring to species' overall size.

Viguiera cordifolia   ASTERACEAE
Golden-eye, sunflower golden-eye, toothleaf
Open shrub and woodlands, rocky slopes,
roadsides. Summer, fall. Locally common.

An erect perennial with rough, multiple stems to 3+ feet
tall. Leaves opposite below, occasionally alternate at tips
of branches, on petioles to ⅓ inch long, ovate to deltate
to lanceolate, to 4 inches long and 2¾ inches wide, margins serrate, surfaces rough. Flowering heads terminal,
in loose corymbs. Heads about 1 inch wide, to 8 yellow ray
florets, 40+ yellow disc florets. Found in upper elevations
in mountains of West Texas, in canyons and along creek
banks. Named after René Viguier (1880–1931), a French
botanist.

Viguiera dentata ASTERACEAE
Golden-eye, plateau golden-eye
Open rocky slopes, canyons, open shrub and
woodlands, roadsides. Summer, fall. Common.

An erect, much-branched perennial with rough stems
to 6 feet. Leaves opposite below, alternate above, on petioles to 2 inches long, ovate to lance-ovate to lanceolate, to 5 inches long and 3¼ inches wide, margins serrate, surfaces rough. Flowering heads in loose corymbs,
yellow-orange ray florets 10–14 per head, disc florets
darker orange-yellow and to 50 per head. Found throughout Chihuahuan Desert to eastern Edwards Plateau and
southern Post Oak Savanna.

Wedelia acapulcensis ASTERACEAE
Zexmenia, hairy wedelia, orange zexmenia
Rocky outcrops, cliffs, roadcuts, brushlands, thornscrub,
roadsides. Spring, summer, fall. Common.

An erect perennial with much-branched stems to 3+ feet
tall. Leaves opposite, deltate to lanceolate to elliptic, to 3
inches long and 1 inch wide, margins roughly dentate to
3-lobed, surfaces rough to the touch. Flowering heads
solitary or in loose corymbs, on peduncles to 12+ inches
long. Heads 1¼ inches wide with 8± orange-yellow ray florets, numerous disc florets of same color. Found in Central Texas, south into Mexico, and west into Chihuahuan
Desert; grows on limestone soils.

Xanthocephalum gymnospermoides ASTERACEAE
San Pedro matchweed
Open meadows, grasslands, stream and creek
bottoms, roadsides. Summer. Rare.

An erect, single-stemmed annual to 5 feet tall, simple branching in upper portion of stem. Leaves alternate, sessile, oblanceolate, to 4 inches long, margins
entire to toothed, teeth may be spine-tipped. Flowering
heads terminal, solitary or in clustered corymbs. Heads
1¼ inches wide with 50 orangish yellow ray florets and
numerous disc florets of same color. Can be found in Jeff
Davis County, with one well-documented population
found along Scenic Loop. Genus name of Greek origin
and means "yellow head." Specific epithet translates to
"descendant of gymnosperm."

227

Zinnia grandiflora   ASTERACEAE
Plains zinnia, Rocky Mountain zinnia
Open grass, brushlands, prairies, open rocky slopes
and hillsides. Spring, summer, fall. Common.

An erect to prostrate, rounded perennial with heavily
branched stems to 9+ inches long. Leaves opposite, sessile, linear, to 1¼ inches long and less than ⅛ inch wide,
margins entire, tips pointed, surfaces rough. Flowering heads solitary on peduncles to ½ inch long. Heads to
1½ inches wide, ray florets yellow with 3–6 per head and
slightly 3-lobed or notched, disc florets orange to reddish.
Found throughout Chihuahuan Desert, often occurring
in vast numbers in creosote–short grass flats.

Amoreuxia wrightii   BIXACEAE
Wright's yellowshow, yellow show
Grasslands, shrublands, roadsides and other open
areas. Spring, summer, fall. Uncommon.

An erect perennial with glabrous stems to 20 inches tall
from tuberous roots. Leaves alternate, on petioles 3+
inches long, orbicular, 5- to 7-lobed, to 2 inches long and
2¾ inches wide, margins serrate. Bilateral flowers on
3-inch-long peduncles originating from upper leaf axils.
Flowers 2½ inches wide, sepals yellow-orange with reddish spots at base, one sepal will not have spots. Found in
gravelly to sandy soils in South Texas, from Val Verde to
Cameron County. Usually flowers after rain events.

Heliotropium torreyi   BORAGINACEAE
Torrey's heliotrope, yellow heliotrope, slimleaf heliotrope
Rocky open brush and woodlands.
Spring, summer, fall. Common.

An erect, open perennial with branching stems to 20+
inches tall, leaves and stem with soft, appressed hairs.
Leaves alternate, sessile or nearly so, linear, to 1¼ inch
long, margins revolute, tips acute. Stems terminating in
scorpioid cymes. Flowers 5-lobed, yellow with a greenish center, corolla deeply lobed, lobes pointed, about ³⁄₁₆
inch wide. Found primarily on limestone, in sparse habitats from Chihuahuan Desert south to far South Texas.
Named in honor of John Torrey (1796–1873), an American
botanist.

Lithospermum caroliniense   BORAGINACEAE
Hairy puccoon, Carolina puccoon
Open shrub and woodlands, grasslands, prairies,
roadsides and other open areas. Spring. Common.

An erect, typically unbranched perennial with pubescent,
grooved stems to 30+ inches tall. Leaves alternate, sessile,
lanceolate, to 3 inches long and ¾ inch wide, margins ciliate, blades pubescent. Stems terminating in scorpioid
cymes. Flowers yellow to yellow-orange, 5-lobed, tubular, about ¾ inch wide. Found in eastern third of Texas,
uncommon in Panhandle and Central Texas, found in
sandy soils. Genus name of Greek origin and means
"stone" (*litho*) "seed" (*spermum*), referring to the hard,
rounded seed.

Lithospermum cobrense   BORAGINACEAE
Smooththroat stoneseed
Open pine-oak-juniper woodlands, meadows, roadsides
and other open areas. Spring, summer. Uncommon.

An erect perennial with a 2-foot single stem, stems occasionally branched. Basal leaves oblanceolate, to 4 inches
long and ¾ inch wide. Stem leaves alternate, sessile, linear to oblong, to 1½ inches long and ¼ inch wide, margins revolute, blades with visible, white hairs. Flowers in
terminal racemes, tubular, 5-lobed, pale yellow to cream
with age, to about ¾ inch wide. Found in mountains of
Chihuahuan Desert, mid to upper elevations; easily seen
along Scenic Loop in Jeff Davis County.

Lithospermum incisum   BORAGINACEAE
Golden puccoon, narrowleaf stoneseed, fringed puccoon
Grasslands, prairies, fields, open brush
and woodlands, roadsides and other open
areas. Winter, spring, fall. Common.

An erect perennial with one or more branching stems
to 16+ inches tall. Leaves alternate, sessile, linear to
lance-linear, to 2½ inches long and ¼ inch wide, margins entire to ciliate, blades pubescent. Stems terminating in cluster of sterile, yellow, trumpet-shaped flowers
to 1½ inches long and ¾ inch wide. Flowers 5-lobed, lobe
margins wavy and fringed. Cleistogamous flowers found
lower on stem, hidden among leaves, and occur after sterile flowers bloom. Most common *Lithospermum* species
found in Texas; weak in deep East Texas.

Erysimum capitatum BRASSICACEAE
Sanddune wallflower, prairie rocket, western wallflower
Grasslands, prairies, pastures, open brush
and woodlands, roadsides and other open
areas. Spring, summer, fall. Uncommon.

An erect biennial or short-lived perennial with branching stems to 3 feet. Basal leaves spatulate to oblanceolate or linear, to 7 inches long and ½ inch wide, margins entire or dentate, tips acute, surfaces with 2- to 4-rayed trichomes. Upper leaves similar, smaller. Flowers in terminal, clustered racemes, elongating throughout season. Flowers 4-petaled, yellow to yellow-orange. Found in West Texas; additional populations in northern Panhandle and East-Central Texas.

Paysonia lasiocarpa BRASSICACEAE
Roughpod bladderpod
Fields, meadows, grasslands, open brush and
woodlands. Late winter, spring. Common.

An erect, decumbent or procumbent annual or weak perennial with slender, pubescent stems to 20 inches. Basal leaves oblanceolate, to 4 inches long and 1¼ inches wide, margins sinuate-dentate or lobed, surfaces pubescent. Stem leaves obovate to elliptic, to 1¾ inches long and ¾ inch wide, margins sinuate-dentate, bases eared, tips rounded, surfaces pubescent. Yellow flowers in terminal racemes, 4-petaled to ¾ inch wide. Fruits inflated, round to elliptic, to ⅓ inch long and as wide on pedicels to 1¼ inches long, with visible hairs, drooping. Found in open areas in South Texas, less common north to Travis County.

Physaria fendleri BRASSICACEAE
Fendler's bladderpod
Grasslands, open shrublands, outcrops, desert
washes and drainages. Spring. Common.

An erect perennial with pubescent leaves and stems, to 10 inches. Basal leaves linear, to 2 inches, margins entire to dentate. Upper leaves linear to oblanceolate, to 1 inch, margins entire to slightly dentate, occasionally involute. Leaves silvery pubescent with rayed trichomes. Stems terminating in racemes. Flowers 4-petaled, yellow to yellow-orange, about ½ inch wide. Fruit spherical, to ⅓ inch diameter. Common during early spring in western Edwards Plateau, Chihuahuan Desert, the Panhandle, and into South Texas. Will flower out of season if rains permit.

Physaria gordonii BRASSICACEAE
Gordon's bladderpod
Open grasslands and prairies, open brushlands, washes, creek bottoms, overgrazed pastures, roadsides and other open areas. Late winter, spring, summer. Common.

An erect annual to short-lived perennial with pubescent leaves and stems to 12 inches. Basal leaves obovate to oblong, to 2 inches long, margins lyrate-pinnatifid or dentate or entire. Upper leaves linear and sickle-shaped, to 1¾ inches long, margins entire or dentate or repand. Flowers in terminal, dense racemes, with 4 petals, yellow to orange, about ⅓ inch wide. Fruits spherical. Common throughout western two-thirds of state, from central South Texas north into Oklahoma, west into New Mexico and northern Mexico.

Helianthemum carolinianum CISTACEAE
Carolina frostweed
Woodlands, forests. Spring. Common.

A low-growing, erect perennial with pubescent, reddish brown stems to 12 inches. Leaves alternate and basal rosettes, on short petioles, spatulate to obovate or elliptic, to 1½ inches long and ¾ inch wide, margins entire, tips obtuse, bases tapering, surfaces pubescent. Stems terminating in scorpioid cymes, 1–3 flowers per cyme. Flowers 5-petaled, yellow, to 1 ⅜ inches wide. Found in sandy, wooded areas with open understory.

Helianthemum georgianum CISTACEAE
Georgia frostweed
Fields, plains, open brush and woodlands, dunes. Spring, summer. Common.

An erect, branching perennial with tomentose stems to 12+ inches tall. Basal leaves spatulate to oblanceolate, to 1 inch long and ⅜ inch wide, surfaces with star-shaped hairs. Stem leaves alternate, on short petioles, oblanceolate to elliptic, to 1 ⅝ inches long and ⅜ inch wide, margins entire, tips rounded. Flowers in terminal cymes, 5-petaled, yellow, to 1 inch wide. Found in sandy soils throughout western half of Texas; frequent along lower coast and in Post Oak Savanna.

Side margin text:

mustard family BRASSICACEAE
rockrose family CISTACEAE

231

Helianthemum rosmarinifolium   CISTACEAE
Rosemary-leaf frostweed
Fields, meadows, grasslands, open brush and
woodlands. Spring, summer. Common.

An erect to ascending multistemmed perennial with
tomentose stems to 16+ inches tall. Basal leaves obovate,
to 1 inch long and ¼ inch wide. Stem leaves alternate, on
short petioles, oblanceolate to lanceolate, to 1¾ inches
long and ¼ inch wide, margins revolute, tips obtuse to
acute. Flowers solitary, terminal, 5-petaled, yellow to ½
inch wide; cleistogamous flowers clustered in leaf axils
and less than ¼ inch long. Found in sandy soils in Post
Oak Savanna and adjacent regions from Oklahoma south
to Coastal Bend.

Cleomella longipes   CLEOMACEAE
Chiricahua Mountain stinkweed
Desert washes, riparian areas. Spring,
summer. Uncommon.

An erect, glabrous annual with multiple branching,
spreading stems to 3 feet. Leaves alternate, palmately trifoliolate. Leaflets oblanceolate to oblong-lanceolate, to
1⅓ inch long and ⅓ inch wide, margins entire, tips acute
to rounded. Inflorescences in terminal racemes with
numerous bilateral flowers. Flowers yellow, 4-petaled,
petals lanceolate, 6 stamens. Fruit rhomboidal, with 15
seeds per capsule. Found in sandy to gravelly soils from
Brewster to El Paso County.

Uvularia perfoliata   COLCHICACEAE
Perfoliate bellwort
Along creeks, slopes, or ravines in deciduous
woodland or forests. Spring, summer. Rare.

An erect, rhizomatous and stoloniferous perennial with
one or many branching stems to 20 inches. Leaves alternate, perfoliate, few, ovate to oblong, to 4 inches long
and 2 inches wide, margins entire, tips acute to pointed,
lower surfaces glabrous and glaucous. Flowers solitary on
peduncles to ¾ inch long, bracted. Bracts perfoliate and
similar to leaves below. Flowers bell-shaped with 6 tepals,
pale tannish yellow, to 1½ inches long. Found around
creeks or streams in deep East Texas.

Lenophyllum texanum   CRASSULACEAE
Texas stonecrop
Lomas, salt flats, Tamaulipan
Thornscrub. Fall, winter. Rare.

An ascending, succulent perennial with branching
stems to 8 inches tall. Leaves opposite, fleshy, obovate to
ovate-lanceolate, to 1 inch long, tips acute to obtuse. Flowers in terminal spikelike racemes, bell-shaped, 5-petaled,
yellow, less than ¼ inch wide. New plants produced veg-
etatively via leaves. Rare but found in South Texas thornscrub (often at base of woody shrubs) and along coast,
from Webb County east to Matagorda County.

Sedum nuttallianum   CRASSULACEAE
Yellow stonecrop
Open areas with shallow soil. Spring, summer. Common.

An erect annual with succulent leaves and stems 4 inches
tall, often forming large colonies. Leaves, lanceolate to
oblong, to ½ inch long and ⅛ inch wide, yellow-green.
Flowers in terminal cymes. Flowers yellow, 5-petaled to
¼ inch wide. Found throughout central portion of state,
north into Oklahoma. This unmistakable species is common on shallow soils in granite, limestone, and sandstone. Can occur in tens of thousands during well-timed
summer rains, creating a yellow mosaic against exposed
bedrock. Genus name dates back to mid-15th century and
is of Latin origin; it means "sedentary" or "to sit," probably referring to plant's habit.

Apodanthera undulata   CUCURBITACEAE
Coyote gourd, melon loco
Creosote and mesquite shrubland.
Spring, summer, fall. Common.

A spreading perennial vine with branching stems to 9
feet long from large, thick, tuberous roots. Leaves reniform, to 6 inches broad, slightly lobed, with undulate
to dentate margins, petioles to 1¼ inches. Male flowers
form in lower axils, female flowers in upper. Flowers
funnel-shaped to 2 inches in diameter with 5 distinct
lobes, erect, extending above foliage. Found in sandy to
gravelly soils in Chihuahuan Desert.

Cucurbita foetidissima CUCURBITACEAE
Buffalo gourd, stinking gourd, calabacilla loca
Fields, roadsides, thickets, disturbed areas, various
shrublands. Spring, summer. Common.

A large perennial vine with spreading, climbing stems to
20 feet long from tuberous roots. Leaves triangular-ovate,
to 12 inches long, with angled lobes, grayish green to
silver-green. Flowers yellow, to 4 inches long. Fruit green
with lighter stripes when young, resembles a small water-
melon, turning yellow at maturity. All portions of plant
emit a foul smell, especially when touched. Widespread
throughout Texas, but absent in far south, coastal, and
eastern regions. Seems to prefer river banks and washes;
may climb over smaller trees and shrubs.

Ibervillea lindheimeri CUCURBITACEAE
Lindheimer's globeberry, snake apple, balsam gourd
Roadsides, fence lines, shrublands,
woodlands. Spring, summer. Common.

Perennial climbing vine from a turnip-shaped root with
slender, branching stems to 10 feet long. Semisucculent leaves are to 3¼ inches long, with 3–5 deep lobes
and toothed margins. Flowers tubular, yellow, 5-lobed,
½ inch wide. Fruit bright red when mature. Common
throughout its range, which is a wide swath through Central Texas, extending from Cameron County north to
Oklahoma, west to Brewster County, and east to just past
Brazos River. Bird dispersed, this species can frequently
be found growing along fence lines.

Ibervillea tenuisecta CUCURBITACEAE
Cutleaf globeberry, slimlobe globeberry
Desert scrub, shrublands, washes,
fence lines. Summer. Common.

Perennial climber with slender, branching stems to 8
feet, from a turnip-shaped root. Leaves to 2½ inches
wide, deeply 5-lobed with linear and slightly lobed divisions, petioles to ¾ inch. Flowers yellow, tubular, about
½ inch wide. Fruit a bright red berry, about ½ inch in
diameter. Very similar to *Ibervillea lindheimeri*; their
ranges overlap in the west. Differences in leaf morphology separate the two. Found from western Edwards Plateau to El Paso.

Melothria pendula CUCURBITACEAE
Meloncito, creeping cucumber, Guadeloupe cucumber
Woodlands, canyons, creek and river banks,
brushlands, thickets. Summer, fall. Common.

A climbing or trailing vine from tuberous roots, with
slender stems to 6+ feet long. Leaves cordate to triangular to 3-lobed, margins entire, surfaces rough. Solitary flowers on slender peduncles, bell-shaped, yellow to
yellow-orange, petals lobed or notched. Immature fruit
is a green-striped pepo, to about 1 inch long, black when
mature. Common throughout most of state. Weak to
absent in Panhandle and to El Paso.

Acmispon oroboides (*Lotus plebeius*) FABACEAE
New Mexico bird's foot trefoil, pine deervetch
Rocky slopes, rocky grasslands, rocky outcrops,
cliffs, ledges. Spring, summer. Locally common.

An ascending perennial with multiple stems radiating from a central root, stems to 10 inches long. Leaves
alternate, pinnately lobed, with 5 leaflets. Leaflets oblanceolate to linear, to ½ inch long, margins entire, bases
tapering, tips acute, surfaces pubescent. Inflorescences
solitary or in small umbels on peduncles originating
from upper leaf axils, calyx brick red. Flowers yellow,
bilateral, wings surrounding keel, banner erect, often
with red veins. Found in mountains of Chihuahuan Desert, at mid to upper elevations.

Aeschynomene indica FABACEAE
Indian jointvetch, budda pea, curly indigo
Marshes, thickets, creek and river banks, roadside
ditches and other wet areas. Summer, fall. Uncommon.

An introduced, erect annual to perennial with hollow
stems to 6+ feet tall, stem surface glabrous to hispid.
Leaves alternate, pinnate, to 4 inches long, to 50+ leaflets.
Leaflets linear-oblong, to ½ inch long, margins entire,
glabrous. Flowers solitary or few, arising from upper leaf
axils. Flowers pale yellow to white, often with red to purple veins near base of banner, banner erect to ½ inch long
and ⅓ inch wide, petal margins ciliate. Found primarily
along Gulf Coast, from Brownsville to Florida, occasional
farther inland.

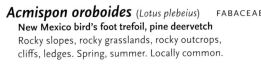

235

Aeschynomene viscidula FABACEAE
Sticky jointvetch
Grasslands, open brushlands, roadsides.
Spring, summer. Locally common.

A prostrate, sprawling perennial with viscid-pubescent stems to 3+ feet long. Leaves alternate, pinnate, to 1 inch long. Leaflets obovate, to ¼ inch long, margins ciliate-glandular, bases tapering, tips rounded. Inflorescences originating from leaf axils on short peduncles, typically paired. Flowers yellow to pale yellow, bilateral, to ⅓ inch long, banner with occasional red veins and ring near base. Found in sandy soils along southern Texas coast, occasional inland to Edwards Plateau.

Astragalus giganteus FABACEAE
Giant milkvetch
Open mountain slopes and grasslands.
Summer. Uncommon.

An erect, robust perennial with pubescent stems to 3+ feet tall. Leaves alternate, pinnate to 14 inches long, 17–35 leaflets. Leaflets elliptic or ovate to oblong, to 2 inches long, margins entire, tips pointed, blades and rachis covered in silky pubescence, soft to the touch. Flowers in racemes, somewhat crowded, papilionaceous, light yellow, nodding, to nearly 1 inch long. Found in open areas in upper elevations of Davis and Chinati Mountains. Large stature and silvery gray pubescence distinguish this species from others.

Astragalus mollissimus var. *earlei*
FABACEAE
Earle's woolly locoweed
Fields, grasslands, pastures, open brush and woodlands, other open areas. Spring. Uncommon.

An ascending, spreading, dense perennial. Leafy, pubescent stems to 12 inches tall and nearly twice as wide, originating from central rootstock. Leaves alternate, pinnately compound, to 8 inches long, with 15–21+ leaflets. Leaflets elliptic, ovate or oblong or rhombic, to ¾ inch long, margins entire, tips pointed, blades greenish gray, soft and visibly pubescent. Flowers in racemes with 20± flowers, creamy yellow, papilionaceous, to just over ¾ inch long. Found in Chihuahuan Desert, east into Edwards Plateau and north into southern Panhandle.

Baptisia bracteata FABACEAE
Longbract wild indigo
Grasslands, prairies, meadows, open brushlands,
roadsides and other open areas. Spring. Common.

An ascending to spreading shrubby perennial with
branching stems to 18 inches tall. Plant to 3+ feet wide.
Leaves alternate, sessile or on petioles 1½ inches long, trifoliolate, leaflets oblanceolate, to 3 inches long and 1 inch
wide, margins entire, bases tapering, tips pointed. Inflorescences in terminal racemes to 9 inches long, racemes
typically horizontal, not erect. Flowers abundant but not
crowded, papilionaceous, pale yellow, to 1 inch long and
nearly as wide, banner erect and somewhat folded backward, keel and wings protruding. From Cameron County,
north into Oklahoma, east into Louisiana; scattered
populations in Panhandle and southwestern Edwards
Plateau.

Baptisia nuttalliana FABACEAE
Nuttall's wild indigo
Woodlands, woodland edges, meadows. Spring. Common.

An erect, branching perennial to 4 feet and nearly as
wide, young stems short-pubescent. Leaves alternate,
on short petioles, trifoliolate, leaflets oblanceolate, to 1½
inches long and ¾ inch wide, margins entire, bases tapering, tips acute to obtuse. Inflorescences in erect, short
terminal racemes. Flowers few, papilionaceous, yellow, to
¾ inch long, wings and keel horizontal and protruding,
banner arched forward. Found in dry, sandy soils in eastern third of Texas.

Baptisia sphaerocarpa FABACEAE
Yellow wild indigo, bush pea, green wild indigo
Fields, grasslands, prairies, open brush and woodlands,
roadsides and other open areas. Spring. Common.

An erect shrubby perennial with branching stems to 3+
feet tall. Leaves alternate, on petioles to ⅝ inch long, trifoliolate, leaflets oblanceolate to obovate, to 3¼ inches
long, margins entire, bases tapering, tips acute to
rounded. Flowers in terminal racemes to 12 inches long,
numerous, somewhat crowded, papilionaceous, yellow,
to nearly 1 inch long, banner erect and folded, keel and
wings horizontal and protruding. Frequent in Southeast
Texas, less common farther north into Oklahoma; generally in eastern third of state in open, sandy soils.

Caesalpinia caudata FABACEAE
Tailed nicker
Open brush and grasslands. Spring. Uncommon.

An erect, branching perennial with wispy branches to 20 inches tall. Alternate leaves, compound with 3–11 pairs of pinnae, lateral pinnae to 1½ inches long, terminal pinnae to 4 inches long, petiole to ¾ inch long. Leaflets opposite, not crowded, broadly ovate to ½ inch long, margins entire, bases slightly cordate, tips acute. Flowers on pedicels to ⅓ inch, widely spaced in terminal racemes to 12+ inches long, bilateral, yellowish orange, to 1½ inches wide, with 4 spreading lateral petals and a horizontal central upper petal with inner red venation. Fruit flattened to 1⅓ inches long and ⅔ inch broad, tip pointed. Prefers sandy soils of deep South Texas.

Chamaecrista fasciculata FABACEAE
Partridge pea, sleeping plant
Fields, meadows, grasslands, prairies, open brush and woodlands, roadsides and other open areas. Spring, summer. Common.

An erect, slender annual with glabrous, branching, reddish brown stems to 4+ feet tall. Leaves alternate, pinnate with 8–15 pairs of leaflets. Leaflets linear-oblong, to ¾ inch long and less than ¼ inch wide, margins entire to ciliate, tips mucronate. Stipules present as well as single gland at base of lower pair of leaflets. Flowers in short racemes originating along upper stem just above leaf axils. Flowers to 1½ inches wide, 5-petaled with lower petal larger and curved inward, petals yellow with red spots at base on upper 4 petals. Common in eastern half of Texas.

Chamaecrista flexuosa var. *texana*
FABACEAE
Texas sensitive pea, Texas senna
Grasslands, fields, pastures, open brush and thornscrub, roadsides and other open areas. Winter, spring, summer. Common.

A prostrate perennial with multiple reddish brown stems originating from a central base, to 18 inches long. Leaves alternate, pinnate, 10–16 pairs of leaflets. Leaflets oblong to lanceolate, to ⅓ inch long and less than 1/16 inch wide, margins entire to ciliate, tips acute, pointed. Stipules present as well as a single gland located just below lowest pair of leaflets. Flowers originating in leaf axils, 5-petaled, petals yellow with red spots on upper 4 petals, to 1¼+ inches wide. Found in South Texas.

Chamaecrista greggii   FABACEAE
Gregg's sensitive pea
Thornscrub, brushlands. Spring, summer. Rare.

An erect, heavily branched perennial shrub, with stems
to 3 feet. Leaves alternate, clustered, pinnate, 2–5 pairs of
leaflets. Leaflets oblanceolate to obovate, to ¾ inch long,
margins entire, tips rounded. Flowers solitary or few, on
short peduncles originating from upper leaf axils, yellow,
5-petaled with lower petal larger and curved inward—giving an overall rounded-ball shape. Currently known from
Jim Wells and Live Oak Counties, perhaps elsewhere
in South Texas, as this species is common in northern
Mexico. Although a woody shrub, *Chamaecrista greggii* is
included here as it is rarely, if ever, found in field guides.

Crotalaria sagittalis   FABACEAE
Rattlebox, arrowhead rattlebox
Fields, grasslands, meadows, open brush
and woodlands, roadsides and other open
areas. Spring, summer. Common.

An ascending annual to short-lived perennial with pubescent stems to 20 inches tall. Leaves alternate, simple, lanceolate or linear-elliptic, to 2½ inches long and to ½ inch
wide, margins entire, bases cuneate, tips acute, blades
visibly pubescent. Flowers in racemes to 4 inches long
originating from leaf axils, yellow, bilateral, to ⅓ inch
long, banner erect and much larger than wings, which
enclose keel. Fruit oblong, to 1½ inches long and ⅜ inch
wide. Found in sandy soils in eastern third of Texas, from
Coastal Bend north into Oklahoma.

Dalea aurea   FABACEAE
Golden dalea, golden prairie clover, silktop dalea
Fields, grasslands, prairies, open shrub
and woodlands, roadsides and other open
areas. Spring, summer. Common.

An erect perennial from a woody base, with one to several canescent stems to 20 inches. Leaves alternate, pinnate to 3 inches long with 5–7 leaflets. Leaflets oblanceolate to obovate, to 1 inch long, margins entire, bases
tapering, tips obtuse to acute, surfaces silky-canescent,
folded. Inflorescences in dense, terminal spikes, peduncles to 4 inches, often with smaller lateral spikes. Flowers
numerous, yellow, bilateral, to about ¼ inch long and as
wide. Common throughout western two-thirds of Texas.
Absent in South Texas.

239

Dalea nana FABACEAE
Dwarf dalea, dwarf prairie clover
Rocky or gravelly open grasslands, shrub
and woodlands, roadsides and other open
areas. Spring, summer. Common.

An ascending to decumbent perennial with canescent
stems to 8+ inches long branching from base. Leaves
alternate, pinnate, to 1¼ inches long with 5–9 leaflets.
Leaflets obovate to ⅝ inch long, margins entire to involute, tips mucronate to rounded, surfaces with silky
hairs. Inflorescences in dense, terminal spikes, spikes
somewhat pubescent. Flowers yellow, papilionaceous,
narrow, small. Found in western two-thirds of Texas,
from Brownsville north through Panhandle, west to New
Mexico.

Dalea neomexicana FABACEAE
Downy prairie clover
Desert scrub, grasslands. Spring, summer, fall. Common.

A prostrate to decumbent perennial with soft, velvety
stems branched from base, to 8 inches long. Leaves alternate, pinnate, to 1¼ inches long with 7–11 leaflets. Leaflets obovate, to ⅓ inch long, margins crenulate, surfaces
velvety. Peduncles short, opposite leaves. Racemes pubescent, dense to ¾ inch long. Flowers small and often hidden by pubescent calyces, pale to creamy yellow, papilionaceous, banner often with a rose-red blotch near base,
wings not spreading. Found in Chihuahuan Desert,
south to Webb County, often overlooked because of small
stature and nonshowy flowers. Crenulate margins on
leaflets are a distinguishing feature.

Genistidium dumosum FABACEAE
Brushpea
Open desert scrub. Spring, summer. Rare.

An erect, shrubby, rounded perennial with heavily
branched stems to 24 inches. Leaves alternate, trifoliolate.
Leaflets oblanceolate, to ½+ inch long, margins involute,
bases tapering, tips pointed, surfaces pubescent. Flowers in short racemes originating from leaf axils, papilionaceous, yellow, about ⅜ inch wide and as long, banner
erect with green streaks near base, wings covering keel,
appearing inflated, horizontal. Found on limestone, in
Brewster County between Lajitas and Terlingua.

Hoffmannseggia glauca   FABACEAE
Pork-nut, hog-plum, Indian rushpea
Open grass and brushlands, flats, river
floodplains, roadsides and other open areas.
Spring, summer, fall. Common.

An erect perennial with slender stems to 12 inches, stems
usually glandular pubescent. Leaves alternate, bipinnate,
to about 4 inches long, with 5–11 pairs of pinnae and 5–11
pairs of leaflets. Leaflets oblong to obovate, to ⅓ inch
long, glabrous or pubescent. Inflorescences in terminal
racemes to 8 inches long, raceme glandular-pubescent.
Flowers to 15, bilateral, yellow-orange, 5-petaled, upper
petal smaller than other 4 and with red blotches in center,
to 1 inch wide, petals and calyx with glandular hairs (a
distinguishing characteristic). Widespread from Panhandle to South Texas, west throughout Chihuahuan Desert,
absent from Central Texas.

Macroptilium gibbosifolium   FABACEAE
Variableleaf bushbean, wild bushbean
Rocky slopes, hillsides and grasslands,
roadsides. Summer, fall. Locally common.

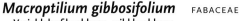

A prostrate to clambering vine with stems to 5+ feet long.
Leaves alternate, trifoliolate. Leaflets rhombic-ovate, often
lobed or widened at base, to 1¾ inches long, margins
entire, bases rounded or tapered or truncate, tips rounded
to acute, upper surface of blade gibbous. Peduncles to 10
inches. Flowers in raceme to 3¼ inches long, orange-red
to salmon, bilateral, wings elongated and scalloplike, keel
twisted, banner with inward-rolled margins. Currently
known from Jeff Davis and Val Verde Counties. Somewhat common along Scenic Loop and drainages in Davis
Mountains.

Medicago arabica   FABACEAE
Spotted medick, spotted burclover, heart clover
Urban and suburban areas, roadsides.
Spring. Locally common.

A decumbent or spreading annual with pubescent stems
to 24 inches long. Leaves alternate, on petioles to 3¼+
inches long, 3-foliolate, leaflets obcordate, to 1 inch long
and 1¼ inches wide, margins weakly serrate, bases tapering, tips rounded to notched. Center of leaflets with dark
chevron. Flowers in racemes originating from leaf axils,
yellow, papilionaceous, to ¼ inch long, banner notched,
lateral wings spreading. Found near human habitation.

241

Medicago lupulina FABACEAE
Black medick, black nonesuch, hop-clover
Fields, pastures, urban and suburban areas,
roadsides. Spring, summer. Locally common.

An introduced, prostrate to ascending annual with pubescent, occasionally branching stems to 30 inches. Leaves alternate, 3-foliolate. Leaflets obovate or oval-ovate, to ⅔ inch long, margins dentate, surfaces pubescent to nearly glabrous. Flowers in rounded and dense racemes originating from leaf axils, peduncles to 3 inches. Flowers ⅛ inch long, yellow, papilionaceous. Fruit is a single-seeded, pubescent, curled pod. Widespread throughout Texas, a common weed of lawns and maintained areas. Native of Eurasia.

Medicago minima FABACEAE
Small bur-clover, little bur-clover
Fields, pastures, roadsides, urban and suburban areas,
other open, disturbed places. Spring. Common.

An introduced, decumbent to erect annual with pubescent stems to 12 inches long. Leaves alternate, 3-foliolate. Leaflets oval to obovate, to ⅜ inch long, margins entire to dentate, tips rounded and mucronate. Peduncles to 1 inch. Flowers solitary or to 5 in rounded racemes, to 3/16 inch long, yellow, papilionaceous. Fruit is a rounded, coiled pod with hooked prickles. Frequent throughout Edwards Plateau, less common north into Panhandle and Oklahoma, east into Louisiana, south to Coastal Bend, west to Pecos County, spreading.

Medicago orbicularis FABACEAE
Blackdisk medick, button medick, button-clover
Fields, pastures, roadsides and other open,
disturbed areas. Spring. Uncommon.

An introduced, decumbent to ascending annual with glabrous stems to 20 inches long. Leaves alternate, 3-foliolate. Leaflets obovate to obcordate, to ¾ inch long, margins serrate, bases tapering to rounded. Flowers few, 1–5 per peduncle, papilionaceous, yellow, about 3/16 inch long. Fruit is an unarmed pod, glabrous, coiled into spirals to ¾ inch wide. Uncommon from Oklahoma south to Coastal Bend, originally from Mediterranean area.

Medicago polymorpha   FABACEAE
Bur-clover, bur medick, toothed medick
Urban and suburban areas, roadsides. Spring. Common.

An introduced, prostrate to decumbent to ascending annual with glabrous to weakly pubescent stems to 20 inches long. Leaves alternate, 3-foliolate. Leaflets obovate, to ¾ inch long, margins toothed, bases rounded, tips notched, blades mostly glabrous. Flowers few, in short racemes, papilionaceous, yellow, to ¼ inch long. Fruit coiled with hooked prickles, surface glabrous. Common throughout South Texas, north into Oklahoma, east into Louisiana, occasional in Chihuahuan Desert.

Melilotus indicus   FABACEAE
Sour clover, alfalfilla, annual yellow sweetclover
Fields, pastures, roadsides, agricultural areas and other areas of human habitation. Spring. Common.

An introduced, erect annual with heavily branched, glabrous stems to 24+ inches tall. Leaves alternate, 3-foliolate. Leaflets oblanceolate to obovate, to 1 inch long and ⅜ inch wide, margins serrate or minutely dentate along upper half, bases cuneate, tips obtuse. Flowers in dense terminal or axillary racemes, yellow, papilionaceous, to ⅛ inch wide. Fruit round, flat to ⅛ inch wide. Frequent throughout majority of Texas. Weak to absent in Panhandle, common along roadsides, especially near agricultural areas.

Melilotus officinalis   FABACEAE
Yellow sweet clover
Fields, pastures, roadsides, agricultural areas, and other areas of human habitation. Spring. Common.

An introduced, erect annual or biennial with branching, angular stems to 5 feet. Leaves alternate, 3-foliolate. Leaflets obovate, ovate, oblanceolate or linear, to 1 inch long and ½ inch wide, margins toothed or serrate. Flowers in terminal or axillary racemes to 6 inches long. Flowers yellow or white, papilionaceous, to ⅓ inch long. Fruit oval and short stalked. Widespread throughout Texas. Oval-shaped fruit distinguishes this species from *Melilotus indicus*.

243

Neptunia lutea FABACEAE
Yellow puff, yellow sensitive briar
Grasslands, fields, prairies, open brush
and woodlands, roadsides and other open
areas. Spring, summer, fall. Common.

A prostrate, sprawling perennial with weak stems to 2+
feet long. Leaves alternate, bipinnately compound, with
4–11 pairs of pinnae and 8–18 pairs of oblong leaflets.
Compact, round to oval flowering heads on peduncles to
5 inches long, to 60 individual yellow flowers. Found in
open areas throughout eastern half of Texas, from Laredo
area north into Oklahoma, east into Louisiana.

Neptunia pubescens FABACEAE
Yellow-puff, tropical yellow-puff
Grasslands, prairies, fields, open shrub and
woodlands, dunes, roadsides and other open
areas. Spring, summer, fall. Common.

A prostrate, sprawling perennial with weak stems to 2+
feet long. Leaves alternate, bipinnately compound with
2–6 pairs of pinnae and 14–40+ pairs of oblong leaflets. Compact, oval to round flowering heads consist of
to 30 yellow flowers on peduncles to 4 inches. Found
along coast and inland, from Brownsville to Louisiana.
Although range of this species and *Neptunia lutea* overlap, leaf morphology differentiates the two.

Rhynchosia americana FABACEAE
American snoutbean
Fields, prairies, grasslands, open brush and
woodlands. Spring, summer, fall. Common.

A prostrate to trailing, twining vine with branching,
pubescent stems to 4+ feet long, multiple stems from
central base. Leaves alternate, on petioles to 2 inches
long, one leaflet, reniform, to 2 inches wide and as long,
margins entire, bases cordate, tips rounded. Flowers in
short racemes originating from leaf axils, papilionaceous,
yellow, to ³⁄₈ inch long, banner erect and creased, keel
extending slightly beyond lateral wings. Found in sandy
soils in South Texas, north into southern Edwards Plateau, east into Southeast Texas.

244

Rhynchosia latifolia   FABACEAE
Prairie snoutbean
Woodlands, thickets, brushlands, fence
lines. Spring, summer. Common.

A trailing or twining, climbing vine with branching, pubescent stems to 3+ feet long. Leaves alternate,
3-foliolate, leaflets widely ovate to rhombic, weakly lobed,
to 3 inches long, bases tapering, margins entire, tips
obtuse. Flowers in racemes to 12 inches long, originating
from leaf axils, papilionaceous, yellow, banner reflexed
and creased, lateral wings and keel horizontal. Found in
eastern third of Texas, often in sandy soils.

Rhynchosia minima   FABACEAE
Least snoutbean
Thickets, brush and woodlands, fence lines.
Spring, summer, fall. Common.

A trailing or twining perennial vine with pubescent
stems to 4+ feet long. Leaves alternate, 3-foliolate, leaflets
rhombic to round, to 1½ inches long, bases tapering to
round, margins entire, tips acute. Flowers in racemes to 6
inches long, originating from leaf axils, yellow, papilionaceous, to ⅓ inch long, banner reflexed, occasionally with
red venation, keel slightly longer than wings, horizontal.
Common along coast from Hidalgo County into Louisiana, throughout Southeast Texas, and west into Edwards
Plateau.

Senna bauhinioides   FABACEAE
Twinleaf senna, two-leaved senna
Open shrub and grasslands, rocky slopes,
river floodplains, washes, roadsides and other
open areas. Spring, summer. Common.

An erect or spreading to ascending perennial with
branching, gray-tomentose stems to 16+ inches tall.
Leaves spirally arranged, leaflets 2, oblong to ovate, to
1¾ inches long and ¾ inch wide, bases asymmetric,
rounded, tips rounded, slightly pointed, leaf surfaces gray
tomentose. Flowers in cymes of 2 or 3 or solitary, yellow
with darker venation, to 1¼ inches wide, with 5 unequal
petals. Fruits ascending, curved. Frequent in Chihuahuan Desert where it is widespread at lower elevations,
less common in South Texas; often found in sandy to
gravelly disturbed soils.

245

Senna durangensis   FABACEAE
Durango senna
Sparse desert scrub, Tamaulipan Thornscrub.
Spring, summer, fall. Uncommon.

An erect or ascending perennial with stems to 20 inches long, stems with gray or yellow pubescence. Leaves spirally arranged, on petioles longer than leaflets. Leaflets 2, nearly round to widely oval, to 2 inches long and 1½ inches wide, bases asymmetrical, rounded, margins entire, tips rounded, blades softly pubescent. Flowers in cymes of to 6 flowers or solitary, yellow with darker venation, to about 1¼ inches wide, with 5 unequal petals. Fruits straight to slightly curved, erect. Found in sandy to gravelly soils along the Rio Grande in the Trans-Pecos and Lower Rio Grande Valley.

Senna lindheimeriana   FABACEAE
Lindheimer's senna
Open brush and woodlands, rocky slopes, outcrops, ledges, gravelly creek and river beds, open grasslands. Summer, fall. Common.

An erect perennial with multiple pubescent stems, rarely single-stemmed, to 6 feet tall. Leaves spirally arranged, pinnate, to 5 inches long and 2 inches wide, with 5–8 pairs of leaflets. Each leaflet oblong to elliptic, to 2 inches long and ¾ inch wide, bases asymmetric, margins entire, tips acute or obtuse, mucronate, blades silky. Flowers in racemes originating from upper leaf axils, light yellow with darker venation, with 5 unequal petals. Frequent in rocky terrain from El Paso west into Edwards Plateau.

Senna obtusifolia   FABACEAE
Java-bean, sicklepod, coffeeweed
Fields, pastures, grasslands, open shrub and woodlands, roadsides, railroads and other open, disturbed areas. Summer. Common.

An erect, branching annual with stems to 30+ inches tall, stems and foliage with foul odor. Leaves spirally arranged to alternate, pinnate, to 1½ inches long and 1 inch wide, 3 pairs of leaflets with each leaflet obovate, bases rounded, margins entire, tips rounded and slightly mucronate. Yellow flowers either solitary or in pairs, originating from axils of upper leaves, to 1 inch wide, with 5 unequal petals. Fruit to 6 inches, curved. Found in eastern third of state, frequent in Southeast Texas.

Senna occidentalis   FABACEAE
Septic weed, coffee senna, stinkingweed
Urban and suburban areas, roadsides and other
disturbed areas. Summer, fall. Common.

An introduced, erect annual with glabrous stems to 6+
feet tall, stems and foliage with foul odor. Leaves spirally
arranged to alternate, pinnate, with 4–6 pairs of leaflets,
each leaflet lanceolate to ovate, to 2½ inches long and 1
inch wide, bases asymmetric, margins entire, tips acute
to acuminate. Flowers in racemes originating from upper
leaf axils, yellow, to 1¼ inches wide, with 5 unequal petals. Fruit slender, linear to 4¾ inches long. Most common
in Southeast Texas, south to Cameron County and into
Mexico; spreading.

Senna pumilio   FABACEAE
Dwarf senna
Open grass and shrublands, rocky slopes and
hillsides, roadsides and other open areas.
Spring, summer. Locally common.

A tufted perennial with leafy stems to 8 inches tall when
in flower. Leaves spirally arranged with one pair of leaflets. Leaflets linear to lanceolate, to 2 inches long and
less than ⅛ inch wide, margins entire, tips pointed,
blades folded with visible appressed hairs. Flowers solitary on pedicels to 6 inches, yellow, to 1 inch wide, with 5
unequal petals. Widespread and locally common. Found
in western portion of state, from Lubbock south into Mexico, east to Coastal Bend, west to Presidio County.

Senna roemeriana   FABACEAE
Two-leaf senna
Grasslands, fields, prairies, open shrub
and woodlands, roadsides and other open
areas. Spring, summer. Common.

An erect to ascending perennial to 2 feet tall with
gray-pubescent stems. Leaves spirally arranged, on petioles shorter than blades, pinnate, with one pair of leaflets, each leaflet linear to lanceolate, to 2½ inches long
and to ½ inch wide, bases rounded and asymmetrical,
margins entire, tips pointed, blades often folded. Flowers
in racemes originating from leaf axils, yellow to orange,
to 1 inch wide, 5 unequal petals. Frequent throughout
Edwards Plateau, north into Oklahoma, west to Culberson County and New Mexico.

Sesbania drummondii   FABACEAE
Rattlebush, rattlebox, poison bean
Creek and river beds, banks of lakes and
ponds, roadside ditches and other low, wet
areas. Spring, summer, fall. Common.

An erect, short-lived perennial shrub with a stout single branching stem to 8+ feet tall. Leaves alternate, pinnate, to 8 inches long, 20–50 leaflets. Leaflets oblong to
1½ inches long, margins entire, tips mucronate. Flowers in hanging racemes originating from leaf axils,
orange-yellow, to ⅝ inch long, papilionaceous. Fruit to
about 3 inches long and ⅜ inch wide, 4-winged. When
mature, seed is loose on inside. Found in South Texas,
northeast to Louisiana, less so in Edwards Plateau and
North-Central Texas; often occurring in large colonies.

Sesbania vesicaria   FABACEAE
Bagpod, bladderpod
Creek and river beds and bottoms, wet prairies
and savannas, roadside ditches and other
low, wet areas. Summer. Common.

An erect annual with a single, branching stem to 6+
feet tall. Leaves alternate, pinnate, to 6 inches long, with
20–40 leaflets. Each leaflet oblong-elliptic, to 1¾ inches
long, bases rounded, tips mucronate. Flowers in hanging racemes originating from leaf axils, to ⅜ inch long,
papilionaceous, banner orange-red with yellow base, margin notched, keel and wings red. Found in eastern half of
Texas, from Coastal Bend north into Oklahoma, east into
Louisiana. Often found in large populations.

Stylosanthes biflora   FABACEAE
Pencil-flower, sidebeak pencilflower
Fields, meadows, grasslands, savannas, open brush and
woodlands, roadsides. Spring, summer. Uncommon.

An erect to ascending perennial with pubescent, branching stems to 18 inches. Leaves alternate, on petioles to ¼
inch long, trifoliolate, leaflets elliptic, to 1½ inches long
and ⅓ inch wide, bases tapering, margins entire to ciliate. Flowers solitary, rarely more than one, occurring in
leaf axils, papilionaceous, yellow, banner round with red
streaks at base, wings horizontal. Found in eastern third
of Texas, from Coastal Bend north into Oklahoma.

Trifolium campestre   FABACEAE
Field clover, hop-trefoil, low hop clover
Shrub and woodlands, roadsides. Spring. Common.

An introduced, decumbent annual or biennial with branching stems to 12 inches, stems pubescent or glabrate. Leaves alternate, 3-foliolate, leaflets ovate to obovate, to ¾ inch long and ⅓ inch wide, bases tapering, margins dentate, tips rounded to notched. Flowers small, in short and rounded to cylindric spikes originating from upper leaf axils, yellow, numerous, papilionaceous, banner large and protruding forward and covering keel, wings cup keel from below. Common throughout eastern third of Texas.

Trifolium dubium   FABACEAE
Suckling clover, little hop clover, lesser trefoil
Fields, meadows, pastures, grasslands, roadsides and other open areas. Spring, summer. Common.

An introduced, erect or decumbent, low-growing annual with pubescent, branching stems to 15 inches. Leaves alternate, 3-foliolate, leaflets obovate to ½ inch long, bases tapering, margins entire, tips notched, middle leaflet with slightly longer stalk. Inflorescences in rounded clusters held above foliage on stalks to 1+ inch long. Flowers small, yellow, papilionaceous, banner longer than keel and wings. Common in Southeast Texas, uncommon farther north into Oklahoma and west into Panhandle. Originally from northern Europe, widely introduced throughout North America.

Vigna luteola   FABACEAE
Hairypod cowpea, yellow vigna
Thickets, brushlands, fence lines, roadsides. Spring, summer, fall. Uncommon.

A perennial climbing vine with stems to 10+ feet long. Leaves alternate, trifoliolate, leaflets ovate to lanceolate, to 3 inches long, bases tapering, margins entire, tips pointed. Flowers in racemes originating from leaf axils. Flowers yellow, to ¾ inch long, banner creased, wings spreading slightly. Only native species of *Vigna* in Texas; found in South Texas and north along coast into Louisiana. In South Texas, it grows along banks of Rio Grande and around resacas; along coast it can be found on edges of freshwater marshes. Pantropical.

Zornia bracteata   FABACEAE
Viperina
Woodlands, fields, meadows, roadsides and other
open areas. Spring, summer, fall. Common.

A prostrate annual with stems to 2 feet long radiating
from a central root. Mat forming in dense populations.
Leaves alternate, palmately compound with 4 leaflets.
Leaflets lanceolate, to 1 inch long, petioles to 1 inch. Flowers in bracted spikes to 6 inches long, papilionaceous,
yellow, ½ inch long, banner with red streaks along veins.
Viperina is found from far South Texas north to Dallas area and east into Louisiana. Genus name honors
Johannes Zorn, a late 18th-century German apothecary.

Zornia gemella   FABACEAE
Dos hoja, zarzaboca de dos hojas, two leaf
Fields, meadows, prairies, roadsides and other
open areas. Spring, summer, fall. Uncommon.

A prostrate annual with stems to 1+ foot long. Leaves
alternate, on petioles 1 inch long, palmately compound,
2 leaflets, to 1 inch long, varying from lanceolate to
lance-ovate. Yellow, papilionaceous flowers about ½ inch
long, upper keel often streaked red along veins, occurring
along bracteate inflorescences, each flower surrounded
by 2 bracts which do not overlap. Found in South Texas,
from Coastal Bend south into Mexico; occasionally hidden among grasses and other herbaceous plants.

Hypericum crux-andreae   HYPERICACEAE
St. Peter's wort
Savannas, meadows, bogs, pond and lake edges, other
areas with wet or damp soils. Summer, fall. Common.

An erect, shrubby perennial with unbranched or weakly
branched stems to 4+ feet tall. Leaves opposite, sessile
to clasping, oblong to elliptic, to 1½ inches long and ¾
inch wide, margins entire, bases somewhat cordate, tips
rounded to obtuse. Flowers in terminal cymes or solitary,
yellow, to 1¼ inches wide, 4-petaled, petals obovate, stamens yellow, numerous. Found in open woodlands in
East Texas.

Hypericum drummondii   HYPERICACEAE
Nits and lice
Fields, meadows, open woodlands,
roadsides. Summer. Common.

An erect, branching annual with slender, leafy stems
to 30+ inches tall. Leaves opposite, sessile, linear to
linear-lanceolate, to ¾ inch long, ascending to erect, margins entire to revolute, tips acute. Flowers in terminal
cymes, yellow to ½ inch wide with 5 ovate petals. Found
in open, sandy areas in eastern half of Texas, from central
Edwards Plateau into Louisiana.

Hypericum hypericoides   HYPERICACEAE
St. Andrew's cross
Forests, woodlands, thickets, grasslands,
bogs. Spring, summer, fall. Common.

An erect to ascending to decumbent shrubby perennial
with reddish brown, leafy, branching stems to 3+ feet
tall. Leaves opposite, sessile, linear to oblanceolate, to 1¼
inches long and ⅓ inch wide, bases narrowed, margins
entire to revolute, tips acute. Flowers solitary, yellow, to
about 1¾ inches wide, 4-petaled, petals oblong-elliptic.
Found in eastern third of state.

Hypericum punctatum   HYPERICACEAE
Spotted St. Johnswort
Fields, meadows, grasslands, open woodlands.
Spring, summer. Uncommon.

An introduced, erect perennial with unbranched or
weakly branched stems to 3+ feet tall. Leaves opposite,
sessile, oblong to elliptic, to 2¾ inches long and ¾ inch
wide, bases clasping margins entire, tips rounded to
obtuse. Flowers in crowded terminal cymes, yellow, often
with small darker spots, 5-petaled, to ½ inch wide, stamens numerous. Currently known from North-Central
Texas east to Texarkana.

Hypoxis hirsuta   HYPOXIDACEAE
Yellow star grass, eastern star grass, common goldstar
Woodlands, forests, stream banks.
Spring, summer. Common.

A perennial with grasslike leaves and appearance, scapes to 10 inches in height. Leaves linear with longest usually 1½ times length of scape, ¼ to ¾ inch wide, varying degrees of pubescence. To 7 flowers in terminal umbels, bright yellow, about ¾ inch in diameter, 6 petals. Found in eastern third of Texas. Genus name of Greek origin and means "under" (*hypo*) "sharp" (*oxys*), referring to pointed ovaries.

Hypoxis wrightii   HYPOXIDACEAE
Wright's star grass
Pine woodlands and forests, meadows, prairies. Spring. Uncommon.

A perennial with grasslike leaves and appearance, to 12 inches tall. Leaves linear, 1½–2 times longer than scape and to ¼ inch wide, rigid, pubescent. Scape to 12 inches, usually shorter. Flowers yellow, to ¾ inch wide, with 6 tepals in a short raceme. Found scattered throughout eastern third of Texas, in pine-oak woodlands that have been well-managed with regard to fire. Named in honor of Charles Wright, a Texas botanist who lived during the 1800s. In *Hypoxis hirsuta*, the pedicel is usually twice as long as bracts on scape; in *H. wrightii*, pedicel length is less.

Iris pseudacorus   IRIDACEAE
Yellow-flag, yellow iris
Swamps, ponds, shores of rivers and lakes, other wet areas. Spring, summer. Uncommon.

An introduced, aquatic, rhizomatous perennial with a single stem to 3 feet tall. Leaves sword-shaped, to 3+ feet long and just over 1 inch wide at largest. Inflorescences terminal on slender stems with 12 flowers per. Flowers yellow with 3 sepals and 3 petals, each sepal to 3 inches long and arches downward, petals just over 1 inch long and spread outward without arching. Native of the Old World; brought here as an ornamental and still available in the nursery trade. Not common throughout Texas, but usually in large colonies when found. Typically around urban areas and other sites where intentionally planted.

Sisyrinchium rosulatum   IRIDACEAE
Annual blue-eyed grass
Fields, meadows, roadsides, disturbed
areas. Spring, summer, fall. Common.

An erect, tufted annual with branching stems to 15
inches tall. Numerous grasslike, glabrous leaves, half the
length of flowering stems. Star-shaped, ½ inch flowers
variable in color and can range from yellow to maroon or
pink, center usually deep purple. Outer tepals flare outward, inner portions form a recognizable bell shape when
viewed from side. Common in southeast and eastern portions of state. Absent elsewhere. Prefers disturbed soils.

Leonotis nepetifolia   LAMIACEAE
Christmas candlestick, lion's ears
Floodplains, urban and suburban areas, roadsides and
other waste places. Spring, summer, fall. Uncommon.

An introduced, erect annual with single stems to about
6 feet tall. Leaves opposite, on petioles 2+ inches long,
ovate to deltate, to 4 inches long and nearly as wide, margins crenate to serrate. Flowers in rounded clusters in
upper stems, clusters to 3 inches broad, orange, to 1 inch
long, bilabiate. Upper lip unlobed and longer than lower
lip which is 3-lobed. An introduced ornamental from
tropical Africa and India which has escaped cultivation.
Found in disturbed areas, generally around populated
areas in East and Central Texas. Specific epithet refers to
leaves, which are like *Nepeta* species.

Monarda punctata   LAMIACEAE
Horsemint, spotted horsemint, spotted beebalm
Fields, grasslands, prairies, open brush
and woodlands, roadsides and other open
areas. Spring, summer. Common.

An erect perennial, typically unbranched, or weakly
branched, with leafy, pubescent stems to 3 feet tall. Leaves
opposite, on short petioles, lanceolate, to 3½ inches long
and 1 inch wide, bases tapering, margins serrate to entire,
tips pointed. Stems terminating in short, crowded spikes
of roundish flowering heads. Flowers creamy yellow to
white, heavily spotted, bilabiate to 1 inch long, lower lip
3-lobed with middle lobe larger than others, bracts dusty
white. Common throughout majority of state. Absent in
far West Texas. Usually found in sandy soils.

253

Utricularia gibba   LENTIBULARIACEAE
Bladderwort, cone-spur bladderwort, humped bladderwort
Edges of and within ponds and lakes, slow-moving
streams, bogs, ephemeral waters. Summer, fall. Common.

A carnivorous annual to perennial, floating aquatic or
rooted in mud, with hairlike branching stems to 10+
inches long. Plants often forming floating mats. Leaves
alternate, thin, to ⅜ inch long and forked. Along leaves
are threadlike extensions and bladders used to trap
micro-organisms. Yellow, bilabiate flowers about ¼ inch
long occur on slender scapes to 5 inches tall, to 3 flowers per scape, lower lip inflated and hiding spur below,
upper lip bannerlike. Most common bladderwort found
in Texas. Absent only in West Texas and Panhandle.

Erythronium rostratum   LILIACEAE
**Yellow trout lily, beaked trout lily, yellow dog-tooth violet,
yellow fawnlily**
Mixed pine woodlands and forests. Spring. Rare.

An erect (when in flower), bulbous and stoloniferous perennial to 8 inches tall. Two basal leaves in
flowering plants; one in nonflowering plants. Leaves
elliptic-lanceolate to ovate, bases tapering, margins
entire, tips pointed, blades glabrous, green, mottled
brown. Flowers solitary, somewhat erect (not nodding) at
end of scape to 8 inches tall, yellow, about 1½ inches long
and as wide with 6 recurved petals. Rare; often found
near streams in far eastern Texas, and like white trout lily,
will often form colonies.

Lilium michauxii   LILIACEAE
Carolina lily
Oak-pine woodlands and forests. Summer. Uncommon.

An erect perennial, from a bulb, with stems to 3 feet
when flowering. Whorled leaves, oblanceolate, to 5½
inches long and 1¾ inches wide, margins undulate. To
4 nodding flowers in terminal umbels. Flowers 4 inches
wide, with 6 heavily reflexed and yellow-orange to reddish
orange petals, often with dark reddish to maroon spots.
Unmistakable; found in deep East Texas.

Linum alatum LINACEAE
Winged flax
Fields, grasslands, prairies, open brush
and woodlands, roadsides and other open
areas. Spring, summer. Common.

An erect annual with glabrous stems to 12 inches tall.
Leaves alternate, sessile, ascending or held close to
stem, linear to linear-lanceolate, to 1¼ inches long, margins entire, tips pointed. Flowers in terminal cymes,
yellow-orange with a darker center, 5-petaled, radial, to 1+
inch wide. Sepals ovate with glandular, toothed margins.
Found in sandy soils throughout South Texas and along
coast to Galveston Bay.

Linum berlandieri LINACEAE
Berlandier's yellow flax
Fields, grasslands, prairies, open brush
and woodlands, roadsides and other open
areas. Spring, summer. Common.

An erect, glabrous annual with leafy stems, branching
from base to 20 inches. Leaves alternate, sessile, ascending to erect along stem, linear, to 1¼ inches long, margins entire, tips pointed to acute. Flowers numerous,
in terminal cymes, yellow to yellow-orange and reddish
below middle, 5-petaled, radial to about 1 inch wide.
Sepals lanceolate to ovate. Most common *Linum* species
found in Texas, only absent in far western and East Texas.

Linum elongatum LINACEAE
Laredo flax
Open shrub and grasslands, rocky outcrops, roadcuts
and roadsides. Spring, summer. Uncommon.

An erect, glabrous annual or perennial with stems
branching from base, to 20 inches though typically
shorter. Leaves alternate, sessile to clasping, ascending
to erect along stem, linear to 1¼ inches long, margins
entire, tips pointed to acute. Flowers solitary or few, terminal or from upper leaf axils, 5-petaled, radial, to about
¾ inch wide, yellow to yellow-orange with reddish purple
banding in center. Sepals lanceolate. A species of South
Texas found from Dimmit County south to Brownsville.

Linum medium   LINACEAE
Stiff yellow flax, common yellow flax
Fields, meadows, grasslands, roadsides and other
open areas. Spring, summer. Common.

An erect, airy perennial with glabrous, branching stems
to 28+ inches tall. Leaves alternate above and opposite
below, elliptic to lanceolate, to 1 inch long and less than
¼ inch wide, margins entire, tips pointed to acute. Flowers in terminal panicles. Flowers yellow, to ½ inch wide,
5-petaled, petals typically notched, rotate. Found in eastern third of Texas.

Cevallia sinuata   LOASACEAE
Stinging cevallia, stinging serpent
Open shrublands, roadsides, washes and other
disturbed areas. Spring, summer, fall. Common.

An erect, multistemmed perennial from a woody base to
18 inches tall, leaves and stems covered in stinging hairs.
Leaves alternate or sessile or on short petioles, lanceolate
to 2½ inches long, margins sinuate or pinnatifid. Flowers
in compact and rounded cymes, either terminal or originating from upper leaf axils. Peduncles to 4 inches long.
Flowers numerous, pale yellow, to ½ inch wide. Common
along roadsides in southern and West Texas, north into
Panhandle; lacking in central and eastern portions of
state. A burning sensation from the stinging hairs can be
quite painful and may last several hours.

Eucnide bartonioides   LOASACEAE
Rock-nettle, yellow rock-nettle, yellow stingbush
Steep slopes, cliffs and bluffs. Winter,
spring, summer, fall. Uncommon.

A trailing annual or short-lived perennial from a semiwoody base, with numerous stems to several feet long.
Leaves alternate, round to cordate, to 4 inches long,
shallowly lobed with toothed to scalloped margins.
Leaf petioles may exceed length of leaves. Bright yellow funnel-shaped flowers to 2 inches in diameter, with
numerous fine stamens exceeding petals. There are 2
varieties in Texas: *Eucnide bartonioides* var. *edwardsiana* is
found in the Edwards Plateau and usually grows around
waterways; *E. bartonioides* var. *bartonioides* is more common along the Rio Grande and its tributaries. Perhaps
best place to spot plants is along Hot Springs Trail in Big
Bend National Park.

rock-nettle family
LOASACEAE
LOASACEAE

Eucnide lobata   LOASACEAE
Lobed-leaf rock nettle, lobed-leaf stingbush
Protected limestone cliffs. Spring, summer, fall. Rare.

An erect, branching, rounded annual to perennial, to 10 inches tall and twice as wide, stems and leaves with visible hairs. Leaves alternate, round to broadly deltate in outline, to 1 inch long and as wide, lobed with ultimate lobe margins roughly toothed, petioles to 1 inch long or more, bases cordate, tips acute. Flowers in upper leaf axils, yellow, about ¾ inch wide, 5-petaled, radial to slightly bilateral with up to 120 stamens. Currently known from Starr County in deep South Texas.

Mentzelia multiflora   LOASACEAE
Stick-leaf, blazing star, Adonis blazingstar
Open fields, shrublands, roadsides and disturbed areas. Spring, summer. Common.

An erect, multibranched biennial with whitish stems to 2½ feet tall. Linear to lanceolate leaves variable in size, but can reach 6 inches long and have lobed margins, leaf undersides with recurved hairs that readily stick to clothing. Inflorescences numerous, 2 inches in diameter, 5 petals and 5 slightly smaller sepals, bright yellow (older flowers may lose their yellow color and fade to white). Flowers are closed in morning and open in afternoon. Found in western portion of state, mostly west of Pecos River, although a few collections have been made in the Panhandle, where its range extends eastward from New Mexico.

Mentzelia oligosperma   LOASACEAE
Chicken-thief, stick-leaf, pegajosa
Fields, meadows, open woodlands and shrublands, other open areas. Spring, summer, fall. Common.

An erect, semiwoody, multibranched perennial with single or multiple stems to 2 feet tall. Leaves alternate, ovate to rhombic, to 2½ inches long and 1 inch wide, margins toothed or lobed, leaf surfaces with rough hairs. Like other members of genus, leaves readily adhere to clothing and fur of animals. Orangish yellow flowers are to ¾ inch in diameter and have 5 petals that taper to a point. Lanceolate calyx lobes can be seen emerging between petals. Widely distributed throughout state, lacking in East Texas. Found in a wide variety of soil types and substrates, most common on limestone.

257

Heimia salicifolia LYTHRACEAE
Mellow-yellow, yellowcrest, willow-leaf heimia
Thickets, riparian areas, lomas. Summer, fall. Rare.

An erect, shrubby perennial with glabrous, leafy stems to 4+ feet tall. Leaves opposite, on short petioles or sessile, linear-oblanceolate to linear-lanceolate or lanceolate, to 2 inches long and ½ inch wide, bases tapering, margins entire, tips pointed. Flowers large, to 1¼ inches wide, 6-petaled, yellow to yellow-orange, in leaf axils of upper stem. Found in Lower Rio Grande Valley, in Cameron and Hidalgo Counties.

Cottsia gracilis (*Janusia gracilis*) MALPIGHIACEAE
Propeller-bush
Sparse desert scrub, open brushlands, rocky outcrops, canyons and other rocky, open areas. Spring, summer. Uncommon.

A twining, climbing vine with thin, pubescent stems to 5+ feet long. Leaves opposite, linear to lanceolate, to 1½ inches long and about ⅓ inch wide, bases tapering, margins entire with several teeth at base, tips acute, blades silky above. Flowers on short peduncles originating from leaf axils at ends of stems, propeller-shaped, yellow to yellow-orange, 5-petaled, petals ovate at end with thin base, to ¾ inch wide. Fruit is either a 2- or 3-winged samara, reddish brown in color. Found in mid to lower elevations in Chihuahuan Desert, often climbing over shrubs.

Galphimia angustifolia MALPIGHIACEAE
Thryallis
Sparse desert scrub, open brush and woodlands, rocky outcrops and slopes, canyons, roadcuts and other open, rocky areas. Spring, summer, fall. Common.

An erect perennial with glabrous stems to 16+ inches tall. Leaves opposite, on short petioles or nearly sessile, linear-lanceolate to oval, to 2 inches long and ½ inch wide, bases tapering, margins entire, tips pointed. Stems terminating in loosely flowered racemes to 6 inches long. Flowers radial, yellow, fading to red, 5 petals, to about ¾ inch wide. Found primarily on limestone throughout southern Edwards Plateau, west to Big Bend, south into Mexico.

Abutilon fruticosum MALVACEAE
Indian mallow, pelotazo, Texas Indian mallow
Grasslands, fields, pastures, open shrub and
woodlands, roadsides and other open areas.
Winter, spring, summer, fall. Common.

An erect, shrubby perennial with tomentose, branching
stems to 5+ feet tall. Leaves alternate, ovate, to 4 inches
long and 2 inches wide, becoming smaller up the stem,
bases cordate, margins serrate, tips acute, blade surfaces
pubescent. Flowers either solitary or in terminal panicles,
radial with 5 petals, yellow to yellow-orange, to nearly 1
inch wide. Found throughout South Texas, north into
Oklahoma; becoming less common farther north and
west to El Paso.

Abutilon malacum MALVACEAE
Yellow Indian mallow
Open desert scrub and grasslands, canyons,
mountain drainages. Summer. Uncommon.

An erect, shrubby perennial with tomentose, branching
stems to 3+ feet tall. Leaves alternate, ovate, to 3 inches
long, bases cordate, margins serrate, tips pointed, surfaces tomentose, fuzzy, pale grayish green. Yellow to
yellow-orange flowers in terminal and compact panicles,
radial, 5-petaled, to 1¼ inches wide. Located in Chihuahuan Desert, from Val Verde County west to El Paso.

Abutilon wrightii MALVACEAE
Wright's Indian mallow
Open brush and woodlands, thornscrub, fields,
canyons, rocky outcrops, roadsides and other
open areas. Spring, summer, fall. Uncommon.

A procumbent to ascending perennial with pubescent
stems to 2+ feet long. Leaves alternate, rounded-cordate,
to 1¾ inches wide and as long, bases cordate, margins
dentate, tips acute to obtuse, lower surface of leaves softly
pubescent, grayish green, upper surface sparsely pubescent, green. Flowers typically solitary in upper leaf axils,
yellow to yellow-orange, to 1¼ inches broad. Occasional
in Chihuahuan Desert, often on limestone, east into
Edwards Plateau, south to Cameron County.

Allowissadula holosericea MALVACEAE

Velvet-leaf mallow, Chisos Mountain false Indianmallow
Open shrub and woodlands, canyons, ravines,
rocky slopes. Spring, summer, fall. Uncommon.

An erect, bushy perennial with branching stems to nearly
6 feet tall. Alternate leaves velvety, sometimes occurring in pairs, ovate to triangular and slightly 3-lobed, to
7 inches long and 5 inches wide, bases cordate, margins
dentate to crenate. Flowers 5-petaled, occur in panicles
of 2+ flowers (rarely solitary), yellow to yellow-orange, to
1½ inches wide. Found throughout Central Texas, west
into mountains of Chihuahuan Desert, where it occurs at
higher elevations.

Hibiscus coulteri MALVACEAE

Desert rosemallow, desert hibiscus, Coulter hibiscus
Rocky slopes, open desert scrub. Winter,
spring, summer, fall. Uncommon.

An erect, slender perennial to 5 feet tall with both leaves
and stems covered with star-shaped hairs. Leaves ovate,
with lower leaves undivided to 1½ inches, upper leaves
divided into 3 (rarely 5) parts, about 2 inches long, bases
cordate, margins roughly toothed to slightly lobed. Pale
yellow flowers, to 1½ inches long and slightly wider, may
have red lines at base of throat (I have never observed
this character in Texas). Found in western portion of
state, often in gravelly soils along alluvial fans. Named
after Thomas Coulter, Irish botanist and physician who
collected in northern Mexico and southwestern United
States in early 1800s.

Malvastrum coromandelianum MALVACEAE

False mallow, threelobe false mallow, prickly false mallow
Brush and woodlands, floodplains, riparian
drainages and other low, wet areas. Winter,
spring, summer, fall. Common.

An erect annual or short-lived perennial with a single,
leafy stem to 5 feet tall, stem weakly branched above.
Leaves alternate, on petioles to 1½ inches long, ovate to
lanceolate, to 2 inches long and nearly as wide, typically
smaller, bases truncate to rounded to cuneate, margins
serrate, surfaces of leaves covered with star-shaped or
simple hairs. Yellow to yellow-orange solitary flowers are
to ½ inch wide and occur in leaf axils at ends of branches.
Found from Big Bend region east into Louisiana, south
into Mexico.

Modiola caroliniana MALVACEAE
Carolina bristlemallow, Carolina modiola
Marshes, banks of canals, ponds, lakes, and
streams, urban and suburban areas, roadsides
and other disturbed areas. Spring. Common.

An introduced, creeping perennial with pubescent stems
to 24+ inches long, stems rooting at nodes. Leaves alternate on petioles the length of blade, rounded-cordate, to
2½ inches long and 1¾ inches wide, 3- to 5-lobed, bases
cordate, margins incised. Solitary flowers on slender
peduncles originating from leaf axils, 5-petaled, radial,
orange to salmon to reddish purple, petals somewhat
erect, ⅓ inch wide. Common along coastal areas and
inland, especially along roads and in urban areas, west to
El Paso, north to Oklahoma; spreading.

Rhynchosida physocalyx MALVACEAE
Bladderpod sida, buffpetal, beaked sida
Thickets, brush and woodlands, forests, fence lines,
urban and suburban areas, roadsides and other
disturbed areas. Spring, summer, fall. Common.

A sprawling perennial from a large taproot, with lax and
sparsely pubescent stems to 16+ inches long. Leaves alternate, on petioles to 1¼ inches long, ovate, to 2½ inches
long and 2 inches wide, bases cordate, margins crenate
to serrate, tips rounded, surfaces visibly pubescent. Flowers radial, 5-petaled, pale yellow, to about 1 inch wide, on
short pedicels originating from upper leaf axils. Frequent
throughout western two-thirds of Texas. Absent in eastern Texas and northern Panhandle. Common weed, often
growing in lawns and residential gardens.

Sida abutifolia MALVACEAE
Spreading sida, creeping sida, hierba del buen día
Fields, pastures, grasslands, open brush and
woodlands, thickets, thornscrub, roadsides and other
open areas. Winter, spring, summer, fall. Common.

A prostrate, trailing perennial with pubescent stems
branching from base, to 2 feet. Leaves spirally arranged,
ovate to oblong, to ¾ inch long and ⅓ inch wide, bases
cordate, margins crenate, tips obtuse, blades pubescent and often folded. Flowers arising from leaf axils on
peduncles to ½ inch long, 5-petaled, radial, yellow to
yellow-orange, to about ½ inch wide. Frequently found in
disturbed areas throughout Texas; absent in far eastern
Texas and northern Panhandle.

Sida lindheimeri   MALVACEAE
Lindheimer's sida
Open shrub and woodlands, fence lines,
roadsides. Spring, summer, fall. Common.

An erect to sprawling perennial with sparsely pubescent
stems to 3+ feet long. Leaves alternate, linear to lanceolate, to 2¼ inches long and ¼ inches wide, bases truncate,
margins dentate, tips acute, lower leaf surface weakly
pubescent, upper surface glabrate. Radial flowers solitary, in upper leaf axils, 5-petaled, yellow, to 1 inch wide.
Found throughout South Texas, north into Edwards Plateau, and in Southeast Texas.

Sphaeralcea coccinea   MALVACEAE
**Scarlet globemallow, common globemallow,
caliche globemallow**
Grasslands, plains, open brushlands, roadsides and
other open areas. Spring, summer, fall. Common.

An ascending or decumbent, rhizomatous perennial
with several stems to 16 inches tall, star-shaped hairs
along stem. Leaves round, deeply 3- to 5-palmately lobed,
each lobe pedately divided, bases truncate, surfaces with
star-shaped hairs. Flowers occur in leaf axils at ends of
stems, orange to reddish orange, about ¾ inch in diameter. Found throughout western Texas and Panhandle.
Weak into Central Texas.

Sphaeralcea fendleri   MALVACEAE
Fendler's globemallow
Fields, meadows, mountain slopes, desert scrub,
dunes. Spring, summer, fall. Uncommon.

An erect or ascending, shrubby perennial with several
grayish white, canescent stems to 4+ feet tall. Leaves
alternate, petiolate, ovate-oblong to ovate, strongly to
weakly 3-lobed, 2½ inches long, bases cuneate, margins
crenate to dentate, tips acute to obtuse, lower leaf surface
usually densely canescent, upper surface green. Flowers
numerous in terminal panicles, 5-petaled, orange, to 1+
inch wide. Found in western Chihuahuan Desert, often
along roadsides.

Sphaeralcea hastulata   MALVACEAE
Spear globemallow
Open brush and grasslands. Winter,
spring, summer. Common.

A decumbent perennial with several or few canescent
stems to 12 inches long. Leaves alternate, oblong-ovate to
ovate-lanceolate, deeply 3-lobed, to 2½ inches long, bases
truncate, margins entire or crenate-dentate, tips acute,
surfaces pubescent (more so on lower surface). Flowers
in terminal and few-flowered racemes, 5-petaled, orange
to red, to ¾ inch tall and 1½ inches wide when fully open.
Widespread throughout Chihuahuan Desert, south to
Rio Grande Valley, west into Edwards Plateau and southern Panhandle.

Sphaeralcea incana   MALVACEAE
Gray globemallow
Open grass, brush and woodlands, rocky slopes
and hillsides, dunes, roadsides and other open
areas. Spring, summer, fall. Uncommon.

An erect, multistemmed, branching perennial with yellowish canescent stems (distinctive) to 5+ feet tall. Leaves
alternate, deltate-ovate, to 3 inches long, 3- to 5-lobed,
margins crenulate, surfaces yellowish green, canescent,
lower surface with prominent venation. Flowers in terminal panicles, 5-petaled, orange, to 1½ inches wide.
Found throughout Chihuahuan Desert, in sandy to gravelly soils.

Sphaeralcea leptophylla   MALVACEAE
Scaly globemallow
Open grasslands and desert scrub, roadsides.
Spring, summer. Locally common.

A decumbent to ascending perennial with numerous
stems to 20 inches long, stems slender with grayish silver
scales. Leaves alternate, sometimes clustered below, linear to oblanceolate, 3-lobed, to 1½ inches long, margins
revolute or entire, apex obtuse to acute, usually with short
pointed tip, surfaces silvery gray. Upper leaves becoming
linear, not lobed or divided and reduced in size. Flowers
in terminal panicles, 5-petaled, orange to reddish orange,
to 1¼ inches wide. Found in Chihuahuan Desert region,
on rocky slopes or hillsides, often mixed with other
globemallows.

Sphaeralcea lindheimeri   MALVACEAE
Lindheimer's globemallow, woolly globemallow
Grasslands, shrub and woodlands, roadsides and other open areas. Winter, spring, fall. Locally common.

A decumbent, multistemmed, branching perennial with soft pubescent stems and leaves, to 28 inches long. Leaves alternate, deltate-ovate, to 1½ inches long and as wide, bases cordate to truncate, margins toothed or 3-lobed, undulate, tips acute to obtuse, blades greenish above and silvery white below. Flowers in terminal racemes, orange with yellow centers, 5-petaled, radial, to 2 inches wide. Found throughout South Texas on sandy soils.

Sphaeralcea pedatifida   MALVACEAE
Palmleaf globemallow, littleleaf globemallow
Fields, meadows, grasslands, open brush and woodlands. Spring, summer, fall. Common.

An ascending to erect, multistemmed, branching perennial with slender, pubescent stems to 18 inches. Leaves alternate, triangular, pedately divided, with each of 5 primary divisions further lobed or roughly toothed, tips pointed, surfaces greenish gray pubescent. Upper, newer leaves greener and less pubescent than lower. Flowers not numerous, in terminal racemes, 5-lobed, orange, to ¾ inch broad. A species of South Texas, common along roadsides.

Waltheria indica   MALVACEAE
Malva del monte, basora prieta, velvet leaf
Thornscrub, dunes, sandhills, prairies, fields, roadsides and other open areas. Winter, spring, summer, fall. Locally common.

An erect, branched perennial with woolly stems to 4+ feet tall. Leaves alternate, on petioles to 2 inches long, ovate to lanceolate, to 4 inches long and half as wide, bases slightly cordate to obtuse, margins serrate to crenate to dentate. Small yellow flowers about ¼ inch wide, in rounded clusters about ½ inch wide, in upper leaf axils. To 30± flowers per inflorescence, usually just a few open on any given day. Found in sandy, sometimes gravelly, soils in far South Texas; a few collections from Brazoria and Harris Counties; expected elsewhere along coast. Named in honor of Augustin Friedrich Walther (1688–1746), a German botanist.

Proboscidea althaeifolia MARTYNIACEAE
Desert unicorn plant, yellow-flowered devil's claw
River floodplains, sandy washes, drainages.
Summer, fall. Uncommon.

A perennial to about 14 inches tall, spreading to 3+ feet
in diameter. Leaves alternate, ovate to 3 inches long and
3½ inches wide, surfaces viscid-pubescent. Flowers
in axillary racemes held above leaves, bell-shaped, to 3
inches long, yellow with a mixture of dark spots around
edge of and leading into tube, yellow fading to white farther inside tube. Fruit green when young, maturing and
drying until it dehisces, hooks spreading outward giving appearance of a claw. Fruit edible when young, seed
edible at maturity. Yellow-flowered devil's claw can be
found in far West Texas, from Presidio County to El Paso
County.

Rhexia lutea MELASTOMATACEAE
Yellow meadow beauty
Wet savannas and open pinelands, roadside
ditches. Spring. Locally common.

An erect, much-branched perennial with pubescent,
4-angled stems to 18+ inches tall. Leaves opposite, sessile, linear-lanceolate to elliptic, to 1 inch long and ⅓
inch wide, bases tapering, margins dentate, tips acute,
surfaces with sparse, visible hairs. Stems terminating in
few-flowered cymes, originating from leaf axils. Flowers
4-petaled, yellow, to just over 1 inch wide, petals elliptic. Distinctively urn-shaped calyx persists after flowering and harbors capsule. Grows in wet soils of Southeast
Texas.

Aletris aurea NARTHECIACEAE
Yellow colic root, golden colic root, colicroot
Wet savannas, bogs, pine barrens, roadsides.
Spring, summer. Uncommon.

An erect perennial from a dense rosette with a slender
scape to 3 feet tall. Basal leaves only, elliptic to lanceolate, to 3½ inches long, ¾ inch wide. Flowers yellow,
bell-shaped, to ¼ inch long, numerous but not crowded
in upper third of scape. Found throughout the Big
Thicket, in scattered populations, west to Bastrop County
and north into Oklahoma.

unicorn-plant family
MARTYNIACEAE

melastoma family
MELASTOMATACEAE

bog asphodel family
NARTHECIACEAE

Nelumbo lutea   NELUMBONACEAE
American lotus, yellow lotus, water chinquapin
Ponds, floodplains, slow-moving bodies of
water. Spring, summer. Common.

Aquatic perennial from rhizomes. Large round leaves, to
27 inches in diameter, from a central stalk, which may be
floating or, more commonly, raised above surface on long
petioles. Yellow flowers to 10 inches wide held on peduncles to 3 feet above surface of water. Perhaps our most
striking aquatic plant, hard to miss and occurring in
large colonies. Look in ponds, stock tanks, and other still
waters from far South Texas north into Oklahoma and
east to Louisiana. Available in the nursery trade. Established elsewhere as an ornamental; however, can become
problematic if left unchecked. Tubers and seeds edible;
woody fruit used for decoration.

Peganum mexicanum   NITRARIACEAE
Garbancillo, limoncillo, Mexican rue
Alluvium soils of West Texas. Summer. Rare.

A prostrate to slightly decumbent perennial, heavily
branched from a single rootstock, to 20+ inches wide,
leaves and stems pubescent to glabrate. Leaves alternate,
highly dissected, lobes linear, blades fleshy and dark
green. Flowers solitary in upper leaf axils, pale yellow to
½ inch wide. Occurs in just a few counties in West Texas,
usually in small populations.

Acleisanthes parvifolia   NYCTAGINACEAE
Big Bend trumpets, littleleaf moonpod
Open desert scrub. Spring, summer, fall. Uncommon.

An erect or ascending, open perennial, stems 24+ inches
tall, with glandular hairs throughout. Leaves opposite,
on short petioles, ovate to rhombic, to 1 inch long and ½
inch wide, reduced farther up stem, few, sparse, bases
tapering, margins entire, tips pointed. Flowers solitary in
upper leaf axils, funnel-shaped, yellow-green, to 2 inches
long. Uncommon to rare in barren, gypseous soils of Chihuahuan Desert. Found between Terlingua and Lajitas,
along roadside near Long Draw. Specific epithet of Latin
origin and means "small leaved."

266

Commicarpus scandens (*Boerhavia scandens*)
NYCTAGINACEAE
Climbing wartclub
Desert shrublands, South Texas scrub, canyons,
among boulders, rocky outcrops and ledges.
Spring, summer, fall. Uncommon.

An erect, clambering, vinelike perennial with glabrous,
branching, slender stems to 6+ feet long. Leaves opposite, on petioles to 1 inch long, ovate to triangular, to
2½ inches long and 1¾ inches wide, bases cordate to
truncate, margins sinuate, tips acute or pointed. Inflorescences in terminal and axillary umbels on peduncles to 2½ inches, to 11± flowers per umbel. Flowers
pale yellow-green, shortly funnel-shaped to bell-shaped,
5-lobed, to about ¼ inch wide and long. Oddly distributed
in Texas, with populations at lower elevations in Big Bend
region and in South Texas from Coastal Bend south into
Mexico.

Nuphar advena (*N. lutea*)   NYMPHAEACEAE
Spatterdock, yellow water lily, cow lily
Ponds, marshes, streams, lakes, and other slow-moving
bodies of water. Spring, summer, fall. Common.

Aquatic perennial with large, rhizomatous roots. Leaves
round with entire margins, usually emersed, upper
and lower surfaces green. Flowers rounded, yellow, to 2
inches in diameter. Found throughout Edwards Plateau,
east into Louisiana, north into Oklahoma, occasional in
South Texas. Absent from Panhandle, South and far West
Texas. Occasionally clogs small waterways and overtakes
small ponds.

Nymphaea mexicana   NYMPHAEACEAE
Mexican water lily, yellow water lily, lampazo amarillo
Ponds, lakes and slow-moving bodies of
water. Spring, summer. Uncommon.

Aquatic perennial with stoloniferous rootstock. Floating
leaves to 7 inches in diameter, typically smaller, green
above and red below with entire or sinuate margins.
Flowers yellow, to 4½ inches in diameter, either floating or extended above surface of water. Found in still or
slow-moving bodies of water in coastal counties. Introduced elsewhere because of its availability in the nursery
trade, and may be encountered farther inland. Tubers are
an important food source for canvasback duck.

267

Menodora heterophylla   OLEACEAE
Red-bud, low menodora
Fields, grasslands, open shrub and woodlands,
rocky outcrops, ledges, roadsides and other open
areas. Winter, spring, summer, fall. Common.

A spreading, decumbent perennial with numerous
pubescent, branching stems to 10 inches tall. Leaves
opposite, crowded, linear to oblong-lanceolate, to 1¾
inches long and 1¼ inches wide, margins entire or with
3–7 clefts or lobes, ciliate, tips acute. Flowers yellow
(red when in bud), terminal and solitary, to 1 inch wide.
Corolla funnel-shaped with 5 broad petals. Common
throughout Central Texas, from southern Panhandle
south to Cameron County.

Menodora longiflora   OLEACEAE
Showy menodora
Rocky slopes, outcrops, ledges, open grass, shrub and
woodlands, drainages. Spring, summer. Common.

An erect, branching perennial with numerous, slender
stems to 3+ feet tall. Leaves opposite below and alternate
above, linear to elliptic-lanceolate, to 2 inches long and ⅓
inch wide, margins entire, tips acute to obtuse. Numerous flowers in terminal cymes, yellow, trumpet-shaped,
to 2 inches long and 1¼ inches wide. Common from El
Paso into Edwards Plateau; infrequent in Starr County.

Menodora scabra   OLEACEAE
Rough menodora
Rocky slopes and grasslands, creek beds,
drainages. Spring, summer, fall. Common.

An erect, scabrous perennial with multiple, slender,
leafy stems to 15+ inches tall. Leaves opposite below and
alternate above, linear to lanceolate or oblong-lanceolate
below, to 1¾ inches long and ¼ inch wide, margins
entire, tips acute. Numerous flowers in terminal cymes,
yellow, 5-petaled, radial, tube less than ¼ inch long, to ¾
inch wide. Found in Chihuahuan Desert.

Ludwigia decurrens ONAGRACEAE
Wingleaf primrose willow, willow primrose, wingstem water primrose
Swamps, bogs, edges of ponds, lakes and other still waters, roadside ditches and other low, wet areas. Spring, summer, fall. Common.

An erect, branched perennial with 4-winged stems to 6+ feet tall. Leaves alternate, sessile or nearly so, lanceolate to elliptic, to 5 inches long and 1½ inches wide, margins entire, tips acute, blades often folded. Yellow flowers solitary in axils of upper leaves, 4 sepals and 4 petals, to 1 inch wide. Capsule to ¾ inch long, 4-angled. Common in wet areas in eastern fourth of Texas, less common west to Edwards Plateau and south along coast.

Ludwigia leptocarpa ONAGRACEAE
Anglestem primrose-willow
Swamps, edges of ponds, lakes, streams, and rivers, roadside ditches and other low, wet areas. Spring, summer, fall. Common.

An erect annual to perennial with branching, softly pubescent stems to 5+ feet tall. Leaves alternate, sessile or on petioles ⅓ inch long, lanceolate to elliptic-oblanceolate, to 6 inches long and 1½ inches wide, bases tapering, margins entire, tips acute. Yellow flowers solitary in axils of upper leaves, radial, to ¾ inch wide with 4–7 sepals and 5 petals, petals obovate and slender at the base, 10 stamens. Capsule slender, to 2 inches long. Most commonly found in Southeast Texas, less common north into Oklahoma and west into Edwards Plateau.

Ludwigia octovalvis ONAGRACEAE
Mexican primrose willow, narrow-leaf water primrose, seedbox
Swamps, edges of ponds, lakes, rivers and creeks, roadside ditches and other low, wet areas. Summer, fall. Common.

An erect, well-branched perennial to 3 feet, stems slightly glabrous or with flattened hairs. Leaves alternate, lanceolate to ovate, to 5½ inches long and 1½ inches wide, margins entire, somewhat wavy, tips acute. Flowers in upper leaf axils, solitary, 4 sepals and 4 petals, yellow, radial, to 1¼ inches wide, 8 stamens. Fruit to 1¾ inches long and ⅓ inch thick. Found in wet areas throughout southern Edwards Plateau, east to Louisiana, south into Mexico.

Ludwigia peploides ONAGRACEAE
Floating water primrose, creeping water primrose, water primrose
Edges of and within ponds, lakes, streams, and rivers, roadside ditches and other areas with still or slow-moving water. Spring, summer, fall. Common.

An aquatic or marginal perennial with floating or sprawling, reddish, glabrous, branching stems to 24 inches. Leaves alternate, on petioles to 1½ inches long, oblong to oblong-spatulate to elliptic, to 3½ inches long and 1¾ inches wide, bases tapering, margins entire, tips acute to rounded, surfaces glossy, upper side of blades glabrous, underside glabrous to slightly pubescent. Flowers solitary in leaf axils, to 1 inch wide or slightly larger, 5 sepals and 5 yellow petals, 10 stamens. Common in eastern half of Texas; occasional in Chihuahuan Desert.

Oenothera berlandieri subsp. *pinifolia*
(*Calylophus berlandieri* subsp. *pinifolius*) ONAGRACEAE
Berlandier's sundrops, square-bud primrose, sundrops
Fields, grasslands, prairies, open shrublands, roadsides and other open areas. Spring, summer, fall. Common.

An erect, slightly bushy perennial with multiple, reddish brown stems to 20+ inches tall. Leaves alternate, on short petioles to nearly sessile, linear to oblanceolate, to 3¼ inches long and ⅓ inch wide, bases tapering, margins toothed, tips acute to rounded. Flowers originating in axils of upper leaves and appearing clustered, nearly sessile, yellow with 4 broad petals, to nearly 2 inches wide, center of flower and stigma black. Common in open areas throughout Central Texas, north into Oklahoma; occasional farther south to Coastal Bend, west into Chihuahuan Desert and East Texas.

Oenothera brachycarpa ONAGRACEAE
Short-fruit evening primrose
Rocky slopes, hillsides, outcrops, open desert scrub. Spring, summer. Uncommon.

An acaulescent perennial with basal leaves radiating to 12 inches in diameter. Leaves on petioles to 2½ inches long, linear to ovate, to 6 inches long and 1¼ inches wide, bases tapering, margins entire to sinuate to dentate, tips acute, blades glabrous. Hypanthium to 6 inches. Flowers yellow, to 4 inches wide, 4-petaled, petals notched. Located in gravelly soils of Chihuahuan Desert; no preference of substrate.

Oenothera drummondii ONAGRACEAE
Beach evening primrose, Drummond's evening primrose
Beaches, dunes and other coastal, sandy
areas. Spring, summer. Common.

A decumbent, spreading perennial from a woody base
with pubescent, branching stems to 3+ feet long. Leaves
alternate, on short petioles to sessile, oblanceolate to obovate, to nearly 3 inches long and ½ inch wide, margins
entire or sinuate to dentate, blades canescent. Hypanthium to 1¾ inches long. Flowers yellow, 4-petaled, to 3
inches in diameter. Found in dunes along Texas coast.

Oenothera grandis ONAGRACEAE
Largeflower evening primrose, showy evening primrose
Fields, prairies, grasslands, open brush and
woodlands, roadsides, river and creek banks
and other open areas. Spring. Common.

An erect to decumbent annual with pubescent stems
to 24+ inches long. Leaves alternate, sessile, elliptic to
oblanceolate, to 3½ inches long and ¾ inch wide, margins sinuate-pinnatifid, deeply lobed or entire, tips acute,
surfaces visibly pubescent with long, soft hairs. Hypanthium to 2 inches long. Flowers yellow, to 2 inches wide,
4-petaled, petals notched to heart-shaped, margins wavy.
Common throughout Texas, in open, sandy soils. Weak to
absent in Chihuahuan Desert and Northeast Texas.

Oenothera hartwegii (*Calylophus hartwegii*)
ONAGRACEAE
Hartweg's sundrops, western primrose
Open grass and brushlands, rocky slopes, roadsides
and other open areas. Spring, summer. Common.

An erect, bushy perennial with multiple stems arising
from a central woody base to 16+ inches tall and wide.
Leaves alternate, linear to oblong-lanceolate, to 2 inches
long and ⅜ inch wide, bases tapering, margins entire to
slightly toothed, tips acute to rounded. Flowers in upper
leaf axils, yellow, to 2+ inches in diameter, 4-petaled, petals wrinkled and wavy and blowsy. A variable species
with 5 subspecies represented in Texas, spread throughout western two-thirds of state.

271

Oenothera jamesii   ONAGRACEAE
River primrose, James's evening primrose
Banks of creeks and rivers, edges of ponds.
Summer, fall. Locally common.

An erect, large biennial, with pubescent stems to 6+ feet tall. Leaves alternate, on petioles to 2½ inches long, elliptic to lanceolate, to 8 inches long and 1½ inches wide, bases tapering, margins entire, sinuate-pinnatifid, or finely toothed, tips acute. Hypanthium to 4½ inches. Flowers yellow, 4-petaled, to 4 inches wide when fully open. Widespread throughout Texas but not common, found in Chihuahuan Desert, Panhandle, Edwards Plateau, and occasionally farther southeast toward coast.

Oenothera laciniata   ONAGRACEAE
Cut-leaf primrose
Fields, grasslands, prairies, open shrub and woodlands, roadsides and other open, sandy areas. Spring, summer, fall. Common.

An erect to decumbent annual with simple or well-branched stems to 24 inches long. Leaves alternate, sessile, elliptic to oblanceolate, to 3½ inches long and ¾ inch wide, margins sinuate-pinnatifid, deeply lobed or entire, tips acute, blades visibly pubescent with long and soft hairs. Hypanthium to 1⅝ inches long. Flowers yellow, to 1¼ inches wide, with 4 notched petals. Similar to *Oenothera grandis,* but with smaller flowers and a shorter hypanthium. Widespread and common throughout majority of Texas. Weak in western Edwards Plateau and Chihuahuan Desert.

Oenothera linifolia   ONAGRACEAE
Threadleaf evening primrose, three-leaved sundrops
Open woodlands, grasslands, meadows, fields. Spring. Common.

An erect annual with slender stems to 12 inches tall, branching (if any) from base, leaves often crowded at base. Leaves alternate, nearly sessile, filiform, slender, to 1 inch long, margins entire, tips pointed. Hypanthium less than ⅛ inch long. Flowers about ¼ inch long on terminal racemes, yellow, 4-lobed, lobes notched. Found on open, sandy soils in eastern third of Texas.

Oenothera macrocarpa   ONAGRACEAE
Missouri evening primrose, bigfruit evening primrose
Fields, grasslands, prairies, brush and
woodlands, roadsides and roadcuts, other open
areas. Spring, summer, fall. Common.

An erect to decumbent perennial with stems to 20+
inches long. Leaves alternate, sessile above, on petioles
2 inches long below, lanceolate to elliptic, to 5+ inches
long and 1¼ inches wide, bases tapering, margins entire
to widely dentate, tips acute. Hypanthium to 6 inches
long. Flowers yellow, 4-petaled, to 5 inches wide, margins
frilled. Fruit large, to 2 inches long, with 4 large wings
about ¾ inch wide each. Common in rocky areas, often
on limestone, from Panhandle and North-Central Texas
south into eastern Edwards Plateau.

Oenothera serrulata *(Calylophus serrulatus)*
ONAGRACEAE
Yellow sundrops, serrateleaf evening primrose
Fields, pastures, grasslands, open shrublands, roadsides
and other open areas. Spring, summer. Common.

An erect, bushy perennial with multiple stems from a
central woody base. Leaves alternate, sessile or on short
petioles, linear to oblong or oblanceolate, to 2½ inches
long, margins serrulate or rarely entire, tips pointed. Yellow flowers, sessile in upper leaf axils, 4 petals, spreading
to 1 inch wide, margins lacerate. Widespread and common in open areas throughout Texas. Absent in Big Bend
region. Found along roadsides in late spring.

Oenothera triloba   ONAGRACEAE
Stemless evening primrose
Fields, grasslands, meadows, rocky outcrops
and slopes, open brush and thickets. Winter,
spring, early summer. Common.

A stemless annual or biennial, with a rosette to 20 inches
broad. Basal leaves on petioles usually ¾ inch long but up
to 3 inches possible, elliptic to oblanceolate, to 12 inches
long and 1¾ inch wide, margins pinnatifid, tips acute to
obtuse. Hypanthium to 4 inches long. Flowers pale yellow, to 1¼ inches wide, 4-petaled, petal margins somewhat frilly. Common in Chihuahuan Desert and Edwards
Plateau, absent in eastern fourth of Texas.

273

Cypripedium kentuckiense   ORCHIDACEAE
Yellow lady's slipper, Kentucky lady's slipper, ivory lady's slipper
Beech hardwood forests. Spring. Rare.

An erect, unbranched perennial to nearly 3 feet. Large, lanceolate leaves, to 5 per plant, to 10 inches long and 6 inches wide. Impressive (to 2½ inches) inflated lower lip of flower can vary from yellow to ivory, and is plant's most striking feature. Found in a few sites in deep East Texas; grows in moist soils, near watercourses. Recently a new population was found in Post Oak Savanna, which is dominated by oak-pine woodlands. Habitat loss and over-collecting has put species at risk in Texas and the United States.

Platanthera chapmanii   ORCHIDACEAE
Chapman's fringed orchid
Bogs, seeps, wet savannas. Summer. Rare.

An erect perennial with stems to 30 inches. Leaves to 3 per plant, linear-lanceolate to lanceolate, to 10 inches long and 1¼ inches wide, sheathed. Flowers in dense spikes, orange to yellow. Lateral sepals reflexed, upper sepal curved. Petals linear to obovate and fringed at tips. Lip ovate, to ⅜ inch long and as wide, heavily fringed. Spur to ⅔ inch, opening round. Rare in Southeast Texas. One of 3 species of fringed, orange-flowered *Platanthera* species in Texas, others are more common; differences in lip and spur length separate species.

Platanthera ciliaris   ORCHIDACEAE
Yellow fringed orchid, orange fringed orchid
Meadows, prairies, pine savannas, open woodlands, marshes, bogs, roadsides. Spring, summer. Locally common.

An erect perennial with glabrous stems to 3+ feet tall. Leaves few, to 4 per plant, lanceolate to lance-elliptic, to 16 inches long and 2⅓ inches wide. Flowers in dense spikes, orange to yellow. Lateral sepals reflexed, upper sepal curved. Petals linear to cuneate, margins fringed at tips, lip to ¾ inch, ovate-spatulate, heavily fringed. Spur cylindric to 1½ inches long. Found in eastern fourth of Texas, with a few isolated populations farther west.

Platanthera cristata ORCHIDACEAE
Crested yellow orchid
Wet meadows, open woodlands, bogs.
Spring, summer. Uncommon.

An erect perennial with glabrous stems to 3+ feet tall.
Leaves few, to 4 per plant, linear-lanceolate, to 8+ inches
long and 1¼ inches wide, spreading to ascending. Orange
flowers in dense, terminal spike. Lateral sepals spreading, upper sepal entire or notched. Petals obovate to
oblong-elliptic, margins fringed to entire. Lip ovate, to
⅜ inch long and ¼ inch wide. Spur cylindric, to ⅜ inch
long, opening triangular to keyhole shape. Found in
Southeast Texas, growing in open pine forests, occasional
along roadsides within wooded areas.

Aureolaria grandiflora OROBANCHACEAE
Largeflower yellow false foxglove
Woodlands, forests, stream and river banks.
Spring, summer, fall. Common.

An erect, hemiparasitic perennial with branching, pubescent stems to 5+ feet tall. Leaves pubescent. Lower leaves
opposite on winged petioles to 1 inch long, ovate, pinnatifid, to 3¼ inches long and 1¾ inches wide, bases tapering, ultimate margins irregular, entire to slightly toothed,
tips of lobes round. Upper leaves reduced, uppermost
leaves entire to toothed, not pinnatifid. Large yellow flowers, pedicels to ½ inch, 5-lobed, bell-shaped, to 2 inches
long, bilateral, lobes rounded at tips. Found in sandy soils
in eastern third of Texas.

Castilleja citrina OROBANCHACEAE
Yellow paintbrush, lemon paintbrush
Fields, prairies, grasslands, open brush and woodlands,
roadsides and other open areas. Spring. Common.

An erect, hemiparasitic perennial with woolly stems to
12+ inches tall. Leaves alternate, with 1–3 pairs of lateral
lobes which are linear to lanceolate, to 3+ inches long and
¼ inch wide, margins entire, blades fuzzy, silvery green.
Flowers in terminal, bracted spikes. Bracts with 1 or 2
lateral lobes, outer lobes linear to lanceolate, middle lobe
wider than lateral lobes. Lower bracts with yellow tips,
color extending toward base on upper bracts. Calyx similar color, to 1½ inches. Flowers bilabiate, galea green,
upper lip extending beyond calyx, lower lip shorter and
usually visible outside calyx lobe. Found in western and
northern Edwards Plateau, north into Panhandle and
Oklahoma.

Castilleja genevievana OROBANCHACEAE
Genevieve's Indian paintbrush
Open brushlands, desert scrub, roadsides.
Spring, summer. Uncommon.

An erect, hemiparasitic, multistemmed perennial with pubescent, leafy stems to 10+ inches tall. Stems often turning reddish brown with age. Leaves alternate, sessile, linear to lanceolate, to 3½ inches long and ⅓ inch wide, bases blunt, margins entire and ciliate, tips acute, blades pubescent and folded. Stems terminating in bracted spikes. Bracts 3-parted, yellow in upper half, green toward base. Calyx 4-lobed, yellow, extending well beyond lower lip. Flowers yellow, tubular, to 1 inch long, bilabiate, upper lip elongated and extending slightly beyond calyx, lower lip reduced. Found on limestone from Upton County south into Mexico.

Castilleja mexicana OROBANCHACEAE
Mexican paintbrush
Fields, grasslands, open brush and woodlands, roadsides and other open areas. Spring, summer. Locally common.

An erect, hemiparasitic annual or weak perennial with pubescent stems, occasionally branching from base, to 12 inches. Leaves alternate, linear near base, 3-parted above, margins wavy, blades with stiff hairs. Inflorescence in terminal, bracted spikes. Bracts 3-to 5-parted, mauve with yellow tips or green, variable, margins wavy. Calyx 4-lobed, green to mauve, to 1 inch. Flowers yellow or pale yellow or mauve, to 2 inches long, bilabiate, lower lip 3-lobed with lobes deeply cut to tube and margins wavy, upper lip curved. Located in mid to upper elevations in mountains of Big Bend region, north into New Mexico.

Pedicularis canadensis OROBANCHACEAE
Canadian lousewort, wood betony, high heal-all
Prairies, fields, meadows, edges of forests, roadsides and other open areas. Spring. Uncommon.

An erect, rhizomatous, hemiparasitic perennial with pubescent stems to 16+ inches tall. Basal leaves mostly, oblong to elliptic, to 6 inches long and 2 inches wide, ultimate margins toothed to rounded or wavy. Stem leaves much reduced, alternate. Yellow flowers in terminal crowded spikes to 4 inches long, bilabiate, white or yellow lower lip reduced and 3-lobed, upper lip elongated and curved at tip. Found in eastern third of Texas.

Argemone aenea PAPAVERACEAE
Yellow prickly poppy, golden prickly poppy
Fields, meadows, prairies, open brush and
woodlands, roadsides and other open areas.
Spring, summer, fall. Uncommon.

An erect annual to short-lived perennial with branching
prickly stems and yellow sap, to nearly 3 feet tall. Leaves
alternate, sessile or nearly so, deeply lobed throughout,
lower leaves to 6 inches long and 2¾ inches wide, upper
leaves much smaller and stiffer, lower leaf surface with
prickles. Flowers yellow to bronze, fragile, to 3+ inches in
diameter, stamens 150+. Found from West Texas southeast to coast. Uncommon most years, but can be numerous with adequate, well-timed rains. Genus name of
Greek origin (*argema*) and means "ulcer" or "cataract."
Similar plant was used to treat cataracts.

Argemone mexicana PAPAVERACEAE
Mexican prickly poppy, hierba loca
Open fields, meadows, brushlands, roadsides,
railroad rights-of-way and other open areas.
Winter, spring, summer, fall. Uncommon.

An erect, single or multistemmed annual branching
from base, to 2½ feet tall. Leaves lobed throughout,
upper leaves smaller and more shallowly lobed than
lower leaves, which can reach 6+ inches long. Petioles
lacking throughout. Prickles, if present, found on veins.
Bright yellow flowers to 2¾ inches broad, relatively few
(fewer than 50) stamens compared to *Argemone aenea*.
Widespread throughout lower half of state from the
Trans-Pecos east to upper Coastal Bend.

Corydalis curvisiliqua PAPAVERACEAE
Scrambled eggs, golden smoke, curvepod
Fields, grasslands, pastures, prairies, open
brush and woodlands. Spring. Common.

An erect winter annual with glaucous, leafy stems to 16+
inches tall. Compound leaves, mostly basal, alternate
along stems, 2 or 3 pairs of leaflets. Leaflets lobed, lobes
oblong to elliptic or obovate, margins entire or incised,
tips rounded. To 18 flowers in terminal racemes. Curved
tubular flowers, yellow to orange-yellow to just over ½
inch long, bilateral, outer petals keeled at opening, upper
petal spurred, inner 2 petals hidden and often overlooked. Common throughout Central Texas, north into
Panhandle and Oklahoma, west into Big Bend region.

Corydalis micrantha   PAPAVERACEAE
Scrambled eggs, slender corydalis, smallflower fumewort
Fields, grasslands, pastures, open brush and woodlands, roadsides and other open areas. Spring. Common.

A prostrate to ascending or erect winter annual with glaucous, leafy stems to 16+ inches long. Leaves twice compound. Basal leaves to 3 inches long and 2 inches wide, on petioles to 3 inches long, lobes ovate to elliptic to obovate, margins incised, tips slightly pointed. Stem leaves alternate, similar to basal, but smaller. To 16 flowers in terminal racemes. Curved, tubular flowers, pale yellow to about ½ inch long, bilateral, outer petals keeled at opening, upper petal ending in spur, inner petals hidden. Smaller, secondary raceme consisting of cleistogamous flowers typically present but inconspicuous and below leaves. Found throughout eastern half of Texas. Weak in Panhandle.

Eschscholzia californica subsp. mexicana
PAPAVERACEAE
Mexican poppy
Rocky to gravelly slopes and flats in desert scrub. Winter, spring, summer. Locally common.

An erect annual to 18 inches tall with glabrous stems and leaves. Leaves heavily lobed, fanlike. Flowers solitary at end of peduncles to 10 inches long, yellow to yellow-orange, about 2 inches in diameter, closing in evening. A subspecies of California poppy, though generally smaller than its western counterpart. Found only in Franklin Mountains of El Paso. Can occur in the tens of thousands during years with well-timed winter rains, often coloring mountain slopes.

Hunnemannia fumariifolia   PAPAVERACEAE
Mexican tulip poppy, arroyo poppy
Canyons, rocky slopes. Winter, spring. Rare.

An erect, round, multistemmed perennial, to 24 inches wide and tall, stems and leaves glaucous. Leaves alternate, on petioles 3+ inches long, each leaf to 4 inches long, round, deeply and thinly 3-lobed, lobes again lobed and linear to elliptic, ultimate margins entire. Flowers solitary at stem ends, bright yellow, to 2½ inches in diameter, outer petal margins wavy, yellow-orange anthers. Known from a few limestone canyons in southern Brewster County. Very similar to *Eschscholzia californica* subsp. *mexicana*.

Passiflora lutea
Yellow passionflower vine
Shaded woodlands, edges of waterways, and
canyons. Spring, summer, fall. Locally common.

Perennial vine to 15 feet, usually smaller. Leaves alternate, 3-lobed, 3 inches wide and long, margins entire,
surfaces glabrous to slightly pilose. Flowers originating from leaf axils on slender peduncles, pale yellow
and sometimes tinged green, to ¾ inch wide. Fruit is
a marble-sized berry, turning deep purple when ripe.
Often seen in cooler, shadier environments in Central or
East Texas. Like others in this genus, an important food
source for many butterflies.

Gratiola flava   PLANTAGINACEAE
Yellow hedge hyssop
Prairies, fields, grasslands. Winter, spring. Uncommon.

An erect, glabrous annual with several slender stems to
4 inches tall, branching in upper stem. Leaves opposite,
sessile or clasping, linear-oblanceolate, to ½ inch long
and ¼ inch wide, margins entire or slightly serrate, tips
obtuse. Flowers solitary at end of short peduncle. Flowers
yellow, tubular to bell-shaped, to ½ inch, bilabiate, lower
lip 3-lobed, upper lip 2-lobed or notched. Found in open,
sandy soils from lower coast northeast into Louisiana,
where it is rare.

Mecardonia procumbens   PLANTAGINACEAE
Baby jump-up, monkey jump-up
Banks and shallow waters of ponds, ephemeral pools,
lakes, slow-moving creeks and rivers, roadside ditches
and other low, wet areas. Spring, summer, fall. Common.

A prostrate to somewhat ascending, spreading annual
with glabrous, branching stems to 16 inches long. Leaves
opposite, sessile, ovate to obovate-oblong, to 1 inch long,
margins serrate, tips obtuse, blades glabrous. Flowers solitary in upper leaf axils on pedicels longer than
leaves below. Sepals covering floral tube. Flowers yellow, to about ½ inch, bilabiate, upper lip erect and somewhat recurved often with reddish purple veins, lower
lip 3-lobed with lobes slightly notched. Widespread and
frequent in wet areas in southern half of Texas, from Big
Bend region east into Louisiana.

Polygala nana   POLYGALACEAE
Candyroot, bachelor's button
Hillside bogs, wet pineland savannas and
other low, wet areas. Spring. Uncommon.

An erect or ascending, single-stemmed annual or biennial, with slender stems to 6 inches. Basal leaves spatulate to obovate, to 1¾ inches long and ¾ inch wide, bases
narrowing, margins entire, tips rounded, occasionally
mucronate. Stem leaves, if present, are similar to basal
leaves but narrower and sessile. Flowers numerous in
compact and crowded racemes. Flowers yellow, less than
¼ inch, lateral wings spreading. Found in deep East
Texas, from Angelina County south to Jefferson County,
east into Louisiana.

Polygala ramosa   POLYGALACEAE
**Pinebarren milkwort, low pinebarren milkwort, yellow
savanna milkwort**
Hillside seeps, bogs, wet pine savannas and other
low, wet areas. Spring, summer. Uncommon.

An erect, single-stemmed annual with glabrous, branching stems to 16 inches. Basal leaves elliptic to obovate,
to ¾ inch long and ¼ inch wide, bases tapering, tips
rounded. Stem leaves alternate, linear, shorter than
basal leaves, ascending. Numerous racemes forming a
dense and flat to rounded head to 6 inches in diameter,
individual racemes loosely flowered. Flowers yellow, lateral petal-like sepals not spreading. Found in Southeast
Texas, from Chambers County north to Houston County,
east into Louisiana.

Heteranthera dubia   PONTEDERIACEAE
Grassleaf mudplantain
Rivers, creeks, ponds, ephemeral pools, ditches and other
bodies of water. Spring, summer, fall. Locally common.

An aquatic, emergent perennial with stems to several
feet long, plants forming mats at water's surface. Leaves
alternate, sessile, linear, grasslike, to 1½ inches long,
submerged leaves to 4 inches long, both less than ¼ inch
wide, margins entire. Solitary yellow flowers occur at end
of stalk to 4 inches above water's surface, about ¾ inch
wide, trumpet-shaped, with 6 equal lobes. In creeks and
rivers, where there is a strong current, leaves are smaller,
and flowers occur at water's surface. Locally common, to
becoming a nuisance in some areas. Found sporadically
throughout state.

Phemeranthus aurantiacus   PORTULACACEAE
Orange flameflower, flameflower, talinum
Open brush and grasslands, rocky slopes, outcrops and
other open areas. Spring, summer, fall. Common.

An erect perennial with slender, slightly branching stems
to 18 inches. Leaves subsessile, linear to lanceolate, to 2½
inches long, margins entire to revolute. Inflorescences
about 1¼ inches wide, orange to yellow, either solitary or
in small terminal clusters arising from upper leaf axils.
Flowers open late afternoon for a few hours. Found in
rocky soils of western Edwards Plateau, west into Chihuahuan Desert. Flower color varies, with mixed populations
occurring.

Portulaca oleracea   PORTULACACEAE
Purslane, little hogweed
Fields, overgrazed lands, urban and suburban
areas, roadsides and other disturbed areas.
Spring, summer, fall. Common.

A spreading, prostrate annual with succulent maroon
stems to 20+ inches long. Leaves alternate, sometimes
opposite, subsessile, obovate to spatulate, to 1 inch long
and ½ inch wide, fleshy, margins entire. Flowers in leaf
axils, 5-petaled, to ⅜ inch wide, yellow to yellow-orange.
Widespread throughout Texas, often found in home
landscapes.

Portulaca suffrutescens   PORTULACACEAE
Shrubby purslane
Grasslands, rocky slopes, open brushlands, canyons,
desert washes and creeks. Spring, summer. Uncommon.

An erect perennial with branching, reddish brown stems
to 12+ inches tall. Alternate, fleshy, succulent leaves, linear, to 1 inch long and ¹⁄₁₀ inch wide. Flowers in axils of
upper stem, 5-petaled, about 1 inch wide, orange or copper or bronze, surrounded by visible trichomes. Typically
found at mid or upper elevations in Chihuahuan Desert.

Anagallis arvensis PRIMULACEAE
Scarlet pimpernel
Urban and suburban areas, roadsides and other
disturbed sites. Spring, summer. Common.

An introduced, erect or ascending annual with glabrous,
branching stems to 20 inches. Leaves opposite, sometimes whorled at stem ends, ovate to elliptic to lanceolate,
to 1¼ inches long and ⅓ inch wide, entire margins, surfaces glabrous. Flowers occur on short pedicels originating from leaf axils, 5-petaled, trumpet-shaped, to about ⅓
inch wide, in orange or red or blue. A common lawn and
urban weed found throughout South Texas, northeast
into Louisiana and north into Oklahoma.

Aquilegia canadensis RANUNCULACEAE
Wild columbine, columbine
Protected canyons, limestone ledges, among
large boulders. Spring. Uncommon.

An erect, multistemmed, leafy perennial to 3 feet tall
when flowering. Stems slightly branched, reddish green,
glabrous or pubescent. Leaves alternate, ternate, lobed
leaflets 3 inches long and 2 inches wide. Flowers nodding, spurred, to about 1½ inches long and 1 inch wide,
petals yellow, sepals and spurs red. Populations in southern and eastern edges of Edwards Plateau appear to be
relict, with their closest neighbors occurring just across
the border in southeastern Oklahoma. Ruby throated
hummingbird noted as a pollinator. Widely available in
the nursery trade; readily hybridizes with other columbine species.

Aquilegia chrysantha var. *hinckleyana*
RANUNCULACEAE
Hinckley columbine
Rocky wet areas along perennial waterways.
Spring, summer, fall. Rare.

An erect, multistemmed perennial to 3 feet tall. Basal
leaves biternate, leaflets to 1½ inches, leaves glabrous
above and glaucous below. Flowers erect, yellow, spurs to
1¾ inches long, sepals 1 inch long and ½ inch wide. Once
ranked as a separate species, now considered a variety.
Named after Leon Carl Hinckley, who taught at Sul Ross
State University. Known from just two locations in Texas,
both on private land in Presidio County.

Aquilegia longissima   RANUNCULACEAE
Longspur columbine
Canyon springs. Spring, summer, fall. Rare.

An erect, leafy, multistemmed perennial to 4 feet tall. Basal leaves glabrous (below) to glandular-pubescent (above), 3-ternate, to 17 inches long, leaflets to 1½ inches. Flowers yellow, erect, rarely nodding, with spurs to 6 inches long. A striking columbine making its way into cultivation. Found in Chihuahuan Desert, around perennial waters, in mountain canyons. Several populations can be found in Big Bend National Park.

Ranunculus fascicularis   RANUNCULACEAE
Early buttercup
Prairies, savannas, woodlands. Spring. Common.

An erect, pubescent perennial to about 8 inches when in flower. Leaves mostly basal, sessile or on short petioles, compound with 3–5 leaflets, each leaflet shallowly or deeply 3-lobed, margins toothed at tips. Stem leaves alternate, similar to basal leaves but few and smaller. Flowers solitary or few, on slender peduncles, radial, yellow, 5 petals and 5 sepals, stamens numerous, to 1 inch wide. Found in eastern third of Texas, west into Edwards Plateau, where it is uncommon.

Ranunculus sceleratus   RANUNCULACEAE
Cursed crowfoot, cursed buttercup, celery-leaved buttercup
Ponds, stock tanks, creek and river banks, ditches and other low, wet areas. Spring, summer. Locally common.

An erect annual with freely branching, hollow, glabrous stems to 2 feet tall. Leaves alternate, reniform to slightly cordate, 3-lobed, to 2 inches long and 2¾ inches wide, bases cordate to truncate, margins crenate. Flowers terminal, each flower about ⅓ inch wide, 5 yellow petals surround a tight cluster of green pistils. Found throughout state.

283

Thalictrum fendleri RANUNCULACEAE
Fendler's meadow-rue
Mountain woodlands, canyons, drainages.
Spring, summer. Uncommon.

An erect, slender, airy, stoloniferous perennial with branching stems to 3+ feet tall, purple stems glabrous. Leaves alternate, 2- or 3-ternate, to 12+ inches long including petiole, leaflets 3–5 cleft or lobed, to about 1 inch long and as wide, margins entire, tips rounded to acute, lower surface lighter than upper. Flowers terminal in loose, open panicles, petals absent, 5 green drooping sepals. Grows in upper elevations in mountains of West Texas, from Presidio County north to Culberson County. Uncommon, but easily found growing in moist, shaded soils along rock faces, at bases of cliffs or boulders.

Duchesnea indica ROSACEAE
Indian strawberry, mock strawberry, false strawberry
Urban and suburban areas, roadsides and other disturbed areas. Spring, summer, fall. Common.

An introduced, stoloniferous, prostrate, spreading perennial with stems to 4 feet long, often forming small colonies. Basal leaves on petioles to 4 inches long, trifoliolate, leaflets ovate, to 1¾ inches long and 1¼ inches wide, bases truncate to widely cuneate, margins serrate to crenate. Flowers on short stalks originating from crown, 5-petaled, yellow, about ¾ inch wide, produce a small ½-inch-long drupe. Found in eastern Texas; thrives in wet, sandy soils. Fruit is edible, but bland.

Ruta graveolens RUTACEAE
Common rue, ruta, herb of grace
Fields, roadsides, and other disturbed areas.
Spring, summer, fall. Uncommon.

An introduced, erect, multistemmed perennial from woody base, plants to 3 feet tall and equally wide. Leaves alternate, aromatic, glaucous, 2 or 3 pinnate, to 5 inches long. Yellow flowers to ½ inch in diameter in panicled cymes. Each flower has 4 or 5 petals, with entire or toothed margins. The fruit, a capsule, has rounded lobes. These latter two characters differentiate *Ruta graveolens* from *R. chalapensis*, which has fringed petals and pointed lobes on the fruit. Widely planted as an ornamental and herb; has escaped in various areas around state.

Thamnosma texana   RUTACEAE
Dutchman's breeches, Texas desert rue,
rue of the mountains
Grasslands, fields, open brush and woodlands,
rocky outcrops, ledges and slopes, desert
scrub. Spring, fall. Common.

An erect perennial with slender, branching stems to 12+
inches tall. Leaves alternate, linear, to ¾ inch long, margins entire, tips pointed, blades glandular, aromatic.
Drooping, urn-shaped flowers in terminal racemes.
Flowers to ¼ inch long with 4 sepals and 4 petals, color
varies from yellow to red throughout its range; western
plants typically red flowered. Fruit is 2-lobed capsule,
thick and leathery, leading to the common name dutchman's breeches. Common, but often overlooked because
of small size. Found in western two-thirds of Texas, from
eastern Edwards Plateau west into New Mexico, south
into Mexico, and north into lower Panhandle.

Sarracenia alata   SARRACENIACEAE
Yellow pitcher plant, yellow trumpets, flycatcher
Hanging bogs, marshes, ditches and other wet areas
with nutrient-poor soils. Spring, summer. Uncommon.

A carnivorous perennial to 2+ feet tall. Leaves modified into inflated vessels, to 28+ inches long, lip rolled,
hood ovate and covering opening of pitcher. Leaves
yellow-green with red venation often and coloring
throughout upper portion. Scape to 28+ inches tall. Flowers drooping, yellow-green with tinges of red, to about
3½ inches wide. Five sepals, ovate to rhombic, curved.
Five petals, drooping, constricted in middle, to 2½ inches
long. Infrequent throughout East Texas, often found in
association with other uncommon or rare plants.

Buddleja scordioides   SCROPHULARIACEAE
Escobilla, butterflybush
Grasslands, fields, open brushlands, roadsides and
other open areas. Spring, summer, fall. Common.

An erect to ascending shrubby perennial with
much-branched, woolly-tomentose stems to 3 feet. Leaves
opposite, linear to oblong, to 1¾ inches long and ⅓ inch
wide, margins crenate to serrulate, tips obtuse, sessile,
surfaces tomentose. Small, 4-lobed, yellow flowers occur
in clusters in leaf axils along upper stems. Each cluster about ⅓ inch wide, often hidden and barely noticeable because of pubescent calyces. Found in Chihuahuan
Desert.

citrus family
RUTACEAE

pitcher plant family
SARRACENIACEAE

figwort family
SCROPHULARIACEAE

Verbascum blattaria SCROPHULARIACEAE
Moth mullein
Fields, pastures, roadsides and other open,
disturbed areas. Spring, summer. Uncommon.

An introduced, erect biennial with multiple, pubescent,
slender stems to 3 feet tall. Seldom branching, weakly
if so. Basal leaves forming a rosette to 20 inches in
diameter, on petioles, oblong, occasionally lyrate. Stem
leaves alternate, sessile above, clasping below, lanceolate, to 5 inches long and 2 inches wide, margins dentate
to crenate to undulate. Flowers well-spaced in terminal
racemes to 18 inches long. Flowers yellow with reddish
purple bases, to 1¼ inches wide, 5-lobed, lobes unequal
with lower lobe larger; filaments pubescent. Often in
seed mixes; most common in Northeast Texas.

Verbascum thapsus SCROPHULARIACEAE
Flannel mullein, common mullein
Stream banks, floodplains, pastures, fields, open
grass and woodlands, roadsides and other open
areas. Spring, summer, fall. Locally common.

An introduced, robust, erect biennial with densely woolly,
stout, occasionally branching stems to 4+ feet tall. Basal
leaves in a rosette to 24+ inches in diameter. Stem leaves
alternate, sessile to clasping above, on petioles below,
crowded, oblong to oblanceolate, smaller farther up stem,
margins entire, tips pointed, blades greenish gray, woolly.
Stems terminating in crowded spikes. Flowers yellow,
5-lobed, bilateral, lower lobe larger, to about 1¼ inches
wide when fully open. Most common in Southeast Texas,
west to Val Verde County.

Chamaesaracha coniodes SOLANACEAE
Gray five eyes
Open grass and brushlands, desert scrub, gravelly
washes and creeks, roadsides and other disturbed
areas. Spring, summer, fall. Common.

An erect to ascending perennial with pubescent branching stems to 12 inches long. Leaves opposite, on short
petioles, lanceolate, to 2¼ inches long and ¾ inch wide,
bases tapering, margins wavy to pinnately lobed, tips
acute to obtuse, surfaces glandular-pubescent. Flowers
originating from upper leaf axils, radial to ½ inch wide,
5-lobed, star-shaped, white to pale yellow with darker centers. Fruit is a berry. Found in western half of state; common in Trans-Pecos and Panhandle.

Physalis angulata   SOLANACEAE
Cutleaf groundcherry
Fields, grasslands, brush and woodlands, rocky
outcrops, ledges, grassy rocky slopes and hillsides,
roadsides. Spring, summer. Common.

An erect annual with branching stems to 24+ inches tall.
Leaves alternate, on petioles to 3¼ inches long, ovate to
ovate-lanceolate, to 4⅓ inches long and 3½ inches wide,
bases wedge-shaped, margins toothed to incised, rarely
entire, tips acute, upper surface usually glabrous, lower
surface pubescent. Flowers solitary on pedicels to 1¾
inches originating from upper leaf axils, rotate, 5-lobed,
yellow, with or without darker centers. Fruit is a berry
surrounded by an inflated calyx with 10 ribs. Found in
eastern half of Texas, with western populations in Big
Bend region.

Physalis cinerascens   SOLANACEAE
Groundcherry, smallflower groundcherry
Fields, grasslands, open brush and woodlands, rocky
outcrops, ledges, roadsides and roadcuts, other open
areas. Winter, spring, summer, fall. Common.

An erect, decumbent, spreading perennial, branching
throughout to 16+ inches tall, leaves and stems pubescent. Leaves alternate, on petioles to 2 inches long, ovate
to kidney-shaped to somewhat triangular, to 2+ inches
long and 1½ inches wide, margins toothed or undulate or
entire, blades pubescent, often slightly folded. Flowers on
short pedicels originating from leaf axils, flowers rotate,
yellow with darker centers, to ½ inch wide. Common and
found throughout Texas in various habitats.

Physalis cinerascens var. spathulifolia
SOLANACEAE
Beach groundcherry, dune groundcherry
Beaches, dunes, sandy grasslands. Winter,
spring, summer, fall. Locally common.

An erect, decumbent, spreading perennial, branching throughout to 16+ inches tall, leaves and stems with
star-shaped hairs. Leaves alternate, on winged petioles,
thick, spatulate to lanceolate or ovate, to 2+ inches long,
margins undulate, blades tapering. Flowers on short
pedicels originating from leaf axils. Flowers rotate, pale
yellow with darker centers, to ½ inch wide. Found along
Texas coast and barrier islands, and farther inland in
coastal counties.

Solanum rostratum   SOLANACEAE
Buffalo bur, mala mujer, Mexican thistle
Fields, pastures, open brush and woodlands, creek
and river beds and banks, roadsides and other open,
disturbed areas. Spring, summer, fall. Common.

An erect annual with prickly stems to 2 feet tall, stems
with star-shaped hairs. Leaves alternate, pinnate, to 4
inches long and 3 inches wide, 1- or 2-lobed, irregu-
larly shaped, margins undulate, veins on lower surface
with yellow spines. Inflorescence in racemes. Flowers star-shaped to 1 inch wide, the 5 lobes typically not
divided, margins wavy to lacerate. Berries to ½ inch
wide and covered by a prickly calyx, splitting open when
mature. Widespread and common throughout Texas,
often in overgrazed pastures.

Viola pubescens   VIOLACEAE
Downy yellow violet
Mixed woodlands and forests. Spring. Rare.

An erect, rhizomatous perennial with 1–3 stems to 10
inches tall. Basal leaves few or absent, on petioles to 5
inches long, ovate to lanceolate, to 3 inches long and 2½
inches wide, margins entire or toothed or crenate. Upper
leaves alternate, similar to but smaller than basal leaves.
Flowers on peduncles to 5 inches long, yellow, about ¾
inch wide, 5 petals, lower petal with darker veins, upper
lobes reflexed. Found in northeast portion of state.

Hemerocallis fulva   XANTHORRHOEACEAE
Orange daylily, tawny daylily
Old homesteads, open woodlands, roadsides.
Spring, summer. Uncommon.

An introduced, clumping, rhizomatous perennial to 4
feet tall when flowering. Basal leaves numerous, arching, grasslike, to 3 feet long and 1 inch wide. Inflorescences on scapes to 4+ feet tall, in terminal cymes, usually 2 per scape, occasionally solitary. Each flower orange,
large and showy, to 6 inches wide, with 6 tepals (or 12 in
double-flowered forms). Originally from Asia, this species and many cultivars were brought in as ornamentals.
Now an escapee, plant is found sporadically in Texas,
most often in northeastern part of state.

Kallstroemia grandiflora   ZYGOPHYLLACEAE
Arizona poppy, desert poppy, giant poppy
Rocky slopes, gravelly washes, sparse
shrublands. Summer, fall. Locally common.

An erect, multistemmed annual to 3 feet tall, often forming large populations when conditions permit. Leaves
opposite, pinnate, to 3 inches long, 4–10 pairs of obovate
leaflets, surfaces pubescent. Flowers in slender panicles, bright orange, to 2 inches wide. Found throughout
Trans-Pecos region, west to California. Look for orange
caltrop in sandy soils, typically along roadsides or desert
washes.

Kallstroemia parviflora   ZYGOPHYLLACEAE
Warty caltrop, small-flowered carpetweed
Desert scrub, open grass, brush and woodlands,
washes, creek and river beds, roadsides and other
open areas. Spring, summer, fall. Common.

A prostrate to decumbent annual to 3 feet long, from a
single taproot, with pubescent to glabrous stems and
leaves. Leaves opposite, pinnate, to 2½ inches long with
3–5 pairs of elliptic to oval leaflets, surfaces usually
pubescent. Flowers on short peduncles originating in leaf
axils, to ¾ inch wide, yellow-orange, 5-petaled. Pubescent
fruits have a beak that is longer than body of fruit. This
characteristic separates *Kallstroemia parviflora* from other
species found in Texas: *K. hirsutissima* and *K. californica*. Widespread throughout Texas. Weak in eastern and
southeast portions of state.

Kallstroemia perennans   ZYGOPHYLLACEAE
Perennial caltrop
Limestone slopes and rocky flat areas in sparse
shrublands. Spring, summer. Rare.

A prostrate to slightly ascending perennial with branching, spreading stems 10 inches tall and 2 feet wide, stems
hispid, grayish green. Leaves opposite, pinnate, elliptic,
to 3 inches long with 4 or 5 pairs of leaflets. Each leaflet
ovate to obovate, to ⅜ inch long and ⅓ inch wide. Flowers
originating in upper leaf axils, to 2 inches wide, orange.
Found in Brewster, Presidio, Val Verde, and Terrell Counties, always on limestone soils close to Rio Grande.

Tribulus terrestris ZYGOPHYLLACEAE
Goat head, puncture vine, abrojo de flor amarilla
Disturbed areas, roadsides, urban areas.
Spring, summer, fall. Common.

An introduced, multibranched, prostrate annual from a single rootstock with stems often reaching 6+ feet long, stems and leaves covered in fine hairs. Leaves opposite, compound, to 1¾ inches long, with 3–7 pairs of oblong to ovate leaflets. Each leaflet to ½ inch long and narrow. Flowers yellow, 5-petaled, to ½ inch wide. Fruits spiny, about ⅓ inch in diameter, eventually splitting into several sections (nutlets), each armed with sharp spines. Introduced from Mediterranean. Considered invasive. An agricultural pest and toxic to livestock.

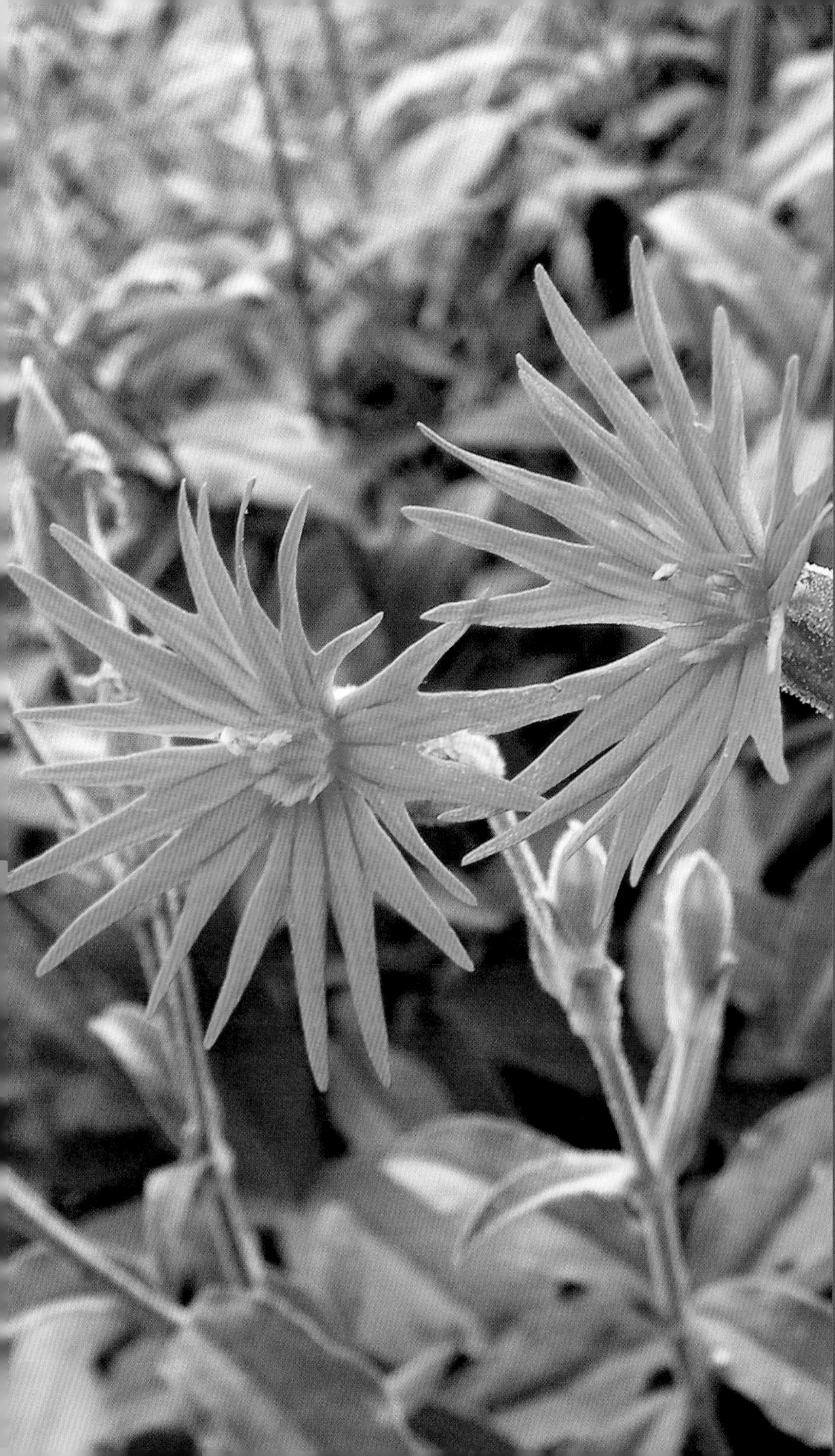

Gomphrena haageana   AMARANTHACEAE
Rio Grande globe-amaranth
Fields, open brush and woodlands,
rocky slopes. Summer, fall. Rare.

An erect perennial with slender, pubescent stems,
branching above, to 30 inches tall. Leaves opposite, sessile or on petioles ¾ inch long, oblanceolate to linear, to
4 inches long and ¼ inch wide, margins entire. Terminal inflorescence a round to cylindric compact spike,
about 1 inch in diameter, consisting of numerous flowers
surrounded by small, bright red bractlets. Known from
Val Verde, Gillespie, and El Paso Counties. Named in
honor of Johann Nicolaus Haage, a 19th-century German
plantsman. Cultivated; expect everywhere.

Asclepias brachystephana   APOCYNACEAE
Bract milkweed
Open brushlands, desert washes, grasslands,
fields, roadsides and other open areas.
Spring, summer, fall. Common.

An erect perennial to 18 inches tall, with multiple stems
from a slender taproot. Leaves opposite, on short petioles, linear to lanceolate, to 5 inches long and ½ inch
wide, margins entire. Inflorescences occur laterally along
upper portion of stems. Individual flowers are 5-petaled,
about ½ inch wide, with reflexed, reddish purple corollas.
Found in western portion of state, primarily in Chihuahuan Desert, north into western Panhandle.

Asclepias curassavica   APOCYNACEAE
Tropical milkweed, veintiunilla, bloodflower
Urban and suburban areas, drainages, bayous, canals,
and other wet areas. Spring, summer, fall. Uncommon.

An introduced, erect, multistemmed annual with non-
branching or weakly branched glabrous stems to 3+ feet
tall. Leaves opposite, on petioles to ½ inch long, elliptic
to lanceolate, to 5 inches long and 1¼ inches wide, bases
tapering, margins entire, tips pointed. Flowers in terminal umbels, 5-lobed, corolla reflexed, reddish orange,
yellow column of fused stamens and pistils. Has escaped
cultivation and naturalized in far South Texas and
around Houston area. It is expected elsewhere, as plants
are widely available in the nursery trade.

Matelea biflora   APOCYNACEAE
Two-flowered milkweed vine, purple milkweed vine, prairie pickle
Fields, meadows, open brush and woodlands, roadsides. Spring, summer. Common.

A trailing, prostrate perennial vine from a central root-stock with stems to 2 feet long. Leaves opposite, on petioles to 1 inch long, round to lanceolate-ovate, to 2 inches long and about 1¼ inches wide, bases cordate, margins entire to wavy. Flowers in leaf axils, typically in pairs, maroonish brown, distinctly star-shaped, with 5 slender corolla lobes and white centers. The large fruit, a follicle to 4 inches long and about 1 inch wide, is covered in warty protuberances and resembles a cucumber when immature. Found throughout Central Texas, north into Oklahoma. Often overlooked because of its creeping habit.

Matelea cynanchoides   APOCYNACEAE
Prairie milkvine
Open woodlands. Spring, summer. Common.

A prostrate, creeping perennial vine from a central rootstock with several stems to 2 feet long. Leaves opposite, on petioles to ⅓ inch if present, slightly round to lanceolate-oval, bases cordate, margins entire and slightly wavy. Flowers occurring in pairs in leaf axils, to ½ inch in diameter, maroonish brown, distinctly star-shaped, corolla lobes ovate to elliptic. Grows in sandy soils throughout eastern portion of Texas with scattered populations in South-Central and North-Central Texas. Absent in Edwards Plateau and far West Texas.

Matelea decipiens   APOCYNACEAE
Oldfield milkvine, climbing milkvine
Open woodlands. Spring, summer. Uncommon.

A climbing, twining perennial vine with pubescent stems to 8+ feet long. Leaves on petioles 2 inches long, heart-shaped, to 5½ inches long, bases cordate, margins entire, surfaces covered in soft, pubescent hairs. Flowers in umbels originating from leaf axils, maroon to brownish purple, star-shaped, to about ¾ inch wide, lobes linear to lanceolate, often curled. Found in East Texas, often in sandy soils of Post Oak Savanna.

APOCYNACEAE
dogbane family

APODANTHACEAE
stem-sucker family

ARISTOLOCHIACEAE
dutchman's pipe family

Matelea radiata APOCYNACEAE
Falfurrias milkvine, Bentsen's milkvine
Thornscrub, fence lines. Spring, summer. Rare.

A slender, twining, climbing perennial vine with softly pubescent stems to 3+ feet long. Leaves opposite, on petioles to ¼ inch long, lanceolate to narrowly triangular, to 1 inch long and ¼ inch wide, bases sagittate to cordate, margins slightly revolute, tips pointed. Flowers distinctly star-shaped, to ½ inch wide, the 5 corolla lobes linear-oblong, greenish brown. Follicles slender, smooth, light gray with green streaks when young, turning brown when mature, to 2½ inches long. Found in far South Texas, among the Tamaulipan Thornscrub. Often difficult to find. Look for this species along fence lines, where it is more exposed.

Pilostyles thurberi APODANTHACEAE
Thurber's stemsucker, pilostyles
Desert scrub and brushlands. Spring. Uncommon.

A stem parasite with the primary, vegetative portion of the plant inside stems of its host, semiwoody species of the Fabaceae. Flowers small, less than ⅛ inch long and as wide, solitary, but often clustered along same stem, brownish red to maroon, inside of flower and tips usually white to creamy yellow. Found in Edwards Plateau and Chihuahuan Desert, north throughout Panhandle. This parasite has been reported on *Dalea frutescens*, *D. formosa*, and *Psorothamnus scoparius*.

Aristolochia coryi ARISTOLOCHIACEAE
Cory's pipevine, Cory's dutchman's pipe
Rocky outcrops and slopes, ledges, cliffs, along rocky, dry washes. Spring, summer, fall. Uncommon.

A prostrate perennial from a succulent root, with many slender stems to 18 inches long. Leaves alternate, on petioles to 1 inch long, triangular, may be lobed at base, to 2 inches long and 1½ inches wide. Solitary flowers, to 1 inch long and ½ inch wide, on peduncles to 3¾ inches long. Curved, one-lobed calyx can vary from reddish brown to creamy yellow. Corolla absent, instead calyx opens to reveal a cream-colored throat with outer portions rimmed in reddish purple and inner portions often spotted with same darker color. Found in western portion of Edwards Plateau, west into the Trans-Pecos. Often overlooked.

Aristolochia erecta ARISTOLOCHIACEAE
Swan flower, upright pipevine, grass-leaf pipevine
Fields, meadows, open hillsides, roadsides and
other open areas. Spring, summer. Uncommon.

A slightly erect to prostrate perennial with pubescent
stems to about 1 foot long. Linear to lanceolate leaves to 5
inches long and ½ inch at their widest, pubescent above,
glandular below. Solitary flowers, to 4 inches long. Tube
is a faint brownish purple, with light green veins and just
over 1 inch long. Opening of limb is cream colored, dotted with deep purple spots, upper portion of limb elongated and linear, reaching 2¾ inches long. Mimics short
grasses and is often overlooked. Easiest to find when pipevine swallowtail butterflies are feeding on foliage. Found
mostly in South Texas, north into southern Edwards Plateau, east to Harris County, west into Val Verde County.

Aristolochia reticulata ARISTOLOCHIACEAE
Texas dutchman's pipe
Woodlands, forests. Spring, summer. Uncommon.

An erect, slender perennial with pubescent, zigzag
stems to 16 inches tall. Leaves alternate, few, sessile and
may appear clasping with basal lobes wrapping around
stem, oval to ovate, to 4¾ inches long and 2¾ inches
wide, bases cordate, margins entire to undulate, tips
obtuse, surfaces somewhat pubescent. Flowers in
racemes originating from lower nodes of stem and
usually lying on ground, to ⅜ inch long, limb reddish dark brown, tube mauve, inflated and curved.
Easily overlooked. Found in wooded areas in eastern
fourth of Texas.

Aristolochia wrightii ARISTOLOCHIACEAE
Wright's dutchman's-pipe, Wright's swanflower
Rocky outcrops and slopes, cliff faces,
roadcuts. Spring, summer. Uncommon.

A prostrate perennial with velvety stems to 18 inches
long. Leaves alternate, on petioles to 1 inch long, triangular to ovate, to 1½ inches long and as wide,
tawny-pubescent, bases cordate, margins wavy or entire,
tips acute. Solitary flowers consist of a 1½-inch-long tube
that continues as a 2-inch-long limb covered with brown
dots and ends in a yellowish green tip. Found in mountains of West Texas.

Manfreda variegata   ASPARAGACEAE
Huaco, amole, Texas tuberose
Shrublands, woodlands, rocky slopes.
Winter, spring, summer. Uncommon.

A perennial with globose rhizomes and underground stem. Leaves linear-lanceolate, to 18 inches long and 2 inches wide, typically erect, channeled with toothed margins. As with most *Manfreda* species, leaves have varying degrees of mottling. Scape to 5 feet tall, with uncrowded flowers in the last 12 inches. Flowers funnel- to bell-shaped, reddish brown, sometimes yellowish green, with wide spreading filaments. Found in far South Texas. Typically blooms prior to *M. sileri*, which, along with differences in leaf and flower morphology, distinguishes the two. Both species available in the nursery trade.

Cirsium turneri   ASTERACEAE
Cliff thistle, Turner's thistle
Exposed cliffs and ledges. Summer. Rare.

An ascending or hanging or horizontal perennial with tomentose, branched or unbranched stems to 2 feet long. Leaves alternate, oblong-elliptic to oblanceolate, to 12 inches long and 2 inches wide, pinnatifid, margins dentate and with spines. Flowering heads either single or to 6, in tight corymbs held just above upper leaves, each head about 2 inches long and 1 inch wide, with numerous red disc florets, ray florets absent. This rare thistle can be found in canyons, on either limestone or igneous substrates, in West Texas from Brewster to Val Verde County. Present in several locations in Big Bend National Park as well as Black Gap Wildlife Management Area.

Emilia fosbergii   ASTERACEAE
Florida tasselflower, Fosberg's pualele
Urban and suburban areas, vacant lots, roadsides, railroad rights-of-way and other disturbed areas.
Winter, spring, summer, fall. Uncommon.

An introduced, erect annual with a single, weak stem to nearly 3 feet tall. May be branched in upper portion. Leaves oblanceolate to pandurate, 5 inches long and 2 inches wide, upper leaves generally smaller than lower, bases clasping, margins entire to toothed to somewhat lobed. Flowers in terminal weak cymes or corymbs, cylindric heads ½ inch in diameter and usually twice as long, ray florets absent, 20–100+ red or purple or pink disc florets. Found mostly in Cameron and Harris Counties.

Gaillardia amblyodon   ASTERACEAE
Maroon blanket flower, maroon fire-wheel
Fields, meadows, prairies, open brush
and woodlands, roadsides and other open
areas. Spring, summer. Common.

An erect annual with a heavily branched stem to 18
inches tall, leaves and stem with rough hairs. Leaves
on 1¼-inch-long petioles, oblanceolate to spatulate, 2½
inches long and 1 inch wide, margins entire or toothed,
upper leaves often lacking petioles and with clasping
bases. Flowering heads solitary, 2½ inches wide, on
6-inch-long peduncles, 12± maroon to red ray flowers
(rarely yellow-tipped), disc florets numerous and yellow
with purple tips. Found along southern edge of Edwards
Plateau, east to Brazos River drainage.

Gaillardia pulchella   ASTERACEAE
Indian blanket, firewheel

Grasslands, prairies, open brush and woodlands, roadsides
and other open areas. Spring, summer. Common.

An erect annual with branching stems to 2+ feet tall,
stems and leaves with stiff hairs. Leaves alternate, lower
leaves on 1-inch-long petioles, upper leaves lacking petioles or clasping, linear to spatulate, to 4 inches long and
1½ inches wide, margins entire, sometimes toothed or
lobed. Flowering heads solitary, 3 inches in diameter, on
slender 8-inch-long peduncles. Ray florets to 14, yellow
to orange along outer half and red to purple along inner
half, disc florets numerous and yellow to purplish brown.
Found throughout state.

Gaillardia suavis   ASTERACEAE
Perfume balls, sweet gaillardia, pincushion daisy
Fields, meadows, grasslands, prairies, open
brush and woodlands, roadsides and other
open areas. Spring, summer. Common.

An erect, clumping perennial to 20 inches tall. Leaves
mostly basal, on petioles to 2¼ inches long, spatulate to
oblanceolate, to 5 inches long and 2 inches wide, margins
pinnatifid or toothed or entire. Fragrant flowers about 1
inch in diameter, solitary at end of slender peduncles to
18+ inches tall, typically rayless but if present only about
½ inch long and usually maroon, disc flowers numerous
and reddish purple to pink. Widespread throughout state,
but absent in far western and eastern portions.

Ratibida columnifera ASTERACEAE
Mexican hat, prairie coneflower, red-spike Mexican hat
Fields, prairies, grasslands, open shrublands
and woodlands, roadsides and other open
areas. Spring, summer, fall. Common.

An erect, multistemmed, taprooted perennial to 4 feet
tall, branching from base and along stem. Basal and
stem leaves to 6 inches long and 2½ inches wide, 1- or
2-pinnatifid, lobes lanceolate to ovate. Flowering heads
numerous, columnar, held above leaves on peduncles
to 18 inches long, ray florets to 12 per head, to 1¾ inches
long, vary in color from maroon to purple or yellow or
maroon and yellow, disc florets in the hundreds and
greenish yellow to purple. Found throughout Texas in
vast numbers along roadsides.

Ratibida peduncularis ASTERACEAE
Naked prairie coneflower, short-skirt coneflower
Prairies, grasslands, fields, open shrublands,
coastal dunes. Spring, summer, fall. Common.

An erect, taprooted, multistemmed perennial to 4
feet tall. Leaves to 5½ inches long and 3 inches wide,
2-pinnatifid to lyrate-pinnate, with up to 10 narrowly
lanceolate to ovate lobes. Flowering columnar heads
to 12 per plant, held on peduncles 18± inches long. Up
to 14 ray florets, about ½ inch long, from maroon to
purple-maroon or yellow to maroon and yellow. Disc
florets in the hundreds, greenish yellow to purple. Found
along lower coast. Less common northeast of Coastal
Bend and farther inland to Edwards Plateau.

Thelesperma burridgeanum ASTERACEAE
Burridge's greenthread
Fields, pastures, grasslands, open brush
and woodlands. Spring. Rare.

An erect annual with slender stems to 18 inches tall,
majority of leaves found in lower half of stem. Leaves
opposite, pinnately lobed, lobes linear, to 1 inch long and
less than $1/_{16}$ inch wide. Flowering heads terminal, ray
florets 8 per head and mostly reddish brown with yellow
margins, disc florets to 20+ per head and reddish brown
to purple. Found in South Texas from San Antonio southwest to Maverick County and south to Rio Grande Valley.

Brasenia schreberi CABOMBACEAE
Water-shield, snot weed
Ponds, lakes, stock tanks, slow-moving bodies
of water. Spring, summer. Common.

An aquatic perennial from a slender rootstock. Leaves
floating, elliptic, to 4 inches long and wide. Flowers reddish purple, held above surface. Young vegetative portions of plant covered in thick, clear mucilage, hence
common name snot weed. Found in eastern third of
Texas, mostly in Southeast Texas.

Lobelia cardinalis CAMPANULACEAE
Cardinal flower
Springs, creek and river banks, marshes, swamps,
edges of ponds and lakes and other open, wet
areas. Spring, summer, fall. Common.

An erect, single-stemmed perennial with a glabrous,
stout stem to 6 feet tall. Leaves alternate, on short petioles or sessile, ovate to lanceolate, to 6 inches long and
1½ inches wide, margins serrate, tips pointed, surfaces
rough. Flowers in terminal racemes to 20 inches long,
held somewhat upright, brilliant red, to 1½ inches long
and 1 inch wide, lower lip 3-lobed, lateral lobes spreading and thin, a slender tube between 2 lateral lobes holds
reproductive structures. Widespread. Frequent in eastern portion of state, less frequent farther west. Absent in
South Texas.

Silene laciniata subsp. *greggii*
CARYOPHYLLACEAE
Mexican pink, Mexican campion, cardinal catchfly
Mountainous oak-pine-juniper woodlands.
Summer, fall. Uncommon.

An erect perennial with branched stems to 3 feet tall.
Upper leaves lanceolate to elliptic, to 1½ inches long and
⅓ inch wide. Lower leaves oblanceolate, larger, entire
margins. Leaf surfaces rough to the touch. Flowers terminal, brilliant scarlet-red, just over 1 inch in diameter,
with 5 deeply 5- to 7-lobed petals. Found in higher elevations of mountains in West Texas. Specific epithet means
"divided into narrow lobes," referencing lobed petals.

water-sheild family
CABOMBACEAE

lobelia family
CAMPANULACEAE

carnation family
CARYOPHYLLACEAE

Silene subciliata   CARYOPHYLLACEAE
Louisiana catchfly, prairie-fire pink, catchfly, silene
Open mixed-pine woodlands. Summer, fall. Rare.

An erect perennial with several weakly branched, glabrous stems to 3 feet tall. Leaves glabrous, opposite, linear to oblanceolate, to 6 inches long and ½ inch wide,
margins entire, leaf blade may narrow to slight petiole.
Flowers solitary or to 3 in loose, airy cymes, brilliant red,
about 1 inch in diameter, petals may be notched at tip.
Rare, but can be seen in Big Thicket National Preserve, in
sandy soils.

Lechea mucronata   CISTACEAE
Hairy pinweed
Fields, prairies, grasslands, margins of and
openings in woodlands, roadsides and other
open areas. Summer, fall. Common.

An erect, branching biennial or perennial with pubescent stems to 3 feet tall. Leaves opposite or whorled, on
short petioles, elliptic to ovate, to 1¼ inches long and ¼
inch wide, bases rounded to cuneate, margins entire to
ciliate, tips acute. Flowers in axillary or terminal inflorescences, reddish, inconspicuous, sepals glabrous, inner
sepals longer than outer, petals shorter than sepals. Fruit
slightly round, ¹/₁₆ inch long. Found throughout eastern
two-thirds of Texas. Less common farther west.

Lechea tenuifolia   CISTACEAE
Narrowleaf pinweed
Fields, prairies, woodlands, forests, river
bottoms. Summer, fall. Common.

An erect, branching biennial or perennial with stems to
16 inches tall. Leaves opposite or whorled, linear to oblanceolate, to ¾ inch long and less than ¹/₁₆ inch wide, top
rounded, upper surface glabrous, lower surface pubescent along midvein. Flowers in axillary or terminal inflorescences, small, reddish maroon. Fruits oval, to ¹/₁₆ inch
in diameter. Most common in eastern third of state. Less
common farther west to Pecos County. Prefers sandy soil,
mostly in shade.

Ipomoea cristulata   CONVOLVULACEAE
Scarlet creeper, Trans-Pecos morning-glory
Canyons, rocky outcrops, creeks.
Summer, fall. Locally common.

An annual twining, climbing vine with glabrous stems
to 8 feet long. Leaves alternate, on petioles to 3¾ inches
long, ovate, deeply 3- to 5-lobed, to 4 inches long and 3
inches wide, bases cordate, margins entire to dentate.
Flowers in 1- to 7-flowered cymes originating from axils,
bright reddish orange, trumpet-shaped, to 1 inch long
and ¾ inch wide. Found in drainages in mountains of
Chihuahuan Desert region. More common in years with
adequate monsoon rains. Specific epithet means "small
crest," referring to tufts on sepals and fruits.

Echeveria strictiflora   CRASSULACEAE
Desert savior, echeveria, tail of dragon
Exposed rocky slopes, cliff faces, canyon
walls. Summer. Uncommon.

A perennial succulent to about 8 inches in diameter.
Leaves forming rosette, each leaf to 5 inches long, oblanceolate to spatulate, fleshy to the touch. When in flower, a
scape to 18 inches tall is produced, typically unbranched,
but may be forked. Flowers bright red, about ¼ inch long,
along upper side of raceme, only 2 or 3 open at any time.
Found only in Brewster, Jeff Davis, and Presidio Counties. On either igneous or limestone formations at mid to
upper elevations. Look for species in Big Bend National
Park, along Window and Boot Canyon trails in Chisos
Mountains, and in limestone canyons of Dead Horse
Mountains.

Acalypha phleoides   EUPHORBIACEAE
Shrubby copperleaf, three-seeded mercury
Creek and river bottoms, canyons, rocky outcrops,
open brush and woodlands, urban and suburban
areas, roadsides. Spring, summer. Common.

An erect, branching, pubescent perennial to 20 inches
tall. Leaves alternate, on petioles to ¾ inch long, ovate
to rhombic, to 2¼ inches long and just over 1 inch
wide, bases rounded, margins serrate, tips acute, surfaces somewhat pubescent. Flowers in dense, terminal
spikes, to 2 inches long, female flowers below with long
red styles, male flowers above with a reddish brown and
grainy appearance. Fruits 3-seeded rounded capsules,
seeds less than ¹⁄₁₆ inch long. Found throughout Central
Texas, west into Chihuahuan Desert.

morning glory family
CONVOLVULACEAE

stonecrop family
CRASSULACEAE

euphorb family
EUPHORBIACEAE

Acalypha radians EUPHORBIACEAE
Cardinal feather
Open grass, brush and woodlands,
roadsides. Summer, fall. Common.

A decumbent, spreading, dense perennial with heavily branched stems to 16 inches tall, often shorter and wider. Leaves alternate, on petioles to ⅝ inch long, kidney-shaped to round, lobed, to ½ inch long and ¾ inch wide, bases rounded to slightly cordate, tips rounded, surfaces fuzzy. Male and female flowers on separate plants. Female flowers in terminal or axillary spikes to ⅝ inch long, styles bright red. Male flowers numerous, in terminal spikes to 2½ inches long, grainy, cream to reddish brown. Found throughout South Texas, north into Edwards Plateau. Generally grows in sandy, open soils.

Euphorbia cyathophora EUPHORBIACEAE
Fire on the mountain, wild poinsettia
Open brush and woodlands, canyons, riparian
areas. Spring, summer. Common.

An erect annual with glabrous, slender, branching stems to 20 inches tall. Leaves alternate, occasionally opposite, on short petioles, linear to linear-lanceolate, or obovate, to 6 inches long, margins entire or weakly serrate, tips and bases acute, larger and wider leaves may be pandurate, upper surface green and glabrous, lower surface silvery white. Bracts similar to leaves, red near base. Inflorescences in terminal clusters, male and female flowers inconspicuous and separate, style greenish yellow. Fruits glabrous, 3-chambered. Found throughout state, especially in southwestern Edwards Plateau and Trans-Pecos.

Euphorbia heterophylla EUPHORBIACEAE
Mexican fireplant, wild poinsettia, painted euphorbia
Open brush and woodlands, riparian areas.
Spring, summer, fall. Uncommon.

An erect annual with slender, branching stems to 30 inches tall. Leaves opposite below, alternate above, with uppermost leaves close to flowers opposite, ovate to elliptic or rhombic-ovate, to 4 inches long, margins entire or slightly toothed and often involute, tips acute to obtuse and often mucronate, blades pandurate. Bracts similar to leaves, but not pandurate, red from base extending to tip, lower surfaces silvery white. Flowers in terminal clusters, greenish yellow, male and female flowers separate. Fruits 3-chambered capsules. Grows in sandy soils in South Texas.

Jatropha cathartica EUPHORBIACEAE
Jicamilla
Open brush, thornscrub, flats and slopes.
Spring, summer, fall. Uncommon.

An erect perennial from a large rounded caudex, with glabrous, somewhat fleshy, branching stems to 18 inches tall. Leaves alternate, 5- to 7-palmately lobed, to 4 inches long, margins lacerate, serrate, undulate, or entire. Flowers in loose cymes extending well beyond foliage, brilliant red, ½ inch in diameter, 5 petals. Often found in spongy saline or clay soils of South Texas, from Val Verde County to Brownsville.

Apios americana FABACEAE
American ground-nut, potato bean, Indian potato
Woodlands. Spring, summer. Uncommon.

A twining, high-climbing perennial vine with slender, deciduous stems to 9 feet long, from tuberous rhizomes. Leaves alternate, on petioles to 3 inches long, pinnate, 5–7 leaflets, ovate to lance-ovate, bases rounded, margins entire, tips pointed. Flowers in dense racemes, originating from leaf axils, papilionaceous, brownish red, to about ⅜ inch long, banner rolled forward, keel arching to tip of banner, wings curved downward. Most common in eastern fourth of Texas. Less common westward throughout Edwards Plateau and into northern Panhandle. Often found around wooded creeks and streams.

Indigofera lindheimeriana FABACEAE
Lindheimer's indigo
Limestone creeks, washes, canyon bottoms, drainages. Spring, summer. Locally common.

An erect, pubescent perennial with branching stems to 3 feet tall. Leaves alternate, pinnately compound, to 3 inches long, leaflets obovate to elliptic, to ½ inch long, opposite or nearly so, bases tapering, margins entire, tips rounded, blades often folded, silver-gray pubescent. Flowers in somewhat loose racemes originating from upper leaf axils, reddish orange to salmon with a yellow patch in banner center, banner erect and reflexed at tip, outer portion visibly pilose, wings outstretched, elongated. Found in Edwards Plateau, west to Brewster County.

Indigofera miniata   FABACEAE
Scarlet-pea, coastal indigo
Fields, pastures, grasslands, open brush
and woodlands, roadsides and other open
areas. Spring, summer. Common.

A procumbent or decumbent perennial with several
branching stems to 16 inches long. Leaves alternate, pinnate, to 1¼ inches long, leaflets oblanceolate to elliptic, to ½ inch long, bases tapering, margins entire, tips
rounded to mucronate, blades often folded, somewhat
pubescent. Flowers in short racemes originating from
upper leaf axils, reddish orange to salmon, bilateral, banner erect and curved, wings projecting, distal ends broad
and rounded. Found throughout South Texas, north
into Oklahoma and eastern Panhandle, west to Brewster
County, east into Louisiana.

Pediomelum rhombifolium   FABACEAE
Brown-flowered psoralea, gulf Indian breadroot
Open grass, brush and woodlands, rocky hillsides and
slopes, creek banks, drainages. Spring, summer. Common.

A prostrate, trailing or clambering vinelike perennial
with branching stems to 3 feet long. Leaves alternate, pinnately 3-foliolate, leaflets round to rhombic to ovate, to 1½
inches long and 1¼ inches wide, tips acute to rounded,
occasionally notched, bases tapering to rounded, blades
pubescent. Flowers in loose spikes on peduncles to 3
inches long, papilionaceous, to ⅓ inch long, banner brick
red with yellow spot at central base, margins slightly
curved backward, lateral wings and keel darker red,
wings horizontal. Widespread in southern two-thirds of
Texas.

Pueraria montana var. *lobata*   FABACEAE
Kudzu
Brush and woodlands, roadsides, fence lines and other
open areas. Spring, summer, fall. Locally common.

An introduced, twining, high-climbing vine with pubescent stems to 60 feet long. Leaves to 5 inches long, alternate, on petioles 5+ inches long, 3-foliolate, middle leaflet ovate-rhomboid, with a rounded base, becoming
lobed, lateral leaflets lobed to one side, margins ciliate
to entire, tips pointed, acuminate. Flowers in 8-inch-
long racemes originating from leaf axils, numerous and
crowded, papilionaceous, 1 inch long, reddish purple to
violet-purple, banner with creamy yellow center at base,
protruding forward somewhat.

Trifolium incarnatum   FABACEAE

Crimson clover, Larry's honey-clover, Italian clover

Fields, meadows, roadsides and other open
areas. Spring, summer. Common.

An introduced, erect, branching or unbranched annual
with pubescent stems to 30 inches tall. Leaves alternate,
on petioles to 4 inches long, 3-foliolate, leaflets obovate
to oblong-cordate, bases tapering, margins entire or
toothed, tips rounded and notched, lower surface of leaflet pubescent, upper surface glabrous. Flowers in cylindric terminal spikes to 2½ inches long, numerous and
densely arranged, crimson-red, papilionaceous, slender,
to ½ inch long and ascending, banner and lateral wings
enclosing keel. Found in eastern fourth of Texas. Often
used as a cover crop; tends to escape.

Iris fulva   IRIDACEAE

Copper iris

Swamps, shallow waters, stream banks, wet meadows,
ditches and other wet areas. Spring. Rare.

A rhizomatous perennial with erect leaves and stems to
just over 3 feet tall. Bright green, linear leaves are slightly
shorter than stems and 1 inch wide. Flowers at ends of
slender stems, 1 or 2 per stem, reddish copper, sepals
downward-arching and 2 inches long and nearly as wide,
petals arching, nearly as long as sepals but only half as
wide at their greatest. Only red iris naturally occurring in
state. Reported from 2 counties in deep East Texas along
Louisiana border.

Krameria lanceolata   KRAMERIACEAE

Ratany, trailing ratany, prairie bur

Meadows, fields, prairies, roadsides, open
woodlands and shrublands, and other open
areas. Spring, summer, fall. Common.

A trailing or prostrate perennial vine from a woody rootstock with numerous stems to 5 feet long. Leaves alternate, silky, linear to oblong, about ½ inch long with entire
margins. Flowers bilateral, about 1 inch in diameter, deep
reddish purple to crimson with 5 unequal petals (upper
3 petals are larger). Fruit is a single-seeded bur covered
in stiff spines. Always a treat to find in flower and often
mistaken for a more glamorous species. Found throughout most of Texas; absent in far eastern Texas. No preference of substrate or soil type. The only vining species of
Krameria in Texas.

305

Salvia coccinea   LAMIACEAE
Red sage, tropical sage, scarlet sage
Open brush and woodlands, riparian areas,
thickets. Spring, summer, fall. Common.

An erect annual to short-lived perennial with pubescent,
branching stems to 3+ feet tall. Leaves opposite, on
petioles to 1¾ inches long, deltate, to 2¾ inches long
and 2 inches wide, bases cordate to truncate, margins
crenate, tips acute to obtuse. Flowers in terminal spikes,
red, 1 inch in diameter, bilabiate, upper lip reduced,
lower lip enlarged, 3-lobed, middle lobe wide and spreading beyond lateral lobes. Widespread from South Texas,
north into Oklahoma. Increasingly less common farther
north and east into Louisiana. Widely available in the
nursery trade and as seed. Expected elsewhere through
introductions.

Salvia greggii   LAMIACEAE
Autumn sage, Gregg's salvia, cherry sage
Open shrub and woodlands, rocky outcrops, canyons,
drainages. Spring, summer. Uncommon.

An erect, multistemmed, branching, semiwoody perennial with leafy stems to 3 feet tall and as wide. Leaves
opposite, on petioles to ¼ inch long, elliptic to obovate,
to 1 inch long, aromatic, margins entire to crenulate,
blades somewhat leathery. Flowers in loose, terminal
racemes, scarlet to reddish pink, bilabiate, upper lip visibly pubescent, lower lip enlarged, lobed. Widespread but
not frequent from Presidio County to eastern portion of
Edwards Plateau. Seems to prefer protected, rocky habitats. Widely available in the nursery trade in various
flower colors.

Salvia penstemonoides   LAMIACEAE
Big red sage
Rocky outcrops, ledges, stream banks.
Spring, summer, fall. Rare.

A large, erect glabrous perennial with stiff, branching
stems to 5 feet tall. Leaves opposite, on petioles below,
becoming sessile above, linear to oblong-lanceolate, to
5 inches long, margins entire to finely dentate, ciliate.
Flowers in terminal racemes, 5 per node, numerous, reddish purple to red, bilabiate, to 1½ inches long, upper lip
extending beyond lower, lower lip 2-lobed. Once thought
to be extirpated, but recently rediscovered in a few areas
in southern Edwards Plateau, where it is endemic. Available in the nursery and seed trade and has been introduced elsewhere.

Salvia regla LAMIACEAE
Mountain sage, royal sage
Oak-pine-juniper woodlands. Summer, fall. Uncommon.

An erect, shrubby perennial with branching stems to
5+ feet tall. Leaves opposite, on petioles to ½ inch long,
deltate-ovate, bases truncate, margins crenate, tips
obtuse, surfaces glabrous, shiny. Flowers originating
from upper leaf axils, solitary or few on a short raceme,
scarlet red, bilabiate, to 1½ inches long, upper and lower
lips about same length. Grows in upper elevations of Chisos Mountains in Big Bend National Park; found along
Chisos Basin Road. Reported from Davis Mountains in
Jeff Davis County as well.

Salvia roemeriana LAMIACEAE
Cedar sage, Roemer's sage
Oak-juniper woodlands, canyons, rocky outcrops,
wooded creek banks. Spring, summer. Common.

An ascending to erect, multistemmed perennial with hirsute leaves and stems to 2 feet tall. Leaves opposite, cordate to roundish, to 2 inches long and as wide, margins
crenate to dentate. Flowers in terminal racemes, scarlet
red, bilabiate, lower lip 3-lobed, middle lobe enlarged and
divided, upper lip reduced. Found from Big Bend region
east throughout lower Edwards Plateau, primarily growing in shade.

Stachys coccinea LAMIACEAE
Texas betony, scarlet hedgenettle
Mountainous rocky outcrops, canyons
and slopes. Summer. Rare.

An erect, rhizomatous perennial with pubescent stems
to 3 feet tall. Leaves opposite, on petioles to 2½ inches
long, triangular to ovate-lanceolate, to 3¼ inches long,
bases rounded to truncate to cordate, margins dentate to
serrate, tips acute to obtuse. Flowers in terminal spikes,
6 per node, scarlet red, bilabiate, to 1 inch long, lower lip
3-lobed, middle lobe larger than lateral lobes, oval upper
lip not lobed, tube cylindric. Reported from mountains
around El Paso. Known to occur in Oregon Mountains
north of El Paso in New Mexico. Widely available in the
nursery trade. Expect introductions elsewhere.

307

Hermannia texana MALVACEAE
Texas burstwort, Mexican mallow
Rocky slopes, open brush and woodlands, fields,
prairies. Spring, summer, fall. Uncommon.

An erect, multistemmed perennial to 2 feet tall with
stems covered in star-shaped hairs. Leaves on petioles to
¾ inch long, ovate-elliptic, to 2½ inches long, bases cordate or rounded or truncate, margins dentate to sinuate.
Flowers nodding, in cymes in upper portion of stem, reddish orange, about ⅜ inch long. Found mostly in South
Texas, north into southwestern Edwards Plateau where it
grows in open areas on rocky or sandy soils. Genus name
honors Paul Hermann, a 17th-century German physician
and botanist.

Hibiscus martianus MALVACEAE
**Heartleaf rose mallow, heartleaf hibiscus,
tulipan del monte**
Open shrub and woodlands, thornscrub.
Winter, spring, summer, fall. Uncommon.

An erect, branching perennial to 4+ feet tall, stems with
gray pubescence. Leaves cordate to ovate, sometimes
weakly 3-lobed, to 3¼ inches long and wide, margins
dentate to serrate, surfaces with star-shaped hairs. Flowers originate in axils of upper leaves, bright red, 2 or 3
inches in diameter. Unmistakable plant can be found
from southeastern Brewster County south into Cameron
County, generally in counties adjacent to Rio Grande.
Flowering throughout year farther south, it is typically
hidden among woody shrubs and difficult to locate unless
in flower.

Malvaviscus arboreus var. drummondii
MALVACEAE
Turk's cap, wax mallow, Drummond's turkscap
Wooded canyons, drainages, riparian areas.
Spring, summer, fall. Uncommon.

An erect perennial, often forming small clonal populations via roots, with pubescent stems to 5+ feet tall.
Leaves ovate, deeply 3-lobed, to 3½ inches long and as
wide, bases cordate, margins dentate to crenate. Bright
red, erect flowers originate in upper portions of stem, to
2 inches long, stigma extending beyond petals. Fruits red
and fleshy when mature, edible, somewhat akin to apples.
Found in southeastern Edwards Plateau, east into Louisiana, south into Mexico.

Trillium gracile MELANTHIACEAE
Sabine River wakerobin, slender trillium
Stream banks and slopes, woodlands
and forests. Spring. Uncommon.

An erect, rhizomatous, perennial with 1–3 flowering
stalks to 15 inches tall. Leaves absent. Scapes slender, reddish brown, topped by 3 leafy bracts. Bracts elliptic-ovate
to obovate, to 3½ inches long and 1¾ inches wide, surfaces mottled light green to dark green. Flower solitary,
linear-elliptic, to 1¾ inches long, sepals lanceolate to 1
inch long and ¼ inch wide, dark purple-reddish brown
and horizontal, 3 petals dark reddish purple, erect, tips
and upper portions touching but not connected. Found in
deep East Texas, from Shelby County south to Jefferson
County, east into Louisiana. Forms colonies.

Nyctaginia capitata NYCTAGINACEAE
Scarlet musk flower, devil's bouquet
Grasslands, fields, prairies, open desert scrub, roadsides
and other open areas. Summer, fall. Common.

An erect to spreading perennial with sticky-pubescent,
branching stems to 3 feet tall. Leaves opposite, unequal
in size, triangular to ovate, to 5 inches long and 4
inches wide, bases truncate to obtuse, margins sinuate to undulate, tips acute to pointed, blades glabrous to
sticky-pubescent below and glaucous above. Flowers in
terminal or axillary umbels on peduncles to 5¾ inches
long, funnel-shaped, scarlet red, fuchsia or reddish
orange, to 1¾ inches long and ⅝ inch wide, from few to
15±. Widespread from Cameron County north through
Edwards Plateau, west throughout Chihuahuan Desert.

Corallorhiza wisteriana ORCHIDACEAE
Spring coral-root, Wister's coral-root, arousing coral-root
Woodlands and forests. Winter,
spring, summer. Uncommon.

An erect, mycoheterotrophic perennial with reddish purple to brownish yellow leafless stems to 18 inches tall.
Leaves absent. Flowers on upper third of raceme, to 25
per raceme, bilateral, 3 sepals and 3 petals, brownish
purple to yellow, sepals lanceolate to ⅜ inch long, lateral
sepals curved-erect and forming a hood over column with
upper sepal and petals, lip white or slightly tinged pink
with reddish purple spots. Widely distributed in Texas,
although scattered.

death camus family
MELANTHIACEAE

four o'clock family
NYCTAGINACEAE

orchid family
ORCHIDACEAE

Dichromanthus cinnabarinus
ORCHIDACEAE
Scarlet ladies' tresses, cinnabar ladies' tresses
Oak-pine forest and woodlands. Summer, fall. Uncommon.

An erect perennial to nearly 3 feet tall with a single flowering stalk. Green leaves sheathing stem, linear to oblanceolate, to 10 inches long and about 1½ inches wide. Flowers in spikes to 7 inches long, 40 per spike, red to reddish orange, curved, sepals flared, upper sepals erect, interior yellow-orange, each flower surrounded by a reddish orange bract. Found in mountains in Big Bend region.

Hexalectris revoluta   ORCHIDACEAE
Curly coral root
Oak-juniper-pine woodlands. Spring, summer. Rare.

An erect, mycoheterotrophic perennial with brownish purple to tannish pink, glabrous stems to 20 inches tall; plants solitary or in groups. Leaves absent. Flowers in racemes, 15± per raceme, sepals and petals similar in color and shape, tan to pinkish brown with dark stripes, elliptic to lanceolate, recurved, sepals to about 1 inch long, petals to about ¾ inch long, lip 3-lobed, middle lobe white or pale pink with darker magenta stripes. Known from mixed woodlands in Brewster and Culberson Counties. Specimen photographed on limestone substrate in oak-juniper canyon.

Hexalectris spicata   ORCHIDACEAE
Spike crested coral root, crested coral root
Juniper-oak or pine woodlands. Spring,
summer. Uncommon.

An erect, mycoheterotrophic perennial with yellow-brown or pinkish brown to purple stems to 2 feet tall. Leaves absent. Flowers in racemes, sepals and petals similar in color and shape, tannish yellow to brownish purple with darker veins, oblong-elliptic, lateral sepals to ¾ inch long, upper sepal to 1 inch long, lateral petals to nearly 1 inch long, lip pink to white with dark magenta stripes, 3-lobed. Widespread throughout Texas. Found in Big Bend region east to Louisiana, typically in rich, organic soils in woodlands, most often in oak-juniper woods. Collections spotty in Texas, and incomplete. Expect elsewhere.

Hexalectris warnockii ORCHIDACEAE
Warnock's coral root
Woodlands, canyons, drainages. Spring, summer. Rare.

An erect, mycoheterotrophic perennial with dark red-dish purple stems to 16 inches long. Leaves absent. To 10 flowers in a raceme, sepals and petals dark reddish pur-ple to maroon, lateral sepals linear-oblong, upper sepal linear-lanceolate, petals oblanceolate, all to about ¾ inch long, not recurved, lip 3-lobed, middle lobe larger and white to cream with purple to maroon veins and mar-gins. Scattered from mountains of West Texas east into Edwards Plateau and North-Central Texas.

Isotria verticillata ORCHIDACEAE
Large whorled pogonia, whorled pogonia, purple fiveleaf orchid
Forests, seeps, bogs. Spring. Rare.

An erect, rhizomatous perennial with brownish green, glabrous stems to 16 inches tall. Leaves 5±, whorled or appearing so, elliptic, oblong-lanceolate, or obovate, to 4 inches long and 2 inches wide, margins entire, tips obtuse. Flowers on peduncles typically shorter than length of leaves, sepals 3, brownish purple at ends and greenish toward base, lanceolate, to 2¾ inches long and less than ¼ inch wide. Petals yellow-green, elliptic-ovate to lanceolate, to 1 inch long and ⅓ inch wide, covering column. Lip yellow-green to white, streaked purple, to 1 inch long and ⅜ inch wide. Found in deep East Texas, in rich woodlands. Often forms colonies.

Neottia bifolia (*Listera australis*) ORCHIDACEAE
Southern twayblade
Moist woods, marshes, bogs. Spring,
summer. Uncommon.

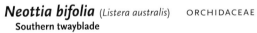

An erect perennial with glabrous, purple-green stems to 12 inches tall. Leaves opposite, 1 pair, ovate to oblong or elliptic, to 1½ inches long and ¾ inch wide, bases slightly cordate, margins entire, tips obtuse to pointed. Flowers in a raceme, to 25 per raceme, reddish purple, less than ½ inch long, narrow, sepals and lateral petals incon-spicuous, lip obvious and to ½ inch long with 2 thin, linear-lanceolate lobes. Found in eastern fourth of Texas, typically in areas with moist soils. Often overlooked because of small size.

Castilleja indivisa OROBANCHACEAE
Texas paintbrush, Texas Indian paintbrush
Fields, meadows, grasslands, prairies, open
brush and woodlands, roadsides and other
open areas. Spring, summer. Common.

An erect, hemiparasitic annual with pubescent stems to
16 inches, stems reddish brown with age. Leaves alternate, sessile, linear to lanceolate, to 3+ inches long and ⅓
inch wide, margins entire to ciliate, occasionally lobed at
base, tips acute, blades pubescent. Inflorescences in terminal bracted spikes, bracts typically 3-lobed with entire
margins, red to orange to salmon to pink, calyx tubular,
ends of lobes pink to red. Flowers bilabiate, about 1 inch
long, upper lip barely extending beyond calyx, lower lip
reduced, calyx interior yellow-green. Found in eastern
half of state.

Castilleja integra OROBANCHACEAE
Wholeleaf Indian paintbrush
Grasslands, plains, open brush and woodlands, roadsides
and other open areas. Spring, summer, fall. Common.

An erect, hemiparasitic perennial with tomentose
stems to 16 inches tall. Leaves alternate, sessile, linear
to linear-lanceolate, to 3+ inches long and ¼ inch wide,
margins entire to ciliate, tips pointed, blades somewhat
woolly on lower surface, folded. Inflorescences in terminal bracted spikes, bracts 3-lobed or entire, ovate to lanceolate, tips red to yellow, calyx 4-lobed, tubular, to 1½
inches long, red to yellow. Flowers greenish yellow, to 1¾
inches long, bilabiate, upper lip barely extending beyond
calyx. Found in Chihuahuan Desert.

Castilleja lanata OROBANCHACEAE
Woolly Indian paintbrush, woolly paintbrush
Fields, grasslands, open brush and woodlands,
roadsides and other open areas. Late winter,
spring, summer, fall. Common.

An erect, hemiparasitic, multistemmed perennial from
a woody base, with woolly stems to 3+ feet tall. Leaves
alternate, sessile, linear, to 3+ inches long, margins
entire, tips acute, blades folded, gray-green, woolly. Inflorescences in terminal, bracted spikes, bracts entire or
3-lobed, oblanceolate, ends red to orange, bases of bracts
woolly, calyx to 1 inch long, tips red to orange, bases
greenish gray, woolly. Flowers almost entirely covered by
calyx, bilabiate, upper lip extending beyond calyx lobes, to
about 1¼ inches long. Found in Chihuahuan Desert.

312

Castilleja lindheimeri
(Castilleja purpurea var. lindheimeri)
OROBANCHACEAE
Lindheimer's paintbrush
Fields, grasslands, open brush and woodlands, roadsides
and other open areas. Spring. Locally common.

An erect, hemiparasitic perennial with villose stems to 12
inches tall. Leaves alternate, to 3+ inches long and ¼ inch
wide, with 1–3 pairs of lateral lobes, lobes linear to lanceolate, margins entire, blades fuzzy, silvery green. Inflorescences in terminal bracted spikes, bracts with 1 or 2
pairs of lateral lobes, outer lobes linear to lanceolate, middle lobe broad, reddish orange to yellow-orange with red
tips on lower bracts, calyx 4-lobed nearly covering flower
within. Flowers bilabiate, lower lip shorter but slightly
protruding from calyx, upper lip longer, galea greenish and visible beyond calyx. Found throughout Central
Texas, southwest into Mexico.

Castilleja rigida   OROBANCHACEAE
Rigid paintbrush
Mountain slopes and ridges, sparse brushlands,
grasslands. Early winter, spring, summer, fall. Rare.

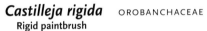

An erect, hemiparasitic perennial with finely pubescent, occasionally branching stems to 2+ feet tall. Leaves
alternate, sessile, oblanceolate to linear, to 3+ inches
long and ⅓ inch wide, margins entire, tips acute, blades
pubescent, grayish green. Inflorescences in terminal,
bracted spikes, bracts obovate to elliptic, tips of lower
bracts bright red to orangish red to reddish purple, margins somewhat rolled inward. Calyx 2-lobed, to 1½ inches
long. Flowers 1¾ inches long, bilabiate, lower lip reduced,
often hidden by calyx, upper lip elongated and extending beyond calyx, galea greenish yellow. Found in mid
to upper elevations in Chihuahuan Desert and western
Edwards Plateau.

Epifagus virginiana   OROBANCHACEAE
Beechdrops
Beech woodlands and forests. Winter, spring. Uncommon.

An erect, parasitic perennial, often found in clumps,
with fleshy, yellowish brown to purplish brown stems
to 18 inches tall, scales along stem to ¹⁄₁₀ inch long, triangular to ovate. Leaves absent. Inflorescences alternate
along stem, bilateral, outer side reddish brown, inner
side creamy white, 4 lobes. Upper flowers to ⅓ inch long,
tubular. Found in Southeast Texas.

Argemone sanguinea   PAPAVERACEAE
Rose prickly poppy, red prickly poppy
Prairies, meadows, fields, open brushlands
and thornscrub, roadsides and other open
areas. Winter, spring, summer. Common.

An erect annual to short-lived perennial with branching stems to 5 feet tall. Lower leaves larger (to 8 inches
long) and deeper lobed than upper leaves, prickles along
veins on leaf bottoms. Flowers to 4 inches broad, in
red, rose, lavender, bronze, white, or variations of these
colors (most populations in Texas are rose to pink).
Found in South Texas, from Coastal Bend west into the
Trans-Pecos.

Papaver somniferum   PAPAVERACEAE
Opium poppy, poppyseed, poppy
Creek and river beds, floodplains, urban
and suburban areas, other areas of human
habitation. Spring. Uncommon.

An introduced annual with stout, glabrous, branching
stems to 3+ feet tall. Leaves alternate, oblong to ovate,
bases clasping, margins dentate to serrate, tips pointed.
Basal leaves to 6+ inches long, typically with lacerate
or pinnate margins. Flowers terminal or from axils of
upper leaves, 3+ inches wide, with 4 delicate petals, colored red, pink, purple, white, or blue; the most frequent
escapee is red with a black center. Fruits large, round to
oval poricidal capsules, glaucous when immature, aging
light brown to tan. Widely planted ornamental that has
escaped cultivation. Found in Hill Country.

Penstemon baccharifolius   PLANTAGINACEAE
Rock penstemon
Limestone ridges, canyon walls, bluffs, roadcuts and
other areas with exposed rock in the Edwards Plateau
and Trans-Pecos. Summer, fall. Locally common.

An erect, multistemmed perennial with pubescent stems
to 18+ inches tall. Leaves opposite, sessile above, on petioles below, oblanceolate to obovate, to 1¼ inches long,
margins toothed, tips rounded. Flowers in terminal panicles, red, to 1 inch long or slightly longer, bell-shaped,
upper lip 2-lobed, erect to slightly reflexed, lower lip
3-lobed, reflexed. Grows on exposed limestone rock in
Hill Country and west to Brewster and Presidio Counties.
Can be located along Highway 90 at Pecos River crossing
and along roadcuts between Junction and Fort Stockton.

Penstemon barbatus PLANTAGINACEAE
Beard-lip penstemon
Mountains of West Texas. Summer. Locally common.

An erect perennial with multiple, glabrous stems to 3+
feet tall. Leaves opposite, sessile, lanceolate, to 6 inches
long, margins entire, tips acute. Flowers in 1½-inch-long
terminal racemes, scarlet red, bilabiate, upper lip 2-lobed
and projecting over lower lip, which is 3-lobed and greatly
reflexed. Commonly seen along scenic loop through
Davis Mountains. Look for this species among boulders
and along roadcuts from Fort Davis to York Ranch. Also
found in Guadalupe and Chisos Mountains at similar elevation and habitat.

Penstemon cardinalis PLANTAGINACEAE
Regal penstemon, cardinal penstemon
Canyons, mountain slopes, rocky
outcrops. Spring, summer. Rare.

An erect perennial with glabrous, reddish stems to 4+
feet tall. Leaves opposite, sessile to clasping, cordate
to elliptic to slightly rounded, to 2½ inches long and 2
inches wide, margins entire, tips acute, blades glaucous,
thick and glabrous. Flowers in terminal racemes, numerous, scarlet red, tubular, bilabiate, to 1½ inches long,
upper lip 2-lobed and projecting, lower lip 3-lobed and
reduced, throat covered in dense, golden hairs. Found in
upper elevations of Jeff Davis and Culberson Counties.

Penstemon havardii PLANTAGINACEAE
Havard's penstemon
Mountain slopes and associated drainages
in the Trans-Pecos. Spring, summer, fall.
Locally common to uncommon.

An erect, glabrous perennial with stems to nearly 6 feet
tall, usually shorter, leaves and stems glaucous. Leaves
opposite, sessile, elliptic, to 4 inches long and 2¾ inches
wide, margins entire, tips rounded or notched. Flowers in
terminal racemes, red to reddish orange, 1¼ inches long,
bilabiate, tubular, with a projecting 2-lobed upper lip and
a 3-lobed lower lip. Commonly seen close to Rio Grande,
especially in gravelly washes and creeks, although it can
occur among boulders along canyon walls.

Penstemon murrayanus PLANTAGINACEAE
Scarlet penstemon
Grasslands, meadows, fields, open brush and
woodlands. Spring, summer. Uncommon.

An erect, glabrous perennial with reddish stems to 6
feet tall. Leaves opposite below, connate above, sessile,
ovate to slightly round to elliptic, to 4 inches long and 2
inches wide, margins entire, tips acute, blades glabrous
and glaucous. Flowers in terminal racemes, bright red, to
1¼+ inches long, bell-shaped, bilabiate, lower lip 3-lobed,
reflexed, upper lip 2-lobed, reflexed to curled. One of the
most beautiful native *Penstemon* species. Worthy of cultivation. Found in sandy soils, mostly East Texas, with
additional populations found in South-Central Texas, to
Victoria County. Can be found at Gus Engeling Wildlife
Management Area in Anderson County.

Penstemon ramosus (P. lanceolatus)
PLANTAGINACEAE
Lanceleaf beardtongue
Desert canyons, washes, rocky slopes
and hillsides. Spring. Rare.

An erect, pubescent perennial with slender stems to 20+
inches tall. Leaves opposite, sessile, lanceolate to linear,
to 4 inches long and ⅓ inch wide, margins entire, tips
acute. Flowers in terminal racemes, somewhat nodding,
bilabiate, bright red, tubular, to 1⅓ inches long, upper lip
erect and 2-lobed, lower lip 3-lobed, lobes slender. Found
on limestone in Big Bend region. Known from Brewster
and Culberson Counties. Also in northern Mexico, southwestern New Mexico, and southeastern Arizona.

Penstemon wrightii PLANTAGINACEAE
Wright's penstemon
Mountain slopes, rocky outcrops, canyons,
ridges, bluffs. Spring, summer. Uncommon.

An erect perennial with glabrous stems to 4+ feet tall.
Leaves opposite, sessile, ovate to elliptic, to 3 inches long
and 2 inches wide, margins entire, tips rounded to acute,
blades glaucous, thick and leathery. Flowers in terminal
racemes, bell-shaped, red, to about ¾ inch long, upper
lip 2-lobed with lobes rounded, lower lip 3-lobed. An
endemic species found in Jeff Davis, Brewster, Presidio,
and Reeves Counties. Look for this species in the Davis
Mountains, typically at lower elevations than *Penstemon
barbatus*. Named after Charles Wright (1811–1885), who
collected in Texas during the mid-1800s.

Ipomopsis aggregata POLEMONIACEAE
Skyrocket, scarlet gilia, scarlet standing cypress
Open woodlands, fields, open rocky slopes,
drainages, creek banks, and other open, seasonally
wet areas. Summer, fall. Locally common.

An erect biennial to short-lived perennial with branching stems to 6 feet tall. Basal leaves to 2½ inches long, finely divided with linear lobes, margins entire, surfaces woolly white. Upper leaves smaller, less pubescent, and with fewer lobes. Flowers in upper leaf axils, scarlet to orange, rarely yellow, trumpet-shaped, to 1½ inches long, 5-lobed with lobes lanceolate. Found in Chihuahuan Desert region; a few collections from upper Panhandle. Often found around where water collects during summer months, such as roadside ditches and roadcuts.

Ipomopsis rubra POLEMONIACEAE
Standing cypress, red gilia, red Texas star
Fields, meadows, grasslands, open brush and
woodlands. Spring, summer. Common.

An erect biennial with a large rosette of leaves and a stout, leafy, branching stem to 5+ feet tall, leaves and stems pubescent. Leaves alternate, pinnate, heavily divided, to 3+ inches long, lobes linear and threadlike. Flowers densely arranged along upper stem, red to orange, rarely yellow, trumpet-shaped, 5-lobed, to 1+ inch long. Found throughout Central Texas, north into Oklahoma, east into Louisiana.

Clematis texensis RANUNCULACEAE
Scarlet clematis, scarlet leather flower, Texas leather flower
Limestone cliffs and ledges, among protected
wooded canyons, along perennial streams and
creeks. Spring, summer. Uncommon.

A climbing perennial vine with reddish stems to nearly 10 feet long. Leaves pinnate, unlobed to 3-lobed, to 3½ inches long and 2⅓ inches wide, margins entire with 6–10 leaflets. Terminal leaflet tendril-like, each leaflet ovate to round. Flowers in loose cymes, 7 per cyme, to 1¼ inches long, urn-shaped to round, interior cream (in plants growing in eastern portion of its range) or same color as exterior. Fruits are achenes with feathery tails to 2¾ inches long. Found in Edwards Plateau, along waterways or in protected, wooded canyons. Not a common species, though when found, it is usually abundant in the area.

317

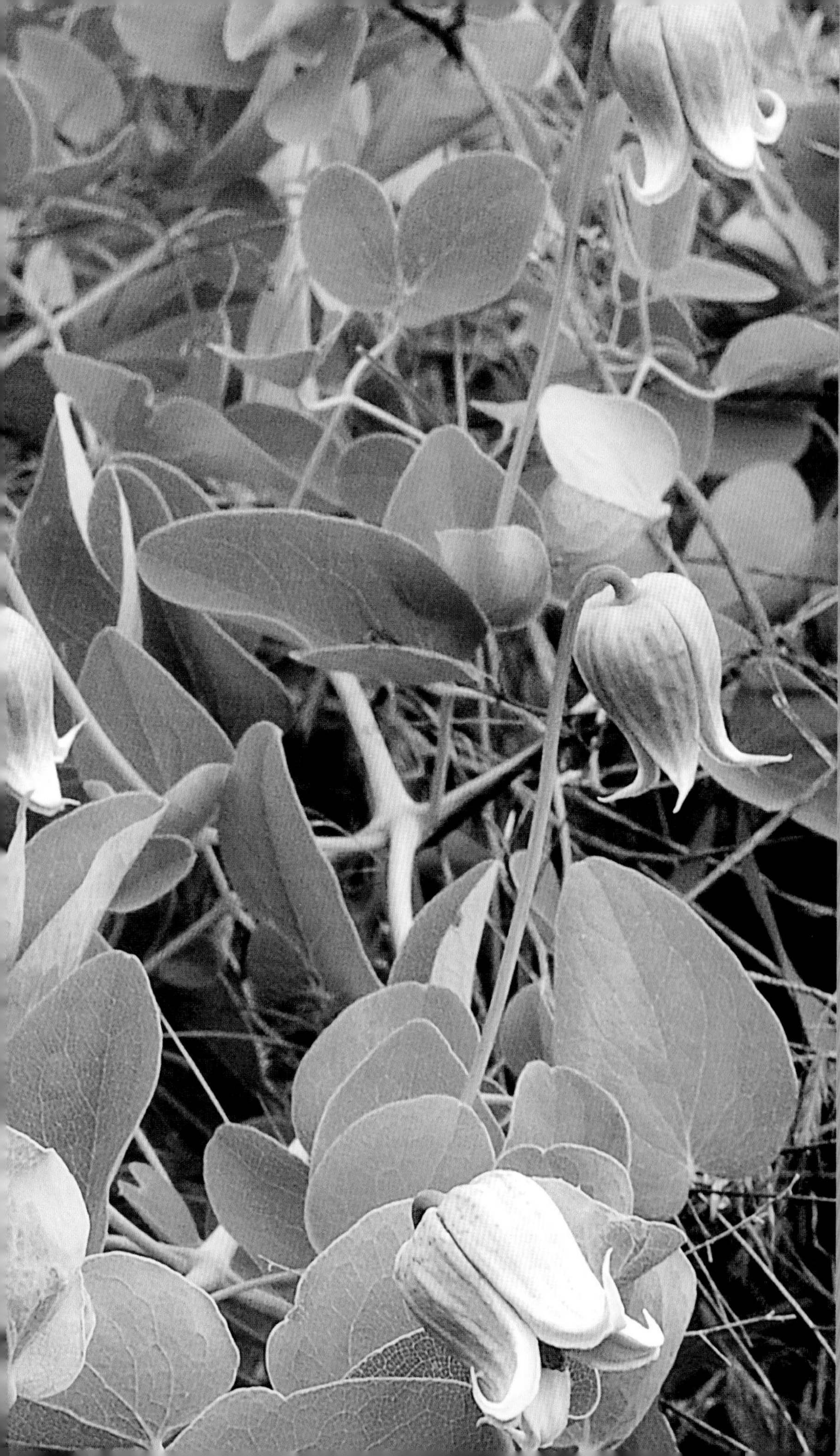

Carlowrightia texana   ACANTHACEAE
Texas wrightwort
Fields, open grass brushlands, thickets, rocky outcrops, roadsides, and other open areas. Spring, summer, fall. Common.

A low, branching perennial with leafy stems to 16 inches tall, usually half this height. Leaves opposite, round to ovate, to about ⅓ inch long, surfaces pubescent. Flowers pink to white with purple veins along lobes, to ½ inch in diameter, bilateral, upper lobe erect and somewhat reflexed, lateral lobes cupping lower lobe. Recurved stem hairs and leaf shape distinguish this species from *Carlowrightia torreyana*, which is similar in size. Found in gravelly soil and disturbed ground in Tamaulipan Thornscrub, Edwards Plateau, and Chihuahuan Desert.

Dicliptera brachiata   ACANTHACEAE
Branched foldwing, branched dicliptera, wild mudwort
Woodland edges, riparian areas. Summer, fall. Common.

An erect perennial to 30 inches tall, with hexagonal stems and numerous branches. Leaves opposite, on petioles over 1 inch long, ovate to lanceolate, to 4 inches long and 2 inches wide. Flowers in axils and distinctly 2-lipped, to ⅝ inch long, pink to purple or white. Frequent throughout central and eastern portions of state, along banks of rivers and other perennial moving bodies of water, usually occurring in colonies.

Justicia ovata var. *lanceolata*
ACANTHACEAE
Looseleaf water-willow, lance-leaved water-willow
Swamps, bogs, marshes, other wet areas. Spring, summer. Locally common.

Erect perennial with glabrous stems to 12 inches tall, stems slightly branched. Leaves linear to lanceolate, to 4 inches long and 1¼ inches wide. Flowers in 4-inch spikes arising from leaf axils, lavender to white, to ½ inch long, bilabiate, lower lip 3-lobed, upper lip 2-lobed. Primarily an East Texas species; however, a few collections have been made farther west and south to Cameron County. Found in wet areas, but not necessarily perennial waters.

Stenandrium barbatum ACANTHACEAE
Shaggy stenandrium, early shaggytuft
Sparsely vegetated shrubland. Spring,
summer. Locally common.

A multibranched, dwarf perennial to just over 2 inches
tall from a central root. Oblanceolate leaves, to 1¾ inches
long and ⅓ inch wide, are covered in fine hairs and soft to
the touch. Density of hairs gives a soft, fuzzy appearance.
Flowers appear out of foliage, strikingly pink, 5-lobed,
½ inch long and ¼ inch wide. Found in Chihuahuan
Desert region, emerges in early spring and after rains
during summer months. Typically grows on loose, open
limestone.

Yeatesia platystegia ACANTHACEAE
Wild shrimp plant, Montell bractspike
Woodlands, shrublands, riparian areas. Summer. Rare.

An erect, slender perennial to 16 inches tall that readily
branches. Leaves lanceolate to linear, on short petioles,
to 2 inches long and ½ inch wide. Most obvious character is flowering spike, to 2 inches long. Flowers on
heart-shaped bracts, light purple, to 1 inch long, slender
tube nearly entire length, lower lip deeply 3-lobed, upper
lip slightly notched. Considered rare, found in southeastern edge of Edwards Plateau, south to Starr County.
Found growing under woody species, or along edges of
thickets. Large populations, with thousands of individuals, during years of well-timed precipitation.

Sesuvium maritimum AIZOACEAE
Slender seapurslane, annual seapurslane
Beaches, sandy shores, and marshes along the
coast. Winter, spring, summer, fall. Uncommon.

A prostrate annual, multibranched with succulent stems
to 16 inches long, yellowing with age, not rooting at
nodes. Leaves on a clasping petiole, fleshy, spatulate to
ovate, 1 inch long. Flowers barely ¼ inch broad when
fully open, calyx lobes pink to purple when open, appearing individually in leaf axils. Found along coast and barrier islands; additional populations in floodplain of Rio
Grande in Hudspeth County.

Sesuvium portulacastrum   AIZOACEAE
Seapurslane, shoreline purslane, seaside purslane
Beaches or inland with sandy or clay soils.
Winter, spring, summer, fall. Common.

A highly branched, prostrate perennial with red, fleshy stems that root at nodes. Leaves succulent or fleshy, oblong to elliptic-obovate, to 2¼ inch long and 1 inch wide. Single flowers arise from short pedicels in leaf axils, to ½ inch wide, 5-lobed calyx green on outside but when in bloom reveals a bright pink interior. Along all of Texas's beaches; a few collections have been made in Webb County. Common name sea pickle arises from taste of edible leaves.

Sesuvium verrucosum   AIZOACEAE
Western seapurslane, verrucose seapurslane
Coastal areas, playas, saline soils. Spring,
summer. Locally common.

A much-branched prostrate perennial. Stems nearly 3 feet long, typically verrucose, do not root at nodes. Leaves fleshy, succulent, linear to spatulate, to 1½ inches long and ¼ inch wide. Flowers appear in leaf axils, pink, 5-lobed, solitary, about ¼ inch in diameter. Found along lower Gulf Coast, typically on clay soils behind dune systems; also West Texas and Panhandle, growing in salt flats, playas, and along waterways.

Trianthema portulacastrum   AIZOACEAE
Horse purslane, verdolaga blanca, desert horse-purslane
Thickets with sandy soil, dunes, playas, river and creek
banks, disturbed areas. Spring, summer, fall. Uncommon.

An annual succulent, prostrate or decumbent, with heavily branched stems to 3 feet. Leaves in unequal pairs along stem, on petioles usually equaling length of leaf, elliptic to orbiculate, 1½ inches long. Solitary pink to purple calyx occurs in leaf axils, 5-lobed, about ⅓ inch wide. Widespread throughout Texas, but lacking in central portion of state and Panhandle.

Gomphrena nealleyi   AMARANTHACEAE
Nealley's globe amaranth
Fields, meadows, grasslands, prairies, open
brushland. Winter, spring, summer. Common.

An erect perennial with pubescent, weak stems to 16
inches tall. Leaves sessile, obovate to spatulate, to 1½
inches long and ½ inch wide, margins entire and ciliate,
upper surfaces visibly pubescent. Inflorescences slightly
round to cylindric, about ½ inch in diameter, consisting of numerous flowers, surrounded by pink to white
bractlets. Found from deep South Texas and northeast
along coast to Houston area and slightly inland, in sandy
soils. Named in honor of Greenleaf Cilley Nealley, a
19th-century Texas plant collector and botanist.

Gomphrena nitida   AMARANTHACEAE
Pearly globe amaranth
Fields, meadows, open woodlands.
Summer, fall. Uncommon.

An erect, slender annual with pubescent stems to 24+
inches long. Leaves opposite, on petioles to ¼ inch long,
obovate or oblong, to 2½ inches long and 1 inch wide,
margins entire, tips acute or obtuse, lower surfaces with
long hairs. Flowers clustered in rounded terminal heads,
pink-tinged and cream to yellow, individual flowers less
than ¼ inch long. Found in Big Bend region, north into
Reeves County, along roadsides, especially near mountain drainages. Specific epithet name *nitida* comes from
niteo, which means "shine" and could refer to glossy
nature of bracts.

Allium ampeloprasum   AMARYLLIDACEAE
Wild leek, elephant garlic, broadleaf wild leek
Old homesteads, roadsides, disturbed
areas. Spring, summer. Uncommon.

An introduced bulbous perennial with a scape to 5 feet
tall. Leaves thick, solid, channeled to 20 inches long and
2 inches wide, margins rough, serrate, with distinct yet
pleasant garlic taste. Flowers appear in globose umbels at
apex of scape, pink to reddish purple or white. Introduced
from Europe as both a landscape plant and an edible.
Typically found near old homesteads, abandoned gardens,
and in other cultivated areas.

Allium drummondii   AMARYLLIDACEAE
False garlic, wild garlic, Drummond's onion
Prairies, meadows, hillsides, roadsides.
Spring, summer. Common.

Bulbous perennial, typically clustered, with a scape to
12 inches tall. Leaves, to 5, are ⅕ inch wide and up to
12 inches long, flat to channeled, margins entire. The
umbel, mostly compact, holds to 25 urn- to open star–
shaped flowers. Each flower about ¼ inch in diameter, usually pink to rose but may be white. Look for this
plant, Texas's most common *Allium* species, throughout
the state; it can occur in populations with thousands of
individuals.

Allium perdulce var. *sperryi*
AMARYLLIDACEAE
Sperry's wild onion
Rocky slopes and hillsides. Spring. Common.

A multibulbous perennial with a scape to 8 inches
tall. Leaves, to 5 per bulb, are longer than scape, to 12
inches long and ¹⁄₁₆ inch wide, with entire margins.
Loose-flowered umbel with up to 25 urn-shaped flowers, pink or white with obvious darker midribs. Found
only in West Texas, from Edwards County west to El Paso
County. A smaller variety, *Allium perdulce* var. *perdulce*, is
found in Panhandle.

Asclepias incarnata   APOCYNACEAE
Swamp milkweed
Creek and river banks, ponds, marshes, and other
low, wet areas. Spring, summer, fall. Uncommon.

An erect, multistemmed, perennial with branching stems to 5+ feet tall. Leaves opposite, occasionally
whorled, lanceolate, to 6 inches long and 1½ inches wide
but typically half this size, margins entire, surfaces glabrous. Inflorescence a terminal umbel, to 3½ inches
wide. Flowers about ¼ inch wide, 5-lobed, corolla pink,
reflexed with ascending tips. Hoods white to pinkish
white. Follicles smooth, elliptic to lanceolate, to 4 inches
long. Uncommon throughout Texas, with localized concentration in southern Edwards Plateau. Absent in Chihuahuan Desert and South Texas.

324

Asclepias nummularia APOCYNACEAE
Tufted milkweed, yerba de cuervo
Open, rocky, mountain slopes. Spring. Locally common.

A decumbent to erect, diminutive perennial with one to several stems, branching from base to 6 inches tall when in flower. Opposite leaves, usually 2 or 3 pairs, rounded to widely ovate-lanceolate, up to 1¾ inches long and as wide, short petiolate to nearly sessile, margins wavy, tips rounded to acute. Upper leaf surface densely tomentose, lower surface with prominent venation. Flowers few to numerous in loose umbels on peduncles to 3½ inches long, corollas with 5 reflexed lobes, tannish brown and tinged pink, hoods rose to pink, extending above white hooks. Follicles to 2½ inches long and smooth. Found in Brewster, Jeff Davis, and Presidio Counties, typically at mid elevations.

Asclepias rubra APOCYNACEAE
Red milkweed, pink milkweed, bog milkweed
Swamps, bogs, wet savannas and meadows, other low, wet areas. Spring, summer. Uncommon.

An erect perennial with glabrous to slightly pubescent, slender stems to 4+ feet tall. Leaves opposite, sessile or nearly so, lanceolate to broadly ovate, to 6½ inches long and 2¾ inches wide, bases cordate or rounded, margins entire to wavy, tips pointed. Inflorescences in umbels on peduncles to 4+ inches long, with 20± flowers per umbel. Flowers pink to rose to purplish red, 5-lobed, corolla reflexed, hood slightly lighter in color. Follicles smooth, elongated oval shape, tapering at both ends, to 4¾ inches long and ¾ inch wide. Found in eastern third of Texas.

Camassia scilloides ASPARAGACEAE
Wild hyacinth, Atlantic camas
Prairies, fields, meadows, woodlands and other open areas. Spring. Common.

Bulbous perennial with clasping leaves and scape to nearly 3 feet tall. Keeled leaves, as many as 8, to 24 inches long and ¾ inch wide. Final 8 inches of scape host numerous light purple to lavender flowers, each about 1 inch in diameter. Flowers have 6 tepals and 6 anthers, which are bright yellow; the green ovary can be seen in center of tepals. Found in central, east, and north portions of state, east to Louisiana, north into Oklahoma; can occur in very large colonies.

dogbane family
APOCYNACEAE

asparagus family
ASPARAGACEAE

Acourtia nana ASTERACEAE
Desert holly, dwarf desertpeony
Shrublands, desert scrub. Spring, summer. Common.

An erect, rhizomatous perennial to about 10 inches tall, with nearly horizontal branching. Leaves sessile, rhombic, to 2 inches long, with heavily dentate margins; resemble holly leaves. Flowering heads solitary and terminal to about 1 inch long, up to 24 pink to bluish pink florets. Common in the Trans-Pecos, especially lower elevations dominated by creosote and mesquite, where it often grows under these and other shrubs; less common in western Edwards Plateau. Usually found in small colonies.

Acourtia runcinata ASTERACEAE
Featherleaf desertpeony
Forests, woodlands, shrublands. Winter, spring, summer, fall. Common.

A perennial consisting of a basal rosette, with scapes to 12 inches tall. Basal leaves on petioles that can be nearly nonexistent to 3½ inches long, oblong to oblanceolate, pinnately lobed, to 9 inches long, margins dentate and spine-tipped. Flowering heads on peduncles to 12 inches long, usually one per, but as many as 3. Florets pink to lavender-pink, to ¾ inch long. Common in South and West Texas, less common in southern Edwards Plateau; often found in shady areas.

Acourtia wrightii ASTERACEAE
Brownfoot, pink perezia
Grasslands, meadows, woodlands, shrublands, roadsides. Spring, summer, fall. Common.

An erect, typically single-stemmed, leafy perennial with glabrous stems to 3+ feet tall. Leaves alternate, sessile, lanceolate to elliptic, to just over 5 inches long and 1 inch wide, margins dentate. Flowering heads in terminal corymbs, to 5 inches in diameter, with numerous pink to lavender florets to ¾ inch long. Common throughout Chihuahuan Desert region, scattered collections in western and southern Edwards Plateau, one collection from Cameron County.

Cosmos parviflorus   ASTERACEAE
Southwestern cosmos
Open mountain brush and woodlands.
Summer, fall. Locally common.

An erect annual with a single, branching stem to 3+ feet
tall. Leaves opposite, on petioles to ¼ inch long, 1- to
3-pinnately lobed with lobes linear, to 2½ inches long,
margins entire to ciliate. Flowering heads either single
or in loose corymbs at ends of stems, individual heads to
1 inch wide, ray florets pink to violet and to 8± per head,
disc florets yellow and numerous. Only native *Cosmos*
species in Texas, found in upper elevations in Big Bend
region.

Echinacea angustifolia   ASTERACEAE
**Narrow-leaf coneflower, black Samson, narrow-leaved
purple coneflower**
Prairies, grasslands, open brush and woodlands, roadsides
and other open areas. Spring, summer. Uncommon.

An erect perennial with greenish to purple stems to
2 feet tall, stems and leaves covered with coarse hairs.
Basal leaves only, on petioles to 3½ inches long, elliptic
to lanceolate, to 12 inches long and 1½ inches wide, margins entire. Solitary heads terminal on peduncles to 12+
inches tall. Ray florets pink to purple and to 1½ inches
long, disc florets numerous and purple. Widespread
from South-Central Texas north into Oklahoma; absent
in western Texas, very weak in the east. *Echinacea* is of
Greek origin (*echinos*) and translates to "hedgehog," a reference to the seedhead. Specific epithet means "narrow
leaves."

Echinacea atrorubens   ASTERACEAE
Topeka purple coneflower
Prairies, fields, meadows, woodlands, open brush and
other open spaces. Spring, summer. Locally common.

An erect perennial to nearly 3 feet tall, pubescent leaves
and stems. Basal leaves only, on petioles 5 inches long,
linear to lanceolate, to 12 inches long and to 1 inch wide,
margins typically entire. Heads about 1⅓ inches in diameter, solitary on peduncles to 20 inches long, drooping ray
florets pink to purple and to 1⅓ inches long, disc florets
green to pink or purple. Populations can number in the
thousands, from Galveston County north-northwest into
Oklahoma. Specific epithet of Latin origin and means
"dark red," referring to petal color.

327

Echinacea purpurea   ASTERACEAE
Purple coneflower, eastern purple coneflower
Open woodlands, grasslands. Spring, summer. Rare.

An erect perennial to 4 feet tall, with pubescent leaves
and stems. Basal leaves, on petioles to nearly 10 inches
long, ovate to lanceolate, to 12 inches long and 1–4 inches
wide, bases rounded or cordate, margins serrate to dentate. Solitary heads on peduncles to 10 inches tall, pink
to purple ray florets to 3+ inches long and about ½ inch
wide, disc florets green to pink to purple in color. Rare in
Texas, but widely available in nursery trade and has been
planted and seeded extensively across state. Several collections may be from introduced plants. Natural populations do exist, in far northeast corner of Texas.

Echinacea sanguinea   ASTERACEAE
Sanguine purple coneflower
Open piney woods, prairies. Spring, summer. Common.

An erect perennial to 4 feet tall, with green to purplish
stems. Stems and leaves pubescent to varying degrees of
density. Basal leaves, on petioles to 4 inches long, elliptic to lanceolate, to 12 inches long and ⅜–1¼ inches
wide, margins entire and ciliate. Heads solitary, about
1¼ inches across, on peduncles to 2+ feet long. Distinctive long, slender ray florets light pink to reddish purple,
reflexed and to 2¾ inches long, disc florets typically purple. Usually found in sandy soils, from Bastrop County
east into Louisiana, northeast into Oklahoma and Arkansas, and well-managed forests of East Texas.

Eutrochium fistulosum   ASTERACEAE
Joe-pye weed, queen of the meadow, hollow joe-pye weed
Bogs, marshes, wet meadows, stream banks, and
other low, wet areas. Summer, fall. Uncommon.

An erect perennial with purple, hollow, mostly
unbranched stems to 9+ feet tall. Leaves in whorls of 4–6
and occasionally more, on petioles to ½ inch long, elliptic, to 9 inches long and 3 inches wide, larger on lower
stem, smaller on upper and lateral stems, margins serrate to crenate. Flowering heads in compound corymbs
at stem ends, with central stem hosting largest infof-
cence, often 10+ inches in diameter. Individual heads
about ⅓ inch long and ⅛ inch wide, to 7 pink to rose disc
florets, ray florets absent. Found in deep East Texas, in
and around Big Thicket, in deep, rich alluvium soils.

Lygodesmia ramosissima   ASTERACEAE
Pecos River skeletonplant, Big Bend skeletonplant, skeletonplant
Grasslands, open brush and woodlands,
roadsides. Spring, summer, fall. Uncommon.

An erect perennial with heavily branched green stems
to 2 feet. Basal rosette leaves linear, to 2¾ inches long,
¹⁄₁₀ inch wide, margins entire or laciniate. Upper leaves
becoming smaller to the point of appearing scalelike.
Flowering heads terminal, about 1 inch wide, on short
peduncles. Florets light purple to lavender, 5–12 per head,
ligulate florets only. Found in Big Bend region, north into
New Mexico.

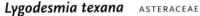

Lygodesmia texana   ASTERACEAE
Skeletonplant, Texas skeleton plant, Texas skeleton weed
Grasslands, open brush and shrublands, roadsides and
other open areas. Spring, summer, fall. Common.

An erect, rhizomatous perennial with green to glaucous
stems to 2 feet tall. Basal leaves linear, to 8 inches long,
⅓ inch wide, margins laciniate, upper leaves becoming
smaller to the point of appearing scalelike. Solitary flowering heads, to 3 inches in diameter with 8–12 pink to lavender to purple florets. Found throughout most of Texas
except far eastern portion.

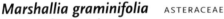

Marshallia graminifolia   ASTERACEAE
Grassleaf Barbara's buttons
Wet savannas, woodlands, bogs.
Summer, fall. Uncommon.

An erect perennial with simple to branched stems to
16+ inches tall. Basal leaves petiolate, oblanceolate, to
10 inches long and ½ inch wide, 3-nerved. Linear upper
leaves sessile, usually flat against stem. Flowering heads
on peduncles to 20 inches, each head just over 1 inch
wide, with numerous lavender to purple disc florets. Frequent in Big Thicket, less common in surrounding areas.
Specific epithet means having grasslike leaves.

Nicolletia edwardsii ASTERACEAE
Edward's hole-in-the-sand plant
Sparse desert scrub. Winter, spring,
summer, fall. Uncommon.

An erect to spreading annual with branching, glaucous
stems to 10 inches tall. Leaves opposite and alternate,
glaucous, to 2 inches long, 3–5 linear lobes tipped with
a yellow band. Flowers on peduncles to just over 1 inch,
light pink to white ray florets, yellow disc florets. Found
throughout year with proper rainfall in rocky, gravelly, or
sandy soils in the Chihuahuan Desert. Genus name in
honor of Jean Nicolas Nicollet (1786–1843), a French geog-
rapher who mapped the Mississippi River and its tributaries during the 1830s.

Palafoxia callosa ASTERACEAE
Small palafox
Fields, pastures, grasslands, open brushlands, roadsides
and other open areas. Spring, summer. Common.

An erect annual to 2 feet with glandular stems that are
weakly branched in upper portions. Leaves linear to 2¾
inches long and ⅛ inch wide. Flowers ½ inch in diameter, held in loose, terminal corymbs, light pink to purplish, fading to nearly white, disc florets only. Found
throughout Central Texas, north into Oklahoma and west
into eastern Chihuahuan Desert, typically on limestone
soils. Similar to *Palafoxia rosea* and *P. texana*, but with
shorter phyllaries (to ¼ inch in *P. callosa*; ¼–⅜ inch in
others). Genus named in honor of Spanish general José
de Palafox y Melzi (1780–1847).

Palafoxia hookeriana ASTERACEAE
Hooker's palafox, sand palafox
Open prairies, grasslands, shrublands, roadsides
and other open areas. Summer, fall. Common.

An erect, typically single-stemmed annual to nearly 6
feet (usually shorter), stems glandular and branching in
upper portions. Leaves lanceolate to 4 inches long and 1
inch wide. Flowers in loose corymbs at stem end, pink to
rose, 1½ inches in diameter, to 13 ray florets, numerous
disc florets. Occurs in sandy soils from far South Texas
north to Edwards Plateau and northeast to Henderson
County, where its range overlaps with *Palafoxia reverchonii*. Named after William Jackson Hooker (1785–1865),
an English botanist.

Palafoxia reverchonii ASTERACEAE
Reverchon's palafox
Grasslands, prairies, meadows, open woodlands,
roadsides and other open areas. Summer, fall. Common.

An erect annual with a single, branching stem to 2½+
feet tall, stem pubescent. Leaves lanceolate, to 2½ inches
long and ¼ inch wide. Flowers in loose, terminal corymbs, to 8 ray florets, 12–30 disc florets, both pink to rose
in color, heads 1 inch in diameter. Like other rayed palafoxias, found in sandy soils from Harris County north to
Upshur County. Named in honor of Julien Reverchon, a
French botanist who lived and collected in Texas during
the late 1800s.

Palafoxia sphacelata ASTERACEAE
Othake, sand palafox
Open brushlands, weak grasslands.
Summer, fall. Common.

An erect annual to nearly 3 feet tall, single-stemmed but
branched below. Stems with glandular hairs above, stiff
hairs below. Leaves lanceolate, to 3½ inches long and
¼ to ¾ inch wide. Flowering heads to 1 inch in diameter. Flowers in loose, terminal corymbs, light to dark
pink to rose with 3–5 ray florets and to 35 darker disc florets. Commonly found in sandy soils of West Texas and
Panhandle. Range does not overlap with ranges of other
ray-flowered palafoxias found in Texas. Specific epithet of
Latin origin and means "with brown or black speckling."

Palafoxia texana ASTERACEAE
Texas palafox
Barrier island dunes, fields, meadows, open
brush and woodlands, roadsides and other open
areas. Spring, summer, fall. Common.

An erect, somewhat scabrous annual, typically
single-stemmed, with branching above, to nearly 3 feet
in height. Leaves ovate to thinly lanceolate, to just over
3 inches long and ¼ to ¾ inch wide. Flowers held on
loose corymbs, ray florets absent, disc florets 10–25, pink
to rose, each head about ½ inch across. Widespread in
South Texas, typically south of Edwards Plateau, east to
Coastal Bend. Similar to *Palafoxia rosea*, but with larger
leaves. *Palafoxia texana* var. *ambigua* common along
southern coast of Texas; *P. texana* var. *texana* found farther inland.

331

Pluchea baccharis (*P. rosea*)   ASTERACEAE
Rosy camphorweed
Edges of ponds, lakes, and creeks, wet
savannas, roadside ditches and other low, wet
areas. Spring, summer. Uncommon.

An erect, somewhat rhizomatous, branching perennial
with soft, pubescent stems to 2 feet. Leaves sessile, ovate
to elliptic-oblong, to 2½ inches long and 1¼ inches wide,
bases clasping to truncate, margins toothed, surfaces
with soft hairs. Flowering heads in terminal corymbs, ray
florets absent, disc florets rose to pink to purple. Number
of individual heads can range from just a few to hundreds
per plant. Found in Southeast Texas, in wet, sunny conditions. Distinguished from other *Pluchea* species by rigid
leaves which are patchy white because of hairs.

Pluchea camphorata   ASTERACEAE
Camphorweed
Edges of ponds, lakes, and marshes, roadside ditches and
other low, wet areas. Spring, summer, fall. Common.

An erect annual to short-lived perennial with branching stems to 5 feet. Leaves on petioles to ¾ inch long,
elliptic to oblong, to 6 inches long and 2½ inches wide,
margins dentate, serrate, or entire, blade surfaces soft.
Flowering heads in panicles, ultimately ending in terminal corymbs. Ray florets absent, disc flowers pink to rose
and numerous. Found in eastern third of Texas, leaves
very aromatic. Genus is named in honor of Noël-Antoine
Pluche (1688–1761), a French naturalist.

Pluchea foetida   ASTERACEAE
Stinking camphorweed
Edges of ponds, lakes, creeks, wet savannas,
roadside ditches and other wet areas.
Spring, summer, fall. Common.

An erect annual or short-lived perennial with branching
stems to 3+ feet tall, occasionally rhizomatous. Leaves
oblong-elliptic to lanceolate or ovate, to 4 inches long,
1½ inches wide, bases clasping, margins finely toothed.
Flowering heads in terminal corymbs. Ray florets absent,
disc florets pink to creamy white and numerous. Number
of individual heads can be few or into the hundreds per
plant. Corymbs can vary from a tight formation to very
loose. Found in eastern third of Texas.

Pluchea odorata ASTERACEAE
Shrubby camphorweed, sweetscent, saltmarsh fleabane
Edges of ponds, lakes, streams, rivers,
roadside ditches, marshes and other low, wet
areas. Spring, summer, fall. Common.

An erect annual or short-lived perennial with branching
stems to 3+ feet tall. Leaves on petioles or sessile, ovate
to lanceolate to elliptic, to 6 inches long and 2½ inches
wide, margins serrate. Flowering heads in terminal corymbs. Ray florets absent, disc florets numerous, pink to
rose to purple or creamy white. Number and density of
heads can vary greatly, from just a few to hundreds per
plant. Most common *Pluchea* species in Texas, found
throughout state.

Pluchea sericea ASTERACEAE
Arrowweed
Stream and river banks, floodplains, desert
washes. Spring, summer. Uncommon.

An erect woody perennial with branching stems to 9+
feet tall, both leaves and stems with a soft, silver pubescence. Leaves alternate, sessile, lanceolate to oblanceolate,
to 2 inches long and ½ inch wide, margins entire. Flowering heads in tight, simple terminal cymes. Ray florets
absent, disc florets few, pink to purple. Found in Chihuahuan Desert region of Texas, where it grows in lower elevations. Specific epithet means "silky," referring to soft
nature of leaves.

Tiquilia canescens BORAGINACEAE
Dog's ear, woody crinklemat, oreja de perro
Open brush and grasslands, rocky outcrops, desert
washes, creek beds, roadsides and other open, rocky
to gravelly areas. Spring, summer. Common.

A prostrate to ascending, spreading perennial from a
woody rootstock, with much-branched stems to 6 inches
tall, leaves and stems tomentose. Leaves alternate, on
short petioles, ovate to elliptic, to ½ inch long and ⅓ inch
wide, bases and tips acute, margins entire. Flowers terminal, clustered, 5-lobed, pink to rose to white, about ¼
inch wide. Most common species of *Tiquilia* found in
Texas, frequent throughout Chihuahuan Desert, western
Edwards Plateau, and south to Cameron County.

Tiquilia gossypina   BORAGINACEAE
Texas crinklemat
Flats, floodplains, creek and canyon bottoms, and
other low, open areas. Spring, summer. Uncommon.

A prostrate, mat-forming perennial from a woody rootstock with stems to 16 inches long. Leaves on short petioles, clustered, oblong to oblanceolate, to ⅓ inch long,
pubescent, tips pointed, surfaces greenish gray with
visible long white hairs. Flowers in terminal clusters,
5-lobed, pink to purple-magenta, less than ¼ inch wide
and about as long. Found on gypseous soils in Chihuahuan Desert; usually grows around drainages. Similar to
Tiquilia hispidissima; differences in leaf morphology distinguish the species.

Tiquilia greggii   BORAGINACEAE
Gregg's tiquilia, plumed crinklemat
Open brush and grasslands, sparse desert
scrub. Spring, summer, fall. Common.

An erect, bushy, rounded perennial with much-branched
stems to 18+ inches tall. Leaves alternate, ovate to elliptic,
to ⅓ inch long and ¼ inch wide, entire margins, tomentose. Flowers in terminal, fuzzy, globular clusters. Flowers 5-lobed, pink to rose or magenta, less than ¼ inch
wide. Grows on limestone soils in Chihuahuan Desert.
Genus name derived from local Peruvian name for this
genus: *Tiquil-tiquil*.

Tiquilia hispidissima   BORAGINACEAE
Hairy crinklemat
Open desert scrub, flats, creek beds.
Spring, summer. Uncommon.

A prostrate, spreading, mat-forming perennial with
much-branched stems to 18 inches long. Leaves clustered, typically linear, occasionally ovate or elliptic, to
½ inch long, less than 1⁄16 inch wide, petioles lasting on
stem after leaves fall off, upper surface green with scattered visible hairs. Flowers terminal, 5-lobed, pink to
magenta, less than ¼ inch wide. Usually found growing
on gypseous soils in the Trans-Pecos. Similar to *Tiquilia
gossypina*; leaf morphology distinguishes the species.

Tiquilia mexicana   BORAGINACEAE
Mexican crinklemat
Sparse desert scrub, washes, creek beds and other dry,
rocky to gravelly areas. Spring, summer. Uncommon.

A prostrate, spreading, mat-forming perennial with
branching, tomentose stems to 20 inches long. Leaves
clustered, elliptic to ovate to lanceolate, to ½ inch long
and ¼ inch wide, margins revolute, ends acute to obtuse,
both surfaces of grayish green blades tomentose with
longer hairs visible on upper surface. Flowers terminal,
surrounded by leaves, 5-lobed, pink to magenta, less than
¼ inch wide. Found in Big Bend region, from Presidio to
Val Verde County. Similar to *Tiquilia canescens*; leaf morphology separates the species.

Petrorhagia dubia   CARYOPHYLLACEAE
Hairy pink, pink grass, windmill pink
Savannas, grasslands, fields, roadsides and other
open areas. Spring, summer. Locally common.

An erect, introduced annual with either simple or
branching stems to 16 inches tall. Leaves opposite, sessile, linear, to 1 inch long, margins entire, upper leaves
ascending. Flowers terminal, radial, with 5 deep lobes,
somewhat cordate, pink to rose to purple with darker
venation to about ¼ inch wide. Common along roadsides
during springtime from Texarkana south to Houston
area, spreading. Originally from southern Europe and
Mediterranean region.

Silene antirrhina   CARYOPHYLLACEAE
Sleepy catchfly, sleepy silene
Open brush and woodlands, fields, meadows, roadsides
and other open areas. Spring, summer. Common.

An erect annual with simple or branched stems, occasional glutinous patches, to 20 inches tall. Leaves opposite, in pairs at nodes, sessile, linear-lanceolate to elliptic, to 2 inches long and about ⅓ inch wide, margins
entire. Terminal flowers, 2–4 per stem, on pedicels to ½
inch. Individual flowers about ¼ inch in diameter, with
5 pink, purple, or white notched petals. Found throughout Texas, grows in sandy or gravelly soils. Common
name comes from viscid patches along stems that entrap
small insects. Genus, originally described by Linnaeus,
is named after Silenus, companion to Bacchus, the Greek
god of drunkenness and winemaking.

Silene gallica CARYOPHYLLACEAE
Common catchfly, small-flowered catchfly, silène de France
Feral fields, roadsides and other disturbed
areas. Spring, summer. Common.

An introduced, erect annual with branched, sticky stems
to 18 inches tall. Leaves opposite, rough, in pairs at nodes,
oblanceolate to lanceolate to slightly spatulate, to 3 inches
long and ½ inch wide, margins entire, petioles (if present) on lower leaves. Flowers terminal, pink, white, or a
combination of the two, about ⅓ inch in diameter, 5 petals unlobed or notched. An Old World species found in
both East and West Texas, usually in sandy or gravelly
soils. Specific epithet means "from France."

Polanisia dodecandra subsp. *riograndensis* CLEOMACEAE
Rio Grande clammyweed
Open shrublands, grasslands, fields, agricultural
areas, drainages, roadsides and other disturbed
areas. Spring, summer, fall. Locally common.

An erect annual with a single, branching stem to 2 feet
tall, leaves and stems covered with sticky glandular hairs.
Leaves alternate, trifoliolate, leaflets rounded to oval, to
1½ inches long and ½ inch wide, margins entire to ciliate, upper leaves not compound. Flowers numerous in a
terminal raceme, bilateral with 4 pink to rose to red petals
that are spatulate to heart-shaped with a thin base. Found
in sandy to gravelly soils in South Texas.

Callisia micrantha COMMELINACEAE
Little-flowered spiderwort, southern coastal roseling
Thornscrub, prairies, grasslands, lomas.
Spring, summer, fall. Uncommon.

A prostrate to climbing perennial with succulent stems
to 12+ inches tall, stems becoming erect when in flower.
Leaves alternate, elliptic to oblong to lanceolate, to 1½
inches long and ⅓ inch wide, bases sheathed on stem,
margins ciliate, tips acute, blades folded, succulent.
Flowers in terminal cymes, with 3 white sepals, pubescent on underside, and 3 pink to rose petals which are
triangular-ovate and about ½ inch wide. Found in South
Texas, along the coast and on mudflats; inland on clay
soils.

Tradescantia brevifolia COMMELINACEAE
Trans-Pecos spiderwort
Rocky outcrops, boulders, cliffs and other protected
rocky areas. Summer, fall. Uncommon.

A prostrate to ascending rhizomatous perennial with
fleshy, semisucculent, branching stems to 12+ inches
long. Fleshy leaves, spirally arranged, ovate to elliptic,
to 3½ inches long and 1¾ inches wide, bases clasping,
margins finely serrate, tips slightly pointed. Flowers in
terminal, sessile cymes, solitary, 3-petaled, pink to reddish purple, to about ½ inch. Found in moist, shady areas
in mountains of Big Bend region, as well as Val Verde
County.

Tradescantia leiandra COMMELINACEAE
Canyon spiderwort
Canyons, mountain drainages and
valleys. Summer, fall. Rare.

An erect, branching perennial with glabrous stems to
20+ inches tall. Leaves spirally arranged, lanceolate to
6 inches long and 1 inch wide, bases rounded, margins
entire or ciliate, tips pointed, leaves sheathed. Inflorescence in terminal cyme. Bracts ovate-lanceolate, to nearly
2 inches long. Flowers 3-petaled, pink to purplish red to
about ¾ inch wide, nearly sessile. Known from a few locations; found around springs, seeps, or perennial creeks,
in mountains of West Texas.

Convolvulus arvensis CONVOLVULACEAE
Bindweed, field bindweed, possession vine
Meadows, fields, open shrub and woodlands, fence
lines, agricultural lands, feral areas, roadsides and other
disturbed areas. Spring, summer, fall. Common.

An introduced, rhizomatous, twining or spreading perennial vine with branched stems to 4 feet long. Leaves alternate, on petioles shorter than 4 inches long, variable in
shape often because of sun exposure, ovate to elliptic, to 4
inches long and 2⅓ inches wide, bases cordate, truncate,
hastate, or sagittate, margins entire to undulate. Inflorescence solitary or as many as 3 in leaf axils, 1 inch long and
as wide, on short peduncles and pedicels to 1½ inches.
Flowers funnel to bell-shaped, pink, lavender, or white; if
white, usually tinged pink or lavender. Considered a noxious weed and found throughout state.

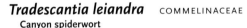

Ipomoea cordatotriloba   CONVOLVULACEAE
Purple bindweed, tievine, sharp-pod morning glory
Fields, meadows, prairies, brush and woodlands,
roadsides and other disturbed, open areas.
Spring, summer, fall. Common.

A twining, climbing perennial vine with stems to 9+
feet long. Leaves cordate to ovate, to 3½ inches long and
2¾ inches wide, margins entire to 3- to 5-lobed. Flowers funnel-shaped, to 2¼ inches long, rose or lavender
or purple with darker centers, one to several flowers on
short peduncles. Common throughout most of Texas
aside from Panhandle and far West Texas. Specific epithet of Latin origin and means "heart-shaped, 3-lobed," a
reference to the leaf.

Ipomoea costellata   CONVOLVULACEAE
Crestrib morning-glory
Fields, meadows, rocky outcrops, among boulders,
canyons, drainages. Summer. Uncommon.

A slender, airy, clambering annual vine with glabrous
stems to 24+ inches long. Leaves alternate, sessile or
nearly so, palmately lobed with 5–9 lobes, each lobe slender, linear to lanceolate, to 1 inch long, margins entire.
Flowers solitary or in pairs on peduncles to 4 inches long,
funnel-shaped, 5-lobed, pink to pale lavender, to ½ inch
long. Found in open, sunny areas in Chihuahuan Desert,
west into Edwards Plateau, south to Lower Rio Grande
Valley.

Ipomoea leptophylla   CONVOLVULACEAE
Bush morning-glory, bush moon-flower, manroot
Prairies, fields, open brushlands, roadsides.
Spring, summer. Locally common.

A multistemmed, bushy, clumping perennial with
stems to 3 feet. Leaves alternate, linear-lanceolate, to 6
inches long, ⅓ inch wide, margins entire. One to several funnel-shaped flowers, pink to lavender-pink to purplish red with darker centers, to 3½ inches long, nearly
as wide. Bush morning-glory is common in open areas
of the Panhandle, south to Midland-Odessa area; historic
collections from Central Texas. Specific epithet means
"thin leaves." Edible, tuberous roots.

Ipomoea pes-caprae   CONVOLVULACEAE
Goat-foot morning-glory, bayhops, beach morning-glory
Beaches, coastal dunes. Winter, spring,
summer, fall. Common.

A prostrate perennial vine, rooting at nodes, with stems
to 100+ feet long. Leaves alternate, thick and leathery,
on petioles 6 inches long, slightly round, notched at tip,
to 4½ inches wide and 3½ inches long, margins entire.
Flowers one to several per peduncle, funnel-shaped, dark
pink to purple, to 3½ inches long and 2½ inches wide.
Frequent along beaches and dunes in Texas; widely distributed on tropical and subtropical beaches. Seeds, 4 per
capsule, are covered in dark, velvety hairs, which aid in
floatation and dispersal. Specific epithet means "goat's"
(*caprae*) "foot" (*pes*) and is of Latin origin.

Ipomoea rupicola   CONVOLVULACEAE
Cliff morning-glory
Desert scrub, thornscrub. Spring,
summer, fall. Uncommon.

A trailing, twining perennial vine with glabrous stems to
6+ feet long. Leaves alternate, cordate to ovate or oblong,
to 3¾ inches long, 2 inches wide, margins entire or lobed
or slightly toothed at the base. Funnel-shaped flowers,
one to several, pinkish lavender to purple with darker
centers, to 3½ inches long. Found in gravelly, rocky soils
of limestone origin in far South Texas, northwest along
border into Big Bend region, occasional collections from
Central Texas.

Ipomoea sagittata   CONVOLVULACEAE
Saltmarsh morning-glory, arrow leaf morning-glory
Marshes, creek and river banks, edges of
ponds, roadside ditches and other low, wet
areas. Spring, summer, fall. Common.

A twining, climbing perennial vine with glabrous
stems to 8+ feet long. Leaves alternate, sagittate,
deltoid-lanceolate or ovate-lanceolate, to 4 inches
long and 2 inches wide, margins entire. Flowers
funnel-shaped, solitary or to 3, dark pink to reddish purple, to 4 inches long and as wide. Mainly found along
coastal Texas; however, it can also occur inland with
proper habitat and has been reported upstream along
Rio Grande, as far as Del Rio.

Drosera brevifolia DROSERACEAE
Dwarf sundew
Open pine woodlands and forests, coastal dunes and flats, and other sandy, wet soils. Spring. Locally common.

A small, carnivorous, rosette-forming annual or perennial to 5 inches tall when in flower, both leaves and stem covered in sticky hairs. Leaves spatulate, about ¾ inch long, width of entire plant about 1½ inches. Flowers solitary on slender 5-inch scapes with glands on short stalks, to ½ inch wide with 5 pink petals. This smallest sundew in Texas can be found in East Texas and farther south along coast. With adequate moisture it will persist; otherwise it will perish after one season.

Drosera capillaris DROSERACEAE
Pink sundew
Pine woodlands, savannas, bogs, and other sandy, wet areas. Spring, summer, fall. Locally common.

A small, carnivorous, rosette-forming perennial to 8+ inches tall when in flower. Leaves on petioles 1½ inches long, spatulate, ⅜ inch long, with obvious glandular hairs throughout. Flowers, 2 to 20, on glabrous scapes to 12 inches tall, pink, 5-petaled, about ⅜ inch wide. Found in sandy soils with poor nutrients in East Texas. Genus name of Greek origin, meaning "dewy," in reference to leaf appearance.

Cologania angustifolia FABACEAE
Longleaf cologania
Rock slopes, outcrops, grasslands, fields, brush and woodlands. Summer, fall. Locally common.

A procumbent, twining vine with pubescent stems to 5+ feet long. Leaves alternate, on petioles 4 inches long, trifoliolate, leaflets slender, linear, to 3¾ inches, margins entire, tips acute, blades folded, pubescent. Flowers solitary or paired in upper leaf axils, rose to reddish purple. Papilionaceous, banner erect and notched with darker venation and white patch at base, lateral wings wider at distal end. Found in mid to upper elevations in mountains of Chihuahuan Desert, frequent along roadsides in Davis Mountains during summer months.

Cologania pallida FABACEAE
Pale cologania
Fields, grasslands, brush and woodlands, rocky
outcrops. Summer, fall. Uncommon.

A procumbent, twining vine with pubescent stems to
4+ feet long. Leaves alternate, on petioles to 1⅓ inches
long, trifoliolate, leaflets ovate to elliptic, bases rounded
to acute, margins entire, tips acute and terminating in
a sharp point, blades pubescent. Flowers solitary in leaf
axils on pedicels to ½ inch long, deep rose to reddish purple, bilateral, banner erect and often with darker venation
and white patch at base, lateral wings wider at distal end.
Found in mid to upper elevations in mountains of Chihuahuan Desert. Wider, shorter leaves distinguish this
species from *Cologania angustifolia*.

Dalea villosa var. *grisea* FABACEAE
Silky prairie clover
Fields, meadows, open woodlands.
Spring, summer. Uncommon.

An erect, leafy perennial with multiple, branching stems
to 24+ inches tall. Leaves alternate, pinnate, to 1¾ inches
long, with 9–17 leaflets that are oblong to oblanceolate or
linear-oblong, to ½ inch long, margins entire, tips mucronate, surfaces pilose. Flowers numerous in dense, terminal, cylindric spikes to 2½ inches long at end of season,
papilionaceous, pink to light purple, less than ¼ inch
long. Found in eastern third of Texas.

Desmodium incanum FABACEAE
Creeping beggarweed, Spanish clover, kaimi clover
Pastures, prairies, grasslands, savannas.
Summer, fall. Uncommon.

A prostrate to erect, shrubby perennial with pubescent,
slender, reddish brown stems to 3+ feet long. Leaves
alternate, trifoliolate, leaflets elliptic, to 3¾ inches long
and 1¾ inches wide, with middle leaflet larger than lat-
erals, bases rounded, tips acute. Flowers in terminal
racemes to 8 inches long, not crowded, papilionaceous,
pink to reddish purple, banner erect and notched with a
red and yellow spot at base, wings somewhat spreading.
Fruit segmented with segments detaching easily, pubescent. Found in open areas with sandy soils, from DeWitt
County south to Coastal Bend and east to Houston area.

341

Galactia canescens FABACEAE
Hoary milkpea
Fields, pastures, grasslands, prairies, open
brush and woodlands and other open
areas. Spring, summer. Uncommon.

A prostrate to trailing perennial vine with slender,
pubescent stems to 8+ feet long. Leaves alternate, trifoliolate, leaflets ovate to elliptic, to 2½ inches long, bases
rounded, margins entire, tips rounded to notched, surfaces pubescent, lower surface with distinct venation.
Flowers in short racemes originating from leaf axils,
papilionaceous, to ½ inch wide, pink to rose, banner
erect and notched, wings and keel darker. In addition
to aerial flowers, cleistogamous flowers are produced
underground, resulting in a small, single-seeded fruit.
Widespread but uncommon from Dallas area south into
Mexico.

Galactia volubilis FABACEAE
Downy milkpea
Shrub and woodlands. Spring, summer. Common.

A twining, climbing perennial vine with slender, pubescent stems to 5+ feet long. Leaves alternate, trifoliolate,
leaflets oblong-ovate to elliptic, to 2 inches long and 1
inch wide, bases and tips rounded, margins entire, surfaces with distinct, visible venation. Flowers in racemes
to 4 inches long originating from leaf axils, papilionaceous, rose to pink to purple-pink, to ½ inch long, banner
erect with yellow spot at base, wings not spreading and
darker in color. Found in eastern third of Texas.

Kummerowia striata FABACEAE
Japanese clover
Fields, pastures, grasslands, open brush and
woodlands, roadsides and other disturbed
areas. Spring, summer. Common.

An introduced, ascending to erect or sprawling annual
with slender branching stems to 16+ inches long. Leaves
alternate, trifoliolate, leaflets oblong-elliptic to obovate,
to 1 inch long and ⅓ inch wide, bases tapering, margins
entire to ciliate, tips rounded and mucronate, surfaces
pubescent. Flowers originating from leaf axils, solitary to
3, papilionaceous, banner erect and pink to purple with
darker venation near base. Found in eastern fourth of
Texas.

Lathyrus hirsutus   FABACEAE
Singletary pea, hairy vetchling, Caley pea
Pastures, fields, roadsides and other open
areas. Spring. Locally common.

An introduced, clambering or trailing annual vine with
slender, winged stems to 3+ feet long, stipules and calyces hirsute. Leaves alternate, one pair of leaflets that are
linear-lanceolate, to 3¼ inches long, entire margins,
tips pointed, tendrils originating from base of leaflets,
3-branched. Stipules linear-lanceolate, to ¾ inch long.
Flowers in short racemes originating from leaf axils,
papilionaceous, to ⅜ inch long, with an erect pink to purple or blue banner, wings horizontal and lighter in color.
Widespread in eastern half of Texas, north of Coastal
Bend.

Lathyrus latifolius   FABACEAE
Perennial pea, everlasting pea, sweet pea
Homesteads and other areas of human
habitation. Spring. Rare.

An introduced, climbing to clambering perennial vine
with winged stems to 6+ feet long. Leaves alternate, on
winged petioles to 2 inches long, one pair of ovate to
oblong leaflets to 3 inches long and 1 inch wide, margins entire, tips pointed, branched tendril originating
from base of leaflets. Flowers in short racemes from leaf
axils, papilionaceous, to 1 inch wide, dark pink to rose
to purplish pink, banner erect, wings horizontal. Native
to Europe and available in the nursery trade; occasionally escapes cultivation. Currently known from Dallas-Ft.
Worth north into Oklahoma.

Lathyrus pusillus   FABACEAE
Tiny pea
Fields, grasslands, prairies, open brush and
woodlands, roadsides. Spring. Common.

A prostrate to clambering annual vine with weakly
pubescent, winged stems to 24+ inches long. Leaves alternate, one pair of linear-lanceolate leaflets to 2¾ inches
long, margins entire, tips pointed, branched tendril originating from base of leaflets. Flowers in short racemes,
solitary or paired, pink to blue, to ⅜ inch long, banner
reflexed, wings horizontal. Throughout eastern third of
Texas, uncommon west to Pecos River and south into central South Texas.

Lespedeza repens   FABACEAE
Creeping lespedeza, creeping bush-clover
Fields, open brush and woodlands, roadsides and
other open areas. Spring, summer. Common.

A procumbent perennial with weakly pubescent stems to
4+ feet long. Leaves alternate, trifoliolate, leaflets ovate to
elliptic, to 1 inch long, bases and tips rounded, margins
entire. Flowers in racemes originating from leaf axils,
to 8, papilionaceous, pink to bluish purple, banner with
dark venation and yellow spot at base, wings spreading.
Found throughout eastern third of Texas, occasional in
eastern Edwards Plateau.

Lespedeza virginica   FABACEAE
Virginia bush-clover, slender lespedeza
Open woodlands, roadsides. Summer. Common.

An ascending to erect perennial with leafy, pilose stems
to 5+ feet tall. Leaves alternate, trifoliolate, leaflets linear
to oblong, to 1¾ inches long, margins entire, tips ending
in sharp point. Crowded flowers in short racemes originating from leaf axils, about ¼ inch wide, papilionaceous,
pink to purple, banner with darker venation near base,
wings horizontal. Inconspicuous cleistogamous flowers
lower on stem. Throughout eastern half of Texas, from
Coastal Bend north into Oklahoma, east to Atlantic coast.

Mimosa nuttallii   FABACEAE
Catclaw sensitive briar, Nuttall's sensitive briar
Fields, grasslands, open brush and woodlands,
roadsides and other open areas. Spring. Common.

A prostrate perennial with stems to 3+ feet long, with
recurved prickles. Leaves alternate, bipinnate with 4 or 5
pairs of pinnae and 10–15 pairs of elliptic to oblong leaflets, to ⅓ inch long, tips terminating in a sharp point,
lower leaf surface with raised venation. Flowers on
peduncles to 4¾ inches long, originating from leaf axils,
pink, numerous, in a rounded inflorescence. Legumes
linear, to 1¾ inches long, covered with prickles. Found
throughout Panhandle, southeast to Coastal Bend and
east to Louisiana. Absent in South Texas and more arid
regions of West Texas. Fruit morphology is best way to
differentiate from other prostrate, vinelike, briars.

344

Mimosa roemeriana   FABACEAE
Roemer's sensitive briar, Roemer's mimosa
Fields, pastures, grasslands, open brush and woodlands,
roadsides and other open areas. Spring. Common.

A prostrate perennial with stems to 3+ feet long, stems
with recurved prickles. Leaves alternate, bipinnate with
2–5 pairs of pinnae and 6–13 pairs of oblanceolate leaflets, to ⅓+ inch long, tips obtuse, lower leaf surface glabrous without prominent venation. Flowers on peduncles
to 2½ inches long, pink, numerous, in a rounded inflorescence. Legumes linear, 1¾ to 2¾ inches long. Found
on limestone soils throughout Edwards Plateau, north
into Oklahoma. Ranges of *Mimosa roemeriana* and *M.
nuttallii* overlap; peduncle length, fruit length, and leaflet
morphology help in identification.

Mimosa strigillosa   FABACEAE
Powder-puff, vergonzosa
Fields, grasslands, open brush and woodlands,
coastal plains and dunes, roadsides and other
open areas. Spring, summer. Common.

A prostrate perennial with pricked stems to 3+ feet long.
Leaves alternate, 2-pinnately compound, with 4–6 pairs of
pinnae and 10–15 pairs of ¼-inch linear leaflets. Flowers
on peduncles to 4½+ inches long, originating from leaf
axils, pink, numerous, in rounded to slightly elongated
inflorescences. Legumes flat, to ¾ inch long, ½ inch
wide, not splitting but breaking apart like a loment. Most
common in Southeast Texas, south along coastal plains
into Mexico, and northwest into Edwards Plateau.

Phaseolus acutifolius   FABACEAE
Tepary bean
Mountain canyons, slopes, among boulders,
ledges, and drainages. Summer. Rare.

A prostrate or trailing or clambering vine with pubescent
stems to 5+ feet long. Leaves alternate, trifoliolate, lanceolate to rhombic-ovate leaflets, to 4+ inches long and 1½
inches wide, bases broadly tapered to nearly truncate, tips
acute. Flowers on peduncles to 1¾ inches long, solitary or
to 4 per raceme, purplish pink, to ½ inch long, papilionaceous, banner erect, wings spatulate, keel contorted. In
canyons in mid to upper elevations in Chihuahuan Desert. While uncommon, can be found in Jeff Davis County
along Scenic Loop.

345

Phaseolus angustissimus   FABACEAE
Slimleaf bean
Rocky slopes, desert canyons and washes.
Summer, fall. Uncommon.

A prostrate or trailing, clambering vine with pubescent
stems to 5+ feet long. Leaves alternate, trifoliolate, linear to lanceolate, to 4 inches long and ⅜ inch wide, bases
wedge-shaped, tips acute, blades glabrous, somewhat
glaucous. Flowers few, on peduncles to 1¼ inches long,
papilionaceous, pink to rose to purple-pink, banner erect,
wings somewhat twisted and elongated and horizontal,
keel contorted. Found in Big Bend region from Presidio
County to Terrell County, also in El Paso County, usually
growing in lower elevations closer to Rio Grande.

Phaseolus filiformis   FABACEAE
Slimjim bean
Rocky mountain slopes, mountain brush and
woodlands. Spring, summer. Uncommon.

A prostrate, trailing, twining perennial vine with pubescent stems to 3+ feet long. Leaves alternate, trifoliolate,
leaflets ovate, to 2¾ inches long, bases lobed, margins
ciliate, tips acute to obtuse, upper portion of blades with
obvious lighter blotches along midvein. Peduncles to 4
inches, racemes to 4 inches long. Flowers pink to light
purple, bilateral, banner margins rolled backward, keel
twisted and contorted, wings widened at distal ends and
somewhat twisted. Found in Chihuahuan Desert region.

Phaseolus maculatus   FABACEAE
Metcalf bean, spotted bean
Rocky slopes, outcrops, cliffs, among boulders and
other rocky areas. Summer. Locally common.

A prostrate to climbing, twining perennial vine with
stems to 9+ feet long. Leaves alternate, trifoliolate, leaflets ovate to obovate to nearly round, to 2 inches long,
bases rounded, margins entire, tips terminating in a
sharp point. Peduncle to 8 inches, raceme to 6 inches
long. Flowers well-spaced, pink to light purple, banner
erect with margins rolled backward and greenish with
pink portions or tinged, lateral wings twisted and mostly
pink with white bases, keel twisted and white to pale
pink. Found in Big Bend region, from Jeff Davis to Terrell
County, mid to upper elevations.

346

Securigera varia FABACEAE
Crownvetch, purple crownvetch
Banks of creeks, rivers, lakes, and creeks,
roadsides. Spring, summer. Uncommon.

An introduced, ascending, rhizomatous, branching
perennial with stems to 3 feet tall. Leaves alternate, pinnately compound, to 6 inches long, 11–25 oblong leaflets
to ¾ inch long and ¼ inch wide, margins entire, tips
mucronate. Flowers in to 6-inch racemes, papilionaceous,
to ½ inch long, banner pink to reddish purple, slightly
curved backward, lateral wings white or pink-tinged and
enclose keel. While uncommon, widespread throughout
state. Originally from Eurasia and Africa.

Strophostyles helvola FABACEAE
Amberique-bean, fuzzy-bean, trailing fuzzy bean
Fields, meadows, grasslands, open brush and
woodlands, roadsides. Spring, summer. Common.

A trailing to climbing annual vine with slender, branching, pubescent stems to 8+ feet long. Leaves alternate, on
petioles to 2 inches long, trifoliolate, leaflets lanceolate
to oval, to 2 inches long and 1¼ inches wide, bases lobed,
margins entire, tips acute. Flowers in racemes originating from leaf axils on peduncles to 12 inches long, floral
bracts blunt and half as long as calyx or shorter, various shades of pink fading to yellow, papilionaceous, to
¾ inch long, banner erect, lateral wings horizontal, keel
curved upward and tip of keel usually darker or purplish.
Throughout eastern half of Texas, from Coastal Bend
north into Oklahoma, also in northeastern Panhandle.

Strophostyles umbellata FABACEAE
Pink fuzzybean, wildbean, perennial woolly bean
Open woodlands. Spring, summer. Common.

A trailing to climbing perennial vine with slender,
branching, pubescent stems to 6+ feet long. Leaves alternate, trifoliolate, leaflets lanceolate to oblong, to 2+ inches
long and ¾ inch wide, bases rounded to tapering, margins entire, tips acute to round. Flowers few, in racemes
originating from leaf axils, peduncles to 12 inches long,
floral bracts acute and as long as calyx, various shades
of pink, papilionaceous, to about ¾ inch long, banner
roundish, wings horizontal, keel curved upward. Found
in pine or mixed-pine woodlands in eastern fourth of
Texas. Thinner and unlobed leaves differentiate from
Strophostyles helvola.

347

Tephrosia lindheimeri   FABACEAE
Lindheimer's hoarypea
Open brush and woodlands, fields, pastures, roadsides and other open areas. Spring, summer. Common.

A decumbent perennial from a woody base, with several pubescent, spreading stems to 3+ feet long. Leaves alternate, pinnate to 6 inches, 7–15 obovate to elliptic or nearly round leaflets to ⅓ inch long, bases cuneate, margins entire, visibly silvery pubescent, tips mucronate. Flowers in racemes to 12 inches long, deep pinkish red to magenta, to ⅝ inch long, papilionaceous, bilateral, banner erect, with white blotch near base, wings not spreading. Found in sandy soils from San Saba County, south into Mexico.

Trifolium pratense   FABACEAE
Red clover
Fields, grasslands, open brush and woodlands, roadsides and other open areas. Spring, summer. Common.

An introduced, decumbent to erect perennial or biennial with pubescent stems to 24+ inches long. Leaves alternate, 3-foliolate, leaflets oval to ovate to oblong, to 2 inches long and ¾ inch wide, bases widely tapering, margins entire, ciliate, tips obtuse, blades pubescent, upper surface usually with obvious light green chevron. Flowers in terminal, roundish heads, papilionaceous, pink to rose, thin, tubular, banner longer than keel and lateral wings. Frequent in Southeast Texas (around Houston area), occasional in North-Central and Central Texas and along Coastal Bend; expect elsewhere.

Trifolium resupinatum   FABACEAE
Persian clover, reversed clover
Agricultural areas, roadsides. Spring. Uncommon.

An introduced, decumbent to ascending annual with glabrous stems to 18+ inches long. Leaves alternate, sessile, 3-foliolate, leaflets obovate to oblanceolate, to ¾ inch long and ⅜ inch wide, bases tapering, margins serrate. Flowers in terminal and axillary roundish heads, papilionaceous, pink to rose, banner larger than keel and wings and turned so that it is on the bottom. An agricultural escapee found in Southeast Texas, mostly around Galveston Bay area to Louisiana and farther north into Oklahoma; expect elsewhere, including maintained parks.

348

Sabatia angularis GENTIANACEAE
Rosepink, common rosepink, rose gentian
Open woodlands, edges of woodlands.
Spring, summer. Uncommon.

An erect annual either branched or unbranched with gla-brous, angled to slightly winged stems to 28+ inches tall. Leaves opposite, cordate-ovate above, roundish below, to 1¼ inches long and 1 inch wide, margins entire, blades clasping, glabrous. Flowers in terminal cymes. Flowers rose-pink to white, greenish yellow in center, to 1½ inches wide, 5 petals, rotate. Found in mixed forest openings in eastern fourth of Texas.

Sabatia arenicola GENTIANACEAE
Sand rose gentian, beach gentian
Beaches, dunes, coastal flats, fields, savannas.
Spring, summer. Locally common.

An erect annual with glabrous stems to 12 inches tall. Stems simple or branching in upper portion. Leaves opposite, succulent, elliptic-ovate to ovate-lanceolate, to 1 inch long and ½ inch wide, margins entire. Flowers ter-minal, rose-pink or white with white and yellow centers, 5-petaled, petals rhombic. Common along Texas Coast from Brownsville to Louisiana, often seen on inland side of dunes. Easily distinguished by its thick, fleshy leaves.

Sabatia campestris GENTIANACEAE
Meadow pink, prairie sabatia, western rose gentian
Fields, meadows, open grass and brushlands,
drainages. Spring, summer. Common.

An erect annual with glabrous, branching stems to 20 inches tall. Leaves opposite, clasping, ovate-elliptic to oblong-elliptic, margins entire, tips acute to obtuse. Flow-ers in terminal cymes, rose-pink with white centers, rotate, 5-petaled, tips of petals pointed, to 1½+ inches wide. Found in eastern half of Texas, west to Val Verde County. Specific epithet of Latin origin; means "of the fields and meadows."

Sabatia gentianoides   GENTIANACEAE
Pinewoods rose gentian
Wet savannas and pine woodlands, bogs.
Spring, summer. Uncommon.

An erect annual, either unbranched or branching in upper portions only, with glabrous stems to 20 inches tall. Basal leaves oblong to roundish spatulate, to 1¼ inches long and ½ inch wide. Stem leaves sessile, linear, ascending or appressed, to 4 inches long and less than ⅛ inch wide, margins entire, tips acute. Flowers solitary or in clusters, either terminal or in upper leaf axils, pink to deep rose with a greenish yellow center, radial, 7–12 petals, to 2+ inches wide. Found in eastern fourth of Texas, in wet meadows and pitcher plant bogs, also along roadsides in Hardin County.

Zeltnera arizonica (*Centaurium arizonicum*)
GENTIANACEAE
Arizona centaury
Fields, meadows, grasslands, open brush and woodlands, drainages, roadsides and other open areas. Spring, summer. Common.

An erect annual or biennial, with glabrous, branching stems to 20+ inches tall. Leaves opposite, sessile, oblanceolate to lanceolate, to 2 inches long and ½ inch wide, bases tapering, margins entire to somewhat revolute, tips acute to obtuse, lower leaves larger and wider than upper leaves. Flowers terminal or originating from upper leaf axils, pink to rose to purple, funnel-shaped, 5-lobed, radial, to about 1½ inches long. Found in wet or damp soils in Chihuahuan Desert region of Texas.

Zeltnera beyrichii (*Centaurium beyrichii*)
GENTIANACEAE
Mountain pink, quinine-weed, rock centaury
Open grass and brushlands, rocky slopes and hillsides, roadsides and other open, exposed areas. Spring, summer. Common.

An erect, much-branched annual with a single stem to 12 inches; plant has a bouquet appearance. Leaves opposite, sessile, linear to linear-lanceolate, to 1¼ inches long, margins entire to revolute, tips acute. Flowers terminal and densely covering top of plant, funnel-shaped, 5-lobed, radial, pink to rose with white centers, to 1 inch wide. Found in open, rocky to gravelly or caliche soils of Edwards Plateau, north into Oklahoma.

Zeltnera calycosa (*Centaurium calycosum*)
GENTIANACEAE
Buckley's centaury
Meadows, fields, edges of streams,
roadsides. Spring. Common.

An erect annual with simple or branching stems to 20+
inches tall. Leaves opposite, sessile, oblong to elliptic to
lanceolate, to 2½ inches long and ½ inch wide, margins
entire to somewhat revolute, tips acute to obtuse, surfaces
glabrous. Flowers in cymes or solitary, funnel-shaped,
pink to rose or rarely white, with greenish white centers,
to ¾ inch long and 1 inch wide. Found in wet soils, especially around perennial and ephemeral creeks and drainages, from Central Texas, west to New Mexico, south to
Cameron County.

Zeltnera glandulifera (*Centaurium glanduliferum*)
GENTIANACEAE
Glandular mountain pink
Grasslands, brushlands, roadsides and other
open areas. Spring, summer. Uncommon.

An erect, much-branched annual with a single stem to
6+ inches tall; plant has an overall bouquet appearance.
Leaves opposite, sessile, linear to linear-lanceolate, to
1 inch long, margins entire to somewhat revolute, tips
acute, leaf surfaces glandular. Flowers terminal, deep
rose to pinkish red-purple with yellowish white centers.
Found in gravelly to rocky soils of Big Bend region, along
highway 90 in Brewster County, west of Sanderson. Similar to *Zeltnera beyrichii*, but smaller and with glandular
leaves.

Zeltnera maryanna (*Centaurium maryannum*)
GENTIANACEAE
Mary Anna's mountain pink, gypsum centaury
Open brushlands in gypseous soils. Spring. Rare.

An erect, much-branched annual with a single stem to
10 inches tall and as wide; plant has an overall bouquet
appearance. Leaves and stems grayish green. Leaves
opposite, sessile, linear to lanceolate, to 1 inch long, margins entire to revolute, tips pointed. Flowers numerous,
terminal, rose to pink, with white and yellow centers,
trumpet-shaped, radial, to about 1 inch wide. Similar to
Zeltnera beyrichii, but ranges do not overlap. Found on
gypseous soils in Culberson County.

351

Zeltnera texensis (*Centaurium texense*)
GENTIANACEAE
Lady Bird's centaury
Fields, meadows, depressions, open brush,
drainages, creek banks and other areas with
seasonally wet soils. Spring, summer. Common.

An erect, slender, airy annual with branching stems to 12
inches tall. Leaves opposite, sessile, linear, to 1 inch long,
margins entire, tips pointed. Flowers in open, loose, terminal cymes, trumpet-shaped, 5-lobed, pink to rose with
white centers, and occasionally all white, to ⅜ inch wide.
Found throughout eastern half of Edwards Plateau, where
it is most common, north into Oklahoma, and southeast to Houston area. Seems to prefer sunny situations
with damp soils, and often found in depressions, around
ephemeral streams, or seeps on slopes; grows in both
limestone and granite soils.

Erodium cicutarium   GERANIACEAE
Redstem filaree, redstem stork's bill, common stork's bill
Pastures, fields, urban and suburban areas, roadsides and
other open, disturbed areas. Winter, spring. Common.

An introduced, ascending to decumbent or prostrate annual to biennial with heavily branched,
glandular-pubescent stems to 20+ inches long. Leaves
alternate, pinnate, ovate to oblanceolate, to 4 inches long,
9–13 leaflets with leaflets deltoid to ovate, to about ⅝
inch long, dissected, pubescent. Flowers in an umbel,
5-petaled, pink to rose, to ⅓ inch wide, radial. A common
weed throughout most of Texas. Absent to uncommon in
East Texas and along coast. Prefers dry and sandy to gravelly soils, often occurring in disturbed soils or lawns.

Erodium texanum   GERANIACEAE
Texas stork's bill, fillaree, stork's bill
Fields, prairies, grasslands, open brush and shrublands,
roadsides and other open areas. Winter, spring. Common.

A prostrate to ascending annual to biennial, stems
branching from base, to 20 inches long; stems canescent. Leaves alternate, on reddish brown petioles double
or triple the length of blade, simple, cordate, to 1¾ inches
long, bases lobed-cordate, margins crenate, tips rounded.
Flowers in umbels, 5 somewhat unequal petals, pink
to rose, to about 1 inch wide. Widespread and common
throughout eastern three-fourths of Texas. Absent in the
Panhandle.

352

Geranium caespitosum GERANIACEAE
Piney Woods geranium, purple cluster geranium
Open woodlands, canyons, drainages.
Summer. Uncommon.

An ascending to erect, occasionally procumbent perennial with reddish brown stems to 28+ inches long, with
stiff or soft hairs. Leaves alternate, round, to 2 inches
wide, deeply 5-lobed, lobes 3-palmately cleft, margins
entire, tips pointed. Flowers in pairs, on terminal peduncles to 2 inches, 1¼ inch pedicels, pink, rose or magenta,
occasionally white with pink streaks, center of flower
frequently faded or white, to 1¼ inches wide. Found in
upper elevations in mountains of West Texas, in mixed
pine-oak-juniper woodlands.

Geranium carolinianum GERANIACEAE
Carolina geranium, Carolina crane's bill
Fields, pastures, grasslands, open shrub and woodlands,
roadsides and other open areas. Spring. Common.

An ascending annual or biennial, with heavily branched
stems to 30+ inches tall, stems with recurved hairs.
Leaves alternate, round to kidney-shaped, to nearly 3
inches wide, deeply 5-lobed, lobes then again once or
twice cleft, margins entire, tips rounded to pointed. Flowers in terminal clusters, 5-petaled, light pink to white,
to ⅓ inch wide. Found throughout eastern half of Texas,
from Brownsville north into Oklahoma, with additional
populations west of Pecos River; often found in residential and urban areas.

Geranium dissectum GERANIACEAE
Cut-leaf geranium, cut-leaf crane's bill
Fields, roadsides and disturbed areas. Spring. Uncommon.

An introduced ascending, spreading annual or biennial,
with pubescent stems to 24 inches long. Leaves alternate,
on petioles to 3+ inches long, round, to nearly 3 inches
wide, deeply 5-lobed, lobes again dissected, segments
becoming linear, margins entire, tips pointed to round.
Flowers in terminal clusters, on short pedicels, pink to
magenta or rose, 5-petaled, notched, unequal, with one
petal much larger than others, to about ⅓ inch wide.
Occasionally found in eastern fourth of Texas, less common elsewhere; native to Europe.

Nama hispidum   HYDROPHYLLACEAE
Hairy nama, bristly nama
Open shrub and woodlands, creek and river bottoms,
canyons, washes, grasslands, prairies, roadsides and
other open areas. Spring, summer. Common.

An erect to ascending annual with branching stems to
12+ inches tall, leaves and stems with stiff hairs. Leaves
alternate, linear-oblong to obovate, to 2¾ inches long
and ⅓ inch wide, margins entire, often heavily revolute. Flowers in terminal clusters or solitary, pink to lavender, 5-lobed, funnel-shaped, to about ½ inch long.
Widespread throughout Texas. Absent in eastern fourth.
Found in disturbed, sandy to gravelly soils.

Nama parvifolium   HYDROPHYLLACEAE
Small-leaf fiddleleaf, small flowered nama
Open brush and woodlands, grasslands, fields,
meadows, roadsides, Spring, summer. Uncommon.

A prostrate annual to short-lived perennial with
much-branched stems to 10 inches tall. Leaves alternate,
occasionally opposite toward tip of stems, oblanceolate to
obovate, to 1 inch long and ⅓ inch wide, margins revolute, occasionally entire. Flowers either solitary or occurring in small terminal clusters, funnel-shaped, ½ inch
long, 5-lobed, corolla pink to lavender, with white throat.
Infrequent in Big Bend region and South Texas.

Nama torynophyllum   HYDROPHYLLACEAE
Matted fiddleleaf
Rocky slopes, desert washes, canyon floors,
sparse desert scrub. Winter, spring. Rare.

A small, prostrate, matted annual with reddish, branching stems to 3 inches tall, leaves and stems densely villose. Entire plant to 4 inches in diameter. Leaves alternate, spatulate, to ⅓ inch long, half as wide, margins
revolute. Flowers found along stems, solitary or in clusters, pink to white, 5-lobed, smaller than widest point
of leaves. Located in Big Bend region, from Presidio to
Val Verde County. Grows in gravelly soils close to Rio
Grande; often overlooked because of small size.

Sisyrinchium minus   IRIDACEAE
Dwarf blue-eyed grass, pink-eyed grass
Prairies, meadows, fields, roadsides and
other open areas. Spring. Common.

An erect, tufted annual with branching stems to 10
inches tall. Linear, glabrous, grasslike leaves are shorter
than stems. Pink- to rose-colored flowers, with yellowish centers, to ½ inch diameter and slightly bell-shaped
in center. Occasionally plants with all-yellow flowers.
Found in sandy soils along coast, north into Edwards Plateau and east to Louisiana; absent in western Texas and
Panhandle.

Brazoria truncata   LAMIACEAE
Rattlesnake flower
Open areas, meadows, fields, woodland
margins. Spring, summer. Uncommon.

Erect annual with a stout, branched, pubescent stem to
20 inches high. Leaves oblong or spatulate, to 4 inches
long. Lower leaves with winged petiole, upper leaves sessile. Flowers pale pink with purple spots inside throat,
forming a dense spike to 6 inches long. Lower lip 3-lobed
with notched margin, upper lip 2-lobed. Endemic species
commonly found on sandy soils from Coastal Bend north
throughout Post Oak Savanna.

Clinopodium brownei   LAMIACEAE
Browne's savory
Marshes, stream banks, roadside ditches and other
wet areas. Winter, spring, summer, fall. Common.

Spreading perennial with weak stems to about 15 inches
long. Ovate leaves to 1 inch long and ¾ inch wide. Pink
to lavender flowers appear on short pedicels from leaf
axils, lower lip is 3-lobed, middle lobe notched, upper
lip reduced compared to lower. Found in wet areas along
southern coast, north into Central Texas, east to Florida.
Semiaquatic plant widely available in the aquatic nursery
trade.

Hedeoma acinoides   LAMIACEAE
Annual pennyroyal, slender false pennyroyal, hedeoma
Meadows, fields, open areas. Spring, summer. Common.

A slender, erect annual with pubescent stems to 1 foot
tall. Leaves on 1/10-inch-long petioles, elliptic to ovate, to
1 inch long and 1/3 inch wide. Bilabiate flowers appear in
terminal multiflowered cymes, slender, pink, to 1/4 inch
long. Crushed leaves and stems very aromatic. Common
along rocky slopes and in soils of limestone origin along
southern and eastern edges of Edwards Plateau.

Hedeoma drummondii   LAMIACEAE
**Limoncillo, Drummond's false pennyroyal, mock
pennyroyal**
Rocky outcrops, open areas, fields.
Spring, summer, fall. Common.

An erect to decumbent annual to perennial (depending
upon latitude), with densely pubescent, heavily branched,
single or multiple stems, to 2 feet tall. Leaves on short
petioles or subsessile, variable, elliptic to ovate, 1/2 inch
long and 1/4 inch wide, margins entire or subsessile. Bilabiate flowers originate in upper leaf axils of stems, pink
to lavender, to 1/2 inch long, upper lip reduced, lower
lip heavily 3-lobed, middle lobe notched. Widespread
throughout most of state. Absent in East Texas and
coastal areas. Commonly found on slopes of limestone
origin. Named after Scottish naturalist, Thomas Drummond, who collected in Texas during the 1830s.

Hedeoma hispida   LAMIACEAE
Rough false pennyroyal
Open prairies, meadows, fields, roadsides and other
open, disturbed areas. Spring, summer. Common.

An erect, densely pubescent annual, usually
single-stemmed with little or no branching, to 16 inches
tall. Opposite, linear leaves are to 3/4 inch long and 1/8 inch
wide, margins entire. Flowers appear in whorls in leaf
axils, 1/4 inch long, bilabiate, rose to light purple, upper lip
notched and lower lip 3-lobed. Found in eastern Central
Texas, east to Louisiana and north into Oklahoma.

356

Hedeoma reverchonii LAMIACEAE
Reverchon's false pennyroyal, rock hedeoma
Rocky slopes, bluffs, roadcuts, roadsides.
Spring, summer, fall. Common.

An erect, densely pubescent, multistemmed, branched perennial from a woody base to nearly 2 feet in height. Leaves linear to ovate, margins entire to crenate, undersides and margins of leaves pubescent. Flowers pink to rose or lavender, ½+ inch in length, lower lip 3-lobed with central lobe toothed, upper lobe shorter and smaller than lower and slightly toothed. Found throughout Central Texas, predominately on limestone soils in Edwards Plateau, north into Oklahoma. Named after Julien Reverchon, a French botanist who lived and worked in Texas during the late 1800s.

Lamium amplexicaule LAMIACEAE
Henbit, henbit deadnettle
Urban lawns, disturbed areas. Spring, summer. Common.

An introduced, spreading annual, often branching freely from base with green or reddish stems reaching 2 feet in length, new growth often erect. Leaves orbicular, about 1 inch in diameter, may have shallow palmate lobes, margins crenate. Upper leaves sessile, lower leaves petiolate. Pink to purple flowers produced in leaf axils; as many as 12 flowers at each axil. Each flower approximately ½ inch long, slightly erect and 2-lobed. Lower lobe twice divided, revealing white center often tinged or dotted purple, upper lip reduced and covered in fine hairs. Found throughout Texas, particularly around populated areas.

Lamium purpureum LAMIACEAE
Purple deadnettle, red deadnettle, purple archangel
Urban and suburban areas, roadsides and other
disturbed sites. Summer, fall. Uncommon.

An introduced, erect, often unbranched glabrous annual to 2½ feet tall, typically half that height. Leaves opposite, deltoid to cordate, to 1½ inches long and nearly as wide, margins crenate, leaf surfaces pubescent. Whorls of flowers along stem, above leaf axils and at apex of stem. Flowers 2-lipped, pink or purple or white, about ½ inch long, lower lip obviously 2-lobed, upper lip unlobed and darker with reddish hairs. Not as common as *Lamium amplexicaule*, but can be found around old homesteads.

Monarda clinopodioides LAMIACEAE
Basil beebalm
Fields, grasslands, meadows, open brush
and woodlands, roadsides and other open
areas. Spring, summer. Common.

An erect pubescent annual with a single branching stem
to 16 inches tall. Leaves opposite, on petioles to ¾ inch
long, oblong, to 2 inches long and ¾ inch wide, bases
tapering, margins entire to serrate at acute tips. Stems
terminating in flowering spikes, heads rounded, leafy
bracts below. Flowers numerous, bilabiate, pink to pale
purple, with darker purple spots on 3-lobed lower lip,
upper lip 2-lobed or notched, bracts purplish. Common
throughout Central Texas from Coastal Bend north into
Oklahoma, east into Louisiana, occasional farther west.

Monarda fistulosa LAMIACEAE
Wild bergamot, long-flowered horsemint
Meadows, open woodlands, fields, roadsides and
other open areas. Spring, summer. Common.

An erect, single-stemmed, rhizomatous perennial with
branching, pubescent stems to 4+ feet tall. Leaves opposite, on petioles to ¾ inch long, triangular-lanceolate to
ovate, to 4 inches long and 2 inches wide, bases truncate,
margins serrate, tips acute. Flowers numerous in terminal, roundish head, about 1½ inches wide, bilabiate,
lavender, lower lip 3-lobed, upper lip erect with stamens
extending well beyond lip. Common in eastern third
of state, uncommon in West Texas, but can be found in
upper elevations in the sky islands.

Monarda pectinata LAMIACEAE
Pony beebalm, plains beebalm
Fields, grasslands, meadows, open brush
and woodlands, roadsides and other open
areas. Spring, summer. Common.

An erect, rounded annual, branching from base, with
pubescent stems to 12+ inches tall. Leaves opposite, on
petioles to ½+ inch long, oblong to lanceolate, to 2 inches
long and ½ inch wide, bases tapering, margins subentire
to serrate at ends, tips pointed, blades usually with visible hairs. Stems terminating in spike of several roundish flowering heads, each with numerous, bilabiate, light
pink flowers, about ¾ inch long, lower lip 3-lobed, middle
lobe rounded, upper lip erect and curved. Most common
in Panhandle and mid to upper elevations of Chihuahuan
Desert, west into Edwards Plateau.

Perilla frutescens   LAMIACEAE
Beefsteak plant, Chinese basil, rattlesnake weed
Grasslands, pastures, meadows, open brush
and woodlands, floodplains, roadsides and other
open areas. Spring, summer, fall. Common.

An introduced, erect, introduced perennial with branching, dark red, pubescent stems to 3 feet. Leaves opposite,
ovate-cordate, to 5 inches long and 3 inches wide, margins serrate, upper surface wrinkled, glabrous, green to
maroon. Flowers in terminal spikes to 7 inches long, bilabiate, to ⅛ inch long, rose to purple or white tinged with
pink, both lips reduced, notched. Common in damp, disturbed soils in eastern quarter of Texas, scattered populations elsewhere. Originally used as an ornamental, but
has escaped cultivation. Edible but toxic to cattle, goats,
and horses.

Physostegia correllii   LAMIACEAE
Correll's obedient plant
River and creek banks, edges of lakes and
ponds. Spring, summer. Rare.

An erect, rhizomatous perennial with either simple or
branched glabrous stems to 6+ feet tall. Leaves opposite, sessile, elliptic to 5 inches long and 2¾ inches wide,
bases tapering, margins serrate to dentate, tips pointed,
blades leathery. Flowers crowded in terminal spikes,
bilabiate, lavender, interior purple spotted or striped, to
1¼ inches long. Floral tube inflated, rounded, lower lip
3-lobed, middle lobe largest, upper lip with wavy margin
tapering to blunt tip. Rare in Texas, but widely scattered
from Val Verde County east to Louisiana.

Physostegia digitalis   LAMIACEAE
False dragonhead, finger false dragonhead
Open woodlands, grasslands, prairies, roadsides and
other open, wet areas. Spring, summer. Uncommon.

An erect, rhizomatous perennial with stout, branching
stems to 6+ feet tall. Leaves opposite, sessile, oblong to
elliptic, to 8½ inches long and 3 inches wide, bases clasping, margins undulate to serrate, tips acute, blades leathery. Flowers in single or branching terminal spikes, light
pink with darker pink to purple spotting inside heavily
inflated and rounded corolla, bilabiate, lower lip 3-lobed,
upper lip 2-lobed or notched. Found in eastern fourth of
Texas, often forming small colonies.

Physostegia intermedia   LAMIACEAE
Marsh obedient plant, slender false dragonhead, spring obedient plant
Seasonally wet grasslands, meadows, river and creek banks, roadside ditches and other low, wet areas. Spring, summer. Common.

An erect, rhizomatous perennial with slender stems to 4+ feet tall. Leaves opposite, sessile, linear to lanceolate, to 4 inches long and ½ inch wide, bases clasping, margins entire to sinuate or occasionally dentate, tips pointed. Flowers in terminal spikes, numerous, lavender, throat pale with dark reddish purple spots, about ¾ inch long, bilabiate, lower lip 3-lobed with each lobe approximately same size, upper lip slightly notched. Found throughout eastern third of state, often forming large colonies.

Physostegia longisepala   LAMIACEAE
Long-sepaled false dragonhead
Bottomlands, marshes, roadsides and other low, wet areas. Spring, early summer. Rare.

An erect, rhizomatous perennial with a single, stout stem to 4+ feet tall. Leaves opposite, on petioles 1½ inches long, lower leaves elliptic or oblong or oblanceolate, to 3½ inches long and ¾ inch wide, bases cuneate, margins wavy to slightly toothed, tips acute to obtuse. Middle and upper leaves similar, but sessile. Flowers in terminal spikes, single or branching, rose to reddish violet to deep lavender, interior lighter or streaked or spotted dark pinkish purple, bilabiate, lower lip 3-lobed, upper lip 2-lobed, corolla inflated, to 1⅓ inches long. Found in southeastern Texas.

Physostegia pulchella   LAMIACEAE
Showy false dragonhead, beautiful false dragonhead
Wet grasslands, fields and prairies, woodland edges, roadside ditches and other low, wet areas. Spring, summer. Common.

An erect, rhizomatous perennial with simple, slender to stout stems to 4+ feet tall. Leaves opposite, lower leaves oblong-lanceolate to elliptic, to 4¾ inches long and 1 inch wide, bases tapering down petiole, margins slightly entire to finely toothed, tips obtuse. Higher leaves similar, smaller, sessile to clasping, margins serrate. Stems terminating in single or branching spikes with pinkish lavender to reddish purple flowers with darker spots or stripes in throat. Flowers to 1¼ inches long, bilabiate, lower lip 3-lobed, upper 2-lobed, tube inflated. Found in eastern third of Texas.

Poliomintha glabrescens LAMIACEAE

Rosemary-mint, leafy rosemary-mint, Corley's canyon-mint
Rocky outcrops, canyons, rocky slopes and
cliffs. Spring, summer, fall. Uncommon.

An erect, shrubby, woody perennial with pubescent, branching stems to 2+ feet tall. Leaves opposite,
linear-oblong, to ¾ inch long and less than ¼ inch wide,
bases rounded, margins entire, tips obtuse, aromatic.
Numerous flowers in terminal, short spikes, pinkish
lavender, ¼ inch long and as wide, bilabiate, lower lip
3-lobed with lateral lobes broad, upper lip notched, interior often with dark purple spots. Known to occur in
Brewster, Pecos, and Presidio Counties.

Stachys drummondii LAMIACEAE

Drummond's betony, pink-mint
Open brush and woodlands, thickets, palm
groves. Winter, spring, summer. Uncommon.

An erect annual or biennial with pubescent, branching stems to 3 feet tall. Leaves opposite, on petioles to 4
inches long, ovate to ovate-oblong, to 4 inches long, bases
cordate to truncate, margins crenate, tips obtuse. Leaves
and petioles smaller farther up stem. Flowers in terminal
spikes or racemes, pink to lavender, bilabiate, lower lip
3-lobed, middle lobe broad, smaller upper lip roundish
and entire. From Houston area south to Brownsville and
into Mexico.

Stachys floridana LAMIACEAE

Florida hedgenettle, Florida betony
Woodlands, forests, thickets, fields.
Spring, summer. Uncommon.

An erect perennial with pubescent stems to 16 inches
tall. Leaves opposite, on petioles to 1½ inches long, elliptic to ovate, to 1½ inches long, margins serrate to dentate. Leaves and petioles progressively smaller farther up
stem. Flowers loosely spaced in terminal spikes, about
½ inch long, pink to purple to violet or white, bilabiate,
lower lip larger and 3-lobed, middle lobe broad, upper lip
reduced and unlobed, exterior of corolla visibly pubescent. Found in sandy soils in Southeast Texas, usually in
colonies. Tubers are edible.

Teucrium canadense   LAMIACEAE

American germander, Canada germander, wood sage
Almost exclusively waterways, creek and river
banks, edges of ponds and lakes, marshes and
other low, wet areas. Spring, summer. Common.

An erect, branching perennial with a stout main stem
to 3+ feet tall. Leaves opposite, ovate to lanceolate, to
5 inches long and 2½ inches wide, margins serrate,
tips acute to pointed, rarely obtuse. Lower leaves with
rounded bases, upper leaves becoming sessile. Stems terminating in crowded spikes of numerous bilabiate, light
pink to lavender to white flowers, often with purple spots
along 3-lobed lower lip, middle lobe greatly enlarged and
spreading, smaller lateral lobes erect to reflexed, upper
lip greatly reduced. Weak in Panhandle and Chihuahuan
Desert regions.

Pinguicula pumila   LENTIBULARIACEAE

Butterwort, dwarf butterwort, small butterwort
Open grasslands, meadows, fields, savannas,
bogs, pine woodlands and forests, roadsides
and other open areas. Spring. Uncommon.

A small, acaulescent, carnivorous perennial to 8 inches
tall when in flower. Basal leaves elliptic to obovate, to
1¼ inches long, bases narrowing to center, margins
entire, rolled upward, tips notched, blades fleshy, bright
yellow-green, covered in sticky, greasy hairs. Scapes to
8 inches tall bear a solitary flower, lavender to pale violet to white, with a yellow center. Flowers 5-lobed, lobes
unequal, bilateral, at base is a single pointed spur to
about ⅛ inch long. Found in Big Thicket region.

Lindernia dubia   LINDERNIACEAE

Yellow-seed false pimpernel, false pimpernel
Banks of ponds, lakes, streams and rivers, playas,
roadside ditches and other wet areas or in shallow
waters. Spring, summer, fall. Common.

An erect annual with glabrous, branching, 4-angled
stems to 8 inches tall, reddish brown. Leaves opposite,
on short petioles or sessile, oval to ovate, to 1½ inches
long and ¾ inch wide, bases tapering, margins entire to
widely dentate, tips acute, blades glabrous. Flowers solitary, originating in upper leaf axils, to ⅓ inch long, tubular, pinkish lavender to white, usually blotchy, bilabiate,
upper lip 2-lobed and protruding, lower lip 3-lobed and
spreading. Common in eastern third of Texas.

Ammannia coccinea   LYTHRACEAE
Scarlet toothcup, toothcup, valley redstem
Marshes, banks of creeks, ponds, rivers, and lakes, wet meadows and grasslands, roadside ditches and other low, wet areas. Spring, summer, fall. Common.

An erect annual with reddish, stout, glabrous stems, branching from base, to 20+ inches tall. Leaves opposite, lanceolate to linear, to 4 inches long and ½ inch wide, bases cordate and clasping, margins entire, tips acute, blades with prominent central vein. Flowers in leaf axils of upper stem, pink to purple, about ¼ inch wide, 4 petals oval and equal in shape. Common throughout Texas.

Cuphea carthagenensis   LYTHRACEAE
Colombian waxweed, tarweed cuphea
Marshes, floodplains, bogs, swamps, roadside ditches and other low, wet areas. Summer, fall. Uncommon.

An erect annual with pubescent, branching stems to 30+ inches tall. Leaves opposite, elliptic to oval, to 2½ inches long, bases tapering, margins entire, tips acute, blades wrinkling with age. Flowers in leaf axils of upper stem, pink to purple, about ¼ inch wide, 6 petals. Nativity uncertain; some sources indicate it is native, others suggest it is introduced. Uncommon in Southeast Texas. Found throughout Gulf Coast states, as well as Central and South America.

Cuphea glutinosa   LYTHRACEAE
Sticky waxweed, Mexican heather
Edges of ponds, lakes, creeks and rivers, wet meadows, grasslands and prairies, roadsides and other low, wet areas. Spring, summer, fall. Common.

An introduced, erect annual with pubescent stems, branching from base, to 10+ inches tall. Leaves opposite, on short petioles or appearing sessile, elliptic to oval or ovate, to nearly 1 inch long, bases rounded, tips acute or slightly pointed. Stems terminating in racemes with loosely spaced, 6-petaled, pink to purple flowers to about ⅓ inch long and as wide. Occasionally veins along petals darker. Found in wet areas throughout Southeast Texas, south to Coastal Bend, spreading.

Lythrum alatum LYTHRACEAE
Winged loosestrife, winged lythrum
Wet meadows and grasslands, roadside ditches and
other low, wet areas. Spring, summer, fall. Common.

An erect perennial with heavily branching, glabrous,
winged stems to 3+ feet tall. Leaves opposite below,
becoming alternate farther up stem, sessile, elliptic to
lanceolate, to 3½ inches long and 1 inch wide, bases
cuneate, margins entire, tips pointed. Stems terminating in leafy spikes with ½-inch-wide, lavender to purple,
6-petaled flowers. Found in wet areas throughout eastern half of state, along coast to Mexico, and in northern
Panhandle.

Lythrum californicum LYTHRACEAE
California loosestrife, purple loosestrife
Wet meadows, prairies, and grasslands, marshes, banks
of ponds, lakes, creeks and rivers, roadside ditches
and other wet areas. Spring, summer, fall. Common.

An erect, spreading perennial with glabrous, branching stems to 3+ feet tall. Leaves alternate, sessile, upper
leaves linear to oblong, lower leaves lanceolate, to 1¼
inches long and ⅓ inch wide, bases rounded to clasping,
margins entire, tips pointed. Stems terminating in leafy
spike, with lavender to purple, 6-petaled, ½-inch-wide
flowers occurring in leaf axils. Common throughout
western two-thirds of Texas, from Mexico north to Oklahoma, west into New Mexico.

Rotala ramosior LYTHRACEAE
Tooth-cup, lowland rotala
Edges of ponds, lakes, creeks and rivers,
marshes, roadside ditches and other wet
areas. Spring, summer, fall. Common.

An erect to sprawling annual, with branching, glabrous,
reddish, 4-angled stems to 18 inches long. Leaves opposite, on short petioles to nearly sessile, linear to elliptic to
oblanceolate, to 1¾ inches long and ½ inch wide, bases
wedge-shaped, margins entire, tips obtuse. Flowers in
leaf axils along upper stem, light pink to white, 4-petaled,
less than ¼ inch wide. Found throughout eastern half of
Texas, from Cameron County north into Oklahoma.

Anoda cristata   MALVACEAE
Crested anoda, violeta
Mountain drainages, wet prairies, roadsides and
other disturbed areas. Spring, summer. Common.

A weakly erect to sprawling annual with branching stems
to 3 feet long. Alternate, pubescent leaves, ovate to triangular to somewhat palmately lobed, to 3¾ inches long,
cordate bases, margins crenate to slightly entire. Flowers
occurring on pedicels to 5 inches long in axils of upper
leaves, solitary, pink to purple, to about ½ inch in diameter. Oddly dispersed: in West and Central Texas, found
along mountain drainages and creeks and in mixed
woodlands; in far South Texas, in roadside ditches and
wet meadows.

Callirhoe alcaeoides   MALVACEAE
Plains poppy mallow, pale poppy mallow
Plains, fields, grasslands, prairies, open
brushlands, roadsides and other open
areas. Spring, summer. Uncommon.

An erect to ascending perennial with multiple stems to
3+ feet tall, stems with star-shaped hairs. Leaves alternate, on petioles to 8 inches long, triangular, cordate
or ovate, unlobed to 5- to 7-lobed, 5½ inches long and
4 inches wide, ultimate margins entire, tips of lobes
acute to rounded. Flowers in terminal racemes, radial,
5-petaled, pink, white, or mauve, to 2+ inches wide.
Found in North-Central Texas, which is southern extent
of plant's range.

Callirhoe involucrata   MALVACEAE
Winecup, purple poppy mallow
Prairies, grasslands, brush and woodlands,
forests, thickets, roadsides. Late winter,
spring, early summer. Common.

A decumbent to erect perennial with multiple, angular stems, forming a mat to 36 inches in diameter and
12 inches tall, stems reddish purple with visible hairs.
Leaves alternate, on petioles to 4 inches long, round, to 4
inches long and as wide, palmately 5-lobed, lobes divided,
ultimate margins toothed, tips of lobes acute. Flowers
originate from leaf axils on pedicels to 6 inches long,
radial, 5-petaled, pink or magenta with white centers or
all white, to 2½ inches wide. Petals may be erect or lax.
Widespread but absent in far western and northeastern
Texas.

365

Callirhoe papaver MALVACEAE
Woodland poppy mallow
Pine-oak woodlands and adjacent open
areas. Spring, summer. Uncommon.

An ascending, weakly erect or decumbent perennial with
pubescent stems to 3+ feet tall. Leaves alternate, on petioles to 10+ inches long, cordate to triangular or ovate, to
4½ inches long and 5 inches wide, 3–5 lobes lanceolate
to linear or falcate, margins entire, tips of lobes acute.
Flowers on peduncles 4 to 8 inches long, 5-petaled, radial,
deep pink to magenta with white centers, to 1¾ inches
wide. Found in eastern fourth of state, historic collections
farther west into Edwards Plateau.

Callirhoe pedata MALVACEAE
Standing winecup, palmleaf poppy mallow
Grasslands, prairies, fields, open brush
and woodlands, roadsides and other open
areas. Spring, summer. Common.

An erect or nearly erect perennial with glabrous stems to 3+ feet tall. Leaves alternate, on petioles to 6 inches long, cordate,
round, or ovate, 3- to 5-lobed, to 3½ inches long and as
wide, lobes oblanceolate, margins entire, tips rounded
to acute. Flowers on peduncles to 6 inches long, 5-lobed,
radial, fuchsia without a white center though occasionally all-white flowers occur, to 1⅓ inch wide. Common
throughout Edwards Plateau, north into Oklahoma.

Hibiscus denudatus MALVACEAE
Paleface rose mallow, paleface, rock hibiscus
Rocky slopes and open desert shrublands.
Winter, spring, summer, fall. Common.

An erect, slender, branching perennial to 2½ feet tall,
with star-shaped hairs on leaves and stems. Leaves oblong
to ovate, unlobed or weakly 3-lobed, to 1¼ inches long and
1 inch wide, dentate to crenate margins, cuneate to truncate bases. Flowers solitary in axils of upper leaves, pale
pink or purple or faded to nearly white, to 2 inches wide
and ½ inch long. Found in West Texas, generally west
of Pecos River, grows in gravelly soils, no substrate preference. Hybrid between this species and *Hibiscus coul-
teri*, named *H. ×sabei*, has been documented in southern
Brewster County.

Hibiscus moscheutos   MALVACEAE
Swamp rose mallow, crimson-eyed rose mallow, marshmallow hibiscus
Banks of streams, ponds, and other bodies of water, marshes, roadside ditches and other wet areas. Spring, summer, fall. Common.

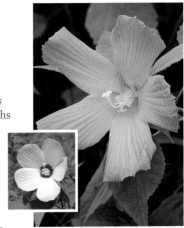

An erect, multistemmed perennial to 8 feet tall, stems mostly glabrous. Leaves on petioles half to three-fourths as long as blade, lanceolate to ovate to orbiculate, unlobed or 3-lobed, to 8 inches long and 5 inches wide, bases cordate to cuneate, margins crenate or dentate or serrate. Flowers in upper leaf axils, pink to white with or without red centers, to 6 inches in diameter. Found in southeastern Texas. Specific epithet means "musk scented" and is of Latin origin. Uncommon west into Edwards Plateau, north into Oklahoma.

Kosteletzkya virginica (*K. pentacarpos*)
MALVACEAE
Saltmarsh mallow, seashore mallow, Virginia fen-rose
Marshes. Summer, fall. Uncommon.

An erect perennial with somewhat pubescent branching stems to 9 feet. Leaves ovate to palmately or hastately 3- to 5-lobed, to 6¾ inches long and 6 inches wide, bases truncate to cordate to hastate, margins serrate to dentate to entire. Flowers occur in axils of upper leaves or along branch stems, solitary, pink, to 4 inches wide. Found along coast from Coastal Bend north into Louisiana. Genus named in honor of Vincenz Franz Kosteletzky, a professor of botany who lived and worked in Prague during the 1800s.

Malva neglecta   MALVACEAE
Common mallow, cheeseweed, roundleaf mallow
Urban and suburban areas, rural homesites, roadsides and other disturbed areas. Spring, summer, fall. Common.

An introduced, spreading annual to perennial vine with pubescent, branching stems to 3 feet long. Leaves alternate, on petioles to 6+ inches long, orbicular to reniform, palmately lobed, to 2½ inches long and 3 inches wide, bases cordate, margins crenate. Flowers solitary or in small clusters in leaf axils, pink to light purple or white, to ¾ inch in diameter. Common throughout Central Texas, west to New Mexico, north to Oklahoma. Less common in East Texas. Absent in South Texas.

367

Malva parviflora   MALVACEAE
Small-flowered mallow, little mallow, least mallow
Fallow fields, agricultural lands, urban and
suburban areas, roadsides and other disturbed
areas. Spring, summer. Common.

An introduced, erect to spreading annual to perennial
vine with multiple stems to 2 feet long. Leaves alternate,
on petioles 2–3 times as long as blade, slightly round to
cordate to reniform, 5- to 7-lobed or angled, to 3½ inches
long and wide, bases cordate, margins crenate. Flowers
solitary or to 4 in leaf axils, pale pink to purple to nearly
white, ¼ inch long. Common throughout southern Texas,
west to Big Bend region, sparsely introduced elsewhere
throughout state.

Malvella leprosa   MALVACEAE
Alkali weed, oreja de ratón, scurfy sida
Sparse brush and grasslands, roadsides, washes,
banks of playas and other low, open areas.
Winter, spring, summer, fall. Common.

A prostrate perennial with pubescent stems to 16 inches
long. Leaves pubescent, reniform to deltate, to 1⅓ inches
long and wide, bases truncate to slightly cordate, margins
serrate. Flowers arise from leaf axils, light pink to cream,
about ¾ inch in diameter. Commonly overlooked, found
throughout West Texas, west of Pecos and in Panhandle, in clay soils with high salt content. Specific epithet
of Latin origin and means "scaly," referring to stems and
leaves.

Malvella sagittifolia   MALVACEAE
Arrow-leaf scurfy sida
Mudflats, basins, drainages and other low, disturbed
areas. Spring, summer, fall. Uncommon.

A prostrate, trailing perennial with scale-covered stems
to 18 inches long. Leaves triangular, to 1⅓ inches long,
entire margins, truncate base typically with several teeth,
both surfaces sparsely covered with silver scales. Flowers light pink to white with a hint of yellow, about ¾ inch
wide. Similar to *Malvella leprosa* in habit, but distinguished by triangular leaf. A third species, *M. lepidota*,
occurs in same areas as others and is distinguished by its
intermediate characters. Primarily found in open areas
in Big Bend region, also in Panhandle and South Texas.

Melochia pyramidata   MALVACEAE
Pyramid flower, pyramid bush, broom wood
Thornscrub, washes, sparse grasslands,
overgrazed fields, roadsides and other disturbed
areas. Spring, summer, fall. Common.

An erect, multistemmed perennial with branching, glabrous to pubescent stems to 5 feet tall. Leaves alternate, on petioles to ½ inch long, ovate to lanceolate, to 1½ inches long and ¾ inch wide, bases rounded to cuneate, margins serrate. Flowers occur singly or in umbels, pink to violet, 5-petaled, about ½ inch wide and as long. Frequent in southern half of Texas, from Big Bend region east to Louisiana, south into Mexico.

Melochia tomentosa   MALVACEAE
Woolly pyramid bush, teabush
Open shrub and woodlands, fields, roadsides.
Spring, summer, fall. Uncommon.

An erect perennial with stems to 6 feet tall. Leaves on petioles to 1 inch long, ovate to lanceolate, to 2¾ inches long and 1¾ inches wide, bases rounded to slightly cordate, tomentose, margins dentate to crenate. Flowers in cymes, pink to purple to violet, to ¾ inch long and about ¾ inch wide. Found in far South Texas. Similar to *Melochia pyramidata*, but with tomentose leaves and stems.

Pavonia lasiopetala   MALVACEAE
Rock rose, Texas swamp-mallow, rose pavonia
Open shrub and woodlands. Summer, fall. Uncommon.

An erect perennial to 4 feet tall and nearly as wide with star-shaped hairs on both stems and leaves. Leaves ovate, on petioles half to equal length of blade, to 2 inches long, bases cordate, margins dentate. Flowers occur in axils of leaves, solitary, pink to lavender, to 1 inch in diameter. Found from Terrell County east to Bastrop, generally following southern edge of Edwards Plateau; may be introduced elsewhere as this species is widely available in the nursery trade. It is peculiar that the common name swamp-mallow is used, as this species does not live in such habitats.

369

Sida ciliaris MALVACEAE
Bracted sida, bracted fanpetals
Fields, grasslands, pastures, open brushlands, roadsides and other open areas. Spring, summer, fall. Common.

A prostrate to ascending to somewhat erect perennial with stems branching from base, to 12 inches tall, stems with star-shaped appressed hairs. Leaves alternate, on short petioles, linear to oblong-lanceolate, to 1 inch long and about ¼ inch wide, bases rounded to cordate, margins toothed with visible hairs, tips acute, blades green with visible hairs. Flowers occur on short pedicels at ends of stems, to 10 flowers per inflorescence, 5-petaled, pink to salmon colored. From South Texas, generally south of Edwards Plateau, east to Houston area.

Sphaeralcea angustifolia MALVACEAE
Globemallow, copper globemallow
Washes, drainages, creek and river beds, roadsides and other disturbed areas. Winter, spring, summer, fall. Common.

An erect, multistemmed perennial with stems to 5 feet tall, stems usually with star-shaped hairs. Leaves variable from linear to lanceolate to angled-ovate, lobed or hastately lobed to angulate, to 6 inches long and 1¾ inches wide, bases cuneate, margins dentate to crenate, surfaces covered in star-shaped hairs. Flowers occur at tips or along upper stems in clusters, pink, orange, lavender, mauve, reddish orange, or white, to 1¼ inches broad. Found in western Texas, south along Rio Grande to deep South Texas, north through Edwards Plateau and into Panhandle.

Proboscidea louisianica subsp. *fragrans*
MARTYNIACEAE
Fragrant devil's claw, unicorn plant
Mountain and desert washes, creeks and drainages, roadside ditches and other low, seasonally wet areas. Spring, summer, fall. Common.

An erect, spreading annual with sticky-pubescent stems to 3+ feet tall and 5+ feet wide. Leaves highly viscid-pubescent, tacky to the touch, ovate, to 10 inches wide. Flowers in terminal spikelike racemes extending above foliage, deep pink to magenta with yellow nectar guides and spots within tube, bell-shaped, 5-lobed. Fruit, as with all devil's claws, is a dry dehiscent pod. Found in mountains and lower basins of Chihuahuan Desert region.

Proboscidea parviflora   MARTYNIACEAE
Doubleclaw, devil's claw
Desert washes, canyons, roadsides and other
disturbed areas. Spring, summer. Uncommon.

An erect, branching annual with sticky-pubescent stems
to 5+ feet tall and 4 feet wide. Leaves opposite to alternate,
on petioles to 10 inches long, triangular-ovate to nearly
round, to 10 inches long, bases cordate, margins entire to
wavy, tips rounded. Flowers on loose racemes below foliage, pink to white to purple-magenta, with nectar guides
near and in tube, 5-lobed and tubular, to 1½ inches long
and ¾ inch wide. Fruit much larger than other *Proboscidea* species, reaching 10 inches long with 2 pairs of claws.
Found in far West Texas from Brewster to El Paso County.
Other collections in Rio Grande Valley.

Proboscidea sabulosa   MARTYNIACEAE
**Sand dune unicorn plant, dune devil's claw,
dune unicorn plant**
Sand dunes, washes and other areas with
deep sand. Summer, fall. Rare.

An erect, branching annual with sticky-pubescent stems
to 4 feet tall and as wide. Opposite and/or alternate leaves,
on petioles to 4+ inches long, triangular-ovate to nearly
reniform, bases cordate, margins undulate, tips rounded
to obtuse. Flowers in loose racemes occurring in leaf
axils, tubular, 5-lobed, pink to white with darker lobes
and often darker spots within tube, to about ¾ inch long,
anthers red. Grows in sandy soils in West Texas from
Midland-Odessa area into Hudspeth County, also in deep
South Texas.

Mayaca fluviatilis   MAYACACEAE
Stream bogmoss
Bogs, swamps in and along streams, ponds, and
lakes. Spring, summer, fall. Uncommon.

An erect or decumbent, mat-forming perennial, either
terrestrial or aquatic, with branching stems to 20+ inches
long. Leaves sessile, crowded, dense, lanceolate to linear,
to ¾ inch long, margins entire. Flowers solitary, originating along stem, pedicels to ½ inch, 3 green ovate to lanceolate sepals, 3 ovate petals, pink to rose to maroon usually
with white bases, to ½ inch wide. Found in wet or damp
soils or submerged in shallow waters in eastern portion
of Texas.

Rhexia mariana   MELASTOMATACEAE
Maryland meadow-beauty, meadow beauty, pale meadow-beauty
Wet grasslands, meadows, and savannas, bogs, woodland edges, roadside ditches and other low, wet areas. Spring, summer. Common.

An erect perennial, branching above, with 4-angled stems to 2+ feet tall. Leaves opposite, on short petioles, elliptic to lanceolate, to 2½ inches long, bases rounded, margins serrate and ciliate, tips pointed. Flowers in terminal cymes, pale pink to lavender, 4-petaled with 8 yellow stamens and sickle-shaped anthers, 1⅓ inches wide. The urn-shaped calyx and capsule within persist after flowering. Most common species of *Rhexia*. Found in eastern fourth of Texas.

Rhexia virginica   MELASTOMATACEAE
Virginia's meadow-beauty
Bogs, hillside seeps, wet meadows.
Spring, summer. Uncommon.

An erect, branching perennial with 4-angled, pubescent stems to 3+ feet tall. Leaves opposite, sessile, ovate-lanceolate or elliptic, to 4 inches long and 1½ inches wide, bases rounded to cordate, margins toothed and ciliate, tips acute, blades pubescent. Central and lateral stems terminate in flowering cymes. Flowers pink to rose-pink, 4-petaled with 8 bright yellow stamens and falcate anthers, about 1½ inches wide. Urn-shaped calyx and capsule within persist after flowering. Found in eastern fourth of Texas.

Nelumbo nucifera   NELUMBONACEAE
Sacred lotus
Retention ponds, cattle tanks, ponds.
Spring, summer. Uncommon.

An introduced, aquatic, rhizomatous perennial to 6+ feet tall when in flower. Leaves and flowers held above surface of water. Leaves peltate, on petioles to 6 feet long, round, to 20+ inches wide, margins entire to undulate. Flowers on peduncles to 6+ feet tall, held above leaves, solitary, pink to light pink, fading to white, to 10 inches wide. Similar to native *Nelumbo*, easily distinguished by pink flowers. Species intentionally introduced around state, primarily as an ornamental. Found in Dallas and Austin and Southeast Texas.

Abronia ameliae   NYCTAGINACEAE
Amelia's sand verbena, heart's delight
Sandy prairies. Late winter, spring, summer. Rare.

A stout, erect to ascending perennial with pubescent, sticky stems to about 20 inches tall. Leaves opposite, to 3 inches long and 2 inches wide, margins sinuate, surfaces with glandular hairs, sticky to the touch. Flowers numerous in terminal rounded heads to about 2 inches wide, trumpet-shaped, pink to magenta, to 1 inch long and ⅓ inch wide. Endemic to Texas, found in the South Texas Sand Sheet in far South Texas.

Abronia carletonii   NYCTAGINACEAE
Carleton's sand verbena
Desert scrub, open brushlands. Spring, summer, fall. Uncommon.

An erect perennial with unbranched or weakly branched sticky stems to 18+ inches tall. Leaves opposite, on petioles to 1¾ inches long, lanceolate to elliptic-oblong, to 2 inches long and 1¼ inches wide, margins entire to undulate, tips acute, blades usually glabrous, thick, and somewhat fleshy. Flowers numerous in terminal rounded clusters, pink to purplish, trumpet-shaped, to ⅝ inch long and ⅓ inch wide. Found in gypseous or limestone soils in the Trans-Pecos.

Acleisanthes chenopodioides
NYCTAGINACEAE
Goosefoot moonpod
Open areas, sparse brush and grasslands, rocky slopes. Spring, summer, fall. Common.

An erect, branched perennial to 18 inches tall, from a thick rootstock. Leaves opposite, on petioles to 2¾ inches long, sparsely scattered along stems, fleshy, ovate to deltate, to 2 inches long and 1½ inches wide, bases rounded to cordate, margins entire to undulate, tips acute, obtuse, or rounded. Flowers in terminal clusters or upper leaf axils, shortly funnel-shaped with 5 notched lobes, pink to rose with lighter centers, to about ½ inch wide. Found in open areas throughout Chihuahuan Desert, at lower elevations or within basins.

Allionia incarnata var. *incarnata*
NYCTAGINACEAE
Trailing four o'clock, trailing windmills
Open areas, rocky outcrops, roadsides.
Winter, spring, summer, fall. Common.

A prostrate perennial vine to 4+ feet long. Leaves opposite, oval to oblong, can vary in size on same stem but usually no longer than 2½ inches or wider than 1⅓ inches, margins entire or undulate. Flowers on 1-inch-long peduncles arising from leaf axils, pink to magenta. Found from South Texas north through Panhandle and west through the Trans-Pecos. Prefers sandy, gravelly, rocky soil. The fruits have 0–4 triangular teeth along their winged lateral ribs.

Anulocaulis eriosolenus   NYCTAGINACEAE
Big Bend ringstem
Open desert scrub. Spring, summer, fall. Uncommon.

An erect, airy annual or short-lived perennial with slender, glabrous stems to 5 feet. Leaves mostly in lower portion of plant, few along stem, opposite, unequal in size, on petioles to 3 inches long, ovate to round, to 4½ inches long and 5¼ inches wide, bases cordate to truncate, margins wavy to entire, tips rounded or obtuse, surfaces pubescent. Flowers solitary or in pairs, widely spaced in terminal panicles, radial, shortly funnel-shaped, pink to lavender with darker streaks where 5 lobes meet, to ⅓ inch long and 1 inch wide. Found in sparse desert scrub in Presidio and Brewster Counties.

Anulocaulis leiosolenus var. *gypsogenus*
NYCTAGINACEAE
Gypsum ringstem
Open, sparse desert scrub. Spring, summer, fall. Rare.

An erect, airy perennial with slender, glabrous stems to 5+ feet tall. Leaves mostly in lower portion of plant, opposite, unequal in size, on petioles to 3 inches long, ovate to round, to 6 inches long and 7¾ inches wide, bases cordate, margins undulate, tips rounded, surfaces glabrous. Flowers few, well-spaced in terminal panicles, funnel-shaped, 5-lobed, faded pink to white with yellow streaks where lobes are joined, to 1¾ inches long and 1 inch wide, tube slender, stamens to twice as long as tube. Found northern Culberson and Loving Counties.

Anulocaulis leiosolenus var. *lasianthus*
NYCTAGINACEAE
Southwestern ringstem
Open, sparse desert scrub. Spring, summer, fall. Rare.

An erect, airy perennial with slender, glabrous stems to
5+ feet tall. Leaves mostly in lower portion of plant, opposite, unequal in size, on petioles to 3 inches long, ovate
to round, to 6 inches long and 7¾ inches wide, bases cordate, margins undulate, tips rounded, surfaces densely
covered by hairs with pustules at their base. Flowers
in umbellate clusters well-spaced in terminal panicles,
funnel-shaped, 5-lobed, pink, to 1¾ inches long and 1
inch wide, tube slender, stamens to twice as long as floral
tube. Found on limestone-based soils, often clay, in Brewster and Presidio Counties.

Boerhavia coccinea   NYCTAGINACEAE
Scarlet spiderling, red boerhavia, hierba del cancer
Open rocky soils, grasslands, desert scrub, desert
washes, dunes, creek and river beds, roadsides and other
disturbed areas. Winter, spring, summer, fall. Common.

A prostrate to decumbent perennial with
sticky-pubescent, branching stems originating from
a central root, ascending when able to climb on other
plants. Leaves opposite, on petioles to 1 inch long,
ovate to broadly lanceolate to nearly round, to 3 inches
long and 2½ inches wide, bases round or truncate or
wedge-shaped, margins sinuate, tips acute or obtuse or
round, blades glabrous to pubescent. Terminal or axillary
inflorescences. Flowers clustered with 13± other flowers in umbels, deep rose to scarlet, about ⅛ inch wide,
bell-shaped. Absent in Panhandle and deep East Texas.

Cyphomeris gypsophiloides   NYCTAGINACEAE
Red cyphomeris
Sparse desert scrub, washes, drainages, canyons, open
brush and woodlands. Summer, fall. Uncommon.

An erect to ascending, open perennial with glabrous, branching stems to 4+ feet tall. Leaves opposite, on petioles to nearly sessile, oblong-lanceolate to
lanceolate-linear, to 4 inches long and 1¼ inches wide,
margins entire, tips acute. Flowers in open, terminal
racemes, funnel-shaped, deep pink to magenta, to ½ inch
long and as wide, 5-lobed, anthers extending well beyond
tube. Found throughout Chihuahuan Desert, east into
western Edwards Plateau.

Mirabilis albida   NYCTAGINACEAE

White four o'clock, hairy four o'clock, pale umbrella-wort
Fields, grasslands, prairies, rocky slopes, open brush
and woodlands, roadsides. Summer, fall. Common.

An erect, single- to multistemmed perennial with pubescent, branching stems to 3 feet tall. Leaves opposite, on petioles to ¼ inch long, linear-lanceolate to ovate-deltate, to 4 inches long and 1 inch wide, bases cordate, tapered, round, or truncate, margins entire, tips acute, blades glabrous or glandular-sticky. Flowers in terminal cymes or originating from upper leaf axils, peduncle to 1 inch, radial, bell-shaped, pink to reddish violet or white, about ½ inch wide, 5-lobed. Found throughout Texas. Genus name of Latin origin and means "wonderful" or "marvelous." Specific epithet refers to light- or white-colored flowers.

Mirabilis linearis   NYCTAGINACEAE

Linear-leaf four o'clock, narrow-leaf four o'clock
Fields, prairies, grasslands, open shrub
and woodlands, roadsides and other open
areas. Spring, summer, fall. Common.

An erect, ascending, or decumbent perennial with glabrous to hirsute stems to 4+ feet long. Leaves opposite, linear-lanceolate, to 4¾ inches long and ⅓ inch wide, bases acute, margins entire, tips sharply tapered or rounded. Flowers in terminal or axillary cymes, radial, bell-shaped, pinkish purple to white, to ½ inch wide. Common throughout most of Texas; absent in eastern fourth.

Mirabilis multiflora   NYCTAGINACEAE

Colorado four o'clock, marvelous many-flowered four o'clock
Grasslands, fields, open shrub and woodlands.
Spring, summer, fall. Uncommon.

An erect, spreading perennial with glabrous or pubescent, leafy, heavily branching stems to 24+ inches tall; forming clumps 3+ feet in diameter. Leaves opposite, ovate, to 4 inches long and 3¼ inches wide, bases rounded to cordate, margins entire, tips acute to obtuse. Flowers terminal, in small leafy clusters, funnel-shaped, radial, pink-magenta, to 2⅓ inches long; showy. Found in open grassy areas throughout Chihuahuan Desert.

Mirabilis nyctaginea NYCTAGINACEAE
Wild four o'clock, heartleaf four o'clock
Pastures, fields, open brush and woodlands, roadsides and other open, disturbed areas. Spring, summer. Common.

An erect, branching perennial with glabrous stems to 4+ feet tall. Leaves opposite, on short petioles, cordate, to 4 inches long and 3 inches wide, bases cordate, margins entire, tips acute or tapering to a point, blades glabrous. Flowers in terminal cymes, numerous, shortly funnel-shaped, radial, pink to magenta to reddish purple, to ½ inch wide. Most common in limestone soils of Central Texas, north to Oklahoma, less common elsewhere. Absent in South Texas.

Oenothera canescens ONAGRACEAE
Spotted evening-primrose
Playas, lake and pond shores, grasslands, plains, fields and other low, open areas. Spring, summer. Common.

An erect, rhizomatous perennial with canescent stems to 8 inches tall. Leaves alternate, on short petioles to nearly sessile, lanceolate, to ¾ inch long and ¼ inch wide, bases tapering, margins widely dentate to entire, tips acute. Hypanthium to ¾ inch. Flowers pink to rose, with darker spots throughout and white near base, petals broadly lanceolate, to 1 inch wide. Common throughout wet areas or in depressions in Panhandle.

Oenothera curtiflora (*Gaura parviflora*)
ONAGRACEAE
Lizard-tail, smallflowered gaura, velvet-leaf gaura
Fields, open brush and woodlands, riparian areas, roadsides and other disturbed areas, often in urban and suburban areas. Spring, summer, fall. Common.

A robust, erect annual with pubescent, sticky, stout stems to 6+ feet tall. Leaves alternate, sessile or nearly so, elliptic to ovate, to 5 inches long and 1¾ inches wide, bases tapering, margins sinuate and/or toothed, tips acute, leaf surfaces velvety. Flowers in dense spikes, bilateral, 4-petaled, pink to nearly white, to ⅛ inch long, sepals strongly reflexed. Found throughout majority of Texas. Absent in eastern fourth.

377

Oenothera speciosa   ONAGRACEAE
**Pink evening primrose, showy primrose,
amapola del campo**
Fields, meadows, grasslands, prairies, open
shrub and woodlands, roadsides and other
open areas. Spring, summer. Common.

An erect to sprawling, rhizomatous perennial with
branching stems to 24 inches long, stems with flattened
hairs. Leaves alternate, on petioles to 1 inch long, lanceolate, elliptic or oblanceolate, to 3 inches long and ¾ inch
wide, margins entire or dentate or slightly pinnatifid, tips
acute to obtuse. Hypanthium to ¾ inch. Flowers originating in upper leaf axils, 4-petaled, to 3½ inches wide, pink
to white, often with white and yellow centers and darker
veins. Common throughout majority of state, weak in
Chihuahuan Desert and northern Panhandle; spreading.

Oenothera xenogaura (*Gaura drummondii*)
ONAGRACEAE
Drummond's beeblossom, scented gaura
Fields, grasslands, open brush and woodlands, roadsides
and other open spaces. Spring, summer, fall. Common.

An erect, rhizomatous perennial with leafy, pubescent
stems branching from base, to 2+ feet tall. Leaves alternate, lanceolate to elliptic, to 2¾ inches long, margins
entire or wavy or toothed, surfaces pubescent. Flowers
in terminal spikes, bilateral, 4 petals clawed, pink to red,
about ½ inch long, 8 stamens, stigma 4-lobed. Fruit is
a sessile capsule. Most common in southern Texas, less
common north to Red River, west to Val Verde County.
Absent in deep East Texas.

Calopogon oklahomensis   ORCHIDACEAE
Oklahoma grass pink, prairie grass pink
Prairies, grasslands, savannas, bogs and other
open, wet areas. Spring, summer. Uncommon.

An erect, glabrous perennial, from a corm, with stems to
14 inches tall. Leaf grasslike, linear, to 14 inches long and
to ½ inch wide, often longer than stem. Flowers in terminal raceme, to 7+ flowers per, bilateral, pink to magenta
or occasionally white, to 2 inches wide and as long, 3
sepals and 3 petals, upper petal rounded triangular, stamens yellow, stigma curved. Uncommon in eastern
fourth of Texas, grows in acidic soils, may occur in large
numbers in proper conditions.

Calopogon tuberosus   ORCHIDACEAE
Tuberous grasspink
Bogs, marshes, savannas, grasslands, pitcher-plant
communities. Spring, summer. Locally common.

An erect, glabrous perennial with flowering stems to
24+ inches tall. Single leaf, grasslike, linear-elliptic to 12
inches long and 1½ inches wide, base sheathed, margin
entire, tip acute. Stem terminates in a spike of to 15 flowers, pink to rose, occasionally white. Flowers bilateral
with 3 sepals and 3 petals, upper petal thin at base and
triangular above with a pale pink to white patch, slightly
muricate, stamens golden yellow, stigma curved. Locally
common in Southeast Texas, north into Oklahoma.

Epipactis gigantea   ORCHIDACEAE
Chatterbox orchid, stream orchid, giant helleborine
Springs, seeps, steep slopes, banks of
creeks. Spring, summer. Uncommon.

An erect, glabrous, leafy perennial with stems to 3+ feet
tall. Leaves alternate, sheathed, ovate-elliptic to lanceolate, to 8 inches long and 3 inches wide, margins entire.
To 30 flowers in terminal racemes. Flowers with 3 sepals
and 3 petals, sepals green to rose and ovate-lanceolate,
petals pink to rose to orange with darker veins, lower
petal 3-lobed with lip protruding to a point. Uncommon
but widespread throughout state, found in Hill Country, west to Chihuahuan Desert, isolated populations
elsewhere.

Hexalectris grandiflora   ORCHIDACEAE
Largeflower crested coral root, giant crested coral root
Oak-pine-juniper woodlands. Spring, summer. Rare.

An erect perennial with reddish brown, glabrous stems
to 20+ inches tall; plants either solitary or colonial.
Leaves absent. To 20 flowers in racemes. Flowers pink
to magenta to crimson, 3 sepals and 3 petals. Sepals
elliptic-lanceolate, 2 lateral and one upper. Lateral petals
both smaller than sepals. Lower lip 3-lobed, with middle
lobe broad and darker, lateral lobes reduced and erect.
Located in mountains of Big Bend region, mid to upper
elevations, in rich, organic soils.

Pogonia ophioglossoides   ORCHIDACEAE
Rose pogonia, snakemouth orchid, beard flower
Bogs, wetland pine savannas, baygalls.
Spring, summer. Uncommon.

An erect perennial with a single stem to 28+ inches
tall. Leaves few, alternate, sheathed, elliptic to lanceolate to oblong, to 4¾ inches long and 1⅓ inch wide.
Flowers solitary or paired, pink to white. Sepals lanceolate to oblong-elliptic, to 1 inch long. Petals elliptic
to lance-obovate to 1 inch long, covering lip below. Lip
spatulate to 1 inch, often with dark purple streaks along
edges, with yellow patch near base, margins fringed to
lacerate. Found in eastern third of Texas, west to Bastrop
County.

Agalinis densiflora   OROBANCHACEAE
**Osage false foxglove, fine-leaf gerardia,
fine-leaf hairy foxglove**
Prairies, grasslands, fields, open brush
and woodlands. Summer, fall. Rare.

An erect annual with pubescent, rough, leafy stems to
30+ inches tall. Leaves opposite, sessile above, on petioles below, pinnatifid with linear lobes to 1½ inches long,
margins with long, well-spaced hairs, tips pointed. Stems
terminating in leafy spikes. Flowers bell-shaped, pink to
light purple, throats lighter in color and with dark spotting, 5-lobed, bilateral, lower lip 3-lobed and spreading,
upper lip 2-lobed and arched. Rare in Central Texas, generally found in a narrow band from San Antonio area,
north into Oklahoma.

Agalinis fasciculata   OROBANCHACEAE
Beach false foxglove
Grasslands, fields, meadows, savannas, open woodlands,
marshes, dunes and other open areas. Fall. Common.

An erect, hemiparasitic annual with stout, rough,
branching stems to 3+ feet tall. Leaves opposite, linear, to 1½ inches long, margins entire, tips acute, blades
folded, bundles of leaves in primary leaf axils. To 30 flowers in terminal racemes. Flowers bell-shaped, pink to
rose, throats lighter in color with dark spotting, pedicels
less than ¼ inch, bilabiate, upper lip 2-lobed, lower lip
3-lobed, corolla pubescent. Common in eastern fourth of
Texas, less common farther west to Edwards Plateau.

Agalinis heterophylla OROBANCHACEAE
Prairie agalinis, prairie false foxglove, prairie gerardia
Prairies, grasslands, fields, pastures, open
brush and woodlands, roadsides and other open
areas. Spring, summer, fall. Common.

An erect, hemiparasitic annual with glabrous, branching
stems to 2+ feet tall. Leaves opposite, on short petioles to
sessile, linear to thinly lanceolate to elliptic, to 1¼ inches
long and ⅛ inch wide, bases tapering, margins entire,
tips pointed to acute. Flowers in terminal racemes, sessile, bell-shaped, pink to rose with lighter throat and dark
purple-red spots within, bilabiate, upper lip 2-lobed and
erect, lower lip 3-lobed and protruding, exterior of corolla
visibly pubescent. Common in East Texas, less common
in eastern Edwards Plateau, south to Cameron County,
north into Oklahoma.

Agalinis maritima OROBANCHACEAE
Boca Chica false foxglove, saltmarsh foxglove
Dunes, marshes, mudflats and other low, wet areas
along coast. Spring, summer, fall. Locally common.

An erect, hemiparasitic annual with glabrous, leafy,
thick, branching, semisucculent stems to 2 feet. Leaves
opposite, linear to 1¼ inches long, tips acute to pointed,
margins entire, blades fleshy. Flowers in terminal
racemes, pedicels to ¾ inch, bell-shaped, rose to purple
with darker spots inside tube, bilabiate, upper lip 2-lobed,
lower lip 3-lobed. Corolla visibly pubescent, to about ¾
inch long. Common along Texas coast.

Agalinis tenuifolia OROBANCHACEAE
Slender false foxglove
Wet meadows, savannas, grasslands,
fields, banks of ponds, streams, and other
bodies of water. Fall. Uncommon.

An erect, hemiparasitic annual with glabrous, branching stems to 20+ inches tall. Leaves opposite, sessile, linear, to 3 inches long and ¼ inch wide, margins entire,
tips pointed to acute. Flowers in terminal racemes, pedicels to ½ inch, bell-shaped, pink to purple, interior with
dark spots and 2 yellow lines, to ¾ inch wide, bilabiate,
upper lip 2-lobed, lower 3-lobed, margins of lobes ciliate.
Uncommon in Northeast Texas, occasional collections
farther south to Coastal Bend.

Castilleja sessiliflora OROBANCHACEAE
Downy painted cup, downy paintbrush
Fields, grasslands, prairies, open brush and woodlands, roadsides and other open areas. Spring, fall. Common.

An erect, hemiparasitic perennial with slightly woolly stems to 12+ inches tall. Leaves alternate, linear or with lateral lobes, to 3 inches long and ¼ inch wide, margins entire, blades silvery pubescent. Inflorescences in terminal, bracted spikes. Bracts with 1 or 2 lateral lobes, ends of bracts mauve to pink to purple, lobes linear to lanceolate. Calyces 4-lobed, lobes linear, similar color to bracts, to 1¾ inches long. Flowers bilabiate, extending beyond calyx, upper lip longer than lower and pointed, galea yellow, lower lip 3-lobed and white. Common throughout Chihuahuan Desert, north into Panhandle, scattered collections elsewhere throughout Central Texas and east.

Oxalis drummondii OXALIDACEAE
Drummond's wood sorrel
Woodlands, fields, meadows, creek and river drainages, brushlands. Spring, summer, fall. Common.

An erect and spreading, stemless perennial to 12 inches tall. Basal leaves only, with 3 leaflets, to 2 inches wide, each leaflet lobed and V-shaped (somewhat cordate), lobes oblong or lanceolate. Inflorescences in scapes surpassing leaves, often twice their length, 3–10 flowers per scape. Flowers bell-shaped, erect to nodding, 5-petaled, pink to light purple or violet with greenish yellow centers and white ring toward base of petals, to 1 inch long. Found throughout Central Texas, west to El Paso, south to Coastal Bend and into Mexico.

Oxalis violacea OXALIDACEAE
Violet wood sorrel
Woodlands, grasslands, brushlands.
Spring, summer, fall. Common.

An erect, spreading, stemless perennial, from a bulb, to 6+ inches tall. Basal leaves only, trifoliolate, to 1 inch wide, leaflets V-shaped, margins entire, lobes rounded. Inflorescences in scapes surpassing foliage, often twice the height of leaves, to 19 flowers per scape (though usually fewer). Flowers bell-shaped, 5-petaled, lavender to purple with greenish yellow centers, to ⅓ inch wide. Most common in eastern third of Texas, less common farther west to Val Verde County.

Passiflora ciliata *(P. foetida* var. *ciliata)*
PASSIFLORACEAE
Corona de Cristo, fetid passionflower, blue passionflower
Shrublands. Spring, summer, fall. Locally common.

A climbing perennial vine to 6+ feet long. Foliage and
stems glabrous to pubescent, often with a tinge of brown.
Leaves 3-lobed, middle lobe larger and less rounded than
outer two. Fruit ovoid, red when mature, often with persisting floral bracts. Petals in varying tints of pink, lavender, purple, white, or cream, 1½ inches long; filament
whorls purplish. Mostly found in South Texas, growing
over shrubs and fences, typically in sandy soil.

Mimulus alatus   PHRYMACEAE
Winged monkeyflower
Creek and river bottoms, wet woodlands,
banks of waterways, and other low, wet,
shady areas. Summer, fall. Uncommon.

An erect or ascending perennial with glabrous, square
stems to 30+ inches long. Leaves opposite, on petioles to
½+ inch long, ovate to lanceolate, to 5 inches long and 2
inches wide, margins dentate or serrate, tips acute. Solitary flowers occur in leaf axils on pedicels to ½ inch
long, may appear sessile, to ½ inch long, pink to pale blue
with yellow patch in center of lower lip, throat pubescent,
bilabiate, lower lip 3-lobed with lobes rounded, upper
lip 2-lobed with lobes erect to reflexed. Found in eastern
third of Texas.

Rivina humilis   PHYTOLACCACEAE
Pigeon berry, rouge plant, coralito
Woodlands, brushlands, thickets, canyons, rocky
outcrops. Spring, summer, fall. Common.

An erect, sprawling perennial with weak, lax, glabrous
to pubescent stems to 4 feet. Leaves alternate, elliptic to
oblong to deltate to ovate, to 4 inches long and 2 inches
wide, bases cordate or truncate or rounded, margins
entire to wavy, tips acute to obtuse. To 50+ flowers in
racemes to 6 inches long, petals absent, 5 pink to white
sepals, about ¼ inch wide. Fruit deep red when mature,
fleshy and juicy. Absent in Panhandle and far eastern
Texas.

passion flower family
PASSIFLORACEAE

phryma family
PHRYMACEAE

pokeweed family
PHYTOLACCACEAE

Penstemon cobaea   PLANTAGINACEAE
Foxglove, prairie penstemon, prairie beardtongue
Fields, pastures, meadows, grasslands prairies,
open brush and woodlands, roadsides and other
open areas. Spring, summer. Common.

An erect perennial to 2 feet tall, with one to several
pubescent stems arising from a woody base. Leaves opposite, stem leaves sessile, basal leaves petiolate, lanceolate to ovate, to 6 inches long and 2 inches wide, margins
toothed, tips acute, blades glabrous or slightly pubescent.
Flowers in terminal racemes, bell-shaped, pink or purple or rose to nearly white, floral tube inflated, bilabiate,
upper lip 2-lobed, lower lip 3-lobed, lobes rounded, to 2+
inches long. A prairie species found throughout most of
state, lacking in far South Texas and far West Texas.

Penstemon jamesii   PLANTAGINACEAE
James's penstemon, James's beardtongue
Rocky slopes, outcrops, canyons, cliff edges,
escarpments. Spring. Uncommon.

An erect, pubescent perennial with stems to 16+ inches
tall. Leaves opposite, sessile, linear to lanceolate, to 5
inches long and ¾ inch wide, margins entire or toothed,
tips acute, blades pubescent. Flowers in terminal
racemes, bell-shaped, throat pubescent, lavender to purple, bilabiate, upper lip 2-lobed, lower lip 3-lobed, to 1
inch long. Found in mountains of Chihuahuan Desert,
north into New Mexico, east into western Edwards Plateau; New Mexico populations extend into western middle Panhandle.

Penstemon tenuis   PLANTAGINACEAE
Brazos penstemon, Gulf Coast penstemon
Coastal prairies, fields, grasslands,
marshes. Spring. Uncommon.

An erect perennial with slender, slightly pubescent stems
to 3+ feet tall. Leaves opposite, lanceolate, to 4¾ inches
long and 1 inch wide, margins toothed to entire, tips
pointed. Lower leaves sessile, upper leaves connate. Flowers in terminal racemes, bell-shaped, pink to rose or light
purple with white throats, about ½ inch wide and slightly
longer, bilabiate, upper lip 2-lobed with lobes erect, lower
lip 3-lobed with lobes rounded. Found in open, damp
areas from Coastal Bend northeast into Louisiana, historic collections farther inland.

Penstemon triflorus   PLANTAGINACEAE
Hill Country penstemon
Rocky outcrops, ledges, cliffs, woodland
openings. Spring, summer. Locally common.

An erect, slightly pubescent perennial with multiple
stems to 26+ inches tall. Leaves opposite, linear to lanceolate to ovate, to 3½ inches long and 2 inches wide, margins toothed. Lower leaves sessile, upper leaves connate.
Flowers in terminal racemes, bell-shaped, pink to rose to
red, often with white stripes along throat, bilabiate, upper
lip 2-lobed, lower lip 3-lobed, to 1½ inches long. Found
on limestone throughout Edwards Plateau, west into Chihuahuan Desert.

Ipomopsis havardii   POLEMONIACEAE
Havard's ipomopsis
Open, sparse brushlands and desert scrub.
Winter, spring, summer, fall. Uncommon.

An erect, rounded to open perennial with heavily branching stems to 20+ inches tall, both leaves and stems covered in visible, stiff, white hairs. Leaves alternate, 1- or
2-pinnate, to ¾ inch long, lobes linear, margins entire,
tips pointed. Inflorescences bilateral, trumpet-shaped
in clusters originating from tips of branches. Flowers 5-lobed, pink to white with patches of rose mottled
throughout, upper middle lobe with faint yellow spot
at base. Can bloom throughout year, after rain events.
Found in Big Bend region, also along lower slopes and
around desert washes near Rio Grande.

Ipomopsis longiflora   POLEMONIACEAE
Long-flowered ipomopsis
Open desert scrub, desert washes, rocky hillsides.
Spring, summer, fall. Locally common.

An erect, wispy biennial with glabrous to pubescent
branching stems to 3+ feet tall. Leaves alternate, deeply
lobed, threadlike to 1½ inches, surfaces glabrous or with
short pubescence. Flowers occur at tips of branches either
singly or to 3, radial, trumpet-shaped, light pink to light
blue and fading to white as they age, more than 1 inch
long and often to 2 inches. Found in gravelly to sandy
soils in West Texas, north into Panhandle.

385

Phlox glabriflora subsp. littoralis
POLEMONIACEAE
Rio Grande phlox
Coastal grasslands and prairies, open brush
and woodlands, roadsides and other open
areas. Winter, spring. Common.

An erect, pubescent, low-growing annual with branching stems to 8+ inches tall; long visible hairs on leaves, stems, and sepals. Leaves opposite below, alternate above, sessile, ribbonlike, to 3¼ inches long and ⅓ inch wide, margins entire, tips acute to pointed. Stems terminating in cymes with inflorescences. Flowers several in number, large, radial, 5-petaled, pink to purple to nearly white, lobes usually lighter or white at base with deep rose to purple center, to 1½ inches wide, tube slender to ¾ inch long. Found in open areas in South Texas, from Coastal Bend west and south into Mexico.

Phlox mesoleuca   POLEMONIACEAE
Threadleaf phlox
Open rocky slopes, open desert scrub and sparse
grasslands. Summer, fall. Locally common.

An erect, branching, glandular-pubescent perennial to 20+ inches tall. Leaves opposite, sessile, linear, 2 to 3¾ inches long and less than ¼ inch wide, margins entire, tips pointed. Inflorescences in loose, terminal cymes on pedicels to 1¾ inches long. Flowers few, pink with white center, 5-lobed, to ¾ inch long and 1 inch wide. Found in rocky to gravelly areas, often on slopes or hillsides in Chihuahuan Desert region. Similar, and closely related, to *Phlox nana*; much thinner and longer leaves of *P. mesoleuca* set it apart.

Phlox nana   POLEMONIACEAE
Dwarf phlox
Open rocky slopes, open grass, brush and woodlands,
canyons, roadsides. Summer, fall. Common.

An erect, branching, glandular-pubescent perennial with stems to 12 inches tall. Leaves opposite, sessile, elliptic to lanceolate, to 1¾ inches long and ¼ inch wide, margins entire, tips pointed. Inflorescences in loose, terminal cymes on pedicels to ¾ inch long. Flowers few, pink with a white center, 5-lobed, to ¾ inch long and 1 inch wide. Found on hillsides throughout Chihuahuan Desert east to Crockett County. Similar to *Phlox mesoleuca*, but with shorter leaves, shorter pedicels, and dense, glandular hairs throughout.

Phlox pilosa POLEMONIACEAE
Downy phlox, prairie phlox
Fields, meadows, grasslands, open brush and woodlands,
roadsides and other open areas. Spring. Common.

An erect, multistemmed, branching perennial with
stems to 24 inches tall. Leaves opposite, sessile, linear
below, lanceolate above, to 5 inches long and ⅜ inch wide,
margins entire, tips pointed. Inflorescences in terminal
panicles. Flowers numerous, 5-lobed with tips of lobes
pointed, pink, lavender to nearly white, to ¾ inch long
and 1¼ inches wide. Common throughout eastern third
of Texas and west through Edwards Plateau. Widely available in the nursery and seed trade, expected elsewhere as
this species tends to escape and persist.

Phlox roemeriana POLEMONIACEAE
Golden-eye phlox
Fields, pastures, grasslands, open shrub and woodlands,
roadsides and other open areas. Spring. Common.

An erect, branching annual, typically single-stemmed
to 15 inches tall though often only a few inches high.
Leaves oblanceolate and opposite below, lanceolate and
alternate above, to 2 inches long and ¼ inch wide, margins ciliate, tips pointed, surfaces somewhat pubescent.
Inflorescences in terminal panicles, pedicels to 1½ inches
long. Flowers 5-lobed with lobes pointed, pink or purple
or rarely white with brilliant yellow center at opening of
tube, to ½ inch long and about 1 inch wide. Common on
limestone and granitic soils of Edwards Plateau, usually
occurring in vast numbers during early spring.

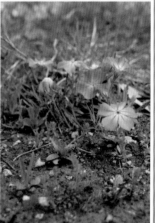

Polygala glandulosa POLYGALACEAE
Glandular milkwort
Thornscrub, open brush, gravelly hillsides and
slopes. Spring, summer. Uncommon.

An erect to ascending perennial from a woody base, with
numerous, pubescent, leafy stems to 8 inches tall. Leaves
crowded, alternate, obovate to oval, to ⅜ inch long, margins entire, tips rounded to acute, occasionally mucronate, blades visibly pubescent. Inflorescences in 1 or 2
flowered terminal racemes, lateral sepals large, spreading. Flowers pink to rose with cream-colored petals, to ⅓
inch wide with lateral wings fully open. Typically found at
bases of or hidden among shrubs in Tamaulipan Thornscrub of South Texas, occasionally in more open areas.

phlox family
POLEMONIACEAE

milkwort family
POLYGALACEAE

387

Polygala incarnata POLYGALACEAE
Procession flower
Open fields, grasslands, savannas, fields
and woodlands, bogs, roadsides and other
open areas. Spring, summer. Common.

An erect, slender annual with simple or branching, glabrous stems to 14 inches tall. Leaf arrangement variable,
opposite or whorled below, upper leaves scattered and
alternate, linear to ⅓ inch long. Stems terminating in
compact racemes to 1½ inches long. Flowers numerous,
pink to rose to purple, to ½ inch long, bilateral, crest variously lobed. Widespread in eastern third of Texas, from
lower coast north into Oklahoma, east into Louisiana.

Polygala lindheimeri POLYGALACEAE
Lindheimer's milkwort, shrubby milkwort
Open grass, brush and woodlands,
roadsides. Spring, summer. Common.

An erect to decumbent perennial with pilose stems to 8
inches tall. Leaves alternate, lower elliptic to oval, upper
obovate to lanceolate, to ½ inch long and nearly as wide,
bases rounded to obtuse, margins entire, tips acute to
obtuse and mucronate, surfaces pilose. Stems terminating in few-flowered, open racemes. Flowers usually to no
more than 8, bilateral, pink to rose to reddish purple, to
½ inch wide, lateral sepal wings spreading and obovate.
Common throughout western Edwards Plateau, south to
Starr County, west into Big Bend region and north into
Panhandle; often overlooked because of small size.

Polygala macradenia POLYGALACEAE
Purple milkwort, glandleaf milkwort
Open grass, brush and woodlands, sparse
desert scrub, rocky slopes, outcrops, ledges,
and caprock. Spring, summer. Common.

An erect to ascending, low-growing, much-branched and
multistemmed perennial with leafy, heavily canescent
stems to 8 inches long or tall. Leaves alternate, sessile,
crowded, linear-oblong to lanceolate, to ⅜ inch long and
⅛ inch wide, blades densely canescent. Inflorescences in
1 or 2 flowered terminal racemes, lateral sepals pink to
rose or purple, crest yellow, to ½ inch wide. Primarily on
limestone, from South Texas north throughout Chihuahuan Desert.

Polygala mariana   POLYGALACEAE
Maryland milkwort
Wet savannas, fields, meadows, bogs and other open areas
with damp or wet soils. Spring, summer. Locally common.

An erect, slender, single-stemmed annual, occasionally branching near top, to 16 inches, upper portion of
stem slightly pubescent. Leaves alternate, sessile, linear
above, spatulate below, to 1 inch long and ⅛ inch wide,
tips acute, pointed. Inflorescences in terminal or axillary
compact, dense racemes. Flowers light pink to pinkish
purple to rose to purple, to ¼ inch wide, bilateral, lateral
wings spreading. Found in East Texas, most common
in Southeast Texas from Montgomery County east into
Louisiana.

Polygala polygama   POLYGALACEAE
Bitter milkwort, racemed milkwort
Open woodlands, bogs and other open areas
within woodlands. Spring. Locally common.

An erect, ascending or sprawling biennial with slender,
occasionally branched, glabrous stems to 12 inches tall.
Leaves alternate, sessile, oblong to oblong-lanceolate,
to 1¼ inches long, margins entire, tips rounded and
mucronate. Inflorescences in loose, terminal racemes to
4 inches long. Flowers pink to rose or purple, ovate lateral sepals spreading. Most common in Southeast Texas,
occasional southwest to Coastal Bend and northwest to
Dallas area.

Persicaria maculosa   POLYGONACEAE
Spotted lady's thumb
Banks of waterways and bodies of water,
roadside ditches and other low, wet areas.
Spring, summer, fall. Uncommon.

An introduced, procumbent, decumbent, ascending or
erect annual with glabrous, reddish brown, branching
stems to 2+ feet long. Leaves alternate, on petioles to ⅓
inch long, lanceolate to ovate, to 4+ inches long and 1
inch wide, bases tapering, tips pointed, upper leaf surface
often with dark crescent-shaped spot. Flowers in spikes
to 2 inches long, radial, 5 tepals, rose-pink occasionally
with greenish white centers, to ¼ inch wide. Ocrea light
brown, to ⅜ inch long, ciliate with hairs about ⅛ inch
long. Widespread throughout Texas.

389

Persicaria pensylvanica   POLYGONACEAE
Pennsylvania smartweed
Banks of waterways and bodies of water, roadside ditches
and other low, wet areas. Spring, summer, fall. Common.

An ascending to erect annual with branching, glabrous
stems to 5+ feet tall. Leaves alternate, on petioles to 1
inch long, lanceolate, to 7+ inches long and 2 inches wide,
bases tapering, tips pointed, surfaces glabrous or slightly
pubescent, with or without dark patch on upper surface. Ocrea brown to tan, to ¾ inch long, papery, bristles
essentially absent. Flowers in terminal spikes to 2 inches
long, radial, rose-pink to greenish white, 5 tepals, to ¼
inch wide. Common and widespread, often weedy.

Phemeranthus longipes   PORTULACACEAE
Pink flameflower
Open, sparse, rocky shrublands.
Summer, fall. Uncommon.

An erect perennial, from a woody base, to 10 inches tall
when in flower. Basal leaves only, succulent, sessile,
cylindric, to 1 inch long. Flowers in cymes on slender
peduncles to 6 inches long. Flowers pink to white, about
⅓ inch wide, 5 petals, radial. Found in western Edwards
Plateau west to El Paso. Grows in rocky open areas with
little vegetation, such as ridges, steep slopes, and along
canyon walls, usually in conjunction with *Selaginella* and
arid-land ferns.

Portulaca pilosa   PORTULACACEAE
Hairy portulaca, pink pigweed, moss rose
Sparse, open brushlands, rocky habitats, outcrops,
roadsides and other open, disturbed areas.
Winter, spring, summer, fall. Common.

A prostrate to ascending annual with succulent, branching stems to 10 inches long. Leaves alternate, sessile,
oblong-lanceolate, cylindric or rounded on top only, to ¾
inch long and 1/10 inch wide, tips pointed, hairs at base
of leaves. Flowers occur at ends of stems surrounded by
a tuft of hairs, 5-petaled, pink to purple, to ½ inch wide.
Widespread throughout Texas with no preference to soil
type. Specific epithet means "hairy."

Clematis carrizoensis   RANUNCULACEAE
Carrizo sands leather flower, sand clematis
Open shrub and woodlands, roadsides,
fence lines. Spring, summer. Rare.

A trailing or low-climbing perennial vine with glabrous
to glaucous reddish brown stems to 9+ feet long. Leaves
pinnate with 8–10 ovate leaflets to 2¾ inches long and 2⅓
inches wide, terminal leaflet with tendril. Flower solitary,
oval to urn-shaped to 1¼ inches long, faint lilac to creamy
yellow, margins of sepals wavy. Achene with feathery
tail to just over 2 inches long. A recent addition to our
flora; limited to Carrizo Sands formation in northeastern
Texas.

Consolida ajacis   RANUNCULACEAE
Doubtful knight's spur, rocket larkspur
Roadsides, suburban and urban areas, along
railroads, vacant lots and other disturbed
areas. Summer. Uncommon.

Introduced annual to 3 feet tall, with 2 or 3 stems that are
slightly branched, stems pubescent when young and glabrous with age. Leaves alternate, round, palmately lobed
with lobes repeatedly divided, giving leaves a feathery
appearance. Flowers numerous in racemes to 12 inches
long, pinkish purple or blue or violet, 2 inches in diameter on pedicels about 1 inch long. Introduced from Eurasia, widespread escapee across United States and elsewhere. Common in wildflower seed mixes.

Houstonia purpurea   RUBIACEAE
Venus' pride, purple bluet
Open woodlands. Spring. Rare.

An erect to ascending perennial with single or multiple
pubescent stems to 12 inches tall. Leaves opposite, sessile,
ovate to lanceolate, to 2 inches long and 1 inch wide, bases
rounded to cordate, margins entire, tips acute. Flowers in
terminal or axillary cymes. Flowers funnel-shaped, pale
pinkish purple to white, 4-lobed, about ¼ inch wide and
as long. Common in eastern United States but rare in
Texas, currently known from Newton County, on border
of Louisiana.

Houstonia rosea   RUBIACEAE
Rose bluet
Fields, pastures, prairies, maintained lawns,
roadsides. Winter, spring. Uncommon.

A low-growing, spreading, rarely erect annual to 5 inches
long when spreading. Leaves opposite, sessile, spatulate,
to ½ inch long, bases tapering, margins entire, tips acute.
Flowers terminal, trumpet-shaped, pink, large compared
to plant, to ¼ inch long and ⅜ inch wide. Found in eastern third of Texas, from Coastal Bend north into Oklahoma, east into Louisiana.

Sherardia arvensis   RUBIACEAE
Blue field-madder, spurwort
Pastures, fields, open brushlands, roadsides
and other open areas. Spring. Uncommon.

An introduced, prostrate or decumbent annual with
glabrous, 4-angled, simple or branching and spreading
stems to 16 inches long. Leaves whorled, sessile, obovate
to elliptic, to ¾ inch long, margins entire and with short
prickles, tips acute. Inflorescences in clustered terminal
heads, lanceolate bracts just below heads. Flowers typically 4–8 per head, trumpet-shaped, lavender to blue,
4-lobed, to ¼ inch wide. Frequent in Southeast Texas and
Houston area, less common farther north into Oklahoma
and west to Gillespie County, expected elsewhere.

Datura quercifolia   SOLANACEAE
Oak-leaf datura, oak-leaf thorn-apple
Canyons, washes, creek bottoms, drainages, roadsides
and other low areas. Spring, summer, fall. Common.

An erect annual with a single, branching stem to 5 feet
tall and nearly as wide, glabrous to slightly pubescent
leaves and stems. Leaves ovate, to 6½ inches long and
4 inches wide, deeply lobed, bases cordate or cuneate,
margins toothed. Flowers occur in upper leaf axils,
funnel-shaped, light purple, about 3 inches long. Spiny
fruits remain erect as they mature. Plant has a slight
burnt-rubber odor, unpleasant. Typically found in disturbed areas such as mountain drainages in Chihuahuan
Desert.

Bouchea linifolia VERBENACEAE
Linear-leaf bouchea, flaxleaf bouchea, groovestem bouchea
Open limestone slopes, canyons,
drainages. Summer. Uncommon.

An erect, shrubby, leafy perennial with branching, glabrous, ridged stems to 3 feet. Leaves opposite, sessile,
linear to lanceolate, to 1¾ inches long, bases narrowed,
margins entire, tips acute. Flowers in terminal spikes
to 6 inches long, not crowded, trumpet-shaped, pink to
purple, 5-lobed with wavy lobe margins, to ¾ inch wide
and as long. Uncommon to rare on limestone in western
Edwards Plateau west to Presidio County; also found in
El Paso.

Glandularia bipinnatifida VERBENACEAE
Prairie verbena, Dakota vervain, purple prairie verbena
Fields, prairies, pastures, grasslands, open
shrub and woodlands, roadsides and other open
areas. Spring, summer, fall. Common.

An ascending perennial branching from base and rooting at nodes with pubescent stems to 20 inches, often
forming rounded clumps. Leaves opposite, bipinnate
to tri-pinnate with ultimate lobes again divided, to 3
inches long including petiole, lobes linear to oblong,
bases tapering, margins revolute or entire, tips acute,
blade surfaces pubescent. Stems terminating in crowded,
rounded spikes, elongating throughout season. Flowers
trumpet-shaped, 5-lobed with lobes unequal, deep pink
to lavender or purple and changing color as they age,
flowers to ⅜ inch wide. Absent west of Pecos County, in
deep East Texas, and most of South Texas.

Glandularia canadensis VERBENACEAE
Rose vervain, rose mock vervain
Fields, grasslands, open woodlands and forests, roadsides
and other open areas. Spring, summer. Common.

An ascending to decumbent perennial, rooting at nodes,
with glabrous to pubescent branching stems to 24+
inches tall. Leaves opposite, ovate to lanceolate, pinnatifid and further divided, to 3 inches long and as wide,
ultimate margins dentate and ciliate, lobe tips acute,
blades pubescent. Stems terminating in spikes to 6
inches long and 2½ inches wide. Flowers numerous,
trumpet-shaped, 5-lobed with lobes unequal, rose or lavender or purple, to ½ inch wide. Common throughout
East Texas.

Glandularia pulchella   VERBENACEAE
South American mock vervain, moss verbena
Fields, meadows, urban and suburban areas, roadsides
and other open areas. Spring, summer. Locally common.

An introduced, decumbent annual to perennial with
branching, pubescent stems to 24 inches, flowering portion of stems ascending. Leaves opposite, sessile, triangular, primary lobes 1- or 2-pinnatifid, to 1½ inches long
and 1¼ inches wide, bases tapering, margins revolute
or entire, tips acute, surfaces pubescent with prominent veins on upper surface. Flowers in terminal spikes
elongating to 1¾ inches throughout season, numerous,
trumpet-shaped, 5-lobed with one lobe larger than others,
pink to lavender to purple with white centers and fading
to a light blue, to ⅜ inch wide. Introduced in Southeast
and far South Texas as well as other urban areas throughout Texas.

Glandularia pumila   VERBENACEAE
Pink vervain, pink mock vervain, dwarf vervain
Fields, grasslands, prairies, open shrub and woodlands,
rocky outcrops, hillsides, roadsides and other
open areas. Winter, spring, summer. Common.

An ascending to decumbent annual with multiple
branching stems from a central base to 12 inches tall,
stems reddish brown and pubescent. Leaves opposite,
on short petioles, triangular, to 1¼ inches long, blades
3-parted, lobes divided or lobed or cut, bases truncate,
margins revolute and wavy and occasionally entire. Flowers in terminal compact spikes, trumpet-shaped, 5-lobed
with lobes unequal, pink to purple, to ¼ inch wide. Common throughout eastern three-fourths of state.

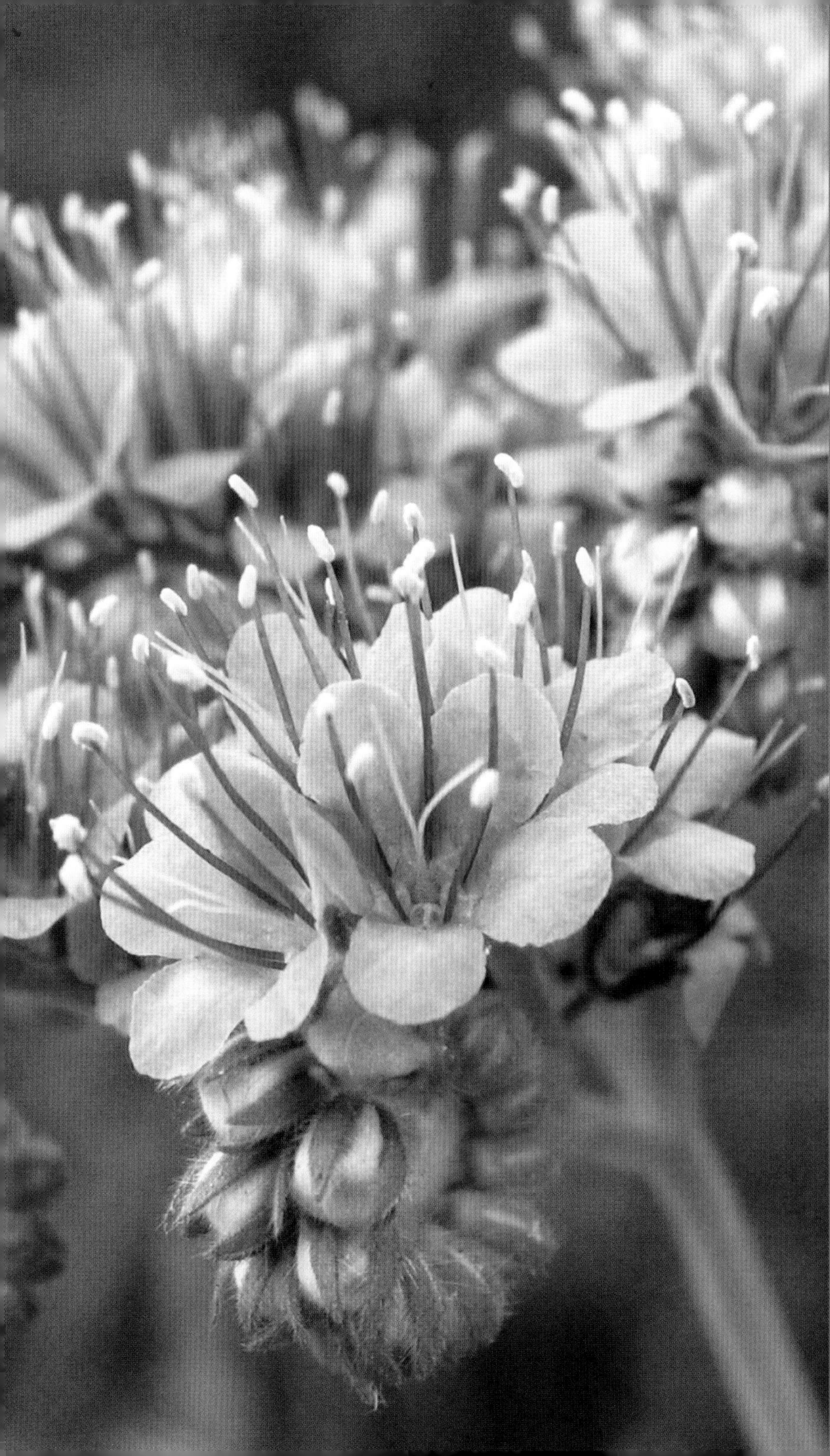

Carlowrightia linearifolia ACANTHACEAE
Heath wrightwort, linear-leaf wrightwort
Gravelly soils along washes, arroyos, and other drainages. Spring, summer, fall. Locally common.

A heavily branched perennial to just over 3 feet tall, usually half that size. Leaves opposite, linear, to 1¼ inches long, surfaces rough to the touch. Flowers in panicles, bluish purple, about ½ inch in diameter, bilabiate, most often appearing after rains. Found in Chihuahuan Desert region, usually in limestone soils, but grows on igneous rock as well.

Carlowrightia serpyllifolia ACANTHACEAE
Trans-Pecos wrightwort
Rocky slopes, hillsides, cliffs and ledges, canyons, among boulders and other rocky areas. Summer. Uncommon.

An erect, shrubby perennial with heavily branched stems to 12+ inches tall. Stems and leaves glandular pubescent. Leaves opposite, on short petioles, oblong lanceolate to ovate, to ¾ inch long and less than ¼ inch wide, bases tapering, margins entire, tips pointed. Flowers purple-blue to pinkish purple, bilateral, in terminal spikes and in upper leaf axils, 4-lobed, upper lobe erect with streaks in center leading into tube, lateral wings spreading, much larger than other lobes, lower lobe curved. Found in Chihuahuan Desert. Currently known from El Paso, Presidio, and Brewster Counties.

Dyschoriste linearis ACANTHACEAE
Snake herb, narrowleaf dyschoriste, polkadots
Open grasslands, rocky slopes, open brushlands. Spring, summer. Common.

A rhizomatous, erect, sometimes relaxed perennial to 18 inches. Leaves opposite, linear to oblong, to 2½ inches long, margins entire. Flowers purple, 5-lobed, to ½ inch in diameter, in axils along stem. Found throughout most of state, aside from East Texas and upper Panhandle.

Justicia pilosella ACANTHACEAE
Hairy tube-tongue, false honeysuckle, Gregg's tube-tongue
Brushlands, edges of waterways, woodland
edges. Spring, summer, fall. Common.

An erect or ascending perennial to 16 inches tall, branching from a semiwoody base. Leaves ovate to oval, to 1½
inches long and ½ inch wide. Flowers purple to white,
usually solitary, about 1 inch long and half as wide, with
a distinctly 3-lobed lower lip which is larger than notched
upper lip. Found in Central, South, and West Texas,
growing in various habitats and preferring protection
from woody shrubs.

Ruellia caroliniensis ACANTHACEAE
Carolina wild petunia
Woodlands, thickets, open prairies, meadows.
Spring, summer, fall. Common.

An erect perennial to 36 inches tall, stems typically covered in fine hairs. Lower leaves are obovate; middle and
upper leaves oval or elliptic or lanceolate or ovate. Flowers resemble petunias, are purple, sometimes white, to
2 inches long and 1 inch wide, in upper axils of leaves
in clusters to 4, opening in morning and falling by early
afternoon. Found in open woods, woodland edges, and
open areas in East Texas.

Ruellia nudiflora ACANTHACEAE
Wild petunia, violet wild petunia, common wild petunia
Meadows, fields, brushlands, woodlands.
Winter, spring, summer, fall. Common.

An erect perennial herb to 2 feet tall, usually half that
height, from a woody base. Both stems and leaves are covered in fine hairs. Leaves may be on short petioles, elliptic, to 2½ inches long, margins undulate to dentate. Flowers purple to lavender, 5-lobed, to 2 inches in diameter
and just over 2 inches long, in leaf axils, opening during
early morning and falling by afternoon. Widespread
throughout South and Central Texas, extending west to
Brewster County. Absent in far western Texas and Panhandle. Found in various habitats, but seems to prefer
shadier areas where overstory provides protection.

Ruellia parryi   ACANTHACEAE
Parry's ruellia, Parry's wild petunia
Limestone outcrops, cliffs, rocky slopes.
Spring, summer, fall. Common.

A small perennial, to 16 inches tall, with branching stems
that become woody with age. Leaves small, oval, to ¾
inch long and just over ⅓ inch wide, margins with obvious hairs, shorter hairs found elsewhere. Flowers in leaf
axils, 5-lobed, to 1½ inches long and about 1 inch wide.
Found in Chihuahuan Desert region, usually in harsh,
exposed conditions. Named in honor of Charles Christopher Parry (1823–1890), a British American botanist who
worked on the United States and Mexican Boundary Survey (1848–1855).

Allium cernuum   AMARYLLIDACEAE
Nodding onion, drooping onion
Mountain woodlands and forests. Summer. Uncommon.

A perennial from several bulbs, typically with a short rhizome, to 20 inches tall. Leaves ¼ inch wide, about half as
long as scape, flat to concave to deeply V-shaped in cross
section. Scape to 20 inches tall, gives rise to nodding,
loose umbel with to 35 blue or pink or white urn-shaped
flowers ¼ inch in diameter. Found in upper elevations of
West Texas. Most easily seen in flower during mid to late
summer in Chisos and Guadalupe Mountains.

Eryngium hookeri   APIACEAE
Hooker's eryngo
Grasslands, fields, prairies, open brush and
woodlands, roadsides. Summer, fall. Common.

An erect, slender annual with branching stems to 24
inches tall. Basal leaves oblong-lanceolate, to 3¾ inches
long and 1¼ inches wide, margins serrate to dentate.
Stem leaves alternate, sessile, lanceolate, margins toothed
and spiny. Upper leaves ovate, 5–7 palmate, to 1⅓ inches
long, lobes spiny. Flowering heads terminal, oval, to ¾
inch wide, bluish purple tinged, narrow, spiny bracts
below. Found in Southeast Texas, north into Oklahoma,
east into Louisiana.

Eryngium leavenworthii APIACEAE

Leavenworth's eryngo

Fields, grasslands, prairies, open brush and woodlands, roadsides and other open areas. Summer. Common.

An erect, branching perennial with glabrous, slender stems to 3+ feet tall. Lower leaves alternate, nearly sessile, oblanceolate, to 2½ inches long and ¾ inch wide, margins entire, tips pointed. Upper leaves opposite, ovate, palmate, tips spiny, blades rigid. Flowering heads large, terminal, to 1½ inches long and 1 inch wide, bluish purple to purple, bracts below, rigid, with 3–7 teeth. Found in Edwards Plateau, west into Brewster County, north into Oklahoma, occasionally in lower Panhandle and Southeast Texas.

Eryngium prostratum APIACEAE

Prostrate eryngium

Prairies, grasslands, fields, open woodlands. Spring, summer. Common.

A prostrate to ascending perennial with glabrous, slender, branching stems to 28+ inches tall. Basal leaves petiolate, ovate to lanceolate, to 2 inches long and 1 inch wide, simple or palmately lobed, margins entire to dentate. Upper leaves similar to basal, smaller and sessile. Flowering heads originating from axils, light blue, oval to cylindric, to ⅜ inch long and less than ¼ inch wide, bracts lanceolate, to ½ inch long, lacking spiny tips or lobes. Found in eastern third of Texas, in wet or damp soils.

Amsonia ciliata APOCYNACEAE

Bluestar, Texas bluestar, fringed bluestar

Grasslands, fields, open brush and woodlands. Spring, summer. Common.

An erect, multistemmed, clumping perennial to 2 feet tall. Leaves alternate, sessile or on short petioles in upper leaves, lanceolate to linear or threadlike, to 3¼ inches long and ⅜ inch wide, margins entire. Numerous light blue, star-shaped flowers atop a trumpet-shaped corolla, each to ½ inch wide, occur in a thyrse and barely exceed the leaves. Found in Edwards Plateau, north into Panhandle and Oklahoma. Specific epithet means "fringed with hairs," referring to pubescent calyx lobes and bracts.

carrot family
APIACEAE

dogbane family
APOCYNACEAE

399

APOCYNACEAE
dogbane family

ASPARAGACEAE
asparagus family

ASTERACEAE
sunflower family

Amsonia tabernaemontana   APOCYNACEAE
Bluestar, blue dogbane, willow amsonia
Open brush and woodlands, prairies, river and creek
banks, bottomlands. Spring, summer. Common.

An erect, clumping, multistemmed perennial with stems
to 3 feet tall. Leaves alternate, on short petioles, ovate to
lanceolate, to 6 inches long and 2 inches wide, margins
entire. Numerous light blue, star-shaped flowers atop a
trumpet-shaped corolla, about ½ inch wide, occur in a
thyrse, barely exceeding leaves. Found in eastern third
of state, from coast north into Oklahoma, east into Louisiana. Usually grows in sandy soils. Genus name honors
Charles Amson, an 18th-century American physician.
Specific epithet means "mountain cottage."

Muscari neglectum   ASPARAGACEAE
Common grape hyacinth
Fields, old homesteads, urban and suburban
areas, roadsides. Spring. Uncommon.

An introduced, erect, bulbous perennial with glabrous
stems to 12+ inches tall. Basal leaves thick, grasslike, linear, to 12 inches long and ⅓ inch wide, ribbed. Scape to 10
inches tall, extending beyond leaves. Flowers in crowded
racemes, 20–40 per raceme, urn-shaped, drooping, dark
blue-purple with white margins, less than ¼ inch long. A
common escapee from gardens, usually spreading locally,
occasionally found in somewhat remote areas. Bulbs persist in and are transported in soil, so expect to see plants
along roadways. Found in North-Central Texas and eastern Edwards Plateau; expect elsewhere.

Carduus nutans   ASTERACEAE
Musk thistle, nodding thistle
Overgrazed pastures, fields, grasslands, river
bottoms, roadsides and other disturbed areas.
Spring, summer. Locally common.

An introduced, erect annual or biennial with winged,
toothed stems to 5+ feet tall. Basal leaves lanceolate, pinnatifid, to 12 inches long and 4 inches wide, margins
with yellow spines. Stem leaves alternate, sessile, lanceolate to elliptic, pinnatifid, to 6 inches long and 1½ inches
wide, margins spine-tipped. Flowering heads solitary or
in corymbs, at ends of stems, to 3 inches wide, nodding,
disc florets numerous (to 1000 per head), purple. Noxious
weed found throughout Texas, mostly in Central to West
Texas.

Carduus pycnocephalus ASTERACEAE
Italian thistle, slender thistle
Overgrazed pastures, fields, creek and river
bottoms, roadsides and other disturbed areas.
Spring, summer. Locally common.

An introduced, erect annual or biennial with spiny,
winged stems to 4+ feet tall. Basal leaves lanceolate to
elliptic, pinnatifid, to 10 inches long and 4 inches wide,
margins with spines, veins milky white, lower side of leaf
grayish white pubescent, upper leaves smaller. Flowering heads in small clusters at ends of stems, occasionally
solitary, each head to ¾ inch wide and about 1 inch long,
ray florets absent, disc florets numerous, purple-pink.
Primarily found in Central Texas, from Val Verde County
northeast into the Dallas–Fort Worth area.

Centaurea cyanus ASTERACEAE
Bachelor's button, cornflower, blue-poppy
Grasslands, fields, meadows, brush and
woodlands, roadsides and other disturbed
areas. Spring, summer. Uncommon.

An erect, introduced annual, typically single-stemmed,
branching to 3 feet tall. Basal leaves lanceolate, to 4
inches, margins entire, surfaces slightly woolly. Stem
leaves linear, to 4 inches, margins entire. Flowering
heads in cymes, with to 35 blue florets, outer florets longer, raylike, heads about 2 inches wide. Found in Central
and East Texas; species is included in wildflower mixes
and is intentionally spread.

Chromolaena odorata ASTERACEAE
Crucita, blue mistflower, Christmas bush
Thickets, palm groves, creek bottoms, woodland
edges. Spring, summer, fall. Common.

An erect to sprawling perennial with a single stem,
much-branched throughout to 6+ feet tall. Leaves opposite, lanceolate to deltate to ovate, to 4 inches long and 1½
inches wide, margins dentate to slightly entire. Flowering
heads in corymbs, as few as 5 or more than 50 heads per
inflorescence, each head less than ½ inch wide, with light
blue disc florets, ray florets absent. Found in deep South
Texas, northeast to Orange County, in thickets and low
areas along the Texas coast.

401

Cirsium carolinianum ASTERACEAE
Carolina thistle
Open shrub and woodlands, fields, roadsides and
other open areas. Spring, summer. Uncommon.

An erect biennial to perennial, typically with a single
stem, slightly pubescent, branching above to 5+ feet tall.
Leaves alternate, upper leaves on short petioles to sessile, lower leaves on petioles 6 inches long, linear-oblong,
slightly lobed, to 6 inches long and ¾ inch wide, margins
with spines. Flowering heads solitary or 10+ in loose panicles at ends of stems, each head about 1¾ inches wide
and about 1¼ inches tall, ray flowers absent, disc florets
numerous, purple to pink, occasionally white. Found sporadically in eastern third of state.

Cirsium horridulum ASTERACEAE
Bastard thistle, horrid thistle, bristly thistle
Fields, meadows, pastures, prairies,
grasslands, open shrublands, roadsides and
other open areas. Spring. Common.

An erect biennial or perennial with single or multiple stout, branching stems to 6 feet tall. Leaves alternate, linear to oblanceolate to elliptic, to 16 inches
long and 4 inches wide, lobed or unlobed, margins
dentate to pinnatifid, with spines. Flowering heads either
single or to 20 in corymbs, each head to 4 inches wide,
disc florets purple to reddish or yellow, ray florets absent.
Formidable plant found throughout eastern Texas, south
into southern Texas, and into Edwards Plateau.

Cirsium ochrocentrum ASTERACEAE
Yellowspine thistle
Prairies, grasslands, fields, pastures, open
brush and woodlands, roadsides and other
open areas. Spring, summer. Common.

An erect perennial with one or several stems, to 3 feet
tall, usually unbranched, stems densely tomentose.
Leaves alternate, elliptic to oblanceolate, pinnately lobed,
margins coarsely dentate, undulate, tips of lobes with
yellow spines to ¾+ inch long. Leaves of middle to upper
stem drooping. Flowering heads solitary or few, in corymbs held above lower leaves, on peduncles to 2 inches
long, disc florets numerous, purple to lavender, sometimes white, to 3+ inches wide, ray flowers absent. Found
throughout Central Texas, north into Panhandle and
Oklahoma, west into New Mexico and northern Mexico.

Cirsium texanum   ASTERACEAE

Texas thistle, purple thistle, southern thistle
Grasslands, prairies, pastures, fields, open brush and
woodlands, roadsides. Spring, summer. Common.

An erect annual or biennial, with single, branching,
tomentose stem to 6 feet tall. Leaves oblong to elliptic, to
12 inches long and 4½ inches wide, becoming smaller
up the stem, unlobed to lobed, margins dentate, spines
along margins, or on tips of lobes. Flowering heads single
or to 10 in panicles to 12 inches long, each head about 2½
inches wide and 2 inches tall, disc florets numerous, purple to pink, occasionally white, ray florets absent. Found
in open areas throughout state; absent in northern Panhandle, far eastern and far western Texas.

Cirsium undulatum   ASTERACEAE

Gray thistle, wavyleaf thistle, plumed thistle
Prairies, fields, meadows, open brush and
woodlands, roadsides and other open areas.
Spring, summer, fall. Common.

An erect perennial with single or multiple branching,
tomentose stems to 3+ feet tall. Leaves alternate, elliptic to ovate, to 16 inches long and 4 inches wide, margins
undulate and dentate or lobed with yellow spines to ½
inch. Flowering heads either solitary or to 10+ in corymbs, each head 2 inches tall and as wide, disc florets
numerous, purple to pink to lavender, occasionally white,
ray florets absent. Found in Central Texas, north into
Panhandle and Oklahoma, west into New Mexico and
northern Mexico.

Cirsium vulgare   ASTERACEAE

Bull thistle, spear thistle, common thistle
Grasslands, prairies, pastures, open brush and
woodlands, fallow fields, roadsides and other open,
disturbed areas. Spring, summer, fall. Locally common.

An introduced, erect biennial with either single or multiple stems to 6 feet tall, stems branching, villose. Leaves
alternate, lanceolate to obovate, to 16 inches long and 6
inches wide, deeply pinnatifid, lobes spine-tipped, final
margins revolute or ciliate or somewhat dentate, upper
surfaces of leaves with spines. Flowering heads in terminal corymbs, each head 2 inches wide, purple to
light purple, disc florets numerous, ray florets absent.
Currently known from southeastern Edwards Plateau,
North-Central Texas, and Brazoria County.

403

Conoclinium betonicifolium ASTERACEAE
Betony-leaf mistflower
Coastal dunes and beaches, edges of creeks and
lakes, marshes. Spring, summer, fall. Common.

A procumbent or decumbent perennial with stems, rooting at nodes, to 3 feet. Leaves opposite, on petioles about
one-third the length of blade, oblong-lanceolate to ovate
to triangular, to 2+ inches long, bases cordate to truncate,
margins crenate to dentate. Flowering heads in dense
corymbs, each head less than ¼ inch wide, disc florets
numerous, light blue. Found in sandy soils along lower
coast, inland to Val Verde County.

Conoclinium coelestinum ASTERACEAE
Blue mistflower, blue boneset, mistflower
Stream and river banks, edges of lakes,
floodplains, woodlands, coastal sands and other
wet areas. Spring, summer, fall. Common.

An erect to decumbent or procumbent, rhizomatous
perennial with stems to 3 feet tall, rooting at nodes.
Leaves opposite, on petioles ¾ inch long, triangular to
deltate to ovate, to 4 inches long, bases cuneate to truncate, margins serrate to dentate to crenate. Flowering
heads in dense corymbs, each head to ¼ inch broad, disc
florets numerous, light blue to violet. Widespread in various habitats throughout eastern third of Texas, south into
Mexico.

Conoclinium dissectum (*C. greggii*)
ASTERACEAE
Gregg's mistflower, palmleaf mistflower
Grasslands, prairies, fields, open brush
and woodlands, roadsides and other open
areas. Spring, summer, fall. Common.

An erect, rhizomatous perennial with stems to 3+ feet
tall, forming small colonies. Leaves opposite, on short
petioles to sessile, deltate to ovate, 3- to 5-lobed, lobes
heavily dissected or toothed, margins entire. Flowering
heads in terminal corymbs, typically just a few inches in
diameter, disk florets numerous, to ¼ inch long, ray florets absent. Found from central South Texas west to El
Paso. Grows in more arid habitats than other *Conoclinium*
species found in Texas.

Elephantopus carolinianus ASTERACEAE
Carolina elephantsfoot, leafy elephantsfoot
Pine or mixed pine forests and woodlands.
Summer, fall. Common.

An erect to ascending perennial with pubescent to glabrous stems to 3+ feet tall. Leaves alternate, sessile, ovate
to lanceolate to elliptic, to 8 inches long and 3½ inches
wide, margins dentate to crenate, surfaces pubescent.
Flowering heads solitary or in terminal clusters held just
above leafy, deltate to lanceolate bracts, heads about 1
inch wide, 4 disc florets per head, light purple. Found in
wooded areas in eastern third of Texas. Grows in wet or
damp sandy soils.

Elephantopus nudatus ASTERACEAE
Smooth elephantsfoot
Open areas or edges in pine or mixed pine forests
and woodlands. Summer, fall. Uncommon.

An erect perennial with mostly basal leaves and slender branching stem to 3+ feet tall. Leaves oblanceolate to
spatulate, to 7+ inches long and 1½ inches wide, margins
entire, leaf surfaces pilose. Flowering heads terminal,
either solitary or in small clusters, held just above leafy,
deltate to lanceolate bracts, heads about 1 inch wide with
5± purple disc florets, ray florets absent. Found in pine
woodlands and forests of Southeast Texas. Similar to *Ele-
phantopus tomentosus*, which is smaller and has densely
pilose lower leaf surfaces and cordate flower bracts.

Eurybia hemispherica ASTERACEAE
**Southern prairie aster, single-stemmed bog aster,
Tennessee aster**
Prairies, meadows, pastures, open woodlands,
roadsides. Summer, fall. Common.

An erect, rhizomatous perennial with branching, reddish
brown stems to 3 feet tall, stems solitary or few. Lower
leaves alternate, petiolate, lanceolate-ovate to linear, to 6
inches long and ½ inch wide, margins entire to weakly
dentate, occasionally revolute, tips acute to obtuse. Upper
leaves similar, smaller, sessile to clasping. Flowering
heads solitary or numerous in spikelike racemes, heads to
1½+ inches wide, 15–30 purple-blue ray florets, to 80+ yellow disc florets. Found throughout eastern third of Texas,
occasionally in small colonies.

405

Liatris acidota   ASTERACEAE

Gulf Coast gayfeather, sharp gayfeather, sharp blazing star
Coastal prairies, wet savannas and pine flats, roadside
ditches and other low, wet areas. Summer, fall. Common.

An erect perennial from a globose corm, with glabrous
stems to 3+ feet tall. Leaves linear to oblanceolate, 3–5
nerves, lower leaves to 15 inches long and ¼ inch wide,
becoming smaller farther up stem, margins entire,
blades glabrous. Flowering heads in dense spikes, with
4± dark purple florets per head. Found from Coastal Bend
northeast into Louisiana. Specific epithet means "sharp
point," possibly referring to pointed leaves.

Liatris aspera   ASTERACEAE

Rough liatris, rough gayfeather, rough blazing star
Prairies, plains, fields, open brush and
woodlands. Summer, fall. Common.

An erect perennial from a globose corm, with rough,
pubescent stems to nearly 5+ feet tall. Leaves oblanceolate to elliptic or lance-spatulate to lance-linear, to 10
inches long and 1 inch wide, 1-nerved, becoming smaller
up stem, margins revolute to entire, blades glabrous or
with rough hairs. Flowering heads well-spaced in spikes,
18–24 dark purple to lavender or pink florets per head.
Found in eastern third of Texas, in open fields and prairies. Specific epithet means "rough," referring to hairs on
leaves and stems.

Liatris elegans   ASTERACEAE

Elegant gayfeather, pinkscale
Fields, meadows, grasslands, open brush
and woodlands, dunes, roadsides and other
open areas. Summer. Common.

An erect perennial from a corm, with hirsute stems to 4+
feet tall. Leaves alternate, sessile, oblanceolate, to 8 inches
long and ⅓ inch wide, becoming smaller up stem, margins entire, tips pointed. Flowering heads numerous and
crowded, in terminal spikes, each head with 4 or 5 florets.
Phyllaries petal-like, purple, pink, white, or yellow, lanceolate, spreading. Found in sandy soils in various habitats
throughout eastern third of Texas, southwest to Lower
Rio Grande Valley.

Liatris glandulosa   ASTERACEAE
Sticky gayfeather, sticky liatris
Rocky outcrops, open brush and woodlands.
Summer, fall. Uncommon.

An erect perennial from a corm, with glandular stems to
2 feet tall. Leaves linear to lanceolate, to 4½ inches long
and 1¾ inches wide, becoming smaller above; 1-nerved,
margins revolute; surfaces with glandular hairs. Flowering heads in dense spikes, each head with 3 or 4 purple to
lavender florets. Endemic to Texas and found in just a few
counties from Travis north to Dallas County, usually on
exposed limestone soils.

Liatris punctata var. *mexicana*
ASTERACEAE
Mexican blazing star
Grasslands, fields, meadows, open brushlands,
roadsides and other open areas. Summer. Uncommon.

An erect, somewhat rhizomatous perennial from an
elongated corm, with glabrous stems to nearly 3 feet tall.
Leaves linear, lower leaves to 5 inches long and ¼ inch
wide, becoming smaller farther up stem, margins entire
to ciliate. Flowering heads widely spaced in terminal
spikes, stem visible between heads, each head with 3–8
purple to lavender to white florets. Found in West Texas,
mostly west of Pecos River. Tends to prefer rocky soils on
open slopes. One of 3 varieties in Texas; not as common
as others.

Liatris punctata var. *mucronata*
ASTERACEAE
Cusp blazing star, gayfeather, liatris
Prairies, fields, meadows, open brush and woodlands,
roadsides and other open areas. Summer, fall. Common.

An erect perennial from a globose corm, with glabrous
stems to nearly 3 feet tall. Leaves linear, lower leaves to
5½ inches long and ¼ inch wide, reduced farther up
stem, margins entire to ciliate. Flowering heads in dense
to loose spikes, each head with 3–8 purple to lavender to
white florets. Both var. *mucronata* (corms globose) and
var. *punctata* (corms elongate to rhizomatous) have dense,
crowded spikes, but former is generally found on eastern
edge of Edwards Plateau and farther east, while latter is
widespread throughout remainder of state.

407

Liatris pycnostachya   ASTERACEAE
Cat-tail gayfeather, cat-tail blazing star, prairie gayfeather
Wet prairies and savannas, woodlands, riparian
areas, bogs, roadsides. Summer, fall. Common.

An erect perennial from corms, with glabrous to densely
pubescent stems to 4+ feet tall. Leaves linear to oblanceolate, to 8½ inches long and 4 inches wide, becoming
smaller farther up stem, each leaf with 3–5 veins, surfaces glabrous or pubescent. Flowering heads in dense
spikes, each head with 5–8 purple to lavender to pink
florets. Found throughout eastern third of state, south to
Coastal Bend.

Plectocephalus americanus
(*Centaurea americana*)   ASTERACEAE
Basket flower, American basket flower, star-thistle
Prairies, fields, grasslands, open shrub
and woodlands, roadsides and other open
areas. Spring, summer. Common.

An erect annual, typically with one branching stem to
5 feet tall. Basal leaves oblanceolate to obovate, sessile
or winged-petiolate, to 8 inches long, margins entire to
toothed. Upper leaves sessile, lanceolate to ovate, to 4
inches long, margins entire to serrate. Flowering heads
to 5 inches wide, outer florets purple to light blue or pink,
inner florets cream to pink. Found throughout Texas;
weak in East Texas, though occurs in vast populations
during wet years.

Rhaponticum repens (*Acroptilon repens*)
ASTERACEAE
Hardheads, Russian knapweed
Canal banks, ditches, roadsides, railroad rights-of-way and
other disturbed areas. Spring, summer, fall. Uncommon.

An introduced, erect, rhizomatous, bushy perennial
with heavily branched stems to 24 inches. Basal leaves
oblong, to 6 inches long, margins dentate to lobed. Upper
leaves alternate, sessile, linear-lanceolate to oblong, to
2¾ inches long, margins entire, tips acute, surfaces usually rough. Flowering heads in terminal corymbs, florets
bluish purple to pink, to 36 florets per head, each head to
1 inch long and ¾ inch wide. Spreading in Chihuahuan
Desert, currently known from Pecos County west to Hudspeth County.

Silybum marianum   ASTERACEAE
Blessed milk thistle, Mediterranean milk thistle, Scotch thistle
Agricultural fields, pastures, roadsides and other disturbed areas. Winter, spring, summer. Uncommon.

An erect, introduced annual to biennial, with a single, unbranched, spiny stem. Basal leaves petioled, lobed, to 2 feet long, margins spiny, blades with white venation. Upper leaves similar to basal leaves, but with clasping bases and progressively smaller. Flowering heads solitary, radial, discoid, to 1½ inches wide, disc florets numerous, purple to purplish red; phyllaries ovate, to 1½ inches long, ends spiny, tannish brown at the tips. Found in the central portion of Texas; cultivated for both medicinal uses and as an ornamental.

Tamaulipa azurea   ASTERACEAE
Blue boneset, tamaulipa, blueweed
Shrublands, palm groves. Winter, spring. Uncommon.

An upright, leggy, shrubby perennial with branching stems to 8+ feet tall, the plants often growing within and on other plants. Leaves opposite, deltate, to 2 inches long and 1¾ inches wide, bases truncate to rounded-tapered, margins toothed, tips acute, upper surface of leaves wrinkled. Flowering heads discoid in terminal corymbs, to ¼ inch wide, to 50 light blue to lavender disc florets. Found in far South Texas in Hidalgo, Cameron, and Willacy Counties, usually seen on edges of thickets and within prickly pear stands.

Vernonia baldwinii   ASTERACEAE
Ironweed, Baldwin's ironweed, western ironweed
Grasslands, prairies, woodland and forest margins. Summer, fall. Common.

An erect, unbranched perennial to 5 feet tall; stems and leaves covered in soft hairs. Leaves mostly on upper stem, elliptic to lanceolate, to 7 inches long and 3 inches wide, margins heavily toothed. Flowering heads in terminal corymbs, each head consisting of numerous purple florets. Found throughout Central Texas, east into Louisiana, and north into Oklahoma, typically in wooded areas along creeks and drainages (especially in shaded areas), although noted in open areas, too. Genus name honors William Vernon, an English botanist who collected in North America in 1698. Species namesake William Baldwin (1779–1819) was an American botanist and physician.

409

Vernonia gigantea   ASTERACEAE
Giant ironweed, tall ironweed
River and creek banks, floodplains and other
riparian areas. Summer, fall. Rare.

An erect perennial to 8 feet tall; stems covered in soft
hairs. Leaves lanceolate, primarily along the upper stem,
to 10 inches long and 4 inches wide, margins toothed,
lower portions of leaf may be scabrous. Flowering heads
in terminal corymbs, held above foliage, with each head
consisting of numerous purple florets. Collected a few
times in Southeast Texas and once in Coastal Bend, but
quite common outside Texas, from Great Lakes south to
Gulf Coast. Specific epithet refers to size of species.

Vernonia larseniae   ASTERACEAE
Larsen's ironweed, Sanderson ironweed
Limestone washes, canyon beds, creek banks
and other low areas where seasonal runoff
collects. Summer, fall. Locally common.

An erect, single to multistemmed perennial to 4 feet tall.
Stems and leaves covered in soft, woolly hairs. Leaves linear, to 4 inches long and ¼ inch wide, margins entire.
Flowering heads in terminal corymbs, crowded or loose,
many or few, each head consisting of 50+ purple florets.
Found in Brewster, Pecos, and Terrell Counties in West
Texas. Specific epithet honors Esther Louise Larsen, a
botanist who originally described this species as *Verno-
nia lindheimeri* var. *leucophylla* in the late 1920s.

Vernonia lindheimeri   ASTERACEAE
Lindheimer's ironweed, woolly ironweed
Rocky hillsides, roadcuts, other open areas with
exposed limestone soils. Summer, fall. Common.

An erect, multistemmed perennial to 3 feet tall. Stems
and leaves woolly to the touch. Leaves mostly along stem,
linear, to 3½ inches long and ¼ inch wide, margins
entire. Flowering heads in clustered, terminal corymbs
consisting of several heads and 25± purple florets. *Ver-
nonia lindheimeri* is similar to *V. larseniae*; however, their
ranges do not seem to overlap, though both species are
only found on limestone. Overall, *V. larseniae* is a much
larger plant and softer to the touch. Specific epithet honors Ferdinand Jacob Lindheimer.

Vernonia marginata   ASTERACEAE
Plains ironweed
Open fields, meadows, mountain slopes, creek banks,
roadsides and other open areas. Summer, fall. Common.

An erect, multistemmed perennial to 3 feet tall, with
pubescent stems. Leaves are mostly along stem, lanceolate to linear, to 6 inches long and ½ inch wide, margins
entire. Flowering heads in compact, terminal corymbs,
consisting of numerous purple florets, each head to ⅓
inch wide. Found in western Central Texas, north into
Panhandle and west into Hudspeth County.

Vernonia texana   ASTERACEAE
Texas ironweed
Woodlands, bottomlands, banks of
waterways. Spring, summer. Common.

An erect, weakly rhizomatous perennial with glabrous
or somewhat pubescent stems to 3+ feet tall. Basal leaves
ovate-lanceolate, becoming linear-lanceolate farther up
stem, 6 inches long and 1 inch wide, margins slightly
toothed to entire. Flowering heads held above leaves
in panicles, each head consisting of 20± purple florets.
Found east of Edwards Plateau, south to Coastal Bend,
and north into Oklahoma.

Xylorhiza wrightii   ASTERACEAE
Terlingua aster, Big Bend aster, gypsum daisy
Rocky hills, slopes, washes, arroyos, roadcuts and
other sparse or barren areas. Spring. Uncommon.

An erect perennial to 20 inches tall with branching in
upper portion of glandular stems. Leaves variable, spatulate to obovate to oblong, to 1 inch wide and 2½ inches
long, margins entire to toothed. Flowers in solitary, terminal heads on peduncles to 4 inches long, each head
consisting of 40–60 blue ray florets fading to white, disc
florets numerous and yellow. A striking spring bloomer
seen in Big Bend region, especially around Terlingua, in
areas with little vegetation and gypseous soils. Only species of *Xylorhiza* found in Texas. Genus name of Greek
origin and means "woody root." Specific epithet honors
Charles Wright.

411

Cynoglossum virginianum BORAGINACEAE
Wild comfrey
Deciduous and mixed woodlands. Spring. Uncommon.

An erect perennial with a single, unbranched stem to 3 feet tall; stem with long, stiff hairs. Basal leaves petiolate, elliptic-oblong, to 8 inches long. Stem leaves smaller but similar in shape to basal leaves, alternate, sessile to clasping. Flowers in terminal racemes, numerous, blue to white, 5-lobed, tubular, about ⅓ inch wide. Found in deep East Texas, with a few collections farther west.

Heliotropium indicum BORAGINACEAE
Turnsole, alacrancillo
Riparian areas, lake and pond banks, roadside ditches and other low, wet areas. Spring, summer, fall. Common.

An introduced, erect, leafy annual with rough, branching stems to 3+ feet tall. Leaves alternate, on petioles 4 inches long, ovate to elliptic, to 6 inches long and 4 inches wide, bases acute to obtuse to slightly cordate, margins undulate, tips acute to obtuse. Stems terminating in scorpioid cymes. Flowers funnel-shaped, blue to violet, 5-lobed, less than ¼ inch wide. Widespread throughout eastern third of Texas, from Cameron County north to Oklahoma, frequent in moist soils. Native of Asia.

Hesperidanthus linearifolius
(*Schoenocrambe linearifolia*) BRASSICACEAE
**Mountain mustard, slimleaf plainsmustard,
hesper mustard**
Open brush and woodlands, rocky hills, mountainsides, canyons, drainages. Summer, fall. Common.

An erect perennial with glabrous, slender stems to 4+ feet tall. Basal leaves absent. Stem leaves alternate, on short petioles, linear, to 5 inches long and ⅓ inch wide, bases cuneate, margins entire to rarely dentate, tips acute. Flowers in open racemes, to 1½ inches wide, actinomorphic, purple, occasionally with dark purple veins, 4 petals, spatulate. Found in mid to upper elevations of Chihuahuan Desert, extending east into western Edwards Plateau.

Streptanthus carinatus subsp. *carinatus*
BRASSICACEAE
Lyreleaf jewelflower
Open desert scrub. Spring. Uncommon.

An erect annual to biennial, with glabrous, branching stems to 2+ feet tall. Basal leaves in a rosette, oblance-olate, pinnatifid, to 6 inches long, margins dentate to entire. Stem leaves ovate to lanceolate, to 5¾ inches long and 2 inches wide, bases clasping, margins entire or pinnatifid or dentate. Flowers in terminal racemes, urn-shaped, to ½ inch long, sepals purple to magenta, petals reduced, recurved, white with purple veins or light purple, on pedicels to 1 inch long. Found in Chihuahuan Desert.

Streptanthus cutleri BRASSICACEAE
Cutler's jewelflower
Desert scrub, desert washes, rocky slopes. Spring. Rare.

An erect annual with glabrous, branching stems to 3+ feet tall. Basal leaves in a rosette, oblanceolate, to 8 inches long, margins pinnatifid. Stem leaves similar, smaller, margins pinnatifid to entire. Flowers in racemes, pedi-cels to 1 inch long, strongly bilateral, to 1½ inches wide, with dark purple sepals and 4 purple to lavender petals, 2 large and 2 greatly reduced, larger petals with obvious dark purple veins. Rare in southern Brewster County during most years; however, during years of adequate rainfall, thousands of plants may be found.

Streptanthus hyacinthoides BRASSICACEAE
Smooth jewelflower
Grasslands, fields, meadows, prairies, open woodlands, roadsides and other open areas. Spring. Uncommon.

An erect annual with glabrous, unbranched or branching stems to 4+ feet tall. Leaves sessile or nearly so, linear to lanceolate, to 6 inches long and 2¾ inches wide, margins entire. Flowers actinomorphic, in somewhat crowded racemes, pedicels to ½ inch long, sepals purple, 4 petals, purple to magenta, occasionally white with purple veins, about 1 inch wide. Found in sandy soils in eastern half of Texas, often in openings in post-oak woodlands. Specific epithet means "resembling hyacinth."

Streptanthus platycarpus   BRASSICACEAE
Broadpod jewelflower
Open brushlands or sparse desert scrub, canyons,
creek bottoms, desert washes. Spring. Uncommon.

An erect annual with glabrous, branching stems to 3+
feet tall. Basal leaves in a rosette, oblanceolate, to 8 inches
long, margins lyrate to sinuate to pinnatifid. Stem leaves
ovate, to 6 inches long and 2½ inches wide, bases clasping, margins entire to dentate. Flowers in racemes on
pedicels to 1½ inches long, each flower about 1 inch wide,
actinomorphic, sepals purple to maroon, 4 petals, blue
to light purple to lavender. Found in western portion of
Edwards Plateau west into Chihuahuan Desert, where it
grows on both limestone and igneous soils.

Tillandsia baileyi   BROMELIACEAE
Bailey's ball moss, giant ball moss
Oak and ebony forests and thickets. Spring, summer. Rare.

An epiphytic perennial reaching more than 12 inches in
diameter. Foliage gray or silver, older leaves turn brown.
Bracts indeterminate, greenish to rose-colored, extending
beyond foliage, eventually yielding tubular violet flowers
during spring. Found in far South Texas; most common
in Cameron County. Prefers shaded canopy offered by
ebony and live oaks, though it may occur on other species
in established, undisturbed systems and has been
noted to occur in full sun. Can be locally common,
but due to urbanization, habitat destruction, and
limited distribution in Texas, is listed as a species
of concern.

Campanula rotundifolia   CAMPANULACEAE
Bluebell, bluebell flower, bluebell of Scotland
Oak-pine woodlands, mountain grasslands
and slopes. Summer, fall. Uncommon.

An erect to arching perennial with multiple, slender, glabrate stems to 18+ inches tall. Basal leaves on long petioles, cordate to slightly round, to 1 inch wide, margins
dentate. Upper leaves alternate, linear, to 2 inches long,
margins entire. Stems terminate in a solitary flower or in
a raceme consisting of 3 flowers, bell-shaped, violet to
blue, to ¾ inch long. Found in upper elevations in mountains of Chihuahuan Desert.

Lobelia berlandieri   CAMPANULACEAE
Berlandier's lobelia
Seeps, marshes, springs, creek and river banks, drainages and other low, wet areas. Spring, summer. Common.

An erect to decumbent annual with a single or a branching stem to 24 inches tall. Leaves alternate, ovate to elliptic to lanceolate, to 2 inches long and 1½ inches wide, bases rounded to cuneate, margins toothed, tips rounded. Flowers in terminal racemes to 10 inches long, not crowded, ½ inch long and as wide, light blue to purplish blue with a yellow and white spot at base of lower lip, 5-lobed, lower lip broadly 3-lobed, upper lip 2-lobed, lobes erect and slender. Most common in South Texas, north into Hill Country, west to Brewster County.

Lobelia fenestralis   CAMPANULACEAE
Fringeleaf lobelia, leafy lobelia
Seeps, springs, wet meadows, in and around creeks and streams. Summer, fall. Locally common.

An erect annual or biennial with leafy, branched or unbranched stems to 4+ feet tall. Leaves alternate, sessile to clasping, lanceolate to oblong or oblanceolate, to 3 inches long and ½ inch wide, margins serrate, tips acute, blades ascending, stiff. Flowers in terminal spikes to 10 inches long, purple to blue, ⅝ inch long, 2 upper lobes recurved and slender, 3 lower lobes joined. Located in Brewster, Presidio, and Jeff Davis Counties, where it grows in wet or seasonally wet areas at mid to upper elevations.

Lobelia puberula   CAMPANULACEAE
Downy lobelia, purple dewdrop
Woodlands and forests, edges of streams, wet savannas and grasslands, swamps, bogs, roadside ditches. Summer, fall. Common.

An erect perennial with a single unbranched stem to 24+ inches tall. Leaves alternate, sessile, oblong to lanceolate, to 5 inches long and 1½ inches wide, margins toothed or slightly entire. Flowers in terminal, dense racemes, to 75± per raceme, each flower bilateral, to 1 inch long, corolla pubescent, purple to blue, 5-lobed with 3 larger lower lobes and 2 reduced upper lobes, which may be reflexed. Found in eastern third of Texas, from Coastal Bend north into Oklahoma, east into Louisiana.

Triodanis coloradoensis   CAMPANULACEAE
Colorado Venus' looking glass
Fields, meadows, brush and woodlands,
roadsides. Spring. Common.

An erect, slender annual, branching or not, with angular stems to 2+ feet tall. Leaves alternate, sessile above,
on petioles below, elliptic to oblanceolate, to 3 inches
long, margins toothed, tips pointed. Flowers originating
in upper leaf axils, broadly bell-shaped to ¾ inch long,
5-lobed, blue to purple with white or lighter centers, lobes
spreading open. Found primarily on limestone soils in
Edwards Plateau, west to Terrell County. Five other *Triodanis* species found in Texas; most of their ranges overlap. Variations in leaf morphology help differentiate
them.

Commelina dianthifolia   COMMELINACEAE
Bird's bill dayflower
Mountainous brush and woodlands, canyons, stream
and creek bottoms, rocky outcrops and other shaded,
rocky areas. Summer, fall. Locally common.

An erect to ascending perennial with unbranched or
occasionally branched, fleshy stems to 18+ inches tall.
Leaves spirally arranged, sheathed, grasslike, linear to
lanceolate, to 6 inches long and ⅓ inch wide, tips pointed,
blades glabrous or slightly pubescent. Flowers terminal,
solitary or few, on short peduncles which may or may not
exceed spathe, blue, 3-petaled, upper petals reniform to
cordate, lower petal smaller and roundish. Grows in mid
to upper elevations in oak-juniper-pine woodlands of Chihuahuan Desert.

Commelina erecta   COMMELINACEAE
Whitemouth dayflower, widow's tears, day flower
Brush and woodlands, canyons, escarpments,
rocky outcrops, roadsides, suburban and urban
areas. Spring, summer, fall. Common.

An erect to ascending, multistemmed, often weedy
perennial with fleshy, pubescent stems to 2+ feet tall.
Leaves spirally arranged, sheathed, linear to lanceolate, to 6 inches long and 1 inch wide, margins entire,
tips pointed. Flowers mostly terminal, originating from
spathe on short peduncles to 1½ inches long, solitary
or in cymes, 3-petaled, 2 upper petals blue, lower petal
white, flowers to 1¼ inches wide. Widespread throughout Texas.

Tinantia anomala   COMMELINACEAE
False dayflower, widow's tears
Rocky outcrops, escarpments, among boulders,
woodland edges, canyons and other shady
areas. Spring, summer. *Common.*

An erect perennial with glabrous, succulent stems to
30+ inches tall. Basal leaves petiolate, linear to spatulate,
to 8 inches long including petiole. Upper leaves spirally
arranged, sessile and clasping, lanceolate, to 4 inches
long, bases cordate, margins entire, tips acute to pointed,
blades glabrous. Flowers in terminal cymes, with uppermost leaf bractlike behind inflorescence, bilateral, about
1 inch wide, 3-petaled, upper 2 petals obovate and blue
(occasionally white), single lower white petal smaller
and hidden. Found throughout eastern Edwards Plateau,
southwest to Val Verde County; less common toward
coast.

Tradescantia humilis   COMMELINACEAE
Texas spiderwort
Open brush and woodlands, creek and river
floodplains, dunes and other open, sandy
areas. Spring, summer. *Common.*

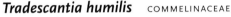

An erect to ascending perennial with multiple stems
branching from base, to 8+ inches tall. Leaves mostly
basal, sessile, clasping, linear-lanceolate, to 8 inches long
and ¾ inch wide, margins ciliate, purple, tips pointed.
Flowers in terminal cymes or on stems originating from
nodes below, on pedicels to 1 inch long, petals 3, blue, to
1 inch wide. Found in sandy soils in southern Texas, occasionally north to Oklahoma.

Tradescantia occidentalis   COMMELINACEAE
Prairie spiderwort, western spiderwort
Prairies, fields, grasslands, brush and
woodlands, thickets, urban and suburban areas,
roadsides. Spring, summer. *Common.*

An erect to ascending perennial with glabrous, occasionally branching stems to 3+ feet tall. Leaves spirally
arranged, linear-lanceolate, grasslike, to 20 inches long
and 1½ inches wide, bases sheathed, margins entire, tips
pointed, blades glabrous, glaucous, upper leaves folded.
Flowers in terminal cymes, with additional flowering
stems originating from axils below, light blue to purple to rose, to 1¼ inches wide, 3 petals, ovate. Frequent
and widespread. Weak in deep East Texas and along Rio
Grande in South Texas.

Evolvulus alsinoides   CONVOLVULACEAE
Slender dwarf morning-glory, ojo de vibora
Rocky slopes, canyons, open grass and brushlands
and other open areas. Spring, summer. Uncommon.

An ascending to prostrate perennial with pubescent
stems to 2 feet long. Leaves sessile or on short petioles,
lanceolate to oblong, to 1 inch long and ¾ inch wide,
margins ciliate. Light blue to deep blue, 5-lobed, radial
flowers, about ⅓ inch in diameter, occur singly on pedicels extending beyond length of leaves. Found from El
Paso to South Texas, generally following Rio Grande. In
South Texas, may bloom throughout year. Specific epithet
means "resembling *Alsine*," an old name for genus now
known as *Stellaria*, which includes chickweeds.

Evolvulus nuttallianus   CONVOLVULACEAE
**Silky evolvulus, shaggy dwarf morning-glory,
shaggy evolvulus**
Open grasslands, prairies and fields, open
brush and woodlands, rocky slopes, canyons
and valleys. Spring, summer. Common.

An erect to ascending perennial with several pubescent,
greenish gray to brown stems to 10 inches tall. Leaves
alternate, sessile or on short petioles, linear-oblong to
lanceolate to oblanceolate, to ¾ inch long and ¼ inch
wide, bases tapering, margins entire, tips acute to obtuse,
blades with silky pubescence, grayish green. Flowers
occur in leaf axils, purple to blue to pink to lavender,
bell-shaped to rotate, to ½ inch wide, 5-lobed, center of
lobes lighter and forming a star in middle of corolla.
Found throughout Central Texas, west to New Mexico,
north through Panhandle and into Oklahoma; absent in
East Texas. Weak in South Texas.

Ipomoea dumetorum   CONVOLVULACEAE
Railway creeper
Mountain slopes. Summer. Rare.

A twining, climbing annual vine with stems to 3+ feet
long. Leaves alternate, on petioles ¾ inches long, triangular, 3-lobed, to 1¼ inches long and nearly 1 inch wide,
bases cordate, margins entire. Flowers trumpet-shaped,
purple, to ½ inch long, in cymes of to 3 flowers. Found
in upper elevations of Davis Mountains. Specific epithet
is of Greek origin and means "of thornscrub or thickets,"
referencing habitat.

Ipomoea hederacea   CONVOLVULACEAE
Ivy-leaf morning-glory
Fields, stream and river banks, roadsides and other
disturbed areas. Summer, fall. Uncommon.

An introduced, twining, climbing annual vine with
branching, pilose stems to 6 feet long. Leaves alternate,
on petioles 2 inches long, cordate to ovate, deeply 3-lobed,
to 4 inches long and 3½ inches wide, margins entire to
undulate. Funnel-shaped flowers, to 3 per axil, 2 inches
in diameter, bluish purple with white centers. Widely
scattered throughout state; weak or absent in Panhandle.
Specific epithet of Latin origin and means "resembling
ivy."

Ipomoea lindheimeri   CONVOLVULACEAE
Lindheimer's morning-glory, blue morning-glory
Rocky outcrops and slopes, canyons, draws, ravines,
roadcuts. Spring, summer, fall. Uncommon.

A twining, climbing perennial vine with pubescent
stems to 8+ feet long. Leaves variable, cordate-ovate to
slightly round, to 5 inches long and 4 inches wide, 3- to
7-lobed, bases cordate. Flowers light blue to lavender,
funnel-shaped, 2½ inches wide and to 4 inches long, with
pale or white centers. Found in central portion of state,
west into New Mexico. While not frequent, this species
can be seen along roadsides, especially in southwestern
Edwards Plateau. Specific epithet honors Ferdinand Jacob
Lindheimer (1801–1879), the father of Texas botany.

Ipomoea nil   CONVOLVULACEAE
Morning glory
Urban and suburban areas, agricultural fields, roadsides
and other disturbed areas. Summer, fall. Uncommon.

A twining, climbing annual vine with pubescent stems
to 10+ feet long. Leaves alternate, cordate-ovate, 3-lobed
to hastate, to 7 inches long and 6 inches wide. Flowers
funnel-shaped, purple to blue to red, with white centers,
rays along limbs can be darker than major color. Widely
cultivated. Many horticultural selections exist in a wide
array of colors. Documentation is sparse, but expect to
find this species throughout state.

Astragalus crassicarpus   FABACEAE
Groundplum milkvetch, ground plum
Prairies, grasslands, open brush and woodlands,
roadsides. Spring, summer. Common.

An ascending or decumbent perennial with multiple
pubescent stems from a central woody base, to 24 inches
long. Leaves alternate, pinnate, to 6 inches long, with
15–29 leaflets, each leaflet elliptic, to ½ inch long, margins entire with visibly silver pubescence, tips mucronate,
blades flat or folded. Flowers in racemes arising from leaf
axils, papilionaceous, to ¾ inch long, purple to lavender.
Banner erect, oval, elongated, cleft. Lateral wings projecting, nearly horizontal. Fruits inflated, nearly round to
oblong, to 1¾ inches long. Absent in South Texas, deep
East Texas, and southern Panhandle.

Astragalus distortus var. engelmannii
FABACEAE
Engelmann's milkvetch
Open grasslands, fields and pastures, open
brush and woodlands, rocky outcrops, roadsides
and other open areas. Spring. Common.

An ascending to decumbent short-lived perennial with
stems from a central base, to 8+ inches long. Leaves
alternate, pinnate, to 4 inches long, with 13–25 leaflets,
each leaflet oval to elliptic-oblanceolate to nearly round,
to ⅜ inch long, margins entire, tips notched. Flowers in
racemes originating from leaf axils, purple to lavender to
pink. Banner erect, to ⅜ inch long, keel to about ⅓ inch
long, wings somewhat spreading and protruding. Found
in eastern third of Texas, from Coastal Bend north into
Oklahoma, east into Louisiana.

Astragalus lindheimeri   FABACEAE
Lindheimer's milkvetch
Open grass and brushlands, rocky slopes, roadsides
and other open areas. Spring, summer. Common.

An ascending, spreading annual with stems to 16+ inches
tall. Leaves alternate, pinnate, to 2¾ inches long with
13–21 leaflets, each leaflet oblong, to ½ inch long, margins entire, tips truncate, notched. Flowers in racemes
originating from leaf axils, papilionaceous, bicolored, to
about ¾ inch long. Banner white with purple margins,
keels purple, wings white. Frequent in North-Central
Texas, south to Coastal Bend, north into Panhandle.

Astragalus lotiflorus   FABACEAE
Lotus milkvetch
Prairies, grasslands, fields, open brush and woodlands, roadsides and other open areas. Spring. Common.

An ascending, leafy perennial with multiple stems to 4 inches tall, from a stout taproot. Leaves alternate, pinnate, to 3 inches long, with 7–17 leaflets, each leaflet lance-elliptic to oblong, to ½ inch long, margins entire, tips pointed, blades occasionally folded, visibly pubescent. Flowers in racemes to 4 inches long, to 8± per raceme, to ½ inch long, papilionaceous. Banner erect, purple to creamy yellow with dark purple central veins. Wings protruding, horizontal, purple to creamy yellow. Frequent in open areas of Panhandle, south into Central Texas, with isolated populations in Big Bend region and far South Texas.

Astragalus mollissimus   FABACEAE
Woolly locoweed, purple locoweed, woolly milkvetch
Fields, grasslands, pastures, prairies, open brush and woodlands, roadsides and other open areas. Spring. Common.

An ascending, spreading, dense perennial with leafy, pubescent stems to 18 inches tall and nearly twice as wide, stems originating from central woody rootstock. Leaves alternate, pinnate, to 10 inches long, with 15–35 ovate to obovate or elliptic-rhombic leaflets, each leaflet to 1½ inches long, margins entire, tips pointed, blades greenish gray, soft and visibly pubescent. Flowers in racemes with to 20± per raceme, purple to magenta, papilionaceous. Found from Panhandle south to western Edwards Plateau and throughout Chihuahuan Desert.

Baptisia australis   FABACEAE
Blue wild indigo, blue false indigo
Prairies, grasslands, fields, roadsides. Spring. Uncommon.

An erect, heavily branched perennial with glabrous, glaucous stems to 3+ feet tall. Leaves alternate, on petioles ¼ inch long, palmately trifoliolate, obovate to obovate-lanceolate, to 3¼ inches long and 1¼ inches wide, bases tapering, margins entire, tips rounded to acute. Flowers in spikelike racemes to 18 inches long, evenly spaced, papilionaceous, light to medium blue, to 1 inch long. Found in northeastern Panhandle and North-Central Texas near Red River.

Centrosema virginianum FABACEAE
Butterfly pea, spurred butterfly pea
Fields, meadows, grasslands, brush and woodlands,
thickets, riparian areas, fence lines, railroads, creek
and river bottoms. Spring, summer, fall. Common.

A trailing or twining perennial vine with stems to 5+ feet
long. Leaves alternate, trifoliolate, to 4 inches long, leaflets linear to ovate, to 2½ inches long, margins entire,
tips acute and terminating in a sharp point. Flowers solitary or in pairs on peduncles shorter than leaves, bluish
purple to pink, to 2⅓ inches long, bilateral, banner white
in center, lateral petals and keel usually lighter in color.
Widespread and often growing on and among herbaceous
plants and grasses. Found in eastern half of Texas, from
Cameron County north into Oklahoma, east to Atlantic
Coast.

Clitoria mariana FABACEAE
Atlantic pigeonwings, pigeonwings, butterfly pea
Brush and woodlands, roadsides, fence
lines. Spring, summer. Common.

An erect to trailing to climbing vine with slender stems
to 3+ feet long. Leaves alternate, trifoliolate, to 5 inches
long, leaflets lance-ovate, to 3 inches long, margins
entire, tips acute. Flowers solitary or to 3 on peduncles
arising from leaf axils, blue to pink with darker venation toward base of standard petal, bilateral, to 2½ inches
long. Found in various habitats, often growing on or in
shrubs or small trees in eastern half of Texas.

Dalea compacta FABACEAE
Compact prairie clover
Fields, grasslands, prairies, open shrub
and woodlands, roadsides and other open
areas. Spring, summer. Common.

A decumbent to ascending perennial with one to several stems to 20+ inches long, stems glabrous to weakly
pubescent. Leaves alternate, pinnate, to 2 inches long,
leaflets 5–7, linear to oblong, to ¾ inch long, margins
involute, tips acute to mucronate. Flowers in terminal
spikes ¾ inch long, numerous, papilionaceous, less than
¼ inch wide and long, purple to pink. Found in eastern
half of Texas, growing in clay soils.

Dalea formosa FABACEAE
Feathery dalea, feather plume
Open shrub and grasslands, rocky outcrops,
ridges and ledges, roadcuts and other rocky
areas. Spring, summer. Common.

An erect, well-branched, shrubby perennial with weak
branches, stems to 3+ feet tall. Leaves alternate, pinnate, less than ¼ inch long, leaflets in 2–6+ pairs, bases
cuneate, margins entire, involute to folded, tips obtuse.
Flowers bilateral in terminal spikes, calyx lobes thin,
feathery. Banner cordate, yellow with white band and
apex matching color of wings. Wings and keel blue,
purple, pink, or white. Found throughout Chihuahuan
Desert, north through Panhandle and south to Zapata
County.

Dalea frutescens FABACEAE
Black dalea
Rocky mountain slopes, open
brushlands. Summer. Common.

An erect, shrubby, rounded perennial with
much-branched, glandular, reddish brown stems to 3 feet
tall and as wide. Leaves alternate, occasionally appearing clustered, pinnate, to 1 inch long with 13–17 leaflets, each leaflet to ⅓ inch long, obovate, margins silvery
pubescent, tips notched. Flowers on terminal peduncles
to 2 inches long, numerous, in rounded spikes, papilionaceous, purple, to ¼ inch long and as wide. Frequent
in western half of Texas, from Lower Rio Grande Valley,
north into Oklahoma, west into New Mexico and northern Mexico.

Dalea lachnostachys FABACEAE
Glandleaf prairie clover
Open desert grass and shrublands, desert
scrub. Spring, summer. Locally common.

An erect perennial with gland-dotted, branching stems
to 12 inches tall. Leaves alternate, pinnate, to 3¼ inches
long, with 9–11 leaflets, each leaflet ovate or obovate, to
¾ inch long, bases and tips rounded, blades silky, folded.
Flowers in terminal, pubescent racemes to 2½ inches
long, blue, bilateral, papilionaceous. Banner erect with a
yellow and white patch at base, wings spreading. Found
in rocky soils in Chihuahuan Desert, usually at mid
to lower elevations. Glandular stems, peduncles, and
rachises easily distinguish this species.

423

Dalea lanata var. *terminalis*   FABACEAE
Woolly prairie clover, woolly dalea
Fields, meadows, grasslands, open brushlands, roadsides and other open areas. Spring, summer. Common.

A prostrate perennial with densely villose stems to 20 inches long, flowering stalks ascending. Leaves, stems, and inflorescence silvery gray. Leaves alternate, pinnate, to 1¼ inches, leaflets 9–13, obovate to cuneate, to ½ inch long, margins entire to rolled, tips notched, surfaces villose. Flowers in elongated spikes, on peduncles along stem opposite leaves and 1¼ inches long, numerous, papilionaceous, bluish purple to reddish purple, less than ¼ inch wide and long, stamens extending beyond petals. Found in sandy soils of Panhandle, south to Pecos River, east along Red River to Arkansas.

Dalea lasiathera   FABACEAE
Purple dalea, purple prairie clover
Grasslands, fields, open brush and woodlands, roadsides and other open areas. Spring, summer. Common.

An erect to ascending multistemmed perennial from a central woody base, with leafy, glabrous stems to 12+ inches tall and 20 inches wide, lower stems spreading along surface. Leaves alternate, pinnate, to 1½ inches long, leaflets 7–13, linear-oblong to oblanceolate, bases tapering, margins entire, tips rounded to notched, blades folded slightly. Flowers in terminal racemes 3 inches long, papilionaceous, purple to reddish purple. Banner round, with a yellow and white patch at base. Common in Central Texas, in far South Texas, Big Bend region, and along Red River.

Lupinus havardii   FABACEAE
Havard's bluebonnet, Big Bend bluebonnet
Desert rocky slopes, desert washes, roadsides. Winter, spring. Locally common.

An erect winter annual with flowering stems to 2+ feet tall. Leaves alternate, palmately compound, to 7 leaflets, oblanceolate, to ¾ inch long. Flowers dense in racemes that are 18+ inches long, blue (occasionally white, pale blue, or pink), about ½ inch wide and as long. Banner with pale yellow blotch on lower center, lateral wings not spreading. Locally common, along Rio Grande from Hudspeth County south to Brewster County. Named after Valery Havard (1846–1927), an American botanist and army surgeon.

Lupinus subcarnosus   FABACEAE
Texas bluebonnet, sandyland bluebonnet, buffalo clover
Grasslands, plains, open brush and woodlands,
roadsides and other open areas. Spring. Common.

An erect winter annual with branching, silky stems to
16+ inches tall when in flower. Leaves alternate, palmately compound, leaflets 5, oblanceolate, to 1 inch long
and ½ inch wide, margins entire, tips rounded. Flowers in racemes to 5 inches long, peduncles to 3½ inches,
bilateral, ½ inch long and as wide, light blue with a white
patch in middle of banner, turning red after pollination.
Banner reflexed, wings inflated. Found in sandy soils
from South Texas northeast into Louisiana.

Lupinus texensis   FABACEAE
Texas bluebonnet, buffalo clover, wolf flower
Fields, prairies, grasslands, open brush and woodlands,
roadsides and other open areas. Spring. Common.

An erect winter annual with branching, silky stems to
16+ inches tall when in flower. Leaves alternate, palmately compound, leaflets 5, oblanceolate, to 1 inch long
and ½ inch wide, margins entire, tips acute to obtuse.
Flowers in racemes 6+ inches long and silky, white at top,
bilateral, dark blue to blue with a white patch in center of
banner which turns red after pollination. Banner spreading to slightly reflexed, wings not inflated. Widespread
and spreading throughout Texas. Absent in Panhandle,
far West Texas, and Northeast Texas.

Macroptilium atropurpureum   FABACEAE
Purple bean, purple-bush bean, aggie bean
Coastal grasslands and plains, rocky mountain
slopes. Spring, summer. Uncommon.

A twining, clambering perennial vine with pubescent
stems to 5+ feet long. Leaves alternate, trifoliolate, ovate
to rhombic to lance-ovate, often widened or slightly
lobed in lower half, to 2¾ inches long and 1¾ inches
wide, bases truncate, margins entire, tips acute. Flowers on 3½-inch-long racemes with 12-inch-long peduncles, bilateral, wings elongated, dark purple to black.
Keel contorted, twisted, pinkish. Banner mauve-pink,
often reflexed. Found along coastal Texas, from Cameron
County to Coastal Bend, as well as in mountains of southern Presidio County.

425

Medicago sativa   FABACEAE
Alfalfa
Fields, agricultural areas, roadsides and other open, disturbed areas. Spring, summer. Common.

An introduced, ascending to erect perennial with slender, leafy, branching stems to 3 feet tall. Leaves alternate, 3-foliolate, leaflets obovate, oblong or lanceolate, to 1¼ inches long and ⅓ inch wide, bases tapering, margins dentate, tips rounded. Flowers in crowded terminal and axillary racemes, papilionaceous, to ½ inch long, purple, with darker venation along banner. Banner notched, lateral wings spreading. Commonly planted and thus widespread throughout Texas.

Orbexilum pedunculatum   FABACEAE
Sampson's snakeroot
Fields, meadows, woodlands. Spring. Common.

An erect, occasionally branching perennial with stems to 30+ inches tall. Leaves alternate, trifoliolate, on petioles 2 inches long, leaflets lanceolate to elliptic-oblong, to 3 inches long and ¾ inch wide, margins entire, tips acute. Flowers in 4-inch-long racemes originating from upper leaf axils, on peduncles to 6 inches long, crowded, bilateral, lavender, to ¼ inch long. Banner with darker center portion near base, keel dark purple, lateral wings projecting. Found in sandy soils in eastern third of Texas.

Pediomelum cyphocalyx   FABACEAE
Turniproot
Open grass, brush and woodlands on limestone hills and slopes. Spring. Uncommon.

An erect, airy, slender perennial with weakly branching, pubescent stems to 28+ inches tall. Leaves alternate, palmately 3- to 5-foliolate, leaflets elliptic-linear to lanceolate, to 3½ inches long and ⅜ inch wide, bases tapering, margins entire, tips pointed, lower leaf surface with flattened hairs, upper surface glandular. Flowers in dense 3-inch-long racemes originating from leaf axils, on peduncles to 3¼ inches long, papilionaceous, lavender to light blue or purple. Banner erect to protruding and margins often rolled, lateral wings horizontal. Found in eastern Edwards Plateau, north to Dallas–Fort Worth area.

Pediomelum hypogaeum var. *scaposum*
FABACEAE
Subterranean Indian breadroot
Open grass, brush and woodlands. Spring. Uncommon.

An acaulescent perennial from tuberous roots, with densely pubescent peduncles and petioles, to 8 inches tall when in flower. Basal leaves on petioles 4½ inches long, palmately 3- to 7-foliolate, leaflets obovate to linear-elliptic, to ¾ inch long and ½ inch wide, bases tapering, margins entire, tips pointed, lower leaf surface densely covered in flattened, white hairs, upper surface less so. Flowers in dense, rounded spikes on 4-inch-long peduncles, papilionaceous. Banner erect, slightly curving backward, lavender to light purple, often with darker streaks. From Dallas–Fort Worth area south into eastern portion of Edwards Plateau.

Pediomelum latestipulatum var. *latestipulatum* FABACEAE
Texas plains Indian breadroot, scurfpea
Open grass and brushlands. Spring. Uncommon.

An erect, slender perennial from tuberous roots, with unbranched, or weakly branched above, pubescent stems to 12 inches long. Leaves alternate, on petioles 2¾ inches long, palmately 5- to 7-foliolate, leaflets elliptic to obovate, to 1¾ inches long and ⅝ inch wide, bases tapering, margins entire, short ciliate, appearing yellowish white, tips pointed, leaf surfaces glandular, blades often folded. Flowers in short, rounded, dense racemes, papilionaceous, dark blue to lavender. Banner erect to angled forward. Found in North-Central Texas, south into northern Edwards Plateau.

Pediomelum linearifolium FABACEAE
Narrowleaf Indian breadroot
Prairies, plains, grasslands, open brush and woodlands. Spring. Common.

An erect perennial with slender, branching stems to 30+ inches tall. Leaves alternate, palmately 3-foliolate, leaflets linear to lanceolate, to 2½ inches long and less than ¼ inch wide, margins entire, tips and bases acute. Flowers in loose racemes, few, papilionaceous, lavender to light purple or blue, ⅓ inch long. Banner protruding, lateral wings spreading, horizontal. Found in Edwards Plateau, north into Oklahoma and throughout Panhandle.

Psoralidium tenuiflorum   FABACEAE
Slimflower scurfpea, scurfpea, scurfy pea
Fields, grasslands, prairies, open brush and
woodlands. Spring, summer. Common.

An erect, heavily branched perennial with glandular
stems to 24+ inches tall. Leaves alternate, 3-foliolate, leaflets oblong-lanceolate to linear, to 2 inches long and ½
inch wide, bases tapering, margins entire, tips pointed,
leaf surfaces gland-dotted, upper glabrous, lower with
short, flattened hairs. Flowers in racemes to 2 inches long
on peduncles to 1¼ inches long, papilionaceous, blue.
Banner with white streak in central base, lateral wings
spreading, exposing curved keel. Widespread throughout
state. Absent only in East and South Texas.

Psorothamnus scoparius   FABACEAE
Broom smokebush, broom dalea, false purple dalea
Open desert scrub. Spring, summer, fall. Uncommon.

An erect, shrubby ephemeral perennial with multiple
branching stems to 3+ feet tall, stems yellowish green,
canescent with obvious glands. Leaves opposite, sessile,
simple or rarely 3-foliolate, leaflets linear to ⅜ inch long,
margins revolute, tips obtuse, surfaces gland-dotted.
Flowers in terminal, rounded spikes that are ¾ inch
wide, dense, papilionaceous, ¼ inch long and as wide,
dark blue with white interiors, often with blue spots. Banner erect, wings spreading. Found in sand dunes of El
Paso and Hudspeth Counties along I-10.

Vicia ludoviciana   FABACEAE
Deer-pea vetch
Fields, grasslands, meadows, shrub- and woodlands,
roadsides, gardens. Spring. Common.

An annual climbing to decumbent vine with glabrous
or pubescent stems to 3+ feet long. Leaves alternate, pinnate, to 4 inches long, leaflets linear-oblong to elliptic,
to 1 inch long, bases round-tapering, margins entire,
tips either pointed or rounded. Flowers in racemes originating from leaf axils, bilateral, blue-lavender, to ⅓
inch long. Banner notched and erect or folded. Widespread throughout state. Weak in Northeast Texas and
Panhandle.

Vicia minutiflora FABACEAE
Pygmyflower vetch, small flower vetch
Fields, grasslands, meadows, open brush and woodlands, roadsides and other open areas. Spring. Common.

An annual vine with slender, branching, glabrous or slightly pubescent stems to 2+ feet tall. Leaves alternate, to 2½ inches long, to 6 leaflets, each leaflet linear to oblong, to 1½ inches long, margins entire, tips acute or rounded-mucronate. Flowers on peduncles to ¾ inch long, solitary or in pairs, pale blue to light purple, bilateral, to about ¼ inch long. Banner erect, with darker veins, lateral wings spreading and often lighter in color than banner. Found throughout eastern third of Texas, from Coastal Bend north into Oklahoma and east into Louisiana.

Vicia sativa FABACEAE
Common vetch, spring vetch
Fields, meadows, grasslands, brush and woodlands, roadsides, residential areas and other open, disturbed sites. Spring. Common.

An introduced, climbing or ascending annual with glabrous or slightly pubescent branching stems to 30+ inches tall. Leaves alternate, pinnate, to 5 inches long with a forked tendril, leaflets oblong, to ¾ inch long, margins entire, tips pointed. Flowers occur in leaf axils, nearly sessile, usually solitary, occasionally paired, bilateral, to ¾ inch long, purplish red. Banner lighter than keel and wings, wings not spreading. Widespread throughout eastern half of Texas and spreading.

Vicia tetrasperma FABACEAE
Lentil vetch, four-seeded vetch, smooth tare
Fields, grasslands, pastures, open brush and woodlands, roadsides and other open, disturbed areas. Spring. Locally common.

An introduced, climbing or trailing annual with pubescent stems to 24+ inches long. Leaves alternate, pinnate, to 3 inches long with a terminal, branching tendril, leaflets linear-oblong, to ¾ inch long, margins entire, tips acute or rounded-mucronate. Flowers occur in upper leaf axils, on short peduncles, usually paired or solitary, to ⅓ inch long, blue-lilac. Banner with darker veins, wings spreading. Found in eastern fourth of Texas, but spreading and expected elsewhere.

429

Vicia villosa FABACEAE
Winter vetch, hairy vetch, fodder vetch
Fields, pastures, grasslands, open brush and woodlands, roadsides and other disturbed areas. Spring, summer. Locally common.

An introduced annual or biennial with branching, pubescent stems to 3+ feet tall. Leaves alternate, pinnate, to 10 inches long, with a terminal, branching tendril, leaflets oblong-lanceolate to linear, to 1 inch long and ¼ inch wide, margins entire, tips pointed. Flowers in racemes to 6 inches long, crowded, blue-violet to purple or pink, to ¾ inch long, nodding. Banner interior and wings lighter in color or white. Widespread and spreading in Texas; most common in eastern half of state. The longer, nodding flowers are key characters.

Eustoma exaltatum GENTIANACEAE
Bluebells, Texas bluebells, catchfly prairie gentian
Fields, prairies, meadows, grasslands, marshes, edges of creeks, ponds and other bodies of water, roadside ditches and other low, wet areas. Spring, summer. Common.

An erect, single or multistemmed annual to perennial with glabrous stems to 24+ inches tall. Leaves opposite, sessile and clasping, ovate to elliptic-oblong or elliptic-lanceolate, to 3¾ inches long and 1¼ inches wide, margins entire, tips obtuse, blades glaucous to green, thick. Flowers terminal, either solitary or in panicles, large, showy, 5-petaled, bell-shaped, 1⅓ inches long and to 2 inches wide, purple to blue to lavender or white. Found throughout Texas. Absent in East Texas Piney Woods north of Houston-Beaumont area.

Hydrolea ovata HYDROLEACEAE
Blue waterleaf, ovate false fiddleleaf, hairy hydrolea
Edges of ponds, lakes, streams, roadside ditches, and other low, wet areas. Summer. Common.

An erect, branching perennial with leafy, stout, spiny stems to 20+ inches tall. Leaves alternate, on petioles, ovate, to 2½ inches long and 1 inch wide, bases tapering, margins entire, tips acute, surfaces with small, stiff hairs. Flowers in terminal corymbs, blue, 5-petaled, distinctly star-shaped, to 1 inch wide, numerous. Found from Coastal Bend, north into Oklahoma, east into Louisiana. Genus name of Greek origin and means water (*hydor*) and olive (*elaia*), referring to habit and leaves.

Nemophila phacelioides HYDROPHYLLACEAE
Baby blue-eyes
Fields, meadows, open brush and
woodlands. Spring. Common.

An erect annual with branching stems to 14 inches
tall. Leaves alternate, pinnately divided with 9–11 divisions, oblong, to 3¼ inches long and 2 inches wide, tips
rounded to acute. Flowers solitary from leaf axils or in
terminal cymes, 5-lobed, light blue to purple with white
centers, to 1¼ inches wide, showy. From Coastal Bend,
east Galveston Bay, north into Oklahoma and west into
central Edwards Plateau.

Phacelia coerulea HYDROPHYLLACEAE
Caterpillar weed, skyblue scorpionweed, skyblue phacelia
Open desert scrub, washes. Spring, summer. Uncommon.

An erect annual with glandular leaves and slender, reddish brown stems to 16 inches tall. Leaves alternate, ovate
to oblong-ovate, to 3¼ inches long and 1 inch wide, lower
leaves pinnatifid, upper leaves scalloped. Flowers occurring in scorpioid cymes, bell-shaped, 5-lobed, light blue
to white. Found in rocky to gravelly soils in West Texas,
often in open creosote-ocotillo scrub.

Phacelia congesta HYDROPHYLLACEAE
Bluecurls, caterpillars, spike phacelia
Brush and woodlands, prairies, grasslands,
canyons, creek and river banks, rocky outcrops,
roadsides. Spring, summer. Common.

An erect annual to biennial with pubescent (sometimes
glandular) leaves and stems, stems to 3+ feet tall. Leaves
alternate, ovate, to 4 inches long and 1¾ inches wide, 1- or
2-pinnate, final margins lobed to crenate-undulate. Stems
terminating in scorpioid cymes, consisting of numerous
blue or purple bell-shaped flowers to about ¼ inch wide.
Widespread through most of Texas. Absent in Panhandle
and far eastern Texas. During dry years it grows in moist,
shady areas.

Phacelia glabra HYDROPHYLLACEAE
Smooth phacelia, smooth scorpionweed
Prairies, grasslands, meadows, open areas in
woodlands, roadsides. Spring. Uncommon.

An erect annual with slender, glabrous stems. Leaves to
10 inches long, alternate, semisucculent, oblong to oval,
to 1¾ inches long and ½ inch wide, 1- or 2-pinnate, lobed.
Stems terminating in scorpioid cymes. Flowers blue to
lavender with a white center, bell-shaped, to ½ inch wide.
Found in eastern third of Texas.

Phacelia integrifolia var. *texana*
HYDROPHYLLACEAE
Texas bluecurls, Texas scorpionweed, Texas phacelia
Desert scrub, grasslands, washes, low areas,
roadsides. Spring, summer. Uncommon.

An erect annual with sticky, glandular leaves and stems
to 2 feet tall. Leaves alternate, lanceolate to oblong, to
5½ inches long and ¾ inch wide, lobed, final margins
crenate or lobed. Stems terminating in scorpioid cymes.
Flowers bell-shaped, 5-lobed, bluish purple to purple to
lavender. Found in Chihuahuan Desert in rocky to gravelly to sandy soils.

Phacelia patuliflora HYDROPHYLLACEAE
Blue phacelia, sand phacelia, sand scorpion-weed
Prairies, grasslands, savannas, open woodlands,
roadsides and other open areas. Spring. Common.

An erect to decumbent annual with slender, pubescent,
branching stems to 12 inches tall. Leaves alternate, upper
sessile, basal petiolate, oblong to oval, to 4 inches long
and 1¾ inches wide, pinnately lobed to pinnatifid, final
margins crenate to lobed, surfaces pubescent. Common
throughout the central portion of Texas, from the Big
Bend region, east to Houston.

Phacelia popei HYDROPHYLLACEAE
Pope's bluecurls
Grasslands, open brush and woodlands, roadsides
and other open areas. Spring. Common.

An erect, branching annual with glandular leaves and
stems to 18 inches tall. Leaves alternate, oblong, to 6
inches long and 1¼ inches wide, once-pinnate, occasionally bipinnate, upper leaves pinnatifid, lobes variable,
lance-ovate to lanceolate to linear, margins entire to revolute. Stems terminating in scorpioid cymes. Flowers
5-lobed, bell-shaped, purple to blue. Found in West Texas
and Panhandle.

Phacelia robusta HYDROPHYLLACEAE
Stout phacelia
Desert scrub, washes, creek and river beds,
open grasslands and other dry, open areas.
Spring, summer. Locally common.

An erect, stout annual or biennial with glandular, sticky
leaves and stems to 3 feet, stems visibly viscid-pubescent.
Leaves alternate, ovate to orbicular, to 6 inches long and
3 inches wide, margins lobed to crenate, upper leaves on
petioles to 1+ inch long. Stems terminating in scorpioid
cymes. Flowers blue to lavender, bell-shaped. Found in
Chihuahuan Desert north into Panhandle.

Alophia drummondii IRIDACEAE
Purple pleat-leaf, propeller flower, prairie iris
Fields, meadows, grasslands, roadsides.
Spring, summer. Common.

A bulbous perennial with a single stem to about 18 inches
tall. Linear leaves from a sheathing base and to 18 inches
long. Flowers about 2 inches in diameter and can be varying shades of purple. Center of tepals lighter in color,
usually cream or yellow with reddish purple spots, 3
inner tepals about half the length of outer tepals. Found
in South Texas and eastern third of state.

Herbertia lahue IRIDACEAE
Prairie nymph
Grasslands, prairies, open areas and
roadsides. Late winter, spring. Common.

A bulbous perennial with single or branched stem to
about 10 inches tall. Leaves linear, about ¼ inch wide, not
as tall as inflorescence, most (to 6) are basal; however, a
few leaves sheath stem. Outer tepals bluish purple, to 2
inches in diameter, cream colored in center with darker
purple spotting. Inner tepals much reduced, often dark
purple to violet. Very early to flower; can easily be seen
along Coastal Bend, north to Edwards Plateau and east to
Louisiana. No preference of soil type.

Iris virginica IRIDACEAE
Southern blue-flag, Virginia iris
Wetlands, marshes, margins of lakes and streams,
ditches and other wet areas. Spring, summer. Common.

An erect, rhizomatous perennial with simple stems to
3 feet tall. Arching, linear leaves shorter than stems, no
more than 30 inches long and just over 1 inch wide. Each
inflorescence yields 2 or 3 blue to lavender flowers with
darker veins. Arching sepals just over 3 inches long and
1½ inches wide, with yellow pubescent patch leading into
floral tube. Petals slightly smaller than sepals, similar in
color, yellow patch much reduced. Found widely scattered
in eastern portion of state, mostly east of Brazos River.

Nemastylis geminiflora IRIDACEAE
Celestial, prairie celestial, celestial lily
Woodlands, fields, prairies and other open
areas. Spring, summer. Common.

A slender, bulbous, erect perennial with branched
stems to 16 inches tall. Leaves along stem linear to
sword-shaped, to ¾ inch wide, usually exceed flowering
stalk. Inflorescence usually produces 2 light blue flowers,
white in center, 2+ inches in diameter. Found throughout
central portion of state, south to Coastal Bend, north to
Oklahoma, and east to Louisiana. Absent in Panhandle,
West Texas, and far South Texas. Celestials open late in
morning or early afternoon and only remain open a few
hours.

Nemastylis tenuis IRIDACEAE
Southwestern pleatleaf
Open pine-oak woodlands. Spring, summer. Rare.

A slender, erect, bulbous perennial with unbranched
stem to 12 inches tall. Three linear basal leaves slightly
shorter than stems and less than ¼ inch wide. Single stem leaf is half the length of basal leaves. Typically
one, rarely 2, radial light blue to lavender flowers, each 2
inches wide, on each stem. Found in upper elevations of
Jeff Davis and Brewster Counties.

Sisyrinchium angustifolium IRIDACEAE
**Blue-eyed grass, Bermuda blue-eyed grass,
narrowleaf blue-eyed grass**
Banks of streams and swamps, wet
meadows and woodlands and other low,
wet areas. Spring, summer. Common.

An erect, clumping perennial with branched stems to 18
inches tall. Numerous, erect, slender, grasslike leaves to
12 inches long and lack hairs. Flowers blue to violet with
yellow centers, ½ inch wide, on peduncles about ¼ inch
above leafy bracts. Found throughout central portion of
state, north into Panhandle and Oklahoma, east to Louisiana. Absent in western and southern portions of state.
About a dozen species of blue-eyed grass in Texas, many
with overlapping ranges. May hybridize, which can make
identification a chore.

Agastache pallidiflora LAMIACEAE
Mountain giant hyssop
Mountain woodlands, rocky outcrops, moist
meadows. Spring, summer, fall. Common.

An aromatic, erect perennial with single branching stem
to 3 feet tall. Leaves opposite, on petioles ¾ inches long,
deltoid-ovate, to 2½ inches long and nearly as wide, margins serrate. Flowers on terminal spikes several inches
long, each flower just ⅓ inch in diameter, color varies
from purple to white. Grows above 6000 feet in woodlands of West Texas.

Ajuga reptans   LAMIACEAE
Common bugle
Old homesteads, urban areas. Spring,
summer. Uncommon.

An introduced, stoloniferous, mat-forming perennial
herb to 1 foot tall. Leaves variable. Basal leaves ovate, to
3 inches long and 1 inch wide. Upper leaves similar in
shape, but smaller. Flowers on terminal, whorled, leafy
spikes, blue, 2-lipped, sessile, lower lip 3-lobed, upper
lobe much reduced. A native of Europe; widely cultivated
and has escaped. Currently known from a few urban
collections.

Monarda citriodora   LAMIACEAE
Lemon horsemint, horsemint, purple horsemint
Fields, prairies, grasslands, open shrub
and woodlands, roadsides and other open
areas. Spring, summer. Common.

An erect, pubescent annual with a single branching,
leafy stem to 2+ feet tall. Leaves opposite, on petioles 1¼
inches long, lanceolate to oblong, to 2½ inches long and
¾ inch wide, bases tapering, margins serrate to subentire, ciliate at base, tips acute. Stems terminating in leafy
spikes, flowers clustered in roundish heads in axils, bilabiate, purple to pink to rose, often with dark purple spots,
nearly 1 inch long, upper lip curved, lower lip 3-lobed,
bracts surrounding flowering heads tinged various
shades of purple. Found throughout state.

Prunella vulgaris   LAMIACEAE
Self-heal
Grasslands, meadows, open shrub and woodlands,
creek and river banks and floodplains, roadsides and
other open areas. Spring, summer, fall. Common.

An erect perennial with unbranching, pubescent stems
to 12 inches tall. Leaves opposite, lanceolate to ovate, to 2
inches long and ¾ inch wide, margins entire to toothed.
Stem terminates in dense spike of light blue to purple or
white bilabiate flowers, to about ½ inch long, lower lip
3-lobed, middle lobe larger and fringed, upper lip large
and not reduced. Flower color can vary; generally lower
lip is lighter than upper. Found throughout eastern third
of Texas.

Rhododon angulatus   LAMIACEAE
Angled sandmint
Open grass and brushlands. Spring, summer. Rare.

An erect annual with pubescent, glandular stems,
branching from base and throughout, to 12 inches tall.
Leaves opposite, sessile, ovate to elliptic, to nearly 1 inch
long and ½ inch wide, bases cordate to rounded, margins
entire to ciliate, tips obtuse to slightly acute, blades glandular. Stems terminating in spikes, 8± flowers per axil, to
10+ clusters of flowers per spike. Flowers bilabiate, light
purple with darker spots along lighter throat, lower lip
3-lobed, middle lobe larger and notched, upper lip erect
and 2-lobed. A geographically isolated species found in
open, sandy soils of Aransas and Refugio Counties.

Salvia arizonica   LAMIACEAE
Arizona sage
Oak-pine-juniper mountain woodlands. Summer, fall. Rare.

An erect, branching perennial with pubescent leaves and
stems to 18 inches long, stems square, somewhat rhizomatous. Leaves opposite, on petioles ⅓ inch long, deltate to
ovate, to 2 inches long and 1½ inches wide, bases cuneate
to rounded, margins serrate to crenate, tips acute. Stems
terminating in loose spikes, with flowers solitary to several at nodes. Flowers bilabiate, blue to purple-blue to
pink (latter rare in Texas), upper lip shorter than lower,
lower lip 3-lobed, middle lip elongated. Grows in upper
elevations in mountains of Chihuahuan Desert.

Salvia azurea   LAMIACEAE
Giant blue sage, pitcher sage, big blue sage
Prairies, fields, grasslands, open shrub and
woodlands, roadsides. Spring, summer. Common.

An erect perennial with a single or branching pubescent
stem to 5+ feet tall. Leaves opposite. Lower leaves lanceolate to oblong, to 5 inches long and 1½ inches wide, margins entire. Upper leaves linear, margins entire to dentate
or serrate at tips. Stems terminating in spikes with flowers in whorls. Flowers bilabiate, to ¾ inch long, blue with
a white throat, lower lip 3-lobed, middle lobe enlarged
and wide, upper lip reduced. Widespread throughout
eastern two-thirds of state, occasional in West Texas.

Salvia engelmannii   LAMIACEAE
Engelmann's sage
Grasslands, prairies, fields, open brush and
woodlands, roadsides. Spring, summer. Common.

An erect, multistemmed, clumping perennial to 18
inches tall with pubescent leaves and stems. Leaves opposite, petiolate, linear-lanceolate, to 3¼ inches long and ½
inch wide, margins entire to dentate. Stems terminating
in compact racemes with to 6 flowers per node. Flowers
bilabiate, light blue, lower lip enlarged, to ¾ inch long. A
Texas endemic. Found in eastern portion of Edwards Plateau. Similar to *Salvia texana*, but easily distinguished by
leaf morphology and distinctive odor of crushed leaves in
S. engelmannii.

Salvia farinacea   LAMIACEAE
Mealy blue sage, mealycup sage, mealy sage
Prairies, grasslands, fields, pastures, open
brush and woodlands, roadsides and other open
areas. Spring, summer, fall. Common.

An erect, multistemmed perennial to 3 feet tall, with
pubescent leaves and stems. Leaves opposite. Lower
leaves on petioles 1½ inches long, linear to lanceolate to
ovate, 4 inches long and 1½ inches wide, bases obtuse to
cuneate, margins serrate. Upper leaves similar, smaller,
margins entire. Stems terminate in many-flowered
spikes. Flowers bilabiate, normally ash-blue to dark
blue to purple, occasionally white, to 1 inch long, lower
lip enlarged. Common throughout majority of Texas.
Absent in Panhandle and far South Texas. Weak in East
Texas. Available in seed mixes. Expected elsewhere and
spreading.

Salvia lycioides   LAMIACEAE
Canyon sage
Mountain woodlands, canyons, slopes,
ledges. Spring, summer. Uncommon.

An erect, ragged, shrubby perennial with branching
stems to 24 inches tall and equally as wide. Leaves opposite, on petioles ¼ inch long, oblong-elliptic to oval, to 1¼
inches long, margins entire to crenulate or serrate. Flowers in terminal, open racemes, in pairs, blue, to ½ inch
long and as wide, bilabiate, lower lip greatly enlarged and
broad at base, notched, upper lip reduced. Located in mid
to upper elevations in mountains of Chihuahuan Desert.
In shady areas, plants tend to be less robust than those
found in open spaces.

Salvia lyrata   LAMIACEAE
Lyre-leaf sage, cancer-weed, wild sage
Grasslands, meadows, fields, open brush and
woodlands. Winter, spring. Common.

An erect, pilose perennial with leaves mostly basal and
rosette, flowering stem to 2 feet tall. Leaves on petioles
4 inches long, obovate to oblanceolate, to 8 inches long,
margins heavily sinuate or lyrate or repand. Stem leaves
opposite, sessile, elliptic, to 3½ inches, margins toothed,
usually only 1 or 2 pairs of leaves along stem. Flowers in
a slender spike, occasionally branched, light blue, bilabiate, in whorls of 3–10 per node, to 1 inch long, lower lip
enlarged, upper lip reduced. Found in eastern third of
Texas, often in maintained areas; readily spreading.

Salvia reflexa   LAMIACEAE
Lanceleaf sage, Rocky Mountain sage, lambsleaf sage
Fields, grasslands, open brush and
woodlands. Spring, summer. Common.

An erect, multistemmed, branching annual with glabrous or slightly pubescent stems to 24+ inches tall.
Leaves opposite, on petioles ⅝ inch long, lanceolate to
linear-oblong, to 2 inches long and ½ inch wide, bases
tapering, margins toothed to entire, tips acute. Flowers
in crowded, terminal racemes, blue to white, bilabiate.
Lower lip 3-lobed with much larger and spreading central lobe, lateral lobes arching backward, reduced upper
lip protruding forward and not lobed. Found throughout
Central Texas, north into Oklahoma and Panhandle, west
through Trans-Pecos. Prefers rocky soils, often on slopes.

Salvia reptans (S. leptophylla)   LAMIACEAE
Slender-leaf sage
Mountain creek beds and drainages.
Summer, fall. Uncommon.

An erect, multistemmed, bunching, somewhat rhizomatous perennial with glabrous flowering stems to 3+ feet
tall. Leaves opposite, linear, to 3½ inches long and less
than ¼ inch wide, margins entire or slightly dentate at
tips of leaves. Stems terminating in slender spikes to
14 inches long. Flowers sky blue to dark blue, bilabiate,
loosely spaced along spike, occurring singly or in pairs,
lower lip enlarged, upper lip reduced. Currently known
from Jeff Davis County. Grows in gravelly to rocky soils
in and along mountain creeks and drainages. Found in
Madera Creek.

Salvia texana   LAMIACEAE
Texas sage
Prairies, grasslands, fields, meadows, open
brush and woodlands, roadsides and other open
areas. Spring, summer, fall. Common.

An erect, multistemmed, clumping perennial with
pubescent, branching stems to 16 inches tall. Leaves
opposite, sessile, obovate-lanceolate to oblanceolate, to
2 inches long, margins entire to dentate, revolute, tips
acute. Stems terminating in a leafy raceme. Flowers purple to bluish purple with a white throat, bilabiate, to 1
inch long, lower lip 3-lobed, middle lobe enlarged, cleft.
Frequent throughout Central Texas, extending south.
Absent in Panhandle, East and West Texas.

Salvia whitehousei   LAMIACEAE
Clustered sage, clustered salvia
Sparse, open, desert scrub. Spring, summer. Uncommon.

An erect, rounded, multistemmed perennial with pubescent stems to 16 inches tall, often half this height. Leaves
opposite, sessile, linear, to 3½ inches long and less
than ¼ inch wide at base, margins revolute, tips tapering to fine point, blades pubescent. Flowers in leaf axils
of upper stem, bilabiate, purple to lavender, to nearly 2
inches long, generally arching upward, lower lip deeply
3-lobed, middle lobe greatly enlarged and notched, upper
lip smaller, 2-lobed, erect. Found in small populations on
limestone soils throughout western Edwards Plateau, east
into Chihuahuan Desert. Grows around roadcuts along
I-10 west of Ozona and Highway 90 west of Del Rio.

Scutellaria cardiophylla   LAMIACEAE
Heart-leaf skullcap, gulf skullcap
Fields, meadows, open woodlands, roadsides and
other open areas. Spring, summer, fall. Uncommon.

An erect, branching annual with pubescent stems to
20+ inches tall. Leaves opposite, upper leaves sessile,
lower leaves on petioles, deltate to cordate, to 2 inches
long, margins crenate to dentate, ciliate on upper leaves.
Flowers occur in leaf axils at end of stem, bilabiate, purple to pinkish purple with white throat (usually spotted),
just under 1 inch long, upper lip helmet-shaped, lower
lip enlarged, neither lobed, interior of flower pubescent.
From Edwards Plateau east into Louisiana, north into
Oklahoma, south to Matagorda Bay.

Scutellaria drummondii LAMIACEAE
Drummond's skullcap
Grasslands, fields, thickets, open brush and
woodlands, rocky outcrops, roadsides and other
open areas. Winter, spring, summer. Common.

An erect, branching annual with pubescent stems to 12+
inches tall. Leaves opposite. Lower leaves on short petioles, ovate, to ¾ inch long, margins crenate, tips acute.
Upper leaves smaller, sessile, margins entire. Flowers
occur in leaf axils along upper stem, bilabiate, about ½
inch long, light to dark blue to purple, throat and middle of lower lip white with blue to purple spots, lower
lip 3-lobed, middle lobe notched, margins wavy, upper
lobe reduced, galea visibly pubescent. Found throughout
Texas. Weak in upper Panhandle and deep East Texas.

Scutellaria integrifolia LAMIACEAE
Helmet-flower, rough skullcap
Edges of and openings in woodlands, fields,
rights-of-way, roadsides and other open
areas. Spring, summer. Common.

An erect perennial with rough, branching stems to 28
inches tall. Leaves opposite. Stem leaves on petioles ½
inch long, oblong to linear-lanceolate, to 2½ inches long
and ¾ inch wide, margins entire. Upper leaves smaller,
sessile. Lowest leaves on petioles as long as leaf blade,
ovate, margins crenate. Stems terminating in raceme or
panicle, with to 40 flowers per raceme. Flowers bilabiate, to 1 inch long, blue to purple, with white throat that
extends onto lower lip, lower lip notched, upper lip visibly
pubescent. Found in eastern fourth of Texas.

Scutellaria muriculata LAMIACEAE
Rio Grande skullcap
Open brush and thickets, fields, flats, roadsides
and other open areas. Winter, spring. Common.

A procumbent to ascending annual with pubescent,
branching stems to 12 inches long. Leaves opposite.
Lower leaves on petioles 13 inches long, ovate to deltoid, about ½ inch long, margins crenate. Upper leaves
smaller, nearly sessile, becoming round, margins entire,
blades with soft, fine hairs, tips rounded. Flowers occur
in axils along upper stem, bilabiate, blue to purple,
throats white with blue to purple spots, to about ½ inch
long, lower lip 3-lobed, lower lobe notched. In South
Texas, south of San Antonio to Cameron County.

Scutellaria ovata LAMIACEAE
Heartleaf skullcap
Open brush and woodlands, canyons, outcrops,
roadsides. Spring, summer. Common.

An erect, rhizomatous perennial with pubescent, branching stems to 3 feet tall. Leaves opposite, on petioles to 2
inches long, cordate to ovate, to 5 inches long, bases cordate, margins crenate to serrate, tips acute, upper surface of blades wrinkled. Flowers in terminal racemes,
numerous, bilabiate, blue with white throat and lower lip,
lower lip slightly 3-lobed, middle lobe notched, upper lip
reduced, to about 1 inch long. From Central Texas, east
into Louisiana, north into Oklahoma. Often found along
woodland edges and near waterways.

Scutellaria parvula LAMIACEAE
Small skullcap
Fields, meadows, edges of and openings in
brush and woodlands, roadsides and other
open areas. Spring, summer. Common.

An erect, rhizomatous perennial with branching stems to
12 inches tall. Leaves opposite, upper leaves sessile, lower
leaves on petioles, deltoid to ovate, to ¾ inch long and ½
inch wide, margins dentate. Flowers occur in leaf axils
along upper portion of stems, bilabiate, blue to purple,
throat white with blue to purple spots, to ½ inch long,
lower lip 3-lobed, middle lobe notched, upper lip reduced,
galea visibly pubescent. Found in eastern third of Texas.

Scutellaria wrightii LAMIACEAE
Wright's skullcap, bushy skullcap, shrubby skullcap
Grasslands, prairies, open shrub and woodlands, roadsides
and other open areas. Spring, summer. Common.

An erect, multistemmed perennial, from a central crown,
with leafy, pubescent stems to 10 inches tall. Leaves opposite, on short petioles, oval, to 1 inch long and ½ inch
wide, bases narrow, margins entire, tips rounded. Flowers crowded in upper leaf axils, blue to purple to violet,
throat white with darker spots, bilabiate, from ½ to 1 inch
long, lower lip 3-lobed, lobe margin undulate to dentate,
upper lobe reduced, galea visibly pubescent. Frequent
throughout Central Texas, north into Oklahoma and eastern Panhandle, with disjunct populations in Big Bend
region and a historic record from Harris County.

Trichostema dichotomum LAMIACEAE
Bluecurls, forked bluecurls, bastard penny-royal
Open woodlands. Summer, fall. Common.

An erect, somewhat weedy annual with pubescent, leafy, heavily branched stems to 2+ feet tall. Leaves opposite, on short petioles, oblong to ovate, to 2½ inches long and 1 inch wide, bases tapering, margins entire, tips acute, leaves and petioles reduced farther up stem. Flowers in cymes originating from axils in upper leaves, to 7± flowers per cyme, each bilateral, blue, to ¾ inch long, 5-lobed, lower lobe largest and extending downward and about twice the length of other lobes which point upward, 4 stamens arch above lower lobe. Found in eastern fourth of the state.

Warnockia scutellarioides LAMIACEAE
Prairie brazoria, prairie brazosmint
Fields, meadows, grasslands, open brush and woodlands. Spring, summer. Common.

An erect, branching annual with glabrous stems to 18 inches tall. Leaves opposite, sessile to clasping, oblong to lanceolate, to 1½ inches long, margins serrate toward ends, tips acute, surfaces pubescent. Flowers in terminal or axillary spikes to 8 inches long, purple to pink with white throat spotted pink, ⅝ inch long, bilabiate, upper lip entire, not lobed, slightly reflexed, lower lip 3-lobed, middle lobe larger than outer 2. Frequent throughout Edwards Plateau, south to Coastal Bend and east into Southeast Texas.

Linum lewisii LINACEAE
Blue flax, wild blue flax, Lewis flax
Grasslands, fields, open shrub and woodlands, roadsides and other open areas. Spring, summer, fall. Common.

An erect, glabrous perennial with slender stems branching profusely from base to 30+ inches tall. Leaves alternate, sessile to clasping, linear to linear-lanceolate, to 1¼ inches long, margins entire, tips pointed. Lower leaves spreading to ascending, upper leaves nearly clasping. Flowers in terminal panicles, light to dark blue with yellow centers and often with darker venations, 5-petaled, rotate, to 1¼ inches wide. Frequent throughout Chihuahuan Desert and eastern Edwards Plateau. Less common in Panhandle and North-Central Texas.

Linum pratense   LINACEAE
Meadow flax, Norton's flax, meadow blue flax
Fields, meadows, creek and river drainages, open shrub
and woodlands, prairies. Spring, summer. Common.

An erect, glabrous annual with stems branched at base to
16 inches tall and with leaves dense in lower half of plant,
scattered above. Leaves alternate, linear to lanceolate, to
¾ inch long, margins entire, tips pointed. Flowers in terminal panicles, light blue to white, to about ¾ inch wide,
rotate, 5-petaled, margins wavy. Found in Central Texas,
north into Panhandle and Oklahoma, west to Pecos River.
Also found in Jeff Davis County. Similar to *Linum lewisii*,
but an annual and smaller overall.

Nymphaea elegans   NYMPHAEACEAE
Tropical water lily, blue water lily, lampazos
Ponds, ditches, low areas where ephemeral
waters collect. Spring, summer. Uncommon.

An aquatic perennial from nonstoloniferous roots, with
floating leaves. Leaves oval to ovate, to 7 inches in diameter, usually smaller, green above, purple below. Flowers blue, fading to white as they age, about 5½ inches
in diameter, extending above water's surface on slender
peduncles. Mostly found in counties along coast in South
Texas, but has been collected farther inland. Historic collections have been made in El Paso and Bastrop Counties,
and, interestingly, there is notation of a collection near
Waco.

Buchnera americana   OROBANCHACEAE
American bluehearts, bluehearts
Wet meadows, fields, grasslands, open woodlands
and marshes. Spring, summer, fall. Common.

An erect, hemiparasitic annual to perennial with single
scabrous stem, occasionally branching above, to 2 feet
tall. Basal leaves lanceolate to obovate, to 10 inches long.
Upper leaves opposite, ovate-oblong to lanceolate, to 2½
inches long and ¾ inch wide, bases uneven, margins
dentate, tips acute, leaf surface with 3 prominent veins.
Flowers in terminal spikes to 6 inches long, 5-lobed,
trumpet-shaped, purple, bilateral, lobes uneven, notched
at tip. Found throughout Texas. Most common in east
and along coast to Mexico.

444

Castilleja purpurea   OROBANCHACEAE
Purple paintbrush
Grasslands, prairies, fields, open brush and woodlands,
roadsides and other open areas. Spring. Common.

An erect, hemiparasitic perennial with woolly stems to
12+ inches tall. Leaves alternate, with 1–3 pairs of linear to lanceolate lateral lobes, 3+ inches long and ¼ inch
wide, margins entire, blades fuzzy, silvery green. Flowers in terminal, bracted spikes, bracts with 1 or 2 lateral
lobes, outer lobes linear to lanceolate, middle lobe broad,
purple to purple-red tips on lower bracts, upper bracts
with more color, calyx 4-lobed, similar in color to bracts,
nearly covering flower within. Flowers bilabiate, lower
lip shorter, upper lip longer. Found in Edwards Plateau,
northeast into Oklahoma.

Orobanche cooperi subsp. *palmeri*
OROBANCHACEAE
Palmer's broomrape
Open grass, brush and scrublands.
Spring, summer, fall. Uncommon.

An erect, parasitic perennial with a leafless, densely flowered, simple or branching stem to 6 inches tall. Leaves
absent, scales present, usually hidden by flowers. Flowers in 6-inch-tall spikes starting at soil surface, bilabiate, about ⅝ inch long, purple or faded (as in photograph), with yellow blotch in center of lower lip. Lower
lip 3-lobed, lobes slender, upper lip 2-lobed, lobes erect
to reflexed with an apical tooth, tube arching. Found on
gypseous and limestone soils in the Trans-Pecos; hosts
are *Viguiera* species.

Orobanche ludoviciana   OROBANCHACEAE
Louisiana broomrape
Open brush and woodlands, desert scrub, thornscrub,
dunes. Spring, summer, fall. Uncommon.

An erect, parasitic perennial with a leafless, densely flowered, simple or branching stem to 8 inches tall. Leaves
absent, scales lanceolate to ovate-lanceolate, to ⅓ inch
long. Flowers in dense spikes, bilabiate, to ¾ inch long,
tubular, purple to reddish purple or yellow to cream, tube
cream to white, upper lip 2-lobed, larger, broader than
lower lobes, lower lip 3-lobed, lobes reflexed. Widespread
and variable throughout Texas. Absent in eastern fourth
of state.

Orobanche multiflora
(*O. ludoviciana* subsp. *multiflora*)   OROBANCHACEAE
Manyflowered broomrape
Open brushlands. Spring, summer, fall. Uncommon.

An erect, parasitic perennial with a leafless, densely flow-ered, silvery gray canescent, stout stem to 10+ inches tall, usually smaller. If branching occurs, it is usually below ground or just at surface. Leaves absent, scales lance-ovate, to ½ inch long. Flowers in dense spikes hid-ing stems, bilabiate, purple with yellow inside throat, corolla visibly pubescent, tube cream colored, arching to 1½ inches long. Lower lip 3-lobed, middle lobe usually protruding, lateral lobes spreading, upper lip 2-lobed, upper lobes erect and arching backward. *Orobanche mul-tiflora* parasitizes *Varilla texana* and can be found in South Texas.

Orobanche ramosa (Phelipanche ramosa)
OROBANCHACEAE
Hemp broomrape
Fields, pastures, agricultural areas, roadsides.
Spring, summer. Uncommon.

An introduced, erect, parasitic annual to perennial with leafless white to tan stems to 16 inches tall. Leaves absent, scales ovate to ovate-lanceolate, to ⅜ inch long. Flowers in spikes to 10 inches tall, usually shorter, bilabiate, to 1 inch long, tubular, violet to blue to pale yellow, white throat. Lower lip 3-lobed, lobes recurved, upper lip 2-lobed, erect, corolla with visible, glandular hairs. Found in Dal-las area, southeast to Houston. Spreading.

Passiflora incarnata   PASSIFLORACEAE
Maypop, passionflower vine, pasionaria
Woodlands, fence lines, roadsides and open areas. Spring, summer. Locally common.

A perennial vine to 20+ feet tall, often taking over smaller shrubs and trees. Leaves are deeply 3-lobed, often with serrated margins. Flowers on short stalks in leaf axils, purple to lavender, about 3 inches in diameter. Fruits large, turning orange when ripe, edible. This unmistak-able vine is easily seen in flower spring through sum-mer in East Texas. A larval host plant for Gulf fritillary butterflies.

Epixiphium wislizeni PLANTAGINACEAE
Balloon bush, large snapdragon vine,
sand snapdragon vine
Open brushlands, dunes. Spring, summer. Uncommon.

A perennial climbing to clambering vine to 8+ feet
long with glabrous stems and leaves. Leaves alternate to
slightly opposite, on petioles 2 inches long, triangular
to hastate, with tips and lobes pointed, to about 2 inches
long, bases cordate, margins entire. Flowers blue to lavender to purple, to 1 inch long, nearly as wide, bilabiate,
bottom lip 3-lobed, upper 2-lobed and reflexed. Overall similar to *Maurandella antirrhiniflora*, but with larger
flowers, stouter stems, and different habitat preferences.
Generally found throughout Trans-Pecos and Pecos River
drainage.

Leucospora multifida PLANTAGINACEAE
Narrowleaf paleseed, obe-wan-conobea
Creek and river beds and banks. Spring,
summer, fall. Common.

An erect, spreading annual with heavily branched, pubescent stems to 8 inches tall and as wide. Leaves opposite,
on short petioles, triangular-ovate, to 1¼ inches long and
½ inch wide, pinnate, lobes linear to oblong, bases tapering, margins entire, tips rounded to acute, blades with
soft hairs. Flowers occur in upper leaf axils, solitary, to ⅓
inch long, violet to pale lavender or white, bilabiate, tubular, lower lip 3-lobed, upper lip weakly 2-lobed. Frequent
along waterways throughout Texas. Absent in Panhandle
and far West Texas.

Maurandella antirrhiniflora
PLANTAGINACEAE
Snapdragon vine, roving sailor, little snapdragon vine
Canyons, ledges, cliffs, among boulders,
creek and river banks, brushlands, fence
lines. Spring, summer, fall. Common.

A perennial multistemmed, branching vine to 6 feet
long. Leaves alternate, on petioles 1¼ inches long, triangular to sagittate, to 1 inch long and as wide, bases cordate, margins entire. Flowers blue, purple, red, or white,
to 1 inch long, bilabiate, with bottom lip 3-lobed, upper
lip 2-lobed. Frequent in Central, West, and South
Texas; often seen growing along fences. Prefers
shady areas. Genus name honors Catalina Pancra-
tia Maurandy, an 18th-century Spanish botanist.

447

Nuttallanthus canadensis PLANTAGINACEAE
Canadian toadflax
Grasslands, fields, meadows, prairies, roadsides
and other open areas. Spring. Common.

An erect, glabrous annual to biennial with leafy stems,
branching at base, and flowering stems to 24+ inches
tall. Leaves alternate above, opposite below, sessile, linear to oblong, to 1½ inches long and ⅛ inch wide, margins entire. Flowers in terminal spikes, to ⅜ inch long,
light blue to violet with a white throat, bilabiate. Upper lip
2-lobed, lower lip evenly 3-lobed, spur ¼ inch long and
curved. Frequent in open areas in eastern half of state,
less so farther west. Smaller flowers and shorter spurs
separate this species from *Nuttallanthus texanus*.

Nuttallanthus texanus PLANTAGINACEAE
Texas toadflax
Grasslands, fields, meadows, prairies, open
brush and woodlands, roadsides and other
open areas. Winter, spring. Common.

An erect annual to biennial with leafy stems branching at
base and with flowering stems to 28+ inches tall. Leaves
alternate along spike, opposite below, sessile, linear, to 1½
inches long, margins entire, tips pointed. Flowers in terminal spikes, light blue to violet, more than ⅜ inch long,
bilabiate, upper lip 2-lobed, lower lip evenly 3-lobed, spur
⅜ inch long and curved. Found throughout Texas. Weak
in western Edwards Plateau and Panhandle.

Penstemon dasyphyllus PLANTAGINACEAE
Cochise beardtongue
Rocky slopes, canyons, open desert scrub
and brushlands. Spring. Uncommon.

An erect, pubescent perennial with slender stems to 18+
inches tall. Leaves opposite, sessile, linear to narrowly
lanceolate, to 2¾ inches long and less than ¼ inch wide,
margins entire, tips acute, blades folded, pubescent.
Flowers in terminal racemes, blue to purple, bilabiate,
bell-shaped, tube inflated, lower lip 3-lobed, upper lip
2-lobed. Found in Big Bend region, east to western edge
of Edwards Plateau. Prefers limestone. Found on roadcuts
near Pecos River between Iraan and Sheffield.

Penstemon fendleri   PLANTAGINACEAE
Fendler's penstemon
Fields, grasslands, pastures, prairies, rocky slopes, open brush and woodlands. Spring, summer. Locally common.

An erect, glabrous perennial with stems to 18+ inches tall. Leaves opposite, sessile, lanceolate, to 4 inches long and ½ inch wide, margins entire, tips acute, blades folded, thick, glaucous, and glabrous. Flowers in terminal racemes, tubular, purple to lilac to pink, bilabiate, to ¾ inch long, upper lip erect and 2-lobed, lower lip 3-lobed. Found in rocky to gravelly or sandy soil in Central Texas, west to El Paso, and north throughout Panhandle. During years with good winter rains, *Penstemon fendleri* grows throughout its range along roadsides.

Stemodia lanata   PLANTAGINACEAE
Woolly stemodia, gray-woolly twintip, stemodia
Dunes, open scrub and grasslands, fields, prairies and other open areas. Spring, summer, fall. Locally common.

A prostrate, sometimes ascending, spreading, matting vine with dense, woolly leaves and stems, rooting at nodes, to several feet long. Leaves opposite, sessile, oblong-elliptic to obovate, to 1 inch long and ⅓ inch wide, margins dentate to serrate or entire on lower leaves. Purple to lavender flowers occur in upper leaf axils, about ¼ inch across and ⅓ inch long. Found primarily along lower coast and slightly inland. Forms large, loose mats.

Veronica anagallis-aquatica
PLANTAGINACEAE
Water speedwell, brook pimpernel
Shallow waters or banks of creeks and streams. Spring. Uncommon.

An introduced, erect to ascending, glabrous perennial with stout, branching stems to 3+ feet tall. Leaves opposite, sessile, oblong-lanceolate or elliptic or lanceolate or ovate, to 4 inches long and 1½ inches wide, bases rounded to clasping, margins entire or serrate to toothed, tips acute. Flowering stems terminating in racemes to 6 inches long, with additional racemes produced from lower leaf axils. Flowers numerous, blue to lavender, 4-lobed, bilateral, lower lobe unequal, smaller than others. Found in Edwards Plateau, north into Oklahoma, in northern Panhandle, Chihuahuan Desert, and Southeast Texas.

Veronica persica   PLANTAGINACEAE
Birdeye speedwell, bird's eye speedwell, Persian speedwell
Urban and suburban areas, and other disturbed
areas. Winter, spring. Uncommon.

An introduced, ascending annual with pubescent,
branching stems to 12+ inches long. Leaves alternate
above, opposite below, on short petioles, oval to orbicular,
½ inch long and ⅓ inch wide, bases truncate to rounded,
margins dentate to crenate. Bilateral flowers solitary in
upper leaf axils, blue to violet with white centers and
darker veins, to ⅓ inch wide, 4-lobed, with 1 lobe smaller
than others. Scattered throughout Texas, primarily found
in areas of human activity, parklands, campuses, and residential areas.

Veronica polita   PLANTAGINACEAE
Wayside speedwell, gray field speedwell
Urban and suburban areas, roadsides and other
disturbed areas. Spring. Uncommon.

An introduced, prostrate to reclining annual with pubescent, fleshy stems, typically branched at the base, to 10
inches long. Lower leaves opposite, on short petioles, oval
to round, to ⅓ inch long and ¼ inch wide, margins dentate to crenate. Upper leaves alternate, similar to lower,
but sessile. Solitary flowers in upper leaf axils, blue to
violet, with white center and darker veins, about ¼ inch
wide, bilateral with one lobe smaller than others. Widespread throughout Texas in areas of human activity.

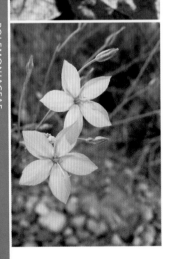

Gilia stewartii   POLEMONIACEAE
Stewart's gilia
Open desert brush and grasslands. Spring. Uncommon.

An erect biennial or short-lived perennial with slender,
branching stems to 12+ inches long, bases becoming
woody, stems and leaves grayish green. Basal leaves bipinnate, to 2 inches long. Stem leaves alternate, pinnate,
lobes linear, to ¾ inch long, tips pointed. Flowers solitary
or terminal on short peduncles, radial, 5-petaled, light
blue to purple to pink, to 1 inch wide. Found in Big Bend
region on rocky, open slopes.

Giliastrum rigidulum POLEMONIACEAE
Bluebowls, blue gilia
Open grass and brushlands, rocky slopes,
hillsides. Spring, summer, fall. Common.

An erect, spreading, rounded perennial with
much-branched stems to 10 inches tall and twice as wide.
Leaves alternate, mostly in lower half, dissected, to 1½
inches long, segments linear to oblong, margins entire
or toothed. Flowers solitary on peduncles to 1 inch long,
rotate, to 1 inch wide, 5 lobes, blue to purple with yellow and white centers, sepals awned. Found in eastern
Trans-Pecos through Edwards Plateau, and into South
Texas. Prefers limestone.

Heteranthera limosa PONTEDERIACEAE
Blue mudplantain
Ponds, creeks, lakes, ditches, ephemeral
pools and other wet areas with shallow
water. Spring, summer, fall. Common.

An aquatic annual with stems submerged or growing in
saturated soils to 10 inches long. Basal leaves sessile, linear to oblanceolate, to 2½ inches long and ¼ inch wide,
margins entire. Emersed leaves on petioles 5 inches long,
ovate, to 2 inches long and 1½ inches wide, truncate
to cuneate, margins entire. Solitary, trumpet-shaped
flowers, with 6 lobes, to 2 inches wide, blue to white.
Most common *Heteranthera* species in state. The tiny
seed is trapped in mud on the feet of birds standing in
shallow water, then transported to next body of water.

Heteranthera mexicana PONTEDERIACEAE
Mexican mudplantain
Ephemeral pools, roadside ditches and other low,
seasonally wet areas. Spring, summer, fall. Rare.

An aquatic annual with stems to 20+ inches long, leaves
and stems with a slight pubescence. Leaves alternate,
sheathed, linear to straplike, to 8 inches long and ½ inch
wide, margins entire. Flowers in terminal spikes, to 24
per spike, trumpet-shaped, pale to deep blue, with white
center, 6 lobes with 5 above and 6th directly below top
middle lobe. Rare, but usually in vast numbers when
found. Prefers shallow waters (approximately 6 inches
deep) with muddy, clay soils. Found in playas in Panhandle, south to Brownsville in association with *Eleocharis*,
Marselia, and *Sagittaria*.

phlox family
POLEMONIACEAE

pickerel-weed family
PONTEDERIACEAE

451

Pontederia cordata PONTEDERIACEAE
Pickerelweed, pickerel rush
Marshes, banks of creeks, lakes and other bodies
of water, roadside ditches and other low, wet
areas. Spring, summer, fall. Common.

An aquatic, rhizomatous perennial with large basal leaves
and flowering stalks to 4 feet tall. Submersed leaves sessile, linear. Emersed leaves on petioles 24 inches long,
lanceolate to cordate, to 8 inches long and 4½ inches
wide, margins entire. Flowering stalks terminate in a
spike consisting of hundreds of dark blue flowers, each
flower ½ inch wide with 6 lobes, upper 2 lobes with small
yellow patches. Found in and along still or slow-moving
waters in southeastern portion of state, becoming less
frequent north into Oklahoma and west to Central Texas.

Anemone berlandieri RANUNCULACEAE
Tenpetal thimbleweed
Roadsides, fields, prairies, open spaces. Spring. Common.

An erect perennial to 14 inches tall from tuberous roots.
To 6 ternate basal leaves. Solitary flowers, 10–20 sepals,
from blue to purple to white, held well above leaves.
Arises in early spring. Common throughout most of
Texas. Weak in far western and far southern Texas and
Panhandle. Specific epithet honors Jean Louis Berland-
ier (1805–1851), a French-Swiss physician who collected
plants in Texas.

Clematis crispa RANUNCULACEAE
Blue jasmine, swamp leather flower
Along streams, edges of woodlands and open
areas within, especially low areas where water
collects. Spring, summer, fall. Locally common.

A perennial vine to 10 feet tall, usually much shorter,
standing alone or climbing on shrubs, trees, or along
fence lines. Leaves compound, with 2–5 pairs of ovate to
lanceolate leaflets, margins entire to 3-foliolate. Blue, violet, pink, or white flowers, bell-shaped to urceolate, to 2
inches long, sepals recurved, margins undulate. Achenes
have a style to 1¼ inches long, glabrate or finely pubescent. Common in Southeast Texas; sporadic collections
west to Brewster County, south to Laredo, and north into
Oklahoma.

Clematis pitcheri RANUNCULACEAE
Purple leather flower
Margins of wooded areas and open areas within,
along creeks and streams, and fence lines, preferably
in shaded areas. Summer, fall. Common.

A clambering perennial vine from a simple stem, slightly
branched above. Stem leaves pinnate with 3 or 5 leaflets,
rachis ending with filament, leaflets simple, slightly to
deeply 2- to 5-lobed or 3-foliolate. Nodding purple flowers
are ovoid to urceolate with thick sepals. Found throughout Texas, sparingly in eastern portion. *Clematis pitcheri*
var. *dictyota* found in mountains of West Texas, while
C. pitcheri var. *pitcheri* is found elsewhere in state. Former has leaflets less than 1⅔ inches long; latter has larger
leaflets.

Clematis reticulata RANUNCULACEAE
Net-leaf leather flower
Woodlands, creek and river banks.
Spring, summer. Uncommon.

A perennial climbing vine with mostly glabrous stems
to 12+ feet long. Leaves pinnate with 6–8 leaflets and
one terminal leaflet or tendril, leaflets elliptic to ovate,
unlobed or 1- to 3-lobed, to 3½ inches long and 2 inches
wide, leathery, margins entire. Flowers urn-shaped, to
1¼ inches long, lavender to reddish purple. Achene with
a plumose tail to 2⅓ inches long. Found in East Texas,
from Houston area north, weakening toward Oklahoma
border. Grows in sandy soils. Specific epithet refers to
reticulate leaves, which are best way to distinguish this
species from *Clematis pitcheri* (ranges overlap).

Delphinium carolinianum RANUNCULACEAE
Larkspur, Carolina larkspur
Open shrub and woodlands, fields,
meadows, prairies, roadsides and other open
areas. Spring, summer. Common.

An erect, unbranched to slightly branched perennial
with pubescent stems to 3+ feet tall. Leaves alternate, on
petioles to 4 inches long. Basal leaves 4 inches wide and
as long, palmately divided into 3–5 lobes, lobes further
divided and about ¼ inch wide, margins entire. Upper
leaves similar to basal, becoming smaller farther up
stem. Spurred flowers occur in terminal raceme, 1 inch
long and as wide, blue to white or varying shades of blue.
Two subspecies occur in Texas: subsp. *vimineum* has
3-parted leaves, while subsp. *virescens* has leaves with
5+ parts.

453

Delphinium madrense   RANUNCULACEAE
Sierra Madre larkspur, Edwards Plateau larkspur
Open brush and woodlands, fields, roadsides and
other open areas. Spring, summer. Locally common.

An erect perennial with reddish stems to nearly 3 feet
tall, stems with short, erect hairs. Leaves alternate on
petioles to 6 inches long, semicircular to cordate, 3- to
5-lobed, lobes divided again, 3¼ inches long and 4 inches
wide, margins entire, leaf surfaces glabrous. Bright blue,
spurred flowers occur on a terminal raceme, about 1 inch
wide and as long, spurs to ¾ inch long. Found on limestone soils throughout western edge of Edwards Plateau,
west into Big Bend region.

Delphinium wootonii   RANUNCULACEAE
Wooton's larkspur
Oak-juniper woodlands, shrublands, grasslands, fields,
prairies, roadsides. Spring, summer. Locally common.

An erect perennial with reddish pubescent stems to 2
feet tall. Leaves alternate, reniform to fan-shaped, to 1¼
inches long and 1½ inches wide, 5-lobed, lobes divided
again 1 or 2 times. Flowers in short, terminal racemes,
30 per raceme, lavender to white, 1¼ inches wide, spurs
to 1 inch long. Found in western portion of Edwards Plateau, west into New Mexico, north into Panhandle. Lark-
spurs are known to hybridize and sometimes proper
identification can be a challenge.

Houstonia pusilla   RUBIACEAE
Tiny bluet
Fields, pastures, prairies, maintained lawns and
other areas, roadsides. Winter, spring. Common.

A small, erect annual with slender, glabrous stems to 5
inches, occasionally cespitose. Leaves opposite, sessile,
spatulate to ovate, to ⅜ inch long and ¼ inch wide, bases
tapering, margins entire and pubescent, tips rounded.
Flowers terminal, trumpet-shaped, blue-violet to lilac
(rarely white), 4-lobed, to ¼ inch long and as wide. Found
throughout eastern half of Texas, from Laredo north into
Oklahoma. Often confused with *Houstonia micrantha*;
H. pusilla has larger flowers and pubescent leaf margins.

Bacopa caroliniana   SCROPHULARIACEAE
Blue waterhyssop, lemon bacopa
Bogs, creek banks, marshes, ponds, roadside ditches and
other low areas. Spring, summer, fall. Locally common.

A prostrate, creeping, rhizomatous perennial with
branching stems to 3 feet long. Leaves opposite, thick
and fleshy, ovate to elliptic, to 1 inch long, bases clasping,
margins entire. Leaves have a fresh, lemon scent when
crushed. Flowers blue, about ⅓ inch wide, bilabiate, with
upper lip slightly heart-shaped, lower lip evenly divided
into 3 lobes. This slightly aquatic species grows in shallow water or along banks of waterways in Southeast
Texas, from Houston area east to Louisiana. A few populations in Northeast Texas.

Quincula lobata   SOLANACEAE
Purple ground cherry, Chinese lantern
Grasslands, fields, prairies, open brush and
woodlands, roadsides, urban and suburban areas
and other open areas. Spring, summer. Common.

A low, procumbent to spreading perennial with stems
branching from base, to 6+ inches long. Leaves mostly
basal or alternate along stems, on winged petioles to 3
inches long, oblanceolate to linear-lanceolate, to 2 inches
long and 1½ inches wide, bases tapering, margins sinuate, pinnatifid, or entire, tips acute. Flowers on short
peduncles in upper leaf axils, 5-lobed, rotate, purple with
darker star radiating out from center, to ¾ inch wide.
Fruit a roundish berry, surrounded by a papery calyx.
Found in western two-thirds of Texas, from Oklahoma
south into Mexico.

Solanum citrullifolium   SOLANACEAE
Melon-leaf nightshade
Fields, grasslands, creek beds, drainages,
roadsides and other open, disturbed areas.
Spring, summer, fall. Common.

An erect annual with branching stems to 30 inches
tall, stems with glandular and star-shaped hairs as well
as prickles. Leaves alternate, 2-pinnatifid, to 5+ inches
long, lobes oddly rounded, margins irregular, angled
to round to entire. Flowers blue to purple, rotate, about
1 inch wide, 5-lobed, lobes forming distinct star shape,
anthers yellow. Fruit covered with prickly calyx, splitting
at maturity. Found in Chihuahuan Desert, less frequent
in Edwards Plateau.

455

Solanum dimidiatum   SOLANACEAE
Western horse nettle, potato weed, robust horsenettle
Fields, pastures, grasslands, river and creek
banks, roadsides and other disturbed areas.
Spring, summer, fall. Common.

An erect, somewhat rhizomatous perennial with prickly
stems to 3+ feet tall. Leaves alternate, ovate, margins
deeply 5- to 7-lobed, to 6 inches long, bases rounded to
truncate, tips acute. Flowers purple to lavender, occasionally white, rotate, 5-lobed, lobes forming a star, corolla
somewhat reflexed. Found throughout Central Texas,
north into Oklahoma and southern Panhandle, east
into western East Texas. Grows in disturbed areas and
sandy-loam alluvial soils of rivers and creeks.

Solanum elaeagnifolium   SOLANACEAE
Silver-leaf nightshade, trompillo, white horse nettle
Fields, pastures, grasslands, rocky slopes and hillsides,
brush and woodlands, roadsides and other open,
disturbed areas. Spring, summer, fall. Common.

An erect, rhizomatous perennial with spiny, grayish green pubescent stems to 2+ feet tall. Leaves alternate, lanceolate to oblanceolate, to 6 inches long, bases
rounded to truncate to tapered, margins entire or sinuate,
tips acute, blades varying from covered with silver hairs
to less so and almost green. Flowers in racemes originating from upper leaf axils, blue to purple, occasionally
white, rotate, star-shaped, 1 inch wide, 5-lobed with lobes
divided to half their length, stamens yellow. Fruit a spine-
less berry, turning yellow when mature. Widespread.

Solanum stoloniferum   SOLANACEAE
Wild potato, Fendler's nightshade
Mountainous woodlands, canyons,
drainages. Summer, fall. Uncommon.

An erect, stoloniferous, tuber-producing perennial with
pubescent, branching stems to 2 feet tall. Leaves alternate, odd-pinnate, to 10 inches long, with 5–9 leaflets,
leaflets oval to elliptic, to 3 inches long and 1½ inches
wide, margins entire to rough, leaflet surfaces and rachis
with visible, curved hairs. Additional smaller leaves occur
along rachis as well. Flowers blue to purple, star-shaped,
1¼ inches wide, with 5 pointed lobes. Fruit globose, to ⅓
inch in diameter. Found in upper elevations of Chisos,
Chinati, and Davis Mountains of West Texas.

Verbena bracteata VERBENACEAE

Bigbract verbena, prostrate verbena, carpet vervain
Fields, grasslands, pastures, open brushlands, roadsides
and other open areas. Spring, summer, fall. Common.

A prostrate or decumbent annual to perennial with several pubescent stems to 18 inches long, radiating from
central base. Leaves opposite, to 3 inches long and 1 inch
wide, 3-lobed, margins dentate or lobed, blades pubescent. Flowers in terminal spikes to 6 inches long, numerous, small, 5-lobed, light blue or purple with lighter or
white interiors, single lanceolate bract which extends
beyond the length of flower. Found throughout Panhandle, Trans-Pecos, Edwards Plateau, and into East Texas
where it is less common.

Verbena brasiliensis VERBENACEAE

Brazilian vervain
Edges of waterways and bodies of water, roadside ditches
and other wet areas. Spring, summer, fall. Common.

An introduced, open, erect, slender annual or short-lived
perennial with slender, 4-angled, branching, hispid
stems to 7+ feet tall. Leaves opposite, sessile, elliptic to
lanceolate, to 4 inches long and 1 inch wide, margins serrate, tips acute, blades rough to the touch. Flowers in terminal spikes, rounded at first, elongating throughout season, small, trumpet-shaped, 5-lobed, light purple to pink
to rose with darker centers. Widespread from lower coast
north through Edwards Plateau and into Oklahoma, east
into Louisiana; spreading.

Verbena canescens VERBENACEAE

Gray vervain
Fields, pastures, prairies, open shrub and
woodlands, rocky hillsides, roadsides and other
open areas. Spring, summer, fall. Common.

An erect, branching perennial with canescent
leaves and stems to 18+ inches tall. Leaves opposite,
oblong-lanceolate, to 2 inches long, bases clasping, margins dentate to pinnatifid, tips acute. Flowers in terminal
spikes, plentiful but not crowded, bilateral, lobes notched,
light blue, lavender, or purple, about ¼ inch wide. Absent
in Panhandle and East Texas, common elsewhere, primarily on limestone soils. Prefers rocky to gravelly soils.

457

Verbena halei VERBENACEAE
Texas vervain
Prairies, grasslands, fields, pastures, open brush
and woodlands, roadsides and other open areas.
Winter, spring, summer, fall. Common.

An erect, multistemmed perennial with branching stems
to 20+ inches long. Leaves opposite. Lower leaves on petioles, oblong to ovate, to 4 inches long, margins dentate. Middle leaves on short petioles, 1- or 2-pinnatifid,
shorter than lower leaves. Upper leaves sessile, thinner, margins dentate to entire. Inflorescences in loosely
flowered spikes, funnel-shaped, to about ⅓ inch wide,
5-lobed, lobes unequal. Found throughout state. Weak in
Panhandle.

Verbena macdougalii VERBENACEAE
MacDougal verbena, hillside verbena, New Mexico vervain
Mountain grasslands, meadows, open
brushlands. Spring, summer. Rare.

An erect, stout perennial with simple or branching
pubescent stems to 3 feet tall. Leaves opposite, on short
petioles to sessile, oblong-elliptic to ovate, to 4 inches
long, bases narrowed, margins serrate-dentate. Flowers
in terminal spikes to 4 inches long, numerous, 5-lobed,
deep purple to blue, to ⅜ inch wide. Found in Texas only
in higher elevations of Guadalupe Mountains, although
common elsewhere in western United States.

Verbena plicata VERBENACEAE
Fanleaf vervain
Fields, grasslands, prairies, open shrub and
woodlands, roadsides and other open areas.
Winter, spring, summer. Common.

An erect, ascending or decumbent perennial with
pubescent stems to 20+ inches long. Leaves opposite, on
winged petioles to 1¾ inches long, elliptic-ovate, to 1¾
inches long, bases narrowed, margins dentate to 3-lobed,
tips obtuse, blades wrinkled (plicate). Blue, purple, or
lavender flowers in terminal spikes, funnel-shaped,
appearing bilabiate, to ⅓ inch wide, 5-lobed, lower middle lobe larger, outer lobes equal, upper 2 lobes appearing
notched. Found throughout western two-thirds of Texas.

Verbena rigida   VERBENACEAE
Sandpaper verbena, rigid verbena, slender vervain
Fields, pastures, grasslands, roadsides.
Spring, summer. Common.

An introduced, erect, spreading perennial with rough, branching stems to 2 feet tall. Leaves opposite, oblong to lanceolate, bases slightly cordate and somewhat clasping, margins serrate and revolute, tips acute. Flowers in short, terminal spikes, numerous, funnel-shaped, purple to rose, to ⅓ inch wide, 5-lobed with lobes notched. Primarily found in Southeast Texas, west to Austin area. An occasional escapee elsewhere. Common in the nursery trade.

Verbena xutha   VERBENACEAE
Gulf vervain
Fields, prairies, grasslands, open brushlands, roadsides and other open areas. Spring, summer. Common.

An erect, airy perennial with angled, rough stems to 6 feet tall, often with multiple stems. Leaves opposite, oblong or ovate, to 6 inches long, pinnatifid or 3-lobed with a large middle lobe and 2 smaller, equal lateral lobes at base, bases clasping, ultimate margins dentate, tips obtuse. Flowers in elongated terminal spikes, bluish purple to pink to lavender, ⅓ inch wide, 5-lobed with lobes unequal. Found in Coastal and Blackland Prairies of Southeast Texas, south to Coastal Bend, less common north to Red River, isolated populations in Big Bend region and far South Texas.

Viola missouriensis   VIOLACEAE
Missouri violet
Stream banks, swamps, woodlands. Spring. Common.

A stemless, rhizomatous perennial to about 6 inches wide and just a few inches tall. Basal leaves only, on petioles to 3½ inches long, cordate, to 3½ inches long and 2½ inches wide, margins crenate. Flowers on stalks to 3½ inches long, solitary, 5-petaled, blue-violet, ¾ inch wide, lower and occasionally side petals with darker veins. Found throughout eastern third of Texas, with additional populations in Davis and Guadalupe Mountains and in upper Panhandle.

459

Viola pedata   VIOLACEAE
Birdfoot violet
Open woodlands, fields, roadsides. Spring. Uncommon.

A stemless, rhizomatous perennial to 6 inches tall. Basal leaves on petioles to 5 inches long, 3- to 5-palmate, each lobe may be further divided, to 1 inch long and as wide, margins entire or slightly toothed. Flowers solitary, dark blue-violet, on peduncles to 5 inches, lower and side petals with darker veins, lower petal white at base. Found in southeastern Texas, east into Louisiana.

Viola sororia   VIOLACEAE
Common blue violet, meadow violet, Missouri violet
Fields, prairies, open woodlands, thickets. Spring. Common.

An erect, stemless, rhizomatous perennial to 10 inches tall. Leaves on petioles to 2+ inches long, cordate, to 3 inches long and as wide, margins crenate to serrate, surfaces glabrous to pubescent. Flowers solitary, 5-petaled, on peduncles that just exceed foliage, about ¾ inch wide, lower and side petals with darker veins, throat white. Found in eastern half of Texas, north into Panhandle where it is uncommon. Prefers dry, sandy soils.

BIBLIOGRAPHY

Ajilvsgi, Geyata. 1979. *Wild Flowers of the Big Thicket: East Texas, and Western Louisiana*. College Station: Texas A&M University Press.

Brown, Paul Martin. 2008. *Field Guide to the Wild Orchids of Texas*. Gainesville: The University Press of Florida.

Correll, Donovan Stewart, and Marshall Conring Johnston. 1996. *Manual of the Vascular Plants of Texas*. Richardson: The University of Texas at Dallas.

Cronquist, Arthur. 1980. *Vascular Flora of the Southeastern United States: Vol. 1: Asteraceae*. Chapel Hill: The University of North Carolina Press.

Diggs, George M., Jr., Robert J. O'Kennon, and Barney L. Lipscomb. 1999. *Shinners & Mahler's Flora of North Central Texas*. Fort Worth: Botanical Research Institute of Texas.

Enquist, Marshall. 1987. *Wildflowers of the Texas Hill Country*. Austin: Lone Star Botanical.

Epple, Anne Orth. *Plants of Arizona*. 1995. Guilford, Connecticut: The Globe Pequot Press.

Flora of North America Editorial Committee, eds. *Flora of North America: North of Mexico*, 20+ vols. New York and Oxford. Vol. 3, 1997; vol. 4, 2003; vol. 5, 2005; vol. 6, 2015; vol. 7, 2010; vol. 8, 2009; vol. 9, 2014; vol. 19, 2006; vol. 20, 2006; vol 21, 2006; vol. 22, 2000; vol. 23, 2002; vol. 26, 2002.

Heywood, V. H., R. K. Brummitt, A. Culham, and O. Seberg. 2007. *Flowering Plant Families of the World*. Ontario, Canada: Firefly Books.

Hickman, James C., ed. 1993. *The Jepson Manual: Higher Plants of California*. Oakland: University of California Press.

Isely, Duane. 1990. *Vascular Flora of the Southeastern United States Vol. 3, Part 2 Leguminosae (Fabaceae)*. Chapel Hill: The University of North Carolina Press.

Jones, Fred B. 1977. *Flora of the Texas Coastal Bend*. Corpus Christi: Mission Press.

Kearney, Thomas H., and Robert H. Peebles. 1951. *Arizona Flora*. Oakland: University of California Press.

Liggio, Joe, and Ann Orto Liggio. 1999. *Wild Orchids of Texas*. Austin: University of Texas Press.

Long, Robert W., and Olga Lakela. 1971. *A Flora of Tropical Florida: A Manual of the Seed Plants and Ferns of Southern Peninsular Florida*. Coral Gables: University of Miami Press.

Poole, Jackie M., William R. Carr, Dana M. Price, and Jason R. Singhurst. 2007. *Rare Plants of Texas*. College Station: Texas A&M University Press.

Powell, Michael A. 1998. *Trees and Shrubs of the Trans-Pecos and Adjacent Areas*. Austin: University of Texas Press.

Richardson, Alfred. 1995. *Plants of the Rio Grande Delta*. Austin: University of Texas Press.

———. 2002. *Wildflowers and Other Plants of Texas Beaches and Islands.* Austin: University of Texas Press.

Richardson, Alfred, and Ken King. 2011. *Plants of Deep South Texas: A Field Guide to the Woody and Flowering Species.* College Station: Texas A&M University Press.

Shreve, Forrest, and Ira L. Wiggins. 1964. *Vegetation and Flora of the Sonoran Desert.* Stanford: Stanford University Press.

Stearn, William T. *Botanical Latin.* 1991. Newton Abbot, Devon, United Kingdom: David & Charles.

Tyrl, Ronald J., et al., eds. 2007. *Keys and Descriptions for the Vascular Plants of Oklahoma.* Nobel, Oklahoma: Flora Oklahoma Incorporated.

Voss, Edward G., and Anton A. Reznicek. 2012. *Field Manual of Michigan Flora.* Ann Arbor: The University of Michigan Press.

Weakly, Alan L., J. Christopher Ludwig, and John F. Townsend, authors; Bland Crowder, ed. 2012. *Flora of Virginia.* Fort Worth: Botanical Research Institute of Texas Press.

PHOTO AND ILLUSTRATION CREDITS

Obtaining all the photographs needed for this book would not have been possible without the help of those who graciously contributed their images. All photographs, aside from the following, are by Michael Eason.

MATT BUCKINGHAM
Arisaema dracontium, 91
Aristolochia reticulata (inset), 295
Asclepias incarnata, 324
Coastal Prairie Harris County, 25
Cypripedium kentuckiense habitat, 11
Epifagus virginiana, 313
Houstonia pusilla, 454
Sarracenia bog Newton County, 27
Tipularia discolor (inset), 155

LAYLA DISHMAN
Achillea millefolium, 93
Agalinis fasciculata, 380
Agalinis heterophylla, 381
Ajuga reptans, 436
Allium ampeloprasum, 323
Alternanthera caracasana, 66
Alternanthera philoxeroides, 67
Alternanthera sessilis, 67
Ammannia coccinea, 363
Ammi majus, 73
Ammoselinum butleri, 74
Amsonia tabernaemontana, 400
Anagallis arvensis, 282
Anemone caroliniana, 168
Anthemis cotula, 94
Aphanostephus ramosissimus, 95
Arisaema triphyllum, 91
Arnoglossum ovatum, 95
Arnoglossum plantagineum, 95
Asclepias curassavica, 292
Asclepias linearis, 81
Asclepias longifolia, 82

Asclepias perennis, 83
Asclepias rubra, 325
Astragalus crassicarpus, 420
Astragalus lindheimeri, 420
Astragalus lotiflorus, 421
Atriplex acanthocarpa, 67
Atriplex semibaccata, 68
Bacopa caroliniana, 455
Baptisia nuttalliana, 237
Baptisia sphaerocarpa, 237
Bidens bipinnata, 195
Bidens tenuisecta, 196
Bifora americana, 74
Boehmeria cylindrica, 180
Boltonia diffusa, 96
Bowlesia incana, 74
Bradburia pilosa, 196
Brickellia eupatorioides, 197
Buchnera americana, 444
Callirhoe involucrata, 365
Callirhoe pedata (inset), 366
Capsicum annuum, 176
Cardiospermum halicacabum, 174
Carduus nutans, 400
Carduus pycnocephalus, 401
Carlowrightia texana, 320
Centaurea melitensis, 197
Centaurea solstitialis, 197
Centella asiatica, 75
Chaerophyllum tainturieri, 75
Chloracantha spinosa, 98
Cicuta maculata, 75
Cirsium vulgare, 403
Clematis crispa, 452

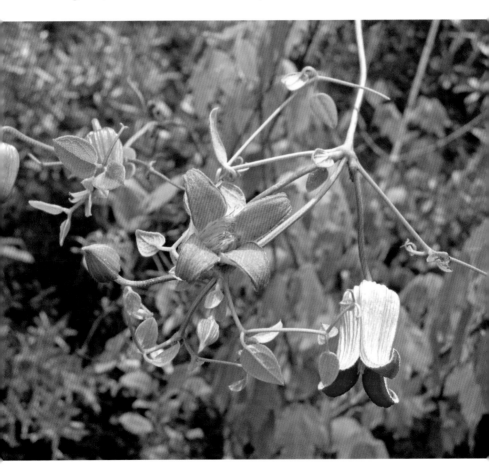

INDEX

Main species entries are in **bold type**.
Species only mentioned in the descriptions are in roman type.

hairy leafcup, 219
hairy mountainmint, 141
hairy nama, 354
hairy pink, 335
hairy pinweed, 300
hairypod cowpea, 249
hairy portulaca, 390
hairy puccoon, 229
hairyseed bahia, 193
hairy sunflower, 206
hairy tube-tongue, 397
hairy vetch, 430
hairy vetchling, 343
hairy wedelia, 227
halberdleaf rose mallow, 145
hammerwort, 180
Haplophyton crooksii, **190**
hardheads, 408
hardy saltbush, 67
hardy swamp lily, 71
Hartweg's sundrops, 271
Havard's bluebonnet, 424
Havard's ipomopsis, 385
Havard's penstemon, 315
heart clover, 241
heartleaf four o'clock, 377
heartleaf hibiscus, 308
heartleaf nettle, 180
heartleaf rose mallow, 308
heartleaf sandmat, 129
heart-leaf skullcap, 440
heartleaf skullcap, 442
heartleaf spurge, 129
heart's delight, 373
heart seed, 174
heart-wing dock, 167
heart-wing sorrel, 167
heath aster, 108
heath wrightwort, 396
hedeoma, 356
Hedeoma acinoides, **356**
Hedeoma drummondii, **356**
Hedeoma hispida, **356**
Hedeoma reverchonii, **357**
Hedyotis acerosa var. *acerosa*, **172**
Heimia salicifolia, **258**
Helenium amarum
    var. *amarum*, **202**, 203

var. *badium*, **203**
Helenium drummondii, **203**
Helenium elegans, **203**
Helenium flexuosum, **204**
Helenium microcephalum, **204**
Helianthemum carolinianum, **231**
Helianthemum georgianum, **231**
Helianthemum rosmarinifolium, **232**
Helianthus angustifolius, **204**
Helianthus annuus, **205**
Helianthus argophyllus, **205**
Helianthus ciliaris, **205**
Helianthus debilis, **206**
Helianthus grosseserratus, **206**
Helianthus hirsutus, **206**
Helianthus maximiliani, **207**
Helianthus mollis, **207**
Helianthus petiolaris, **207**
Heliomeris longifolia, **208**
Heliotropium angiospermum, **112**
Heliotropium confertifolium, **112**
Heliotropium convolvulaceum, **112**
Heliotropium curassavicum, **113**
Heliotropium greggii, **113**
Heliotropium indicum, **412**
Heliotropium molle, **113**
Heliotropium tenellum, **114**
Heliotropium torreyi, **228**
Heller's plantain, 162
helmet-flower, 441
Hemerocallis fulva, **288**
hemp broomrape, 446
henbit, 357
henbit deadnettle, 357
Herbertia lahue, **434**
herb-of-grace, 158
herb of grace, 284
Herissantia crispa, **144**
Hermannia texana, **308**
Hesperidanthus linearifolius, **412**
hesper mustard, 412
Heteranthera dubia, **280**
Heteranthera limosa, **451**
Heteranthera mexicana, **451**
Heterotheca canescens, **208**
Hexalectris grandiflora, **379**
Hexalectris revoluta, **310**
Hexalectris spicata, **310**

ABOUT THE AUTHOR

MICHAEL EASON heads the rare plant conservation department at the San Antonio Botanical Garden. Through his consulting business, Texas Flora, he also works as a conservation botanist, performing plant identification service, botanical inventories, and rare plant surveys on private and public lands. He serves on the boards of the Native Plant Society of Texas and the Chihuahuan Desert Research Institute. Previously, he worked for the Lady Bird Johnson Wildflower Center, where he managed the Millennium Seed Bank Project, and was lead botanist and program manager for several projects, including the vegetation survey of Big Bend National Park and survey of arid-land ferns of the Trans-Pecos. In his spare time, Michael continues to volunteer his time for various organizations such as the Wildflower Center and the Nature Conservancy.

LORI GOLA

LEAF FORM

simple

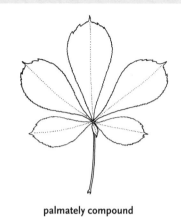

palmately compound

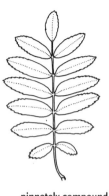

pinnately compound

LEAF SHAPE

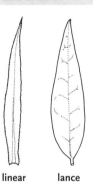    

linear   lance   oval   elliptical   spoon   heart

LEAF MARGINS

entire   toothed   lobed

LEAF ARRANGEMENT

alternate